Lecture Notes in Artificial Intelligence 4659

Edited by J. G. Carbonell and J. Siekmann

Subseries of Lecture Notes in Computer Science

T0241067

Vladimír Mařík

Valeriy Vyatkin   Armando W. Colombo (Eds.)

Holonic and Multi-Agent Systems for Manufacturing

Third International Conference on Industrial Applications
of Holonic and Multi-Agent Systems, HoloMAS 2007
Regensburg, Germany, September 3-5, 2007
Proceedings

 Springer

Series Editors

Jaime G. Carbonell, Carnegie Mellon University, Pittsburgh, PA, USA
Jörg Siekmann, University of Saarland, Saarbrücken, Germany

Volume Editors

Vladimír Mařík
Czech Technical University
Department of Cybernetics
Faculty of Electrical Engineering
16627 Praha 6, Czech Republic
and Rockwell Automation Research Center
Pekařská 10a/695, 15500 Prague 5, Czech Republic
E-mail: marik@labe.felk.cvut.cz

Valeriy Vyatkin
The University of Auckland
Department of Electrical and Computer Engineering
Auckland Mail Centre, Private bag 92019, Auckland 1142, New Zealand
E-mail: v.vyatkin@auckland.ac.nz

Armando W. Colombo
Schneider Electric GmbH
Steinheimer Str. 117, 63500 Seligenstadt, Germany
E-mail: armando.colombo@de.schneider-electric.com

Library of Congress Control Number: 2007933411

CR Subject Classification (1998): I.2.11, I.2, J.1, D.2, I.6

LNCS Sublibrary: SL 7 – Artificial Intelligence

ISSN   0302-9743
ISBN-10   3-540-74478-9 Springer Berlin Heidelberg New York
ISBN-13   978-3-540-74478-8 Springer Berlin Heidelberg New York

Springer is a part of Springer Science+Business Media

springer.com

© Springer-Verlag Berlin Heidelberg 2007
Printed in Germany

Typesetting: Camera-ready by author, data conversion by Scientific Publishing Services, Chennai, India
Printed on acid-free paper   SPIN: 12113279   06/3180   5 4 3 2 1 0

Preface

The research of holonic and agent-based systems is developing rapidly, as is the community around this R&D topic. Despite the fact that real-life practical implementations of such systems remain surprisingly rare, the leaders in different branches of industry feel that the holonic and agent-based systems represent the only way to manage and control very complex, highly distributed systems in the future. The relevant R&D gains more and more support from both industry as well as academic sources. Quite naturally, the number of scientific events aimed at the subject field is also growing rapidly. We can see new lines of conferences like INDIN, while we can observe a strong focus of the already well-established conferences, like INCOM or ETFA, being shifted toward holonic and agent-based manufacturing systems. This is a good sign of the increasing recognition and importance of the field.

We are convinced of the worth and importance of the continuation of the HoloMAS events, which have served as pioneering melting pots for ideas connected with distributed decision making and control in industry and which have already gained international reputation. The first five HoloMAS events held under the DEXA-event umbrella (three workshops, particularly HoloMAS 2000 in Greenwich, HoloMAS 2001 in Munich and HoloMAS 2002 in Aix-en-Provence as well as the 1st HoloMAS 2003 conference held in Prague and the 2nd HoloMAS 2005 held in Copenhagen) helped to bring together the research communities focused on agent-based industrial solutions, to realize the joint principles of agent-oriented applications on different levels of manufacturing, factory and supply chain management and to integrate better their research activities and results. Now, with HoloMAS 2007, we would like to document the feasibility and viability of the initial ideas, to show the current trends in the industrial agent-oriented research and to make the progress in the field clearly visible.

The HoloMAS community has started to cooperate with the IEEE System, Man and Cybernetics (SMC) Society, especially with its Technical Committee on Distributed Intelligent Systems (TC-DIS). We have decided to organize the HoloMAS conference bi-yearly, on even years, under the DEXA umbrella and to focus attention on specific IEEE SMC events on odd years. So, the IEEE DIS workshop with a special track covering the "obvious" HoloMAS topics was organized in Prague in June 2006. Similarly, the IEEE SMC Conference on Distributed Human-Machine Systems (DHMS 2008) which has absorbed the HoloMAS field, will be held in Athens, Greece in March 2008 (http://www.action-m.com/dhms2008/). This approach will help the HoloMAS community to be better integrated with both the information society-oriented DEXA community as well as the IEEE Society aimed at human-machine systems and cybernetics.

We are happy to announce that the HoloMAS 2007 conference was held under the technical co-sponsorship of the IEEE SMC Society in cooperation with the OOONEIDA network and the I*PROMS EU Network of Excellence.

OOONEIDA (http://www.oooneida.info/index.html) is a non-profit corporation incorporated in Canada, registered as O³neida Inc. It operates as a network of networks focused on fostering distributed industrial automation based on open standards. After closing down the activities of the HMS Consortium within the IMS initiative, ending the EU funding of the AgentLink Network of Excellence and the transfer and weakening the influence of the FIPA community, OOONEIDA is becoming the most important and strongest international body in the field.

The I*PROMS EU Network of Excellence (http://www.iproms.org) is aimed mainly at research and development of advanced systems for manufacturing and control. Holonic and agent-based solutions represent one of the latest trends in this area and are a focus of the I*PROMS activities.

We are very glad to declare that there were 63 papers submitted to HoloMAS 2007, prepared by the most important, core research bodies engaged in holonic and agent-based manufacturing and supply chain management world-wide. The PC chose 39 papers to be presented and included in this volume. They contain the most representative results of the corresponding research and provide an excellent overview of what is the current state of the art.

Moreover, there were two invited talks specially tailored for the HoloMAS 2007:

The first one was given by a group of prominent researchers in the area of the IEC 61499 Standard led by Alois Zoitl from the Vienna University of Technology under the support of the PROFACTOR and Rockwell Automation leading experts. This paper can be considered as the key IEC 61499 "summary report" providing an interesting expert view on the past and future of this standard deployment.

The second invited speech was prepared by Peter van Staa, Vice-President of Robert Bosch GmbH. It steps into a completely new area of applying the multi-agent approach in the IC design with the goal of increasing IC design productivity. This talk opened a special session, PIHolS "Performance in Industrial Holonic Systems," within the framework of the HoloMAS 2007 Conference. This session was prepared by Vadim Ermolayev from The Zaporozhye National University, together with Wolf-Ekkehard Matzke from CADENCE Design Systems, GmbH Munich under the strong support of the CADENCE company. This session brought real enrichment of the content and, perhaps, a new stream in agent-based research as the *performance management* domain is a fast growing multi-billion market which drastically lacks reliable means for measuring, assessing, and optimizing the performance of industrial systems.

The HoloMAS 2007 conference created an excellent, highly motivating environment, and helped to continue integration of the community. The conference contributed to a better clarification of the goals and to a more efficient coordination of the research in the subject fields. Furthermore, this conference continued to serve as a display window of holonic and agent-based manufacturing research, offering information about the state of the art to specialists in neighboring, knowledge-processing research fields covered by the DEXA multi-conference event. We are very thankful to the DEXA Association for providing us with this excellent opportunity and to Gabriela Wagner for all her organizational efforts which were of key importance for the success of this event.

We would like to express our thanks to Vadim Ermolayev and Wolf-Ekkehard Matzke for their proactivity in organizing the special PIHolS session.

We would like to thank to IEEE SMC Society for its technical co-sponsorship as well as to both the OOONEIDA and I*PROMS EU Networks for their support and cooperation.

June 2007

Vladimír Mařík
Valeriy Vyatkin
Armando Walter Colombo

HoloMAS 2007

3rd International Conference on Industrial Applications of Holonic and
Multi-agent Systems, HoloMAS 2007

Applications of Holonic and Multi-agent Systems

Regensburg, Germany, September 3–5, 2007

Program Co-chairs

Vladimír Mařík — Czech Technical University in Prague and Rockwell Automation, Czech Republic

Valeriy Vyatkin — University of Auckland, New Zealand

Armando W. Colombo — Schneider Electric, Germany

Program Committee

José Barata — Universidade Nova de Lisboa, Portugal

Vicente Botti — Universidad Politecnica de Valencia, Spain

Jeff Bradshaw — University of West Florida, USA

Robert W. Brennan — University of Calgary, Canada

Monique Calisti — Whitestein Technologies, Switzerland

Luis M. Camarinha-Matos — Universidade Nova de Lisboa, Portugal

Vadim Ermolaev — Zaporozhje State University, Ukraine

Kurt Fassl — Profactor, Austria

Klaus Fischer — DFKI GmbH, Germany

Martyn Fletcher — Defense Science and Technology Lab, UK

Georg Frey — University of Kaiserslautern, Germany

Motohisa Funabashi — Hitachi, Japan

William Gruver — Simon Fraser University, Canada

Kenneth Hall — Rockwell Automation, USA

Toshiya Kaihara — Kobe University, Japan

Kari Koskinnen — Helsinki University of Technology, Finland

Dilip Kotak — Simon Fraser University, Canada

Jose L.M. Lastra	Tampere University of Technology, Finland
Francisco Maturana	Rockwell Automation, USA
Duncan McFarlane	Cambridge University, UK
Gerard Morel	CRAN, France
Michal Pěchouček	Czech Technical University, Czech Republic
Gregory Provan	Cork College, Ireland
Milan Rollo	Czech Technical University, Czech Republic
Leonid Sheremetov	Mexican Oil Institute, Mexico
Alexander Smirnov	SPIIRAS, Russia
Thomas Strasser	Profactor, Austria
Shinsuke Tamura	Fukui University, Japan
Ambalavanar Tharumarajah	Buddy Co. Ltd, Australia
Paul Valckenaers	Katholieke Universiteit, Leuven, Belgium
Antonio Valentini	OOONEIDA, Canada
Hendrik Van Brussel	Katholieke Universiteit, Leuven, Belgium
Tomas Vlček	Czech Technical University, Czech Republic
Pavel Vrba	Rockwell Automation, Czech Republic
Alois Zoitl	Vienna University of Technology, Austria

External Reviewers

Petr Bečvář	CertiCon, Czech Republic
Petr Benda	Czech Technical University, Czech Republic
Jiri Hodík	Czech Technical University, Czech Republic
Pavel Jisl	Czech Technical University, Czech Republic
Jiri Lažanský	Czech Technical University, Czech Republic
Lenka Lhotská	Czech Technical University, Czech Republic
Wolf Matzke	Cadence Design Systems Inc., Germany
Filip Macurek	Rockwell Automation, Czech Republic
Marek Obitko	ProTys, Czech Republic
Martin Rehák	Czech Technical University, Czech Republic
David Šišlák	Czech Technical University, Czech Republic
Pavel Tichý	Rockwell Automation, Czech Republic
Jan Tožička	Czech Technical University, Czech Republic
Jiří Vokřínek	Czech Technical University, Czech Republic

Organizing Committee

Petr Benda	Czech Technical University, Czech Republic
Hana Krautwurmová	Czech Technical University, Czech Republic
Jiří Lažanský	Czech Technical University, Czech Republic
Gabriela Wagner	FAW, University of Linz, Austria

Table of Contents

New Technologies and Techniques

Planning and Scheduling

Design Issues

Applications

PIHolS Workshop

The Past, Present, and Future of IEC 61499

Alois Zoitl[1], Thomas Strasser[2], Ken Hall[3], Ray Staron[3], Christoph Sünder[1], and Bernard Favre-Bulle[1]

[1] Automation and Control Institute, Vienna University of Technology, Gusshausstr. 27-29/376, 1040 Vienna, Austria
{zoitl, suender, favre}@acin.tuwien.ac.at
[2] PROFACTOR Produktionsforschungs GmBH, 4407 Steyr-Gleink, Austria
thomas.strasser@profactor.at
[3] Rockwell Automation, Inc., 1 Allen-Bradley Drive, Mayfield Heights, OH 44124 USA
{khhall, rjstaron}@ra.rockwell.com

Abstract. In 1991, Technical Committee 65 (TC65) of the International Electrotechnical Commission (IEC) approved a New Work Item (NWI) for the development of an international standard for the use of software objects known as Function Blocks (FBs) in distributed Industrial-Process Measurement and Control Systems (dIPMCS). The need for this new standard resulted out of several studies and research programs that have been started or conducted in the late eighties and early nineties of the last century. IEC 61499 got finally standardized in January 2005. Before that, since 2000, it was available in the form of a so-called Public Available Specification (PAS). Although IEC 61499 has been available for so long, up to now most published work on it has been academic or resulted only in prototypical test cases. Most activities around the IEC 61499 standard have been in standardization of the execution environment and definition of semantics. Some current research is in pursuing design and coding tools. This paper gives and overview about the past and present activities and implementations related to IEC 61499 and discusses the potential of this new standard for future application scenarios.

Keywords: Holonic Systems, Distributed Control, Next Generation Automation and Control Systems.

1 Introduction

In 1991, Technical Committee 65 (TC65) of the International Electrotechnical Commission (IEC) approved a New Work Item (NWI) for the development of an international standard for the use of software objects known as Function Blocks (FBs) in distributed Industrial-Process Measurement and Control Systems (dIPMCS). The need for this new standard resulted out of several studies and research programs that have been started or conducted in the late eighties and early nineties of the last century. One of the two most famous are the "21st Century Manufacturing Enterprise Strategy: An Industry-Led View" from the Iacocca Institute [4] and the Holonic

V. Mařík, V. Vyatkin, A.W. Colombo (Eds.): HoloMAS 2007, LNAI 4659, pp. 1–14, 2007.
© Springer-Verlag Berlin Heidelberg 2007

Manufacturing Systems (HMS) project from the Intelligent Manufacturing Systems (IMS) consortium [3]. The first of these developed the visionary "Agile Manufacturing" concept. This concept envisages not only a dynamic reconfiguration of control applications but also a physical reconfiguration of production resources. The second developed means and methods for self-adaptable production systems. HMS required a new lower level control architecture.

IEC 61499 started out as an extension to IEC 61131-3 for distributed function blocks based on concepts taken from Foundation Fieldbus. Through an affiliation of TC65 members with the HMS project the design of IEC 61499 was strongly coupled with the HMS project. The main idea was to get an agile and adaptive lower level control architecture as a basis for an HMS-like control system [5]. Therefore, adaptability and reconfigurability were main requirements for developing the new IEC 61499 architecture by TC65. The result of about 14 years of definition and standardization work is a family of four standards. The concepts of IEC 61499 are based on an adopted standard in the domain of IPCMS, the IEC 61131-3 [2]. The four standards are:

IEC 61499-1 (2005): *Function blocks – Part 1: Architecture*
This part describes the general architecture and all general models behind this standard.

IEC 61499-2 (2004): *Function blocks – Part 2: Software tool requirements*
Part 2 gives rules and concepts for software tool developers implementing an engineering tool for IEC 61499. Most of the information given is rather general. The most important definition of this part is an exchange data format for the software models defined in IEC 61499-1. This is a main requirement for vendor independent software libraries.

IEC 61499-3 (2004): *Function blocks for industrial-process measurement and control systems – Part 3: Tutorial information*
This part is no full standard but a technical report. It contains application examples explaining how to use the IEC 61499 models and frequently asked questions.

IEC 61499-4 (2005): *Function Blocks – Part 4: Rules for compliance profiles*
IEC 61499 leaves several points open to its implementation. How these items are solved should be described in related compliance profiles. IEC 61499-4 defines the structure of such compliance profiles.

A full description of IEC 61499's architecture may be found directly in the standard IEC 61499-1 [1] or in a more concise form in the books from Lewis [38] or Vyatkin [6].

This paper is organized as follows: Section 2 gives an overview on the work that has already been done in the field of IEC 61499. In section 3 it shows the current adoption of the standard in industry and in section 4 it discusses the development needs to help IEC 61499 to more successful industrial adoption. This paper concludes with an outlook on the future of IEC 61499.

2 Existing Work on IEC 61499

IEC 61499 got finally standardized in January 2005. Before that, since 2000, it was available in the form of a so-called Public Available Specification (PAS). Although IEC 61499 has been available for so long, up to now most published work on it has been academic or resulted only in prototypical test cases. Most activities around the IEC 61499 standard have been in standardization of the execution environment and definition of semantics. Some current research is in pursuing design and coding tools. Vyatkin [35] has presented a further study about the potential impact of the IEC 61499 standard on the progress of distributed intelligent automation.

2.1 Execution of IEC 61499 Applications

The first implemented IEC 61499 execution environment is the FBRT[1] (Function Block Run-Time Environment) from James H. Christensen. The FBRT is considered to be a reference implementation and was also used to test the standard during its development. Therefore this implementation features nearly all elements of the standard. The FBRT is implemented in Java and the IEC 61499 elements are represented as Java classes. The main point which is a concern for the practical adoption of the FBRT in industry is its Java implementation. Tests showed that Java will not achieve the required performance and real-time requirements on small embedded control platforms [7].

To achieve a better scalability for small and resource restricted control platforms a C++ implementation based on the FBRT has been undertaken by us [8]. This implementation is able to work without an underlying operating system. The active FBs are implemented as interrupt routines. An Event Dispatcher Concept (EDC) has been introduced for the event delivery. This concept queues all sent events and delivers them according to a First-In-First-Out (FIFO) principle. On the event delivery a FB gets time for processing its internal actions (e.g. computation of algorithms) the event has triggered. The event dispatcher decouples the FB's execution resulting in a more deterministic execution behaviour. The drawback of this solution is that it lacks full featured reconfiguration support.

Nearly at the same time as the work on the FBRT was started, another execution environment was under development at the University of Calgary. This execution environment is called DCOS (Distributed Controller Operating System) and is a fully functional distributed Real-Time Operating System (RTOS). In addition to standard RTOS features like preemptive real-time scheduling, memory management, timing services, and control application support, DCOS provides services for integrated network management and location transparent distribution services. The control applications are modelled in IEC 61499. The modelled FBs are transformed into C++ classes and compiled to a binary format suitable for DCOS. At execution time each FB acts as an active component and gets its own DCOS thread. Events are realized as message ports provided by DCOS allowing communication between threads. For achieving real-time execution the DCOS threads can have assigned priorities and are scheduled

---

[1] Freely available at http://www.holobloc.com

according to these priorities [9]. Because of missing support for dynamic reconfiguration a new execution environment has been started at the University of Calgary that will overcome the limits of DCOS. Due to different reasons, however, the designers never went further than a rough design of the new execution environment (called FBOS for Function Block Operating System) and a compilation of requirements for such an operating system [10].

The Archimedes Execution Environment is an approach with a limited set of supported IEC 61499 elements. Within Archimedes resources are not supported and Service Interface Function Blocks (SIFBs) are handled in a special way. They are automatically generated by the engineering environment and the control engineer accesses the process inputs and outputs in a pre-processed way through so-called Industrial Process Parameters (IPP). Currently there are two implementations of the Archimedes Execution Environment available. The first is designed to work on a real-time enhanced version of Linux and is written in C++ [11]. The second is implemented in Java targeting a real-time enhanced Java virtual machine [12]. Again FBs are represented as classes. If a Function Block Network (FBN) has to fulfil real-time constraints each of the FBs in the FBN gets its own priority assigned. The priority is derived from a modelling element called an event path. An event path is equal to an execution sequence originating from a process input and ending at a process output. Tests showed that following this approach can achieve real-time execution for small applications.

A completely different approach to achieve predictable and real-time execution is the scan-based approach. This approach builds on an overall execution cycle with a predefined cycle time. Within this cycle time a defined sequence is executed. This approach is currently used in state of the art industrial Programmable Logic Controller (PLC) systems based on the IEC 61131-3 standard. To execute IEC 61499 models with the scan-based approach, input events are transformed to Boolean data values and the sending of output events results in setting the connected inputs to true. In each scan cycle of the device each FB gets execution time. If one of the FB's input events is true the FB will process the event, send appropriate output events, and will switch to the next FB in the list. If no input event has occurred the next FB will be checked. This approach has the advantage that each FB will get execution time during each cycle. Therefore it can be predetermined how long a cycle has to last so that all FBs can execute. The main drawback is that each FB will check its input events during every cycle; therefore, execution time is needed even if no event has arrived. Currently three scan-based implementations for IEC 61499 have been developed: one at the German company Softing [13], one at the Tampere University of Technology [14], and the only commercial available runtime environment from ICS Triplex, their ISaGRAF 5.0 product [15].

Cengic et al. [16] found a further problem with scan-based implementations of IEC 61499 execution environments. Scan-based implementations may lose events if they occur close together. Therefore they developed an execution environment where events can not be lost. To achieve this each FB gets an event input FIFO. This FIFO stores each event occurrence together with its associated data. For the execution within a resource they use two threads. The first thread is in charge of handling the event connections and the ECCs. The second thread is in charge of executing the algorithms and sending the output events. Currently this execution environment supports only one resource per device. This approach's main novelty is the queuing of events but this is also its main drawback since the queues need lots of memory and processing resources that are typically not available on small control devices.

Khalgui et al. [17] proposed a temporal validation for the execution of IEC 61499 applications, but limited the scope by their assumptions. First of all they assumed to only have periodic external events. Second each of their resources gets an operating system task and in this task the FBN of the resource is scheduled in a non-preemptive way. In their approach they analyze only the internal structure of the basic function blocks. Based on this analysis an activation trace for the FBN is derived that can be compared to the Event Chain developed in this work. The FB activation trace results in an acyclic task graph that gives a rule describing how to execute the FBs within a resource after an external event has arrived. With this rule in advance of the application deployment a schedule is generated offline.

The most recently presented execution approach is a migrated execution approach for the CNet modeling language. CNet is derived from colored Petri Nets with timed arcs. The so-called handler based execution model introduces event handlers that are notified on event occurrences of the events that they are monitoring. The notification mechanism is similar to the EDC of the approaches described above. Event handlers are not interrupted until they have finished their execution. At the moment the presented approach describes a mapping for resources, CFBs, and BFBs [18].

2.2 Engineering Distributed Control Applications with IEC 61499

The component oriented approach of IEC 61499 allows the reuse of application parts (FBs, sub-applications) in different applications. Software reuse is a complicated problem and depends not only on the means provided by the modeling language but also on the overall application structure. Thus there has been research on structured approaches to control software development carried out. James Christensen developed several design patterns for common problems in the domain of discrete control systems [19] and provided the first IEC 61499 engineering tool—the FBDK.

Apart from this first IEC 61499 engineering tools currently the following IEC 61499 engineering environments are currently available: O3NEIDA Workbench, CORFU ESS, TUT-IPE Visio™ Template, TORERO IDE and the εCEDAC Engineering Environment from the research community and the only commercial product ISaGRAPH 5.0 from ICS Triplex [40].

Ferrarini et al. [20] provide a method based on hierarchical decomposition of the system behavior. The overall system is considered as an object, with the expected behavior as its main method. This method makes use of the functionality (again methods) of sub-modules. The implementation is based on physical components that are capable of operating their control functions by themselves. Therefore, a distributed automation system is the basis for this approach. Each physical component includes a manager that accepts requests from other components. The aggregation of the components based on the functional structure of the overall system is considered with respect to different approaches. The arrangement of several components defines a new component with some common functionality. Depending on the method of aggregation, different hierarchical architectures occur.

Thramboulidis [21] considers the system development for manufacturing systems from a more general viewpoint. He claims an architecture that promotes model integration not only for implementation of space artifacts but also in artifacts of the early analysis and design phases of the development process. The key concept in this architecture is the mechatronic component, composed of the mechanical part, an electrical part, and a software part. These parts collaborate through appropriate links to achieve the system's objectives and build components of the mechatronic system. The proposed architecture consists of four layers. The mechatronic layer is on the top of this architecture and is projected into the three lower layers, namely, the application, the resource, and the mechanical process. The four layers are intersected vertically with the development phases.

Based on mechatronic components a hierarchical application model for control software development has been proposed by [22]. This approach considers equally structured software components in a hierarchical structure that is built up the same way as the mechanical structure of the plant. Through a defined component structure and a strong decoupling of the components the reusability of the software components is increased.

Čengić et al. [23] present a framework for component-based distributed control software, with primary application for distributed control systems. They introduce automation components as software components for implementation of control software applications. The architecture for an automation component is described by subcomponents. There may be as many subcomponents as necessary; an example is given using four subcomponents with different roles: model (basic functions of a unit), controller (functions for some automated behavior of the model), interfaces (interaction with the automation component) and services (human automation component interaction). Automation components may encapsulate other automation components; therefore, a hierarchical architecture arises. The components at higher hierarchical levels are connected by their back-end to the front-end of automation components at lower hierarchical levels.

2.3 Verification of IEC 61499 Applications

Several approaches exist for the formal description of IEC 61499 control logic that has been described within the recent years. They can be separated according to one significant property: whether they include, in addition to the model for FBs, a model for the runtime environment (event propagation within the FBN).

Formal Description of Pure Function Blocks

Vyatkin and Hanisch [24] have published the first approach for a formal description of FBs according to IEC 61499. They use net condition event systems (NCES) which have a number of direct similarities with IEC 61499. NCES modules can be interconnected by event and condition arcs to bigger modules. Event propagation is modeled directly by event arcs; therefore, the runtime scheduling is assumed to be concurrent and instantaneous. Further work based on this approach uses closed-loop verification of the controller and the plant. The work of Vyatkin and Hanisch also provides the basis for current work from Lüder et al. [25].

Wurmus and Wagner [26] present an approach for the formal description by use of interpreted Condition/Event Petri Nets. An event is represented by the flow of markings. Event FBs like E_DELAY are modeled without regard to a concrete implementation within a runtime environment.

Schnakenbourg et al. [27] propose to model FBs using the synchronous language SIGNAL. They use clocks to assure the synchronization between the Execution Control Chart (ECC) and the input events. There is no model included for the propagation of events according to a concrete runtime implementation. Physical time is also not included, but the authors claim that this can be overcome by giving a value to the gap between two instances of a clock.

A rather new approach uses the verification engine of the Prolog language of logic programming, whose implementations contain a built-in deductive inference engine [28]. Therefore, the class of properties that can be checked is extended to more substantial queries providing in return not only "yes" or "no", but also the parameters explaining the reasons. For instance, questions like "at which values of parameter X does parameter Y belong to an interval [a,b]." This approach is limited to basic FBs at the moment, but planned for further investigations are models of service interface FBs, a concept of time, or distributed configurations .

Formal Description of Function Blocks and Their Execution Behavior
Vyatkin [29] describes the modeling of execution semantics of IEC 61499 FBs by use of NCES. These are enhancements of [24] and concentrate on the correct order of actions within a FB as well as the propagation of events over the network by use of a scheduler that provides sequential operation of events. There is no runtime environment available for these models; further efforts include a software implementation as well as a hybrid hardware/software implementation using Field Programmable Gate Arrays (FPGA).

Stanica [30] provides a very simple model of the runtime behavior of an IEC 61499 execution platform. His approach is based on Timed Automata and takes into account the physical time of algorithm execution. Further the formal description restricts the execution of algorithms to only one algorithm at any one time. But there are no models included to describe the propagation of events and further runtime behavior.

Khaligui et al. [31] propose a state machine model compliant to the standard IEC 61499. To avoid unpredictable behavior in the case of simultaneous occurrences of events, they propose to design offline scheduling of FB execution. They verify the schedule correctness using the state machine model. By use of this scheduler, a hard-coded execution model of a runtime environment can be implemented.

Čengić et al. [23] describe their formal model of the runtime environment FUBER, which they have developed based on interacting finite automata in Supremica. In this case the formal description includes many aspects of the runtime behavior. For instance, the event execution model specifies that each FB instance must wait for another instance to finish its event handling before it can begin its own event handling. Incoming events of a FB instance are stored in a queue; all FB instances waiting for execution are also handled in another queue. By use of such a detailed formal description of the runtime behavior, they are able to prove in much detail the behavior of the FUBER implementation. Physical time is not mentioned in their approach. As the implementation of FUBER is based on Java, the virtual machine, as well as the underlying operating system, needs to be included in the models for the consideration of physical time.

Sünder et al. [32] investigate the introduction of the runtime behavior and real-time constraints into the verification process of IEC 61499 based automation systems. In detail, the event propagation policies as well as the necessary execution time for all actions within the automation system are described by the use of NCES. The basis of the formal description provides an analytic methodology for the event propagation policy of an IEC 61499 runtime implementation. By use of this methodology within the formal model of the runtime environment, the overall system behavior and properties, including reactive systems, can be described.

2.4 Reconfiguration of Control Applications

The design of IEC 61499 was strongly coupled with the Holonic Manufacturing Systems (HMS) project. The main idea was to get an agile and adaptive lower level control architecture as a basis for an HMS [5]. Therefore adaptability and reconfigurability were the main requirements for developing the IEC 61499 architecture. Nonetheless a full support for dynamic reconfiguration is beyond the scope of the standard.

The main part of the existing work on dynamic reconfigurable control systems based on IEC 61499 has been done at the University of Calgary. Their work focuses on automatic reconfiguration to react to system disturbances. Zhang et al [33] developed a system architecture for dynamic reconfiguration through the introduction of an orthogonal adaptation framework. This framework consists of additional data and event flows arranged orthogonal to the FB monitoring and controlling the configuration of the control program. The additional control flow is used by configuration control elements in each FB. In a more recent work they utilized a second approach called the contingencies approach [34]. In this approach several applications are programmed in advance and downloaded to the devices at system start-up. Depending on the system state the appropriate application is used. As the whole application is replaced it is rather similar to the functionality provided by state of the art industrial control based on IEC 61131-3.

The real-time Java implementation of the Archimedes Execution Environment also provides support for online reconfiguration [12]. They split the reconfiguration process into two phases. The first phase is the preparation part and runs at low priority. In this phase FB definitions are downloaded to the device, FB instances are created, and data connections are established. This phase may be interrupted at any time by higher priority control elements.

Strasser et al. [39] proposed a method for the reconfiguration of IEC 61499 applications by the use of special IEC 61499 applications—called Evolution Control Applications. The reconfiguration steps can also be directly implemented into IEC 61499 control application but the ECA is especially used to encapsulate these reconfiguration steps into a separate special control application. This makes the presented approach for a control engineer more useable otherwise the control application will be overloaded with reconfiguration parts. The ECA is built of special IEC 61499 compliant management FB types that encapsulate runtime reconfiguration services for dynamic reconfiguration of control application in a distributed system. The trigger to execute an ECA can either be initiated by the user, the control application or by the underlying controlled process.

3   Current Industrial Adoption of IEC 61499

As far as our investigation showed were the first adoptions of IEC 61499 mainly case studies and prototypes. The starting point of several test cases was the development of the FBDK/FBRT package from Rockwell Automation. With this environment it was possible to test the features of IEC 61499. Currently it is still the main environment used for IEC 61499. Other companies also tested IEC 61499 but never got beyond the prototype stage. For example, two published results are Softing [13] or Yamatake with their famous Lego testbed[2]. The result of these investigations was that currently two companies offer control equipment based on the FBDK/FBRT environment. The first one is Tate Control[3] from New Zealand. They offer a small controller with several communication interfaces and I/O ports. The first test application will be product tracking in a meat processing facility. The second company is Western Reserve Controls[4] located in Ohio USA. Their product is called HoloCon ("Holonic Controller"). This HoloCon device is a small control device equipped with a configurable set of I/O ports, Ethernet, and CAN. Currently no industrial use case is publicly available.

A complete self-developed IEC 61499 based product is the IEC 61499 support of the ISaGRAF environment from the company ICS Triplex[5]. They enhanced their IEC 61131-3 environment with support of IEC 61499 elements. This support includes event driven basic and composite function blocks and an application view. Instead of the ECC in ISaGRAF, IEC 61131-3 sequential function chart is used to program basic function blocks. The application view is only for documentation purposes as the distribution model is not implemented. A further shortcoming of this environment can be seen at the execution side. There the event based IEC 61499 is handled on top of the scan based IEC 61131-3 execution environment. Therefore all the drawbacks of scan based execution approaches identified above apply. Up to now no performance values have been available since the product is currently in a beta phase.

Apart from a direct adoption of IEC 61499 two approaches to distributed control systems also exist based on the concepts and definitions of IEC 61499. The first one published was the Interface for Distributed Automation (IDA) approach by a group of hardware and software vendors under the lead of Schneider Electric, Phoenix Contact, and Jetter AG. Within IDA nearly all elements of IEC 61499 have been adopted. Only

---

[2] http://www.holobloc.com/stds/iec/tc65wg6/presentations/feed_carry_test.pdf
[3] http://www.taitcontrols.co.nz
[4] http://www.wrcakron.com/holocon.html
[5] http://www.icstriplex.com

the internals of the basic function block has been left to the specific vendor the block will be executed on. IDA combines events with their associated data and uses only one connection connected to a so-called IDA port. There are three types of connections (i) Data distribution for cyclic exchanged data, (ii) event notifications for single events, and (iii) remote method invocation where another block is called and a return is generated. Because of the strongly industry driven approach, IDA had good chances in the beginning but none of the core members of the IDA group acted as driver of the technology. The merger with the Modbus User Group to become the Modbus-IDA Group was the final end of the IDA technology.

The second approach is the PROFInet Component Based Automation (CBA) approach from Siemens. It can be seen as a mapping of the IEC 61499 elements to the world of traditional scan based PLC systems. The main element within PROFInet CBA is the component. A component represents some control functionality and interacts with other components through its interface. Currently each component is equal to a control device in the PROFInet environment. PROFInet CBA allows one to model the components interface and the interaction between the components. For the interaction DCOM-based middleware handles the data exchange. Only data connections are supported. The components themselves are programmed in the engineering tool of the device vendor. Although several control companies adopted PROFInet CBA (e.g. Hilscher, KW Software) currently there is only small market adoption of PROFInet CBA primarily because the system is complicated to use and several core features of IEC 61499 are missing (e.g. the application model and the composite function block).

4 Open Issues Hindering the Adoption of IEC 61499

Considering the whole life cycle of an automation system, existing work on IEC 61499 tackled only a small part of it: namely the engineering and execution aspects. These are important topics but for technology adopters in the domain of industrial automation it is also important to get the system up and running, keep it running, and in case of problems (e.g. breakdowns) get the system back to operation fast again. To overcome these problems research and development in the following areas will be necessary:

- How to conduct the start-up and the shutdown phase in a distributed system
- Monitoring and debugging of distributed control applications: how to acquire the data, how to present it in the tool, how to locate errors
- Up to now all showcases had between 1 and 4 control devices. How will a system with many nodes (up to hundreds) behave?
- Analysis and tests on the system behavior and stability (e.g. will one node always be down)
- Handling the complexity of a distributed system. Distributed systems are more complex than centralized. Methods and tools are needed that assist the control engineer to make the complexity manageable.

A point not directly related to the operation of the plant is the intended heterogeneous system IEC 61499 targets. Although in a compliance profile the portability, interoperability, and the configurability are regulated there is a problem with executing control applications on devices of different vendors. The reasons for this are gaps and semantic loopholes in the standard that may be interpreted differently. Therefore the execution semantics of IEC 61499 control applications need to be further defined [36].

5 Conclusion: Future of IEC 61499

The world of industrial automation and control has largely changed since the work on IEC 61499 has been started. Distributed controllers, programmable I/O modules and intelligent drives are getting more and more state-of-the-art in automation systems. Their increase in processing power and increased memory hold control applications of a useful size. A second key technology that became popular in recent years is the use of Ethernet technology in industrial automation and control. This technology now allows communication between any members of the communication system. An additional element is the growing complexity of control applications. For example, large modular machines are equipped with 60 or more small control devices (e.g. wood working machines, printing machines...), or in case of building automation there are even more control devices. Currently available engineering methodologies and engineering tools are not designed for handling such systems. A main reason for this is that IEC 61131-3 targets central tightly coupled control systems. Therefore it is cumbersome to get such distributed plants running and keep them running. The software costs of automation systems explode and exceed the cost of the machine's mechanical parts [37].

IEC 61499, as an architecture targeting distributed control systems, could solve several of these problems (e.g. manage distribution, reusability of software components, concurrent software development...). The basic foundation for IEC 61499 is laid by the recent technology changes and development in the domain of industrial automation and control systems. An important point is to get it out soon for solving current customers need. Otherwise IEC 61499 will be a nice concept doomed to die. Vyatkin came to a similar finding in his study on the usage of IEC 61499 [35]. But what he also mentioned is a great increase in published work and articles on IEC 61499 in the last 5 years. This can be a sign for future IEC 61499 adoption.

One driver for getting IEC 61499 products out in the market is to help device vendors integrate this technology into their products. Therefore PROFACTOR and the Automation and Control Institute (ACIN), Vienna University of Technology have founded an open source initiative providing an IEC 61499 runtime environment and an IEC 61499 engineering environment. This open source initiative is called "Open Distributed Embedded Control Environment (ODECE)" and is running under the patronage of O3NEIDA[6]. With this support we hope to get IEC 61499 out in the industry within the next several years.

---

[6] http://www.oooneida.org/

References

1. IEC, Geneva. IEC 61499-1: Function Blocks - Part 1 Architecture (2005)
2. IEC, Geneva. IEC 61131-3 Programmable controllers - Part 3: Programming languages (1993)
3. Holonic Manufacturing Systems Project Consortium. HMS Project Homepage (January 2007), Online Available: http://hms.ifw.uni-hannover.de
4. Iacocca Institute: 21. Century Manufacturing Enterprise Strategy: An Industry-Led View. Technical report, Iacocca Institute, Bethlehem, PA (1991)
5. Christensen, J.H.: Holonic Manufacturing Systems: Initial Architecture and Standards Directions. In: Consortium, H.M.S. (ed.) Proceedings of the 1st Euro Workshop on Holonic Manufacturing Systems, Hannover (December 1994)
6. Vyatkin, V.: IEC 61499 Function Blocks for Embedded and Distributed Control Systems Design, ISA-o3neida, USA (2006)
7. Haidler, J.: Implementing IEC 61499 on embedded systems and distributed control of an assembly testbed. Master's thesis, Vienna University of Technology (June 2002)
8. Zoitl, A.: Development of an IEC 61499 based embedded control platform and integration in a distributed automation system. Master's thesis, Vienna University of Technology (October 2002)
9. Balasubramanian, S.: A Metamorphic Control Architecture for Holonic Systems. PhD thesis, University of Calgary (1997)
10. Fletcher, M., Norrie, D.H.: Real-time Reconfiguration using an IEC 61499 Operating System. In: IEEE Parallel and Distributed Processing Symposium. IEEE Computer Society Press, Los Alamitos (2001)
11. Doukas, G.S, Thramboulidis, K.: A Real-Time Linux Execution Environment for Function Block Based Distributed Control Applications. In: Proc. of the 3rd IEEE Int. Conf. on Industrial Informatics, Perth (2005)
12. Thramboulidis, K., Zoupas, A.: Real-Time Java in control and Automation: A Model Driven Development Approach. In: 10th IEEE Conf. on Emerging Technologies and Factory Automation. IEEE Computer Society Press, Los Alamitos (2005)
13. Blume, R.: Function Block Architecture Runtime Engine and Engineering Toolset: Deliverable D1.3-1 of HMS consortium. Technical report, Softing GmbH, Munich Germany (2000)
14. Martinez Lastra, J.L., Lobov, A., Godinho, L., Nunes, A.: Function Blocks for Industrial-Process Measurement and Control Systems: IEC 61499 Introduction and Run-time Platforms. Tampere University of Technology, Tampere (2004)
15. ICS Triplex: ISaGRAF Webpage (January 2007), http://www.isagraf.com
16. Cengic, G., Ljungkrantz, O., Akesson, K.: Formal Modeling of Function Block Applications Running in IEC 61499 Execution Runtime. In: Proceedings of the 11th IEEE Conference on Emerging Technologies and Factory Automation, ETFA'06, Praque (September 2006)
17. Khalgui, M., Rebeuf, X., Simonot-Lioin, F.: A Schedulability Analysis of an IEC-61499 Control Application. In: Proceedings of the 6th IFAC International Conference on Fieldbus Systems and their Applications, FET, Publa, Mexico (November 2005)
18. Hagge, N., Wagner, B.: Applying the handler-based execution model to IEC 61499 basic and composite function blocks. In: Proceedings of the 4rd IEEE International Conference on Industrial Informatics, INDIN'06, Singapore (August 2006)

19. Christensen, J.H.: Design patterns for systems engineering in IEC 61499, Verteilte Automatisierung - Modelle und Methoden für Entwurf, Verifikation, Engineering und Instrumentierung (VA2000), Otto-von-Guericke-Universität Magdeburg, Germany (March 22-23, 2000)
20. Ferrarini, L., Veber, C., Lorentz, K.: A case study for modelling and design of distributed automation systems. In: Proceedings of IEEE/ASME Int. Conference on Advanced Intelligent Mechatronics (AIM) (2003)
21. Thramboulidis, K.: Model Integrated Mechatronics-Toward a New Paradigm in the Development of Manufacturing Systems. IEEE Transactions on Industrial Informatics 1(1), 54–61 (2005)
22. Sünder, C., Zoitl, A., Rainbauer, M., Favre-Bulle, B.: Hierarchical control modeling architecture for modular distributed automation systems. In: Proc. of the IEEE Int. Conf. on Industrial Informatics (INDIN'06) (2006)
23. Čengić, G., Ljungkrantz, O., Åkesson, K.: A Framework for Component Based Distributed Control Software Development Using IEC 61499. In: Proceedings of the IEEE Int. Conference on Emerging Technologies and Factory Automation (ETFA) (2006)
24. Vyatkin, V., Hanisch, H.-M.: A modeling approach for verification of IEC61499 function blocks using net condition/event systems. In: Proceedings of IEEE Int. Conference on Emerging Technologies and Factory Automation (ETFA'99), pp. 261–270 (1999)
25. Lüder, A., Schwab, C., Tangermann, M., Peschke, J.: Formal models for the verification of IEC 61499 function block based control applications. In: Proceedings of IEEE Int. Conference on Emerging Technologies in Factory Automation (ETFA'05), pp. 105–112 (2005)
26. Wurmus, H., Wagner, B.: IEC 61499 konforme Beschreibung verteilter Steuerungen mit Petri-Netzen, Fachtagung Verteilte Automatisierung (2000)
27. Schnakenbourg, C., Faure, J.-M., Lesage, J.-J.: Towards IEC 61499 function blocks diagrams verification. In: Proceedings of the IEEE International Conference on Systems, Man and Cybernetics, vol. 3 (2002)
28. Dubinin, V., Vyatkin, V., Hanisch, H.-M.: Modelling and Verification of IEC 61499 Applications using Prolog. In: Proceedings of IEEE Int. Conference on Emerging Technologies and Factory Automation (ETFA'06), pp. 774–781 (2006)
29. Vyatkin, V.: Execution Semantic of Function Blocks based on the Model of Net Condition/Event Systems. In: Proceedings of the IEEE Int. Conference on Industrial Informatics (INDIN'06), pp. 874–879 (2006)
30. Stanica, M.: Behavioral Modeling of IEC 61499 Control Applications, PhD report, Universite de Rennes (2005)
31. Khaligui, M., Rebeuf, X., Simonot-Lion, F.: A behavior model for IEC 61499 function blocks. In: Proceedings of the 3rd Workshop on Modelling of Objects, Components, and Agents, pp. 71–88 (2004)
32. Sünder, C., Rofner, R., Vyatkin, V., Favre-Bulle, B.: Formal description of an IEC 61499 runtime environment with real-time constraints. (accepted for). In: IEEE Int. Conference on Industrial Informatics (INDIN'07), Vienna, Austria (2007)
33. Zhang, X., Brennan, R.W., Xu, Y., Norrie, D.H.: Runtime Adaptability of a Concurrent Function Block Model for Real-Time Holonic Controller. In: IEEE Int. Conf. on Systems, Man, and Cybernetics (2001)
34. Olsen, S., Wang, J., Ramirez-Serrano, A., Brennan, R.W.: Contingenciesbased reconfiguration of distributed factory automation. Robotics and Computerintegrated Manufacturing 21 (2005)

35. Vyatkin, V.: The Potential Impact of the IEC 61499 Standard on the Progress of Distributed Intelligent Automation. International Journal of Manufacturing Technology and Management 8(1/2/3) (2006)
36. Sünder, C., et al.: Usability and Interoperability of IEC 61499 based distributed automation systems. In: Industrial Informatics, 2006 IEEE International Conference, pp. 31–37 (August 2006)
37. Kuppinger, S.: Die Schlüssel zur Effizienz, IEE Industrie Elektrik+Elektronik, 1 (2006)
38. Lewis, R.W.: Modeling control systems using IEC 61499. IEE Publishing (2001)Number ISBN: 0 85296 796 9.
39. Strasser, T., Müller, I., Zoitl, A., Sünder, C., Grabmair, G.: A Distributed Control Environment for Reconfigurable Manufacturing. In: 1st I*PROMS Virtual Conference on Intelligent Production Machines and Systems (2005)
40. Strasser, T., Müller, I., Schüpany, M., Ebenhofer, G., Mungenast, R., Sünder, C., Zoitl, A., Hummer, O., Thomas, S., Steininger, H.: An Advanced Engineering Environment for Distributed & Reconfigurable Industrial Automation & Control Systems based on IEC 61499. (appears) In: 2nd I*PROMS Virtual Conference on Intelligent Production Machines and Systems (2006)

Can Multi-Agents Wake Us from IC Design Productivity Nightmare?

Peter van Staa and Christian Sebeke

Robert Bosch GmbH
Peter.vanStaa@de.bosch.com, Christian.Sebeke@de.bosch.com

Abstract. Integrated Circuits (ICs) development fuels the whole semiconductor industry with ever complex designs. They are created in the microcosms of design teams, embedded in a demanding environment made up of customers, research, manufacturing, marketing and accounting. Best productivity wins in the market place, and therefore it is key to optimise the work that is left when the small deterministic part of it has been done. In this talk we will outline boundary conditions and external influences as well as specific characteristics of this world, and emphasise the particular challenges of automotive microelectronics. We will show how far our classic approaches regarding modelling and analysis go and highlight the potential for Multi-Agent Systems (MAS), to finally gain a common understanding and work out the prospective links.

The lion's share of the development work is creative space with levels of freedom that is not available for product solutions only. Unfortunately it is absorbed by activities to bridge the black design chasm that is torn open by growing complexity from price/performance/reliability pressure on the one side and insufficiency of design tools and design flow to cope with this on the other. As complexity grows, there is a need for new tools to manage and assess design flows, to select the right methodologies and stay at the leading edge. The choice of appropriate design flows for the product portfolio results in an increase of design efficiency and therefore is a key differentiator for competitiveness. To realise this, Multi-Agent approaches seem to be a viable way to go, but first we have to learn from each other and match needs and requirements with capabilities and methods.

At a first glance, today's design teams could be modelled by a MAS. Not that people look like popular movie MAS modelled creatures, but as a group of individuals that has learned to solve very complex tasks in a short timeframe. Room to manoeuvre is sparse, and manager's options to deliberately shift resources from one type of task to another, e.g. from analogue to digital design is hardly possible. Approaches to assess and predict productivity in semiconductor design have been explored in the past (e.g. with own tools and by Numetrics [1]), but these lack the option to work in detail on the variants of tool flow and methodology. Leaving it up to the design teams leads to local optimisations and point solutions, not necessarily applicable for several teams and inefficient to maintain. Consequences are lack of support, delays, budget overshoot and overall sub-optimal product solutions. Design process simulations may be possible, but from Monte-Carlo simulations in analog

V. Mařík, V. Vyatkin, A.W. Colombo (Eds.): HoloMAS 2007, LNAI 4659, pp. 15–16, 2007.
© Springer-Verlag Berlin Heidelberg 2007

design we have learned that trial and error approaches can be very time consuming and structured approaches are in high demand, available commercially only today in Electronic Design Automation (EDA) with very limited scope. Therefore, a simulation model for the design environment is required which allows for modulation of the design flow and comes with an optimisation strategy. The room for modulation will be very small initially, such that the simulation environment can simulate and replay a strictly bound design flow, as we have it today. In a second step, the proven to be good model shall get limited amounts of freedom for optimisation. Our vision is to realise this and drive towards a structured solution in either of two ways:

- Create a system that can search for the solution by itself (which may be a MAS-like approach)
- Create a system that works on sensitivities and gradients (based on Data Mining techniques) to structurally find a solution for the best methodology.

For automotive semiconductors the problem is even more a challenge due to a very specific variety of functional blocks for electrical, micromechanical and power electronic systems with highest demand for product quality and reliability. Design effort is not in the complexity of the product itself (simply represented by the number of components like in a microprocessor) but in the call for a heterogeneous, safe system.

Our current research in the frame of the BMBF project PRODUKTIV+[1] is driven by the need to assess and optimise the efficiency of semiconductor design process. We will show the current automotive design flow and our approach to analysis. For a more precise planning, we will describe advanced design project characteristics analysis results as well as simulation and optimisation, potentially with MAS, currently under development in PRODUKTIV+.

Reference

[1] Collett, R.: Benchmarking IC Development Capability – What to Measure? Fabless Forum. Fabless Semiconductor Association 11(2) (2004)

---

[1] PRODUKTIV+ (project label 01M3077) is partly funded by the German government.

From Intelligent Agents to Intelligent Beings

Paul Valckenaers, Hadeli Hadeli, Bart Saint Germain, Paul Verstraete,
Jan Van Belle, and Hendrik Van Brussel

K.U. Leuven, Department of Mechanical Engineering,
Celestijnenlaan 300 B, B-3001 Leuven, Belgium
Paul.Valckenaers@mech.kuleuven.be

Abstract. This paper puts forward a novel concept: *the intelligent being.* Intelligent agents emphasize action and decision-making, which is strongly reflected in the results of agent research. However, real-world applications require much more than decision-making and the intelligent being addresses a crucial part of this: reflecting reality into the agent world. Importantly, reflecting some part of reality offers significant benefits for software developers. Indeed, properly designed intelligent beings inherit the coherency and consistency of the corresponding reality. This allows the development of systems with unprecedented complexity and size. This paper discusses the novel concept and its implications for software development. Importantly, the intelligent agents themselves may be considered as part of the corresponding reality, resulting in short-term forecasting services.

1 Introduction

Nowadays, *intelligent agents, software agents, autonomous agents and multi-agent systems* designate a notable research domain [1]. In this domain, the decision-making capabilities of an agent are central. This is reflected in the linguistic roots of the word agent. Its Latin origin – agere – means *to act.* Likewise, in everyday English, an agent represents a person or an organization to act on his/her/its behalf. An agent mediates, negotiates, manages... Research results reflect this, emphasizing goal-oriented reasoning, game theory, negotiation protocols and alike.

However, real-world applications comprise much more than decision-making. This has prompted researchers to put forward *the environment in a multi-agent system* as a primary design concern. Failure to address this issue in the past causes important classes of valuable applications to escape today's mainstream agent technologies. Fortunately, ongoing research on multi-agent environments and architectures for multi-agent systems is addressing the issues [2]. Within mainstream agent research, ontology technologies address the static aspects only.

Yet, *addressing non-agent dimensions and aspects explicitly* merely begins answering the complexity issue: how to avoid and/or resolve conflicts in software design? Importantly, possible answers must address the integration of software that has been developed by different parties, at different times and locations. Often, software

V. Mařík, V. Vyatkin, A.W. Colombo (Eds.): HoloMAS 2007, LNAI 4659, pp. 17–26, 2007.
© Springer-Verlag Berlin Heidelberg 2007

components are developed by developers that are unaware of the actual applications in which they are later deployed.

Part of the answer, to be revealed below, is given by Shakespeare's most famous writing: "To be or not to be…" The Latin word *essere*, which translates in *to be*, precedes *agere* in a fundamental manner: to exist is a necessary precondition for being able to act. Today, much remains to be explored in software development regarding *essere*. I-Beings – intelligent beings – represent an unexplored research path.

2 I-Beings Prevail

A simple tale often communicates more effectively than intricate explanations. A renowned example is H. Simon's *parable of the two watchmakers*, illustrating why nontrivial systems in dynamic environments must be holonic [3]. The story in this paper recaps a conversation over the maritime radio waves between an intelligent agent and an intelligent being:

- *Intelligent being*: "Ship ahoy. This is CL273. You are on a collision course with us. Please change your heading immediately."
- *Intelligent agent*: "This is USS129. This is the United States Navy. You change your course."
- *Intelligent being*: "This is Canadian Lighthouse 273…"

Intelligent beings de-emphasize and try to avoid the decision-making issues and aspects. They emphasize existence; they are reflecting (some part of) reality. In conflicts, intelligent beings are sheltered by their corresponding reality. As long as the intelligent being reflects reality correctly, resolving conflicts needs to be performed elsewhere in the system. In many ways, maps used for navigation purposes are the best-known precursors of the software beings discussed in this paper.

The attractiveness of intelligent beings, as software components, over intelligent agents becomes clearer now. The reality, which is providing shelter, is always coherent and consistent itself – if not necessarily in a desirable state. This coherency and consistency is inherited by the intelligent beings. The resulting software can be significantly more sophisticated and elaborate, without causing conflicts or creating problems, because of this. Moreover, some key issues emerge:

- Is it possible to develop useful functionality if the intelligent beings are confined to functionality in which reality provides adequate shelter in case of conflicts? In the above story, a navy vessel clearly offers 'superior services' over a lighthouse.
- Which are the proper intelligent beings in a software development context? E.g. what's the intelligent being that is sheltered by the navy vessel?

3 Intelligent Beings

First of all, note that our ambition, as mere mortals, is to render existing beings intelligent, not to create the beings themselves. Intelligent beings are not some form of artificial existence; they add artificial intelligence to something that exists already.

Therefore, the creation of an I-being comprises the identification of the corresponding reality (the being) followed by the development and maintenance of the corresponding intelligence. This section starts with a discussion of the historic predecessor for software beings: maps. Subsequently, the discussion reveals the additional functionalities and services made possible by modern ICT relative to the paper and ink of conventional maps.

3.1 Historical Precursors of I-Beings: Maps

Intelligence mostly refers to the intellect, cleverness and brainpower. However, the word intelligence may also denote the gathering of information (as in Central Intelligence Agency). Maps add intelligence to some part of the world in the latter sense. Nonetheless, maps share a number of key properties with the software beings that are put forward by this paper:

- Maps correspond to some part of the real world. Depending on the kind of map, they reflect road infrastructures, the available depths in the water near the coast, the topology of a mountain range, the location of conduits in a sewage system, etc.
- Maps provide useful information (services, functionality) about the corresponding part of the real world. Maps serve a purpose and this is reflected in choices concerning the information that is (not) represented – e.g. level of detail – and in choices about the representation itself – e.g. the symbols. Nonetheless, most of the map is choice-free where reality already has determined what the map must be.
- The corresponding part of the real world is sufficiently stable (i.e. slow-changing). The map and, possibly, its supporting organization are able to track all relevant changes in the real world. A nautical navigation map typically will be updated annually – i.e. physically replaced by the humans involved – to account for shifting sands on the bottom of the sea. In contrast, route descriptions are easily invalidated by road construction activities.
- A map is robust relative to its correctness, usage/interpretation and completeness. Small errors do not render a map useless; a skilled navigator will spot the error and compensate. In contrast, a route description is like a chain in which a broken link easily causes the whole chain to become worthless. Likewise, when a map user makes a small mistake, the map assists in repairing the situation. Again, route descriptions provide no assistance short of some lucky coincidence. Furthermore, if a map does not exist for some section of the world or if it fails to provide relevant information, it suffices to add this; such extension activity does not invalidate what already exist and the required effort is unaffected by the existing map's size.
- Maps are conflict-free. Information can be missing, outdated, wrong, etc. and representations can be differing – e.g. color-codes versus dashed lines. But, there will be no conflicting choices embedded in maps relative to the real world. When multiple maps are available, any contradiction can be resolved by observing the corresponding reality. People are able to use multiple maps, retrieving information from the most convenient source. In contrast, traffic

rules can be conflicting and it is impossible to use them simultaneously or merge them without undoing embedded choices.

- Maps offer only interim solutions. Some centuries ago, the research community on navigation might have used a Paris-to-Rome benchmark to evaluate and rank scientific contribution and merit. Map technology did not fare well on this benchmark; its score would have to be "did not finish". There exist theoretical indications that "benefiting from the shelter offered by a stable part of reality" and "offering a final and complete solution to a problem" are inherently incompatible objectives [4].

Because maps reflect reality, they are amongst the most successful, complicated and feature-rich artifacts, created by men, that have no integration problems worth mentioning. This is the prime motivation to develop intelligent beings next to intelligent agents. Like maps, I-beings will be interim solutions only. They do not replace agents; they provide additional services that, among others, significantly augment internal agent components such as utility functions and world models.

Overall, maps constitute a good example of where I-beings are going. The main difference is the information technology that is available to build useful cyber-brains for suitable stable parts of reality. This is discussed below.

3.2 From Maps to Intelligent Beings

Modern information and communication technologies, software and hardware, offer significantly more opportunities to transform a "being" into an "intelligent being" than the paper, ink and printing press available to Mercator and his contemporary colleagues some centuries ago. This section discusses these novel opportunities and their implications.

The superior expressive power of ICT is a substantial plus. It permits reflecting reality without distortions if so desired. The deceiving pictures of world maps, e.g. exaggerating the surface near the artic, can be avoided without the inconvenience of a spherical medium. It supports aggregation, specialization, association, numerical expressions, symbolic manipulation, etc. In other words, the information that can be represented, the way it can be structured and the convenience offered to its users, jointly represent a quantum leap over old-fashioned map technologies.

In principle, this expressive power makes it easier to reflect reality in a choice-free manner. The corresponding reality is better able to provide shelter against future conflicts when it is more accurately reflected in the information. A precondition is of course to refrain from including services that require some inherent decision-making, which are to be left to associated intelligent agents. Indeed, the expressive power of ICT can be a temptation and impels numerous developers to include useful services violating this precondition.

ICT enables the intelligent being to provide novel services. Intelligent beings offer services beyond the presentation of simple information concerning their corresponding part of reality. For instance, virtually no real-world application has unlimited access to its world-of-interest (sensor data, user interaction). Intelligent beings may provide virtual sensors to compensate the lack of sensor data or to reduce the cost of sensing. E.g. an intelligent vehicle may compensate a momentary absence of the GPS signal by means of its odometer and route matching software.

ICT allows associating information in a networked fashion. This, for instance, allows capturing the design and usage history of an artifact. The intelligent being corresponding to a milling machine may provide (controlled) access to the user manual, the maintenance log, the CAD drawings, etc. Likewise, this I-being provides links to the other I-beings corresponding to its constituents (spindle, turning table, tool magazine), its neighbors (transport system delivering and fetching products on pallets), its environment (section of the factory infrastructure), its visitors (products on pallets on the turning table, repair men) and residents (tools in the magazine, operators). Furthermore, ICT may turn the intelligent being into an information storage location for other software entities (e.g. like a cyber version of the signposts on road crossings or a post-it note on an office desk) typically resulting in a stigmergic infrastructure. An exhaustive discussion of this aspect is out of the scope of this paper [2].

Sensing, tracking and tracing technologies enable automated updating and storage activities. Whereas sailors will annually update their maritime maps manually, intelligent beings may use sensors and communication services to estimate their state and log their history in real time. E.g. an intelligent windmill measures its rotation speed and output continually. It may also receive a suitable weather forecast to estimate the feasibility of near-future power production alternatives. Note that this intelligent being refrains from decision-making activities: it does not decide how much power will be produced within the available margins. In addition, the intelligent mill may log this information for analysis purposes and possibly for the updating of a self-model.

Tracking increases the collection of parts of reality providing suitable shelter tremendously. If the intelligent being is able to observe and track changes in the corresponding reality, and to adapt itself correspondingly, adequate shelter can be guaranteed in the face of such moderate dynamics. As a consequence, intelligent beings can be developed and maintained in much more situations than simple maps.

The creation and sustaining of holonic I-beings, corresponding to large and complex parts of reality, become feasible [3]. Suitable tracking allows the holonic I-being to adapt by replacing subsystems, mirroring the corresponding reality. Here, on-line, real-time and networked ICT makes a decisive contribution, enabling substantial scaling.

3.3 Mature Intelligent Beings

Today, research only commences to understand and discover what functionalities and services I-being technology may deliver. An initial sample list is discussed below.

An intelligent being supports management functionality. As a full-fledged citizen in cyber space, an intelligent being can be submitted to IT and IPR management. A suitably developed intelligent being accepts the prevailing rules as an input and helps to enforce them. This can be access control, authorization enforcement, inducing social norms, ratification compliance, containment inside an operational envelop, etc. Often, this happens in a suitable environment provided by an operating system, an electronic institution [4] and alike.

Importantly, the choices (rules) imposed to implement management functionalities are external to the intelligent being. These rules typically are stable but do not reflect a corresponding reality, only conventions. Importantly, such conventions fail to reflect a reality that guarantees consistency and coherency. In human society, rules and norms sometimes are occasionally violated for the right reasons. Hard-coding such rule enforcement in the intelligent beings will eventually destroy their shelter and is likely to immobilize software applications in extreme or novel situations. Indeed, the introduction of ICT frequently renders organizations more rigid and less responsive because current practice gets hard-coded into (legacy) software. Hence, a change of the management policy or of the norms imposed by an e-institution must not require any software maintenance to touch on the intelligent beings.

Agents can be made part of the corresponding reality. I-beings need agents to make choices for them; such nearby agents are part of their reality. Hence, an intelligent being may reflect the agent and especially its mental state. In the windmill example, the windmill agent decides about the settings determining the power output of the mill over time (within the available margins of course). Given a suitable weather forecast and a windmill agent's mental state determining control inputs to the equipment, the intelligent being, probably in cooperation with neighboring intelligent beings, will generate a short-term forecast of the expected behavior of the windmill. To generate this forecast, the intelligent being may need to present the intelligent agent with fictive virtual system states and solicit its response.

In this situation, the agent's mental states do not cause coherency or consistency problems. If the agents have mutually inconsistent states, the intelligent beings will render them consistent. This is analogous to what happens if two cars follow intersecting trajectories (i.e. a car crash resulting in two car wrecks). It is not the duty of intelligent being to compensate for poor agent performance; it is even strictly prohibited. Evidently, if the agent and I-beings cooperate to generate short-time forecasts, properly designed intelligent agents change their minds in time to avoid disaster.

Concerning stability, it is advisable to focus on reflecting the more stable aspects of an agent's mental state, or in other words, the serious commitments of the agent. Nonetheless, for the intelligent being it suffices to reflect how much commitment exist, not to enforce it. Evidently, the agent society may enforce commitments, through providing suitable rules to the I-beings, in the agents themselves or by combining both.

Interactions can be represented and reflected. In the natural world, masses interact through gravity, rays of light transfer energy from one location to another... In the cyber world of intelligent agents and intelligent beings, coordination fields can implement interactions [2], a delegate MAS can explore scenarios and make bookings at resources [6]. For obvious reasons, interactions propagate at more moderate speeds than nature's speed of light.

As an example, in a futuristic intelligent traffic system, a network of agents and I-beings may explore possible usage of a traffic infrastructure where agents reflect how users intend to travel and I-beings reflect what would happen. Thus, a near-future image of the implication of the current agent intentions is generated, in time for these agents to reconsider their intentions if indicated.

Importantly, the combination of reflecting agents as part of the corresponding reality and calculating what interactions will follow from their mental states (intentions) produces a short-term forecast accounting for internal system dynamics. Such system design is subject of ongoing research [6].

4 Developing Intelligent Beings

This section discusses what a development approach for I-Beings entails. Software development serves a purpose, i.e. user requirements. From these requirements, a development process guides the creation of software, which in this paper implements one or more intelligent beings. In addition, the shelter-providing reality triggers and guides the development of I-beings. Finally, this section addresses the issue whether and why intelligent beings and agents ought to be distinct software components.

4.1 From User Requirements to I-Being Requirements

Use cases and a business case. Modern software development methodologies do not require complete and correct specifications of the user requirements. They rightly recognize that user requirements change and that complete specifications necessitate too much effort to be viable. Instead, a concise business case situates and justifies the envisaged software development in more general terms. In addition, "use cases" provide specific scenarios that are points in a space of problems that the software needs to handle in its entirety. The software architecture and design approach ensures that the space surrounding and in between the use cases will be covered as well. It is the manner in which the use cases are addressed that ensures proper software functionality, not a meticulous elaboration of all-encompassing specifications.

Models of the problem domain are created in a subsequent software development activity. This activity elaborates models of the world-of-interest for the envisaged application. It refrains from modeling the software itself; the solution itself is absent in these models. Evidently, these problem domain models are relevant for the identification of the candidate intelligent beings; they record which parts of reality are involved in the software development effort.

As I-beings developers aim to avoid making choices in the world-of-interest, the problem domain models are solely used to identify range and scope. The range determines which part of the world provides the candidate beings that may become intelligent, both in space and time. The scope determines which aspects are relevant and which level of detail.

Overall, from the problem domain models, the software development team derives a set of candidate beings where the models specify which part of the world (e.g. a logistic distribution center with its visitors), the relevant aspects (e.g. the presence but not the color of a truck at a docking station), and the level of detail (e.g. weight in kilograms not milligrams).

Iterative development characterizes the subsequent core development activities in a state-of-the-art methodology. Typically, the process generates a series of executables, called constructs or builds. Intelligent beings are constructed as part of this process, and usually their construction is spread over multiple iterations.

Because of their decision-avoiding nature, intelligent beings are well suited for iterative development. Looking at their historical precursor, extending the (geographical) range of a map, adding new aspects (e.g. location of petrol stations, one-way streets), or increasing the level of detail rarely invalidates earlier efforts. Intelligent beings offer similar benefits, except when an iteration (especially increasing the level of detail) uncovers an embedded decision-making activity. This necessitates the elaboration of suitable agents (or user interfaces), thus outsourcing this activity from the perspective of the intelligent being.

Within the overall software development process, the development of intelligent beings is one of many activities. There will be a preference for intelligent beings over other software entities because the efforts spend on intelligent beings yield more durable results. In contrast, quick-and-dirty alternatives to intelligent beings deliver short-term results faster and cheaper. There exists however an alternative source from which the development of intelligent beings is triggered and guided. This is discussed below.

4.2 From Beings to I-Beings

The existence of valuable and stable artifacts (resources) is, next to user requirements, a second source for the development and maintenance of intelligent beings. User requirements are most likely to trigger the initial development. In contrast, numerous subsequent maintenance and enhancement activities are likely to be coordinated and triggered from the part of reality (and its stakeholders) that is reflected by the intelligent being.

For instance, intelligent milling machines or windmills are likely to be more valuable than their mindless competitors. Since, by definition, the intelligent being is able to serve in any situation where its counterpart (machine or mill) is present, the equipment vendors have access to the largest market for the corresponding software. Co-locating the brain with the body is therefore possible and logical. In contrast, decision-making intelligent agents have much more dispersed markets, and their development trigger is likely to remain with original business cases.

The development of an intelligent being also highlights that it belongs together with its counterpart in reality. Indeed, to ensure proper shelter, an intelligent being is essentially an implementation of a model of (the invariants of) its counterpart. The intelligent windmill knows its operating range, its power output in function of wind and control settings, etc. An advanced implementation is even able to coordinate with the (intelligent beings in the) grid to which it is connected and to determine what the resulting interactions and resulting behaviors will be.

In other words, whereas a normal software development process determines which intelligent beings may be useful, the actual and subsequent development of intelligent beings is driven by their corresponding part of reality and the available expert knowledge on this counterpart. The intelligent being captures the laws (of the artificial and nature) that govern the corresponding part of reality. As software benefits tremendously from maximizing its user mass, the stakeholders and owners of the counterpart in reality are the natural community to maintain and enhance an intelligent being.

4.3 Intelligent Agents, Electronic Institutions and Intelligent Beings

In nature (people, animals), intelligent agents are embedded and constitute a part of an intelligent being. However, in many application domains, successful manmade systems have a more modular design. Birds have integrated propulsion and lift devices (flapping wings). In aircraft, the engines (propulsion) and wings (lift) are separate subsystems. Such dissimilarity is quite common and reflects the difference in 'operating conditions' between the two domains. In particular, the modularity permits specialization and reuse in manmade systems.

For this reason, software designs benefit from an explicit separation into agents, beings and institutes. Intelligent agents address respectively application- and situation-specific choices (decision-making and action). Electronic institutes handle stable group choices (norms). Intelligent beings bring (reflect) the world-of-interest into the cyber world. Further environment entities complete the picture [2]. Each of these types of software entities faces radically different user communities, requirements, opportunities and time windows, calling for separate development and life cycle support.

Intelligent beings enjoy the shelter of a corresponding reality. Furthermore, in a holonic design, each individual I-being enjoys a comparatively long useful life. This warrants substantial investments in their software development and enhancement. The main challenge is the need for a multidisciplinary development team. Indeed, profound knowledge of the shelter-providing reality, in combination with software skills, is required. Today, this is lacking in virtually every application domain and naïve views on the world-of-interest prevail.

5 Conclusion

In mainstream agent research, a shared model of the real world is contained in an ontology, which captures only static and invariant aspects. In addition, agents may maintain a non-shared internal world model (their beliefs). This paper adds a novel entity to software systems: the intelligent being. Intelligent beings reflect the real world into the software world. They account for the dynamics in the real world (e.g. through sensors) and they are accessible to all (shared). Moreover, they constitute a 'normalized' world model, analogous to database normalization, in that information is only represented once.

The key advantage of intelligent beings is the shelter provided by reality, which these intelligent beings reflect. If properly designed, an intelligent being inherits the coherency and consistency of the real world. Moreover, holonic designs benefits from stable counterparts in reality, rendering their development economically viable.

In contrast to ontologies, intelligent beings are capable of interaction with each other, with the real world and with intelligent agents. In these interactions, they may account for properties of the real world and mental states (intentions, commitments) of the intelligent agents. In advanced designs, this results in a short-term forecasting capability. Similarly, intelligent being are able to implement, through interactions, advanced services such as virtual sensors and restriction to safe states/trajectories for real-world systems. In some way, these interactions are the artificial counterpart of physical interactions (e.g. colliding masses) in the real world: they reflect facts and/or their implications.

Finally, there exist undeniable reasons to develop and maintain intelligent beings and intelligent agents separately. Indeed, whereas in nature intelligent agents and beings are embodied in single entities (animals, humans), the artificial counterparts are able to exist as separate entities, thus benefiting from decoupled user groups, life cycles, etc. This distinction – artificial systems being more modular – is quite commonly observed (birds versus airplanes, fish versus ships).

Overall, this paper puts forward a novel software artifact, which is a modern generalization of maps. As with maps, the intelligent being is unable to deliver end-user functionality but delivers a valuable contribution nonetheless. Intelligent beings are able to create an infrastructure on which intelligent agents may deliver end-user solutions. And, the potential of intelligent beings concerning the complexity, size, durability of the infrastructure, which they may deliver, is obviously out-of-reach for regular agent technologies.

Acknowledgements

This paper presents work funded by the Research Council of the K.U. Leuven – Concerted Research Action on Autonomic Computing in Decentralized Production Systems.

References

1. WWW.AgentLink.org
2. Valckenaers, P., Sauter, J., Sierra, C., Rodriguez, J.: Applications and environments for multi-agent systems. Journal of Autonomous Agents and Multi-Agent Systems 14(1), 61–85 (2007)
3. Simon, H.A.: The Sciences of the Artificial. MIT Press, Cambridge Mass (1990)
4. Valckenaers, P., Van Brussel, H., Hadeli, Bochmann, O., Saint Germain, B., Zamfirescu, C.: On the design of emergent systems: an investigation of integration and interoperability issues. Engineering Applications of Artificial Intelligence 16, 377–393 (2003)
5. Noriega, P., Sierra, C.: Electronic institutions: Future trends and challenges. In: Klusch, M., Ossowski, S., Shehory, O.M. (eds.) CIA 2002. LNCS (LNAI), vol. 2446. Springer, Heidelberg (2002)
6. Valckenaers, P., Hadeli, Saint Germain, B., Verstraete, P., Van Brussel, H.: Emergent short-term forecasting through ant colony engineering in coordination and control. Advanced Engineering Informatics 20, 261–278 (2006)

Multi-agent Reflection in Autonomic Systems

Jan Tožička[1], Michal Pěchouček[1], Martin Rehák[2], and Magdalena Prokopová[1]

[1] Gerstner Laboratory
[2] Center for Applied Cybernetics
Department of Cybernetics, Czech Technical University
Technická 2, Prague, 166 27, Czech Republic
{tozicka,pechouc,rehakm1,prokopova}@labe.felk.cvut.cz

Abstract. Increasing complexity and scales of computing systems bring growing demands on their designers and administrators. These issues have been explored from different viewpoints. While the multi-agent system researchers focus on the coordination and theoretic properties of distributed system, the researchers from the field of autonomic computing focus on the deployment of self-adapting systems in real domains. This contribution tries to bring together both domains and presents the multi-agent reflection from the autonomic computing point of view.

We show that proposed architecture of reflective agent covers all the characteristics of an autonomic computing system and furthermore, we describe some properties of reflective agents that can further extend the autonomic computing system, especially its self-optimizing abilities. All the characteristics of autonomic computing system are demonstrated on three use cases, where the reflective agents have been deployed, together with the results of experiments.

1 Introduction

Besides *proactiveness*, *reactivity* and *social capability*, the key property of intelligent agents, members of multi-agent communities, is their decision making *autonomy* [1]. Agents can autonomously initiate actions that are based not only on the impulses from the environment (and other agents) but also on the agents internal metal models (such believes, goals, intentions, commitments, coalition memberships etc.) [2]. An important aspect of agents' autonomy is the fact that the agent's decision making process does not need to be transparent to other agents. Thus, it is difficult to predict behavior of the other agents.

In this article, we intend to discuss yet another important aspect of intelligent software agent - *reflectivity*. Multi-agent reflection provides agents with an ability to observe and understand their behavior, to reason about their behavior and revise the behavior accordingly, so that e.g. unexpected situations can be handled efficiently. We will focus on the relation between the agent reflectivity and autonomic computing.

In this section we will introduce the principles of multi-agent reflection. Then we will describe our architecture of reflective/cognitive (RC) agent in second section. In Section 3 we show how the RC agents correspond to autonomic system and show how they extend the features of autonomic system in next section. In the end of this article we present results of several experiments demonstrating autonomic features of RC agents.

V. Mařík, V. Vyatkin, A.W. Colombo (Eds.): HoloMAS 2007, LNAI 4659, pp. 27–36, 2007.

1.1 Multi-agent Reflection

In our research, we will refer to the term **reflection**, similarly to the common meaning used in computer science ([3], [4]), as a very specific quality of any computational system. A reflective system is capable of acquiring knowledge about its computational state, data and execution processes. Such data can be used in order to built a model of its own computation that can be further used to change the process of its own computation.

Reflective computation is made of three rather complicated reasoning processes: (i) acquiring relevant data about computation, (ii) creating a symbolic model of the computational model and (iii) revising the computational process. Standard way of referring to these process used in present-day literature is introspective integrity for the former process, introspective force for the latter and building the symbolic model is referred to as meta-reasoning. Similarly to [4], we understand reflection not only in the sense of agent's self-awareness and collective mutual awareness, but also as a capability to reason about and to act as a result of this awareness.

A multi-agent reflection can be observed from different points of view - as a single agent capability or as a feature of whole community of agents. This is why we distinguish between three different types of reflection in multi-agent systems. We may have a very *individual agent* that does no or very little social reasoning. Such agent manipulates its own internal knowledge structures by means of internal reasoning mechanisms.

More sophisticated agents – *social agents* – carry out social reasoning for which they need a collection of the information about other agents (mutual awareness). This knowledge structure is referred to as agent's **acquaintance model** and is a part of the agent's interaction wrapper (built-in interface between the agent's reasoning core and the reminder of the multi-agent community). Different types of reflection in multi-agent system change different knowledge or reasoning components of the individual agents. We distinguish between: *individual reflection, mutual reflection* and *collective reflection*.

Individual reflection is a revision of agents' isolated behavior that does not necessarily need to result from agents' mutual interaction. Process of individual reflection takes into account agent's awareness of its own knowledge, resources, and computational capacity.

Mutual reflection is a revision of agent's interaction with another agent. This revision is based on agent's knowledge about the other agent, trust and reputation, knowledge about the other agent's available resources and possibly opponent's (or collaborator) long term motivations and intentions. All these kinds of knowledge are referred to as *social knowledge* and are stored in agents' acquaintance models.

Collective reflection is a revision of agents' collective interaction. This is the most complex kind of reflection. Collective behavior of the group of agents is revised as a result of their complex interaction. Collective reflection can be achieved either by: (i) a **single reflective agent** (e.g. a meta-agent) that is responsible for monitoring the community behavior and updating agents' behavior or (ii) **emergently** by collective of agents, each carrying out its specific cognitive/reflective reasoning. In the collective reflection the agents update not only their social knowledge bases and reasoning processes, but also they make attempts to revise other agents acquaintance models and possibly reasoning (unlike in the case of mutual reflection).

1.2 Distributed Reflective Systems

We will concentrate on the notion of autonomous adaptation using the reflection process described above, as this notion is critical for future open ubiquitous (pervasive, ambient) ad-hoc systems. Once we deploy the diverse elements of these systems, they must be able to integrate themselves into the functional organism and to maintain themselves operational even in a long-term perspective. Autonomous adaptation to the changing environment is critical, as it will significantly increase the usability of ubiquitous systems by (i) extending the system lifespan by increasing collaboration efficiency, (ii) extending the average lifespan as system will remain operational even after significant environmental or device changes, (iii) limiting or minimizing the human maintenance operations, (iv) enabling an easy extension of system functionality using the collective reflection process or (v) facilitating the transfer of the knowledge from the existing system into the new one during the replacement phase.

While we have specifically addressed the embedded, highly distributed multi-agent systems in the overview above, most points apply to all types of multi-agent systems.

2   RC Architecture

In a layered structure of the Reflective-Cognitive (RC) agent, the common agent architecture forms the lower half of the new structure – the *Reasoning Layer*. On the top of this layer, we add the *Reflective-Cognitive Layer*, that includes cognition, meta-reasoning and reflective capability. The whole structure is shown in Figure 1. *Reasoning Layer* handles general agent operation – it performs agent-specific actions (interaction

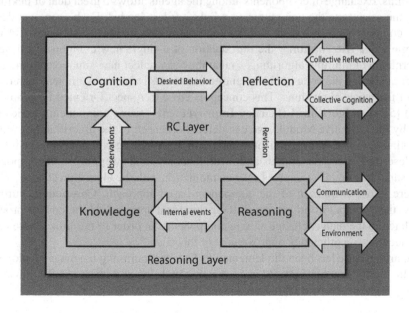

Fig. 1. Reflective-Cognitive abstract architecture

with agent-specific technical resources, environment sensing), social interactions and finally planning and resource management. The *RC Layer* uses two main modules to implement the reflective behavior – *Cognitive Module* that maintains the model of the agent in its environment and identifies the possible improvements, and a *Reflective Module* that performs the modifications in the Reasoning Layer's data changing the data structures and the code to implement these improvements.

One of the goals of the architecture is to introduce a new approach to implementing agent's algorithms. The algorithms, which were previously forming one big block, are shattered into smaller parts we refer to as *components*. The code splitting of the algorithm is done with respect to component's functionality (and reuse) or with respect to the data flow in the whole algorithm. Each component is a self contained java class. Properly chained components form an algorithm which we call a *plan, algorithm or sequence*. To build the plan, Reflective Layer uses the components as *black boxes* described by their inputs, outputs and meta-data. Plans can be triggered by an external or internal event and they implements agent's reaction to the event.

Let us summarize advantages and disadvantages of component approach to algorithm sharing and decomposition.

Advantages of component approach are as follows. (i) **Programme Code Sharing** – the code which is shared across several algorithm can be concentrated in a single component which can be instantiated only once. This saves an important amount of memory and processing time. (ii) **Programme Code Assembly** – using components to assembly algorithm gives us a great portion of freedom when trying to adjust the algorithm to the current state of the environment. Building blocks in the form of components are easy to understand and to manipulate. (iii) **Programme Code Exchange** – smaller portions of the code in the form of components are easier to exchange among agents than complex algorithms. Exchange of components among the agents allows a great deal of flexibility and at the same time the communication links are less loaded. Each agent can decide which components to integrate and combine them with its local code-base. (iv) **Programme Code Alternation** – the introduction of a single new component can result in alternation of multiple algorithms so that they can reflect new situations in the environment. Altering the code on the level of components is far more efficient than on the level of the whole algorithms. This concept is close to Aspect Oriented Programming (AOP) [5]. (v) **Algorithm Efficiency Improvement** – using component metrics provided by the Cognitive Module, we can detect bottleneck of the algorithm and initiate a negotiation to find more efficient substitution. Considering component to be a black box (described by inputs, outputs and meta-data only) and swapping with components of the same functionality, enables easy manipulation with the algorithm code.

There is one *drawback* of the component-based approach. **Component running costs** – the principal disadvantage of the component approach is the cost of processing related to the data exchange among components. In order to minimize these costs, we concentrate on efficiency improvement of this code.

The architecture has been implemented in Java programming language, deployed in $\mathcal{A}$-**globe** multi-agent platform [6] and evaluated in different domains [7][8]. Several of the most relevant results are presented in the Section 5.

3   Autonomic Systems and Reflective Agents

In this section we will show how reflective agents fulfill eight basics characterizes of autonomic system [9].

Self-Monitoring. An autonomic computing system is aware of its state, its behavior and its performance. "It knows itself."

RC Agent: The cognition module is responsible for the monitoring of agent's behavior and performance in the RC agent architecture. Moreover it is responsible for weakness and failures detection. Detected problems together with the high-level description of desired state are sent to the reflective layer that takes appropriate action. This process is part of all other characteristics and therefore we will omit example for this case.

Self-Configuration. An autonomic computing system is able to configure and reconfigure itself to fit changing and unpredictable conditions.

RC Agent: Reasoning layer responsible for performing all agent operations is empty when the agent starts. It is populated by components on first call of the reflective process according to the local conditions. If there is a need reflective process can switch components to reflect changes in the environment or it can also create a new component.

Self-Optimization. An autonomic computing system detects its non-optimal behavior and improves it.

RC Agent: Reflective process can change agent's components to perform better using newly acquired knowledge about the environment or resources. An example of this implementation is described in the Section 5.

Self-Healing. An autonomic computing system detects its malfunctional parts and re-configures them to keep the entire system functional.

RC Agent: Cognition module monitors the execution of components and if any of them fails (i.e. throws an exception) the component can be restarted or even removed from the system if the failure persists. The cognition also observes behavior of the entire agent and if the agent does not perform well the components are changed in similar way as during the changes in the environment.

Self-Protection. An autonomic computing system protects its resources from both the internal and the external attacks. It also maintain overall system security and integrity.

RC Agent: In addition to common components necessary for agent's functionality reflective agent can use other components to protect these primary components. Even the system as a whole can be the part of protection by filtering the incoming data.

Context Awareness. An autonomic computing system is aware of its environment and is able to interact with other entities in the environment to perform global optimization.

RC Agent: Known component can be offered to other agents so that they can integrate it into their reasoning layers. In several cases some problems may arise: (i) component contains some private (e.g. patent protected) knowledge, (ii) component functionality is directly connected to some piece of hardware, (iii) targeted agents has not sufficient resources (memory, CPU) to deploy this component. In this cases, RC agent can decide to provide the component as a service accessible to other agents. Using our framework, each component can be used as a service in a transparent way.

Openness. An autonomic computing system can work in heterogeneous environment and therefore has to be build on open standards and protocols.

RC Agent: The multi-agent system naturally allows heterogeneous agents to live and cooperate together. All agents use FIPA [10] interaction protocols for the communication and the messages are exchanged in the XML format. Moreover, components are exchanged between agents as a java source code and therefore agents running on different hardware platforms can use them. The $\mathcal{A}$-**globe** multi-agent platform allows agents also to migrate from one computer to another. This migration is fully supported by the reflective architecture and each agent can completely change its behavior to adapt to local conditions especially local computational resources.

Anticipation. An autonomic computing system anticipates possible extensions of its behavior and searches for these extensions proactively.

RC Agent: RC agents can exchange components and proactively look for components with desired characteristics. Generally these agents can describe component functionality using its inputs (data driven agents), outputs (goal oriented agent) and eventually also describing desired properties (e.g. component with low computational requirements, or non-communicating component. For more detailed description of negotiation about components see [11]. The same can be said about the self-optimization case since acquired components can be included into the agent reasoning process.

4   Extra Features of Reflective Agents

In this section we will describe what are the additional properties of reflective agents that can be, in our opinion, useful for autonomic systems. We will focus mainly on distributed autonomic systems.

4.1   Collective Reflection

As described above, RC agents are aware of their environment and of other agents. In addition they can negotiate about the adaptation process to improve the quality of the system as a whole. Well known problem of finding some locally optimal state can arise when each agent tries to maximize the quality of the system on its own. Agents can get trapped in local optimum (e.g. Nash equilibrum). This can happen in the case when agents try to achieve different goals (e.g. optimizing different properties of the system) or have different knowledge which is typical for distributed systems.

4.2 Collective Learning

System that is aware of its environment can profit from mining more general knowledge from previous observations. This knowledge can be used for prediction of future states of the environment and thus for the optimization. In addition to the cooperation on achieving globally optimal behavior of the system, agents can collaborate also in searching these generally true properties. This behavior is addressed by multi-agent learning. The agents can exchange knowledge on different levels of abstraction: from observations to created models or meta-knowledge describing the learning process. For this purpose we have designed the multi-agent learning framework MALEF [12].

5   Use Cases, Experiments

In this section we will illustrate the use of the RC agents on three use cases. They will demonstrate the implementation of described autonomic system characteristics while focusing on the value brought by reflective agents.

5.1 Adaptation to Unknown Situations

In this case, the system has to adapt to the situation that has not been known in the design time. The agents fulfilling given tasks know only that if the task fails it should be caused by some state of the environment or observable events in the history. RC agent tries to predict these situations and tries to avoid them. We use ILP machine learning method [13] to find relational dependencies between the failures and observations. Created model is then used for evaluation of risk of possible future failures. This model is created in the form of Prolog program and it is perfectly adapted to actual environment. Unlike common learning agents, RC agent creates a component with predictive abilities and incorporate it into its reasoning layer that can be designed without any learning ability. Such a component can be offered to other agents in the same way as any other component.

Experimental results of this case are shown on the Graph 2. We can see that tasks start to fail as soon as the conditions for failures have been added to the system. When the adaptation have been allowed the agents create new components predicting and avoiding risky situations and the number of failures decrease while the time needed for task completion slightly grows. This experiment have been performed in the logistic simulation scenario A-cross where we have also explored the cooperation between heterogeneous group of adapting agents [7].

5.2 Adaptation to Changing Environment and Resources

As stated above, the adaptation to changing environment and available resources is one of the key properties of both the autonomic system and the reflective agents. In

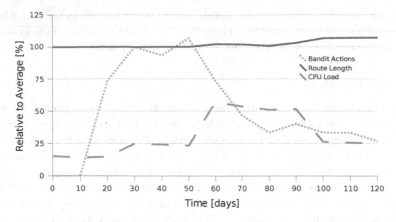

Fig. 2. In the simulation time 20 we have changed the environment in such manner that some tasks can fail. In time 50 we have allowed agents to use ILP system to create new component that predicts such failures and helps agents to avoid them. We can see that adapted agents decrease the number of failures while the quality of service measured in task accomplishment time slightly grows. Dash line shows increased CPU consumption during both the adaptation process and the better task performing.

this experiment, we want to demonstrate how the reflective process can help the RC agent to decrease its CPU consumption on system with limited computational resources. We have created a scenario which changes dramatically CPU consumption during runtime. At the beginning there is very limited number of contracts and the agents have to compete for them. Agents with low CPU resources cannot use components that are very CPU resource-consuming. An example of such a component is task price evaluation from the simulation described in the previous case. The price requires agent's awareness of the competitors as well as the number of available tasks because they compete for these tasks in auction. The price is composed of fixed expenses and adjustable margin. Then the margin can be adjusted to beat other offers while maximize agent's profit. If the agents on slow machines would use too sophisticated evaluation, they would block the whole CPU and would not be able to finish their tasks in required time. Therefore, in such a case, it is better for them to use simpler evaluation instead.

During the experiment we have changed the number of running agents as well. At simulation cycle 60 we have dramatically increased the number of task providers. This caused that the environment becomes less competitive and the agent can increase their prices without the lost of contracts.

We have compared agents running on the systems with limited computational resources with the ones running on the system with enough resources. All agents start with the same margin set up to 1.3.

Form the results illustrated on the Figure 3 we can see the trend in margins during the simulation. This graph illustrates that the agent can decrease its margin in very competitive scenario while in the less competitive scenario it is able to raise it again. As we can see in Figure 3, in both very or little competitive environments the RC agent with *Margin Updater* has higher profit than its competitors.

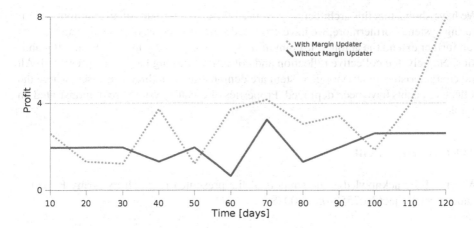

Fig. 3. Comparison of margins and profits of RC agent with sufficient computational resources to update its margins and an agent without needed resources. The environment changed significantly to be less competitive in the simulation cycle 60. We can see that the reflective agent having enough resources (i.e. able to use *Margin Updater*) is able to well adapt to the changes while the agent running on slow machine turned off the *Margin Updater* component to have at least some profit.

5.3 Self-protecting Network

We have deployed reflective agents to network elements (such as switches and routers) to implement the intrusion protection, namely against the network worms. The primary task of these network elements is naturally to operate the traffic. To the components taking care about the traffic, we have added components that can identify possible attacks and filter out the suspicious one. The filters are obviously created and deployed without the human intervention. The agents negotiate about the distribution of these filters to maximize the network security while taking into account limited computational and communication resources.

As the agents negotiate with other agents they can find out that the protection component is already deployed on the adjoining node. In such a case, the RC agent can decide to forward the traffic through this node instead of deploying the filter itself. This feature of delegation, that is novel in the network protection, will be used in the cases where the agent has not sufficient resources to deploy all the filters that are necessary to protect the network, while the protection of the network is much more important than small decrease of the network throughput.

6   Conclusions

Self-aware and self-adapting system design is important topic in both the reflective multi-agent system and autonomic computing system research fields. In this contribution we have presented reflective systems and an abstract architecture of reflective agent.

We have shown that this architecture covers all the characteristics of an autonomic computing system. Furthermore, we have proposed some properties of reflective agents that can further extend the autonomic computing system, especially its self-optimizing abilities. Namely, the collective reflection and collective learning have been presented. All the characteristics of autonomic system are demonstrated on three use cases, where the reflective agents have been deployed. Properties of created system are demonstrated on graphs.

Acknowledgement

We gratefully acknowledge the support of the presented research by Army Research Laboratory project N62558-05-C-0028.

References

1. Wooldridge, M., Jennings, N.R., Kinny, D.: The gaia methodology for agent-oriented analysis and design. Autonomous Agents and Multi-Agent Systems 3(3), 285–312 (2000)
2. Rao, A.S., Georgeff, M.P.: BDI-agents: from theory to practice. In: Proceedings of the First Int. Conference on Multiagent Systems, San Francisco (1995)
3. Maes, P.: Computational reflection. Technical report 87-2, Free University of Brussels, AI Lab (1987)
4. Smith, B.: Reflection and semantics in lisp. In: Proc. 11th ACM Symposium on Principles of Logic Programming, Salt Like City, Utah, Also Xerox PARC Intelligent Systems Laboratory (1984)
5. Elrad, T., Filman, R.E., Bader, A.: Aspect-oriented programming: Introduction. Commun. ACM 44(10), 29–32 (2001)
6. A-Globe: A-Globe Agent Platform (2006),
   http://agents.felk.cvut.cz/aglobe
7. Tožička, J., Jakob, M., Pěchouček, M.: Market-inspired approach to collaborative learning. In: Klusch, M., Rovatsos, M., Payne, T.R. (eds.) CIA 2006. LNCS (LNAI), vol. 4149, pp. 213–227. Springer, Heidelberg (2006)
8. Rehák, M., Pěchouček, M., Prokopová, M., Foltýn, L., Tožička, J.: Autonomous protection mechanism for joint networks in coalition operations. In: Knowledge Systems for Coalition Operations 2007, CTU, Prague 2007 (accepted to be published)
9. Autonomic computing: IBM's perspective on the state of information technology (2007),
   http://researchweb.watson.ibm.com/autonomic/
10. FIPA: Foundation for intelligent physical agents (2004), http://www.fipa.org
11. Foltýn, L., Tožička, J., Pěchouček, M., Jisl, P., Szabó, R., Rollo, M., Rehák, M.: Collective adaptation of reflective agents. In: Proceedings of Engineering Societies in the Agents World VII, Doublin, 2006. LNAI, Springer-Verlag, Heidelberg 2007 (Accepted to be published)
12. Tožička, J., Rovatsos, M., Pěchouček, M.: A framework for agent-based distributed machine learning and data mining. In: Autonomous Agents and Multi-Agent Systems (AAMAS 2007). ACM Press, New York 2007 (Accepted to be published).
13. Muggleton, S., Raedt, L.D.: Inductive logic programming: Theory and methods. Journal of Logic Programming 19/20, 629–679 (1994)

Auctions with Arbitrary Deals

Tamás Máhr[1,2] and Mathijs de Weerdt[2]

[1] Almende BV, Westerstraat 50, 3016DJ Rotterdam, The Netherlands
[2] Delft University of Technology, Electrical Engineering, Mathematics and Computer Science, PO Box 5031, 2600GA Delft, The Netherlands
tamas@almende.com,
M.M.deWeerdt@ewi.tudelft.nl

Abstract. To come to a deal, a bargaining process can sometimes take a long time. An auction may be a faster, but existing auction models cannot cope with situations where money is not an issue, or where it is difficult to express the utility of all participants in a monetary domain.

We propose a modified Vickrey auction based only on preferences over the possible bids. This approach also allows for situations where a bid is not just a price or some fixed set of attributes, but can be any possible offer. We prove that in this flexible, generalized setting, the Vickrey mechanism is still incentive compatible and results in a Pareto-efficient solution.

1 Introduction

In some trading situations, the discussion about a deal does not concern the price, but only other qualitative attributes. The price may be fixed, or money might not play an important role. A common approach is to map all such attributes to a cost value, leading to direct relation between these attributes and price. However, it can be difficult to express qualitative attributes in price. For example, a preference for a certain color, or for a certain befriended relation can be difficult to formulate as a price. In such situations, one may try to use a negotiation technique to find the right attribute values, but negotiation methods tend to take a long time [1]. Auctions can be more efficient (especially one-shot auctions) [2][3], but they rely on utility functions. The main contribution of this paper is a model and some auction protocols for which utilities do not need to be expressed in money anymore; only a preference order is required.

To illustrate the basic ideas behind the model and the mechanisms, we use an example where a travel agency specializes in the organization of corporate day-trips. Corporate day-trips are team-building events, where employees of a company engage in some group activities of leisure. The kind of activity actually chosen depends on, among others, the type of people, their number, and on the budget. In our example, the budget is fixed, and the travel agency has to provide the best choice of activity for that given amount. Suppose there is a company of approximately 40 persons, but not all of them can participate on the same day. The two most popular days are a Tuesday (with 30 people) and a

V. Mařík, V. Vyatkin, A.W. Colombo (Eds.): HoloMAS 2007, LNAI 4659, pp. 37–46, 2007.

Wednesday (with 35 people). Unfortunately, the preference over the activities of choice is different in the two groups. The people who are available on Tuesday prefer indoor skiing, while those available on Wednesday, being of older age, would rather visit a museum. The company wishes to take as many employees as possible to the day-trip, so there is a slight preference towards the museum visit on Wednesday.

One could try to model this case as a negotiation scenario, or alternatively as a multi-attribute auction, where the attributes cover all possible dimensions of a deal [4][5]. In the latter setting, the attributes in our case would be the type of activity, the number of participants, the date, and whether an additional lunch is included or not. The company should provide an evaluation function that expresses the value of a certain bid in money. Day-trip service providers would then submit bids in the predefined format of higher and higher value. Given the fixed budget, the combination that has the highest value would be selected in the end. If the company decides to follow the Vickrey auction protocol [6], then the competing day-trip service providers should submit one closed bid, of which the one with a higher value is selected as winner. The service provider submitting the winner bid can then provide the day-trip service, and the value of the provided service should be equal to the highest non-winning bid. This allows the winner to choose a combination of attribute values that maximizes his utility. In such traditional approaches, like at Parkes and Kalagnanam [7], the utility of the winner bidder and the buyer is supposed to be opposing in all attributes. The buyer should want higher quality and lower price, while the service provider prefers to sell low quality for high price. In reality, however, the preferences may have a more complex relation: sometimes opposing, sometimes being the same. Moreover, since the attributes have to cover all possible offers, it might very well be, that certain attributes are meaningless for the winner (for example he can never offer additional lunch).

The model we introduce in this paper generalizes the traditional multi-attribute auctioning model in two ways. It does not assume that the bidders and the auctioneer have fully opposing preferences, and it does not require that all bids have the same dimensions. These changes make modeling of some real-world cases possible (and others easier), while certain properties of the original model and mechanisms stay valid.

In Section 2 we will introduce our model as a generalization of the traditional auctioning model. This is exemplified by showing how the preferences of the company and the tour operators can be represented. Then the applications of different auction protocols to this model are discussed (Section 3), along with the decisions made by the service providers and the company in the example. Section 4 analyzes the Vickrey mechanism, and proves that the most elementary properties of a Vickrey mechanism still hold in our general model. Advantages, disadvantages and consequences of the proposed model are discussed in Section 4, related work can be found in Section 5, and concluding remarks in Section 6.

2   Model

Let us consider the situation where an auctioneer sells a certain item. Each bidder has a set of possible *bids* he can offer to the auctioneer. Let β be the set of all possible bids and $\beta_i \subseteq \beta$ be the subset of bids that bidder i can offer. In the process of setting the deal, each bidder i sends bids to the auctioneer from β_i. In the general model presented in this section, a bid is not necessarily a price, but can be any description of a possible deal. The auctioneer prefers some of the offered bids over others, and he uses his preferences to select the winning bid.

A bid $(b \in \beta)$ may consist of simply the price, in which case the payment of the winner depends on the set of submitted bids. In a more complex case, when bids consist of multiple attributes, it is common to assume a valuation function that can convert a combination of attribute values to a price. The payment is then again dependent on the value of the other submitted bids. This valuation function plays a central role in the different auction models: it converts the bids to money.

In contrast to this traditional auction model [2], we suggest to generalize the selecting the "payment" to selecting a bid. The consequence of this change is that there is no need to have a valuation function to express the values in money. It is possible to select one of the bids as a contract even without assigning a monetary value to it. We show that the same selection rules can be used as in the original algorithms.

In the traditional model, utility functions of the players use the valuation function to express the utility in money: $U(p) = V - p$, where V is the valuation of the good, and p is the price. In a multi-attribute case, it is $U(a_1, \ldots, a_n, p) = V(a_1, \ldots, a_n) - p$, where $a_1, \ldots, a_n$ are the attributes and p is the price. In our model, the utility function expresses a total *order* over the possible bids and by that over the bids for any participant. Such preference orders make the distinction between more and less preferred bids just as the traditional utility functions do. But in this case, the bid is not expressed in money to make this comparison, allowing us to hold an auction without any money involved. The utility function can be defined as a mapping from bids to integer numbers: $U : \beta \to \mathbb{Z}$. Such a function expresses a preference order as follows: for any two bids c_1, c_2, $c_1 \preceq c_2$ if and only if $U(c_1) \leq U(c_2)$.

A bid in the simplest form contains only the price of a well-defined good or service. Alternatively, a bid may define multiple attributes of a deal, for example the multiple attributes of the good on auction, plus the price. From the most abstract point of view a bid defines everything both parties have to deliver to fulfill the deal. In principle, price is simply one of the attributes of the deal, not even indispensable as existing auction models may let us think. The utility function as we defined it is indifferent of the actual form of the bid. As a consequence, the submitted bids may consist of different attributes.

Even though the structure of the possible bids may be different, the preference orders induced by the utility functions put the bids in a well-defined order (per agent). It is also possible that some bids are equally preferred, thus the utility function assigns the same integer value to different bids. We call such a set of equivalent bids an *equivalence class*. Especially in a multi-attribute setting where some attributes have a continuous domain, there are often infinitely many of such equivalent classes, having often infinitely many members. Consequently, given a utility value, the bid is not uniquely determined.

In the price-only case a utility value of zero means that the bidder (or the auctioneer) neither gains nor loses on the deal. The price level that makes the utility to be zero is called the *private value*. Analogously, we define our utility function to be zero for bids that are indifferent for the player (either a bidder or the auctioneer), positive for bids that are desired by the player, and negative for bids that he will never agree to. The class of bids that belong to utility zero we call the *private class*.

In the corporate-day-trip example, we assume two competing day-trip-service providers: *bidder₁* and *bidder₂*. Our company asks the travel agency (the *auctioneer*) to find the best option given the preferences. The bidders have different contracts to offer. *Bidder₁* has good connections to an indoor-ski facility. He can offer the indoor skiing activity any day for any number of persons, and due to the good business relations he can also offer lunch at the skiing facility. In terms of museum, he can only offer the standard museum visit activity without lunch. *Bidder₂* is in a similar situation, except that he has a good connection to museums, so he can offer the museum visit in connection to lunch, while the skiing stays without lunch. Unfortunately, the museum restaurant has booked a lot of guests for Wednesday already, therefore on that day only 30 persons are accepted. The possible contracts of *bidder₁* and *bidder₂* are listed in Table 1 in separate tables in decreasing order of preference. Just as the preference order of the auctioneer, which, however, contains all possible bids. The auctioneer, on behalf of the company, prefers skiing on Tuesday, museum on Wednesday, having

Table 1. Preference orders of the bidders and the auctioneer over the possible contracts in decreasing order. Equivalence classes are grouped by the same shade of gray.

$Bidder_1$	activity	# people	date
b_6^1	ski	30	any
b_5^1	ski	35	any
b_4^1	museum	30	any
b_3^1	ski + lunch	30	any
b_2^1	museum	35	any
b_1^1	ski + lunch	35	any

Auctioneer	activity	# people	date
b_2^1	museum	35	any
b_1^1	ski + lunch	35	any
b_3^1	ski + lunch	30	any
b_5^1	ski	35	any
b_2^2	ski	35	Tuesday
b_6^1	ski	30	any
b_4^2	ski	30	any
b_1^2	museum + lunch	35	Tuesday
b_3^2	museum + lunch	30	any
b_5^2	museum	35	Tuesday
b_6^2	museum	30	any
b_4^1	museum	30	any

$Bidder_2$	activity	# people	date
b_6^2	museum	30	any
b_5^2	museum	35	Tuesday
b_4^2	ski	30	any
b_3^2	museum + lunch	30	any
b_2^2	ski	35	Tuesday
b_1^2	museum + lunch	35	Tuesday

lunch, and prefers contracts that incorporate more people (even if there are less participant expected on a certain day, because it gives them more flexibility in accepting more people last minute). In this example, the private class of $bidder_1$ is $\{b_1^1, b_2^1\}$, that of $bidder_2$ is $\{b_1^2, b_2^2\}$ and that of the auctioneer is $\{b_4^2, b_6^1\}$.

To properly see the difference of the proposed model and the traditional auction models, let us make two observations. Firstly, in our model, the preference orders of the auctioneer and the bidders are not opposing. Usual utility functions are required to be opposing, but this does not always hold in practise. Secondly, we do not assume that the bids submitted by the bidders are of the same type. Every bidder can offer the type of contracts he likes, and there is no need to define utility functions that expect values of attributes that are not interpreted by the bidder. With these extensions our model is capable of describing trading scenarios that are more realistic than those described by the traditional models.

Having seen the model, in Section 3 we show how one-shot auctions can be extended to handle arbitrary bids.

3   A One-Shot Mechanism

An auctioneer can choose between many different auction protocols to find the best deal in a set of possible bids. The English (best bid, ascending) or Dutch (best bid, descending) auctions are popular in practice. The one-shot Vickrey offers several theoretical advantages, and therefore it is popular among scientists. In the following we show how a Vickrey auction protocol fits in our auctioning model and illustrate its workings by our corporate-day-trip example.

3.1   Generalizing the Vickrey Auction

A Vickrey auction is a one-shot mechanism, where every bidder submits only one bid. The auctioneer selects the best bid according to his preference order and the bidder who submitted that bid is the winner. In case there are more bids that are best, a random choice is made. Since the auction is a second-best bid mechanism, the deal is not defined by selecting the winning bid. For the case when bids consist of a single price, Vickrey has suggested that the second-best price should define the deal [6]. Along the same lines of thoughts, we propose that in the case when bids may consist of any attributes, the protocol consists of the following steps:

1. Every $bidder_i$ selects the bid b_i^0 that is highest according to the auctioneer's preference order $\preceq_a$, but not lower than the bid(s) in his private value class C_i^0: $b_i^0 = \max_{\preceq_a}\{b \mid C_i^0 \preceq_i b\}$. This bid is sent to the auctioneer.
2. The auctioneer selects the bid that scores highest in his preference order as the winning bid. The bidder to whom this bid belongs is the winner of the deal. In case of more than one equally preferred bids, one is chosen at random as the winning bid, and another as the second-best bid.

3. The contract attributes are defined by the auctioneer's equivalence class of the second-best bid b_2. The winner $bidder_w$ selects the bid b_3 that scores highest according to his own preference order, and does not score lower than the bid(s) in the equivalence class of this second-best bid in the auctioneer's order, i.e., $b_3 = \max_{\preceq_w} \{b \mid b_2 \preceq_a b\}$. If the winner has bids that are equal to b_3, then the bid (b_3') that scores highest in the auctioneer's preference order is selected ($b_3' = \max_{\preceq_a} \{b \mid b_3 =_w b\}$).

In the example, the private class of $bidder_1$ consists of the offer of skiing and lunch for 35 persons and the offer of museum for 35 persons ($C_1^0 = \{b_1^1, b_2^1\}$). The private class of $bidder_2$ also contains two offers, both on Tuesday for 35 persons: museum and lunch or skiing ($C_2^0 = \{b_1^2, b_2^2\}$). The two submitted bids are the museum for 35 persons (b_2^1) and the skiing for 35 persons on Tuesday (b_2^2). Since the auctioneer prefers the museum for 35 persons (b_2^1) over skiing with 35 persons on Tuesday (b_2^2), $bidder_1$ is the winner. To set the deal, $bidder_1$ has to select a bid that is not worse for the auctioneer than the equivalence class with contracts for skiing with 35 persons on Tuesday or any other day ($\{b_2^2, b_5^1\}$). Since $bidder_1$ does not have a bid that is better for the auctioneer as well as for himself, the contract made will be skiing with 35 persons (b_5^1).

If all the usual assumptions of a price-only auction holds (especially the pseudo-linear utility functions), this mechanism reduces to the well-known Vickrey auction protocol. In that case equivalence classes consist of only one element, and the winner does not have a choice. In case of the more general preference orderings, however, it is possible that the auctioneer's equivalence class of the second-best bid consists of several possible bids, which are equivalent for the auctioneer, but may make a difference for the winner bidder. By allowing the winner to choose one of these bids a better deal can be made.

Other auction protocols can be generalized in a similar manner. In the Dutch auction the auctioneer announces contracts from more preferred toward less preferred contracts until a bidder stops him. The bidders consider every bid based on their preference orders and private classes. Similarly in the English auction protocol bidders use their own and the auctioneer's preference order to always submit better bids. The auction stops when there are no new bids. It is easy to see (via playing an example auction in all three protocols), that the outcome of the English and the Vickrey protocol is the same, while that of the Dutch is different, just like in traditional model.

The main advantage of the original Vickrey protocol is that it is *incentive compatible*. That is, the dominant strategy of the bidders is to bid according to their private value. We will prove that this property also holds for our modified auction mechanism, thus their dominant strategy is to submit a bid according to their private class.

4   Properties

An auction mechanism is called *optimal*, if the utility of the auctioneer is maximized by the deal it provides. In general it means that the deal is defined by the private value that is most preferred by the auctioneer. Vickrey mechanisms are not optimal, because the deals they result in are defined by the second-most preferred private value. This is true regardless of the existence of any valuation function, also in our case.

Multi-agent researchers are usually concerned about building systems that provide *Pareto-optimal* or *Pareto-efficient* solutions. A deal is Pareto efficient if it cannot be changed in a way that it provides higher utility for one party while not decreasing the utility of the other one.

Proposition 1. *The deals provided by the Vickrey mechanism in the proposed general auctioning model are Pareto efficient.*

Proof. Pareto efficiency follows from the last step in the auction algorithm. It prescribes that the winner chooses a deal that is the best of the bids that are better for him than the second best bid, but not worse for the auctioneer. This ensures that it is not possible to have a deal that is better for the winner, but not worse for the auctioneer.

Due to the selection of b_3' over b_3 it is ensured that the auctioneer cannot have a better deal without violating the winner's preferences. If there was a b_4 that is not worse than b_3' for the auctioneer ($b_3' \preceq_a b_4$), but better for the winner ($b_3' \prec_w b_4$), then in the final step of the protocol b_4 would have been chosen instead of b_3.

Note that in case of a price-only auction, the equivalence classes always contain only one element, therefore the last step of the protocol does nothing.

Beside Pareto efficiency, *incentive compatibility* is one of the most important properties of Vickrey mechanisms. Incentive compatibility means that if the bidder submits a bid according to his private class, then his expected utility is not less then in case of any other bid. This is equivalent to saying that the dominant strategy of the bidders is to bid according to their true valuation.

Proposition 2. *The Vickrey mechanism in the proposed general auctioning model is incentive compatible.*

Proof. The incentive compatibility of the traditional Vickrey mechanism originates from the fact that deviation from the true value either decreases the chance of winning the auction without increasing the expected price, or increases the chance of winning the auction while decreasing the expected price due to a risk of paying more than the true value.

Similar reasoning holds for the Vickrey mechanism in our model. According to this protocol, a $bidder_i$ should submit the bid b_i^0 that is highest according to the auctioneer's preference order, but not lower than the bid(s) in the his private value class C_i^0 (we repeat from the protocol description: $b_i^0 = \max_{\preceq_a} \{b \mid C_i^0 \preceq_b b\}$). Bidders can deviate from this protocol in two ways.

1. The submitted bid b_1 can be higher than (or in) its private value class, but *not the highest according to the preference order of the auctioneer a*, i.e.,

$C_i^0 \preceq_i b_1$ and $b_1 \preceq_a b_i^0$. In this case the bid b_1 has a smaller chance of winning, and if it wins, the bid values are not going to be better than they would be when the truthful bid b_i^0 was submitted, because those are based on the same second-best bid.

2. The bidder may also choose to submit a bid b_1 that he prefers *less than the bids in his private value class* C_i^0, i.e., $b_1 \preceq_i C_i^0$. If the bidder then still loses, this is clearly not a good idea. However, if the bidder wins it may select a bid b_3 based on the second-best bid $b_2 \preceq_a b_3$. We show that even then, the bidder is not better off than with bidding b_i^0. Consider the following proof by contradiction.

Suppose that the bidder is strictly better off bidding this bid b_1 than bidding b_i^0. In that case, there should be a bid b_3 for which the following holds: $b_2 \preceq_a b_3$, because it must be at least as good as the second-best bid b_2, and also $C_i^0 \preceq_i b_3$, because otherwise the bidder would have a bid with less than zero utility. Clearly, the bid b_3 lies in the set $\{b \mid C_i^0 \preceq_i b\}$, and since b_i^0 is the maximum of this set according to the auctioneer's ordering, it holds that $b_3 \preceq_a b_i^0$. With $b_2 \preceq_a b_3$ it thus holds that $b_2 \preceq_a b_i^0$. Thus b_i^0 is also higher than the second-best bid, and if the bidder had followed the protocol, it would also have won, and have been allowed to choose a bid based on b_2. Contradiction. Consequently, a bidder is not better off by bidding lower than its private value class.

Since a bidder is never better off by not bidding according to the protocol, it is a weakly dominant strategy for the bidders to do so. Consequently, the modified Vickrey mechanism is incentive compatible.

5   Related Work

Auctions are well-studied allocation mechanisms that are used in a wide range of areas from e-markets [8][9] to resource allocation [10]. The Vickrey auction mechanism [6] is particularly interesting for use in multi-agent systems because it possesses several desired properties like incentive compatibility and efficiency. However, the Vickrey mechanism has also certain limitations. Humans tend not to use this auction very often, because the auctioneer needs to be fully trusted, people's private values in real-life scenarios are often not (completely) private, or because it gives a lower revenue for the auctioneer. Sandholm [11] also showed some limitations of the Vickrey auction for computational agents. For example, when agents have local uncertainty, or when several auctions are held for items that are interrelated.

The situation where such multiple related items are auctioned is studied as a so-called combinatorial auction [12]. In this case a combination of bids is selected as a winner. The resulting *winner selection problem* is NP-hard, and the focus of some interesting research (see e.g. [3]).

Another extension of the original (single-issue) auction model is to allow bids to contain multiple attributes beside the price. In such auctions, an item with configurable attributes is auctioned. The bidders submit bids that specify the attribute values and the price. Che analyzed an auction mechanism with two attributes: price and quality [13]. He compared different second-price methods and concluded that the one where the winner can select a deal in the end (in contrast to implement exactly the second-best bid) can implement an optimal trade. We generalize this result for non-opposing preferences that order arbitrary bids.

Later David, Azoulay-Schwartz and Kraus extended Che's work to more dimensions, and analyzed the mechanism from the auctioneer's point of view (revenue maximization, rather than efficiency) [5]. In their case utility functions also express the value of bids in money. Although the value of a certain bid might be different for every bidder, these utility functions represent the same preference order for every bidder.[1] In this paper, we generalize their setting on two levels. On the conceptual level, we generalize the notion of bids to not only contain price versus a good or price versus attributes of a good, but to contain arbitrary attributes of a deal. On the practical level this means that the bid selection is not based on money, so we do not require the existence of utility functions that convert all attributes to money. Another difference is that we allow the utility functions of the bidders to represent different preference orders.

Recent research on multi-attribute auctions includes the work of Parkes and Kalagnanam [7], who have introduced iterative mechanisms for multi-attribute Vickrey auctions with pseudo-linear and non-linear utility functions. Teich et al. have recently extended their earlier work on multi-attribute e-auctions by a bidder-support module that can suggest new value combinations to help the bidders to elicit the auctioneer's utility function [4]. For a general overview of existing work on multi-attribute auctions, please see the review paper of Teich et al. [14].

6   Discussion

In this paper we have introduced a generalized model of auctioning that can handle bids with different, possibly non-monetary, attributes submitted by bidders who may have different preferences. The preferences in the model are expressed as orderings instead of the usual utility functions. We have shown how a standard Vickrey auction needs to be modifed to cope with arbitrary bids and not-strictly opposing preferences, and have proved that the mechanism is still incentive compatible and that it is Pareto effcient.

An advantage of preference orders over multi-attribute utility functions is that the bids do not have to consist of the same attributes. It is possible to

---

[1] Actually the requirement is that the utility functions of the bidders should be diametrically opposed to the utility function of the auctioneer. In terms of the order this is equal to requiring strictly opposing orders. Since all bidders have to have a strictly opposing order to the auctioneer's, their orders are then necessarily the same.

order different kinds of bids because preference orders in general do not depend on the structure of the bids.

Another advantage is that here, in contrast to using a utility function, we do not have to express the value of a bid in money. Sometimes it might be diffcult to express certain attributes in money, while a preference order can still be defned. In case the attributes include monetary as well as non-monetary attributes it is possible to mix the preference order model with the traditional model. If a valuation function exists that can summarize the value of some of the attributes, then this summarized value can substitute the attributes it is derived from. Then the preference orders have to consider this single value instead of the multiple original attributes.

A practical issue with the new auctioning model is the representation of the preferences. The auction protocols assume that the preference order of the auctioneer is known by the bidders. How such orders can be expressed in a compact form, however, is left for future work.

References

1. Conitzer, V., Sandholm, T.: Complexity of constructing solutions in the core based on synergies among coalitions. Artificial Intelligence 170, 607–619 (2006)
2. Krishna, V.: Auction Theory. Academic Press, London (2002)
3. Sandholm, T.: Algorithm for optimal winner determination in combinatorial auctions. Artificial Intelligence 135(1-2), 1–54 (2002)
4. Teich, J.E., Wallenius, H., Wallenius, J., Zaitsev, A.: A multi-attribute e-auction mechanism for procurement: Theoretical foundation. European Journal of Operational Research 175, 90–100 (2006)
5. David, E., Azoulay-Schwartz, R., Kraus, S.: Protocols and strategies for automated multi-attribute auctions. In: Proceedings of the First Joint Conference on Autonomous Agents and Multiagent Systems, pp. 77–85 (2002)
6. Vickrey, W.: Counterspeculation, auctions, and competitive sealed tenders. Journal of Finance 16, 8–37 (1961)
7. Parkes, D.C., Kalagnanam, J.: Models for iterative multiattribute Vickrey auctions. Management Science 51, 435–451 (2005)
8. Rosenschein, J.S., Zlotkin, G.: Rules of encounter: designing conventions for automated negotiation among computers. MIT Press, Cambridge, MA, USA (1994)
9. Varian, H.R.: Economic mechanism design for computerized agents. In: Proc. of Usenix Workshop on Electronic Commerce (July 1995)
10. Smith, R.G.: The contract net protocol: high-level communication and control in a distributed problem solver. In: Distributed Artificial Intelligence, pp. 357–366. Morgan Kaufmann Publishers Inc., San Francisco, CA, USA (1988)
11. Sandholm, T.W.: Limitations of the Vickrey auction in computational multiagent systems. In: Lesser, V. (ed.) Proceedings of the First International Conference on Multi–Agent Systems. MIT Press, Cambridge (1995)
12. MacKie-Mason, J.K., Varian, H.R.: Generalized Vickrey auctions. Technical report, University of Michigan (July 1994)
13. Che, Y.K.: Design competition through multidimensional auctions. RAND Journal of Economics 24, 668–680 (1993)
14. Teich, J.E., Wallenius, H., Wallenius, J., Koppius, O.R.: Emerging multiple issue e-auctions. European Journal of Operational Research 159, 1–16 (2004)

Service Composition in Holonic Multiagent Systems: Model-Driven Choreography and Orchestration

Christian Hahn and Klaus Fischer

German Research Center for Artificial Intelligence (DFKI)
Stuhlsatzenhausweg 3, 66123 Saarbrücken
Germany
{Christian.Hahn,Klaus.Fischer}@dfki.de

Abstract. Services provide a universal basis for the integration of business processes that are distributed among entities, both within an organization and across organizational borders. Service-oriented Architectures (SOA) include service composition, management and monitoring, billing and security. This paper presents a model-driven approach to design interoperable holonic multiagent systems in a SOA. Thereby, we mainly concentrate on providing a foundation for how to define the composition of services in holonic multiagent systems and discuss how this integragtion could be done in a MDD manner[1].

1 Introduction

Service-oriented architectures (SOA) have become a very active research area. An interesting and demanding challenge is to generate dynamic composed services in a flexible manner by assembling existing atomic or complex services. New design methodologies and robust development tools for the service composition are needed. Additionally, the complexity of the composition task is further aggravated by the heterogeneous nature of the participating services, as they can be described in different ways, use different interfaces, and most likely deployed by different providers. Thus, the second challenge is to develop modeling techniques to implement flexible, reliable, inter-operating services. Service composition addresses the situation when a client request cannot be satisfied by a single pre-existing service, but can be satisfied by suitably combining some available, pre-existing services. The necessity to explore flexible agent-based mechanisms for service composition is currently discussed as specific challenge in the AgentLink RoadMap [1]. For several reasons, approaches basing on agent technologies are an interesting opportunity when dynamically combining services: Firstly, agents are self-aware and through the possibility of learning they

---

[1] The work published in this paper is partly funded by the European Commission through the ATHENA IP (Advanced Technologies for interoperability of Heterogeneous Enterprise Networks and their Applications Integrated Project) (IST- 507849).

V. Mařík, V. Vyatkin, A.W. Colombo (Eds.): HoloMAS 2007, LNAI 4659, pp. 47–58, 2007.
© Springer-Verlag Berlin Heidelberg 2007

acquire the awareness of other agents and their attitudes. Secondly, they are communicative, whereas services are passive until invoked. Thirdly, in contrast to services, agents act in an autonomous manner that is required by many Internet applications. Lastly, agents are cooperative, and by forming organizations they can provide higher-level and more comprehensive services. In accordance to [2], current standards do not provide any composing functionalities.

As business processes, specified as workflows and executed with services, need to be adaptive and flexible, approaches are needed to facilitate this evolution. The methodology of this paper will outline this concern by designing interopable holonic agents able to adapt on the functionalities and requirements of services in a flexible manner adopting the principles of model-driven development. Agent technology and in particular the holonic approach allows to establish a loose coupling between agents, the implementation is neutral and does not depend on particular technologies as requested in [2]. Additionally, holons are flexible to configure and further the interaction and cooperation between agents.

This paper is structured as follows: In Section 2, the basic concepts of SOAs are discussed. Followed by basic principles of a holonic multiagent system (MAS) in Section 3. Section 4 discusses how to describe a choreography and orchestration in holonic multiagent systems. Section 5 illustrates related metamodels and Section 6 addresses the question on how to use these metamodels to derive transformations. Section 7 concludes this paper.

2   Service-Oriented Architectures

In accordance to the Oasis reference model [3] SOA are a paradigm for organizing and utilizing distributed capabilities that may be under the control of different ownership domains. A distributed entity communicates and interacts with another to perform a unit of work or a service. Each interaction is self-contained and loosely coupled, so that it is independent of any other interaction. Communication can involve either simple data exchange or two or more services coordinating some activity. Thereby, a service is the mechanism to enable access to a set of one or more capabilities, where the access is provided using a prescribed interface and is exercised consistent with constraints and policies as specified by the service description. In a SOA, three basic roles interact:

Service provider: A service provider is the party that provides software applications for specific needs as services. Service providers publish, unpublish and update their services so that they are available on the Internet.
Service requester: A requester is the party that has a need that can be fulfilled by a service available on the Internet. A requester could be a human user accessing the service through a desktop; it could be an application program; or it could be another service. A requester finds the required services via a service broker and binds to services via the service provider.
Service broker: A service broker provides a searchable repository of service descriptions where service providers publish their services and service requesters find services and obtain binding information for these services.

In this paper, we mainly concentrate on the interaction between service providers and requesters and show how the interaction between these roles can be described in holonic multiagent systems. Often, a service may be constructed by aggregating services provided by other entities. Two styles of composing a single service from multiple services can be distinguished:

Choreography: In accordance to [4], a choreography model describes a collaboration between a collection of services in order to achieve a common goal. It captures the interaction in which the participating services engage to achieve this goal and the dependencies between the interactions, including control-flow dependencies, data-flow dependencies, message correlations, time constraints, transactional dependencies, etc. A choreography does not describe any internal action then occurs within a participating service that does not directly result in an externally visible effect. It captures interactions from a global perspective, i.e. all participating services are treated equally, the control is shared among the participating partners.

Orchestration: In accordance to [4], an orchestration model describes both the communication actions and the internal actions in which a service engages. Internal actions include data transformations and invocations to internal software modules (e.g., legacy applications that are not exposed as services). An orchestration may also contain communication actions or dependencies between communication actions that do not appear in any of the service's behaviour interface(s). Orchestrations are also called executable processes since they are intended to be executed by an orchestration engine. In contrast to a choreography, an orchestration describes the control flow of a single partner.

Even if orchestration and choreography are mutually exclusive high-level process management patterns, it is important to note that a real-life system may use a combination of both. For example, it is not uncommon for choreographed services to consist of orchestrated participants. In this case, the global business process is defined by the choreographed interaction, but each participant may be defining an internal business process through orchestration. In this scenario, the choreographed process would likely be multi-organizational, while the orchestrated process would be within an organization.

3 Holonic Multiagent Systems

A MAS consists of a collection of individual agents that are persistent computational entities capable of perceiving and acting upon their environment, in an autonomous manner, in order to meet their design objectives. They interact and communicate with other agents and incorporate reasoning techniques (e.g., planning, decision making, and learning) together with sophisticated interaction to achieve flexible rational behaviour.

It is a widely supported assumption in the multiagent community that the development of robust and scalable software systems requires autonomous agents that can complete their objectives while situated in a dynamic and uncertain environment. To this end, these agents need to be able to engage in rich, high-level social interactions, and operate within flexible organizational structures. Organizational-based agents are a special kind of intelligent agents with distributed expertise (i.e. knowledge)—characterized by domain-specific roles the organizational members possess—and emphasize on cooperativeness and proactiveness in collaboratively pursuing their common goals. In the domain of service composition, organizational-based agents can facilitate a distributed approach to dynamic composition that can be scalable, facilitate learning about specific types of services across multiple compositions and allow proactive failure handling. Holonic multiagent systems provide terminology and theory to realize the dynamically organizing of agents. They are a common example for an organisational-based approach to design cooperative behaviour as those can (i) encapsulate complexity of the subsystems by simplifying representation and design and (ii) modularize functionalities providing the basis for rapid development and incremental deployment.

Holonic concepts are inspired by the idea of recursive or self-similar structures in biological systems (cf. [5]). A formal definition of the tern holonic mulitagent system was given in [6].

A MAS containing *holons* is called a *holonic multiagent system*. The set $\mathcal{H}_t$ of all holons in the MAS $\mathcal{MAS}_t$ is defined recursively:

- for each $a \in \mathcal{A}_t$, $h = (\{a\}, \{a\}, \emptyset) \in \mathcal{H}_t$, i.e. every instantiated agent constitutes an *atomic* holon, and
- $h = (Head, Subholons, C) \in \mathcal{H}_t$, where $Subholons \in 2^{\mathcal{H}_t} \backslash \emptyset$ is the set of holons that participate in h, $Head \subseteq Subholons$ is the non-empty set of holons that represent the holon to the environment and are responsible for coordinating the actions inside the holon. $C \subseteq Commitments$ defines the relationship inside the holon and is agreed on by all holons $h' \in Subholons$ at the time of joining the holon h.

Given the holon $h = (Head, \{h_1, ..., h_n\}, C)$ we call $h_1, ..., h_n$ the *subholons* of h, and h the *superholon* of $h_1, ..., h_n$. The set $Body = \{h_1, ..., h_n\}\backslash Head$ is the set of subholons that are not allowed to represent holon h. Holons are allowed to engage as subholons in several different holons at the same time, as long as this does not contradict the sets of commitments of these superholons.

A holon h is observed by its environment like any other agent in $\mathcal{A}_t$. Only at closer inspection it may turn out that h is constructed from a set of agents. As any head of a holon has a unique identification, it is possible to communicate with each holon by just sending messages to their addresses. C specifies the organizational structure. As long as subholons intend to keep their commitments and as long as subholons do not make conflicting commitments, cycles in holon memberships are possible. A holon h may have capabilities that emerge from the composition of $h_1, ..., h_n$ and it may have actions at its disposal that none of its agents could perform alone.

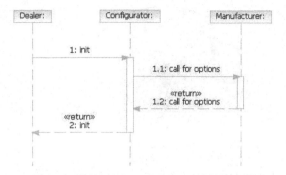

Fig. 1. A simple choreography between three roles

4   Choreography and Orchestration in Holonic Multiagent Systems

As already discussed in Section 2, choreography and orchestration are basic elements for service composition. In this section, we exemplarily show how these composition mechanisms could be modeled in holonic multiagent systems.

Assume, a dealer software provides the service to list options different car manufacturers offer with respect to the consumers' desires and requirements (i.e. price, equipment, etc.). The dealer software evaluates the consumer's request and selects those car manufacturers that offer products that fulfill the consumer's requirements, followed by sending a request to the responsible services on the car manufacturers' side (see Figure 1). The car manufacturers' internal legacy system evaluates the service request and replies by sending a list of options. After receiving the manufacturers' list of options, the dealer software collects and evaluates the responses and illustrates the set of options on its web site. The consumer then may evaluate the options and may proceed by for instance further restricting its requirements or selecting special models it would be interested in getting detailed information.

In Figure 1, we only specify an abstract role *Manufacturer*, instead of characterizing all feasible car manufacturers. By receiving a request, the *Configurator* dynamically decides to which concrete manufacturer it forwards the request. We define two elementary mappings.

Service Requester⟶Holon Head: Each service requester represents a holon as head, the body agents are represented by the service provider the requester interacts with.

Service Provider⟶Holon Body: Each service provider represents a holon as head if the set of service provider it interacts with is not empty. Those service providers again represent the holon bodies.

Both mapping rules allow to mirror a complex service composition inside a holon that may consist of several subholons. The number of subholons depend on how

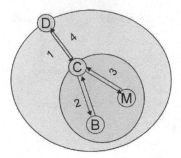

Fig. 2. The resulting holon. Dealer (D) delegates the incoming user request to configurator (C) that requests two manufacturers, B and M, for options.

many entities act as both service provider and requester. The generated holonic agents can engage in a complex nested structures and nested structures of arbitrary depth are possible and meaningful (depending on the complexity of the service composition). Furthermore, each interaction in the holonic agent is self-contained and loosely coupled and thus fulfills the requirements of SOA. Figure 2 illustrates the resulting holonic agents. Messages are sent only between the head agent and its corresponding body agents. The messages are sent in accordance to the specified choreography (see Figure 1), the orchestration defines when a message is sent. In the case of the *Manufacturer*, the *Configurator* dynamically selects two services that offer the requirements specified by the consumer and sends a corresponding message to them. The service orchestration is used to describe the holons behaviour. The configurator's behaviour indicates in which order the requests are sent to the manufacturer. As the manufacturers' answers do not depend on each other, message 2 and 3 in Figure 2 can be sent in parallel. Otherwise, the configurator would have to request the manufacturer in a sequential order.

The Web services are then finally invoked by the body agents representing the manufacturers' side. We refer to [7] for detailed information regarding the interaction of Web service and agents in our scenario.

5   Model-Driven Development of Holonic Multiagent Systems

Model-driven Development (MDD) is emerging as the state of practice for developing modern enterprise applications and software systems. MDD frameworks define a model-driven approach to software development in which visual modeling languages are used to integrate the huge diversity of technologies used in the development of software systems. Furthermore, the MDD paradigm provides us with a better way of addressing and solving interoperability issues compared to earlier non-modeling approaches [8]. From our point of view, SOA is an ideal platform to use the principles of MDD, as the high level description can be translated into the interaction between different services.

In our case, we base our approach on a metamodel for SOA [9] (called platform independent model for SOA, PIM4SOA) which has been developed by IBM, the European Software Institute (ESI) and SINTEF. From a top-down perspective it starts with the PIM4SOA that specifies software services and required interfaces independent of concrete software technology platforms. Using a horizontal transformation, we map the related concepts of the SOA to a PIM for agents that is further refined to a platform specific model (PSM) which describes the realization of the software systems with respect to JACK (cf. [10]), the software technology we have selected for demonstration purpose in this paper. A mapping to JADE is discussed in [11].

The development of systems is fundamentally based on the use of languages to capture and relate different aspects of the problem domain. The benefit of metamodeling is its ability to describe these languages in a unified way. A metamodel describes the concepts and their relationships for the purpose of building and interpreting models. Metamodels can be developed for describing different business domains and different software technology platforms (e.g. Web services and agent systems). In contrast, a model transformation defines the mapping between concepts of the source and target metamodel. In the following, we show how to define platform independent languages for SOAs (PIM4SOA) and agents (PIM4Agents).

5.1   The Platform Independent Model for SOA

The PIM4SOA metamodel covers four important aspects: service, process, information and quality of service. To discuss how choreography and orchestration are defined in the PIM4SOA, we restrict ourselves on discussing the *service* and *process* aspect.

Service Aspect. The service aspect of the PIM4SOA presents services modeled as collaborations that specify a pattern of interaction between the participating roles. A subset of the metamodel for this aspect is presented in Figure 3. The Collaboration specifies the involved roles and their responsibilities and could possibly be constrained by the specification of a process. This process mainly describes how messages are exchanged between the collaborating roles and could thus be considered as a choreography description in the PIM4SOA.

A CollaborationUse specifies the application of a Collaboration in a specific context and includes the RoleBindings to entities in that context. Collaborations are composable and the responsibilities of a role in a composite Collaboration are defined through CollaborationUses by binding roles from the composite to roles of its subcollaborations. Collaborations describe always binary relationships, i.e., a requester that provides the input, and a provider that produces the output parameters. A Role represents how a partner participates

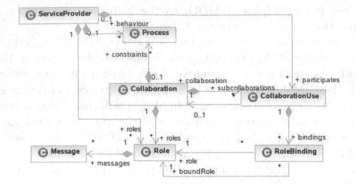

Fig. 3. Service concepts of the PIM4SOA metamodel

in the `Collaboration` by providing services and parameters and using services provided by other partners in its service collaboration. `Messages`, a `Role` sends specify which parameters are sent to which `Role` in a `Collaboration`.

`ServiceProvider` represents a service specification containing the specification of other strategies. Like the `Collaboration`, a `ServiceProvider` is constrained also by a `Process` that presents the orchestration description. A `ServiceProvider` may participate in a set of `CollaborationUses` and could take different role types in the collaboartion. Thus, a `ServiceProvider` may play the role of a requester in one collaboration and may take the role of a provider in an other collaboration. For a more detailed discussion we refer again to [11].

Process aspect. The process elements of the PIM4SOA metamodel are shown in Figure 4. The process aspect is closely linked to the service aspect, the primary link being the abstract class `Scope` above, which can be instantiated as a `Process` belonging to a `ServiceProvider` from that aspect.

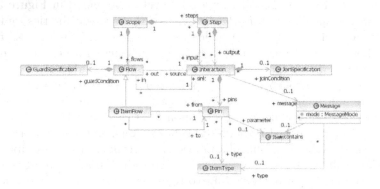

Fig. 4. Process concepts of the PIM4SOA metamodel

The process contains a set of Steps (generally Tasks), representing actions carried out by the Process. A Process consists of StructuredTasks (sub-processes), Steps (atomic tasks and actions, at the PIM level), and Interactions, Flows inking the tasks together. These essentially fall into two categories, interactions with other ServiceProviders, or specialised actions requiring implementation beyond the scope of this model. The Process also contains a set of Flows between these actions, which may be specialised (ItemFlow) to indicate the transfer of specific data identified in the information aspect. For a detailed description, we refer to [11].

5.2   A Metamodel for Agents (PIM4Agents)

The metamodel of the agent aspect (see Figure 5) is centered on the concept of Agent, the autonomous entity capable of acting in the environment. Each Agent has access to a set of Resources from his surrounding Environment like for instance Web services that are offered by particular agents. The Capability represents the set of Behaviours the Agent can possess. It allows to group Behaviours that, conceptually, have a correspondence with regard to what they allow the Agent to do. Each Behaviour can be simple or composed by sub-behaviours, therefore a whole hierarchy of specific Behaviours can be created. Each Behaviour may also send or react to a Message according to a given Protocol and could thus be easily compared with an orchestration. The Role is an abstraction of the social behaviour of the Agent in a given social context, usually a Cooperation. This Role specifies the responsibilities of the Agent in that social context. Correspondingly, the Cooperation represents the interaction between the Agents performing the required set of Roles. The detailed realisation of this interaction is described by a Protocol that indicates what are the Messages to be expected from each of the Roles at each point in time. The execution of the Protocol is performed by a set of Behaviours, each of which sends and/or reacts to messages in accordance to its Role. Agents can take part in an Organisation, a special kind of Cooperation that also has the

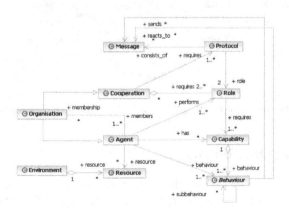

Fig. 5. The service aspect of the platform-independent metamodel for agents

same characteristics of Agent. Therefore, the Organisation can perform roles and have Capabilities which can be performed by its members, be it Agents or suborganisations. Due to the recursive structure between the concepts Agent and Organisation, holonic mulitagent systems can easily be defined using the PIM4Agents. To the outside, a holon is represented by an atomic agent as the Protocol defines the interaction between agents only. The multiple inheritance of the Organisation, from Agent and Cooperation, allows it to have its own internal protocol that specifies how the Organisation coordinates its members. This enables us to define protocols that define how tasks are assigned from the head to the body agents in a choreography manner.

5.3   A Metamodel for BDI-Agents

A partial metamodel of JACK (JackMM) is presented in Figure 6. The most relevant concepts in JackMM is the concepts of a Team which specifies the structure of one or more entities (teams/agents) that is formed to achieve a set of desired objectives. A Team could be either atomic, in which case we can refer to it simply as an Agent, or a set of required roles—subteams—that all together form the Team. The structure how teams are defined matches nicely with the requirements we have to fulfill when developing holonic multiagent systems. The tasks a given Team is able to work on are defined by the roles that it is able to fulfil. How a team actually reacts to an incoming request is specified by a set of TeamPlans, each specifying the behaviour of a team in reaction to a specific event. In general, a team plan is a set of steps specifying how a particular task is achieved by particular roles. Each team plan has an explicitly defined objective for which this team plan is responsible. Role definitions are a further important concept to define teams because a role specifies which Events the role fillers are able to react to and which Events they are likely to send.

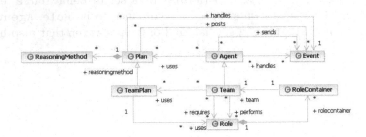

Fig. 6. The metamodel (JackMM) reflecting the JACK framework

6   Model Transformations

A model transformation explains which concepts of a source metamodel are mapped to particular concepts in the target metamodel. In this section, we bring together the metamodel and its concepts described in the previous sections and relate them to one another in a transformation derived from it.

6.1   Transforming PIM4SOA to PIM4Agents

Comparing the PIM4SOA and PIM4Agents metamodels, we derive a set of transformations that are discussed in [11] in more detail. The main transformation is to initialize an `Organization` for each requester and the service providers it interacts with. Service requester and provider act as organizational members. All `Behaviours` that constraint any `Collaboration` the requester participates are mapped to the organizational protocols. The requester acts as Initiator, the service providers act as Participant. This introduces the relationship between head and body agents. The requester's behaviour is mapped to the head's behaviour to describe in which order the protocols are executed. At this stage, we do not specify the behaviour's elements in all details. How its concrete concepts might look like is illustrated in [12].

6.2   Transforming PIM4Agents to JackMM

A basic transformation is the mapping of `PIM4Agents:Organisation` to a `Team` in JackMM. The organisational behaviour is mapped to a `TeamPlan` used by the team. Events a team `sends` or `handles` are defined in the organisational protocol. The team `performs` and `requires` roles that are generated by mapping the organisational performed and required roles. The role of the holon head is performed, the roles of the holon bodies are required by the `Team`. Due to the fact that an agent in the PIM4Agents performs a role, it is recommended to assign `PIM4Agents:Agent` to a `Team` in JackMM (instead of using an `Agent`). The team's `performed` roles are generated by mapping the roles the agent performs. Furthermore, the team `requires` the roles specified in the `PIM4Agents:Organisation`, in which the agent participates. The concept behaviour of the PIM4Agents is directly mapped to a `TeamPlan`. We refer again to [12] to give insights in the `TeamPlan`'s elements. The roles a `TeamPlan` uses are extracted from the organisational required roles. Furthermore, the messages specified by a `Protocol:PIM4Agents` are mapped to `Events` in JackMM. Depending on whether the agent receives or sends a message, it is handles or sent by the `Team` in JackMM. Any performed and required role defined in the PIM4Agents is transformed to JACK-related roles a `Team` `requires` or `performs`.

7   Conclusion

In this paper, we described how holonic mulitagent systems can be used to define service composition within a SOA. Therefore, we showed how the composition of services as defined by a orchestration and choreography could be realized in holonic multiagent systems. The binary collaboration between service requester and service provider as described for instance by a choreography can easily be transformed to implement generic holonic multiagent systems, i.e. the provider requester relationship is mapped to the binary relationship between holon head and body. Therefore we map (i) each service requester to a holon head and (ii) each service provider requested by it to its holon bodies.

Beside the conceptual integration, we showed how to solve technical interoperability issues by defining a model-driven development approach to generically design holonic multiagent systems. Therefore, a SOA description is mapped to a platform independent model for agents (PIM4Agents) and further mapped to JACK where it could be executed. The PIM4Agents could further be used to define holonic mulitagent systems in a platform independent manner to use this description and the PIM to PSM transformation to build executable code in JACK that finally implements the holonic multiagent system.

References

1. Luck, M., McBurney, P., Shehory, O., Willmott, S.: Agent Technology Roadmap (A Roadmap for agent based computing). AgentLink (2005)
2. Singh, M., Huhns, M.: Service Oriented Computing: Semantics, Processes, Agents. John Wiley & Sons, Chichster, West Sussex, UK (2005)
3. MacKenzie, M., Laskey, K., McCabe, F., Brown, P., Metz, R.: Reference Model for Service Oriented Architecture (2006)
4. Barros, A., Dumas, M., Oaks, P.: A critical overview of the web services choreography description language (WS-CDL) (2005)
5. Koestler, A.: The Ghost in the Machine. Hutchinson & Co. (1967)
6. Schillo, M., Fischer, K.: Holonic multiagent systems. Zeitschrift für Künstliche Intelligenz 17(4), 54–55 (2003)
7. Kahl, T., Zinnikus, I., Kahl, T., Roser, S., Hahn, C., Ziemann, J., Müller, J.P., Fischer, K.: Architecture for the design and agent-based implementation of CBPs. In: Proceedings of the third International Conference on Interoperability for Enterprise Software and Applications (I-ESA) (2007)
8. D'Souza, D.: Model-Driven Architecture and Integration - Opportunities and Challenges, Version 1.1, Kineticum (2001)
9. Benguria, G., Larrucea, X., Elvesæter, B., Neple, T., Beardsmore, A., Friess, M.: A platform independent model for service oriented architectures. In: Proceedings of I-ESA Conference (2006)
10. AOS: JACK Intelligent Agents, The Agent Oriented Software Group (AOS) (2006), http://www.agent-software.com/shared/home/
11. Hahn, C., Madrigal-Mora, C., Fischer, K.: Interoperability through a platform-independent model for agents. In: Proceedings of the third International Conference on Interoperability for Enterprise Software and Applications (I-ESA) (2007)
12. Hahn, C., Madrigal-Mora, C., Fischer, K., Elvesæter, B., Berre, A.J., Zinnikus, I.: Meta-models, Models, and Model Transformations: Towards Interoperable Agents. In: Fischer, K., Timm, I.J., André, E., Zhong, N. (eds.) MATES 2006. LNCS (LNAI), vol. 4196. Springer, Heidelberg (2006)

Flexible Roles in a Holonic Multi-Agent System

Emmanuel Adam and Rene Mandiau

LAMIH (UMR CNRS 8530)
Universite de Valenciennes
Le Mont Houy, F-59313 Valenciennes - Cedex 9
emmanuel.adam@univ-valenciennes.fr,
rene.mandiau@univ-valenciennes.fr
http://www.univ-valenciennes.fr/LAMIH/?perso=adam_emmanuel,
http://www.univ-valenciennes.fr/LAMIH/?perso=mandiau_rene

Abstract. Holonic Multi-Agent organisations are particular pyramidal organisations where agents of a layer (having the same coordinator) are able to communicate and to negotiate directly between them. In order to benefit from control allowed by the hierarchical structure of a holonic organisation and from dynamic roles, we propose a holonic multi-agent organisation inspired from working mechanisms of the complex human organisations. We have implemented this architecture by offering a role management capacity to a hierarchical multi-agent platform.

Keywords: holonic multi-agent organisation, roles.

1 Introduction

Our researches aim at integrating multiagent organisation into human organisation, which are more and more based on data exchanges, in order to help actors these system to manage data, to communicate and cooperate between them. We started our works on holonic system 10 years ago, when a patent department of a large company asked us to help its actors to manage distributed data. In order to analyse and model this kind of complex administrative systems (pyramidal, composed of service units and whose actors own roles and differents levels of responsibility), we turned to holonic model [1]. We have designed a method (AMOMCASYS) to model these human organisations, and we reuse this method to design and set-up some information multi-agent systems (IMAS) [2]. We focus in this article on the definitions and concepts that underlie the holonic multi-agent systems that we have set-up.

A holonic organisation has specific workings mechanisms. In order to respect initial definition of holonic systems [3], we propose a particular definition of roles, based on set of rules associated to goals.

Pyramidal structure of a holonic organisation is not frozen, it has to adapt itself to changes. For our holomas, these changes are due to: the agents losses; the agents overloading; the modification by migration of agents between parts of a holomas.

V. Mařík, V. Vyatkin, A.W. Colombo (Eds.): HoloMAS 2007, LNAI 4659, pp. 59–70, 2007.

This article describes firstly our definitions of holonic agents and of the roles played by them.

Then, our propositions to the problem of our holonic multiagent system dynamic, necessary for the robustness, are presented, by: the regeneration of an agent; the organisation growing; and the roles modifications.

A prototype of our platform is finally shown. This one is realized by implementing a layer on a existing muli-agent hierarchic platform.

2   Proposition of a Holomas Using Roles

In our works, we use holonic principles in order to understand the workings mechanisms of the human organisations, in which we plan to set up information multi-agent systems having a holonic architecture.

If holonic model is not suitable for all the organisations, it is particularly adapted to an organisation having a flexible and hierarchic architecture (whose parts have a relative autonomy), where notion of roles, responsibilities and cooperation are important.

We use the social rules defined in the holonic concept in order to simplify and to accelerate the design of a multi-agent society, they provide a framework to build a fixed multi-agent society (which does not imply rigidity). Indeed, hierarchical structure is not sufficient for model actual administrative organisation: "the degradation of hierarchy is a necessity for organisation to prosper" [4]; organisations are, or must be, flexible, more decentralized, and based on roles.

Rules proposed in [3] can be grouped in five sets: the first one is relative to necessary equilibrium between properties of cooperation and autonomy of holons; the second one is about the arborescent structure of a holonic system; the third one describe activities and control mechanisms; the fourth one is relative to communication between holons; the last one presents adaptation of holonic systems to their environment. From these rules, we propose a first set of formal definitions of a holonic multi-agent system, having a pyramidal architecture and whose agents have to reach global objective of the system while having a personal goal to reach.

world definition: We define world as being constituted of the MAS and the environment:
$$world = (environment, mas)$$
environment definition: This environment is constituted of active objects:
$$environment : E = \{object_0, object_1, ..., object_n\}$$
active object definition: An active object can execute functions on it-self or on objects with which is in relation. An object is composed of states and properties, each of these ones can modify states of the object or activate a property of an object with which it is in relation.
$$object_o = (name_o, states_o, properties_o, relations_o)$$
mas and agent definition: MAS is simply defined as a set of agents. Each agent (cf def. 1) is composed of: states; knowledge (social KS, environmental KE and personal KP); messages (dynamic list of objects); a perception function; behaviour rules (functions modifying agent states according to

current states, knowledge and received messages in order to reach the collective goal while moving toward its personal goals (the collective constraints having a priority more important than the personal constraints)).

Notion of roles is necessary to an agent (see for example [5], [6], [7] and [8]). We consider a role as: a set of knowledge (environmental and social); and a set of actions to do to reach goals to which it is dedicated. The definition of a role R (cf def. 2) is relatively similar to agent definition. Indeed, a role gives to an agent: the data (environmental knowledge) necessary to accomplish the role; acquaintances (responsible and assistants) that are linked to the role; working rules (*hardRules*) in which the agent has to choose a rule in order to be considered as playing this role; a set of rules (*flexibleRules*) able to complete the role (for example, a person is considered as a hairdresser *ssi* he/she cuts hair. He/she can sell products, books reservation, but it is not the core of the role).

So, an agent includes a dynamic list of roles. Indeed, an agent can: receive a role; leave a role; delegate a role or goal to its assistants or neighbours (our principle of delegation is inspired from the works of [9]). An acquaintance is added, relative to the agent having the role of responsible of roles played by the team of holonic agents (it is called HRA for Holonic Roles Agent). This one knows roles'list and the relations between agents and roles (cf. figure 1).

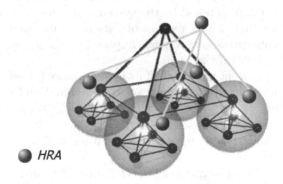

HRA

Fig. 1. Role management on holomas parts

Distribution of roles and rules follows holonic mechanisms: the more the agent is at the bottom of the system, the more its number of roles and rules is reduced, and the more the choice of the rule to use in each role is limited. Conversely, the more the agent is at the top of the system, the more the number of roles/rules is large, and the more the choice of the rule to used in each role is important.

$$agent_a = \begin{pmatrix} KP, KE, KS, HRA, messages_a, \\ perception_a, rules_a, roles_a \end{pmatrix} \qquad (1)$$

$$roles_a = \{R_0, \ldots, R_{nr}\}$$

$$role = \begin{pmatrix} name^{role}, priority^{role}, KE^{role}, KS^{role}, \\ hardRules^{role}, flexibleRules^{role} \end{pmatrix} \tag{2}$$

Personal knowledge (KP) of an agent or role are composed of: a name; its current state (represented by a dynamic set of objects); and its individual goal, GI, composed of a set of constraints on states of the agent/role. Each constraint has a priority in order to avoid conflicts.

Environmental knowledge (KE) of an agent/role (cf def. 3) are partial representations, sometimes erroneous according to the perception function of the agent and its activation, of objects of the environment. We note $o1 \lhd o2$ the fact that $o1$ is a partial representation and lightly different of $o2$. $o1$ is an object image, it is represented as an object having an attribute indicating its update date with the object $o2$ that it represents.

$$KE = \{o_0^{env}, \ldots, o_{nke}^{env}\}$$
$$\forall o_i^{env} \in KE, \exists o \in E : (o_i^{env}.name = o.name) \wedge o_i^{env} \lhd o \tag{3}$$

Social knowledge (KS) of an agent/role are composed of the acquaintances and collective constraints imposed by the system. An agent has a partial image of its acquaintances that are its responsible, its assistants and its neighbours. Collective constraints correspond to goals imposed by the group, and are stored in the collective goal GC of the agent.

The image that an agent has of one of its acquaintance (cf def. 4) is composed of: its name; a part of its states; a part of its individual and collectives goals. We note $imgAgent_a \lhd agent_a$ the fact that $imgAgent_a$ is a partial view of the $agent_a$. Likewise, we note $E_{img} \lhd E$ the fact that the set E_{img} is a partial view of the set E. The image has its update date with its model.

$$imgAgent_a = \begin{pmatrix} name_a, states_a^{img}, GI_a^{img}, GC_a^{img}, rules_a^{img}, \\ roles_a^{img}, responsibles_a^{img}, assistants_a^{img} \end{pmatrix} \tag{4}$$
$$etats_a^{img} \lhd etats_a, \ldots, responsibles_a^{img} \lhd responsibles_a$$

The perception function of an agent allows it to update its knowledge (KP, KS and/or KE) and to supplement them, and to receive messages.

The agent behaviour (cf alg. 1) consists in acting as long as the collective goal and the individual goal of an agent and of its roles are not reached. That is to say, when the states of the agent and its roles correspond to the constraints in GI and GC.

The action (cf alg. 2) consists in realizing tasks that allows the agent to reach the collective goals, the roles goals and its personal goals. This order is arbitrary but we think that it is in adequation with order of priorities used in most of enterprises.

---

algorithm 1. Behaviour of an agent a

---

procedure BEHAVIOUR($KP_a, KE_a, KS_a, messages_a$)
    while ($\exists o \in states_a$: $\neg$RESPECT(o, GI) $\vee$ $\neg$RESPECT(o, GC) AND ($\exists role \in$
$roles_a$: $\neg$COMPLETED($role$))) **do**
        ACT($KP_a, KE_a, KS_a, messages_a$)
    end while
end procedure

Applying a rule task can lead: to the modification of the personal, environmental and/or social knowledge; to the sending of a message; to the creation of an agent; to the delegation of roles and goals; and to the change of responsible.

---

algorithm 2. Action of an agent a

---

procedure ACT($KP_a, KE_a, KS_a, messages_a$)
    for all $goal^{GC} \in GC$ **do**
        if $\neg$REACHED($goal^{GC}$) **then**
                            $\triangleright$ return a rule corresponding to the not reached goal
            $R \leftarrow$ CHOOSERULE($goal^{GC}, GC$)
            APPLY($R.tasks$)
        end if
    end for
    for all $role \in roles$ **do**
        if $\neg$COMPLETED($role$) **then**
            $R \leftarrow$ CHOOSERULE($role$)
            APPLY($R.tasks$)
        end if
    end for
    for all $goal^{GI} \in GI$ **do**
        if $\neg$REACHED($goal^{GI}$) **then**
            $R \leftarrow$ CHOOSERULE($goal^{GI}, GI$)
            APPLY($R.tasks$)
        end if
    end for
end procedure

Holonic concepts allow us a precise definition of an multi-agent organisation, but if each agent is free to choose a rule among several to reach its goals, the structure of the system is relatively rigid. It is necessary to add flexibility to allow the system to be more adaptable to the environment.

3 Dynamic in Holonic Multi-agent Organisation

The holonic multi-agent organisation must be able to regenerate it-self in order to repair the loss of an agent or a agents' branch, following a fault, and it must also be able to grow.

3.1 Robustness by Replication in Holonic Multi-agent Organisation

In order to correct faults, we propose the replication and regeneration of agents. However, replication of all the system is not conceivable, it is more pertinent to recreate only critical entities (for example, see DARX platform (Dima Agent Replication Extension)[10]).

The more critical agents of our holomas are: the responsible of the holomas and the agent responsible of the roles, that we note $RHRA$ (for responsible of the holonic role agents). In our proposition, only these agents are physically replicated and update theirs clones.

It should be interesting to evaluate the criticality of each agent to check if they have to be replicated or not. But we propose a bilateral watch, based on "ping" messages, between an agent and its responsible allows them to detect faulty agent. Each responsible is able to create a clone of agents it manages by using the images that it owns of them.

These principles are stored in the role 'holonicAgent' that owns all agents of a holomas. HRA agents own an additional role 'roleManagement'. Agent at the head of a holomas receives the role 'supervisor' that allows to the agent to update the replicant, and to watch the agent $RHRA$. By the same way, a $RHRA$ agent plays also the roles supervisor role ('rolesSupervisor') that allows it to update its replicat and to survey the head of the holomas.

The goal of the roles responsible agents is not only the regeneration of agents, but also to allow the system to grow, horizontally or vertically.

3.2 Growth in Holonic Multi-agent Organisation

The growth of a holomas appears necessary:

- to lighten the tasks of a holonic agent overloaded by a set of roles, and so by a set of goals. We have in this case a vertical growing: the overloaded agent creates assistants in order to delegate most required roles.
- to acquire complementary competences. We have then a horizontal growing: the agent that needs a competence, can either ask to receive the associated role, or if its number of roles is important, ask to its responsible to create a neighbour having the required role.
- to coordinate agents activities acting in a same goal. The agent creates an intermediate assistant to which it delegates supervision of a set of its assistants.

These growth rules are defined in the 'holonicAgent' role.

Let us note that the pruning in a holomas of an agent or a agent branch poses the problem of the loss of personal knowledge and of action strategies. We think that it is more pertinent to just "deactivate" agents that do not participate anymore to the collective goal, and that have accomplished their roles, and that have reached their individual objectives, in case they should be necessary again.

3.3 Roles Dynamic

In order to answer to a goal linked to one of its roles, each agent chooses a rule among the set $hardRules^{role}$ (cf def. 2) and can choose a rule among the set $flexibleRules^{role}$. The priority of a role's rule increases each time the agent chooses it to reach its goal.

Periodically, HRA agents update agents images whose they are responsible. They own then individual redefinition of roles (modification of priority on the rules) for each holonic agent. Each HRA agent checks if there are differences between prescribed roles and roles really played by agents. If a sufficient number of agents (number that is greater than a critical threshold fixed in the 'roleMan-agement' role) have modified a role in the same way, the new definition of the role is kept. So, when, another agent asks to play the role, it receives the new local definition of the role. A same role can so have been defined in different ways on different parts of a holomas.

The first prototype of this platform has been developed using the MAGIQUE [11] multi-agent platform and we have built an application that allows us to deploy into a network a holonic multi-agent system from its description (by a XML file). We are currently developing our holonic platform as an extension to JADE [12]. This first implementation allows us to develop some holomas whose one dedicated to information retrieval.

4 Application to the Information Retrieval

4.1 Holonic Multiagent Platform

We generally use the MAGIQUE [11] platform to build our prototypes. This platform provides libraries dedicated to hierarchical multi-agent systems development: a MAGIQUE agent is an empty shell having only communication capacities (with its supervisor and its team (agents under it)). It is possible to give skills to an agent by associating it with Java classes, composed of functions or sub-processes. Messages exchanged between agents consist in calls to functions or to sub-processes that are located in the skills. We use this notion of skill to implement rules.

In order to generate holonic multi-agent systems, we have defined seven rules/skills linked to roles played by holonic agents:

- to the (*holonicAgent*) role, that own all agents, are associated the rules/skills: *HolonSkill* that allows it the definition of the acquaintances and the roles oriented communication; *SupervisedSkill* that allows an agent to be survey by its acquaintances in order to detect a fault; *RegenerationSkill* that allows an agent to regenerate its acquaintances; *LearnAndTeachSkill* that allows an agent to learn (receive) rules/skills from other agents and to transmit them.
- to the (*supervisor*) role is linked the rule *HolonicorganisationSkill* that owns: the roles' list; the rules' list linked to roles; and the list of images of the agents that compose the holomas.

– to the (*roleManagement*) role is linked the rule *HRSkill* that allows an agent to transmit roles to agent that ask them and to restore the roles and acquaintances of a regenerated agent.
– to the (*rolesSupervisor*) role is associated the rule *BossHRSkill* that allows the roles supervisor: to create roles responsible agents; to regenerate the holomas supervisor; and to regenerate the whole holomas in case of fault (the running tasks are not regenerated).

The first prototype of our platform do not deal with collective and individual goals, only the goals linked to roles are taken into account.

To implement a holomas, we "just have to" develop only rules that compose roles, as well as knowledge of roles and agents. The relations between roles and rules, agents and roles, and between agents are defined in a XML file. We have built an application [11] that allows us to deploy into a network a holonic multi-agent system from this XML file that describes it and from the java classes corresponding to the roles (cf. Annexe A).

4.2   Case Study

The case study that is presented in this article started in a technological watch department of a large company, which asked for a multi-agent based solution to its information retrieval problem. Following the analysis and the modelling of the tasks realized by actors of this small department (composed of 5 persons), we proposed a first IMAS, composed of sub-IMAS (CIASTEWA, for CO-operative Information Agents' System for the TEchnological WAtch) associated with each actor of the watch team (cf fig. 2). A CIASTEWA is a sub holonic multi agent system, which has to search information, to collect it, to sort it and to communicate relevant information to others CIASTEWA. Interaction between CIASTEWA go through their coordinators, to compare data found by the different actors.

Each of this sub system is made up of:

– a local database that contains the user requests, their results and information on the user,
– an interface agent that assists the users to express their requests and allows them the interaction with the results provided by information agents, or with the other users of the group,
– a coordinator agent that has to coordinate actions of the other agents,
– an information responsible agent, which distributes the requests, which are recorded in the local database, to the request agents that it creates according to a search strategy,
– request agents that distribute the request whose they are responsible to search engine agents that they create,
– search engine agents that have to find information on the Internet.

So, we have dynamic holonic multiagent systems that grow temporarily to achieve theirs tasks. The following code is an extract of the LaunchSearchSkill skill of the Information Responsible Role; it represents the creation of request agents, in Java, by using the MAGIQUE platform.

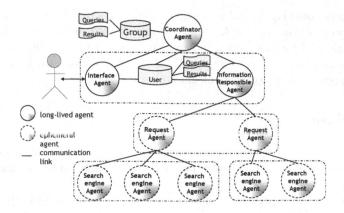

Fig. 2. Architecture of a CIASTEWA

```
for (int i=0; i<reqToLaunch.size(); i++)
{
 Request req = (Request)reqToLaunch.elementAt(i);
 Agent a = platform.createAgent(req.getName());
 a.connectToBoss(getName());
 // add of the holonic behaviour to the new empty agent
 a.addSkill(new holon.skill.HolonSkill(a));
 // set its supervisor
 perform(a.getName() ,"setMySupervisor", new Object [] {getName()});
 // ask to the new agent to retrieve the role "requestSearcher"
 // from the role manager
 a.askNow("requestRole", new Object [] {a.getName(), "requestSearcher"});
 // ask to the new agent to init itself
 a.askNow("initSearchSkill",
    new Object[]{req,externalData,archivedData,localData,deletedData});
 // ask to the new agent (having the request name) to manage the request
 perform(req.getName(), "launchSearch");
}
```

Each request can start immediately by an order of the user (through the interface agent) or be launched at a date recorded in it by the user. Each user has defined between ten and twenty requests to launch on one to five search engines, generally during an interval of one hour in the night. This architecture implies the launch of a maximum of 100 agents on each computer associated to a user, this load has been accepted without problem by the computers.

In the second version of our IMAS, it was asked us to bring the MAS at the end of a third part architecture [11]. The importance of the main agents led us to propose and develop the agents regeneration principles presented in this article. However, if agents are created to replace dead agents, and if they are able to restart the interrupted work (we have killed voluntarily some agents to analyze theirs behaviours), some information are lost. Moreover, it is to the developer to define the knowledge to be stored in a reconfiguration file, no backup copy of the knowledge has been developed in our platform at the moment. The "ping" messages exchanged, about 500 for 5 users, are important but are not carried out at the same time, and on a same computer. Moreover, no necessity of real time reply is required in our applications.

Holonic concepts help us and to agentify problem of distributed data management; our propositions and its first developments allow us to easily design and set-up holonic multi-agent system in a relatively short time. Some development are in progress in our team to apply all of our propositions to the design of a decision support system for users of manual wheelchairs.

5   Conclusion

Our works use the holonic concepts to understand and analyse human organisations and design multi-agent system particularly adapted to the human organisations that we study.

From this work, we propose a multi-agent organisation using both notion of role and notion of hierarchy.

We have developed a first prototype of holonic platform that allows us to automatically deploy a holomas into a network. This platform allowed us to develop easily several IMAS, but need to be improved.

Indeed, the step of the roles definition obliges us to check "manually" that no roles could lead to an interblocking situation. This constraint could be resolved by the addition of the capacity to detect non-cooperative actions (like in [12] for example) in the holonicAgent role that is owned by all the agents. To anticipate, to avoid and to repair a non cooperative situations should slow down the decision making at the personal level of the agents, but should speed up the convergence on the global goal for the holomas.

Another perspective that we have is to develop all of our proposition by using the JADE platform [13]. This platform lends itself to implementation of our concept, by its notions of empty agent receiving behaviours, that can be composed of sub-behaviours, and by the use of yellow pages agents, which are close to our roles management agents.

Acknowledgments. The present research work has been supported by the European Community, the Délégation Régionale à la Recherche et à la Technologie, the Ministére de l'Education Nationale, de la Recherche et de la Technologie, the Région Nord-Pas de Calais, the Centre National de la Recherche Scientifique and the SOLVAY Company. The authors gratefully acknowledge the support of these institutions.

References

1. Adam, E., Mandiau, R., Kolski, C.: Application of a holonic multi-agent system for cooperative work to administrative processes. JASS 2(1), 100–115 (2001)
2. Adam, E., Mandiau, R.: Design of a mas into a human organization: application to an information multi-agent system. In: Giorgini, P., Henderson-Sellers, B., Winikoff, M. (eds.) AOIS 2003. LNCS (LNAI), vol. 3030, pp. 1–15. Springer, Heidelberg (2004)
3. Koestler, A.: The Ghost in the Machine (1969)

4. Schwarz, G.M.: Organizational hierarchy adaptation and information technology. Information and Organization 12, 153–182 (2002)
5. Kendall, E.A.: Role modeling for agent system analysis, design, and implementation. In: First International Symposium on Agent Systems and Applications (ASA'99) (1999)
6. Wooldridge, M., Jennings, N., Kinny, D.: The gaia methodology for agent oriented analysis and design. Journal of Autonomous Agents and Multi-Agent Systems (2000)
7. Ferber, J., Gutknecht, O.: Aalaadin: a meta-model for the analysis and design of organizations in multi-agent systems. In: Demazeau, Y. (ed.) ICMAS 98 (International Conference on Multi-Agent Systems), pp. 128–135. IEEE Press, Los Alamitos (1998)
8. Mathieu, P., Routier, J.-C., Secq, Y.: Rio: Roles, interactions and organizations. In: Mařík, V., Müller, J.P., Pěchouček, M. (eds.) CEEMAS 2003. LNCS (LNAI), vol. 2691. Springer, Heidelberg (2003)
9. Saidani, O., Nurcan, S.: A role based approach for modeling flexible business processes. In: The 7th Workshop on Business Process Modelling, Development, and Support (BPMDS'06), June 2006, pp. 111–120. Springer, Heidelberg (2006)
10. Guessoum, Z., Briot, J.P., Hamel, A., Marin, O., Sens, P. In: Dynamic and Adaptive Replication for Large-Scale Reliable Multi-Agent Systems, pp. 182–198. Springer, Heidelberg (2003)
11. Adam, E., Mandiau, R.: Web interface between users and a centralized information multi-agent system. In: CAiSE Workshops, vol. 2, pp. 340–354 (2004) ISBN 9984-9767-2-6
12. Bernon, C., Camps, V., Gleizes, M., Picard, G.: Engineering adaptive multi-agent systems: The adelfe methodology. In: Giorgini, P. (ed.) Agent-Oriented Methodologies, pp. 172–202. Idea Group Pub. USA (2005)
13. Bellifemine, F., Caire, G., Poggi, A., Rimassa, G.: Jade - a white paper. Technical report, TiLab (2003), http://jade.tilab.com/papers/WhitePaperJADEEXP.pdf

Annexe A : Extract of a XML File Describing a OMAH

```xml
<?xml version="1.0" encoding="ISO-8859-1" ?>
<sma>
<!-- roles descriptions-->
<role>
 <name>BigBoss</name>
 <Knowledge/>
 <skillList>
  <skill>
   <nameSkill>AgentBossSkill</nameSkill>
   <parameter />
  </skill> </skillList> </role>
<role>
 <name>supervisor</name>
 <Knowledge/>
 <skillList>
  <skill>
   <nameSkill>SupSkill</nameSkill>
   <parameter>
    <type>java.lang.String</type>
    <value>agent-config.xml</value>
   </parameter>
  </skill> </skillList> </role>
<role>
 <name>searcher</name>
 <Knowledge/>
 <skillList>
  <skill>
   <nameSkill>InformationResponsibleSkill</nameSkill>
   <parameter />
  </skill>
```

```xml
  </skillList>
 </role>
<role>
 <name>RequestResponsible</name>
 <Knowledge/>
 <skillList>
  <skill>
   <nameSkill>RequestSearchSkill</nameSkill>
   <parameter />
  </skill> </skillList> </role>
<role>
 <name>SearchEngineResponsible</name>
 <Knowledge/>
 <skillList>
  <skill>
   <nameSkill>SearchEngineSkill</nameSkill>
   <parameter />
  </skill> </skillList> </role>
<!-- agents descriptions-->
<agent>
 <name>BOSS</name>
 <roles><name>BigBoss</name></roles>
 <Knowledge/>
 <localisation>192.168.6.51 4444</localisation>
 <boss />
 <subordinates />
 <neighbours />
</agent>
<agent>
 <name>supervisor</name>
 <roles> <name>supervisor</name> </roles>
 <Knowledge/>
 <localisation>192.168.6.51 4444</localisation>
 <boss>BOSS@192.168.6.51:4444</boss>
 <subordinates />
 <neighbours />
</agent>
<agent>
 <name>SearchResponsibleAgent</name>
 <roles> <name>searcher</name> </roles>
 <Knowledge/>
 <localisation>192.168.6.51 4444</localisation>
 <boss>supervisor@192.168.6.51:4444</boss>
 <subordinates />
 <neighbours />
</agent>
<!-- methods to launch at the begining-->
<method>
 <nameAgent>supervisor</nameAgent>
 <nameMethod>initAgent</nameMethod>
 <parameter />
</method>
<method>
 <nameAgent>searcher</nameAgent>
 <nameMethod>go</nameMethod>
</method>
</sma>
```

Agent-Based Inter-Organizational Workflow Management System

Paulo Leitão and João Mendes

Polytechnic Institute of Bragança, Quinta Santa Apolónia, Apartado 1134,
P-5301-857 Bragança, Portugal
{pleitao,jmendes}@ipb.pt

Abstract. An Electronic Institution is a computational framework that provides a set of services supporting the lifecycle of Virtual Organizations. In a virtual organization, different business partners cooperate in order to achieve a common goal (the established contract), being the co-ordination of the corresponding inter-organizational workflow an important issue. This paper describes an inter-organizational workflow management architecture, based in multi-agent systems principles, aiming to orchestrate the contract execution and to obtain feedback from the shop floor level. Aiming to validate its correctness and applicability, a special focus is devoted to its implementation, using the JADE agent development framework, and its operation under different scenarios.

1 Introduction

A Virtual Organization (VO) is a paradigm that can be defined as a temporary consortium of different organizations that "pool their resources to meet short-term objectives and exploit fast-changing market trends" [1], and whose co-operation is supported by computer networks [2]. An Electronic Institution, concept originality introduced by [3] to represent the virtual counterpart of real-world institutions, is a computational framework that may effectively assist the lifecycle of a VO by providing an appropriate set of services, which include [4]: i) assistance to the formation of VOs through negotiation mediation and contract templates, ii) validation and registration of the agreed contracts, and iii) monitoring of the partners' compliance to contractual commitments.

The complexity and heterogeneous nature of the internal partners systems, either business or shop floor systems, require the introduction of a service to coordinate/synchronize the contract execution, demanding a close perception of what is going on at the shop-floor level, in an inter-organizational perspective. This service will obtain feedback from the shop floor level, supporting the detection in advance of unexpected deviations from the plan, allowing the implementation of corrective actions to minimize the impact of these deviations in the contract execution. This service is addressed by an inter-organizational workflow management platform.

This paper describes an inter-organizational workflow management architecture based in multi-agent systems principles. A special focus will be devoted

V. Mařík, V. Vyatkin, A.W. Colombo (Eds.): HoloMAS 2007, LNAI 4659, pp. 71–80, 2007.

to the implementation of the proposed concepts into a case study using JADE (Java Agent Development Framework), and to its operation under different environmental conditions aiming to validate their correctness and applicability.

The paper is organized as follows: first, Section 2 introduces the agent-based inter-organizational workflow management architecture, as part of the Electronic Institution platform. Section 3 describes the implementation of the inter-organizational workflow management system and Section 4 presents the implemented system operating in practice and discusses the achieved results. Finally, Section 5 rounds up the paper with conclusions.

2   Agent-Based Architecture for Inter-Organizational Workflow Management

A contract established during the VO formalization is composed of clauses that define each parties' obligations, together with associated sanctions in case of deviation [5]. Besides specifying explicit behavior norms they also describe a coarse-grained specification of the underlying multiparty business process.

The supervision of the contract execution, demanding a close perception of what is going on at the shop-floor level, in an inter-organizational perspective, requires the existence of an inter-organizational workflow management system, that checks, in a pro-active manner, each partner's compliance to cooperation efforts, and acts accordingly. The main functions associated to this platform are the creation of the coarse-grained work-plan resulted from the contract, the synchronization of tasks during the contract execution, the detection in advance of deviations to the contract and the re-planning in advance aiming to minimize the impact of the disruption, maintaining the terms defined in the contract.

2.1   Architecture Components

The proposed inter-organizational workflow approach is an agent-based architecture [5], illustrated in Fig. 1, that distributes the functionalities, knowledge and competencies by a community of autonomous and cooperative agents. The architecture, focusing the IO-WfM level of Fig. 1, comprises two distinct components that have different roles in the system: IO-WfM and Partner agents.

The *IO-WfM* agents act as coordinators, synchronizing and monitoring the execution of the contract, embodying the following main competencies:

- Synchronization/coordination of the inter-organizational workflow, by enforcing the synchronization among individual workflows. This function is implemented using an orchestration engine embedded in the agent.
- Dynamic update of the workflow, originated by unexpected situations (e.g. delays, deviations or unaccomplished tasks), in order to minimize the impact of such deviations in the contract.
- Provide feedback to the *Contract Monitor* agent about the execution stage of the contract, namely useful inputs for reputation handling and for the redefinition of future contracts.

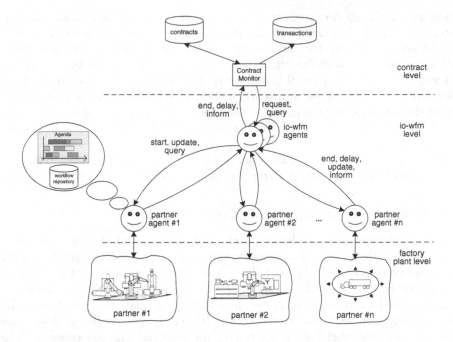

Fig. 1. Inter-Organizational Workflow Management Architecture

The first step in activating pro-active monitoring is to translate the contract into a coarse-grained work-plan, respecting precedence restrictions and deadlines. It is the responsibility of the *IO-WfM* agent to elaborate a fine-grained work-plan, articulated with the contract participants, and employing local-dependent knowledge regarding the execution of each higher-level task.

After building the inter-organizational work-plan, the *IO-WfM* agent starts its synchronization, by determining whether the process is ready to move to the next task according to the work-plan. The *IO-WfM* agent delegates the task control to the partner responsible for its execution and waits for the end of its execution. If an exception occurs, provoking delays in the execution of the work-plan, the *IO-WfM* agent tries to recover by re-scheduling and finding a new plan for the workflow execution. The aim of this re-scheduling is not to re-allocate the tasks to alternative partners, because this implies a modification of the established contract, but to propagate the deviation to the partners in charge of executing posterior tasks. Having, in advance, the information about the deviation, each partner can handle it locally, trying to minimize the impact caused by the original deviation. In case of success, the *IO-WfM* agent will notify the partners about the modification in the work-plan; otherwise, it will notify the *Contract Monitor* agent about the occurrence of the unrecoverable exception, which should then trigger the contract-predicted corrective measures.

The *Partner* agents monitor the local workflow of each VO partner and are responsible to be the first entities to detect, as soon as possible, eventual deviations in the execution of the tasks that may cause contract violations. The detection, executed dynamically and in advance, can be implemented using a rule-based mechanism, that detects, i) the tasks that are in execution but whose estimated end date is earlier than the current date, and ii) the tasks that are yet waiting to start its execution and whose estimated start date is earlier than the current date. In case of occurrence of unexpected situations, the information about the deviation is propagated to the other entities of the system.

These agents are connected to the planning and control system of each partner, which will act as a "black box" as far as the whole system is concerned. The *Partner* agent has a strong connection with the partner itself, often requiring the development of proprietary wrappers and integration mechanisms.

2.2   Interactions Among System Components

The goals defined for the global system will be achieved through the interaction among the several distributed components, each one contributing with its local behavior, knowledge and skills. The interaction between the *IO-WfM* and *Partners* agents allows to implement the functions associated to the inter-organizational workflow management, namely to coordinate the execution of the inter-organization workflow, to detect in advance the occurrence of deviations and to re-plan the workflow aiming to contain potential damages caused by the deviation. Besides the interaction between these two types of agents, the *IO-WfM* agent also interacts with the *Contract Monitor* agent, receiving the contract to orchestrate and providing information about its execution.

This cooperation is regulated through a proper set of interaction protocols (see [5] for a deeply specification of the information exchanged between the system components). As an example, the interaction diagram represented in Fig. 2 illustrates the supervision and synchronization of the contract execution.

Briefly, after the allocation of the tasks to the *Partner* agents, the *IO-WfM* agent orchestrates the execution of the obtained work-plan, taking in consideration the precedence graph of the tasks contained in the contract and the real

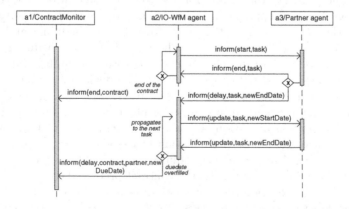

Fig. 2. Interaction Diagram for the Supervision of the Contract Execution

evolution of the agendas of the VO partners. In case of detection of some un-expected problem occurred during the execution of the task causing its delay, the *IO-WfM* agent, based on the estimated end date proposed by the partner entity, triggers a new round to find a new work-plan for the workflow execution that minimizes the impact of the disturbance. For this purpose it may notify all dependent partner entities about the changes in the work-plan, using the inform-update message.

3   Implementation of the IO-WfM System

The concepts described in the last section were implemented into a software application to validate the proposed architecture. The multi-agent system ap-plication was developed using the JADE agent development framework, which simplifies the development of multi-agent systems by providing a set of sys-tem services and agents in compliance with the FIPA (Foundation of Intelligent Physical Agents) specifications: naming service and yellow-page service, message transport and parsing service, and a library of FIPA interaction protocols ready to be used [6]. Since it is based on Java programming language, the whole appli-cation was coded in Java, with the support of development tools, such as Eclipse software framework [7] and Subversion version control system [8].

Both types of agents (i.e. *IO-WfM* and *Partner* agents) are extensions of JADE's Agent class, providing the necessary functionalities to set up an agent (e.g. registration services and mechanisms for sending/receiving messages). The added features are specific to each type of agent, reflecting the requirements of the inter-organizational workflow management architecture. Such characteristics include the use of behavior models that respond to specific events (e.g. messages from the interaction among the *IO-WfM*, *Partner* and *Contract Monitor* agents) according to the actual state of the agent.

Besides the startup and cleanup methods of an agent, it contains a set of behaviors that describes a particular behavior model, specific to each type of agent. A particular behavior corresponds to the execution of a set of actions representing an activity of the agent, that is triggered when a corresponding event occurs. A behavior may change the agents state and may send messages to other agents (an important remark: these states have nothing to do with the internal state used by JADE to represent the agent life-cycle). As an example, the behavior model of a *Partner* agent includes a behavior, triggered in case of detection of a delay in the execution of a task, which predicts the new end date, re-schedules its agenda and notifies the *IO-WfM* agent.

Each agent provides a graphical user interface to assist the user with useful information about the contract execution and the local agenda of each partner. Mainly it consists of a table showing the current state of specific tasks: the *IO-WfM* agent interface represents the tasks of the associated contract and the *Partner* agent exhibits the tasks of the partner that it stands for. The Swing GUI toolkit for Java was used to set up these interfaces.

The communication between *IO-WfM* and *Partner* agents is done via message passing over the network. The messages are encoded using the FIPA-ACL communication language [10] specified by the FIPA organization. Agents may register their functionalities in form of services, so they can be discovered by other agents. For this purpose, JADE offers a Directory Facilitator (DF) agent, specified by FIPA, which acts in a similar way to the yellow pages.

In distributed and heterogeneous environments, the communication between autonomous agents requires a common understanding of the concepts of their knowledge domain, i.e. the usage of a proper ontology. An ontology defines the vocabulary that will be used in the communication between agents, and the knowledge relating to these terms. This knowledge includes the definition of the concepts and the relationships between these concepts. The meaning of the message content is captured in the message ontology. The developed ontology was designed using the Protégé tool [9] and translated into Java classes using the OntologyBeanGenerator plug-in, according to the JADE guidelines that follow the FIPA Ontology Service Recommendations specifications [10].

A major problem when dealing with practical applications in industrial domains is related to the integration of the control application with the real systems, due to the highly heterogeneous nature of existing systems. In fact, the shop floor system of each VO partner will have a particular system architecture and a particular protocol for information exchange. For this purpose, each *Partner* agent will comprise a wrapper, developed case-by-case according to the partner system specifications.

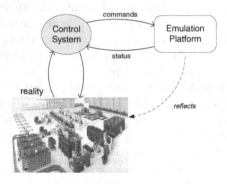

Fig. 3. Emulation and the Correspondent Real System (adapted from [11])

In the experimental phase, the use of the real systems is quite impracticable due to the long development time associated to the development of wrappers for each individual factory plant. Additionally, it would also be impossible to reproduce the same conditions for a number of experimental tests when trying to compare alternative control systems [11]. One way to overcome this problem is to use an emulation platform that behaves like the real system, as illustrated in Fig. 3. For the inter-organizational workflow management platform it is indistinguishable to be connected to the emulation platform or to the real system.

The emulator, one for each shop floor operation of individual VO partners, is an agent which behavior uses a finite state machine and manages a set of Java threads (one for each local task), comprising a stochastic model that will allow us to analyze the system's response to unexpected situations.

4   IO-WfM System in Operation

An experimental case study has been used to validate the correctness and applicability of the proposed agent-based inter-organizational workflow management system. The experimental case study uses a contract defining the agreements established between four consortium partners. The contract is represented by the structure defined in the XML-schema illustrated in Fig. 4. Taking in account the precedences of each task, it is possible to build a Petri net that describes the workflow (see also Fig. 4). Only for simulation purposes it was used small time intervals for the tasks execution that do not correspond to real processes.

The experimental scenario considers two different plant scenarios: i) the first plant scenario considers that no unexpected deviation will occur, and ii) the second plant scenario considers the introduction of disruptions in each partner with the following probability: Philip - 20%, Smith - 10%, Turner - 25% and Scott - 30%. In case of disruption, the deviation introduced in the task execution is proportional to the associated disruption probability. Additionally, the partners also have a set of allocated tasks from other contracts in their agendas, to create possible date overlays when allocating new tasks.

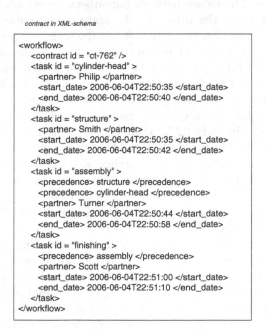
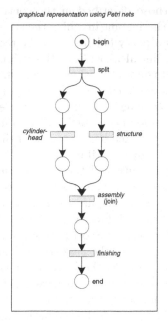

Fig. 4. Representation of the Contract used in the Case Study

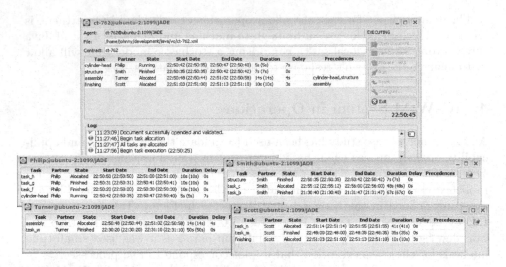

Fig. 5. Prototype of the Inter-organizational Workflow Management System

The developed agent-based inter-organizational workflow management prototype system for the described case study is illustrated in the Fig. 5. It shows the several agents presented in the system and also their graphical user interfaces.

These GUIs facilitate the interaction with the user and show useful information about the ongoing processes, namely related to the list of tasks allocated to each agent and their current status. The values between parenthesis corresponds to those described in the contract, and the others to the real-time execution. At the instant in which the screen-shot was taken (22:50:45), the task *structure* has already finished, but the task *cylinder-head* is still running, because during the initial allocation, the partner Philip was unavailable to respect the commitments established in the contract. This situation originated a delay since the task *assembly* can only be executed after the end of the both previous tasks. The *Partner* agent Philip already detected the deviation, predicted that the end of execution of the task *cylinder-head* will be at 22:50:47 and notified the *IO-WfM* agent, which had propagated the delay to the Turner and Scott partner agents.

However, as illustrated in Fig. 6 another deviation occurs with the delay in the execution of the task *assembly*. The *IO-WfM* agent propagates this delay to the subsequent tasks, in this case to the Scott partner, which has the possibility to anticipate the deviation occurrence and to minimize the impact of the unexpected deviation in its local agenda.

In fact, the Scott partner makes re-adjustments in its agenda anticipating the execution of the task *Task-N*, after verifying the precedences in the associated workplan. At the end, the deviation was partially contained, and even if the delays in the contract execution were not avoided, the system had minimized the impact of the original deviation in the local execution of other tasks.

The results achieved in the experimental test allowed to verify the applicability of the agent-based platform, as well its correctness to implement the functions

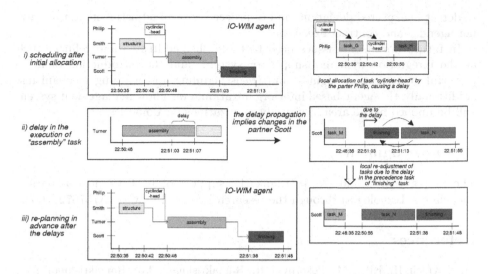

Fig. 6. Experimental Results (Evolution of the Agendas during a Contract Execution)

related to the inter-organizational workflow management, either in normal or unexpected situations. In fact, in a scenario without the presence of deviations, the system is able to synchronize/coordinate, in an inter-organizational point of view, the execution of the contract resulted from the establishment of the virtual organization. In case of a scenario with the presence of disturbances, the system is able to detect, in advance, unexpected deviations in the execution of the tasks belonging to the contract, and to trigger, in advance, a re-planning of the contract workplan minimizing its impact.

5   Conclusions

The business value associated with a VO requires a set of institutional services supporting its lifecycle, and especially a close monitoring of an inter-organizational workflow, allowing that possible problems can be anticipated and their potential damages minimized.

This paper introduced an agent-based inter-organizational workflow management architecture to supervise the contract execution, providing a close perception of what is going on at the shop-floor level in an inter-organizational perspective. The validation of the proposed concepts, to analyze their correctness and applicability, requires their implementation and experimental test in a prototype. For that purpose, a prototype was implemented using the JADE agent development framework. The experimental tests allow verifying that the proposed agent-based inter-organizational workflow management works as specified, either in normal operation or in presence of disturbances. Namely, they show the ability of the system to orchestrate the inter-organizational workflow, to detect unexpected deviations and to proceed with re-adjustments in the partner agendas and contract execution.

In future work, some issues need to be further addressed and refined, such as the integration with real shop floor systems and the introduction of more powerful orchestration engines, and (re-)scheduling and learning mechanisms. Additionally, the agent-based inter-organizational workflow management system will be applied in the area of virtual organizations for domotics.

Acknowledgments

The first author would like to thank the support of FCT (Fundação para a Ciência e a Tecnologia) through the research Project POSC/EIA/57672/2004.

References

1. Davulcu, H., Kifer, M., Pokorny, L.R., Ramakrishnan, C.R., Ramakrishnan, I.V., Dawson, S.: Modelling and Analysis of Interactions in Virtual Enterprises. In: Proc. of the 9th Int'l Workshop on Research Issues on Data Engineering: Information Technology for Virtual Enterprises, pp. 12–18. IEEE Computer Society, Los Alamitos (1999)
2. Camarinha-Matos, L.M., Afsarmanesh, H.: Infrastructures for Virtual Enterprises: a Summary of Achievements. In: Camarinha- Matos, L., Afsarmanesh, H. (eds.) Proceedings of the PRO-VE 99 - IFIP International Conference On Infrastructures for Virtual Enterprises, pp. 483–490. Kluwer Academic Publishers, Dordrecht (1999)
3. Dignum, V., Dignum, F.: Modelling Agent Societies: Co-ordination Frameworks and Institutions. In: Brazdil, P.B., Jorge, A.M. (eds.) EPIA 2001. LNCS (LNAI), vol. 2258, pp. 191–204. Springer, Heidelberg (2001)
4. Cardoso, H., Malucelli, A., Rocha, A.P., Oliveira, E.: Institutional Services for Dynamic Virtual Organizations. In: Camarinha-Matos, L., Afsarmanesh, H., Ortiz, A. (eds.) Collaborative Networks and Their Breeding Environments - 6th IFIP Working Conference on Virtual Enterprises, pp. 521–528. Springer, Heidelberg (2005)
5. Cardoso, H., Leitão, P., Oliveira, E.: An Approach to Inter-Organizational Workflow Management in an Electronic Institution. In: Proc. of the 12th IFAC Symposium on Information Control Problems in Manufacturing, France, pp. 429–434 (2006)
6. Bellifemine, F., Poggi, A., Rimassa, G.: JADE, A FIPA Compliant Agent Framework. In: Proceedings of 4th International Conference on the Practical Application of Intelligent Agents and Multi-Agents, pp. 97–108 (1999)
7. Eclipse: (March 2007), http://www.eclipse.org/
8. Subversion: (March 2007), http://subversion.tigris.org/
9. Protégé: (March 2007), http://protg.stanford.edu/
10. FIPA: Foundation for Intelligent Physical Agents (2007), http://www.fipa.org/
11. Saint-Germain, B., Valckenaers, P., Brussel, H.V., Hadeli, Bochmann, O., Zamfirescu, C., Verstraete, P.: Multi-agent Manufacturing Control: An Industrial Case Study. In: Proc. of the 7th IFAC Workshop on Intelligent Manufacturing Systems, Hungary, pp. 227–232 (2003)

Co-operative Co-evolutionary System for Solving Dynamic VRPTW Problems with Crisis Situations

Rafał Dreżewski, Łukasz Dronka, and Jarosław Koźlak

Department of Computer Science
AGH University of Science and Technology, Kraków, Poland
{drezew,kozlak}@agh.edu.pl

Abstract. Vehicle routing problems with time windows are NP-hard problems. Additional difficulties are introduced by dynamic client requests and crisis situations. One of the techniques used in order to solve such problems are evolutionary algorithms. In this paper a co-evolutionary algorithm with spatial population structure is presented. The system is verified with the use of dynamic vehicle routing problems with time windows and crisis situations.

1 Introduction

In the current economic climate, transportation of cargo and delivering services to the homes of clients is playing a very important and ever-increasing role. One of the most widely researched transport problems today is the Vehicle Routing Problem with Time Windows (VRPTW). The idea of the problem is to realize a given set of transport requests while maintaining the lowest possible costs with the number of used vehicles and the total distance travelled. Each vehicle is described by: a location which has to be visited, a period of time when this location should be visited (called *time window*), a capacity needed for transporting the parcel picked-up/delivered from/to a given location. The vehicles are described by their total capacity (the total size of parcels that may be transported at the same time) and a speed. The formal model of VRPTW problem may be found, for example, in [14].

VRPTW is a NP-hard problem [9]. It means, that the time needed to solve it using algorithms finding strict solutions grows exponentially with the size of the problem. For problems like this approximate solutions which could be found fast enough and would be strict enough need to be searched. NP-hard problems can be solved with the application of various heuristics and meta-heuristics—the point is that they make use of problem internal properties.

It is possible to distinguish two kinds of VRPTW: static and dynamic. In static, all transport requests are known before starting the process of assigning

V. Mařík, V. Vyatkin, A.W. Colombo (Eds.): HoloMAS 2007, LNAI 4659, pp. 81–92, 2007.

them to the vehicles, while in the dynamic case, requests arrive continuously during the simulation process. In such case the modeling of the respective vehicle's location and the status of realizing requests is necessary.

For the analysis of the practical problems associated with the planning and realization of transport requests an important element is taken into consideration, namely, the occurrence of different crisis situations and an attempt trying to limit their consequences. Crisis situations analyzed in this paper, are the following: traffic jams appearing on the routes of vehicles, vehicle breakdowns, delays of starting the request realization, prolonging the time of request realization in a given customer location and premature time windows closing.

2   Previous Research on Dynamic VRPTW Problems and Crisis Situations

The VRPTW has been the focus of analysis by many researchers because of its far-reaching and wide range of practical application. Especially, a particularly high number of solutions of its static version have been worked out. To verify the quality of algorithms, sets of transport requests tests, prepared by Solomon and extended by Gehring and Homberger [1], are used.

The heuristic methods used are usually made up of two stages. In the first one, the initial solutions are generated using different kinds of construction heuristics (for example route first cluster second, saving method, I1 heuristic, parallel I1 heuristic, sweep heuristic). Then, optimization heuristics are used to improve the initial solutions. Different approaches are used, e.g. tabu search, simulated annealing, evolutionary algorithms or ant colony approach. The algorithm proposed by Gehring and Homberger [7], based on evolutionary strategies, obtained especially good results. The overview of best VRPTW solving metaheuristic is presented in [4].

The dynamic versions of VRPTW were also studied [8,3], but less work was done than for static version. In [3] an analysis of problem having mixed static-dynamic features and methods of request generation for such problem as well as measures of its dynamic degree is described.

When modeling crisis situations the the most often researched are the appearance of traffic jams, for this case a multi-agent approach was applied [6].

The analysis of the consequences of critical situations is also the subject of this work. The paper [5] contains an overview of various systems for solving VRPTW and PDPTW (Pickup and Delivery Problem with Time Windows—this problem is similar to the mentioned VRPTW, it is characterized by the fact that with each transport request two locations are associated: the location of pickup and the location of delivery, and these locations are assigned separate time windows) developed in our research group. The pilot version of the platform presented in this paper and the preliminary results of experiments (without crisis situations) obtained with the use of the platform were also described in [5].

3   Algorithms for Solving Dynamic VRPTW Problems

In the system presented in this paper, co-operative co-evolutionary algorithm (CCA) [11] is used to solve dynamic VRPTW problem. The basic CCA algorithm may be described by the following pseudo-code:

```
For each subpopulation S Do:
   Initialise population Ps(0)
   Evaluate all individuals from Ps(0) (by forming groups
      composed of the given individual from S and the chosen
      representants of all other subpopulations)
End_For
While termination condition not met Repeat:
   For each subpopulation S Do:
      Select a set of parents Xs(t) for next generation
      Apply genetic operators to the individuals of Xs(t)
         obtaining a set of descendants Ds(t)
      Evaluate individuals from Ds(t) (in the same way
         as in the case of Ps(0))
      Combine Ps(t) and Ds(t) obtaining Ps(t+1)
   End_For
End_While
```

The algorithm is based on the co-evolutionary algorithm for VRPTW problems proposed in [10]. In such an approach two subpopulations (species) are used. Individuals from the first subpopulation represent the number of clients in each route. Information encoded in the genotypes of individuals from the second subpopulation controls which clients, and in what order, appear in every single route. An individual from the first subpopulation is correct if the sum of all his genes' values is greater or equal to the number of clients. An individual from the second subpopulation is correct if it contains permutation of all clients. Combination of two individuals coming from opposite subpopulations results in a complete solution. The reverse of this process is a separation of a complete solution, which results in two individuals from the opposite subpopulations.

Figure 1 illustrates two individuals from the opposite subpopulations. A value of the first gene of individual from the first subpopulation is the number of clients of first vehicle's route. As we can see, the route of the first vehicle consists of three clients and the first three genes of the individual from the second subpopulation strictly describe the shape of the route: $\{0, 3, 2, 7, 0\}$. The other routes are created in the analogical way. The data contained in the genotype of the individual from the second subpopulation is used to create three routes only. However this is not a problem, because a complete solution is created. Genes which are not used in the complete solution are considered being redundant and they are ignored.

Because it is not possible to predict the number of routes in advance, it is assumed, that the number of genes of individuals from the first subpopulation is half of the number of clients. A maximum length of a route is also limited to this

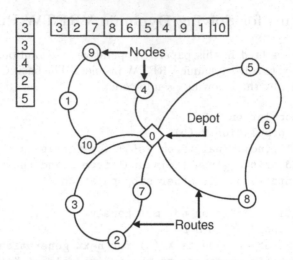

Fig. 1. The individuals from the first (left) and the second (top) subpopulation. Graph illustrates the solution, which is the result of combining given individuals [10].

value. With these assumptions, it is possible, that a shortage of clients during the process of complete solution constructing will occur. In this case the strategy of filling up missing genes with random numbers from the range $\langle 2; n/2\rangle$ (where n is the number of clients) is used.

The co-evolutionary algorithm described above was used together with an island model parallel evolutionary algorithm [2]. In such a model the whole population of individuals is divided into subpopulations living on different islands (computation nodes). The individuals can migrate between islands. In our case also different fitness function on each island is used.

4 Prediction Techniques for Preventing and Avoiding Crisis Situations

The function approximation approach is used as the main prediction technique in the presented system. The goal of approximation is finding dependence between the analyzed continuous attributes and other continuous attributes of the analyzed phenomenon. After computing such a dependence we are able to predict a value of interesting attributes for new sets of attributes of the analyzed phenomenon. The application of this method is based on the assumption that the occurrence and length of crisis situations probably depends on a well formed set of continuous parameters. The key issue in obtaining a good quality of prediction with the use of approximation techniques is the selection of an appropriate set of parameters. Both ignoring important parameters and taking into account unimportant parameters often results in a slow learning process and the decrease in prediction quality. In real conditions, correlation should be analyzed to define which parameters are significant.

We tested two function approximators:

- Multilayer perceptron with a backpropagation algorithm [12]. The number of artificial neurons in the input layer is equal to the number of continuous parameters, on which a crisis depends. Single hidden layer consists of 15 neurons with sigmoid activation function. The output layer consists of a single neuron with a sigmoid activation function—the output is a predicted crisis length. Learning rate decreases while the learning process progresses.
- Tile Coding [13]. The number of tile dimensions is equal to the number of continuous parameters, on which the crisis depends. The size of tiles and number of tilings depend on the type of crisis—both the requirement of strict predictions and memory limitations are taken into consideration. In order to update function values for tiles the delta rule is used [15]:

$$w_i(x) = w_i(x) + \beta(value - w_i(x)) \tag{1}$$

where $w_i(x)$ is the function value for tile, β is the learning rate, and the value is the value returned by environment.

5   System for Solving Dynamic VRPTW Problems with Crisis Situations

The system presented in this paper was implemented with the use of more general, Java based component platform for solving VRP problems. The platform consists of several components, of which the most important are:

- Static problems component.
- Dynamic problems simulation component.
- Soft time windows component—soft time windows allows us to expand time windows for clients and depot. Expanding time windows results in penalties during solutions evaluation.
- Crisis situations simulation component.
- Computational component—algorithms for solving VRP problems are loaded as plugins. Although for this platform there were mostly implemented evolutionary algorithms, the component architecture of the platform allows us to add also non-evolutionary algorithms, like tabu search, etc.
- Operators loaded as plugins—operators are all processes, which input and output is an individual (or a set of individuals). These include all genetic operators like recombination, mutation, etc.

In all experiments presented in this paper the CCA algorithm with the island model—as described in section 3—was used as the computational component (see fig. 2). In order to exchange the best individuals between islands the set of individuals from each island was copied to repository. Individuals from the repository were then sent to other islands, where they replaced the worst individuals. Computations on distinct islands can take place on a single machine or on several network connected machines. Distributed computing uses Java RMI technology.

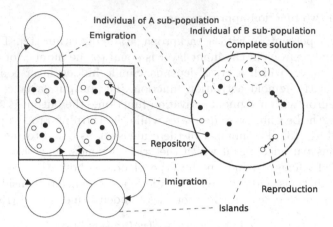

Fig. 2. Computational component: co-evolutionary algorithm and island model

5.1   Dynamic Problems Simulation

The component for dynamic problem simulation realizes an event-driven simulation model with discrete time. Dynamic problems are generated on the basis of static Solomon's test problems. Part of the clients' service requests are declared before the beginning of the simulation—the remaining requests are declared during simulation in two sets of requests. First one arrives when the 1/3 of the simulation has passed and the second when 2/3 of the simulation has passed.

The way of solving the dynamic problem is performing alternate simulations of vehicle movement and the static problem planning algorithm for the set of unserved clients. During the simulation of vehicle movement, vehicle locations and cargo amounts are updated. This updated information is then taken into account during the planning of the next static solution. Clients already served are removed from the set of unserved clients during the simulation of vehicle movement.

The solution of dynamic problem can also be described by the following pseudo-code:

```
Schedule requests declarations
The unserved clients set is empty
While(there are undeclared requests in the schedule)
   Declare requests
   Add clients declaring requests to the unserved clients set
   Run the static problem planning algorithm for
       the set of unserved clients
   Simulate vehicles movement
End_while
```

5.2 Simulation of Crisis Situations

Five types of crisis situations were implemented within the component responsible for simulating such situations. These situations differ from each other in the following ways:

- Place where crisis situations appear—clients or sections of routes between clients.
- Parameters, on which probability of the occurrence of crisis situations and its length depends. Dependence between particular types of crisis situations and their parameters is essential to predict the crisis situations properly. Selecting a set of parameters for the given type of crisis situation means, that there is a high probability, that the crisis situation of a particular type depends on every parameter of the chosen set;
- Time of the crisis situation occurring.

Implemented crisis situations, include (only selected are described in more details):

- Occurrence of traffic jams within some sections of the route, between two clients—depends on two discrete parameters: clients, which identify the particular section of route and one continuous parameter: occurrence time (we assume that the occurrence of traffic jams depends on the time of the day).
- Vehicle breakdowns.
- Delayed readiness of the client (time window opening delayed).
- Prolongation of the service time—depends on one discrete parameter: a particular client, and two continuous parameters: the cargo weight to unload and the occurrence time.
- Premature time window closure.

For each set of values of discrete parameters of crisis, separate crisis length generators were created and used. For each generator and for each continuous parameter a random function was selected and used to compute the probability of crisis situation occurrence and its length. Several types of functions can be used, for example trigonometric, linear, or power with random parameters. The random parameters of the function were selected in such a manner that the function had values from the range $\langle 0, 1 \rangle$ in the whole domain (possible values of crisis' continuous parameter). We assume that the probability of a crisis situation occurring is equal to the geometric mean of crisis' continuous parameters' values. The length of the crisis is equal to the geometric mean of the crisis' continuous parameters' values multiplied by the absolute value of a random number from the normal distribution and some chosen factor.

For each set of values of crisis discrete parameters separate approximators were created and used. Attributes of approximation are continuous parameters of crisis and the crisis length. The latter one is attributed to the prediction. During the phase of vehicles movement simulation, each time when a crisis situation occurring is possible, the crisis length is computed in the manner described in the previous paragraph. When a crisis does not occur it is set to zero. A crisis length is used to correct the parameters of simulation (eg. traffic jam—time of passing the road is made longer). Then the approximator responsible for predicting the crisis length for the crisis type and the set of values of discrete parameters is determined. The chosen approximator is trained: training attributes are the set of values of continuous parameters of crisis and computed crisis length.

The use of separate approximators for each set of values of discrete parameters of a crisis disqualifies the trivial assumption that there is a straight road between every pair of clients. When considering traffic jams, it would mean that we have to create squared clients number of approximators. Thus we provide the possibility of limiting the number of roads in such a way that the road net is the connected graph (accessibility of all clients from the depot is assured). The crisis situations component includes the algorithm for generating the set of roads between clients in such a way that the distance between any particular two clients is close to a straight road length. The predicted delay caused by the traffic jams between two particular clients is the sum of predicted delays caused by traffic jams on all roads between the mentioned clients.

Two methods of avoiding crisis situations with the application of predictors were implemented:

– Correction of routes with the use of predicted crises' lengths during the stage of combining two individuals from opposite populations into a single solution—clients, where a successful service is doubtful because of the high risk of crisis situations occurring are moved to another position in the route or even to another route.
– Correction of fitness function values with the use of predicted crises' lengths—fitness value for a solution, where the risk of the crisis situation occurring is high, is decreased.

6   Experimental Results

The most significant consequence of the crisis situations occurring is the appearance of vehicle delays. Because of these, vehicles arrive at the client later than the planned algorithm assumed, often after closing the clients' time windows. In the last case the client is not served and it greatly decreases the solution quality. For this reason the number of unserved clients is considered as a main optimization parameter—apart from the number of routes. Experiments have been carried out on the set of dynamic problem tests with the diversified dynamism level, generated on the basis of Solomon's static problems set.

Results for R2 Solomon's problem class are listed in fig. 3. Very good results have been achieved with Tile Coding predictor (TC). The number of unserved clients has been reduced by more then half (when compared to algorithm without any predictor—"Basic") and only the small increase of the route numbers has been observed. Good results have also been achieved with the use of soft time windows (SW). In this case, time windows are expanded by 50% (SW = 0.5) of its initial width. The best results however can be observed in the case of using

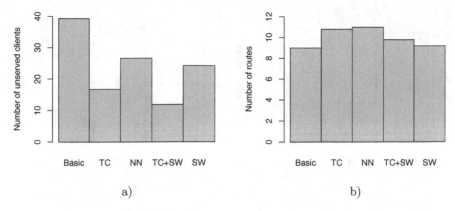

Fig. 3. Average results of 33 experiments carried out on every configuration, for R2 Solomon's problem class: unserved clients (a), and routes (b) for different prediction techniques

Tile Coding predictor and soft time windows simultaneously (TC+SW) with SW = 0.5. This results in over three times reduced values of the unserved number of clients parameter.

Worse results than in the case of using Tile Coding predictor have been achieved with the use of the neural network predictor (NN). The number of unserved clients was reduced by about 30%. This is a result of the fact that the crisis situations generators generate very dispersed crises lengths (values of approximators target functions). If most of these lengths are zeros then the crisis situations do not appear. The neural network often learns incorrectly in the case of such an input data and then it approximates target functions erroneously. The neural network learns much better when input data is less dispersed. In order to verify this thesis the set of experiments was carried out. Crisis generators were simplified in such a manner that crisis situations always appear, but factors used to compute crisis length were reduced by 50%. Results of such experiments are presented in fig. 4.

Results show that Tile Coding and neural network approximation qualities are similar. Although neural network appears to be a considerably less versatile approximator than Tile Coding, it has an important advantage—it does not demand as much memory as the Tile Coding, which is the property that could be decisively significant when function with many continuous parameters is approximated.

Results for other Solomon classes are listed in the table 1. It appears that the most efficient and the most versatile method of avoiding crisis situations is the application of Tile Coding approximation to predict crisis' lengths in order to correct routes and fitness function values. This technique has achieved best effects for each experiment configuration, resulting in 46%–60% (it depends on Solomon's problem class) reduction of the number of unserved clients and the insignificant increase of the number of routes.

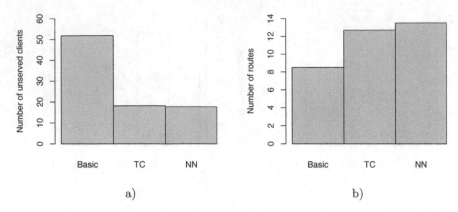

a) b)

Fig. 4. Average results of 33 experiments carried out on every configuration, for R2 Solomon's problem class: unserved clients (a), and routes (b) for different prediction techniques. Crisis situation always appears.

Good results have been also achieved with the use of soft time windows, resulting in 46%–60% reduction of the number of unserved clients (when the time window was expanded by half of its initial width—SW = 0.5) and 25%–47% (when the time window initial width was doubled—SW = 1). Additionally, described method results in the route number reduction, because it expands the interval of time in which the client can be served and thus relaxes the constraints of the problem. It is worth paying attention to the worse results achieved in the case of experiments with Solomon's class 1 problems in comparison to corre-

Table 1. Average results of 30 experiments carried out on every configuration, classified by Solomon's problem classes

Class		Basic	TC	SW = 0.5	SW = 1
C1	Number of routes	15.3	19.9	13.9	13
	Number of unserved clients	32.1	14.3	26.5	23.8
C2	Number of routes	9.9	11.6	9.7	9.8
	Number of unserved clients	30	12.1	22.7	18.6
R1	Number of routes	23.6	27.4	17.8	15.6
	Number of unserved clients	39.7	20.6	32.2	29.5
RC1	Number of routes	23.9	26.9	19.1	16.2
	Number of unserved clients	35.8	16.9	29.4	26.9
RC2	Number of routes	10.4	11.4	9.6	9.3
	Number of unserved clients	31.5	17	20.3	16.6

sponding Solomon's class 2 problems. The reasons of such behavior are narrower time windows in Solomon's class 1 problems. Because of the assumption that the possibility of expanding time window depends on its initial width, narrow time windows are less extensible. Despite the good results being achieved, it is worth remembering, that expanding time windows is the simplification of the problem conditions and it is harmful for clients. That is the reason why these results are considered inferior to others.

7   Concluding Remarks

In the paper the system for solving dynamic vehicle routing problems with time windows and crisis situations was presented. The results of experiments, carried out on test sets for dynamic problems (generated by implemented algorithm on the basis of the well-known and frequently used Solomon's static problems set) have proved that methods of avoiding crisis situations can limit the negative influence on the quality of the VRPTW dynamic problem solution. The main goal of experiments was to verify the quality of implemented techniques of predicting and avoiding crisis situations. The presented results clearly show, which one of the methods is the best and the most versatile. Additionally they determine, in what conditions other methods, less successful in a general case, could be used.

Of course these are only preliminary results and further research and experiments are needed in order to additionally verify proposed mechanisms and compare them to other prediction techniques. Also the agent-based realization of the presented system is included in the future plans. It seems that such decentralized co-evolutionary multi-agent system would have even stronger adaptive capabilities what could be the great advantage—especially in the case of hard dynamic real-life problems.

References

1. Benchmarks: vehicle routing and travelling salesperson problems, http://www.sintef.no/static/am/opti/projects/top/
2. Adamidis, P.: Parallel evolutionary algorithms: A review. In: Proceedings of the 4th Hellenic-European Conference on Computer Mathematics and its Applications (HERCMA 1998), Athens, Greece (1998)
3. Bent, R., Hentenryck, P.: Scenario-based planning for partially dynamic vehicle routing with stochastic customers. Operational Research 52(6), 977–987 (2004)
4. Braysy, O.: Genetic algorithms for the vehicle routing problem with time windows. Arpakannus. Special issue on Bioinformatics and Genetic Algorithms 1, 33–38 (2001)
5. Dreżewski, R., Kisiel-Dorohinicki, M., Koźlak, J.: Agent-based and evolutionary planning techniques supporting crises management in transportation systems. In: A. Dolgui, G. Morel, and C. Pereira, editors, Proceedings of 12th IFAC symposium on INformation COntrol problems in Manufacturing (INCOM'2006), Ecole Nationale Supérieure des Mines de Saint-Etienne and IFAC, vol. 1, Saint-Etienne, France (May 2006)

6. Fischer, K., Muller, J., Pischel, M.: Cooperative transportation scheduling: an application domain for DAI. Applied Artificial Intelligence 10, 1–33 (1996)
7. Homberger, J., Gehring, H.: Two evolutionary meta-heuristics for the vehicle routing problem with time windows. INFORMS Journal in Computing 37(3), 297–318 (1999)
8. Larsen, A.: The dynamic vehicle routing problem. PhD thesis, Department of Mathematical Modelling, The Technical University of Denmark (2000)
9. Lenstra, J.K., Kan, A.R.: Complexity of Vehicle Routing and Scheduling Problems. Networks 11, 221–227 (1981)
10. Machado, P., Tavares, J., Pereira, F.B., Costa, E.: Vehicle routing problem: Doing it the evolutionary way. In: Langdon, W.B., et al. (eds.) Proceedings of the 2002 Genetic and Evolutionary Computation Conference, San Francisco, CA, Morgan Kaufmann, San Francisco (2002)
11. Potter, M.A., De Jong, K.A.: Cooperative coevolution: An architecture for evolving coadapted subcomponents. Evolutionary Computation 8(1), 1–29 (2000)
12. Rumelhart, D.E., Hinton, G.E., Williams, R.J.: Learning internal representations by error propagation. In: Parallel distributed processing: explorations in the microstructure of cognition, Foundations, vol. 1, MIT Press, Cambridge (1986)
13. Sutton, R.S., Barto, A.G.: Reinforcement Learning: An Introduction. MIT Press, Cambridge (1998)
14. Thangiah, S.: Vehicle routing with time windows using genetic algorithms. In: Application Handbook of Genetic Algorithms: New Frontiers, vol. II, pp. 253–277. CRC Press, Boca Raton (1995)
15. Widrow, B., Hoff, M.E.: Adaptive switching circuits. In: Neurocomputing: foundations of research, MIT Press, Cambridge (1988)

Anonymity Architecture for Mobile Agent Systems

Rafał Leszczyna

European Commission, Joint Research Centre,
Institute for the Protection and Security of the Citizen,
Via Enrico Fermi 1, 21020 Ispra (VA), Italy
`rafal.leszczyna@jrc.it`

Abstract. The paper presents a new security architecture for MAS, which supports anonymity of agent owners. The architecture is composed of two main elements: Module I: Untraceability Protocol Infrastructure and Module II: Additional Untraceability Support. Module I is based on the recently proposed untraceability protocol for MAS and it forms the core of the anonymity architecture, which can be supported by the elements of the second module. This part of architecture was implemented and provided to MAS users. Module II instead, is defined in abstract way, through high-level description of its components.

1 Introduction

Agent based Internet environments are an interesting alternative to existing approaches of building software systems. They allow building software systems, which work as human societies, in which members share products and services, cooperate or compete with each other. Organisational, behavioural and functional models etc applied into the systems can be 'imported' from the real world[1].

However, with the emergence of the new paradigm, came also new challenges. One of them is that agent environments, especially those which allow for mobility of agents (Mobile Agent Systems – MAS), are much more difficult to protect from intruders than conventional systems. Agent environments still lack sufficient and effective solutions to assure their security. Researchers agree that this is one of the main obstacles preventing wide popularisation of agent based systems [3,4,1].

This paper presents a new security architecture for MAS, which supports anonymity of agent owners. *Anonymity* is the property of users enabling them to use resources or services (the *items of interest*) without disclosing their identity [5]. It plays crucial role in many activities conducted in the Internet. For example users may be reluctant to engage in web-browsing, message-sending and file-sharing, unless they receive guarantees that their anonymity will be protected to some reasonable degree [6]. Ceki Gülcü and Gene Tsudik [7] describe

---

[1] Some descriptions of case studies illustrating this software design and development approach are available at `http://www.agentlink.org/resources/webCS/` (last access: Feb, 27, 2007). Other motivations for using agents can be found in [1,2,3].

V. Mařík, V. Vyatkin, A.W. Colombo (Eds.): HoloMAS 2007, LNAI 4659, pp. 93–103, 2007.

four categories of internet applications where anonymity is required[2]: discussion of sensitive and personal issues, information searches, freedom of speech in intolerant environments and polling/surveying.

The paper starts with the statement of the architecture goal and the description of its threat model. Next, two main components of the architecture are presented: Module I: Untraceability Protocol Infrastructure and Module II: Additional Untraceability Support. Module I forms the core of the anonymity architecture, which can be supported by the elements of Module II. It is based on the recently proposed untraceability protocol for MAS [8,9,10,11,12] and it was implemented and provided to MAS users. Sections 2.3 and 2.4 describe the protocol and its implementation, while the abstract architecture of the Module II is introduced in Section 2.5. Section 3 concludes on the paper findings.

Because of space limitations some introductory parts of the paper were removed. Thus, for the terminology of anonymity and privacy the reader is directed to the work of Pfitzmann and Hansen [13]. A comprehensive (and up-to-date) bibliography of anonymity is located at http://www.freehaven.net/anonbib/. A reader not familiar with mobile agents will find the useful information in [14,15,16,17,18,19,20,2,4].

2 Architecture

2.1 Objective and Threat Model

Objective. The aim of the architecture is to allow agent owners to hide (make unreadable to unauthorised parties) the address of the agent's base station. This obfuscation should not constrain autonomy of the agent in planning and following its route. Despite the obfuscation the agent should be able to come back to the base station.

In other words, the architecture is required to provide standard level of untraceability (the level which is established by most untraceability protocols) with the guaranty that autonomy of agents is not constrained.

Model of Adversary. The described level of security should be guaranteed for the model of adversary which takes into account all known types of attackers. Thus the following types of adversaries are considered [21]:

- Internal / external. The *internal* adversary is the adversary who succeeded in compromising a container. The *external* adversary is the adversary who gained control over communication links between containers [22].
- Omnipresent / k-listening. The adversary may succeed in attacking all nodes (*omnipresent* adversary), or k of them (*k-listening* adversary [23]). In particular, the *single* adversary is the adversary who managed to compromise only one node [24].
- Active / passive. An *active* adversary can arbitrarily modify the computations and data (by adding and deleting) whereas a *passive* adversary can only listen (read data) [22].

---

[2] It is important to note that the authors don't claim this set to be exhaustive.

- Static / adaptive. *Static* adversaries choose the resources they compromise before start of security protocol and are not able to change them once the protocol has started. *Adaptive* adversaries are able to change the resources they control while the protocol is being executed [22,25]. They can, for example, 'follow' agents [22].
- Hybrid. Hybrids and alliances of attackers may occur, such as external-active or colluding internal and external. Syverson (et al) [24], for example, distinguish between *multiple adversary* and *roving adversary*, which are subsequently: k-listening static and k-listening adaptive adversary.

More detailed description of the adversaries is presented in [12].

Network model. The architecture should interoperate with any agent platform complying to the FIPA specification [26]. Additional assumptions, which must be satisfied in order to allow correct operation of the architecture are described in [12]. These assumptions are related to cryptographic key distribution, characteristics of cryptographic functions, isolation of containers[3] and operational data sharing [12].

2.2   Architecture Components

The proposed anonymity architecture which satisfies the requirements and objectives is composed of the two modules (see Figure 1) [12]:

- Module I: Untraceability Protocol Infrastructure.
- Module II: Additional Untraceability Support.

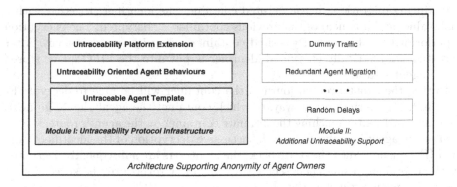

Fig. 1. Anonymity Architecture is composed of two modules: Module I: Untraceability Protocol Infrastructure and Module II: Additional Untraceability Support

---

[3] Just to recall, in MAS a *container* is an instance of a virtual machine which forms a virtual node in the MAS network. On each computer device (PC, PDA, etc) at least one container may be set up. Mobile agents are able to migrate from one container to another.

Module I provides functionality of untraceability protocol with the advantage of not imposing restrictions on agents autonomously selecting their route [8,12]. It forms the core of the anonymity architecture, which is supported by the elements of the second module.

Module II addresses the complex issue of the extended untraceability of agents. It takes into account less probable attacks against untraceability based on traffic analysis[4]. The decision of including this module to the architecture was influenced by the results of a security study of the untraceability protocol [11]. The study proved the satisfaction of the security requirement stated for the protocol [11], i.e. that the protocol protects agents from being traced through their address data. However it also exposed the fact that powerful adversaries have at their disposal a large variety of traffic analysis attacks. These attacks can break security provided by untraceability protocols.

It must be underlined though that since these attacks require very powerful adversaries, they are significantly less probable than the attacks based on reading of the unprotected address of the agent's base station. Moreover, protection from these attacks requires possession of numerous computational and communication resources. For these reasons, Module II was specified as an abstract architecture, through functional descriptions of its components. The implementation questions were left open[5] [12].

2.3   Module I: Untraceability Protocol

Module I represents an infrastructure implementing the recently proposed untraceability protocol for MAS [8,12]. Formal specification of the protocol (in pseudocode) can be found in [8,12], while in brief, the idea of the protocol is that, during migration, at each visited container the identifier (together with a hash value, and a nonce) of the previous container is encrypted. The encryption is performed by the currently visited container, using its own secret key. After that, the symmetrically encrypted identifier is put into the LIFO queue stored in the agent's data.

During the agent's return journey, the container will be able to decrypt the identifier, discovering in this way, to which container the agent should go next. Another words, after reaching the ultimate container on the agent's route, the return of the agent is realised through successive decryption of the identifiers from the LIFO queue. Down the route back, the identifiers are subsequently decrypted by the containers using their secret keys, in order reverse to the succession in which the agent arrived at the ultimate container [8,12].

Before starting the migration the LIFO queue is filled with a number of random values to disallow an adversary to recognise which part of the queue contains

---

[4] *Traffic analysis* is a process of intercepting and examining agents in order to deduce information from their patterns of communication (see [12] for more details).

[5] The decision of implementation and application of the components to a particular MAS should be made by designers and/or administrators of the concrete agent system, based on the cost-benefit analysis.

the encrypted identifier of the base [20,27]. These random values remain in the LIFO queue, and the encrypted identifiers are attached after them.

To detect illegitimate alterations of the data stored in the queue, at each visited container a hash function is computed. The function is calculated on the binary concatenation of three identifiers: of the previous, the current and the following – container. The result is added to the identifier of the previous container before it is encrypted. This method was proposed by Karjoth and is called *hash chaining* [27]. It aims at protection from attacks based on removing identifiers of intermediate containers.

Also before encrypting the identifier, a random value (a *nonce*) is added to it (this operation is called *salting*), so as a result the encrypted identifier (actually this is now, after adding the hash and the nonce, a portion of data which includes the identifier) is *sealed*. This is to assure that the the encrypted packet will have a unique value [28]. Finally the symmetric encryption is performed on the following data: hash function, the identifier and the nonce.

The protocol was designed to utilise the least resources. Encryption is employed only when necessary and only to an essential content [12]. Performance analysis of the protocol (see [10]) proved that this is the time of agent migration, not the time of encryption being the principal component impacting the time complexity of the protocol.

2.4   Protocol Implementation: Untraceability Protocol Infrastructure

Module I was designed to be easily integrated with agent platforms and to facilitate development of applications which take advantage of untraceability. Thus a structure based on the three key elements was proposed [12,29]:

1. An extension to the agent platform providing untraceability service.
2. A set of untraceability-oriented agent behaviours.
3. A template of an untraceable agent.

Adding the new untraceability feature to an agent platform requires registration and launching of the extension. Development of applications which take advantage of untraceable agents involves use of the template and adding the agent behaviours[6] [29].

The agent platform extension is designed as a plug-in (add-on) for agent platform containers. This form of implementation gives freedom in choosing which containers should provide the untraceability function. When an agent arrives at a container, it can check whether the service is available (the container's owner enabled the plug-in) and if it is, then the agent may take advantage of it. The agent calls the service and provides as an input the identifier of the container which it has chosen as a next on its route. Based on this, the plug-in compiles

---

[6] To recall, the agent's *behaviour* is a set of actions performed in order to achieve the goal. It represents a task that an agent can perform [30].

the identifier into a string of the three identifiers: the previous–, the current– and the next– container. Then it computes a MD5 message digest of the string, and accompanies with a generated nonce and the identifier of the previous container. Finally it is all encrypted using AES algorithm and returned to the agent (according to the specification). To provide this functionality each installed plug-in has to maintain a unique secret key for the AES algorithm [12,29].

Because the protocol was implemented as a service add-on for JADE (an agent platform implemented in Java [31], motivations for choosing this platform for the experiments can be found in [12]), the architecture components are realised as Java classes [29]. This means for example that employing the agent template involves inheritance from the UntraceableAgent class, and further development of untraceable agents requires instantiation of the classes GoAheadBehaviour and ComeBackBehaviour – which are responsible for agents migration. In the same way other functionalities can be developed [12,29].

The implemented add-on for JADE is publicly shared under the terms of LGPL license [29]. The open source package including all the necessary classes for enabling the untraceability service at a JADE agent platform, together with documentation and examples is available at the JADE community portal (http://jade.tilab.com/; section: *Add-ons and 3rd party software*).

The architecture was successfully applied to an eHealth[7] case study aiming at provision of anonymous eHealth counseling service. The service embraces all functionalities and activities necessary to provide a user with a comprehensive medical, pharmaceutical, and dietetical knowledge related to the user's health problem. At the same time all users of the service are provided with option of anonymity.

In the implementation, users (both the service users and providers) are represented by agents called Virtual Egos which exist permanently in the agent platform. The Virtual Egos of patients are implemented based on the Untraceable-Agent template (as classes extending the UntraceableAgent class). Users contact them by Support Agents. The Support Agents can be activated from any agent enabled architecture (currently a PC, but since lightweight JADE platform – JADE Leap – is available, in the future this might be done from a mobile phone, a hand-held device etc). Patients describe their cases and the descriptions are passed to the untraceable Virtual Egos which arrived at the users' devices. Then the Virtual Egos untraceably migrate to containers of doctors, taking advantage of untraceability-oriented behaviours. There they present the health problem descriptions to the doctors' Virtual Egos. The doctors give their counsels, and the patients' Virtual Egos move further to contact Knowledge Agents in order to accompany the advices with domain-specific information (dietetic and pharmaceutical). After completing the data, the Virtual Egos return to the patients' containers to present the full counsel. On all containers likely to be visited by patients' Virtual Egos, the Untraceability add-on is activated.

---

[7] The eHealth application was chosen because in eHealth high priority is assigned to user anonymity.

The case study demonstrated the applicability and usefulness of the architecture [9,12].

2.5   Module II: Additional Untraceability Support

Module II: Additional Untraceability Support, aims at protecting agents from Traffic Analysis attacks and from tracing through reading data held by agents. For the reasons mentioned in Section 2.2 i.e. because attacks which it protects from are of low probability of occurrence, and because enabling the module requires numerous resources, the module is specified in abstract way i.e. through high-level descriptions of its components. These descriptions include the objective, the operating principle and the list of attacks from which the component protects from [12].

The Module II components were mainly derived from analogous protection methods already developed for the traditional message-based communication. In the progress of the research they were adapted to MAS. Additionally three new techniques for untraceability in MAS were proposed: Redundant Agents, Agent Migration and Failure Neutral Behaviours [12].

Redundant agents are the specialised agents similar to *dummy agents*[8], different from them in that they are meant to be used. Redundant agents are executed on random containers and then roam around the network, so a user could pick them up and assign their task. When a task is given to an agent, the agent is let to migrate again in order to fulfill the task. After the agent comes back with the results, the results are read, and the agent goes back to its base container. Because the agents start their migration on a container different to the one where it was picked up, this previous container is the agent's base container. Thus this method prevents from discovering the agents' base stations, and can be applied against brute force attacks and timing attacks [12,11].

Redundant agent migration is a method similar to redundant agents, which to the contrary aims at misleading an observer in identifying the destination container. This is obtained through forcing agents to traverse additional containers, so the agents go further than to the original containers. If redundant agent migration is applied to an agent returning to the base container, then it may result in hiding the base station. This method addresses brute force traffic analysis attacks, timing attacks and active traffic analysis attacks exploiting user reactions [12,11].

Failure-neutral behaviours is a technique which helps preventing traffic analysis using denial of service and active traffic analysis attacks exploiting user reactions [12,11]. It is based on designing agent behaviours in the way that an external observer can not distinguish between agents operating in system-failure conditions and agents operating in normal system conditions. Another words,

---

[8] Dummy agents are the agents which function is to be present and to roam in the network of MAS, to intensify the network traffic. They are indistinguishable from functional agents from the point of view of an observer [12].

if an agent encounters a system failure, it must continue its operation *showing* behaviour indifferent to the one it had before the failure occurrence. In this way an attacker trying to identify a traced agent through arranging system-failure conditions (and provoking the agent to behave in a certain way) will not achieve his/her objective, because the agent will not change its behaviour.

This technique is different however to much more restricted – *fault-tolerance* – since the agent is not required to continue its *proper* operation and to provide a *proper* result of its computation. Failure neutral behaving agents may stop their functions. The key requirement for them is that they maintained a 'neutral look'.

Finally, the abstract architecture of Module II specifies the following components [12]:

- Data obfuscation [32,33].
- Batch processing [28].
- Reordering [28].
- Random delaying [34].
- Content uniformising [12].
- Dummy traffic [12].
- Redundant agents [12].
- Redundant agent migration [12].
- Agent size uniformising [12].
- Fault-neutral behaviours [12].
- Authenticated timing information [12].
- Replay detection [28,7].
- Tamper detection [35].
- Nondeterministic routing [12].

Additionally users must be informed about privacy issues related to their distinctive behaviours, see [12].

3   Summary

One of the main obstacles preventing wide popularisation of agent based systems is lack of sufficient and effective solutions to assure their security. This paper presented a new security architecture for MAS, which supports anonymity of agent owners. The architecture is composed of two main elements: Module I, which is responsible for obscuring agents' base addresses and Module II, which protects agents from traffic analysis. Module I forms the core module of the architecture and it implements the specification of the recently proposed untraceability protocol [8,12]. This part of the architecture was developed and proposed as a ready-to-use solution for users of JADE agent platform [29]. It has been also successfully applied to an eHealth case study [9,12]. The case study demonstrated the applicability and usefulness of the proposed architecture.

The second part of the anonymity architecture is based on optional components, which implementation and application to a particular agent system is left to the designers and administrators of the system. These components are specified through high-level descriptions including the objective, the operating principle and the list of attacks from which they protect from [12]. The components are based on protection methods developed for traditional message-based communication and they were adapted to MAS in the progress of this research. Three methods, namely Redundant Agent Migration, Redundant Agents, and Failure Neutral Behaviours are a new proposal for MAS [12].

The architecture offers a solution for protecting mobile agents and it can contribute to wider popularisation of mobile agents. Although it was implemented for JADE, its design can be easily applied to other agent platforms.

References

1. Luck, M., McBurney, P., Preist, C.: Agent Technology: Enabling Next Generation Computing (A Roadmap for Agent Based Computing). AgentLink (January 2003)
2. Gray, R.S., Kotz, D., Cybenko, G., Rus, D.: Mobile agents: Motivations and state-of-the-art systems. Technical Report TR2000-365, Dartmouth College, Hanover, NH (2000)
3. Farmer, W.M., Guttman, J.D., Swarup, V.: Security for mobile agents: Issues and requirements (1996)
4. Jansen, W., Karygiannis, T.: Nist special publication 800-19 - mobile agent security (2000)
5. National Institute of Standards and Technology (NIST): Common Criteria for Information Technology Security Evaluation - Part 2: Security Funtional Requirements. U.S. Government Printing Office (1998)
6. Halpern, J.Y., O'Neill, K.R.: Anonymity and information hiding in multiagent systems. Journal of Computer Security (2004)
7. Gülcü, C., Tsudik, G.: Mixing email with Babel. In: Proceedings of the 1996 Symposium on Network and Distributed System Security (SNDSS '96), vol. 2, IEEE Computer Society, Los Alamitos (1996)
8. Leszczyna, R., Górski, J.: Untraceability of mobile agents. In: Proceedings of the 4th International Joint Conference on Autonomous Agents and Multiagent Systems (AAMAS '05), New York, vol. 3, pp. 1233-1234. Association for Computing Machinery (ACM) Press, New York (2005)
9. Leszczyna, R.: The solution for anonymous access of it services and its application to e-health counselling. In: Proceedings of the 1st 2005 IEEE International Conference on Technologies for Homeland Security and Safety (TEHOSS '05) Gdańsk, Poland, Gdańsk University of Technology, pp. 161-170 (September 2005)
10. Leszczyna, R., Górski, J.: Performance analysis of untraceability protocols for mobile agents using an adaptable framework. In: Stone, P., Weiss, G. (eds.) Proceedings of the 5th International Joint Conference on Autonomous Agents and Multiagent Systems (AAMAS '06), New York, pp. 1063-1070. Association for Computing Machinery (ACM) Press, New York (2006)
11. Leszczyna, R., Górski, J.: An untraceability protocol for mobile agents and its enhanced security study. In: 15th EICAR Annual Conference Proceedings, Hamburg, Germany, pp. 26-37 (April 29 - May 2, 2006)

12. Leszczyna, R.: Architecture supporting security of agent systems. PhD thesis, Gdańsk University of Technology, Gdańsk, Poland (June 2006)
13. Pfitzmann, A., Hansen, M.: Anonymity, unlinkability, unobservability, pseudonymity, and identity management - a consolidated proposal for terminology (version v0.25). Website (December 2005)
14. Chess, D., Harrison, C., Kershenbaum, A.: Mobile agents: Are they a good idea? In: Technical Report RC 19887 (December 21, 1994 - Declassified March 16, 1995), Yorktown Heights, New York (1994)
15. Chess, D., Grosof, B., Harrison, C., Levine, D., Parris, C., Tsudik, G.: Itinerant agents for mobile computing. IEEE Personal Communications 2(5), 34–49 (1995)
16. Franklin, S., Graesser, A.: Is it an agent, or just a program?: A taxonomy for autonomous agents. In: Jennings, N.R., Wooldridge, M.J., Müller, J.P. (eds.) Intelligent Agents III. Agent Theories, Architectures, and Languages. LNCS, vol. 1193, Springer, Heidelberg (1997)
17. Carzaniga, A., Picco, G.P., Vigna, G.: Designing distributed applications with a mobile code paradigm. In: Proceedings of the 19th International Conference on Software Engineering, Boston, MA (1997)
18. Fuggetta, A., Picco, G.P., Vigna, G.: Understanding code mobility. IEEE Transactions on Software Engineering 24(5), 342–361 (1998)
19. Milojicic, D.S.: Trend wars: Mobile agent applications. IEEE Concurrency 7(3), 80–90 (1999)
20. Yee, B.S.: A sanctuary for mobile agents. In: Proceedings of the DARPA Workshop on Foundations for Secure Mobile Code, Monterey, USA (March 1997)
21. Leszczyna, R.: Anonymity architecture for mobile agents. Technical report, European Commission, Joint Research Centre, Institute for the Protection and security of the Citizen, Ispra, Italy (April 2006)
22. Raymond, J.F.: Traffic analysis: Protocols, attacks, design issues and open problems. In: Federrath, H. (ed.) Designing Privacy Enhancing Technologies. LNCS, vol. 2009, pp. 10–29. Springer, Heidelberg (2001)
23. Dolev, S., Ostrobsky, R.: Xor-trees for efficient anonymous multicast and reception. ACM Transactions on Information Systems Secururity 3(2), 63–84 (2000)
24. Syverson, P., Tsudik, G., Reed, M., Landwehr, C.: Towards an analysis of onion routing security. In: Federrath, H. (ed.) Designing Privacy Enhancing Technologies. LNCS, vol. 2009, pp. 96–114. Springer, Heidelberg (2001)
25. Lindell, Y.: Foundations of cryptography 89-856. Electronic document (April 2006)
26. Foundation for Intelligent Physical Agents (FIPA): Fipa abstract architecture specification (2002)
27. Karjoth, G., Asokan, N., Gülcü, C.: Protecting the computation results of free-roaming agents. In: Rothermel, K., Hohl, F. (eds.) MA 1998. LNCS, vol. 1477, pp. 195–207. Springer, Heidelberg (1998)
28. Chaum, D.: Untraceable electronic mail, return addresses, and digital pseudonyms. Communications of the ACM 4(2) (1981)
29. Leszczyna, R.: Untraceability I Add-on for JADE. European Commission, Joint Research Centre, Institute for the Protection and security of the Citizen, Via Enrico Fermi 1, Ispra, Italy. 1 edn. (September 2005)
30. Bellifemine, F., Caire, G., Trucco, T., Rimassa, G.: Jade programmers guide (February 2003)
31. Telecom Italia Lab: Java Agent DEvelopment Framework. Website

32. Sander, T., Tschudin, C.F.: Protecting mobile agents against malicious hosts. In: Vigna, G. (ed.) Mobile Agents and Security. LNCS, vol. 1419, pp. 379–386. Springer, Heidelberg (1998)
33. Borselius, N.: Mobile agent security. Electronics & Communication Engineering Journal 14(5), 211–218 (2002)
34. Kesdogan, D., Egner, J., Büschkes, R.: Stop-and-go MIXes: Providing probabilistic anonymity in an open system. In: Aucsmith, D. (ed.) IH 1998. LNCS, vol. 1525, Springer, Heidelberg (1998)
35. Meadows, C.: Detecting attacks on mobile agents. In: Proceedings of Foundations for Secure Mobile Code Workshop, Monterey, CA, pp. 64–65 (March, 1997)

SitCom – Development Platform for Multimodal Perceptual Services

Pascal Fleury, Jan Cuřín, and Jan Kleindienst

IBM Voice Technologies and Systems, V Parku 4/2294, Praha 4, Czech Republic
{pascal.fleury,jan_curin,jankle}@cz.ibm.com

Abstract. In this paper we introduce SITCOM, a novel software utility
for developing context-aware services, editing and deploying context situation models, and simulating perceptual components. SITCOM, which
stands for *Situation Composer*, is constructed as an open and extensible
framework with rich graphical rendering capabilities, including 3D visualization. One of SITCOM's main goals is to simulate interactions among
people and objects in various settings such as presentation rooms, meetings halls, social places, homes, or car cockpits. Moreover, SITCOM captures and models such environmental context and delivers the abstracted
information to context-aware user services. Contextual models are designed as pluggable modules. They can be configured to build hierarchies
of contextual models and deployed and reused across applications, agent
systems or cognitive architectures. SITCOM allows plugging-in various
multi-modal sensing components such as body trackers, face detectors,
speech recognition engines, gesture recognizers, etc. Therefore, switching
from simulated to real components with SITCOM is seamless, typically
involving no change in the contextual models and the services.

1 Introduction

The concept of ubiquitous computing [1] opens a new era of computer science.
Embedding computers into mobile or wearable appliances, and blending them
into physical environment is breaking the paradigm of static desk-bound computers. This leads to a new quality of relationship between the user and the
machine. Context-awareness – the ability to sense relevant states of the environment – plays an important role in facilitating this new relationship.

Two waves of context-aware systems have already ran over the industry. The
first one started in early nineties with Want's Active Badge [2], Pascoe's CIS [3]
and Xerox's PARCTAB prototype [4]. Closely linked to mobile and wearable
computing, these systems primarily utilized the location context to improve application's time-spatial intelligence. Context was perceived as a vector of physical
and conceptual states of objects.

The next wave has surfaced several years ago with works of Thevenin et al. on
Plastic User Interfaces [5], of Dey et al. on Context Toolkit [6], and MIT's Oxygen [7]. Here context is defined as any information that can be utilized by an
application, including sensed and synthesized knowledge on users, the objects
of the scene, situations, the application itself, environment, and world. While

V. Mařík, V. Vyatkin, A.W. Colombo (Eds.): HoloMAS 2007, LNAI 4659, pp. 104–113, 2007.
© Springer-Verlag Berlin Heidelberg 2007

building toolkits around context, the underlying motive is to find a solid operational definition of context that allows its efficient representation and modeling. The search is also after a proper programming model that facilitates the reuse of context across applications, environments, and users.

However, there is a topic that seems to be highly neglected: tools and development environments for building these contextual services [8]. Application builders moving from design to actual implementation need new methods and techniques in prototyping, debugging, and deployment of contextual services. SITCOM, our context-aware application design tool, shows how we addressed these new challenges in such situations.

In the light of the above motivation, this paper introduces SITCOM (*Situation Composer*), a tool for development of multimodal perceptual services, and reports on our experience in deploying it in real systems. In Section 2 we introduce three roles of developers, and show how SITCOM can support them in their activities. Section 3 is devoted to the description of SITCOM's key abstractions and building blocks. The design of an example application called *Connector Service* is described in Section 4.

2   Contextual Services Developers Perspective

The construction of contextual services demands an interdisciplinary effort because the context-modeling layer typically sits between two infrastructure parts: the environment sensing part called *Perceptual Components* [9], and the application logic. Thus, even a simple service built for an intelligent room requires at least three different roles, each with a different set of skills:

- **Perceptual Technology Providers** supply sensing components such as person trackers, sound and speech recognizers, activity detectors, etc. to see, hear, and feel the environment. The skills needed here include signal processing, pattern recognition, statistical modeling, etc.
- **Context Model Builders** make models that synthesize the flood of information acquired by the sensing layer into semantically higher-level information suitable to user services. Here, the skills are skewed towards probabilistic modeling, inferencing, logic, etc.
- **Service Developers** construct the context-aware services by using the abstracted information from the context model (the situation modeling layer). Needed skills are application logic and user interface design; multi-modal user interfaces typically require yet an additional set of roles and skills.

Now let's take a small tour on how these roles are exercised during the process of service construction. Imagine for a moment a service developer creating a new context-aware service, with this goal: *Once people have gathered in a meeting room, determine when they are taking a break for coffee.* This would for example let staff enter the room only when they do not disturb.

The service developer does not, typically, have access to a fully-equipped room with sensors, nor does she have the technology for detecting people and

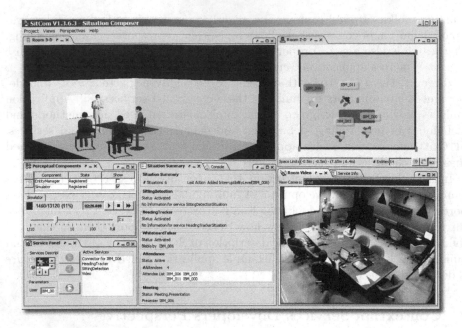

Fig. 1. GUI of SITCOM environment with 3D visualization

meetings. But for an initial prototype of such a service, pre-recorded input data may suffice.

A service developer then talks to context-model builder to define what new contextual abstractions will be needed, and which can be reused from an existing catalogue. The context-model builder in turn talks to technology providers to verify that capturing the requested environment state is within state-of-the art of the sensing technology. If not, there is still a possibility to synthesize the requested information from other sensors under a given quality of service; for example, the number of people in a room may be inferred through sound and speech analysis in case no video analysis technology is available.

SITCOM is the development environment where all these roles meet. SITCOM rationalizes the above process and makes the communication between those roles more efficient and straightforward. It also facilitates the design of the entire system with partially complete and manually designed scenario data, helping with the boostrapping of the entire context-aware application. It also presents most of its information and tools through a user-friendly GUI, as shown in Figure 1.

3   Architecture and Key Abstractions

SITCOM is an extensible Java toolkit to help in all phases of the development of context-aware applications. It presents a set of functionalities that have been shown to be useful for all roles in the development of such applications.

3.1 Information Flow

Sensors deliver their information in a streaming fashion, as do video camera for video data or noise level detectors for a given value of the noise level. The perceptual components, which do some combination of the sensor data to render it at a higher semantic level, still propagate this information, after processing, in a streaming fashion. A body tracker will update the number of detected bodies, and their locations. A room noise classifier will deliver the new label as soon as it has processed the information. In that sense, the data is going through the layers as in a pipeline. As depicted in Figure 2, the information flows through the following layers: sensors, perceptual components, situation modeling, and services.

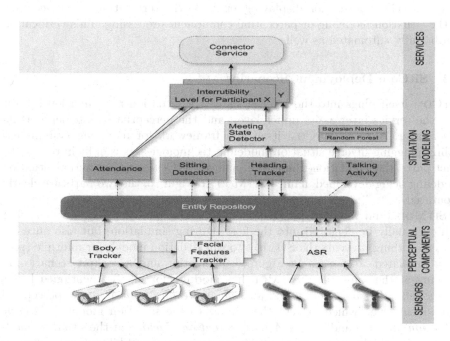

Fig. 2. Schema of data flow in the meeting scenario

Perceptual components provide information about *entities*, which are mapped one-to-one to real world things. These entities have a set of attributes, which may change over time. These attributes are modeled as *streams*, with an update frequency which depends on the type of attribute. For example, a person's ID will most likely change only a couple of times, depending on the accuracy of the person identifier technology, whereas the person's location will most likely be updated often.

The situation modeling layer is where the transformation of a set of facts about the environment into a set of situations is taking place [9]. The situation model will provide information about *situations*, which consist of a set of *states* and their associated transition. The detection of the current state and the detection of state changes is implemented using several techniques, and is extendable. Currently, we have a rule-based engine, several statistical methods, and a very simple hardwired logic. Each situation is embodied in a *situation machine*, which is a Java module in SITCOM, and only the external hull of the situation machine is visible. This uniformity of public interface for situation machines is a key aspect for the flexibility of the simulation environment. The actual set of used situation machines is application dependent, we provide samples in Section 4.2.

The service layer, managing the set of actions corresponding to state changes in the environment model, is also depicted Figure 2. Its output is highly application dependent. SITCOM has a flexible enough framework to accommodate for service-specific information displaying, enabling the verification of the accuracy of the situation modeling or perceptual component processing. This verification can be fully automated as well.

3.2 SitCom Deployment Scenarios

SITCOM itself plugs into the layer stack at the situation modeling level. So it sees the service layer as its upper layer, and the perceptual components as its lower layer. Also, as SITCOM itself is a framework for modeling systems enabling plugging diverse situation modeling technologies, it is split into two distinct parts: the simulation framework, named SITCOM, and the actual situation modeling being developed, named SITMOD. In Figure 3, the two parts are clearly separated.

SITMOD (and modules plugged into it) is the portion of the system that will eventually be deployed into the field. During simulation, but also once deployed, nothing prevents the SITMOD to run situation models for multiple (possibly unrelated) scenarios. In Figure 3, a meeting and a cockpit scenario are running at the same time. SITMOD has modules for all the mentioned layers we model: a *Person Tracker* and an *Engine Health Monitor* at the perceptual component level, which present their input to the situation model; a *Meeting Situation Machine* and a *Pilot Activity Situation Machine* at the situation modeling level, which are scenario specific; and an *Interruptibility Service* and an *Incoming Alarm Service* at the service level, presenting the visible output of the system.

3.3 Experiment Management

Through its GUI, SITCOM can also enable the easy setup of the experiment in loading the situations, perceptual components and services through its set of *manager components* for services, situations and perceptual components (on the right of Figure 3).

It can then feed SITMOD with its *simulator* component, sending either synthetic or recorded data from script files, having semi-simulated components, or handling the activity of real components. This way, we can use partial recorded

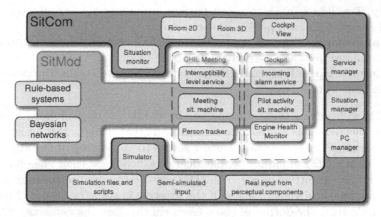

Fig. 3. Architecture diagram overview of SITCOM, the Situation Composer, and SITMOD, the Situation Model framework

data, and run experiment where for example one person is missing, and test that the meeting detector is still working even if the audience is slimmer.

The GUI views can show many details of the inner states of these components, and can render them in raw form, as for example the *Situation Summary* of Figure 1, or in a more scenario specific display, as the *Room2D* or *Room3D* for the meeting scenario or the *Cockpit View* for the Cockpit scenario.

We found it very useful to have these simulation and recorded data possibilities, as for debugging some situations, we can run the experiment up to a point, and then we can interfere with the recorded data using synthetic data, so as to test the situation machine and/or the service. This makes the test of *what if* scenarios very quick and simple. Some of the GUI components, e.g. the Room views, are also useful in demos, to display to the public the current internal representation of the situation.

4   Designing with SitCom

Let us describe the SITCOM framework on a connector scenario proposed and exploited in [10]. The connector service is responsible for detecting acceptable interruptions (phone call, SMS, targeted audio, etc.) of a particular person in the smart room. During the meeting, for example, a member of the audience might be interrupted by a message during the presentation, whereas the service blocks any calls for the meeting presenter. It therefore uses the context-aware service outlined in Section 2.

4.1   Perceptual Components

Our smart room is equipped with multiple cameras and microphones on the *sensor* level. The audio and video data are streamed into the following *perceptual components*, as depicted in Figure 2:

- **Body Tracker** is a video-based tracker providing 3D coordinates of the head centroid for each person in the room;
- **Facial Features Tracker** is a video-based face visibility detector, providing nose visibility for each participant from each camera;
- **Automatic Speech Recognition** is providing speech transcription for each participant in the room.

SITCOM will present these components in its GUI, if they already exist, and will use artificial data as well as data recorded on other sites to start designing the context models. For room data, Figure 1 shows the rendering of the aggregated information in a $2D$ fashion for people locations, headings, their speech activity as well as if they are sitting or not. The $3D$ is useful when annotating information, as it's a more natural view to assess if the meeting is going on or not. Note also the view indicating the output of the sensors (in this case the cameras), which is useful for perceptual component developers to assess the quality of their output.

A key aspect of the perceptual components is that they implement a specific API. This API is defined along *functional* aspects of the perceptual components, e.g. *body location tracker API*, so that a body tracker may do its tracking based on video signals, audio signals, or even be a combination of other mono-modal trackers. The important part is that the API represents the type of information that we can get from the component, not how it got computed.

Such an API also presents the advantage that certain components that may deliver multiple types of information (e.g. speaker ID and audio transcription) will implement multiple simple APIs (e.g. a speaker ID API and a transcription API) instead of one single-purpose combined API. This simplifies the situation model, as it can then requests information from only one aspect of such a component. It also reduces the set of APIs we have to deal with, directly benefitting the integration and deployment of the system.

4.2   Situation Modeling

To plug into the architecture outlined in Section 3, we have designed a few situation machines to detect if there is an ongoing meeting in the room:

- **Attendance** tracks the number of participants in the room;
- **Motion Detection** reports how many participants have moved over a certain distance threshold in a given time period;
- **Heading Tracker** infers the head orientation for each person from her position and face visibility for all cameras;
- **Attention Direction** tracks the number of participants looking towards the same spot, using their heading information;
- **Sitting Detection** infers whether a particular person is sitting or not from the Z (height) coordinate;
- **Crowd Detection** searches for groups of at least 3 people whose relative distance does not exceed a threshold;
- **Talking Activity** tracks duration of speech activity and number of speaker changes in a given period;

- **Meeting State Detector** infers the current state of the meeting in the room;
- **Interruptibility Level** selects the level of *interruptibility* of a particular participant according to the current meeting state and the current speaker.

The actual implementation of particular situation machine can be part of the Java runtime or it can be a standalone module using a remote API. We had investigated the use of statistical classification module for meeting state recognition previously in [11], and have re-used it here.

Again, through its GUI, we can see all the situation machines and their state, for any particular time in the simulation data. In Figure 1, we can see the middle lower panel showing the currently active set of situation machines, along with their state information. Later, we could use the same status information to follow live what our system is doing, all while recording the additional real data.

4.3 Services

The architecture of SITCOM allows for many situation machines (SMs) to be registered with the situation model, but only the SMs that are needed are actually loaded. In Figure 1, we run the connector service for a participant named *IBM_006* that will pull in the necessary set of situation machines. It can be seen that at this time, he is presenting, so his interruptibility level is set to *no interruptions*. The service will use this information and match it to the importance of the incoming interruption request, so that only very important requests get through at this particular time.

SITCOM provides a good infrastructure for plugging components, so that we have used it for other helper services, like the *Video* service, that open a view showing the sensor information from a relevant camera for the current simulated time of the meeting.

4.4 Experiences and Uses

After some initial hiccups of the tool, mainly due to the then immature communication protocol between remote components, we have successfully used the tool in meeting room detection, car cockpit situational analysis and it has also been used in the IST'06 EU projects showcase in Helsinki to display tracked people in the exhibition booth.

In many ways, having an integrated tool specialized for context-aware applications has been helpful to identify necessary pieces for the application, like the needed room information, specific sensor information, or the definition of the whiteboard talker as a useful situation machine for our task. Also, we have used its rendering capabilities for annotation purpose, as there was no available corpus of annotated meeting data containing also multi-modal non-meeting parts.

Our tool is in use on at least 8 sites, and has seen plugins written by multiple developers, who have integrated a rule-based situation modeling, as well as multiple perceptual components. SITCOM is also used to provide contextual

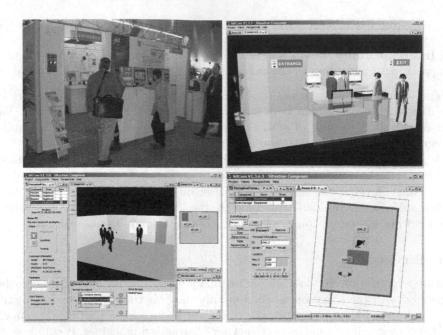

Fig. 4. Some of the deployments of SITCOM: The top row shows the booth at IST'06 in Helsinki along with its model representation, the bottom left shows SITCOM at the first attempt to exchange perceptual components across sites, and the bottom right shows the manual editing of a scene with the entity manager GUI

information and a GUI to an agent-based service architecture, and is used as a manual trigger for some events in scenario-based experiments.

5   Conclusions

We have introduced a development environment that has already been exercised by several developers. SITCOM, working on the division of concerns principle, supports different developer roles, and thus fosters shorter and more efficient development of contextual services.

The SITCOM framework is currently used by more than 8 sites around Europe and it was part of successful demonstrations of technologies, for example on CHIL Technology Day in Berlin in April 2006 or on the IST Event in Helsinki in November 2006. One of the foreseen usage of SITCOM, especially its 3D visualization, is to make real recording anonymous to comply privacy rights.

There are several research and development directions where we see added value in improving the SITCOM utility. One of the development directions is the introduction of ontologies into the process of acquiring and exporting the contextual information. Having the environmental information modeled in an application-independent way is the key prerequisite towards achieving interoperability and autonomy.

Another direction is toward better *tooling* capabilities of the utility. The prospect of having full-fledged Contextual IDE, including the *Situation Debugger* is very appealing for many developers. Part of this effort is making SITCOM a pluggable module into Eclipse, to increase its GUI configurability.

Acknowledgments

This work has been developed as part of the IST FP6 CHIL project (IP 506909), co-funded by EC. The authors would like to thank CHIL colleagues for valuable feedback that results in improved SITCOM's look and functionality.

References

1. Weiser, M.: The computer for the twenty-first century. Scientific American, 94–104 (September 1991)
2. Want, R., Hopper, A., Falcao, V., Gibbons, J.: The active badge location system. ACM Transactions on Information Systems (TOIS) 10(1), 91–102 (1992)
3. Pascoe, J.: Adding generic contextual capabilities to wearable computers. In: The Second International Symposium on Wearable Computers, Pittsburgh, pp. 92–99. IEEE Computer Society, Los Alamitos (1998), Online proceedings available from http://iswc.gatech.edu/
4. Schilit, W.N., Adams, N.I., Want, R.: Context-aware computing applications. In: IEEE Workshop on Mobile Computing Systems and Applications, Santa Cruz, California, pp. 85–90 (December 1994)
5. Calvary, G., Coutaz, J., Thevenin, D.: Supporting context changes for plastic user interfaces: A process and a mechanism. In: HCI'2001 and IHM'2001, pp. 349–363. Springer, London (2001)
6. The context toolkit, http://www.cc.gatech.edu/fce/contexttoolkit/
7. The Oxygen project, http://oxygen.lcs.mit.edu/Overview.html
8. Bowles, K.L.: Problem Solving Using PASCAL. Springer, New York (1977)
9. Crowley, J.L., Coutaz, J., Rey, G., Reignier, P.: Perceptual components for context aware computing. In: Borriello, G., Holmquist, L.E. (eds.) UbiComp 2002. LNCS, vol. 2498, Springer, Heidelberg (2002)
10. Danninger, M., Robles, E., Takayama, L., Wang, Q., Kluge, T., Nass, C., Stiefelhagen, R.: The connector service - predicting availability in mobile contexts. In: Renals, S., Bengio, S., Fiscus, J.G. (eds.) MLMI 2006. LNCS, vol. 4299, Springer, Heidelberg (2006)
11. Fleury, P., Curín, J., Kleindienst, J., Kessl, R.: On handling conflicting input in context-aware applications. In: Renals, S., Bengio, S. (eds.) MLMI 2005. LNCS, vol. 3869, Springer, Heidelberg (2006)

An Ontology-Based Reconfiguration Agent for Intelligent Mechatronic Systems

Yazen Al-Safi and Valeriy Vyatkin

University of Auckland, School of Electrical and Computer Engineering,
Auckland, New Zealand
y.alsafi@ieee.org, v.vyatkin@auckland.ac.nz

Abstract. This paper discusses an ontology-based reconfiguration agent that uses ontological knowledge of the manufacturing environment for the purpose of reconfiguration without human intervention. The current mass customization era requires increased flexibility and agility in the manufacturing systems to adapt changes in manufacturing requirements and environments. Our configuration agent minimizes the overheads of the current reconfiguration process by automating it. It infers facts about the manufacturing environment from the ontological knowledge model and then decides whether the current environment can support the given manufacturing requirements.

Keywords: Ontology, Reconfiguration Agent, OWL, Pellet.

1 Introduction

The current mass customization era demands the manufacturing industry to produce multiple variations of customized products at the price of standardized mass products. In order to meet this demand, the manufacturing industry need to increase the flexibility and agility of their manufacturing processes by adapting new and changing requirements or changes in the manufacturing environment without disturbing the work flow[1].

This paper proposes an ontology-based reconfiguration agent that attempts to reconfigure the manufacturing system after realising changes in the requirements or the manufacturing environment. It forms a new reconfiguration by analysing the new requirements and inferring facts about the environment to deduce whether the current environment can handle the given requirements. The benefit of our approach is minimizing the overheads of the reconfiguration process by achieving rapid reconfiguration with minimum human intervention.

This paper is organised as fellows: Section 2 defines the reconfiguration challenge in the manufacturing industry and introduces our proposed solution to this challenge while Section 3 introduces the notion of ontological knowledge representation and discusses the knowledge model of our simple manufacturing environment model. Section 4 introduces a reconfiguration agent and then discusses its architecture and

V. Mařík, V. Vyatkin, A.W. Colombo (Eds.): HoloMAS 2007, LNAI 4659, pp. 114–126, 2007.

implementation, while Section 5 gives an insight on our current research. Finally in Section 6 conclusions are drawn.

2 Reconfiguration Challenge

One of the main challenges faced by the manufacturing industries is rapid reconfiguration of the manufacturing system to adapt new and changing requirements and environment without human intervention. The flexibility characteristic of a manufacturing factory producing multiple variations of customised products is a very important criteria. The factory must be flexible enough to support different sequences of production in addition to the ability of changing over the production system to offer new products [1].

We illustrate some reconfiguration ideas and challenges on a laboratory example of a modular machine which is a representative model of a simple work cell that can be found in various manufacturing environments. The machine is shown in Figure 1. It consists of two parts: Machine I (Processing Machine) and Machine II (Handling Machine). Each machine is built from some mechatronic devices for performing manufacturing or logistic operations.

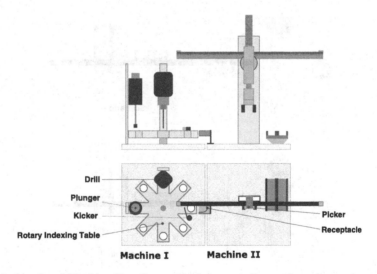

Fig. 1. Machine I and Machine II work together form a small manufacturing environment. Machine I (Processing Machine) is used for processing work pieces while Machine II (Handling Machine) is used for handling and sorting work pieces.

The Machine I consists of four mechatronic devices: rotating indexing table, plunger, drill and kicker performing respectively rotating, hole checking, drilling and kicking. The Machine II consists of two devices: receptacle and picker. The receptacle performs presence detection while the picker performs picking and sorting.

This work cell supports multiple production scenarios resulting from change of product, its features, availability of components, orders, etc. An example of supporting multiple sequences of production resulting from change in the availability of components is shown in Figure 2. It illustrates the complying of two different scenarios with the same given requirement: hole testing followed by sorting according to the presence of a hole. In scenario (i), following the hole testing process, the rotating indexing table moves the work piece towards the kicker in which it get kicked to the receptacle. The picker picks the work piece after being detected by the receptacle and at the same moment sorts according to the presence of a hole. Whereas in scenario (ii), either the kicker or the receptacle is faulty which means the picker has to pick the work piece from the rotating table after that it does the sorting.

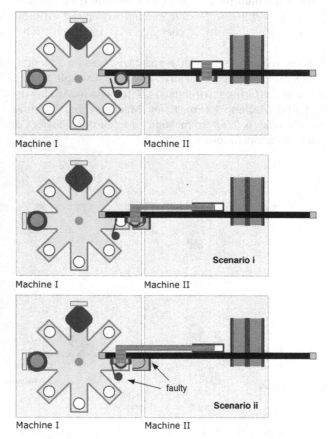

Fig. 2. Two different production scenarios are shown in this figure: scenarios (i) with all functional mechatronic devices, and scenario (ii) with faulty mechatronic devices. Both scenarios satisfy the requested requirements.

Addition of a new device or the replacement of a faulty device with a new one requires deactivation of the system. Moreover, after physically connecting and allocating the device, it may require the adjustments of some lower level controls and, production plans and reprogramming parts of the control system.

In this paper we present a methodology that can reduce some of the overhead mentioned above by rapidly reconfiguring the system via utilising the ontological descriptions of the manufacturing environment and using reconfiguration agent that infer useful facts from these descriptions. Moreover the reconfiguration agent analyses the given requirement to check if the manufacturing environment can handle it.

3 Ontological Knowledge

The knowledge of the manufacturing environment can be formalised along with the rules and the relationships between the objects. The reason behind formalising is to form a reliable and interoperable description of the manufacturing s domain. Hence ontologies can be used as a mean of formalising this knowledge using a common vocabulary or a standard common language like OWL to ensure interoperability [2] [3].

Ontology as defined by Thomas Gruber is "formal specification of a conceptualisation" [4]. An ontology specification is a formal description of a domain of interest, used for a particular purpose and expressed with a controlled vocabulary. The computer scientists have made a clear distinction between the terminological components (Tbox) and assertional components (Abox). The Tbox vocabulary specifies concepts that have associated Abox facts. Figure 3 shows the relationship between an Abox and Tbox. The combination of both represents a knowledge base for the domain [2]. In our case the manufacturing industry is our domain of interest; Tbox describes the concepts in the manufacturing industry whereas Abox represents the instances of these concepts.

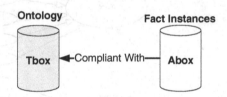

Fig. 3. The knowledge base of a particular domain

There were a few efforts towards forming a common manufacturing ontology during the last decade such as the work [3] done by the National Institute of Standards and Technology, followed by a recent proposal of a common manufacturing upper ontology for manufacturing system (MASON). The proposal was built upon three head concepts: entities, operations and resource [5]. The principle behind that is to provide shared and common understanding of the manufacturing domain. MASON has already been used across many useful applications such as multi agent systems for manufacturing [6].

3.1 Our Simple Environment Knowledge Model

The knowledge model of our simple manufacturing environment is expressed using OWL – Web Ontology Language developed by W3C (World Wide Web Consortium). OWL is an interoperable language through a standardized formal language

(XML) used for defining and instantiating web ontologies. It supports knowledge sharing and reuse which is very important for adding new facts to the knowledge model and keeping it up to date [7][8]. These features have been recently utilised in forming an OWL representation of the Automation Object Reference model for Industrial-Process Measurement and Control Systems [9].

OWL-DL, one of the OWL dialects, is used for expressing our knowledge model for the reason that it ensures reasoning will be computable and decidable [3]. Protégé [10], an open source platform for creating knowledge models, is used for creating the Tbox (formal specification of the environment) and the Abox (instances of machines that comply with Tbox) of our environment. Each machine has an OWL document with instances of all the class (operations and resources) propertied related to the machines. Our knowledge model is based on MASON. Figure 4 shows the main important head concepts that have been identified: Resource and Operation.

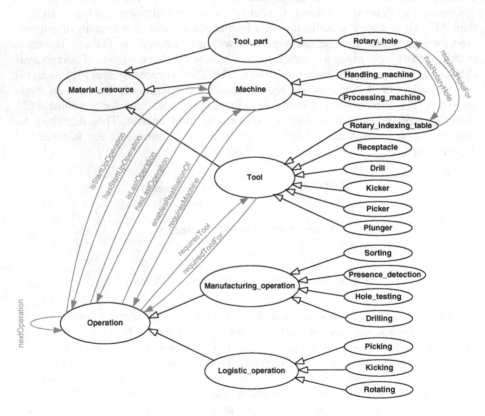

Fig. 4. Ontology describing the knowledge model of our testbed (Tbox)

For the sake of simplicity, we ignored the entity concept in MASON and assumed that our current available machines represent the whole domain of the manufacturing industry. The Operation concept consists of two sub-concepts: Manufacturing

Operation and Logistic Operation. Most of the time, the logistic operations are acting as a link between manufacturing operations.

Table 1 shows some of the important properties that we identified in the environment based on MASON [5]. These properties play a crucial role in helping in inferring useful facts about the environment.

Table 1. Important properties in our environment

Property	Description
nextOperation	This property determines the next feasible operation that can follow the current operation.
isLastOperation	This property classifies the feasible last operation(s) in a machine
isStartUpOperation	This property classifies the feasible start-up operation(s) in a machine

Figure 5 shows some instances (Abox facts) of our manufacturing system and the relationship between them. The two main important instances are the processing machine instance (Processing_machine_1) and handling machine instance (Handling_machine_1). The other instances are the operations instances performed by these machines. As seen in this figure, the nextOperation property links the operations forming a graph like structure. Section 4.6 will show the decision engine of the configuration agent uses this structure in the process of generating a new configuration. There are other instances which are not shown in this figure like instances of the tools that perform these operations.

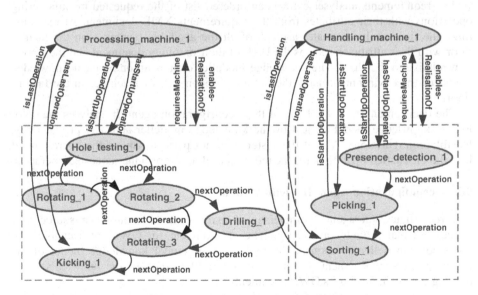

Fig. 5. Facts instances (Abox) of our model environment

4 Reconfiguration Agent

Our reconfiguration agent may generate an alternative or a new configuration if it is feasible to adapt the change in requirements or environment. It analyses the extracted information from the floor specification and requirements. Moreover, it utilises the ontological knowledge of the manufacturing environment to infer facts about the environment.

4.1 Reconfiguration Agent Architecture

The reconfiguration agent consists of four main components: requirements analyser, floor analyser, knowledge modeller, and decision engine. Figure 6 shows a high level architecture of the reconfiguration agent with its components.

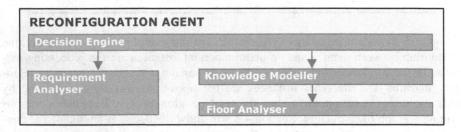

Fig. 6. High level architecture of the reconfiguration agent

The requirements analyser extracts an ordered list of the requested manufacturing operations with their attributes from the requirements XML document. At the same time, the floor analyser creates a graph of all the available machines on the factory floor with their attributes such as the URL of their ontology document and their position relative to the floor. The knowledge modeller creates an ontological knowledge model of the environment using the ontology documents of machines in the factory floor.

The decision engine is the brain of the reconfiguration agent. It analyses the ontological knowledge model created by the knowledge modeller and may produce new feasible configurations. Also if the system can not perform any of the operations, it lists the unsatisfied operation and the required tool to perform the requested operation.

4.2 Reconfiguration Agent Implementation

Our reconfiguration agent is implemented using Jena [11], an open source java framework that provides a programmatic environment for OWL. Jena enables the knowledge modeller component to create an ontological knowledge model of the manufacturing environment. It constructs a tree-like graph of the knowledge from reading the given machine's OWL documents.

Pellet [12], an open-source Java based OWL-DL reasoner is used as our rule-based reasoner to work in conjunction with Jena framework. It is used by the decision engine for inferring facts about our ontology model of the environment. Also, it is used by the knowledge modeller for checking the consistency of the OWL documents.

JDOM [13], a java representation of XML documents is used by the requirement analyser and floor analyser components for reading the requirements XML document and floor specification XML.

Figure 7 shows a more detailed illustration of the main components of the reconfiguration agent. The knowledge modeller constructs the environment knowledge model using JENA from reading the given machines' owl documents. The owl documents' URLs are inside the machine objects extracted by the floor analyser. The decision engine checks if the system can satisfy the given required operations via Pellet inference engine. Firstly it checks if the requested operations can be performed by the available machines, and then ensures that the logistic operations can link them. Finally if it satisfies the requirements, it returns the feasible configuration otherwise it displays the failed operations and the failed connections with the needed tools and machines.

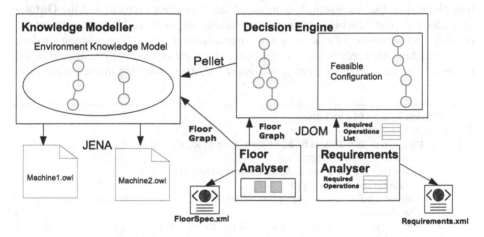

Fig. 7. Detailed illustration of reconfiguration agent's main components

4.3 Requirements Analyser

Requirements analyser extracts all the required operations from the Requirements document. As seen in Figure 8, the root element of the requirements document is **Requirements**. For the sake of simplicity, we only considered Requested Operations as the only element of requirements. It consists of at least one or more Requested Operation element. The options attribute of the Requested Operation is used to state further specification of the requested operation. Different requested operation has different options. E.g. Drill options can include the depth of the hole and speed of the drill while Sorting options can include the criteria of the sorting methodology. The requirement analyser creates an ordered list of required operations object. Each object contains the name and the options of the requested operation. This list is used later on by the decision engine component of the system.

```
<Requirements>
 <ReqOperations>
  <ReqOperation>Hole_testing</ReqOperation>
  <ReqOperation depth=2cm, speed=12>Drilling</ReqOperation>
  <ReqOperation criteria=hole_presence>Sorting</ReqOperation>
 </ReqOperations>
</Requirements>
```

Fig. 8. Requirements XML document

4.4 Floor Analyser

The floor analyser captures all the needed floor specification about the machines in the manufacturing system from the floor specification document. This includes the location, orientation, OWL ontology document of each machine and the connections of one machine to another. As seen in figure 9, the Floor Specification element is the root element of the document. It consists of the **Machines** element and the **Ontologies** Element. The **Machines** element can contain one or more Machine element depending on the number of machines in the manufacturing floor. The position attribute of the machine elements is used to determine the location and the orientation of the machine. For the sake of simplicity, we assumed that any machine in our environment

```
<FloorSpecification>
 <Machines>
  <Machine ID=1 initial=true pos={x0:2 y0:2 x1:2 y1:2}>
   <MachineOntology>
    http://localhost/ProcessingMachine.owl
   </MachineOntology>
  <ConnectedTo startupOp = "Rotation" >2</ConnectedTo>
  </Machine>
  <Machine ID = 2 initial=false pos={x0:2 y0:2 x1:2 y1:2}>
   <MachineOntology>
     http://localhost/HandlingMachine.owl
   </MachineOntology>
   <ConnectedTo
     startupOp = "Picking,Presence_detection">
     1
   </ConnectedTo>
  </Machine>
 </Machines>
</FloorSpecification>
```

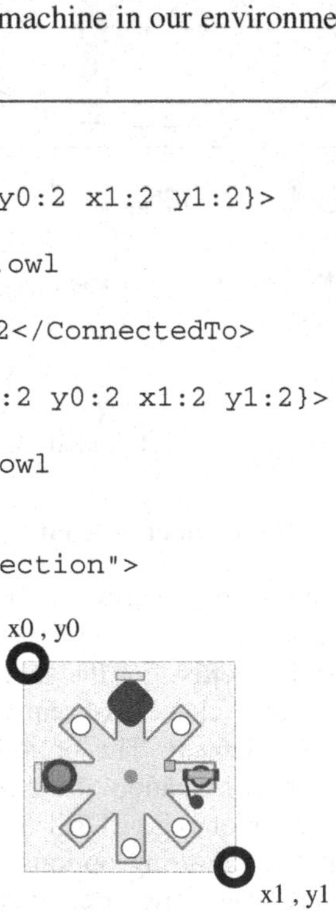

Fig. 9. Floor specification XML document

can fit in a squared shape frame. 'x0' and 'y0' determines the position of the top left hand corner point of the machine while the 'x1, and y1' is the position of the bottom right corner point of the machine. The ID attribute of the machine is used for identifying the machine while the initial attribute is used to determine the startup machines. The Machine element contains two sub- elements: one MachineOntology and at least one ConnectedTo Elements. The MachineOntology has the URL of the machine's OWL document while the ConnectedTo states the machines that this machine connects to. The attributes of ConnectedTo determine the startupOperation in that connection. The floor analyser creates a graph of the available machines objects and provides methods for accessing this graph. Each object includes all the extracted information (location and Ontology URL). This list is used later on by the knowledge modeler component.

4.5 The Knowledge Modeler

It constructs ontology knowledge model of the manufacturing environment using the machines list extracted by the floor analyser. This list contains vital information about the machines for the operation of the knowledge modeller: The URL of the OWL document and the location of each machine. The modeller uses Jena model factory and Pellet inference engine (given by the decision engine) to construct an Ontology model of the factory floor by reading each machine's OWL document. The model factory converts each OWL document to a graph which is the primary data structure in Jena. This graph is wrapped by a model that provides convenient methods for the decision engine to access the contents of the graph.

4.6 The Decision Engine

The decision engine produces a feasible configuration that satisfies the given requirements using the floor graph and the ontology knowledge model. Firstly it uses Pellet inference engine for merging the graphs of the machines to form one graph of the environment. It does that by connecting the last operations of one machine the initial operations of another machine in the factory floor via the nextOperation property.

Secondly it inspects whether the requested operations exist in our ontology knowledge using the inference engine. If all of them exist, it tries to find the logistic operations that can connect the requested operations with each other using depth-first search. It accesses the first satisfied requested operation and marks it as current operation. At the same time it performs a search until it finds the next satisfied requested operation. If it can not find one or a series of logistic operations that connects the current operation to the next one, it indicates that it can not connect the two operations. After that it moves to the next satisfied operation and tries to do the same searching process until it finds next requested operation.

Figure 10 shows an example of two different requirements and the results produced by the decision engine. The facts about our environment (see figure 5) show that the drilling operation comes after the hole testing and not vice versa. We were able to infer that by performing a search through the graph like structure of the operations.

Requirements I can be satisfied because the operations are available and a logistic path exists between them while Requirements II can not be satisfied because there is no logistic connection between hole testing and drilling. Also this figure shows that the system can produce two different configuration in the (Drilling_Sorting section) and (Hole_testing -Sorting section). The reason behind that is, the decision engine decided that the picker is able to pick from the given range of picking in the ontology and also from position of the two machines.

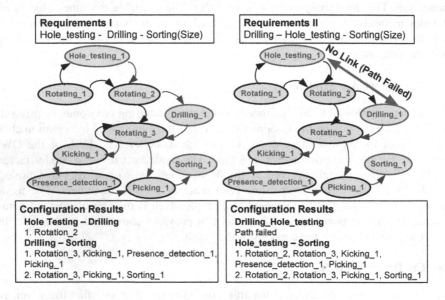

Fig. 10. An Example of two different requirements

5   Future Research

Our current research is moving towards integrating the reconfiguration agent with the distributed controllers of our system's low level components. This will enable the agent to interact and communicate directly with the controllers of the components for the purpose of immediately deploying the new configuration.

The distributed low level controllers of our system have been developed in compliance with the 61499 standard [14]. In [15] a standard component called the 'Interface' function block has been implemented to represent an arbitrary mechatronic actor and integrate it with higher levels of intelligent control We are currently working on the development of a library of service interface function blocks [16] that will allow the reconfiguration agent to communicate with the controllers of the devices in order to deploy the new configuration. Hence this will achieve our main goal of fully reconfiguration of the system without human intervention.

6 Conclusions

An ontology based reconfiguration agent has been developed with the purpose of forming new configuration that adapts changes in manufacturing requirements and environment. It analysis the given requirements and deduce facts about the factory floor environment. Then it creates a new feasible configuration using the deduced facts if it possible

An ontological knowledge model of our simple manufacturing environment based on MASON was created. The configuration agent uses the knowledge model to infer facts about the environment. The 'decision engine component' of our agent uses pellet (an OWL-DL reasoner) to infer facts about the environment. A new configuration is formed if the engine concludes that the environment can satisfies the given requirement or else.

Our current research involves the integration of our reconfiguration agent with the software of the distributed controllers compliant with the new international standard IEC 61499. Achieving the integration will lead to achieving rapid reconfiguration without human intervention.

Acknowledgements

This work has been supported by the research grant 3606588/9273 of the University of Auckland.

References

1. Leitão, P.: An Agile and Adaptive Holonic Architecture for Manufacturing Control, PhD Thesis, University of Porto (2004)
2. Gruber, T.R.: A translation Approach to Portable Ontology Specifications. Knowledge Acquisition 5, 199–220 (1993)
3. Lacy, L.: OWL: Representing Information Using the Web Ontology Language, Trafford Publishing (2005)
4. Schlenoff, C., Ivester, R., Knutilla, A.: A robust process ontology for manufacturing systems integration. In: Proceedings of 2nd International Conference on Engineering Design and Automation (1998)
5. Lemaignan, S., Siadat, A., Dantan, J.-Y., Semenenko, A.: MASON: A Proposal For An Ontology Of Manufacturing Domain Distributed Intelligent Systems. In: Proceedings of International IEEE Workshop on Distributed Intelligent Systems (DIS 2006), Collective Intelligence and Its Applications, pp. 195–200 (2006)
6. Obitko, M., Marik, V.: Ontologies formulti-agent systems in manufacturingdomain. In: DEXA 2002 Proceedings of the 13th International Workshop Database and Expert Systems Applications, pp. 597–602. IEEE Computer Society, Los Alamitos (2002)
7. Web Ontology Language (OWL), W3C Recommendation, http://www.w3.org/TR/owl-ref/
8. Aref, M.M., Zhou, Z.: The Ontology Web Language (OWL) for a Multi-Agent Understating System (2005)
9. Martinez Lastra, J.L., López Orozco, O.J.: Semantic Extension for Automation Objects. In: IEEE Conference on Industrial Informatics, Proceedings, Singapore (2006)

10. Stanford Protégé Website, The Protégé Project (2004), http://protege.stanford.edu/
11. Jena, A.: Semantic Web Framework for Java, http://jena.sourceforge.net
12. Pellet: An OWL-DL Reasoner, http://pellet.owldl.com/
13. JDOM - (Java Document Object Model) Java Toolkit for working with XMLFB Book, http://www.jdom.org
14. Function blocks for industrial-process measurement and control systems - Part 1: Architecture, International Electrotechnical Commission, Geneva (2005)
15. Sardesai, A.R., Mazharullah, O., Vyatkin, V.: Reconfiguration of Mechatronic Systems Enabled by IEC 61499, Function Blocks. In: Proceedings of the 2006 Australasian Conference on Robotics & Automation (2006)
16. Vyatkin, V.: IEC 61499 Function Blocks for Embedded and Distributed Control Systems Design, O3NEIDA - Instrumentation Society of America (2007)

Methods to Observe the Clustering of Agents Within a Multi-Agent System

Raymond J. Staron[1], Pavel Tichý[2], Radek Šindelář[2], and Francisco P. Maturana[1]

[1] Rockwell Automation, 1 Allen-Bradley Drive, Mayfield Hts., OH 44124-6118, USA
[2] Rockwell Automation s.r.o., Pekarska 10a, 15500 Prague 5, Czech Republic
{rjstaron, ptichy, rsindelar, fpmaturana}@ra.rockwell.com

Abstract. Cohesion and coupling are standard concepts in computer science. As in classic software, multi-agent systems (MASs) strive for high cohesion and low coupling. But MASs, by definition, do have some coupling, i.e., the agents seek out and discover other agents, and negotiate and cooperate with them, to accomplish some overall goal. Moreover, as different events occur, and different agents and different agent behaviors are called upon, the coupling values for the system change. This paper proposes a methodology for viewing these changing coupling relationships and clustering behaviors. In addition, the methodology is described as implemented as part of a standard agent monitoring tool.

Keywords: multi-agent systems, clustering, visualization.

1 Introduction

Users of control systems require sophisticated software to design, deploy, operate, and maintain these systems. Suppliers of control system equipment have always supplied the software that is compatible with its hardware. In particular, vendors supply integrated programming environments (IDEs) to assist the customer in designing, programming, and deploying the control programs to the controllers. Moreover, these same IDEs often provide tools that animate the control program as it executes, giving the user a real-time window into the program's changing data and evolving operation. With such views of the program, a user can both monitor and diagnose problems in both his process and his control program itself.

Any IDE for control systems must be usable in the industrial automation marketplace. In particular, typical users are quite knowledgeable about their problem domain but somewhat less so on average about computer science and high level programming languages. The IEC 61131 control languages [3] have been staples in programmable controllers for decades, but they are inadequate on their own for specifying the behavior of intelligent agents within a control system. Though we have, in our Agent Development Environment (ADE) [6], hidden much of the complexity of programming agent behavior in C or C++, the controller still executes it as C++ code. Debugging such a system requires well known capabilities such as viewing the code and its data as it is executed, single stepping, stepping into

V. Mařík, V. Vyatkin, A.W. Colombo (Eds.): HoloMAS 2007, LNAI 4659, pp. 127–136, 2007.
© Springer-Verlag Berlin Heidelberg 2007

functions, using breakpoints, etc. A distributed agent system adds the need for system-wide visualization tools that can be used to monitor and diagnose problems both in the process and the combined control/agent program itself.

To enable visualization and debugging of communication in a multi-agent system, we created a tool called the Java Sniffer [8]. This tool receives messages from all agents in both our Autonomous Cooperative System (ACS) [5], [9] and standard JADE [4] systems simultaneously, reasons about the information, and presents it from different points of view. This tool has proven invaluable in developing agent-based control systems.

If we extend the classical computer science notions of cohesion and coupling [11] to multi-agent systems, cohesion describes the extent to which all the behaviors of an agent (or an agent class) are related and provide some well defined functionality to the system, and coupling measures the extent to which an agent (or an agent class) is connected to another. As in the classic case, in multi-agent systems we strive for high cohesion and low coupling. But multi-agent systems, by definition, do have some coupling, i.e., the agents seek out and discover other agents, and negotiate and cooperate with them, to accomplish some overall goal. In any suitable visualization tool, the cluster of agents that agree together on a plan to solve some problem or react to some event should be evident on the display. Moreover, as different events occur within the control system and different agents and different agent behaviors are called upon, the coupling values for the system change.

This paper suggests a methodology for viewing these changing coupling relationships and clustering behaviors. Information about this coupling or agent clustering can be used by a system developer or integrator in various ways. For example, the structure of agent clusters can be mapped to agent execution hardware. Placing agents that belong to one cluster into one computation unit can improve system performance if cost of communication within a computation unit is lower than communication outside of it. The opposite question that can be answered is how to place agents into a given number of computation units such that communication among these units is minimized.

The paper is organized as follows. Section 2 defines the proposed dynamic model for agent clustering. Section 3 explains how a static analysis using a full set of messages can extend the results of the dynamic analysis. Implementation of these analyses and their visualization within the Java Sniffer are presented in Section 4, and Section 5 shows experimental results on a real MAS application from the material handling domain.

2 Proposed Dynamic Model for Agent Clustering

We suggest a dynamic model that considers a collection of agents as a system of masses exerting forces on one another, observing the changes in each agent's position and velocity. For attraction, the force is proportional to the number of messages sent between any pair of agents, acting for a short time. The repulsive force can be likened to that experienced by two like electrical charges, except that it is formulated as a "reverse gravity". The kinetic frictional force is used to help bring the system into a steady state.

2.1 Definitions

Given A, a collection of agents $\{a_i\}$, with $i = 1...N$, where N is the number of agents. Each a_i has constant mass m_i and time-dependent vectors of position and velocity, $\vec{p}_i(t)$ and $\vec{v}_i(t)$, respectively.

Within each time interval ΔT, acquire or compute some measure of attraction between each pair of agents. Use these values to, first, compute the total force on each agent in the system, and second, using the computed forces and current positions and velocities of the agents, update each agent's position and velocity.

For our purposes we choose for the measure of agent attraction the number of messages, M_{ij}, sent between agents a_i and a_j in each ΔT interval. Thus a value of zero represents no attraction at all. The investigation into other measures of attraction is a future research topic.

2.2 Calculating Forces

The force on any agent a_i is the sum of

1. an attractive force to any other agent that a_i has communicated with in the ΔT interval;
2. a repulsive force to all other agents based on an inverse square law of the distance between them; and
3. a frictional force acting in the direction opposite to the current motion of a_i.

Thus in any ΔT interval the force on an agent a_i is:

$$\vec{F}_i = \sum_{\substack{j=1 \\ j \neq i}}^{N} \vec{f}_{ij}^{\,a} + \sum_{\substack{j=1 \\ j \neq i}}^{N} \vec{f}_{ij}^{\,r} + \vec{f}_i^{\,f} \tag{1}$$

where the summations and additions are vector additions, and:

$$\vec{f}_{ij}^{\,a} = k_a M_{ij} \vec{u}_{ij} \tag{2}$$

$$\vec{f}_{ij}^{\,r} = -k_r \frac{m_i m_j}{d_{ij}^2} \vec{u}_{ij} \tag{3}$$

$$\vec{f}_i^{\,f} = -k_f \vec{v}_i \tag{4}$$

where:

- k_a, k_r, and k_f are constants for the attractive, repulsive, and frictional forces;
- M_{ij} is the number of messages between agents a_i and a_j;
- m_i is the mass of agent a_i;
- d_{ij}^2 is the square of the distance between a_i and a_j;
- $\vec{u}_{ij}$ is the unit vector pointing from agent a_i to a_j; and
- $\vec{v}_i$ is the velocity of agent a_i.

2.3 Calculating Velocities and Positions

Once the force on each agent has been computed for a particular time interval ΔT, the classic equations of motion can be used to compute new velocities and positions. Note that these equations functions are of discrete time, $(n\Delta T)$.

Given the force, $\vec{F}_i(n\Delta T)$, on an agent at some time interval, $n\Delta T$, plus its mass m_i, its current velocity, $\vec{v}_i(n\Delta T)$, and current position, $\vec{p}_i(n\Delta T)$, its new velocity and position are:

$$\vec{v}_i((n+1)\Delta T) = \vec{v}_i(n\Delta T) + \frac{\vec{F}_i(n\Delta T)}{m_i}\Delta T, \tag{5}$$

$$\vec{p}_i((n+1)\Delta T) = \vec{p}_i(n\Delta T) + \frac{1}{2}\frac{\vec{F}_i(n\Delta T)}{m_i}(\Delta T)^2 + \vec{v}_i(n\Delta T)\Delta T, \tag{6}$$

3 Static Analysis of Agent Clustering

Static agent clustering analysis can be used to further support the dynamic model presented in the previous section. Two static analyses are presented: topological agent clustering that uses as input the current positions of the agents as generated from a dynamic analysis, and static agent clustering from a full set of messages. Fuzzy clustering algorithms [2] seem to be most appropriate method for this purpose.

3.1 Topological Agent Clustering

The positions of the agents at a given time as generated by the dynamic model of agent clustering can be further analyzed to identify and display agent clusters. Each agent is associated with one agent cluster and displayed accordingly. We use methods based on the minimization of the objective function; specifically we have used in this paper the Gustafson-Kessel algorithm.

3.2 Static Agent Clustering from Messages

The dynamic model is based on computation of each agent position in each ΔT interval; thus, all agent positions are updated continually. A different type of analysis can be obtained by considering simultaneously all messages sent among agents and directly forming agent clusters using a predefined criterion without directly computing their positions. The criteria are to minimize communication among agent clusters and maximize communication within each agent cluster.

Objective function-based algorithms work with pattern positions while our task is given by the matrix of messages. The number of messages sent between two agents is indirectly proportional to an agent distance but the transformation into pattern positions is not straightforward. Hence the objective function based methods can not be used for the static analysis. But there is a variety of methods that can be utilized for this purpose, e.g., heuristic clustering algorithms and genetic algorithms. These algorithms are able to work with other measures as well, in our case the number of messages. The modified fuzzy clustering algorithm from [7] used in this paper handles the input data set sample by sample.

4 Implementation in the Java Sniffer

The Java Sniffer that is used for logging, visualization, and analysis of agent communication [8] has been extended to visualize both the dynamic and static agent clustering analyses.

4.1 Visualization of Dynamic Clustering

For dynamic agent clustering a two-dimensional world is used for computation and visualization. It is possible to randomly place agents within the grid, replay a log of some communication sequence, compute one ΔT step at a time or switch to online analysis in which incoming messages are analyzed on the fly. An agent filter can be used to analyze and display only selected agents. It is also possible to specify the constants ΔT, k_a, k_r, and k_f, and to initialize the grid size. In addition, all these variables can be changed on the fly during the analysis.

As agents update their own positions, two or more can compute their position on the square grid to be very close so that the repulsive force between them becomes quite large. Therefore, the limit for repulsive force has been set such that for distances smaller than 1 the force is computed for distance equal to 1 in grid units.

Agents are visualized as circles with the agent name appended, where the size of a circle is proportional to the mass of an agent. The mass can be either set to 1 kg. for all agents or calculated based on the communication activity of each agent as in equation (7).

$$m_i = 1 + \log(1 + N \sum_{\Delta T} \sum_{j=1}^{N} \frac{M_{ij}}{\sum_{k=1}^{N} M_{kj}}) \tag{7}$$

Communication between each pair of agents in a given ΔT is visualized as a segment with a given thickness slowly fading away with each time step. Message direction can be depicted as an arrow and both message description and color can be shown. Zooming is either computed automatically or can be set manually.

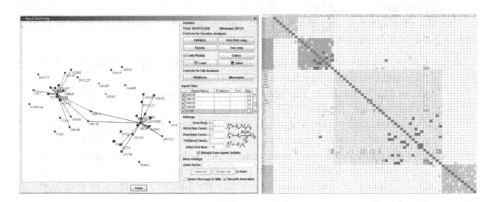

Fig. 1. Dynamic and Static Agent Clustering in Java Sniffer

An agent in the clustering analysis can be configured to be not moveable and after the user changes its position it stays on this point. This feature is useful, for example, when the user wants to see possible clusters around each of the selected agents.

4.2 Visualization of Static Clustering from Messages

Static clustering computed from messages is visualized as a table having the agent names listed in both column and row headers. The number of messages sent and received can be visualized either separately or combined. If they are combined the table becomes symmetric along its main diagonal. If they are treated separately, each row contains the number of messages that the agent in the given row sent to agents identified by the columns. The color saturation of the background under each number in the table is proportional to its value for better visibility of higher numbers.

As a result of the static agent clustering analysis, agents are reordered in such a way that agents belonging to the first cluster are placed at the beginning, agents from the second cluster follow, and so on. Clusters are depicted as squares along the diagonal of the table. Since the criterion for static agent clustering is to maximize communication within clusters, the sum of the numbers in the corresponding squares is maximized and sum of the numbers outside of the squares is minimized.

5 Experimental Results

We now present experimental results on one real MAS. Agents in this MAS are used for control of the transportation of products or discrete materials on the factory's shop floor using a network of conveyor belts [10].

5.1 Description of Material Handling Application

The MAST environment simulates all the components of the holonic packing cell of the Center for Distributed Automation and Control (CDAC) at the University of Cambridge, U.K. This laboratory provides a physical testbed for experiments with the Radio Frequency Identification (RFID) technology and the agile and intelligent agent-based manufacturing control [1].

The MAST's agent library contains the following set of agents to represent and control particular components of the lab's equipment:

- *Conveyors* (B) – transport the shuttles with boxes (there is one main feeding loop and two subsidiary loops leading to robots);
- *Gates* (G) – navigate the shuttles out of the main loop to the subsidiary loops and vice versa;
- *Docking stations* (D) – the shuttles are held here while a box is packed;
- *RFID readers* (R) – that read the IDs (EPC codes) of passing boxes and provide them to the gates to be able to properly direct the shuttle;
- *Fanuc M6i robots* (Robot) – that pack the boxes;
- *Storage units* (Storage) – for temporary holding of the items in four vertical slots (each for a particular type of item);
- *Rack storages* (RS) – (not shown) that store shuttle trays;

- *Gantry robot* (GR) – picks the box out of the rack storage and drops it to the shuttle and vice versa;
- *Shuttles* (id) – that provide transportation capabilities;
- *Orders* (Order) – responsible for fulfilling packaging user requests.

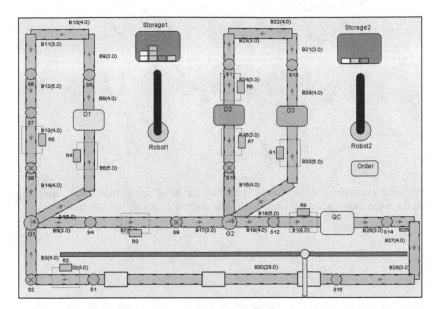

Fig. 2. MAST with CDAC Material Handling application

5.2 Results of Dynamic Analysis

The first set of experiments were performed on the CDAC material handling application with four moving shuttles and four orders fulfilled by both robots; there were 74 agents total. The parameters for the clustering analysis were set to $\Delta T = 0.5$ seconds, $k_a = 0.3$, $k_r = 0.7$, and $k_f = 1$. The mass of each agent has been set according to equation (7).

The agent clustering shows mainly that:

- The main feeding loop and the two subsidiary loops were discovered correctly with G1 and G2 agents connecting them.
- Chains of B, D, and S agents are formed according to their physical distribution in the real system.
- RFID reader agents R are close to corresponding docking stations D and gates G since they are suppliers of RFID readings for them.
- Order and id agents are in the middle and moving around since id agents represent shuttles that move around and Orders contact all other agents.
- Robot agents are close to their corresponding Docking stations.
- Rack Storage (RS) agents are close to id and Order agents since the order starts/ends by getting/placing a shuttle from/to rack storage.

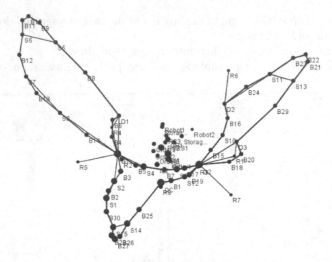

Fig. 3. Agent clustering of the CDAC material handling application after analyzing one hundred thousand messages at the point where the system discovers the shortest paths

Fig. 4. Creation of agent clustering of CDAC material handling application

Clustering starts from a random state depicted in the top left most diagram of Figure 4. From left to right the state of analysis after each subsequent 5000 messages is shown, depicting the gradual discovery of shortest paths. The bottom rightmost diagram shows the state after one hundred thousand messages.

5.3 Results of Static Analysis

Agent clustering can be further analyzed by using the topological agent clustering method. Four agent clusters have been selected for the clustering of the CDAC application. The result of topological agent clustering can be different for each run since the initial position of empty agent clusters is randomly selected. Therefore, the two most common results are shown.

The topological agent clustering method identifies the main feeding loop and the two subsidiary loops. The last identified cluster contains Order, id, RS, and Storage agents. The placement of G agents that represent a connection between the loops and the agents close to them can vary since they can functionally belong to multiple groups. The number of messages sent within clusters divided by the total message count for the left graph is equal to 0.876 and for the right graph is 0.884, indicating relatively high intra-cluster communication.

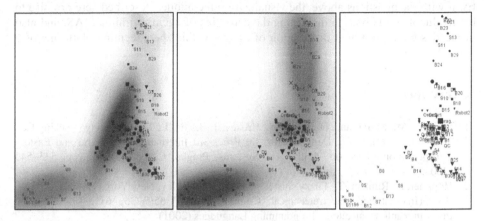

Fig. 5. Two results of topological agent clustering of CDAC material handling application with four clusters and clustering from messages on the right. Agents belonging to one group have the same symbol. Each cluster in the topological agent clustering is approximated by a two-dimensional Gaussian distribution depicted as ellipses with the same center.

The static clustering from messages using the modified fuzzy clustering algorithm with a limit of four clusters gives the ratio of 0.911. This association of agents with clusters is depicted in the rightmost graph of Figure 5. We had expected that clustering methods that have messages in their objective function would produce a better communications ratio. The comparison indicates that the results from pure topological clustering, which in turn are based on the results of dynamic clustering analysis, are close to results obtained from message based methods.

6 Conclusions and Future Work

The dynamic clustering demonstrated its ability to reveal functional structure of the system solely from an analysis of message passing in a MAS. It can also reveal the topology of the hardware equipment if the functional structure of the MAS corresponds with this topology.

This paper has proposed a visualization technique to aid the designer and user of MASs to view the complex changing interactions of the agents within such systems. The experiments indicated some areas that need further study. They are:

1. The attractive force on an agent is directly proportional to the number of messages. Will that number, in any ΔT, become so large that the computed forces on the agents are large enough to push the system into an unstable state? Perhaps there should be a limit to the force on any one agent.

2. Would a repulsive force based on inverse distance (as opposed to the current inverse distance squared) result in a better visualization?
3. What effects does varying the frictional constant (as well as the other constants) have on the visualization?

Even with the questions above, the visualization techniques described here promise to be invaluable tools both in discerning the activities of agents within a MAS, and also in the design and optimal distribution of agents within the executing platforms of a control system.

References

1. Fletcher, M., McFarlane, D., Lucas, A., Brusey, J., Jarvis, J.: The Cambridge Packing Cell - A Holonic Enterprise Demonstrator. In: Proc. 3rd International / Central and Eastern European conference on Multi-Agent Systems, Prague, Czech Republic, pp. 533–543 (2003)
2. Höppner, F., Runkler, T.: Fuzzy cluster analysis. John Wiley, New York (1999)
3. IEC (International Electrotechnical Commission), TC65/WG6, 61131-3, 2nd edn. Programmable Controllers - Programming Languages (2001)
4. JADE: Java Agent DEvelopment Framework (2004), website http://jade.cselt.it
5. Maturana, F.P., Tichý, P., Šlechta, P., Discenzo, F., Staron, R.J., Hall, K.H.: Distributed multi-agent architecture for automation systems. Expert Systems with Applications 26, 49–56 (2004)
6. Staron, R.J., Maturana, F.P., Tichý, P., Šlechta, P.: Use of an Agent Type Library for the Design and Implementation of Highly Flexible Control Systems. In: The 8th World Multiconference on Systemics, Cybernetics and Inform. SCI 2004, Orlando (2004)
7. Šindelář, R., Babuška, R.: Input selection for nonlinear regression models. IEEE transactions on Fuzzy Systems 12(5), 688–696 (2004)
8. Tichý, P., Šlechta, P., Staron, R.J., Maturana, F.P., Hall, K.H.: Multiagent Technology for Fault Tolerance and Flexible Control. IEEE Transactions on System, Man, and Cybernetics – Part C: Applications and Reviews 36(5), 700–705 (2006)
9. Tichý, P., Šlechta, P., Maturana, F.P., Balasubramanian, S.: Industrial MAS for Planning and Control. In: Mařík, V., Štěpánková, O., Krautwurmová, H., Luck, M. (eds.) ACAI 2001, EASSS 2001, AEMAS 2001, and HoloMAS 2001. LNCS (LNAI), vol. 2322, pp. 280–295. Springer, Heidelberg (2002)
10. Vrba, P.: Simulation in agent-based control systems: MAST case study. International Journal of Manufacturing Technology and Management 8(1/2/3), 175–187 (2006)
11. Yourdon, E., Constantine, L.L.: Structured Design: Fundamentals of a Discipline of Computer Program and Systems Design. Prentice-Hall, Yourdon Press (1979)

Distributed Director Facilitator in a Multiagent Platform for Networked Embedded Controllers

Omar J. López Orozco and Jose L. Martinez Lastra

Tampere University of Technology, Institute of Production Engineering,
Korkeakoulunkatu 6, 33720 Tampere, Finland
{omar.lopez, jose.lastra}@tut.fi

Abstract. FIPA-compliant agent platforms must include an Agent Management System, an Agent Communication Channel and a Director Facilitator (DF). The DF is centralized and it administers a register of agents which previously had been registered. Every agent could perform a search for an agent(s) that has specific characteristics or provides a determined service. A centralized DF is a potential point of failure and could cause network overload. The DFs could be distributed through the networked embedded controllers. This paper describes the development of a Distributed Director Facilitator (DDF) which keeps a local register of service providers including the name of the agents and the services provided, this means that every controller could have its own DDF, and agents hosted within a controller could query over the list of service providers.

Keywords: Multiagent systems, agent platform, embedded controllers, Director Facilitator.

1 Introduction

The new generation of reconfigurable manufacturing systems will need new and effective tools to adapt rapidly to continuous product changes, and short runs without seriously impairing production. In order to rapidly adjust production capacity and functionality within part families, the assembly system should be designed capable to face possible changes in structure, as well as in hardware and software components [1].

Intelligent software components are necessary in order to achieve effective reconfiguration, key issues that will bring dynamism are:

1) Software that can help to select the best equipment, in base of their skills, capabilities, physical and working dimensions. Additionally, the selection of appropriate pieces to be used in order to assembly any particular component,

2) Hardware modules or mechatronic devices enhanced by multiagent systems capable of seamless setting up and tackle continuous changing conditions. Devices and machines that automatically adapt to appropriate transporting/moving speeds, and process/operation sequencing,

3) The process of each ID coded part could be automatically tracked through the various assembly stages, allowing assembly/machine and cost analysis at every stage of production.

V. Mařík, V. Vyatkin, A.W. Colombo (Eds.): HoloMAS 2007, LNAI 4659, pp. 137–148, 2007.
© Springer-Verlag Berlin Heidelberg 2007

Conventional process control planning is commonly done off-line, causing a delay in the reconfigurability of the production line. The process control planning has three phases [2]: (1) Task decomposition, (2) Task assignment, (3) Task execution. During the task/operation assignment each operation is delegated to a mechatronic device/module, which would proceed to execute such operations in a coordinated sequence dictated by the product process plan. Multiagent systems and semantic web technologies could tackle the challenges that reconfigurable manufacturing systems are facing concerning to points (1) and (2). The task execution could be improved by the use of multiagent systems; this is by integrating control algorithms along with decision mechanisms in the same embedded controller. This represents a step moving towards loosely decoupled software entities.

The aim of this work is to describe the requirements and development process of a distributed director facilitator. The test bed is the JADE-LEAP platform adapted in order to allow software agents to run within embedded controllers. The next section includes the justification and motivation of this work. Third section is a brief overview of the related work which has motivated this work. The fourth section describes technologies of java-based embedded controllers. The fifth section highlights the importance of agent-based control in the domain of factory automation. In section six there is a short description of agent communication language and the FIPA-compliant platform used as a testbed. Seventh section describes the DDF developed and section eight includes a messaging performance of registration and searching, the last section concludes the paper.

2   Justification of the Work

There are some requirements to distribute the coordination of tasks execution (known as control coordination). The when and whom are important information for agents coordinating the process, the former refers to the triggering of sequences and it is a problem of scheduling, the lather refers to the provider or consumer of a service and it requires service discovery and matching. After service discovery the agent requester knows the names of the agent providers. There are two factors which encourage to perform service discovery in a less constrained platform, the first is that service discovery and matching demand processing capabilities not present yet in most of the current industrial embedded controllers, the second is that the discovery is required only at the bootstrap or when changes/reconfiguration occurs.

Therefore, after the service discovery performed by an agent hosted in a personal computer, a Distributed Director Facilitator (DDF) will receive a registration message with all the potential agent providers for the local agent hosted in the mechatronic module. The local agent should search for a service provider in the DDF every time it requires a service provider. A multiagent system with only one DF would have some issues which could decrease the performance of the system, these are: a single DF will receive all the requests from the agents, and it represents a single point of failure.

The DDF would favor decoupling and scalability of reconfigurable manufacturing systems. After an agent orchestrator matches every service provider to service requesters a message is sent to the agent requesters or directly to the DDF. In order to contact its potential providers the message includes agent providers and service provided. A previous approach used distributed director facilitator across different containers [16], nevertheless, the hardware platform was a personal computer, and the scenario is shown in Figure 1.

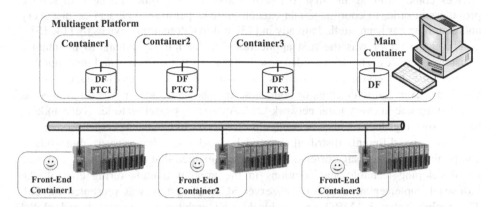

Fig. 1. Distributed Director Facilitator trough different containers hosted in a personal computer

3 Related Work

The Future manufacturing systems have to evolve rapidly due to continuous changing production requirements. Reconfigurable manufacturing systems must be provided with interoperable modular hardware and software components. Hardware modularity has already certain level of maturity considering mechanical (mechanisms) [3] and computational (embedded controllers) components. On the other hand, and in order to obtain software modularity, it is possible to extend concepts from areas such as artificial intelligence and the semantic web. The software agent paradigm is currently one of the best candidates to bring artificial intelligence's mechanisms such as decision and coordination into different levels and areas of manufacturing systems [4], there are already a considerable number of industrial applications of agent-based control and supervision like documented in [5, 6, 7] and a detailed list is presented in [8].

In agent-based control, the nature of Multiagent systems allows the decoupling and distribution of peers. These loosely decoupled entities could be hosted in networked embedded controllers, favoring with this the distribution of decision mechanism along with the control algorithms as proposed by Christensen in [9]. The algorithms for controlling the process can be found at the lowest control level, modularity can be obtaining encapsulating the algorithms in function blocks either according to the IEC 61131-3 [10] or the IEC61499 [11].

Modular design of hardware and software could bring valuable benefits to different players within the value creation chain such as device vendors, machine vendors, system integrators and industrial enterprises. The fact is that if they have components from the previous stage vendors the integration process may cost less time and effort, and save money [12]. Therefore Mechatronic device/modules and automation objects could bring valuable benefits to both the creation chain and the reconfiguration processes along the life-cycle of production cells/lines.

Using semantic web services to describe the functionality/skills of mechatronic devices could allow agents first to discover and then to communicate with service providers in order to coordinate and execute a task/operation. The service discovery and matching has been studied already in [13] and in automation devices by [14, 15].

The name server was the first applications in distributed systems to maintain a register of services. The server's database keeps a register of names and node number of processes and services, the system is partitioned in sub-networks for huge services which are extended over cities or countries, and the name server was distributed as well having one in every local network [25]. Another approach is to let every node to have its own register of names or context prefix server like in the V kernel project.

There are different distribution models such as client/server, blackboard, component-based, message-oriented and service oriented that has been used as a base for developing technological solutions in the area of manufacturing control. An industrial implementation of a client/server SCADA system was presented in [26]. The mobile robot KAMRO uses a blackboard architecture for its shared global database where different elements of the planning and the executive of assembly control interact [27]. Component-based technologies like CORBA or DCOM facilitates the distribution of components hiding to the developer the complexity of configuring distributed application, nevertheless, they have limitations such as cross-platform interoperability and changes or introduction of new components require considerable programming effort.

4 Networked Embedded Controllers

A networked embedded system is a collection of decoupled physically and functionally distributed nodes interconnected via network (i.e. wireline), interacting with the environment by means of sensors and actuator. There are too many options currently on the market, in general they can be grouped according to the programming language, the most popular are: C, C++ and JAVA. Regarding with the JAVA-based controllers two are the most known options of compilers: Just-In-Time and Java Processor Unit.

4.1 Just-in-Time (JIT)

Just-in-time (JIT) compilers are fast dynamic adaptive compilers that translate the Java technology bytecodes into native machine code on the fly. A JIT running on the end user's machine actually executes the bytecodes and compiles each method the first time it is executed [28].

4.2 Java Processor Unit (JUP)

A JUP adds the Java VM's instruction set to a CPU's instruction decoder; this processor can improve the performance of Java code execution. This statement although valid, sometimes lead to a misconception that this hardware acceleration will also out-perform or even have similar performance than VM JITs, for a detailed discussion of the topic refer to [29].

5 Agent-Based Control of Mechatronic Devices

An agent is a physical or virtual entity, which is capable of perceiving its environment and could act upon it. Software Agents can communicate in cases such as task execution coordination, service advertisement/discover, information querying about certain domain. Agents can potentially solve problems generated by changing conditions in distributed processes. By enabling networks of autonomous yet interacting reasoning elements, agent technology provides an alternative to traditional centralized systems. Agent-based solutions are being developed for three problem domains in industrial environments: real-time production control, manufacturing operations management, and the coordination of virtual enterprises [4]. Agent-based applications might improve system's qualitative attributes such as scalability, flexibility, robustness and reconfigurability. On the other hand, their deployment faces such barriers as cost and performance guarantees.

In the domain of factory automation, Multiagent technology is targeting distributed autonomous systems with embedded intelligence, networked autonomous and fault adaptive production control modules. Agents hosted within networked embedded devices convert them into a loosely coupled peers facilitating scalability. This software modularity could facilitate the distribution of control algorithms and logic intelligence together with the Mechatronic module.

Agents have to obtain information about agent service providers hosted or representing Mechatronic modules/devices; in order to interact with the selected peers, agents should request/obtain the names of FIPA interaction protocols, module's physical features such as the working dimensions and/or physical dimensions. They should be able to negotiate in order to organize a task, to solve a problem, to query and update information. Thus, agents should carry out with the requirements of to whom, where and how. This information, in the case of JADE could be found searching on the Director Facilitator, unfortunately the information lacks of semantic meaning and it could lead to a wrong selection of similar service providers. The use of semantic web services to describe devices/modules' capabilities, communication interaction protocols, and physical features could give certainty to the discovery, orchestration and collaboration of agents as coordinator of the service execution.

5.1 Ontology Modeling of Assembly Process

Goods are the final goal of production lines which provides the required processes to accomplish it. Assembly processes have been classified Vos in [17], and refined by Lastra in ABAS® in order to define the functional operations of mechatronic devices [18]. The ontology of Assembly Process should be semantically described in order to provide agents with machine interpretable descriptions. Semantic descriptions of assembly process and equipment were used by Delamer in [15] in order to allow services to be discovered.

5.2 Ontology Modeling of Mechatronic Devices

Mechatronic devices can be classified according to the operative functionality they can provide, thus, it is possible to describe their skills which represent the capability of the device to perform a task, and the service(s) the device could provide by means of its skills. If mechatronic devices/modules are classified and semantically described, therefore could be possible to find out a suitable device to accomplish a required assembly operation.

6 Multiagent Platform

6.1 Agent Communication Language

Agents should interact in order to solve problems; there are different kinds of interactions: cooperation, negotiation and coordination, for all of them standard protocols may be used to favor interoperability. Agents should be able to organize themselves forming societies or clusters in order to face complex problems that require collaboration among them [18]. Thus, agents within a society might communicate with each other, and decide the relevant information to share or the physical action to order. The mechanism for this exchange of information is the Agent Communication Language (ACL). Agents can communicate with each other if they have a common representation language and a framework of knowledge in order to interpret messages they exchange. The most known Agent Communication Language is FIPA-ACL.

Agent Communication Language (ACL) is the mechanism for the exchange of information. Thus, agents can communicate if they have a common representation language, and a framework of knowledge in order to interpret messages they exchange, this is not a share semantics, but a shared ontology [19]. Two of the most known ACLs are KQML and FIPA, there are many similarities between them, for a more detailed description refer to [20].

SOAP is the de facto standard for invocation of web services. It is XML-based and provides a standard framework for the interoperability of heterogeneous applications. JADE being FIPA-complaint utilizes the Agent Communication Language (ACL). FIPA could get interoperability through SOAP but this is a very simple model and has things missing which requires further research and consensus [21], or the development of interfaces like the ACL-SL0/tModel-SOAP Codec which bidirectionally translates FIPA ACL messages into SOAP messages [22].

6.2 Foundation for Intelligent Physical Agents

The FIPA interaction protocols facilitate the interoperability among agents using same protocols. They provide agents with simple protocols for different aspects such as request and inform, or more complex negotiation and coordination such as Contract-Net. Due to the fact that JADE-LEAP is FIPA-compliant platform, it includes message templates that could be used to interact with other agents.

6.3 Agent Platform

JADE is a FIPA-compliant platform which implements two types of registers: white and yellow pages. The former is the Agent Management; the later is the Director Facilitator (DF). The DF is an agent which main functionality is to keep a register of other agents within the same platform. Agents could send a registration message to the DF, the slots of the message template are language, ontology, service, protocol. The information registered by agents has no semantics, therefore, standalone terms could no be enough to completely match requested services, even more applications outside the agent platform would need an interface in order to find a service and which has no the same structure (profile, process, grounding). Nevertheless, agents could register the service and the URI where it could be find the entire service description. So, an agent orchestrator would get a list of services with a list of URIs to find out more details.

6.4 Light Extensible Agent Platform

Development of an Agent platform for networked embedded controllers faces problems such as processing constraints and limited footprint. The JADE-LEAP has been implemented in the industrial embedded controller PTC5800 [24], the main features are described briefly. The Pointe Controller is a Java-Based controller for real-time control and with networking and IO's connectivity. The Pointe controller uses the CLDC configuration of Java Micro Edition JME. The LEAP platform is composed of front-end container(s) and only one back-end container. A front-end container could be host in the PTC5800, it offers limited functionality to agents, in order to overcome this limitation it is necessary to interact with the back-end hosted in a PC.

The LEAP Run-time environment provides to agents the basic services; it must be active on the device before agents can be executed. Each instance of the LEAP run-time is called container and the group of container is known as platform. The container is an agent by itself which provides basic functionality for agents that will be running on it. Deployment of multiagent systems on embedded controllers such as the Pointe Controller requires an agent container running within the embedded controller. The containers of LEAP can work either as Stand-alone or as a split configuration. In the Stand-alone execution mode a complete container is executed on the target device. On the other hand, in the Split execution mode the container is separated into a Front-End (meant for running on the embedded device) and a Back-End (for running on a host with J2SE) linked together through a permanent connection. The back-end location acts as a dispatcher for messages coming and going to other platforms [23], this allows the use of proprietary protocols. This execution mode is particularly suited for resource constrained and wireless devices.

Neither the front-end nor the back-end has Agent Management System (AMS) and Directory Facilitator (DF); these functionalities are provided by the main container of the platform.

7 The Distributed Director Facilitator

Yellow page register is where agents advertise their capabilities, making it available for other agents in the system. An agent may query the register in order to find a service provider, as a reply the register will send a list of agents that match the requested service. The register acts as an information broker on behalf of agents, in the JADE-LEAP platform it is maintained by an agent called Director Facilitator. Since centralized DF would become a single point of failure and a performance bottleneck it is more advantageous to have more than one DF in the system [16].

7.1 Registering on the Distributed Director Facilitator

An agent as initiator of an interaction has to know the name of the potential participants (i.e. responders, providers) In order to communicate with them. The embedded controller has too limited capabilities to perform the entire process of service discovery and matching; therefore these activities are performed by an agent with more computational resources (i.e. agent running in a personal computer). The agent orchestrator would obtain the services available, and could inform either to the agent requester or to the DDF the providers that could be contacted by the local agent. Thereafter, local agents have a faster access to the name of the agents and the service provided.

The Director Facilitator is meant to work in an unconstrained device such as personal computers. Implementing a DF in an embedded device like the PTC5800 requires the simplification of the parsing process in order to adequate to the constrained resources of the controller. Therefore, the agent responsible to receive the message with the data of the agent service providers would parse the message content and obtain the name of agent provider(s) and store within its own local register.

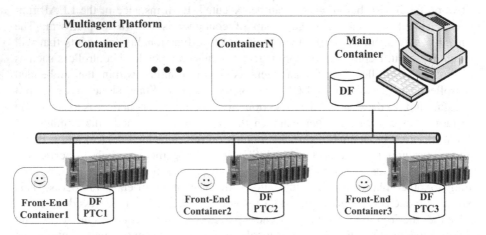

Fig. 2. Director Facilitator distributed across the containers running within the embedded controllers

The static methods in the class provided by the JADE API jade.domain.DFService allow agents to register, deregister, modify and perform searches on DF. Thus, this class provides the required FIPA messages that will be sent to the DF agent, and it is the class that the DDF uses when propagates a registration to its parent DF.

7.2 Searching on the Distributed Director Facilitator

The local agents embedded in the Pointe Controller would query the DDF every time they need a service, and then the DDF will search its register and reply if it found the service. If the DDF hasn't registered the service before, it will propagate the query to its parent DF. The propagation keeps going until the query is answered or it arrives to the highest DF in the hierarchy. If the service is found in a parent DF, it will propagate the answer backwards and every child DF will keep the service registered hereafter.

8 Performance Tests

8.1 Registration

The first test performed is the registration round trip message. The test is divided in two scenarios, no propagation and propagation, Figure 3. The former scenario is as follows, an agent within a container hosted in a PC sends registration messages to the director facilitator embedded in the controller; every message includes the name of an agent which provides a service and the type of service. The DF gets the message, parses it and obtains service and name of the agent provider, this information is stored in a register in the controller, and at the end the DDF sends a confirmation message.

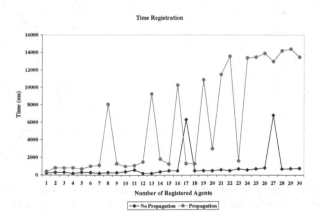

Fig. 3. Round Trip messaging time performance for registration, (a) within the director facilitator embedded in the controller, (b) in both DFs, the DF embedded and the DF in the PC

The propagation scenario includes the previous explained process, in addition the embedded DDF sends a registration message to a DF running in a PC, and finally the last DF sends confirmation backwards to the embedded DDF and this to the agent which first sent the registration message.

The two picks around the 6000 ms are caused by the garbage collector in the no propagation scenario. It means that these registrations took that among of time because the thread representing the embedded DDF was preempted during the occurrence of the garbage collection. Naturally, in the propagation scenario takes more time to receive the confirmation message, too many parsing process have to be done and takes more time to communicate agents in different containers. In a realistic scenario in which mechatronic devices would have various service providers, it wouldn't be too common to have more than 6 service providers, for instance a cross-conveyor which is a shared resource could lead a pallet to the center, right, or left direction (3 services). This could allocate most of the cases in the first part of the graphic.

8.2 Searching Service

The second test has two scenarios as well, no propagation and propagation. In the first scenario is measured the round trip time that takes to the DDF respond to a query for information message sent by an agent within the same front-end container. The round trip time for a message under normal conditions (no garbage collection) is about 57-50 ms. In the second scenario, the agent running in the same container where the DF is running, it sends a query to the embedded DDF, if no information is found the embedded DF forwards the query to the DF running in the PC, if the information was found then the DF in the PC sends backwards the requested information.

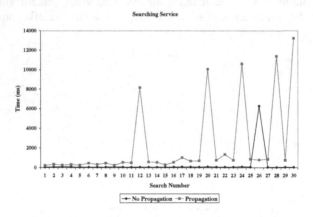

Fig. 4. Round Trip messaging time performance for searching service, (rhombus) only within the director facilitator embedded in the controller, (squares) in the director facilitator hosted in the PC

In the no-propagation scenario only one pick occurs within 30 searches. The times of searching with propagation under normal conditions are 500% bigger than the time with no-propagation.

9 Conclusions

With director facilitators distributed along different containers the network is not overloaded with unnecessary messages every time the requester needs to search for a service. The time for services' registration in a director facilitator running in an embedded device is short enough to be considering as a viable option. Even more, the registration process is not executed continuously in short periods of time, the DFs' information is updated only when the specification of the product or the configuration of the production line changes.

On the other hand, searching for services would be required often. Nevertheless, the average of 58 ms under normal condition could be enough to fulfill demanding time conditions. Next stage includes tests for an agent querying the distributed DF and performing some negotiation/coordination by means of FIPA interaction protocols (i.e. contract-net).

Acknowledgments. This work was supported by the National Technology Agency of Finland (TEKES) and the participant companies of the IMPRONTA applied research project: Nokia Mobile Phones, Perlos, FlexLink Automation, Cencorp and Photonium.

References

1. ElMaraghy, H.A.: Flexible and reconfigurable manufacturing systems paradigms. International Journal of Flexible Manufacturing Systems 17(4) 44–88 (2005)
2. Berbers, Y., Steegmans, E., Holvoet, T.: Agent-based Shop Floor Control Using Jini. Applied Informatics-Proceedings- (2002)
3. Aarnio, J.: Modularization by Integration: Creating Modular Concepts for Mechatronic Products. Doctoral thesis, publication 421, Tampere University of Technology (2003) ISBN 952-15-1027-7
4. Mařík, V., McFarlane, D.: Industrial Adoption of Agent-Based Technologies. Intelligent Manufacturing Control. Computer Society, pp. 27–35 (January/February 2005)
5. Vasko, D., Maturana, F., Bowles, A., Vandenberg, S.: Autonomous Cooperative Factory Control. In: Soo, V.-W., Zhang, C. (eds.) PRIMA 2000. LNCS (LNAI), vol. 1881, pp. 156–169. Springer, Heidelberg (2000)
6. Schoop, R., Neubert, R., Colombo, A.W.: A Multiagent-based Distributed Control Platform for Industrial Flexible Production Systems. In: IECON'01: The 27th Annual Conference of the IEEE Industrial Electronics Society, pp. 279–284 (2001)
7. Bussman, S., Schild, K.: Self-Organizing Manufacturing Control: An Industrial Application of Agent Technology. In: Fourth International Conference on Multiagent Systems, pp. 87–94 (2000)
8. Shen, W., Norrie, D.H.: Agent-Based Systems for Intelligent Manufacturing: A State-of-the-Art Survey. Knowledge and Information Systems, an International Journal 1(2), 129–156 (1999)
9. Christensen, J.: HMS/FB Architecture and its Implementation. In: Deen, S.M. (ed.) Agent-Based Manufacturing: Advances in the Holonic Approach, pp. 53–87. Springer, Heidelberg (2003)
10. IEC SC65B/WG7/TF3, IEC 61131-3, International Standard

11. IEC TC65/WG6. Standard IEC 61499, Function Blocks for Industrial-Process Measurements and Control System
12. Vyatkin, V., Christensen, J., Lastra, J.: OOONEIDA: An Open, Object-Oriented Knowledge Economy for Intelligent Industrial Automation. IEEE Transactions on Industrial Informatics 1, 4–17 (2005)
13. Paolucci, M., Kawamura, T., Payne, T.R., Sycara, K.: Semantic Matching of Web Services Capabilities. In: Yu, C. (ed.) High-Dimensional Indexing. LNCS, vol. 2341, p. 333. Springer, Heidelberg (2002)
14. Jammes, F., Smit, H.: Service-Oriented Paradigms in Industrial Automation. IEEE Transactions on Industrial Informatics 1(1), 62–70 (2005)
15. Delamer, M.: Event-Based Middleware for Reconfigurable Manufacturing Systems: A Semantic Web Service Approach. Doctoral Thesis, Publication 631, Tampere (2006)
16. Hussein, I.: Tampere University of Technology, Master Thesis, Tampere (2007)
17. Vos, J.A.W.M.: Module and System Design in Flexible Automated Assembly. Doctoral Thesis, DUP Science (2001)
18. Martinez, J.L.: Lastra. Reference Mechatronic Architecture for Actor based Assembly Systems. Doctoral Thesis, Publication 484, Tampere (2004)
19. Finin, T., Fritzson, R., McKay, D., McEntire, R.: KQML: as an Agent Communication Language. Association of Computing Machinery (1994)
20. Chaib-draa, B., Dignum, F.: Trends in Agent Communication Language. In: Computational Intelligence, vol. 2(5), Blackwell Publishers, Malden (2002)
21. Laclavík, M., Balogh, Z., Babík, M., Hluchý, L.: AgentOWL: Semantic Knowledge Model and Agent Architecture. Computing and Informatics 25, 419–437 (2006)
22. Greenwood, D.: JADE Web Services Integration Gateway. Available online, http://xopennet.org/netdemo/demos2005/aamas2005_netdemo_2pg.pdf
23. Bergenti, F., Poggi, A.: LEAP: A FIPA Platform for Handheld and Mobile Devices. In: Meye, J.-J.Ch., Tambe, M. (eds.) Intelligent Agents VIII, pp. 436–446. Springer, Heidelberg (2002)
24. López, O., Martinez-Lastra, J.: Performance Measurement of a Multiagent System in Java-Based industrial Embedded Controllers. In: On proceedings of INCOM 06, Saint-Etienne, France (May 2006)
25. Tanenbaum, A., Van Renesse, R.: Distributed Operating Systems. Computing Surveys 17(4), 419–470 (1985)
26. Marcuse, J., Menz, B., Payne, J.: Servers in SCADA Applications. IEEE Transactions on Industry Applications 33(5), 1295–1299 (1997)
27. Hormann, A., Rembold, U.: Development of an advanced robot for autonomous assembly. In: On proceedings of IEEE International Conference on Robotics and Automation, pp. 2452–2457 (1991)
28. available online (07.03.2007), http://java.sun.com/products/hotspot/whitepaper.html#3
29. available online (07.03.2007), http://weblogs.java.net/blog/mlam/archive/2007/02/when_is_softwar_1.html

Agent Methods for Network Intrusion Detection and Response

Martin Rehák, Michal Pěchouček, David Medvigy, Magda Prokopová,
Jan Tožička, and Lukáš Foltýn

Department of Cybernetics, Czech Technical University in Prague
Technická 2, Prague 6, 166 27 Czech Republic
{mrehak,pechouc,prokopova,tozicka,lfoltyn}@labe.felk.cvut.cz

Abstract. While the need to build the Intrusion Detection Systems (IDS) based
on on a distributed and cooperative (P2P) paradigm is being generally acknowledged, the field has been disconnected from the recent advances in the multi-agent
research, most notably the field of trust modeling. Our contribution reviews recent implementations of IDS systems and presents them from an agent research
perspective. We also identify the opportunities where the agent approaches can
be successfully used. Agent techniques can make the IDS more adaptive, scalable and reliable while increasing their autonomy and reducing the maintenance
requirements. Besides trust modeling, we propose that the distributed decision-
making and planning techniques can be used to shorten the detection-response
loop, making the system more robust while facing worm attacks.

1 Introduction

The use of the agent paradigm to develop and deploy an efficient distributed Intrusion
Detection and Protection System on the computer network seems natural and the idea
has appeared relatively early [1]. However, since then, the agent technology and IDS
field have largely ignored each other, possibly at the detriment of the research quality.
This contribution explains how to use the concepts from the agent technology to make
the IDS systems able to efficiently counter the new types of threats as presented in the
suite. While introducing the topic of network security to agent research community, this
paper is also relevant for network security researchers, as it presents a wide choice of
useful techniques applicable to their field.

1.1 The Threat

In the past most of the attacks targeted a single system, in an attempt to disable it or to
gain an unauthorized access to the data in the system. Today, the most dangerous threats
no longer attack hosts, but rather the network infrastructure: worms and Distributed
Denial of Service (DDOS) attacks launched from bot nets are currently a significant
threat, and the protection options remain limited. These attacks are currently used to
extort the money from service providers for not launching DOS attacks against their
sites [2].

V. Mařík, V. Vyatkin, A.W. Colombo (Eds.): HoloMAS 2007, LNAI 4659, pp. 149–160, 2007.

The main danger of worm attacks is similar to that of DDOS, but with a significant difference of not being aimed towards a specific system. Instead, they are designed to spread across the Internet, infect as many vulnerable hosts as possible and use these hosts for further propagation. Typically, they use well known vulnerabilities to infect hosts [3]. As many of the systems connected to the Internet were vulnerable (unpatched), the *CodeRed I* worm infected more than 250 000 systems during the 9 hours of July 19, 2001 [4]. *CodeRed I* and *II* worms exploit the same vulnerability of the Windows IIS server. On the other hand, these (distinct) worms differ by their spreading strategy – while the *CodeRed I* (and *SQL-Snake* that targets the Microsoft MS-SQL servers) uses a random IP generator, the *CodeRed II* worm uses a more local approach, with an increased probability of local spreading. A similar spreading strategy is also used by the *Nimda* worm.

The *Slammer* worm, that has attacked in January 2003 exploited a vulnerability (discovered in June 2002) in the MS-SQL server and MSDE, its desktop database engine. It's spread was very fast, resulting in an infection of 90% of vulnerable hosts in 10 minutes, following the classical exponential growth curve limited only by the size of the vulnerable population [5]. The main cause of disruption was not the benign payload of the worm, but its propagation. In contrast to previous, TCP based worms, the horizontal UDP scan aimed at port 1434 was faster and allowed a better concurrency model. The worm was also able to attack wider range of hosts, due to its ability to use multiple exploits for infection. Therefore, the spread of the worm was limited only by the available bandwidth, and its propagation disrupted the connection of the infected database servers.

Many systems are considered safe from worm attacks as their configuration is not typical and the random spread of the worm is unlikely to find a vulnerable host. When we examine an attack of the *Witty* worm in 2004 [6], we can see a somewhat different image. This worm begun to spread on March 19, 2004, targeting a buffer overflow flaw in RealSecure ISS family of security products. This vulnerability was a very recent one, disclosed only a single day before the worm has appeared. Besides proving that even a less widespread system is prone to attack, the *Witty* worm case have shown that even a very rapid reaction by human standards is insufficient to protect the vulnerable networks, stressing the need to make the protection process automatic (see Section 4).

Using the selected cases mentioned above, we can realize that the security paradigm has changed significantly between the year 1999, when the DARPA data set [7] didn't include any worm-like attacks and the situation today, when self-propagating code (e.g. worms) is considered a major threat. When analyzing the worm's behavior, we shall clearly distinguish between the two components of any worm: its *propagation mechanism* (or strategy) and its *payload*. The propagation mechanism is essentially a code that exploits a particular vulnerability of the targeted group of hosts, combined with the IP scanning strategy. Worm propagation strategies were theoretically modelled [8] and experimentally verified [5]. Therefore, besides the specific vulnerability exploit, most worms differ by their payload. The payload is the code that affects the infected machine, and its effects can range from doing nothing (Slammer) through opening backdoors (CodeRed II) and exposing the sensitive information (Nimda) to malicious acts like data corruption (Witty) or DoS attacks (Code Red I). We argue that the payload evolutions will be the biggest threats in the future, making the worms a vector of spread and obfuscation of the well targeted attacks. Introduction of backdoors for future exploitation, recruiting the systems for zombie networks or launching distributed DOS attacks are only some of the options for the attacker. A mere launch of the worm with several distinct payloads or with mutation capabilities can allow the attacker to hide a specific, well-directed attack in the mass, making its detection and tracking more difficult. The scanning strategies of worms evolve as well - some recent worms perform pre-scanning to identify vulnerable population, spread slowly to a large group of seed hosts and only then launch an Internet wide attack, making the containment of such widespread threat more difficult.

Bot (*zombie*) [9] networks are a significant threat today: they are composed of infected hosts with a running malicious process (bot) that are able to receive orders through a command infrastructure, and perform an attack, ranging from various types of DDOS to spam sending. Zombie networks are typically controlled through IRC channels, and their detection and suppression is extremely difficult due to their number, distributed nature, slow propagation and the fact that most internet-connected computers lack adequate protection.

We argue that the current IDS systems (Section 2) lack a capability to efficiently detect and counter the worm attack without relying on the human to make a decision. Given the characteristics of the attacks, we perceive this as a weakness and we propose a survey of methods from the multi-agent research (Section 3) to address this vulnerability. Instead of relying on human operator to take a critical decision in real-time, we propose to let the intrusion detection/prevention system to take this decision autonomously, albeit within the strict policy-specified bounds defined by the operator [10]. The automated decision process outlined in Section 4 can (arguably) take into account more factors than human and automatically select the best solution from a wide scope of techniques, making the networks more robust and hands-off human supervision more efficient.

2   Brief Overview of Intrusion Detection Systems

Currently, intrusion detection systems can be roughly split into two distinct categories. Most commercial and existing open-source products fall into the *signature-detection* category: these systems match the packets in the network with the predefined set of rules [11]. While this system can be valuable in detecting known attack patterns, it provides no protection against novel threats, or even new permutations of known attack, that are not represented in its knowledge base. Furthermore, as the rules are typically sparse to achieve efficiency, the signature-based IDS have a non-negligible false positives ratio. Another major disadvantage of the existing systems is a high computational cost of reasonably complete set of rules – currently, complete SNORT database is not typically entirely deployed due to the computational power limitations.

The *anomaly detection* approaches in NIDS (Network IDS) are typically based on classification/aggregation of sessions or flows (unidirectional components of sessions) into classes and deciding whether a particular class contains malicious or legitimate flows. While these approaches are able to detect novel attacks, they suffer from comparably high false-positive (or false negative depending on the model tuning) rate. Most research in the NIDS area currently delivers a combination of signature and anomaly detection and aims to improve the effectiveness and efficiency of intrusion detection. In the following paragraphs we are going to present a brief overview of selected (N)IDS systems [12].

MIDAS [13] is an early intrusion detection system which uses heuristic intrusion detection employing both anomaly and misuse detection. MIDAS builds on P-BEST expert system which is written in Lisp and its improved version was used also in other IDS systems - IDES [14] and NIDES [15]. The rule-based expert system uses alarm events generated by the system (such as attempts to run special `suid` commands or number of bad logins) which are matched against primary rules describing some pre-defined action corresponding to the intrusion detection. The secondary rules determine system reaction to alert, typically an alert to the operator. MIDAS is considered to be the first system employing misuse detection.

EMERALD [16] project was developed as for large enterprise networks and combines signature analysis with statistical profiling. EMERALD provides a real-time protection of the network services and infrastructure against external attackers. The analysis scheme of EMERALD is hierarchically layered and extensible by new monitoring modules. Using well-defined interfaces, EMERALD enables incorporation of third-party IDS engines. The analysis scheme is used for correlation of local analysis of results obtained at multiple lower-level monitoring modules by a more abstract upper layer.

IDA system [17] uses the concept of mobile agents to track intruders among various hosts involved in an intrusion attack. IDA uses sensors (e.g. log search) which are present at each target system, in combination with event-specific mobile agents that migrate across the network and gather the information about the attack from local sensors.

MINDS system [18] is an IDS system incorporating signature and anomaly detection suitable for host and network protection. As an input for traffic analysis it uses flow information which is aggregated in 10 minutes intervals. It extracts time-window and connection-window based features, from the traffic, to detect both fast and stealth attacks. The signature detection is used for protection against known threats. Anomaly detection uses a local outlier factor by which an unusual traffic is discovered. The human operator then decides which anomalous traffic is actually malicious and can use the captured information do define the signatures for subsequent traffic filtering.

SABER [19] combines both detection (anomaly and signature) and protection mechanisms. It incorporates a DoS-resistant network topology that shields valuable resources from the malicious traffic, and supports a business process migration to the safe location upon the attack. Real-time host-based IDS monitors program's use of Windows Registry and detects the actions of malicious software. The analogous approach has been used for file-based anomaly detection in Unix environment, when the IDS monitors a set of information about each file access. SABER is completed by autonomic software patching mechanism [20] which tries to automatically patch vulnerable software by identifying and correcting buffer overflows in the code, using the information from specialized honeypots operated alongside production machines.

The Achilles' heel of most intrusion detection and prevention systems is their efficiency and effectively. High number of false positives/negatives requires labor-intensive incident analysis and discourages the administrators from system deployment or use. It also makes the deployment of any automatic protection mechanism highly problematic, as it might cause more harm than good by filtering-out the legitimate traffic, or creating a false sense of security if tuned too liberally. In the next section, we present a selection of techniques from the multi-agent field that can help to alleviate the problem.

3   Relevant Multi-agent Techniques

The biggest threat of the computer network attacks is given by the fact that the attackers operate a collective of loosely coupled, highly autonomous, often collaborating, migrating (and reproducing) computational processes. The success of such collective attacks is given by the fact that they attack uniform computational processes and hardware elements, with identical widespread vulnerabilities. In order to protect the computational resources, information and network as such, we propose to exploit the techniques, algorithms and theoretical results available in the field of multi-agent system, a branch of computer science investigating the collective behaviors of collaborative as well as self-interested, autonomous, intelligent, computational processes.

3.1   Distributed Task Allocation

Balanced allocation of the monitoring process within the network as well as an efficient placement of the intrusion response processes need to be decided and reconfigured locally, in a peer-to-peer interaction among the network components. That is valid because there is a desire to limit centralized decision making processes and centralized collection of data in the network.

Distributed task allocation is a typical problem that is solved in its different variations in the multi-agent research communities for years now (e.g. [21]). The distributed task allocation algorithms are based on different auctioning approaches (e.g. English, Vickery, Dutch, Seal-bid, All-pay [22]), each having different properties in different environments. The most widely used approaches to distributed task allocation are based on the CNP (*contract-net-protocol*) [23] (based on single round Seal-bid auction), iterated CNP, its $OSCM$-CNP optimality improvements [24] and other combinatorial auctions. These techniques have been successfully used in a number of network oriented applications. In more complex task allocation and distributed planning scenarios, more elaborate negotiation techniques and protocols need to be used. Another CNP extension is the ECNP [25,26] protocol which allows partial bid, provisional accepts and refusals in order to decompose the task into subtasks that can be allocated to the agents in the system. Therefore, it merges planning and task allocation phases.

3.2   Adaptation Methods

The field of multi-agent system provides also very specialized approaches towards achieving run-time revisions of the collective of autonomous computational processes: agent migration and multi-agent reflection.

Agent Migration. Changing the location of the agents code and state (data), without any change of its identity is denoted as agent migration [27]. We consider two types of migration: (*i*) weak mobility – an agent migrates from one host machine to another by its own intention and (*ii*) strong mobility, when an agent is forced to migrate from one host machine to another. Both weak and strong agent mobility are suitable mechanisms for network intrusion observation and response as they enable physical reallocation of critical data and computation.

Multi-agent Reflection. Inspired by classical works in computational reflection [28], an ability of agent to understand its running program and to reflect its operation by runtime program modification is understood as a multi-agent reflection. We distinguish between three different types of reflection in multi-agent systems: (*i*) *Individual Reflection* takes into account only the strictly local, internal information: agent's knowledge, resources, and computational capacity. (*ii*) *Mutual Reflection* extends the individual reflection by **unilaterally** taking into account agent's knowledge about other agents, such as trust and reputation, resources, deduced or communicated long-term motivations and intentions. This knowledge is referred to as *social knowledge* [29]. (*iii*) *Collective Reflection* - a revision of agents' collective behavior is not an individual process, but an interaction between multiple agent's reflective layers. The collective reflection can be achieved either by: *(a)* introduction of a single reflective agent (e.g. a meta-agent) that monitors the community behavior and suggests individual agents to alter their behavior or *(b)* emergently by the collective of agents, each carrying out its specific cognitive/reflective reasoning. Unlike in the case of the mutual reflection, the agents update not only their own knowledge and algorithms, but they also influence the changes inside other agents.

Key use cases of the multi-agent reflection deployment are adaptation to changes, system resilience, code sharing, automated programme code assembly, runtime code exchange, run-time code alteration or various performance improvements [30].

3.3   Trust and Reputation Modeling

Trust modeling is the primary approach to the high-level security in the field of the multi-agent systems. Trust models use in the scope of the IDS is two-fold: to model the trustfulness of the individual traffic sources (e.g. applications), and to protect the IDS system against infiltration and misuse.

There are many definitions of trust – the one we will use was proposed by Marsh in [31]: Agent x trusts the agent y if *"Agent x expects that y will behave according to x best interests, and will not attempt to harm x"*. In the open multi-agent systems with self-interested agents, it is necessary to (i) maintain knowledge regarding the trustfulness of one's collaborators, in order to avoid the untrustful agents and to (ii) motivate the agents to behave in a trustful manner.

Trust models [32,33,34,35] are efficient and specialized knowledge structures, that help the agents to accomplish the above goals by efficiently organizing the past experience of the agent and other relevant information [36]. In the current body of work, most systems are based on the following principles (or their stronger modifications): (*i*) The trustfulness of the partner agent is always associated with an *identity* of a particular agent. (*ii*) The trustfulness value associated with the partner depends on the past behavior of the agent in question, as well as the past experience of the other trusting agents (i.e. reputation) and past experience with similar agents. A notable exception in this context is a model developed by Andreas Birk [37], where the trustfulness values are associated with a physical feature of the trusted agent (robot), rather than with its identity. (*iii*) The trustfulness of the partner may be wither general, aggregated for all roles and situations, or situational, depending on task and environment.

Current trust models use a variety of techniques to hold the trustfulness data: some models use a *probability estimate* based on the time-weighted past experience [37]. The REGRET [38] and other models [34] also provide a formal framework used to integrate the observations of the agent with the opinions of the others. However, a simple probabilistic approach seems to be insufficient as it fails to capture the uncertainty of the trust estimate.[1] Therefore, Yu and Singh [39] use a Dempster-Shafer theory to capture the uncertainty in the reputation opinions and Josang et al. [40] use subjective logic for the same goal. The concept can be further extended by use of linguistic categories [32] or by representing the trustfulness as a fuzzy number [35] or a probability distribution. On the other hand, the issues of memory and computational requirements can not be ignored and the efficiency of the inference process is one of the main criteria for the model selection.

Regarding the deployment of the model, two basic options are possible. Many, mainly older architectures [33] rely on a centralized model, where all agents in the system share a single trust model. While this architecture offers some advantages, like fast learning (crucial in large domains, e.g. eBay) and memory efficiency, it requires the agents to share their private knowledge with the reputation manager, requires communication both at the observation and query time and doesn't allow the specialization of the model for individual agent's needs. Therefore, recent architectures rely on the model where each agent maintains its own model, and can combine its own observations with the data obtained from the others by means of reputation sharing.

Both the centralized approach and reputation models can suffer from the disinformation, aimed to maliciously improve or harm a reputation of one or more of the evaluated agents. While such attacks can never be ruled out entirely, the trust model itself can be used to evaluate the trustfulness of other agents in the recommender role [39], making the repetitive false opinions easy to eliminate. This feature is especially important when the system is deployed in a potentially insecure environment, e.g. network under attack.

Most current trust models are well suited for high-level security, with clearly defined and authenticated actors. In the next section, we will discuss the necessary modifications of the trust models in the context of broader network security architecture.

4   Reference Architecture

This Section defines reference architecture that combines the properties of the current generation of the Intrusion Detection systems as presented in Section 2 and appropriate multi-agent techniques briefly outlined in Section 3. The goal of the proposed architecture is to provide a near-real time autonomous attack discovery and response, replacing the direct human decision-making by well defined policies regulating autonomous runtime system decisions. Such rapid response is necessary to counter the threats outlined

---

[1] Many of the cited models do provide the uncertainty as a separate value.

in Section 1.1. The architecture is distributed, based on a peer-to-peer cooperation of autonomous agents:

- **Detection and Reaction Agents (DRA)** are the intelligent core of the system. They are located on appropriate hosts or network elements in the protected network and are responsible for collaborative traffic analysis, attack detection and planning of the reaction. They incorporate the trust model (or similar technology) used for attack detection and classification. Their decision-making in the reaction phase is governed by user-defined policies.
- **Network Sensors (NS)** are specialized agents that observe the traffic on the network, perform the low level analysis and feature extraction and inform the DRA's about their observations. They may also directly detect known malicious traffic (by means of signature detection) and raise an alarm. If appropriate, they may be collocated with DRA's.
- **Host Sensors (HS)** are the agents that reside on the host and are able to raise an alarm when they suspect an intrusion attempt. This alarm is then used for evaluation of the past traffic towards the host by the DRA's.
- **Reconfigurable Network Elements (NE)** are used by DRA agents to implement the protection mechanism when a new kind of attack is detected.

The agents in the community operate in three conceptual phases. In the **first phase**, the NS agents observe the traffic on the network and report the features of the relevant observed network flows to the DRA. The DRA agents then use their trust model to classify unknown traffic by matching it with a reaction from the Host Sensors.

To perform the match in the **second phase** of the detection, the existing trust models must be considerably extended. The match with the current state of the art is much less obvious, as we seriously relax the trust model assumptions from Section 3.3. Instead of a well-defined agent identity, we must define the evaluated connection by its features (e.g. [18]). These features will be then used to model the identity of the observed connection in the same manner as the context of the trusting decision is modeled in [41], by using metric spaces for identity and context representation. Trustfulness values are therefore no longer relative to the real identities or individual connections, but are attached to the centroids of the clusters created in the metric space of the features. When a new connection appears, we use a clustering algorithm to either attach it to an existing cluster, or to create a new cluster altogether. To update the trustfulness of the individual clusters, we rely on a feedback of the HS agents. Once aggregated, the aggregated feedback from related HS is used as a new observation of connection trustfulness for all open and recent relevant connections. One of the important assumptions we make is that the protected system contains many heterogenous hosts with a variety of Host Sensors. Therefore, given the random propagation strategy of typical worm attacks, we shall be able to identify the attack on the hosts that are not vulnerable and are appropriately protected.

Each DRA maintains its own instance of the trust model, and can extend the basic shared feature space with unique features of its own. To communicate these values between the DRA's, the agents use a reputation mechanism in both the subscribe-inform and query mode. Such mechanism will ensure that once the attack is suspected by a single DRA, its classification will spread through the system and allow the other DRA to react faster. On the other hand, they are still autonomous to react differently, reducing the risk of false positives.

In the **third phase**, occurring after the attack detection, the DRA's need to create its description from the model, typically using generalizing machine learning methods. The extracted classifier shall be simple enough to be re-inserted into the reconfigurable Network Elements.

Once the DRA's have generated the description, they need to react swiftly in order to protect the network. By its nature, the proposed mechanism detects most of the new attacks when a part of the network has already been compromised. Therefore, we need to ensure that all connections between any two hosts on the network (including the internet gateway) will be inspected using the filter with the generated description. If such goal can't be achieved for a part of the network, such part must be handled as a single system (and potentially considered unsafe). Taking the distributed decision where to deploy the filters and how to shape the network traffic to inspect most of the connections is a distributed task allocation problem, solvable by the methods from Section 3.1.

Once we have a patch for the exploited vulnerability (possibly generated automatically [20]), we can protect & clean the vulnerable hosts, while removing their protection at network level. This approach requires careful replanning, in order to be able to return to the nominal network configuration as fast as possible, without compromising the network security. Once the protection is no longer necessary, we only keep the generated filter rule on few specialized nodes for the future network-based detection of the external attacks of the same type.

Mechanism Protection. Trust modeling method proposed for attack detection also fulfills the requirement to protect the cooperation between the distributed nodes of the IDS against disinformation, false observations and system misuse in general – the compromised or faked node can be detected and eliminated from the community. Currently, some IDS concepts [42] include this functionality, but with a relatively low level of sophistication. The IDS infrastructure presents a very valuable target for future attacks [6] due to the high level of access rights and the fact that it can not be efficiently shielded from the suspicious traffic. Therefore, an efficient auto-protection mechanism is a necessary prerequisite of the deployment of the autonomous systems that we need to counter the worm-type attacks.

5   Conclusions and Future Directions

This contribution presents a focused overview of the current and relevant IDS systems and proposes the integration of several selected families of agent technologies to address the threat from the Worm-type attacks. We argue that any efficient response mechanism against worm epidemics must be automatic, without including the human reaction into the loop. Direct human supervision can be replaced by policies regulating the system operations [10].

The distributed system, as presented in our reference architecture (see Section 4), shall act in three phases: (i) **Observation**, when the network and host sensors gather the information. This phase relies on a web of heterogenous hosts and sensors. (ii) **Detection**, when the Detection/Reaction agents use the data as an input for their trust models and detect the attacks in the traffic. (iii) **Reaction**, when the DRA's use their trust models to extract a filtering rule for the attack and modify network devices in order to enforce the rule on the bulk of the network communication, preventing the further worm spread.

In order to implement the abstract architecture outlined above, we propose to integrate a wide range of agent techniques to address the inherently distributed nature of all phases of the problem. We also argue that these techniques will require additional development to match the challenging performance requirements of the network security field, and our text specifies several relevant areas and targets, most notably in the field of trust modeling.

In our current and future work, we are experimentally evaluating presented agent techniques in a simulated computer network [43], in order to validate the reference architecture and its implementation before the integration with the real network components.

Acknowledgment

We gratefully acknowledge the support of the presented research by Army Research Laboratory projects N62558-05-C-0028, N62558-07-C-0001 and N62558-07-C-0007.

References

1. Jansen, W., Mell, P., Karygiannis, T., Marks, D.: Mobile agents in intrusion detection and response. In: 12th Annual Canadian Information Technology Security Symposium, Ottawa, Canada (2000)
2. Pappalardo, D., Messmer, E.: Extortion via ddos on the rise (2005)
3. Yegneswaran, V., Barford, P., Ullrich, J.: Internet intrusions: global characteristics and prevalence. In: SIGMETRICS, pp. 138–147 (2003)
4. CERT: Overview of attack trends. Technical report (2002)
5. Moore, D., Paxson, V., Savage, S., Shannon, C., Staniford, S., Weaver, N.: Inside the slammer worm. IEEE Security and Privacy 01, 33–39 (2003)
6. Shannon, C., Moore, D.: The Spread of the Witty Worm. Technical report, CAIDA - Cooperative Association for Internet Data Analysis (2004)
7. McHugh, J.: Testing intrusion detection systems: a critique of the 1998 and 1999 darpa intrusion detection system evaluations as performed by lincoln laboratory. ACM Trans. Inf. Syst. Secur. 3, 262–294 (2000)
8. Moore, D., Shannon, C., Voelker, G.M., Savage, S.: Internet quarantine: Requirements for containing self-propagating code. In: INFOCOM (2003)
9. Cooke, E., Jahanian, F., Mcpherson, D.: The Zombie Roundup: Understanding, Detecting, and Disrupting Botnets. In: Workshop on Steps to Reducing Unwanted Traffic on the Internet (SRUTI), pp. 39–44 (2005)

10. Sierhuis, M., Bradshaw, J., Acquisiti, A., van Hoof, R., Jeffers, R., Uszok, A.: Human-agent teamworks and adjustable autonomy in practice. In: Proceedings of the 7th International Symposium on Artificial Intelligence, Robotics and Automation in Space: i-SAIRAS - NARA, Japan (2003)
11. : SNORT intrusion prevention system (Accessed in January 2007) (2007), http://www.snort.org/
12. Axelsson, S.: Intrusion detection systems: A survey and taxonomy. Technical Report 99-15, Chalmers Univ (2000)
13. Sebring, M.M., Shellhouse, E., Hanna, M.E., Whitehurst, R.A.: Expert systems in intrusion detection: A case study. In: Proceedings of the 11th National Computer Security Conference, Baltimore, Maryland, NIST, pp. 74–81 (1988)
14. Lunt, T.F., Tamaru, A., Gilham, F., Jagannathan, R., Jalali, C., Neumann, P.G., Javitz, H.S., Valdes, A., Garvey, T.: A real-time intrusion-detection expert system (ides). Technical report, SRI International (1992)
15. Anderson, D., Lunt, T.F., Javitz, H., Tamaru, A., Valdes, A.: Detecting unusual program behavior using the statistical component of the next-generation intrusion detection expert system (NIDES). Technical Report SRI-CSL-95-06, Computer Science Laboratory, SRI International, Menlo Park, CA (1995)
16. Porras, P.A., Neumann, P.G.: EMERALD: Event monitoring enabling responses to anomalous live disturbances. In: Proc. 20th NIST-NCSC National Information Systems Security Conference, pp. 353–365 (1997)
17. Asaka, M., Okazawa, S., Taguchi, A., Goto, S.: A method of tracing intruders by use of mobile agents. In: INET'99 (1999)
18. Ertoz, L., Eilertson, E., Lazarevic, A., Tan, P.N., Kumar, V., Srivastava, J., Dokas, P.: Minds - minnesota intrusion detection system. In: Next Generation Data Mining, MIT Press, Cambridge (2004)
19. Keromytis, A.D., Parekh, J., Gross, P.N., Kaiser, G., Misra, V., Nieh, J., Rubenstein, D., Stolfo, S.: A holistic approach to service survivability. In: Proceedings of the 2003 ACM Workshop on Survivable and Self-Regenerative Systems (SSRS), pp. 11–22 (2003)
20. Sidiroglou, S., Keromytis, A.D.: Countering network worms through automatic patch generation. IEEE Security & Privacy 3, 41–49 (2005)
21. Walsh, W.E., Wellman, M.P.: A market protocol for distributed task allocation. In: In Third International Conference on Multiagent Systems, Paris (1998)
22. Sandholm, T.: Distributed Rational Decision Making. In: Weiss, G. (ed.) Multiagent Systems: A Modern Approach to Distributed Artificial Intelligence, pp. 201–258. MIT Press, Cambridge, MA (1999)
23. Smith, R.G.: The contract net protocol: High level communication and control in a distributed problem solver. IEEE Transactions on Computers C-29, 1104–1113 (1980)
24. Sandholm, T.W., Lesser, V.R.: Coalitions among computationally bounded agents. Artificial Intelligence 94, 99–137 (1997)
25. Perugini, D., Lambert, D., Sterling, L., Pearce, A.: Agent-based global transportation scheduling in military logistics. In: AAMAS '04: Proceedings of the Third International Joint Conference on Autonomous Agents and Multiagent Systems, pp. 1278–1279. IEEE Computer Society, Washington, DC (2004)
26. Rehak, M., Pechoucek, M., Volf, P.: Distributed planning algorithm for coalition logistics in semi-trusted environment. In: DIS '06: Proceedings of the IEEE Workshop on Distributed Intelligent Systems: Collective Intelligence and Its Applications (DIS'06), pp. 265–272. IEEE Computer Society, Washington, DC (2006)
27. Suri, N., Carvalho, M.M., Bradshaw, J.M., Breedy, M.R., Cowin, T.B., Groth, P.T., Saavedra, R., Uszok, A.: Enforcement of communications policies in software agent systems through mobile code. In: POLICY, pp. 247–250 (2003)

28. Maes, P.: Computational reflection. Technical report 87-2, Free University of Brussels, AI Lab (1987)
29. Pěchouček, M., Mařík, V., Bárta, J.: Role of acquaintance models in agent's private and semi-knowledge disclosure. Knowledge-Based Systems, 259–271 (2006)
30. Foltýn, L., Tožička, J., Rollo, M., Pěchouček, M., Jisl, P.: Reflective-cognitive architecture: From abstract concept to self-adapting agent. In: DIS '06: Proceedings of the Workshop on Distributed Intelligent Systems, IEEE Comp. Soc. Los Alamitos (2006)
31. Marsh, S.: Formalising trust as a computational concept (1994)
32. Ramchurn, S., Huynh, D., Jennings, N.R.: Trust in multiagent systems. The Knowledge Engineering Review 19 (2004)
33. Sabater, J., Sierra, C.: Review on computational trust and reputation models. Artif. Intell. Rev. 24, 33–60 (2005)
34. Huynh, T.D., Jennings, N.R., Shadbolt, N.R.: An integrated trust and reputation model for open multi-agent systems. Journal of Autonomous Agents and Multi-Agent Systems 13, 119–154 (2006)
35. Rehák, M., Foltýn, L., Pěchouček, M., Benda, P.: Trust model for open ubiquitous agent systems. In: Intelligent Agent Technology, 2005 IEEE/WIC/ACM International Conference. Number PR2416, IEEE, Los Alamitos (2005)
36. Castelfranchi, C., Falcone, R., Pezzulo, G.: Integrating trustfulness and decision using fuzzy cognitive maps. In: Nixon, P., Terzis, S. (eds.) iTrust 2003. LNCS, vol. 2692, pp. 195–210. Springer, Heidelberg (2003)
37. Birk, A.: Boosting cooperation by evolving trust. Applied Artificial Intelligence 14, 769–784 (2000)
38. Sabater, J., Sierra, C.: Regret: reputation in gregarious societies. In: AGENTS '01: Proceedings of the fifth international conference on Autonomous agents, pp. 194–195. ACM Press, New York (2001)
39. Yu, B., Singh, M.P.: Detecting deception in reputation management. In: AAMAS '03, pp. 73–80. ACM Press, New York (2003)
40. Josang, A., Gray, E., Kinateder, M.: Simplification and analysis of transitive trust networks. Web Intelligence and Agent Systems 4, 139–162 (2006)
41. Rehak, M., Gregor, M., Pechoucek, M., Bradshaw, J.M.: Representing context for multiagent trust modeling. In: IEEE/WIC/ACM Intl. Conf. on Intelligent Agent Technology (IAT'06), pp. 737–746. IEEE Computer Society, USA (2006)
42. Janakiraman, R., Waldvogel, M., Zhang, Q.: Indra: A peer-to-peer approach to network intrusion detection and prevention. In: Proceedings of IEEE WETICE 2003 (2003)
43. Rehák, M., Pěchouček, M., Prokopová, M., Foltýn, L., Tožička, J.: Autonomous protection mechanism for joint networks in coalition operations. In: Knowledge Systems for Coalition Operations 2007, Proceedings of KIMAS'07 (2007)

Detecting Intrusions in Agent System by Means of Exception Handling

Eric Platon[1,3], Martin Rehak[2], Nicolas Sabouret[3], Michal Pechoucek[2],
and Shinichi Honiden[1]

[1] National Institute of Informatics
Sokendai and University of Tokyo
2-1-2 Hitotsubashi, 101-8430 Tokyo
[2] Gerstner Laboratory
Czech Technical University
Technická 2, Prague, 166 27
[3] Laboratoire d'informatique de Paris 6
Université Pierre et Marie Curie
104, Avenue du Président Kennedy, 75016 Paris
{platon,honiden}@nii.ac.jp, {mrehak,pechouc}@labe.felk.cvut.cz,
Nicolas.Sabouret@lip6.fr

Abstract. We present a formal approach to conception of a dedicated security infrastructure based on the exception handling in the protected agents. Security-related exceptions are identified and handled by a dedicated reflective layer of the protected agent, or delegated to specialized intrusion management agents in the system if the local reflective layer fails to address the problem. Incidents are handled either directly, if a known remedy exists or indirectly, when an appropriate solution must be identified before response execution. The cooperation between the intrusion management agents and aggregation of their observations can make the system more resilient to misclassification than a solution based purely on signature matching.

1 Introduction

Between their other advantages, the multi-agent systems aim to achieve robust and reliable failover behavior by openness, runtime reconfiguration, dynamic replanning and partner selection and higher agent autonomy in general. Therefore, their application can significantly improve the reliability of the system when it encounters random failures, e.g. hardware malfunction, communication problems, failed battery/power sources and others [1].

On the downside, the very same features that make multi-agent systems resilient against random failures can be leveraged by the adversary to intentionally and efficiently harm the system. The administration of multi-agent systems is notoriously difficult, and when we impose restrictive policies that make the system more resilient against intentional, external intrusions, we restrict its capability to cope with random failures. Therefore, we seek an alternative to such restrictive approach, by using the same features that make the system resilient to natural faults and leveraging them for intrusion observation, detection and response.

V. Mařík, V. Vyatkin, A.W. Colombo (Eds.): HoloMAS 2007, LNAI 4659, pp. 161–172, 2007.

The aim of this paper is to present a new approach to intrusion management based on a model of intrusion detection as exception, the collaboration of *self-protected agents* (or protection-aware agents) running on network hosts, and dedicated network-based Intrusion Detection System (IDS). We argue that the collaboration is crucial for autonomic and timely reactions to intrusions with low level of errors and acceptable performance. While we argue that the integration with a wide range of protected (and potentially vulnerable) agents is crucial, we do not impose any special restrictions on the type of alerts to provide to IDS, making the integration effort easier to standardize and implement.

We propose a distributed, layered architecture where the deployed network elements employ their autonomic properties tailored to manage external attacks, based on the exception-generated feedback from the protected agents. The contribution of the paper is to improve network intrusion management schemes by introducing an overlay of IDS agents, referred to as **CIME** (Collaborative Intrusion Management Element), on a network of autonomic, ***protection-aware*** agents. The protected agents have a reflective architecture allowing them to encompass legacy software and they are able to detect intrusions with an appropriate exception handling model.

The next section (2) presents a model of exception adapted to the detection of intrusion in the cases we are focusing on. Section 3 describes the reflective architecture of in-network agents and the structure of CIME agents. The collaboration scheme and protocols followed by protected agents and CIME on intrusion detection are detailed in section 4. Section 6 concludes the paper and presents our current and future work.

2   Model of Intrusion Detection as Exception

In the scope of this work, we will use the term *network intrusion* to denote situations when an adversary (human, software, or mixed groups) external to the multi-agent system has accessed a restricted data or functionality of the system or has disrupted the system use for legitimate users. Intrusion prevention requires appropriate monitoring of the protected system. Low-level monitoring of the communication network searches for irregularities, such as specific intrusion signatures or unusual traffic. On a conceptually higher level, we can model the the intrusions as *exceptions* [2]in the behavior of agents in the system. An exception may trigger a collaborative exception handling mechanism that detects and possibly manages the intrusion.

2.1   Model

The exception model is related to the usual notion of exception in programming languages [3,4], as the aim is to provide a fault tolerance mechanism, where 'faults' to recover from are network intrusions instead of software or hardware problems. The semantics of the exception model differs consequently as the software involved in the exception handling has not encountered any programming issue, but it still has to handle the (potential) symptoms caused by an intrusion.

The state-chart on Fig. 1 describes the exception model in the system, whose different activities will be allocated to either protected agents or CIME in the system. The

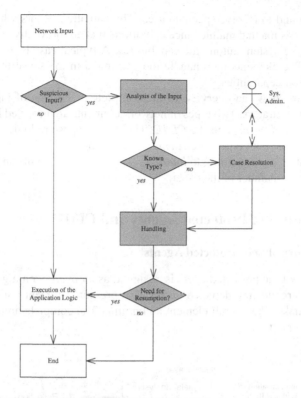

Fig. 1. State-chart for the intrusion in-network management process

state-chart defines the behavior of network elements (either network devices, specialized agents or agent platform security services) when they receive inputs from outside the system. The state-chart features two colors, namely white and gray, to describe respectively the fundamental functionalities and the exception handling stages on intrusion detection.

When an element receives a message, it first screens it do detect the *suspicious* ones, according to standard criteria (e.g. signature) and to additional ones generated by the system or introduced by administrators. If an input is not considered suspicious, it is processed in the application logic of the element, and the state-charts ends on completion of this processing. Any input deemed suspicious is further analyzed to determine the way to handle it. If it is a known intrusion, the element encompasses a handling mechanism and executes it. After completion of the handler, the input can be either processed or discarded, and the state-charts ends. Finally, if the type of intrusion is unknown, the agent attempts to resolve the case by collaborating with other elements and, if needed, with system administrators. The case resolution attempts to automatically find a remedy to the situation, with human decision in the last resort depending on degree of autonomy of the system. The result of the resolution is a command for handling, optionally followed by the resumption of the application logic, and the completion of the state-chart. The system administrator can alternatively initiate the state-chart by sending a command to resolve specific cases. This situation occurs whenever the administrator initiates manual maintenance operations that are preventive or might be out of the scope of the system autonomic capabilities. A typical case is to deploy a patch in the system. The elements then handle the command in the sense that they update automatically their capabilities.

The state-chart shows an overview of the complete processing of inputs and commands from administrators. Two types of network elements are involved in this process, namely the *protected agents* and the *CIME*. These two types are logical and one platform is likely to host both types of elements. Agents and CIME deal with the different stages of the state-chart according to *interaction protocols*. Elements and protocols are introduced in the remainder of the paper.

3   Architectures of Protected Agents and CIME

3.1   Architecture of Self-protected Agents

The architecture of the protected agent is designed as an overlay on a generic application agent. The architecture depicted on Fig. 2 represents an agent with the reflective extension that makes the overall element autonomic. The complete architecture forms a *self-protected agent*.

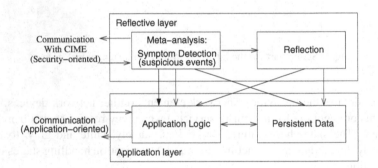

Fig. 2. Architecture of self-protected agents in the network

The architecture has two threads of executions, each in a different layer of the agent. The application layer encompasses the *application logic* (e.g. a legacy application) and its *persistent local data*. Application logic and persistent data components interact to fulfill the functions of the agent, including replying to requests received through the communication link. The reflective layer [5] encompasses two components for a second thread of execution. The *meta-analysis* refers to mechanisms that aims to detect the intrusions, signal the exceptional situations to other components and protect the agent against suspicious input (thus the 'self-protection'). It corresponds to most stages of suspicion evaluation process in Fig. 1. The *reflective* component contains the mechanisms that actually handles the suspected threats and oversees the modification of the agent's code. The meta-analysis commands the reflective mechanisms to achieve the necessary reactions against attacks (unidirectional link). It observes the application layer components to detect suspicious inputs, and it overrides the application logic component (bold arrow) to prevent any execution of suspicious data while it is analyzed. The reflection component receives commands from the meta-analysis to apply a variety of mechanisms on the application logic and the persistent data, such as patching the agent or performing roll-backs on a database. The meta-analysis has additional communication capabilities to contact CIME components in the system. When the meta-analysis encounters a new situation that it cannot handle or decides to inform other elements in a collaboration, it contacts CIME according to an interaction protocol introduced in section 4.

The architecture treats an intrusion detection even as an exception in programming languages. It has some differences however (see Section 2), notably the termination and resumption models. The architecture allows the application layer to continue executing, even though some activities can be blocked by the reflective layer. Typically, a highly-solicited agent can continue serving clients, while the suspicious requests or events are blocked until the reflective layer returns a decision. This 'flexibility' between the components of the architecture increases the dependability of the agent facing exceptional situations as intrusions.

The architecture allows deployment self-protected agents in the network, where the protection is ensured by the reflective layer. When this protection reaches its limits, the reflective layer then collaborates with CIME.

3.2 Architecture of CIME

CIME (Collaborative Intrusion Management Elements) are dedicated intrusion handling elements in the network. They concentrate relevant information from the self-protected agents, agent platform and other sensors, process it to detect the intrusions in the network and assist the reflective layers of protected agents in their self-protection tasks. CIME consist of two functionalities for direct support of protected agents and for

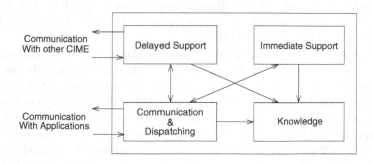

Fig. 3. Architecture of CIME in the network

collaboration with other CIME in the network. CIME receive requests and feedbacks from agents that initiate the first functionality. In reply to requests, CIME can provide two types of support.

- **Immediate support.** CIME provide agents with an immediate solution to their requests. This type of support targets particularly known intrusions. For example, CIME can confirm or dis-confirm that an entry is a phishing attempt.
- **Delayed support.** CIME collaborate with other CIME and, in last resort, with the system administrator to provide agents with solutions when available and possible. This type of support targets unknown intrusions, i.e. new suspicious signature, unusual traffic, etc.

A directory service allows CIME and agents to discover each other, and it also allows CIME to coordinate, share knowledge about intrusion history and possible remedy, and engage in their collaboration protocols. The immediate support is built on the current knowledge of CIME. When this knowledge is sufficient to reply to the agent, the CIME does not need collaborate and can reply immediately. The delayed support is triggered whenever the contacted CIME lacks knowledge for an immediate reply and requires additional knowledge from other CIME or, in last resort, the system administrator. The support actions from CIME can finally be of two distinct kinds, namely *consumable* and *persistent*. Consumable actions are direct fix such as a yes/no reply to a question about phishing attempts. Consumable actions are dynamic in the sense that they are contextual fix: A phishing attempt against a web-site is not permanent, and the web-site URL might change from a 'reputable' address to potential danger. Conversely, persistent support actions are typically permanent patch that are deployed in agents, e.g. to fix a buffer overflow. Their deployment prevents the escalation of a contamination by runtime permanent introduction of remedy.

4   Collaboration Schemes

CIME agents support the self-protected agents in case of intrusion attempts, and their strength is in the collaboration with other CIME executing on the network to share knowledge and services related to intrusion history or new remedy manually injected in the network by system administrators. The present section aims to describe the main interaction protocols involved. The different protocols show how the different actors of the network interact in realizing the high-level process described in Fig. 1. The notation follows the UML 2.0 specification [6].

We assume that self-protected agents register on startup with a CIME agents on the network, and that all CIME agents register with a directory service, also on startup. These registration protocols are also not represented in this paper, as they can rely on standard directory services of agent platform. The registration of agents with CIME agents is static in the following, but a dynamic version could be considered as well. CIME agents provide the directory service with information to publish, so that they are visible to other CIME agents when collaborations are required. The published information is a list of pairs *(id,symptom)*, where *id* is the identifier of the registered CIME and *symptom* is a specific type of intrusion the CIME is capable to deal with.

4.1   Protocol Between Protected Agent and CIME

Fig. 4 shows the interaction protocol between the agent that has detected a suspicious input and the corresponding CIME agent. When an agent receives an input, it

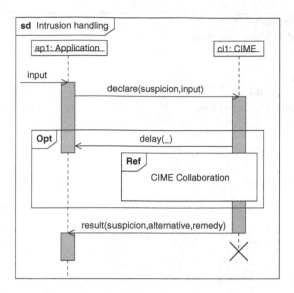

Fig. 4. Interaction protocol between protected agent and CIME

first checks for suspicious clues among the type of intrusions supported in this framework. The finding of such suspicious clue triggers the protocol in Fig. 4. The agent declares the suspicion to the CIME with the appropriate message. If the CIME can provide immediate support, it does not execute the optional sequence (`Opt`) and directly provides the protected agent with a resulting remedy. For the declared suspicion, the field `remedy` is `nil` if the declared suspicion is a false positive. Otherwise, `remedy` is not nil and points to a handling procedure (e.g. deploy a patch, yes/no for phishing). The `alternative` parameter serves to inform the agent that an intrusion attack occurred, but that the type of attack differs from the original suspicion, as piggy-back acknowledgment. The `remedy` parameter then also points to the appropriate handling procedure. If the CIME is unable to provide immediate support, it will first enter the optional sequence to inform the agent of a delay in the support, and initiate the `CIME Collaboration` protocol. This latter protocol describes how CIME collaborate and is described in the next section. Upon the completion of collaboration, the CIME sends a result to the agent. In case the collaboration did not produce any outcome, the `remedy` informs the agent to apply a default handling procedure, i.e. to block the activities related to the suspicious input. The case is then escalated to human operator.

Algorithm 1 sketches the evaluation process of the CIME agent which decides between immediate and delayed support. This algorithm is executed on reception of a `declare` message, and its output determines whether the optional sequence will be executed. The algorithm assumes that the knowledge base KB of the CIME is consistent (i.e. one handler and only one for a type of intrusion), and each entry of KB contains a type of intrusion and the corresponding handler. The algorithm takes the suspicion and input parameters from the agent message as input, and it provides a remedy, alternative and message as its output. After initialization of the output parameters, the CIME

```
Input: suspicion,input
Output: remedy,alternative,message
1  remedy ← nil;
2  alternative ← nil;
3  message ← nil;
4  foreach entry ∈ KB do
5  |    if applicable(input,entry) then
6  |    |    remedy ← entry.handler;
7  |    |    if match(suspicion,entry) then
8  |    |    |    alternative ← entry.type;
9  |    |    end
10 |    |    Break for loop;
11 |    end
12 end
13 if remedy is nil then
14 |    message ← 'delay';
15 else
16 |    message ← 'result';
17 end
```

Algorithm 1. Evaluation Algorithm of CIME

browses its KB in search for appropriate handling procedure. The search tests whether the current entry is applicable to the input. If the test is positive, the reference to the handler of the entry is stored in *remedy*. However, the applicable entry can correspond to another type of suspicion. If such situation occurs, the type of the entry is stored in *alternative* to inform the agent and entail a revision of its evaluation process. When an entry is applicable, the *for* loop is ended. A final test verifies whether the *remedy* has changed. If unchanged (*nil*), the *message* becomes 'delay', i.e. the algorithm ends with a delayed support and the CIME will execute the optional collaborative sequence in the protocol. If *remedy* has changed, the *message* becomes 'result' and the algorithm ends with an immediate support. The CIME will then not execute the optional sequence in the protocol.

Besides addressing the immediate requests from the agents, two more trivial interaction protocol exists between the self-protected agents and CIME elements. The **alarm** protocol is used when the reflective layer of an agent encounters a known threat, resolves the situation locally and informs the CIME about the attack occurrence, so that the suspicious traffic can be identified by the CIME. In case of the above protocol, the suspicion declaration message received from the agent constitutes an implicit alarm.

The **patch** protocol allows the CIME elements to act proactively, and to dispatch the corrections of agent's vulnerabilities before any individual agent is attacked. Such behavior is typically triggered by the attack on a single agent from a multitude of similar agents running in the network, and the CIME may decide to protect all vulnerable agents before they get attacked. This protocol can also be triggered by CIME collaboration or a manual intervention from system administrator. This protocol is simply a simplified stand-alone action from Fig 4, when the result (with a permanent solution) is sent without any previous suspicion declaration message. This protocol, as well as the alarm, can both be implemented using simple broadcasts, or more complex subscribe-inform type protocols, based on the directory information.

4.2 Protocol Among CIME

The protocol in Fig. 5 describes the collaboration patterns between CIME. The collaboration starts when a CIME agent needs the information from others. The first fragment (Opt) is optional and serves to discover other CIME in the network when none are

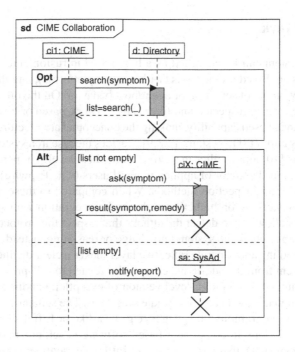

Fig. 5. Collaboration protocol among CIME

known. The CIME contacts the directory service available in the network with a *symptom* parameter. The parameter serves to compile a *list* of CIME that can deal with the particular known symptom[1] (which is related to the type of suspicion and input received by the agent). When the CIME already knows the identity of the peer to contact, it starts with a non-empty *list* parameter. If the *list* of acquaintance is not empty, the CIME will ask to a member of the list for a remedy to the symptom. Different heuristics exist for choosing the member in the list, and we were not concerned with the choice of a particular one. The peer CIME eventually replies with an appropriate remedy. In such case, the requesting CIME revises its knowledge to refer directly to this peer for the same symptom (local storage is also possible, but we would like to avoid overloading

---

[1] Using the standardized identification, for example from: http://cve.mitre.org/

network nodes with redundant information). The CIME can then return to the interaction protocol with the protected agent to provide the freshly acquired remedy. If the *list* is empty, the CIME cannot automatically process the intrusion case, and it is safer to refer to the system administrator by notifying a report based on the identity of the protected agent, the symptom, and a time-stamp for tracking. In addition, the CIME will consistently terminate the protocol with the agent by asking to apply a default handling procedure. The agent should interrupt the activity related to the flawed input, waiting for human intervention. The agent can then proceed with other activities to avoid blocking a network element.

5   Related Work

The proposed system can be classified as a host-based intrusion detection system. Its protected agents are based on the hosts (within agent platforms), and the CIME agents are based mostly on the observation of agent/host behavior. On the other hand, the fact that the messages can be inspected and filtered by network-based or low-level elements represent a network-based capability, making the conceptual architecture essentially hybrid, as are many current IDS systems [7,8,9]. Besides the research systems, many commercial solutions [10] aim to filter the traffic on the host level (i.e. personal firewalls), to analyze suspicious behavior of application and users (e.g. Tripwire), or to combine these tasks with other inspection methods. When compared to these approaches, our system differs by working on higher level due to its integration with specific application agents – this allows us to detect the attacks that respect the protocol and low-level system integrity, but attack the system knowledge or reasoning instead. The integration via exception handling and separate reflective layer makes a clear distinction and spares the baseline system from the additional complexity related to self-protection tasks.

The exception model is an high-level version of exception handling mechanisms in programming languages, with an appropriate semantics. The semantics differs from the ones developed in programming languages (e.g. Java-like or Eiffel-like) and it is more related to the work done in component-based software development and architecture description languages. Dellarocas proposed to introduce 'sentinel components' in the development process of a component-based system to cope with exceptions that can occur in the composition of COTS [11]. Similarly to our approach, this work deals with exceptions that result from inter-component events (e.g. RPC, message). The major difference is the set of collaborative capabilities that introduces more functionalities in our model of exception, and potentially expands the panel of intrusions that can be handled. Architecture-based exception handling introduces another semantics of exception, where the architecture of a system evolves at runtime to compensate exceptional situations [12]. This semantics of exception is also related to the one presented here, but it also does not include the collaborative functionalities. Intrusion detection techniques are being standardized by the IETF [13]. The related working group has defined a message format for information about intrusions [14] and specific protocols between peers on a network to cope with intrusion detections [15]. The interaction protocols proposed in this paper are application-oriented and they were designed so that they can be deployed on top of standard lower-level protocols, notably the ones developed by the IETF.

6 Conclusion

Intrusion detection and handling is a significant security issue for distributed multi-agent systems. As these systems often fulfill mission-critical functions [16], the resistance to intentional attack shall be an integral part of the design. Intrusions must be identified, contained and thwarted in real-time, even though they may use complex strategies or distributed threats. The system we propose offers a close integration with application logic it protects, therefore being able to detect the attacks by means of exception handling, but in the same time uses proven exception handling techniques to make a clear separation between the application code and meta-algorithm in the protection layer. The distributed CIME agents can gather and correlate the information from several sources and increase the quality of system output by partially eliminating the false positive/negative results. In such cases, the additional information about the overall system status is used to complement the suspicion declaration received from the protected agent. CIME agents can provide immediate and delayed support to protected agents, and they are able to supply either direct feedbacks (yes/no answers) or long-term remedies (permanent patches). Delegation of exception handling to the dedicated CIME agents is an essential characteristics of the system (it allows CIME to reason globally) with sufficient data and with the knowledge of the associated network traffic. This more complete vision allows CIME to react more efficiently when encountering threats with no known solution: A CIME can use its knowledge base to generate a filtering rule that can remove the malicious messages before they reach vulnerable agents.

In our future work, we will extend the presented approach in two directions – we can generalize the approach to gather wider range of alarms from protected hosts, and to correlate these alarms with the network traffic observations in order to automatically prevent the spread of malicious code in computer networks [9]. On the other side of the application spectrum, we intend to deploy the solution to protect a resource-constrained sensor networks against misuse.

Acknowledgment

Martin Rehak and Michal Pechoucek gratefully acknowledge the support of the current project by Army Research Laboratory projects N62558-05-C-0028, N62558-07-C-0001 and N62558-07-C-0007. Martin Rehak would also like to acknowledge the support of the National Institute of Informatics in Tokyo during his inspiring visit.

References

1. Šišlák, D., Pěchouček, M., Rehák, M., Tožička, J., Benda, P.: Solving inaccessibility in multi-agent systems by mobile middle-agents. Multiagent and Grid Systems 1, 73–87 (2005)
2. Platon, E.: Model of Exception Management in Multi-Agent Systems. PhD thesis, National Institute of Informatics, Sokendai, Tokyo, Japan (2007)
3. Goodenough, J.B.: Exception Handling: Issues and a Proposed Notation. Commun. ACM 18, 683–696 (1975)
4. Parnas, D.L., Würges, H.: Response to undesired events in software systems. In: International Conference on Software Engineering, pp. 437–446 (1976)

5. Rehák, M., Tožička, J., Pěchouček, M., Železný, F., Rollo, M.: An abstract architecture for computational reflection in multi-agent systems. In: Intelligent Agent Technology, 2005 IEEE/WIC/ACM International Conference. Number PR2416 IEEE, Los Alamitos (2005)
6. : Unified Modeling Language Specification, UML version 2.0 (August 2005) (Accessed in December 2006), http://www.omg.org/docs/formal/05-07-04.pdf
7. Axelsson, S.: Intrusion detection systems: A survey and taxonomy. Technical Report 99-15, Chalmers Univ (2000)
8. Keromytis, A.D., Parekh, J., Gross, P.N., Kaiser, G., Misra, V., Nieh, J., Rubenstein, D., Stolfo, S.J.: A Holistic Approach to Service Survivability. In: Workshop on Survivable and Self-Regenerative Systems (SSRS), pp. 11–22 (2003)
9. Rehák, M., Pěchouček, M., Prokopová, M., Foltýn, L., Tožička, J.: Autonomous protection mechanism for joint networks in coalition operations. In: Knowledge Systems for Coalition Operations 2007, Proceedings of KIMAS'07 (2007)
10. Northcutt, S., Novak, J.: Network Intrusion Detection: An Analyst's Handbook. New Riders Publishing, Thousand Oaks, CA (2002)
11. Dellarocas, C.: Toward Exception Handling Infrastructures in Component-based Software. In: Proceedings of the International Workshop on Component-based Software Engineering (1998)
12. Issarny, V.: Banâtre, J.P.: Architecture-based Exception Handling. In: Hawaii International Conference on System Sciences (2001)
13. : IETF Intrusion Detection Exchange Format Working Group (2007) (Accessed in January 2007), http://www.ietf.org/ids.by.wg/idwg.html
14. : IETF Intrusion Detection Message Exchange Format (2007) (Accessed in January 2007), http://www.ietf.org/internet-drafts/draft-ietf-idwg-idmef-xml-16.txt
15. : IETF Intrusion Detection Exchange Protocol (2007) (Accessed in January 2007), http://www.ietf.org/internet-drafts/draft-ietf-idwg-beep-idxp-07.txt
16. Maturana, F.P., Tichý, P., Staron, R.J., Slechta, P.: Using dynamically created decision-making organizations (holarchies) to plan, commit, and execute control tasks in a chilled water system. In: Hameurlain, A., Cicchetti, R., Traunmüller, R. (eds.) DEXA 2002. LNCS, vol. 2453, pp. 613–622. Springer, Heidelberg (2002)

Smart Caching Algorithm for Software Agents Based on Re-execution Probability

Jarogniew Rykowski

The Poznan University of Economics, Department of Information Technology,
60-854 Poznan, Poland
rykowski@kti.ae.poznan.pl

Abstract. In this paper we propose a new, smart strategy for efficient caching of user-defined software agents. The strategy is based on setting up minimum and maximum caching time for individual agents. These timings are formed on the basis of a way of calling an agent (type of input/output gateway serving a call, previous calls to the same agent, etc.), on the one hand, and past/current/predicted system load, including waiting calls to be served in the near future for the same and other agents, on the other hand. As proven by the tests in real applications, the strategy is efficient, especially in the case of a mass-scale system with thousands and even millions of agents owned (and possibly programmed) by different users.

Keywords: Software agents, caching, human-agent interfaces.

1 Introduction

Together with an expansion of modern information and communication technologies (ICT), a trend is observed of personalization of system functionality and accessibility [7]. Recently, software agents have been proposed to provide flexible, at-the-place and just-in-time, user-centric personalization support [3]. In the proposed solutions, particular attention is paid to user-defined functionality and communication means, as well as trade-off between overall system safety and security, on one hand, and system efficiency, on the other hand [4]. However, so far, in the existing proposals little attraction is observed of testing system efficiency, including one of the most crucial efficiency problems – agent cache. Efficient caching is of particular importance in a case of a mass-scale system, with many agents working in parallel for achieving different goals of different users.

So far, classical algorithms were applied for agent-cache management. Most of the approaches are based on a mutation of the classical Last-Recently-Used (LRU) algorithm. In this algorithm, a time of last serving a call to a given agent is taken into consideration while taking up the decision to leave the agent in the cache, or send it back to the agent repository. The algorithm is not able to cover such important system futures, as for example details of a way of communication (i.e., sending a message) with an agent, CPU and memory resources consumed both by the agent and the system software while the agent is sent to/from the repository, costs of frequent

V. Mařík, V. Vyatkin, A.W. Colombo (Eds.): HoloMAS 2007, LNAI 4659, pp. 173–184, 2007.

updates of internal agent variables, etc. This is due to the fact that the LRU algorithm was originally proposed for unified system parts such as memory pages and system applications, to be invoked and served in the same manner. This is no more true for the user-defined, heterogeneous, asynchronically and remotely called software agents. One may say that the LRU algorithm is hard to personalize, and thus hardly applied in a personalized environment.

In this paper we propose a new, smart strategy for efficient caching of user-defined software agents. The strategy is based on setting up minimum and maximum caching time for individual agents. These timings are formed on the basis of a way of calling an agent, on one hand, and past/current/predicted system load, on the other hand. Taking into account such parameters, as a type of input/output gateway serving a call, previous calls to the same agent, and waiting calls to be served in the near future for the same and other agents, a probability is computed stating whether the agent is to be called in the near future. Based on the probability, at the very end of serving a call, above-mentioned timing is set up for each agent, and a decision is made if this agent should remain in the cache, or send back to the agent repository (if so – when: immediately or in a certain period of time). As proven by the tests in real applications, the strategy is efficient, especially in the case of a mass-scale system with thousands and even millions of agents owned (and possibly programmed) by different users.

The remaining of the paper is organized as follows. In Section 2, overall system architecture is presented, with particular attention paid on implementation issues: agent-based framework, agent types, input-output gateways and data flow, and agent states and transitions between states. Next, basic problems are discussed related with agent cache, and a new algorithm is proposed based on "smart caching" approach. In Section 3 some results are given of system tests and efficiency benchmarks. Section 4 provides a comparison with similar work and concludes the paper.

2 System Architecture

In our approach, we define software agents in classical way [9], as autonomous entities executed at a given place, able to communicate with the environment and other agents or humans. As the implementation base, we propose to use imperative, distributed software agents and the Agent Computing Environment ACE [5]. The ACE framework is based on a set of distributed Agent Servers, each of them capable of storing and executing software agents. The agents may be moved among Agent Servers. There are "light" Agent Servers with limited functionality to be executed in a "thin" hardware/software environment (e.g., mobile phones), and "thick", massively used Agent Servers located in stationary network hosts. The "light" servers are mainly used for executing individual agents of an owner of a mobile device, while the "thick" ones are used by many users in parallel, usually to access certain services, external systems, and public communication channels.

There are two basic classes of ACE agents: Private Agents, and public System Agents. The Private Agents PAs are created and controlled by their human owners. Unless directly ordered by its owner, the agent cannot be accessed by any other agent. For private agents, the main problem is to achieve a reasonable trade-off between overall system security and a need for remote (i.e., server-side) execution of user-defined, thus „untrusted" (from the local administrator point of view) code. Several restrictions and limitations must be applied to user-defined code, protecting the system from (intentional or accidental) damages. Thus, a specialized language is proposed, called Agent Shell Language (ASL), to program agent behavior, based on XML and equipped with several non-standard mechanisms like run-time monitoring of CPU time and memory allocation. ASL-programmed private agents may invoke huge library of on-site, residential, Java-based system agents: communicators, services, brokers to external software systems, tools and utilities, etc. Usually, a small private agent, being a "light" mobile entity, is able to use (i.e., execute) several system agents, to achieve different goals.

Public System Agents SAs are created by trusted users (usually system designers), to be used in a mass manner by many users, providing information in a standardized form and with optimum effort. As overall efficiency is of primary concern, SAs are programmed in Java. A way of usage of a given SA cannot be changed by an ordinary user; however, it may be parameterized during the invocation. A typical Agent Server is equipped with several specialized SAs, so called input/output gateways, able to communicate with an external world (including other Agent Servers, local and remote software, and humans) via communication channels of different type and purpose. In general, two basic types of human-agent communication gateways are available: textual (connection-less) and Web-based (connection-aware approach). A textual gateway is able to exchange unformatted text messages, usually among humans and agents. Physically, textual gateways may use such means as an e-mail SMTP/POP3 connection, SMS (Short Message System)/MMS connection with a telecom network, a voice gateway, etc. Once sent by a textual message, an ACE agent may act as a chatterbot, analyzing the message via keyword extraction and analysis [6]. The chatterbot interface is especially useful for non-advanced users, and for users temporary handicapped due to limited hardware/communication possibilities.

Web-based gateways are used to access an agent via a WWW/WAP page, and from specialized ACE applications. For semi-automatic formatting of both contents and presentation of the data to be sent, XSL-T technology was adopted with XSL transformations defined in a personal manner and stored in private agent variables [5]. To this goal, specialized Session Servers are used to keep track about the history of the traffic among the agents and their users. To improve data formatting and presentation, automatic detection of end-user device may be applied, allowing auto-adjustment to the availabilities and technical possibilities of both communication means and end-user devices.

The number and types of the gateways used (including some specific parameters, e.g., a phone number for an SMS center) is local-administrator dependent. Note that the gateways are implemented as system agents, thus one may easily extend a given Agent Server by some non-standard communication means.

We used classical approach to represent agent states (Figure 1). An agent is moved/created in an agent repository ("asleep" state). To be ready to serve a call, an agent is promoted to the "ready" state by the use of restore() function. As soon as the agent is called and therefore scheduled to be immediately executed, a promotion is made to the "active" state by the use of execute() function. Once the execution is

finished, the agent is moved back to the "ready" state, by the use of stop()
function. After some time, the agent may be shifted back to the repository, to the
"asleep" state, by the use of the store() function. An agent in the "asleep" state
may be moved among several repositories. All the agents in the "ready" and "active"
states compose agent cache.

Fig. 1. Agent states, and transition functions between the states

We do not discuss here important problems of scheduling the calls to the agents
and avoiding/detecting possible deadlocks – these problems are out-of-the-scope of
this paper. A deeper discussion on serializing, prioritizing, and serving the agent calls
may be found in [4, 5].

As mentioned above, before and after the execution, ACE agents are moved from a
repository (agent database) to an execution place (operational memory), and vice-
versa. This movement is related with changing the agent representation. For the
system agents, to execute such an agent, a serialized instance of a Java class is fetched
from the repository and loaded to the instance pool of the local Java Virtual Machine.
For the private agents, ASL-compliant definition of an agent is read from the
repository, changed into the tree representation by an XML parser and loaded to the
agent execution place. For efficiency reasons, frequent flicking of the agents between
the execution places and the repositories should be avoided, especially for the ASL-
based private agents. Thus, if possible, agent representation that already served an
execution should be cached at the execution place for some time, as long as there is a
free space for this representation, and there is a chance the agent will be called once
again in the near future.

As agents are being invoked asynchronously, it is hard to predict if an agent should
be kept (i.e., cached) at the execution place in the "ready" state, or rather send back to
repository in the "asleep" state. For several reasons the LRU algorithm that is the base
for standard cache management systems is not adequate for controlling the agent
cache. First, this algorithm takes into consideration only the last activity time of the
cached element (i.e., last-access-time, last-update moment, etc.). As some invocations
of an agent are grouped into a session (e.g., while contacting an agent via a Web
page), session information should be used that is related with several consecutive
agent invocations rather than the last request only. Second, some gateways, due to
their (tele)communication nature, force an agent to be (in)active for a certain period of
time. For example, an SMS may be sent by a user every two to five minutes[1], while

---

[1] Mainly due to the fact that each message must be manually entered by a user via a mobile
keyword. However, some telecommunication restrictions apply as well, such as querying
SMS messages in base stations of a GSM network, prioritizing the messages with system-
defined messages delivered faster than user-defined ones, etc.

WWW requests to complete a single page may be counted in tens per second[2]. Third, an execution of some agents (e.g., gateways and system agents) is more important from the system point of view than an execution of the private agents owned by ordinary users. Moreover, for efficiency reasons, the gateways should be active all the time, to accept incoming (tele)communication requests addressed to the agents. As in the LRU algorithm it is assumed that each cached entity is equal to the others, and only the last-activity period is taken into account, such algorithm cannot be the base for caching ACE agents.

To efficiently cache ACE agents at the execution places, we propose a new caching strategy assuming that the caching policy is steered not only by the moments of agent executions, but also by the ways the agents are called. We take into account an information that is provided in the call context, mainly characteristics of a gateway that was used to initiate the call, and the session information coming from a Session Server, if any. Based on this information, we compute a probability of calling the agent once again in the near future. Based on this probability, we keep an agent in the ready state regardless other agents. Once the probability drops below certain limit, an agent is sent back to the repository in the asleep state.

As we do not force temporarily inactive agents to be sent back once there is no room for a new agent in the cache memory, there may be a temporal overload of an execution place due to large number of cached (and not executed) agents. To detect such overload, available local system resources such as CPU load and memory utilization are continuously monitored. If the amount of currently available system resources drops under certain limit (e.g., resource-occupation factor above the level of 90%), just-scheduled agent executions are temporary delayed. More the local computer system is overloaded, fewer agents have a chance to execute, thus such agents are temporarily suspended. Usually, for most of the (tele)communication gateways, such execution delay has no importance. For example, a delay counted in seconds for an SMS/MMS gateway is not notified by the users, due to the message delivery time that is counted in minutes and may vary, depending on current overload of the network. After some time, some cached agents that caused the overload are sent back to the repository, and the Agent Server continues to execute agents at the normal speed. Our industry tests proved that such heuristic strategy is efficient enough, and system overload occurs quite rarely. Each time an overload was detected, in few seconds the cache was free of agents and the system resumed its normal activity. The temporal-overload delays were notified only by those users who used a Session Server and a WWW/WAP gateway. However, the longest delays were counted in seconds that was acceptable for most of the users.

Out approach consists in defining two periods for each cached agent and just-executed agent – *minimum* caching period, and *maximum* caching period. The first parameter reflects a minimum period the agent must remain in the agent execution place after the execution. The second period reflects the deadline that forces the cached agent to be sent back to the repository. These periods are set individually for each agent based on history of agent invocations, mainly timings of the calls and the

---

[2] Page layout, buttons, menu, information to be displayed – these are separate page elements, and each of them may be accessed in a separate request to be sent in parallel to the Session Server and, indirectly, to an ACE agent.

characteristics of a gateway that served the last call to the agent. It is up to the local administrator to define a policy of computing the minimum and maximum caching periods. Usually, the policy is based on gateway type. For textual gateways related with such communication channels as SMS and e-mail, the minimum caching time is set to zero, and the maximum caching time is counted in seconds. For the gateways related with Session Servers and WWW/WAP invocations, the minimum caching time is set to be no longer than a minute, and maximum caching time – no more than five minutes. Based on our industry tests it was proven that such strategy is efficient enough to serve large population of the agents and their human owners.

The detailed algorithm for caching ACE agents is the following. The algorithm controls the caching process at a single Agent Server.

A_CACHE – controlling agent cache

1. Let at τ_0 all the agents be placed in the repository in the *asleep* state.

    Let *as* be an Agent Server the algorithm is executed for.

    Let *GW* be a set of all the gateways (gtw_n) of this Agent Server.

    Let *P* be a set of 3-tuples (gateway identifier, gateway minimum caching period, gateway maximum caching period). Detailed values of caching periods related with the gateways are to be set by the administrator of the Agent Server:

    $P = \{(gtw_n, p_{min}, p_{max})\}$

    Let p_{dmin} be the default minimum caching time, to be used when no gateway may be found in the P_{as} set of gateway priorities.

    Let p_{dmax} be the default maximum caching time, to be used when no gateway may be found in the P_{as} set of gateway priorities.

    Let *RA* be a set of all the agents stored in any repository of the Agent Server.

    Let *EA* be a set of all currently executed agents:

    $EA \subseteq RA$ such that each agent from *EA* is in the *active* state.

    Let *CA* be a set of all currently cached and non executed agents:

    $CA \subseteq RA$ such that each agent from *CA* is in the *ready* state.

    Let *MI* be a set of pairs (agent, moment) to store minimum caching periods for the cached agents:

    $MI = \{(a_n, \tau_n)\}$ such that τ_n is a moment, $\forall a_n, n=1...\mathcal{I}, a_n \in CA$

    Let *MA* be a set of pairs (agent, moment) to store maximum caching periods for the cached agents:

    $MA = \{(a_n, \tau_n)\}$ such that τ_n is a moment, $\forall a_n, n=1...\mathcal{I}, a_n \in CA$

    Let *SL* denote current system load. Detailed way of determining current system load depends on the administrator of the Agent Server, usually is collected from the underlying operating system as a percentage of available system resources.

    Let $TSL_{max}(SL)$ be an integer function computing maximum number of agents to be qualified for immediate execution under current system load. A way of computations of the function values depends on the Agent Server administrator.

    Let τ_{now} denote current moment.

2. Create temporally an empty set of agents to be stopped $EAS = \varnothing$. This set contains pairs composed of agent identifier and agent identifier that initiated the call.

3. Based on the *A_SERVE* algorithm of serving incoming calls, determine all the agents belonging to the *EA* set for which maximum execution time is over. Add

these identifiers to the *EAS* set of pairs, registering a name of this agent as the first element of a pair, and a name of a calling agent as the second element of the pair.

4. Based on the *A_SERVE* algorithm of serving incoming calls, determine all the agents belonging to the *EA* set for which the execution is just finished. Add these identifiers to the *EAS* set of pairs, registering a name of this agent as the first element of a pair, and a name of a calling agent as the second element of the pair. By this moment, the *EAS* set contains the pairs of identifiers of just-called and calling agents:

$$EAS = \{(a_i, gtw_i)\} \text{ such that } a_i \in EA \land gtw_i \in GW$$

5. For each element from the *EAS* set, determine maximum and minimum caching period (based on the calling agents) and move this element from the *EA* to the *CA* set, adjusting also *MI* and *MA* sets according to the just determined caching periods. By this moment, the *EA* set is narrowed, and the *CA*, *MI* and *MA* sets are broadened by the identifiers of just-finished agents. To determine maximum and minimum caching time, use the *P* set of gateway priorities. If the identifier of the calling agent (the second element of each pair of the *EAS* set) points to any element from the *P* set of gateway caching periods, fetch this element and apply the second and the third parameters to determine the elements of *MI* and *MA* sets (second elements of the pairs).

6. For each element from the *MA* set, examine the maximum caching period (the second element of the pair of this element). If this caching period exceeded τ_{now}, remove the corresponding agent from the agent execution place and send the agent back to the repository. Remove the corresponding entry in the *CA* set of all the cached agents.

7. Determine current system load *SL*. Based on this value, compute the load factor *lf* as a real value of domain $(0, 1)$ exclusive, by the use of the following formula: $lf = (100-SL)/100$. Lower the load factor, more the system is overloaded.

8. For each element from the *MI* set, examine the minimum caching period (the second element of the pair of this element). If this caching period exceeded τ_{now}, consult the corresponding element (i.e., an element pointing the same agent) from the *MA* set. If the maximum caching period multiplied by the load factor is reached, remove the agent from the agent execution place and send the agent back to the repository. Remove the corresponding entry in the *CA* set of all the cached agents. By this moment, the agent cache is optimized towards current system load and a probability of using any cached agent in the near future.

9. Determine maximum number of agents ma to be qualified for the immediate execution, based on current system load *SL* and the $TSL_{max}(SL)$ function. If $ma <= 0$, go back to step 2.

10. Determine a set of all waiting calls. If this set is empty, go back to step 2.

11. Sort the set of all waiting calls taking into account minimum caching periods for the calling agents. If the calling agent is a gateway, fetch the minimum caching period and the maximum caching period from the *P* table. Otherwise, assume minimum caching period equal to p_{dmin}, and maximum caching period equal to p_{dmax}. For the calls with equal minimum caching periods, take into account the time of registering the call – sooner the call is registered, earlier this call is put to the list of waiting calls.

12. Remove all the elements from the sorted list except for first ma elements. According to the *A_SERVE* algorithm, start the execution of the agents pointed by the list. Register the identifiers of the just-executed agents in the *EA* set as well as *MI* and *MA* sets, taking into account the minimum and maximum caching periods determined in step 11.

13. Go back to step 2 to optimize the set of cached agents and to deal with next calls.

Note that the cached agents are not automatically updated in the agent repository as long as the minimum caching period is not passed. Thus, any meanwhile changes to the agent variables are not permanently saved. To minimize data lost in the case of a system crash, the minimum caching time should be reasonably small.

Note also that by setting the minimum and maximum caching period to zero (either globally, or for selected gateways only), a local administrator may transform the above algorithm to a standard LRU-like algorithm for cache management, for all or selected agents and/or input-output gateways (communication means).

3 Tests and Benchmarks

In order to verify practical usefulness of the ACE framework and the proposed caching algorithm, the framework has been implemented in Java, and further tested in two real-life industrial applications: first, as a general support for the owners of mobile phones to facilitate access to Internet information sources and services, and second, as a support for clients of an e-bank. There were two basic goals of these industrial tests. The first goal was to prove an ability of the ACE framework to serve large number of calls to the agents in a long time without degradation of system efficiency, functionality, and availability. The second goal was to measure system throughput and to estimate average periods of agent waiting, execution, and response.

The tests were split into two groups: functionality tests, and efficiency tests. The functionality tests were performed with real users equipped with real end-user devices, as well as with real information sources – Internet-located sources in the case of the mobile-phone-owner support (weather forecast, sport and culture news, stock exchange information, group-communication support, etc.), and Intranet-based sources in the case of the e-bank (user's bank accounts, investment funds, money exchange, etc.). The main goal of the functionality tests was to determine users' needs and preferences. To this end, we collected and further analyzed information about individual requests, private agent functionality and usage, usefulness and usage of the collection of system agents provided by the administrators, etc.

To test ACE framework efficiency, we measured system performance under maximum system load. To this end, basing on log information of real user activities, we artificially cloned users' agents and users' requests obtained during the functionality tests, resulting in a population of approximately 100 000 agents, being independent copies of a hundred of real users' agents. The request log was used to prepare several test requests that were supposed to be sent to the cloned agents.

In general, we put stress on maximum-overload testing with randomly chosen requests and agents involved. We applied two basic test types: continuous-overload COT test, with certain number of agents being requested per second, and peak-test

PT, aimed at sending large number of requests at once. With the COT test, we were able to verify average system response under maximum stress. With the PT test, we also measured average waiting time (i.e., a period from detecting a request to starting the execution of the agent code). During the tests, we particularly monitored the agent cache, in order to detect the situation the system is temporarily overloaded and unable to accept new requests.

As two basic ways of accessing the agents were preferred by the real users during the functionality tests – SMS messaging and WWW/WAP access – we decided to choose these communication channels as a basic way of the automatic and randomized requests. Due to the fact that the SMS traffic is connection-less, rather than the connection-aware WWW traffic realized via a Session Server, we chose the SMS messaging as the primary communication channel. Thus, we were able to measure agent waiting, execution, and response periods for each separate request rather than the whole session composed of several consecutive requests. However, WWW-related session information was logged and further analyzed off-line.

In order to measure system parameters on-line in a way that does not interfere with monitored software, we distributed the testing system over three hosts: Agent Server host, Session Server host with a WWW server and a simulator of a WAP server, and SMS-Center host, capable of serving SMS/MMS traffic generated by mobile-phones and phone simulators (Figure 2). We also developed specialized system agent able to monitor current system status. The system-monitoring agent was equipped with a graphical user interface GUI implemented in Java, capable of on-line displaying of several system parameters, e.g., number of currently cached agents, average waiting and execution periods, gateway status, etc.

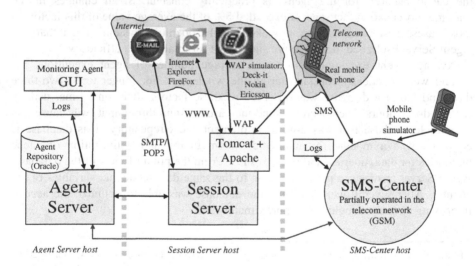

Fig. 2. Architecture of the testing workplace composed of three hosts

The tests were performed on Sun SPARCstation (Enterprise Server 330) and several PC-compatible computers equipped with Pentium III and Pentium IV processors, with Solaris, Open BSD and Windows operating systems. The following

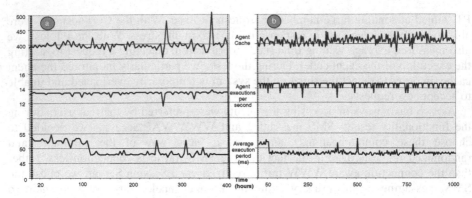

Fig. 3. Test results: (a) twenty-million-messages-long PT test, number of requests: 20 000 000, average agent execution period: 48.7 ms, average number of at-the-moment cached agents: 396 (b) one-month-long COT test, number of requests: 52 781 671, average execution period: 47.2 ms, average number of at-the-moment cached agents: 410

system parameters were continuously inspected and logged: number of the agents in the agent cache, average throughput, i.e., number of agent executions per second, and average agent execution period. The results of sample tests are presented in Figure 3.

Based on the test results, some conclusions were drawn. The most important conclusion is related with the proper behavior of the algorithm for caching the agents. As follows from the tests, even under the maximum system load, the occupation of the cache memory for the agents is practically constant. Small changes in the maximum occupation factor never exceeded 5% of the average value of this factor. In most cases, these changes were provoked by the operating system[3] rather than the Agent Server itself, and they were not significant for total system efficiency.

Average agent execution period and average number of agent executions per second were practically constant during the whole test. For longer tests (two-three days and more) a decrease was observed of these factors after some time, usually several dozen hours. Such decrease (and increased system throughput) was caused by the Oracle database that was used to implement agent repository. This database is equipped with a module for automatic system tuning and optimization of cache memories for data, queries, and query results. From the point of view of the database, Agent Server provokes a periodic access to the same data (code and variables of the agents). After several queries served, the database was able to optimize the access, improving system throughput by approximately 5%.

---

[3] It was detected during the tests that some operating systems (such as Windows 95/98/2000) were not ready for executing an application under maximum load for more than two-three days. For some systems (especially Windows family) an activity was detected every few days related probably with internal system management (memory allocation, task optimization, etc.). Such activities provoked a few-second-long interruptions in the execution of the Agent Server. However, the longest delays detected (2-3 seconds) were not important in the context of sending and receiving SMS messages, due to the long delays caused by the telecommunication network and SMS-Centers (20-30 seconds and more).

We also measure percentage hit, i.e., a percentage ratio for each agent to be requested either from agent repository, or from the agent cache. For SMS gateways, the hit ratio was almost 0%, i.e., extremely rare SMS invocations were reported to be addressed to currently cached agents. This is due to the nature of SMS messaging and long telecommunication delays (a minute and more). For WWW gateways with approximately 20 page elements to be requested at once (i.e., composing a single page), the hit ratio was greater than 95%. This means that only the "preliminary" request related with the page was addressed to a non-cached agent, while the succeeding requests were related with the just-cached agent. An approximate caching time for a single agent was usually kept within the range of one-two minutes, and the longest delays related with "preliminary" page requests were counted in a few seconds. However, such test results are quite difficult to measure and present as figures and numbers, as they strongly depend on manual interaction with the users and individual tolerance to interaction delays – these parameters and variables are hard to measure/repeat.

The tests proved high stability of the system: the Agent Server was executed for more than a month without any break under maximum load. During the tests, even a single message was not lost, and all the requests were served. Even after the longest test, no degradation of system performance was detected.

4 Similar Work, Conclusions

As already mentioned in the Introduction, the problem of efficient caching of the agents has not been deeply analyzed so far. Instead, some problems related with agent mobility took the attention of the researches, including searching for and addressing mobile agents, agent copies, remote agent representatives, routing messages and redirecting calls, etc. Once included, the discussion about the efficiency of agent caching is usually restricted to a mutation of a typical LRU algorithm (cf. Section 2). To our best knowledge, no agent-based system takes into consideration a probability of agent execution in the near future, together with execution details related with the ways of serving the incoming calls by the agents. We found no real discussion on agent flicking between the memory (execution place) and agent repository. Such flicking is of particular importance in the case of XML-based definitions of the agents, as a process of generating an XML tree by the parser is usually time-consuming. However, even for Java-based agents, the CPU-time spent on loading and preparing the corresponding .class file for the execution might be meaningful for overall system efficiency [8], once such calls are counted in thousands and millions.

We could not find any references to functionality tests related with mass-scale usage of user-defined, mobile and distributed agents. Usually, such tests are related with mass, parallel access to a single server/site. However, in such case the software serving the user calls is shared by all the calls. In the case of the ACE system, each separate call is to be served by a separate, individually programmed code. Thus, any evaluation strategy used for a centralized approach cannot be applied directly for our user-defined agents. In addition, what is the most important in the case of the ACE agents is the fact that these agents use real telecommunication devices and channels for the interaction with the users. Except for a very few tries (e.g., [1, 2]), using mobile telecommunication means as a base for a software agent interface has not been considered so far.

Some researchers proposed to use standard HTTP and Java caching to serve software agents (e.g., [10]). However, these solutions are based on standard LRU algorithm with no possibility to predict a probability of future re-execution of selected agent(s). Thus, an efficiency of these solutions in a mass-scale agent environment is disputable.

The efficiency and flexibility of the ACE framework was proven during industry tests (cf. Section 3). We found that our smart-caching strategy improves overall system performance and is transparent to the agent owners.

References

1. AMASE: Agent-based Mobile Access to Information Services, ACTS project homepage (2002), from
   http://www.cordis.lu/infowin/acts/analysys/products/thematic/agents/ch3/amase.htm
2. Farjani, P., Gorg, C., Bell, F.: A Mobile Agent-Based Approach for the UMTS/VHE Concept, Aachen University of Technology, Germany, in CAMELEON project (2002), from
   http://www.cordis.lu/infowin/acts/analysys/products/thematic/agents/ch3/cameleon.htm
3. FIPA Personal Assistant Specification (2006), from
   http://www.fipa.org/specs/fipa00083/XC00083B.html
4. Rykowski, J.: ACE Agents – Mass Personalized Software Assistance. In: Pěchouček, M., Petta, P., Varga, L.Z. (eds.) CEEMAS 2005. LNCS (LNAI), vol. 3690, pp. 587–591. Springer, Heidelberg (2005)
5. Rykowski, J.: Management of information changes by the use of software agents. In: Cybernetics and Systems, vol. 37(2-3), pp. 229–260. Taylor & Francis Publishing, Philadelphia (US) (2006) (ISSN 0196-9722)
6. Rykowski, J.: Using software agents to personalize natural-language access to Internet services in a chatterbot manner. In: Proceedings of the 2nd International Conference Language And Technology (L&T'05) (April 2005) Poznan, Poland (2005)
7. Rykowski, J.: Who should take care of the personalization? In: Suomi, R., Cabral, R., Hampe, J., Felix, H.A., Jarvelainen, J., Koskivaara, E. (eds.) IFIP International Federation for Information Processing, Project E-Society: Building Bricks, vol. 226, pp. 176–188. Springer, Boston (2006)
8. Voyager SOA Platform Recursion Software (2005), from
   http://www.recursionsw.com/Voyager/2005-09-13-Voyager_SOA_Platform.pdf
9. Wooldridge, M.: An Introduction to MultiAgent Systems. Wiley &Sons, Chichester (2002) (ISBN 978-0-471-49691-5)
10. Greenwald, D., Andresen, J.: Integrating Software Agents into the HTTP Caching Infrastructure. In: Proceedings of the 10th International WWW Conference, pos. 1102, Hong-Kong, PDF file (2001), from http://www10.org/cdrom/papers/frame.html

Metaheuristic Agent Teams for Job Shop Scheduling Problems

Mehmet E. Aydin

University of Bedfordshire, Dept. of Computing and Information Systems,
Luton, UK
mehmet.aydin@beds.ac.uk

Abstract. This paper addresses and introduces an overview on various multi-agent architectures applied to teams of metaheuristic agents for job shop scheduling applications, whose developed and examined on distributed problem solving environments. We reported a couple of topologies; ATEAM is a centrally coordinating method, which provides very good results when well-studied, on the other hand, architectures based on peer-to-peer technology provide wider flexibility in implementing various fashions. The experimentation for each targeted topology has revealed more details and attracts more attentions.

1 Introduction

Metaheuristic agents are multi agent systems identified to describe teams of search agents used to operate for optimisation. This type of multi agent systems is specific to implementations of metaheuristics to solve large optimisation problems [16]. One of the major problems with metaheuristics is that there is no guarantee provided to hit optimum solutions within a reasonable time, as they usually provide with local optimum, which may not be very desirable most of the time. One way to overcome this problem is to diversify the search conducted with the heuristics.

Distributed problem solving is mainly expected to bring simplicity and reduction in computational time. In addition, there is a hope to provide with more diversity so as to obtain a reasonably useful solution. That is the case if a well studied multi agent system can tackle multiple regions of the search space simultaneously. Multiple independent runs of the algorithms, which offer distributing the systems over the particular metaheuristic agents, have a potential of carrying out concurrent search within search spaces. We have not come across any study focusing on the topologies of multi agent systems implemented for job-shop-scheduling problems with metaheuristics in an overall view point. That will close the gap that appears in mind of new researchers with bringing forward multiple approaches for the issue. Throughout this paper, a couple of multi agent topologies applied to metaheuristic agent teams for solving job shop scheduling are introduced. Each topology provides with different benefits in tackling search and problem solving. The applications are developed to solve the classical job shop scheduling problems, which are known as

V. Mařík, V. Vyatkin, A.W. Colombo (Eds.): HoloMAS 2007, LNAI 4659, pp. 185–194, 2007.
© Springer-Verlag Berlin Heidelberg 2007

very hard combinatorial optimisation problems [5]. We have tackled the benchmarks that are very well known by the researchers in field.

The paper is organized as follows: various topologies of metaheuristic agent teams are introduced in Section 2 after a brief description of metaheuristic agents. Section 3 provides more experimental details of various metaheuristics applications. The last section provides with the conclusions.

2 Metaheuristic Agents

The concept of metaheuristic agents is identified to describe multi agent systems equipped with metaheuristics to tackle hard optimisation problems. The idea of multi agency is to build up intelligent autonomous entities whose form up teams and solve problems in harmony. The agents equipped with metaheuristics aim to solve hard problems with their own intelligent search skills. Since standalone heuristic search usually face with local minima, ideas such as memetic algorithms, hybrid algorithms etc. have received intensive attention to overcome such shortcomings. On the other hand, the virtue of multi agency brings forward usefulness to exploit for this issue.

Metaheuristic applications have been implemented as mostly standalone systems in ordinary sense and examined under the circumstances of their own standalone systems. Few multi agent implementations in which metaheuristics have been exploited are examined in the literature. In this paper, various implementations of metaheuristic agents have been overviewed with respect to topologies and achievements. All implementations introduced have tackled classical job shop scheduling problems, and examine the systems on distributed problem solving environments. DRAEM [10, 13] software is one of such environments in which a variety of agent topologies can be implemented.

2.1 Topologies of the Agents

Metaheuristic agents have mostly been implemented with different variations of genetic algorithms, tabu search, simulated annealing and hill climbing methods with various topologies. In the following subsections, a couple of multi agent topologies are presented, whose is equipped with various metaheuristics. Among the topologies introduced, some are centrally controlled, while the others are based on peer-to-peer technologies. On the other hand, the implementation of metaheuristics varies with the use of the algorithms exploited. They are mostly hybrid systems of various metaheuristics, where either different algorithms or variations of one algorithm come together to make up the ultimate system. They can be listed as follows:-

1. A framework of ATEAMS applies the idea of teams of asynchronous agents [2] (ATEAMS), which implies co-ordinating a set of autonomous agents to share experiences and advantages of the algorithms over a population of solutions. Each agent runs a particular heuristic algorithm picking up an individual from the population shared, manipulating it for a while, and putting it back into the population. By doing this, the system optimises solutions in such a hybrid way that prevents getting stuck into local minima by utilising the algorithms to be the complementary of one another. In a particular application, implementations of genetic algorithms (GA),

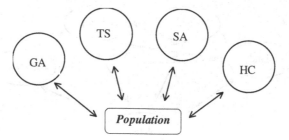

Fig. 1. The framework for ATEAMS architecture

tabu search (TS), simulated annealing (SA) and hill climbing (HC) methods can be utilised to form up an ATEAM of metaheuristic agents. The idea is sketched in Fig. 1.

This is a client-server application in which a population of solutions is kept in a server for providing the metaheuristics agents running on clients with fresh solutions on request each time. The population can be evolved by a particular selection policy, which may imply ranking the solutions with respect to solution quality and removing a number of worst solutions of the population. Illustrative experimentation is reported in the experimental study section.

2. Multi Island Metaheuristic Agents introduces an idea that implies to create identical agents equipped with particular metaheuristics and organised in a peer-to-peer fashion. This topology entails to create each agent as an island, where a population of solutions accommodate on the island, which means that each agent functions via not only operating on solutions but also holding a number of solutions. Fig. 2 sketches this approach as there is a root island takes initiative of launching applications and performing some administrative duties. As reported in experimental study section, we have developed Multi Island Genetic Algorithm (MIGA) and Multi Island Simulated Annealing (MISA) for the purpose of solving job shop scheduling problems. MIGA dictates basically multiple genetic algorithm agents as in the fashion shown in Fig. 2. The idea here is to build up some equivalent GA islands to run in parallel search on their own population. It is also allowed to employ migration operators alongside the crossover and mutation. The islands periodically report their best to the root island (the one with 'r' indices) to keep the system updated.

MISA is another implementation of multi island metaheuristic agent team, which has the same architecture with MIGA; here an evolutionary simulated annealing (ESA) has been implemented [1,3] instead of GA. All islands have been equipped with ESA to evolve a small size population of solutions, where ESA is the main operator to evolve the population. Besides, a special selection rule has been activated to make decision which solution to survive. Similar to MIGA model, migration operator can also operate, to keep the population of the islands diverse. A deeper investigation of this model is reported in experimental results section.

3. Variable Neighbourhood Search Agents is another sort of metaheuristic agent organisation, which mainly furnished with variable neighbourhood search (VNS) algorithms. In this paper, two central and two non-central VNS implementations are introduced for the same purpose. The centrally coordinating approaches work in the way sketched in Fig. 1. Below are the approaches introduced.

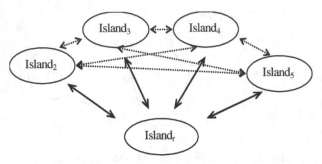

Fig. 2. The frame work for Multi island architecture

a. Centrally coordinated VNS agents are implemented in two sorts. The **synchronised** one is the framework proposed in [12], which implies centralism in coordinating the agents, where each agent is equipped with a VNS algorithm and a coordinating agent serves for collaboration among all. Each particular agent executes the algorithm in which the solution supplied is going through the basic steps of a standard VNS, which are shaking the solution first and then passing it into the local search algorithm to complete one run. Once each agent completes a run, it reports the result found to the coordinating agent, and then it compares all the results collected for the best to be considered for the next generations. Once the coordinating agent identifies the best of all, then it assigns that to every agent for the next generation.

On the other hand, the **asynchronous topology**, proposed in [11] to be applied to multi agent systems, implies a central coordination among the agents, but with an asynchronous point of view. The only difference in between this approach and the previous one is the way of coordination via synchronisation, where this approach does not wait for arrival all the results from the agents to find the best of the time, but whenever one agent contacts the coordinating agent, it finds the best of that time and provide with it for the next generation. It allows each agent to report its result and receiving the best of the time for the next run regardless of whether all agents reported or not. That enables to run various VNSs with different initial solution, while the previous one restricts all agents to run with the same initial solution. Therefore, this method diversifies more.

b. Non-centrally coordinated VNS agents are implemented in two different peer-to-peer ways; the **ring topology** and **mesh topology**. The framework of ring topology as presented in Fig. 3 requires to organise the agents in a ring topology, where the all agents enumerated in a descending order and are to be in a scheme of ring order in which the succeeding numbers are to be adjacent of each other and the first agent is adopted to be the successor of the last one. The idea is to feed a particular agent with the outcome of the previous adjacent for the next generation, while the first agent is fed by the last one. On the other hand, the mesh topology, as indicated in Fig. 4, is another peer-to-peer organisation framework. The agents are labelled in the same scheme as in the ring topology. A particular agent receives three different solutions; one from the previous adjacent, one from itself and one from the next adjacent. Then, each agent compares all three results arrived for the solution to go with in the next iteration.

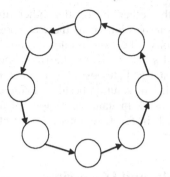

Fig. 3. The framework proposed for ring topology

What is expected from the teams of metaheuristic agents is to bring a breakthrough in parallel and distributing problem solving, as it provides complementariness of various metaheuristics in achieving high quality of solutions. Besides, it brings a massive computational time saving as well. That is happening with all teams of metaheuristics with various level of achievement. ATEAM framework offers better results taking the advantages of the complementariness of the heuristics, as one heuristic may get stuck with some certain conditions while another may rescue it. The teams of metaheuristic agents exploit the possibility of running simultaneous search on various regions of the search space. The further benefits are acquired with abovementioned multi island methods, as both methods (MIGA and MISA) evolve the population with various evolutionary operators (crossover, mutation and selection).

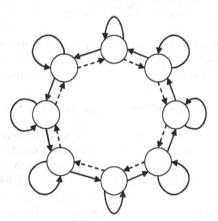

Fig. 4. The framework proposed for mesh topology

On the other hand, the VNS agent teams bring different impressions. The first method enforces all agents to go with the same initial solutions with the only expectations that the randomness in the search may diversify the solutions. Therefore, the performance of such a topology is expected to be with respect to saving computational time. On the other hand, the other three schemes have more fruitfulness for diversification of solutions as there are possibilities to run the agents with different initial solutions. The asynchronous central approach has the lowest likelihood for various initial solutions while the ring topology has the highest. The mesh topology looks in an intermediate position. Hence, the ring topology is expected to provide with a better quality of solution besides saving computational time since it carries out a simultaneous search in multiple regions of the search space, while the other methods conduct search in fewer regions concurrently. All methods are set to complete a pre-defined numbers of iterations (generation).

3   Experimental Results and Discussion

The experimental studies conducted are of different times as each methodology introduced has been done separately. Therefore, the following results should be considered independently. We first provided some results obtained with various metaheuristics and their collaborative performance in the fashion of ATEAM. Secondly, the results obtained with MISA approach for hard JSS benchmarks. Lastly, we provided the performance of VNS agents with framework of ring topology. All the applications are developed using DREAM software, which is a parallel and distributed problem solving environment developed in Java by using multi agent technology. All benchmarks are picked up from OR-Libraray [7].

The measures considered in this study are mainly about quality of solution and/or computational time. The success of the algorithms regarding the quality of solution has mainly been accounted with respect to the relative percentage of error (RPE) index, which is calculated as follows:

$$RPE = \frac{(bf - opt)}{opt} \times 100 \qquad (1)$$

where *bf* is the best makespan found and *opt* is either the optimum or the lowest boundary known for unknown optimum values. Obviously, RPE is calculated based on the best value found, and also it can be measured benchmark-by-benchmark.

3.1   Distributed Resource Evolutionary Algorithm Machine (DREAM)

DREAM is a parallel and distributed problem solving environment, whose consists of a core (DRM) and an evolutionary algorithm library. Distributed Resource Machine (DRM) is an infrastructure that provides a distributed problem solving environment based on mobile agents. It is the distributed infrastructure of DREAM software [10, 13], which was developed to solve problems through distributed evolutionary algorithms spread over a massive network of nodes on the Internet. The main aim of this system is to solve the problems based on multi agent systems, where each runs evolutionary algorithms. The system consists of a scalable network of resources, which works as a peer-to-peer network of nodes spread on physically distributed computers. Each node has incomplete knowledge about the rest of the network and works as the container of all the agents running on a particular computer. The environment has very good functionalities to develop applications such that the agents have good communication and limited mobility. (See [10] for more information on DRM).

The way of distributing the evolutionary processes over the resources throughout DREAM is to implement the island model. Islands are designed and furnished with various properties, data and algorithms, and then distributed over the DRM network. The DRM environment is developed based on multithread programming in Java. It runs the islands as multiple independent run (MIR) technology and provides it with a message passing system (MPS) using connectionist sockets based on TCP/IP protocols. It is required to partition the problem into subparts to be solved through multi island models.

3.2 ATEAM Application for JSS Problems

Talukdar [15] proposed an architecture for autonomous agents operating asynchronously on a shared population of solutions, which they call "ATEAM" standing for asynchronous team. Basically, each agent contributing the team operates independently, selecting a particular solution from the population shared. It places back the solution manipulated by itself to the population. The cooperation is achieved by sharing the solutions in which one adopts the outcome of another as the initial solution. The population is controlled by a subset of destroyer agents, which evaluate solutions according to some certain selection criteria and remove unwanted solutions. In this particular application, we made up an ATEAM of four well-known metaheuristics, namely genetic algorithms, simulated annealing, taboo search and hill-climbing. All have been implemented in the standard way. One destroyer agent operates to evolve the population towards the objective, which is to minimise the makespan of the schedule.

Table 1. Results obtained from various algorithms and ATEAM

Problem	Opt.	SA	HC	TS	GA	ATEAM
ft10	930	5.16	11.22	8.01	13.15	3.05
abz5	1234	1.19	2.00	2.51	2.76	0.32
abz6	943	0.46	0.53	0.53	3.50	0.53
la16	945	2.19	4.68	3.60	4.34	0.50
la17	787	0.76	3.18	0.59	5.12	0.00
la18	848	1.61	4.17	1.34	1.97	1.02
la19	842	2.97	3.64	2.77	3.92	1.19
la20	902	1.03	4.51	1.26	3.58	0.52
orb1	1065	5.01	8.83	7.67	9.98	4.04
Average		2.26	4.75	3.14	5.37	1.24

Table 1 presents the results obtained with each metaheuristic agent running standalone and together in ATEAM fashion. All results are presented in RPE index, which indicates the relative error percentage. The last column of the table indicates the performance of ATEAM as significantly the best. In the bottom line of the table, the performance of each algorithm is provided in average. Obviously, the minimum figure is 1.24 appears in the column of ATEAM. That proves the power of well-studied cooperating metaheuristic agents over the standalone ones.

3.3 MISA Application of JSS

In this application, we developed a team of metaheuristic agents; each runs a simulated annealing algorithm operating completely independent with a non-central coordination. The approach is based on multiple independent run parallelisation technology, where independent agents are running on a network of virtual nodes geographically distributed over WAN. Each agent runs an evolutionary SA algorithm [3] to evolve a small size population of solutions via another simulated annealing like selection policy. The results obtained with MISA for hard JSS benchmarks are presented in Table 2 in comparison with some other methods reported in very recent publications. MISA, which is named as dESA in [1], provides very reasonable level of the quality of the solution in a very short time, as it holds the second best performance. Similar to Table 1, the last row of Table 2, provides the performances in an averaged figures, where MISA gives the second best as well. Moreover, Aydin and Fogarty [1, 3] present achievements of distributed SA (MISA) over the standard ones with respect to both the quality of the solution and the computational time.

Table 2. Results obtained from various recent algorithms for hard benchmarks of JSS problems

Problems	Optimum	MISA	ACO [8]	GRASP [4]	HGA [9]	Satake [14]	VNS Agents
abz07	656	2.44	2.74	5.49	NA	3.51	0.91
abz08	665	2.41	3.61	6.02	NA	2.86	0.75
abz09	679	2.95	3.39	8.98	NA	2.80	0.29
la21	1046	0	0.1	1.05	0	0.00	0
la24	935	0.32	0.96	2.03	1.93	0.11	0
la25	977	0	0	0.72	0.92	0.31	0
la27	1235	0.4	0.65	2.75	1.7	1.05	0
la29	1152	2.08	1.39	4.43	3.82	1.30	1.03
la38	1196	0.42	2.59	1.84	1.92	0.50	0
la40	1222	0.49	0.49	1.8	1.55	0.90	0.16
Average		**1.15**	**1.59**	**3.51**	**1.69**	**1.33**	**0.31**

3.4 VNS Agents with Ring Topology

As mentioned above, we have attempted to solve JSS problems with variable neighbourhood search agents as well. We attempted four different coordination schemes and found the best as the one organized with ring topology. The main idea has been described above. The idea was to improve the performance of the heuristics via multi agent systems while cutting the computational time. In fact, ring topology provided the best as it allows to run multiple independent VNS agents in various regions of the search space simultaneously. The performance of VNS with ring topology is presented in the last column of Table 2, where it provides with the best overall.

The other schemes of VNS agent teams propose less distributedness and more serial-like processing. Fig. 5 indicates the benefit gained with ring topology over the scalability. The figure shows the level of improvement in the quality of solutions with the increased number of agents running independent VNS algorithms. The x-axis of the graph indicates the number of agents with the number of iterations, while y-axis gives the level of RPE averaged over the repetitions. Evidently, the more agents, 10 agents, each runs 20 generations, provides the best performance, which is lower than 0.6% of RPE, while the one runs over a standalone agent provides with 0.8%. That proves another handiness of the teams of metaheuristic agents.

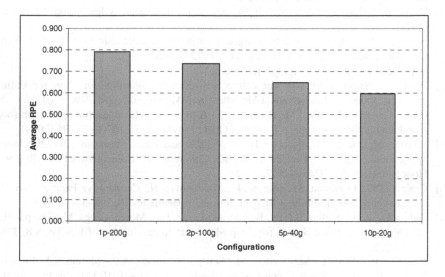

Fig. 5. The solution quality against scalability of VNS agents for JSS

4 Conclusions

In this paper, we revealed the benefits of teams of metaheuristic agents in problem solving. We examined a couple of coordination topologies. ATEAM is a centrally coordinating method, which provides very good results when well-studied. The main difficulty is balancing the metaheuristics to be complementary to each other. Multiple island models provide wider flexibility in implementing various fashions as long as they tuned up with respect to communication load. On the other hand, VNS agents do much better when more multiple independent runs are provided. The best topology found is the ring topology as it keeps diversity higher, and allows search in multiple regions simultaneously. In the future, we are going to focus on this notion to retrieve more information for conveniences.

References

[1] Aydin, M.E., Fogarty, T.C.: A distributed evolutionary simulated annealing algorithm for combinatorial optimisation problems. Journal of Heuristics 10(3), 269–292 (2004)

[2] Aydin, M.E., Fogarty, T.C.: Teams of autonomous agents for job-shop scheduling problems: An experimental study. Journal of Intelligent Manufacturing 15(4), 455–462 (2004)

[3] Aydin, M.E., Fogarty, T.C.: A simulated annealing algorithm for multi-agent systems: a job shop scheduling application. Journal of Intelligent Manufacturing 15(6), 805–814 (2002)

[4] Aiex, R.M., Binato, S., Resende, M.G.C.: Parallel GRASP with Path-Relinking for Job Shop Scheduling. Parallel Computing 29, 393–430 (2003)

[5] Baker, K.R.: Introduction to Sequencing and Scheduling. John Wiley & Son, Chichester (1974)

[6] Beasley, J.E.: OR-Library: distributing test problems by electronic mail. Journal of the Operational Research Society 41(11), 1069–1072 (1990), http://people.brunel.ac.uk/ mastjjb/jeb/info.html

[7] Blum, C., Sampels, M.: An ant colony optimization algorithm for shop scheduling problems. Journal of Mathematical Modelling and Algorithms 3, 285–308 (2004)

[8] Goncalves, J.F., Mendes, J.M., Resende, M.: A hybrid genetic algorithm for the job shop scheduling problem. European Journal of Operations Research 167(1), 77–95 (2004)

[9] Jelasity, M., Preuβ, M., Peachter B.: A scalable and robust framework for distributed applications, CEC'02: The 2002 World Congress on Computational Intelligence, Honolulu, HI, U.S.A. (May 12-17, 2002)

[10] Crainic, T.G., Gendreau, M., Hansen, P., Mladenovic, N.: Cooperative Parallel Variable Neighborhood Search for the p-Median. Journal of Heuristics 10, 293–314 (2004)

[11] Garcia-Lopez, F., Melian-Batista, B., Moreno-Perez, J.A., Moreno-Vega, M.: The parallel variable neighbourhood Search for the p-Median Problem. Journal of Heuristics 8, 375–388 (2002)

[12] Peachter, B., Back, T., Schoenauer, M., Sebag, M., Eiben, A.E., Merelo, J.J., Fogarty, T.C.: A distributed resource evolutionary algorithm machine (DREAM). In: Proc. of the Congress of Evolutionary Computation 2000 (CEC200), IEEE, pp. 951–958. IEEE Press, Los Alamitos (2000)

[13] Satake, T., Morikawa, K., Takahashi, K., Nakamura, N.: Simulated annealing approach for minimising the makespan of the general job-shop. International Journal of Production Economics, 60–61, 515–522 (1999)

[14] Talukdar, S.: Asynchronous teams. In: Proc. of 4th International Symposium on Expert Systems Applications in Power Systems, LaTrobe University, Melbourne, Australia (1993)

[15] Hammami, M., Ghediera, K.: COSATS, X-COSATS: Two multi-agent systems cooperating simulated annealing, tabu search and X-over operator for the K-Graph Partitioning problem. In: Khosla, R., Howlett, R.J., Jain, L.C. (eds.) KES 2005. LNCS (LNAI), vol. 3684, pp. 647–653. Springer, Heidelberg (2005)

Distributed Production Scheduling Using Federated Agent Architecture

Jayeola Femi Opadiji[1] and Toshiya Kaihara[2]

[1] Graduate School of Science and Technology, Kobe University, Japan
femi@kaede.cs.kobe-u.ac.jp
[2] Graduate School of Engineering, Kobe University, Japan
kaihara@cs.kobe-u.ac.jp

Abstract. Making a production system readily reconfigurable in a bid to adapt to very fluid demand profile is pertinent to cost reduction and facility utilization objectives of the system. We consider a production scheduling methodology based on federated agent architecture designed for a flexible job shop with dynamic demand. The interaction protocol within the social network is based on a facilitated auction mechanism. This model employs competition at job centers to maximize financial returns and uses cooperation among facilitator agents to minimize weighted tardiness.

Keywords: Multiagent System, Production Scheduling, Auction-Based Scheduling, Federated Agent Architecture.

1 Introduction

The need for more flexible manufacturing systems is a strong motivation for researchers in agent-based and Holonic manufacturing systems. In the recent past, a number of production system architectures have been built based on these paradigms as can be found in literature [1, 3, 8]. Representing facilities in a manufacturing system as intelligent agents that are capable of decision making and are aware of their environment makes it possible to apply some basic social interaction rules to provide a more pragmatic approach to problems in shop level production system scheduling.

One very important attribute of agent-based manufacturing models is the ease with which they can be reconfigured to meet specific objectives of a system by redefining environmental parameters and/or specifying new objectives to agents in the social network. Manufacturing system models designed using the Multiagent System (MAS) paradigm essentially consist of autonomous agents which are capable of rational behaviour and have objectives that may be competitive (selfish) or cooperative (global). The manufacturing system is modeled as a social network which allows agents to interact with one another as well as with the environment based on certain guidelines referred to as interaction protocol. To date, a lot of efforts have been devoted to developing such protocols geared at efficient performance of the system under consideration. These social network protocols range from market-oriented protocols as discussed in [4, 10, 11, 12] to social negotiation protocols [2, 6] as exemplified in different definitions of the contract net protocol [7, 9]. In the next subsection, we briefly consider the auction protocol on which our model is based.

V. Mařík, V. Vyatkin, A.W. Colombo (Eds.): HoloMAS 2007, LNAI 4659, pp. 195–204, 2007.
© Springer-Verlag Berlin Heidelberg 2007

1.1 Auction Protocol

Auctions are employed to resolve perceived deadlocks among a set of agents competing for limited resources. The objective is often to allocate value to the most deserving bidder. However, the problem lies in determining the most deserving bidder because it is possible to have more than one parameter, which are often conflicting, to put into consideration in determining the bid winner; this is often the case in shop level production scheduling. As rightly pointed out in [3], application of an auction protocol to production scheduling problem results in a dilemma of making competitive agents cooperate in such a way as to achieve a global objective. This is due to the fact that these agents seek to maximize an economic objective while the global objective of the system relates to achieving the highest possible system performance. These two objectives are inherently conflicting ones.

A way out of this problem is to institute a kind of autonomous environmental parameter adjustment mechanism which induces participating bidders to make their resources available to meet system needs in exchange for financial rewards. The contractual side of the protocol however preserves the autonomy of agents by respecting the wishes of agents to either bid or not bid for tasks. Thus, we are able to create a kind of dynamic balance between agent autonomy and system redundancy.

Another point that is worth mentioning in the use of an auction protocol is the level of privacy that agents enjoy within the social network which is treated in [5].

2 Scheduling Problem Definition

The target production system in our research is a flexible job shop with a set of job centers W each having a unique set of uniform machines M_w for $w \in W$. The machines $m_{wi} \in M_w$ (for $i = 1, 2... n$) are parallel machines with the same processing

Table 1. List of Notations

Terms	Notation	Terms	Notation
Set of job centers	W	Task Sequence	S
Job center	w	Number of tasks in sequence	$|S| = m$
Set of machines in job center	M_w	Task	J
Machine i in job center w	m_{wi}	Volume of task j	v_j
Machine capability label	L	Task release time	$r_j(t)$
Availability of machine at time t	$x(t)$	Task due time	$d_j(t)$
Speed of machine i in w (volume/unit time)	ω_{wi}	Assumed speed vector for job centers (volume/unit time)	Ω
Processing cost of machine i in w per unit time	c_{iw}	Assumed processing cost vector at job centers	P
Set of orders	Q	Tardiness weight of order q	k_q
Number of orders	$|Q| = n$	Tardiness of order q	τ_q
Order in time bucket t	$q(t)$	Total weighted tardiness	Z
Payment for q(t)	$p_q(t)$	Makespan of order q(t)	T
Delay Penalty cost for order q(t) per unit time	$c_o(t)$	Slack time for task j	φ_j

capability but different speeds ω_i. The processing capability refers to the kind of processing a machine can perform on a task. Table 1 shows a list of notations used in this paper.

2.1 Environment Specification

The flexible job shop environment under consideration is modeled under the following operational conditions:

(a) Once an order is accepted, it must be fulfilled regardless of the cost of production
(b) It is possible to reject orders if projected capacity is not available within the order lead time.
(c) Orders are fulfilled by executing a sequence of tasks.
(d) The environment does not permit preemption of tasks.
(e) A task cannot be started until the preceding task has been completed.
(f) Recirculation is permitted in the task sequence

Next, we define the optimization problem of the production system in equations (1) – (4). The objective function implies the desire to reduce the total weighted tardiness of accepted orders. The first constraint is the production possibility constraint with respect to task processing time for all tasks in the order while the second constraint is the machine availability constraint. The last constraint is the production profitability constraint.

$$\min Z = \sum_{q=1}^{n} k_q \tau_q \tag{1}$$

$$subject\ to:$$

$$v_j(q)/\Omega_j(q) \le d_j - r_j \quad for\ all\ j \in q \tag{2}$$

$$\sum_{t=r_w}^{v_w/\Omega_w} x(t) = v_w/\Omega_w; \quad x(t) = \{0,1\} \tag{3}$$

$$\sum_{j=1}^{m} \rho_j *(v_j(q)/\Omega_j(q)) \le (p_q - c_q \tau_q) \tag{4}$$

Orders come into the manufacturing system as a dynamic stream. They are presented in the form of aggregated data and contain information about sequence of tasks that make up the order, task volumes, proposed price of order and the penalty cost per unit time delay of order fulfillment. Orders are accepted based on capacity availability and profitability of orders. It is possible to accept orders even when delays may occur in a particular process if it is expected that some order tasks might make up for lost time or if tardiness is within tolerance level. All of these conditions are environmental settings in the manufacturing system and can be tuned to modify the behaviour of the entire system.

3 Federated Agent Architecture

This model is based on federated agent architecture as shown in Fig. 1 below. Each job center is modeled as a federation of agents. The agents in each group have identical features (processing capability) but are different with respect to their processing speeds. As a whole, the production system is made up of three types of agents: Controller, Facilitator and Processor.

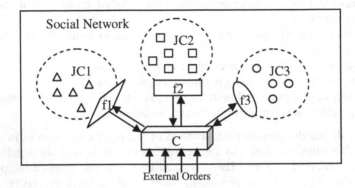

Fig. 1. Federated agent architecture – f1, f2 and f3 are facilitators; C is controller and JC1, JC2 and JC3 are job centers containing processor agents

Fig. 2 below shows a time line of the interaction between agents in the federation once an order is received.

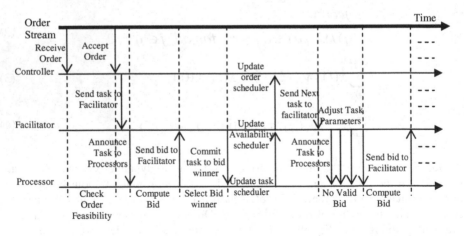

Fig. 2. Time line of scheduling protocol with federated agent architecture

The controller agent has the responsibility of receiving orders from the external world and processing the orders for acceptance or rejection. The processor agents represent machines in the shop floor grouped into job centers based on their processing capabilities. Interaction between the controller agent and processors in a job center is made possible by the facilitator agent. This is to allow for robustness in the system by providing machine agents with more autonomy. Once orders are accepted, the controller begins dispatching of tasks to different job centers in a sequential order. Task information is transmitted to a facilitator agent in a format containing processing specifications: $\{v_j, \rho_j, \varphi_j, r_j, d_j, c_j\}$. Processors bid for tasks to satisfy their private objective function which is a profit maximization function. In bidding, they supply their facilitator agent with a proposal containing $\{c_i, r_i, d_i\}$. The facilitator then selects the bid winner based on cost and lead time criteria. In our model, we take into account earliness of task completion by processors because, the idle time provided by a given machine provides the next task with a slack time for processing in case the estimated lead time for that task is shorter than the processing time of any available machine. It is also important because tasks can be inserted on a machine that provides enough idle time.

3.1 Agent Description

Controller Agent. This agent behaves in such a ways as to maximize the overall utilization of production facilities. The controller agent is the only agent that is aware of the external world. It achieves this by accepting as many orders as possible subject to availability of machines at job centers. The controller dynamically adjusts some environmental parameters like the assumed processing speeds at job centers (Ω_w) and assumed processing cost of each task (ρ_j). These two parameters allow it to determine whether it should accept a task or not. The adjustment of the parameters is based on previous scheduling results. The controller agent has a schedule bank where it stores schedules of all orders that have been fulfilled. Fig. 3 shows a pictorial representation.

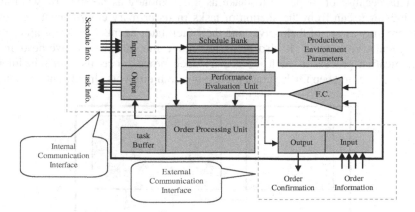

Fig. 3. Pictorial representation of the controller agent

Facilitator Agent. The facilitator agent, shown in Fig 4, provides a transaction interface between the controller and processors the job centers it represents. In order to perform its task, a facilitator agent has complete information about the status of processors in its domain with regards to processing capacities and availability. A facilitator agent also has information about a pending task from an accepted order once a request for processing is transmitted to it by the controller. As an auctioneer, the facilitator agent is responsible for coordinating auctioning activities among its processors. The facilitator agent has an availability schedule which it maintains for each processed task. This schedule keeps track of the number of machines that are available at every instance of time. The facilitator agent takes care of equations (2) and (3) in the optimization problem defined earlier.

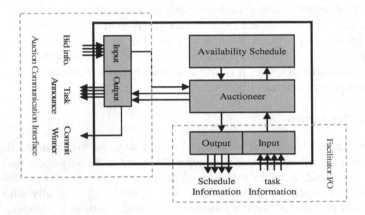

Fig. 4. Pictorial representation of the facilitator agent

Processor Agent. The actual processing of tasks is carried out by processors. Processors in the same job center are *uniform*. A processor agent has a competitive behaviour because of its desire to make as much money as possible by winning as many bids as it can from the auction of tasks in its primary environment. Processor agents are only aware of themselves and their facilitator agent. This keeps all of them from speculative bidding. It also helps to reduce the information overhead in the communication process at each job center. Each processor as its own scheduler as shown in Fig. 5, to keep track of task processing commitments already entered into.

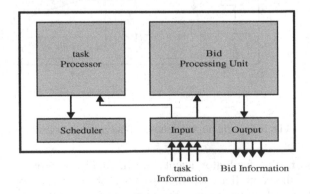

Fig. 5. Pictorial representation of the processor agent

3.2   Agent Interaction and Task Scheduling

Agent Interaction. Communication between controller and facilitator is executed on an agent-to-agent basis. The controller agent transmits and receives messages from facilitator agents individually and sequentially made possible because of the uniqueness of job centers. At the job centers, facilitator agents announce task auctions using a simple *contract net* protocol which eliminates the need for complex agent-to-agent negotiation by broadcasting auctions. Only available processors respond to auctions and in a situation where there is no bidder, a facilitator agent re-evaluates its bid and announces the task again. After selection of an auction winner, the facilitator agent simply notifies the winner while it hides the award information from the other processor. The other processors get notified of their bid loss by the announcement of a new task. This method helps minimize information clog in the social network.

Agent Interaction Algorithm

```
0:   Initialize agents
1:   Controller receives order if exist(order) = true
2:   Controller runs feasibility(environment parameters)
3:   If not feasible, reject order and go to 1
4:   Organize order into tasks
5:   Post pending task to appropriate facilitator
6:   Facilitator auctions task among processor agents
7:   Processors bid for task based on cost and
     availability
8:   If bidders = NULL, adjust task parameters and go to 6
9:   Bid winner is selected and processor commits to task
10:  Winning processor updates its processing schedule
11:  Facilitator updates job center availability schedule
     and posts auction results to controller
12:  Controller updates order processing schedule
13:  Controller: If exist(pending task) = true, go to 5
14:  Go to 1
```

Task Scheduling. When an auction winner is selected by the facilitator agent of a job center, the selected winner proceeds to commit to the task and update its schedule to reflect changes in its available capacity. It also informs the facilitator agent of its unavailability within this time span so the facilitator can update its own availability schedule. When a new task is auctioned, a processor searches for an available slot in its schedule that meets the lead time requirement of that task. Once a task as been committed to by a machine, it is mandated to complete the task. After the processor has scheduled a task, the facilitator informs the controller of the result by sending information containing $\{r_w, d_w\}$ and slack time to it. Slack time is $\max\{0, (d_j(q) - d_w)\}$. The controller agent updates its order schedule bank and sends information about the next task to be processed to the appropriate facilitator agent. The slack time from a previous task gives the active facilitator some latitude to alter task release dates.

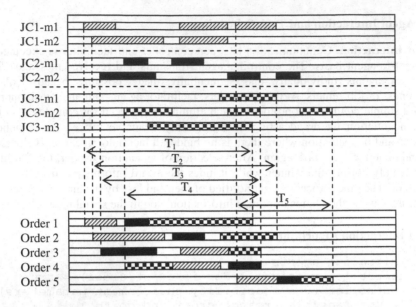

Fig. 6. Gantt chart of five orders processed by a 3 job center shop

Fig. 6 shows an example of a Gantt chart from 5 orders processed by a production system with 3 job centers.

When an auction winner is selected by the facilitator agent of a job center, the selected winner proceeds to commit to the task and update its schedule to reflect changes in its available capacity. It also informs the facilitator agent of its unavailability within this time span so the facilitator can update its own availability schedule. When a new task is auctioned, a processor searches for an available slot in its schedule that meets the lead time requirement of that task. Once a task as been committed to by a machine, it is mandated to complete the task. After the processor has scheduled a task, the facilitator informs the controller of the result by sending information containing $\{r_w, d_w\}$ and slack time to it. Slack time is $\max\{0, (d_j(q) - d_w)\}$. The controller agent updates its order schedule bank and sends information about the next task to be processed to the appropriate facilitator agent. The slack time from a previous task gives the active facilitator some latitude to alter task release dates.

4 Experiments and Result

We conducted experiments with a model production system consisting of five job centers. An order stream containing 100 orders were placed by a random sequence of tasks and task volumes. We ran simulations under three conditions:

Case 1: The lowest speeds of the job centers are taken as the initial assumed speed vector for the controller agent. This is to give every machine the opportunity to bid at the initial stage. The speeds are then changed in response to tardiness situation in the system.

Case 2: The lowest speeds of the job centers are taken as the initial assumed speed vector for the controller agent and this speed vector is held constant all through the simulation process.

Case 3: The highest speeds of the job centers are taken as the initial speed vector for the controller agent and the speeds are held constant for all order conditions.

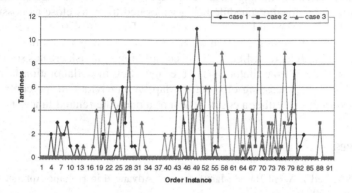

Fig. 7. Tardiness variation for the three simulation conditions

Table 2. Performance Indices under different simulation conditions

Simulation Condition	Total Tardiness	Total Profit from orders	Total Inventory Cost	No. of Processed orders
case 1	101	4738.5	648.7	83
case 2	48	6268.7	572	92
case 3	131	4803.3	117	80

Fig. 7 shows variations in tardiness as orders are being processed for the simulation conditions we considered in our model. From Table 2, it can easily be seen how that it is better to maintain a constant speed selection policy under varying order conditions. When the lowest speed policy is used by the controller agent as in case 2, the system is able to process more orders and incur less tardiness thereby yielding a better total profit than the other cases. In the case of implementing the highest speed policy, the system performance is only better in inventory cost incurred. Methodically adjusting speed parameters as in case 1 may not exactly yield good system performance as seen from the results. It is therefore suggested that to make the most of the cooperation dynamics among the facilitator agents, the controller agent must maintain a constant speed policy over a given period of time depending on the order profile. If work-in-process inventory cost is very high, it is better to adopt the highest processing speed policy while the lowest processing speed policy is advantageous when the work-in-process inventory cost is low as compared to the cost of delayed orders. Therefore the adaptive behaviour which the controller requires is in recognizing the order profile over a long period of time and not a constant speed adjustment mechanism.

5 Conclusion

In the scheduling model proposed, a target schedule is computed by the controller agent based on information about the environment available to it. The actual schedule is then generated by a competitive auction process among the processor agents and a cooperative behaviour among facilitator agents. Facilitator agents adjust task parameters in order for the schedule being generated to be as close as possible to the objective schedule proposed by the controller. The controller's target schedule is generated bearing in mind the global objective of the system which in our case is the minimization of weighted tardiness. Early completion of a task creates some slack for the next task since the facilitator agents are operating in collaboration to reduce the overall tardiness in processing of orders. Adaptive behaviour in the controller agent can be biased to favour either a cost function or a due-date related function.

References

1. Deen, S.M. (ed.): Agent-Based Manufacturing: Advanced in Holonic Approach. Springer, Heidelberg (2003)
2. Huhns, M.N., Stephens, L.M.: Multiagent Systems and Societies of Agents. In: Weiss, G. (ed.) Multiagent Systems: A Modern Approach to Distributed Artificial Intelligence, pp. 79–118. The MIT Press, USA (1999)
3. Markus, A., Vancza, T.K., Monostori, L.: A Market Approach to Holonic Manufacturing. Annals of CIRP 45, 433–436 (1996)
4. Pinedo, M.: Scheduling, Theory Algorithms and Systems, 2nd edn. Prentice Hall, USA (2002)
5. Sandholm, T.: Distributed Rational Decision Making. In: Weiss, G. (ed.) Multiagent Systems: A Modern Approach to Distributed Artificial Intelligence, pp. 201–258. The MIT Press, USA (1999)
6. Sandholm, T.: An Algorithm for Optimal Winner Determination in Combinatorial Auctions. IJCAI, 542–547 (1999)
7. Sandholm, T.: An Implementation of the Contract Net Protocol Based on Marginal Cost Calculations. In: Proceedings of the Eleventh National Conference on AI, pp. 256–262 (1993)
8. Shen, W., Norrie, D.H., Barthes, J.A.: Multi-agent system for concurrent intelligent design and manufacturing. Taylor & Francis Inc. USA (2001)
9. Smith, R.G.: The Contract Net Protocol: High Level Communication and Control in a Distributed Problem Solver. IEEE Transaction on Computers 29, 1104–1113 (1980)
10. Vancza, J., Markus, A.: An Agent Model for Incentive-Based Production Scheduling. In: Computers in Industry, vol. 43, pp. 173–187. Elsevier, Amsterdam (2000)
11. Walsh, W.E., Wellman, M.P.: A Market Protocol for Decentralized Task Allocation. In: Proceedings of the Third International Conference on Multi-Agent Systems, pp. 325–332. IEEE Computer Society, Los Alamitos (1998)
12. Wellman, M.P.: A Market-Oriented Programming Environment and its Application to Distributed Multi-commodity Flow Problems. Journal of Artificial Intelligence Research 1, 1–23 (1993)

A Study on Real-Time Scheduling for Holonic Manufacturing Systems – Simulation for Estimation of Future Status by Individual Holons

Koji Iwamura, Atsushi Nakano, Yoshitaka Tanimizu,
and Nobuhiro Sugimura

Osaka Prefecture University, Graduate School of Engineering, 1-1 Gakuen-cho,
Nakaku, Sakai, Osaka, 599-8531, Japan
{iwamura, tanimizu, sugimura}@me.osakafu-u.ac.jp

Abstract. This paper deals with a real-time scheduling system of the holonic manufacturing systems (HMS). In the previous papers, real-time scheduling processes based on the utility values have been proposed and applied to the HMS. A simulation based procedure has also been implemented to estimate the future status of HMS and to determine the utility values aiming at improving scheduling method. However, it was assumed that only one holon in the HMS carries out the estimation for the ease of the estimation process. A simulation based real-time scheduling method is newly proposed, in the paper, to improve the estimation process which enable all the holons to estimate the future status of the HMS. An estimation process is developed for the individual holons to estimate the future status of HMS through the simulation. Some case studies of the real-time scheduling are carried out to verify the effectiveness of the proposed method.

Keywords: Holonic Manufacturing Systems, Real-time scheduling, Coordination, Estimation of future status.

1 Introduction

Recently, new architectures of manufacturing systems have been proposed to realize flexible control structures of manufacturing systems, which can cope with dynamic changes in volume and variety of products and also unforeseen disruptions, such as malfunctions of manufacturing resources and interruptions by high priority jobs. They are so called as autonomous distributed manufacturing systems [1], biological manufacturing systems [2], random manufacturing systems [3] and holonic manufacturing systems [4] [5] [6] [7].

In the previous paper [4], a real-time scheduling method based on utility values has been proposed and applied to the holonic manufacturing systems (HMS). The holons in the HMS are divided into three classes, in the research, based on their roles in the manufacturing processes and the scheduling processes.

V. Mařík, V. Vyatkin, A.W. Colombo (Eds.): HoloMAS 2007, LNAI 4659, pp. 205–214, 2007.

(a) Resource holons: They transform the jobs in the manufacturing process. In the scheduling process, they evaluate the utility values for the candidate combinations of the resource holons and the job holons which carry out the machining operations in the next time period.

(b) Job holons: They are transformed by the resources from the blank materials to the final products in the manufacturing process. In the scheduling process, they evaluate the utility values for the candidate combinations of the resource holons and the job holons which carry out the machining operations in the next time period.

(c) Coordination holon: It selects a most suitable combination of the resource holons and the job holons for the machining operations in the next time period, based on the utility values sent from the resource holons and the job holons.

A simulation based procedure has also been proposed and implemented for the job holons and the resource holons, in the previous papers [5] [6], to estimate the future status of the HMS through the simulation and to determine the utility values, aiming at improving the scheduling method. However, the following conditions are assumed, in the previous research, for the ease of the estimation process.

(1) Only one job holon or resource holon in the HMS carries out the estimation.

(2) The holon, which carries out the estimation, has the complete simulation model of the HMS. The complete simulation model means that the model includes the decision criteria of all the job holons, the resource holons, and the coordination holon.

A new estimation process is proposed, in this paper, aiming at realizing estimation of the future status of the HMS under the following conditions.

(i) All the job holons and the resource holons, estimate the future status of HMS through the simulation, in order to evaluate the utility values.

(ii) The holons, which carry out the estimation, do not have any information about the decision criteria of all the job holons, the resource holons, and the coordination holon.

2 Simulation Based Real-Time Scheduling Method

One of the important objectives of the HMS is to provide the holons with the flexible and robust capability against the unforeseen disturbances of the manufacturing systems, such as failure of manufacturing resources and interruption by high priority jobs. A real-time scheduling system is therefore proposed to control the holons of the HMS. The real-time scheduling means that the manufacturing schedules of the resource holons and the job holons are determined dynamically only when the status of the HMS and its holons are changed due to some events occur in the HMS. Therefore, the scheduling system only determines the schedules of the resource holons and the job holons in the next time period. The time period means the period between the time when one event occurs and one when another successive event occurs.

Figure 1 shows the simulation based real-time scheduling method proposed here. In the figure, t shows a time when some machining operations are finished, and some

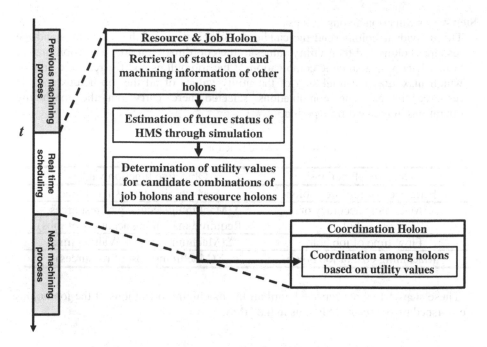

Fig. 1. Simulation based real-time scheduling method

resource holons and job holons change their status from 'operating' to 'idling'. At the time t, all the 'idling' holons select their machining schedules in the next time period. The real-time scheduling method consists of following four processes.

Step 1. Retrieval of status data and machining information of other holons

The individual job holons and resource holons initially obtain the status data and the machining information from all the other holons. Status data means the 'operating' or 'idling' of the other holons. The machining information includes the machining operations of the job holons which will be executed from time t, and the candidate resource holons for the machining operations.

Step 2. Estimation of future status of HMS through simulation

The individual job holons and resource holons firstly setup the initial time T_0 and the termination time T_n for the simulation. The individual job holons and resource holons carry out the estimation of the HMS from time T_0 to T_n through the simulation and generate the feasible future status of the HMS at the time T_n.

Step 3. Determination of utility values

The individual job holons and resource holons determine the utility values for the candidate combinations of the job holons and the resource holons which can carry out the machining operations in the next time period, based on their own objective functions. It was assumed that the individual job holons and resource holons have one of the objective functions shown in Table 1 for evaluating the utility values. In the table, Σ means that the individual holons calculate objective function values after all machining operations are finished in the HMS. The details are given in the previous paper [4].

Step 4. Coordination among holons

The individual holons send the candidate combinations of the job holons and the resource holons and their utility values to the coordination holon. The coordination holon determine a suitable combination of the job holons and the resource holons, which maximize the total sum of the utility values of all the job holons and the resource holons. The combinations selected here carry out the machining operations in the next time period.

Table 1. Objective functions of holons

Objective functions	Objective function values
Efficiency of resource holon	Σ Machining time / Total time
Machining accuracy of resource holon	Σ(Machining accuracy of resources – Required machining accuracy of jobs)
Flow-time of job holon	Σ(Machining time + Waiting time)
Machining cost of job holon	Σ(Machining cost of resources)

These steps 1 to 4 are repeated until all the machining operations of the job holons are finished by the resource holons in the HMS.

3 Estimation Process by Simulation

The individual job holons and resource holons carry out the estimation of the HMS through the simulation. Figure 2 shows an example where a resource holon 1 carries out the estimation of the future status of the HMS through the simulation. In the figure, $S(t)$ represents the status of the HMS at time t. The status $S(t)$ includes the status data and the machining information of all the constituting holons of the HMS, as shown in the followings.

$$S(t) = (u_1(t), u_2(t), ...). \tag{1}$$

where, $u_i(t)$ represents the status data and the machining information of the holon i at the time t.

The simulation process by the holon is summarized in the followings. The holon which carries out the simulation is called the "simulating holon".

Step 1: Generation of candidate combinations

At the time T_0, which is the start time of the simulation, the simulating holon generates all the candidate combinations of the job holons and the resource holons which can start the machining operations in the next time period from the initial status of HMS $S(T_0)$.

The future status of the HMS is affected by the candidate combinations of the job holons and the resource holons generated here. Therefore, m different simulations from the time T_0 are required to estimate the future status of the HMS for the cases where the simulating holon generates m candidate combinations at the time T_0, as shown in Fig. 2. In other words, m branches are generated here for the

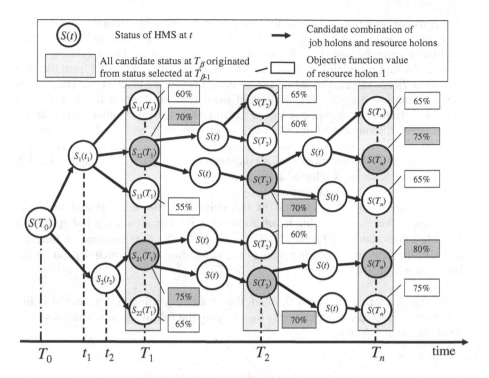

Fig. 2. Estimation of future status of HMS by simulation

future status of the HMS. In this case, number of the candidate combinations m is 2, as shown in Fig. 2.

Step 2: Simulation from T_0 to t_α

The simulating holon starts the simulation of the HMS from the time T_0 by putting the simulation clock forward to t_α ($\alpha = 1, 2, \ldots, m$) for the cases where the individual candidate combinations are used for the next machining operations in the HMS. The t_α is the time when the some machining operations are finished, and some resource holons and job holons change their status from 'operating' to 'idling'. As the simulation results, m future statuses of the HMS are generated, which are represented by $S_\alpha(t_\alpha)$ in Fig. 2.

Step 3: Simulation to β-th machining operations of simulating holon

The simulation process presented in STEP2 shall be repeated to the termination time T_n, in order to get all the future status of the HMS at the time T_n. However, a set of the candidate combinations of the resource holons and the job holons are generated at time t_α, and the status branches to the next status at the time $t_{\alpha+1}$, as shown in Fig. 2. The total number of the branches of the status is rapidly increased as the time progresses. Therefore, the number of branches is reduced at the time T_β ($\beta = 1, 2, \ldots, n-1$). T_β is the time when simulating holon finishes its β-th machining operation.

Let us consider the case where the number of the branches from the initial status at T_0 is m and a set of the candidate status at T_1 are generated through the simulation from the time T_0 to T_1. Where, T_1 is the time when the simulating holon finishes its first machining operation. In the case, m status originated from the first branch at T_0 are selected based on the objective function values at T_1. This means that the simulation system selects a set of most suitable status at the time T_1, and that the selected status has one to one relationship with the initial branch at T_0. In this case, the number of the candidate combinations m at T_0 is 2, therefore two suitable status are selected at time T_1, as shown in Fig. 2. After selecting the suitable status at T_1, the simulation is continued from T_1 to T_2 by applying STEP2, and the suitable status is selected at the time T_2.

Step 4: Simulation to termination time T_n

The simulation and the selection of the suitable status are repeated until the simulation time reaches to the termination time T_n. The simulating holon obtains feasible future status $S_\alpha(T_n)$ ($\alpha = 1, 2, \ldots, m$) of HMS at the termination time T_n, and also the objective function values of the simulating holon which depend on the final status $S_\alpha(T_n)$.

After the simulation process is finished, the simulating holon i evaluates the utility values for the candidate combinations j by applying the following equations, based on its own objective functions.

(1) Efficiency

$$UV_i(j) = 1 - \frac{\max\limits_{j=1,\cdots,m} \{S_j(T_n)_{OF}\} - S_j(T_n)_{OF}}{\max\limits_{j=1,\cdots,m} \{S_j(T_n)_{OF}\} - \min\limits_{j=1,\cdots,m} \{S_j(T_n)_{OF}\}}. \tag{2}$$

(2) Machining accuracy, Flow-time, and Machining cost

$$UV_i(j) = \frac{\max\limits_{j=1,\cdots,m} \{S_j(T_n)_{OF}\} - S_j(T_n)_{OF}}{\max\limits_{j=1,\cdots,m} \{S_j(T_n)_{OF}\} - \min\limits_{j=1,\cdots,m} \{S_j(T_n)_{OF}\}}. \tag{3}$$

where, $S_j(T_n)_{OF}$ represents the objective function value of the simulating holon i at time T_n for the cases where the simulating holon selects the candidate combination j at the initial time T_0.

After the utility values are evaluated, the individual holons send the candidate combinations of the job holons and the resource holons and their utility values to the coordination holon. The coordination holon determine a suitable combination of the job holons and the resource holons, which maximize the total sum of the utility values of all the job holons and the resource holons, as shown in Section 2.

4   Case Study

Some case studies have been carried out to verify the effectiveness of the proposed methods. The HMS model consisting of 6 resource holons is considered for the case

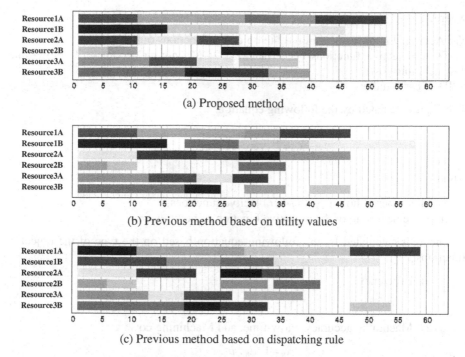

(a) Proposed method

(b) Previous method based on utility values

(c) Previous method based on dispatching rule

Fig. 3. Gantt chart of scheduling results

study. The individual resource holons have the different objective functions and the different machining capacities, such as the machining time, the machining accuracy, and the machining cost.

As regards the job holons, 8 job holons are considered in the case study, which have the different objective functions and the machining sequences. 10 cases are considered, in the case study, by changing the objective functions of the individual resource holons, and the machining sequences of job holons.

Figure 3 shows examples of the real-time scheduling results in the form of the gantt chart. Figure 3 (a), (b) and (c) show the results of the proposed method, that of the previous scheduling method based on utility values [4], and that of the previous scheduling method based on dispatching rule [7].

Figure 4 (a) and (b) summarize the comparison between the proposed scheduling method and the previous scheduling method, from the viewpoint of the objective function values of the individual holons. Figure (a) shows the comparison with previous scheduling method based on utility values, and (b) shows the comparison with previous scheduling method based on dispatching rules. In the figure, the horizontal axis gives the termination time of the simulation T_n. For example, T_1 means that the termination time of simulation is T_1. The vertical axis shows the averaged improvement λ calculated by the following equation.

$$\lambda = \sum_{g=1}^{10} X_{fg} / 10 \quad f = 1, 2, 3, 4. \tag{4}$$

where,

X_{fg}: Averaged improvement of the f-th objective functions of holons,
f: ID of objective functions (1: Efficiency, 2: Machining accuracy, 3: Flow-time, 4: Machining cost),
g: ID of case studies.

The X_{fg} is calculated by the following equation.

$$X_{fg} = [\sum_{h=1}^{H} x_h / H]_{fg}. \tag{5}$$

where,

H: Total number of holons with f-th objective functions,
x_h: Improvement ratio of the objective function of holon h.

The x_h is calculated by the following equation based on the type of the objective functions.

(1) Efficiency

$$x_h = a_h / b_h - 1. \tag{6}$$

(2) Machining accuracy, Flow-time, and Machining cost

$$x_h = 1 - a_h / b_h. \tag{7}$$

where,

a_h: objective function values of holon h obtained by the proposed method,
b_h: objective function values of holon h obtained by the previous method.

As shown in Fig. 4, the proposed scheduling method is effective to improve the objective function values of the individual holons from the view point of the average of all the objective functions. However, proposed method is not so effective from the view point of the objective function of the machining cost and the machining accuracy. It is because that the machining cost and machining accuracy are reduced by a very simple methods in which the job holon only selects a most cheap resource holon, and ones in which the resource holon only selects a most high accurate job holon.

The termination time does not affect the improvement ratio λ, as shown in Fig. 4, and the computation time of the simulation is increased as the termination time is increased. Therefore, T_1 seems to be most suitable and enough for improving the objective function values.

Computation time of the simulation is important for implementation of the proposed real-time scheduling method to the real manufacturing systems. The individual holons take less than 1 minute on average to carry out the simulation for the cases where the termination time of simulation is T_1, and it is sufficient for the practical implementation of the proposed real-time scheduling method.

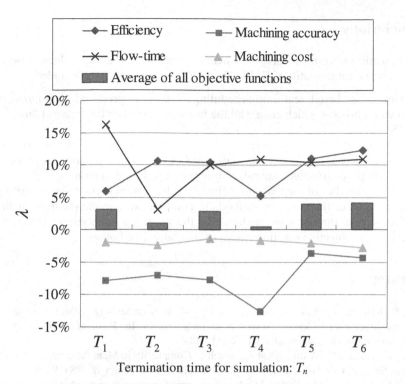

(a) Comparison with previous method based on utility values

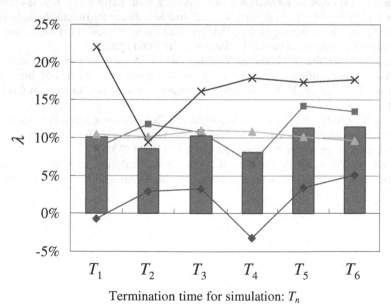

(b) Comparison with previous method based on dispatching rules

Fig. 4. Results of case study

5 Conclusions

New systematic methods are proposed here to evaluate the utility values, based on estimation of the future status of HMS. The following remarks are concluded.

(1) A simulation based real-time scheduling method is proposed to improve the estimation process which enable all the holons to estimate the future status of the HMS.
(2) An estimation process is developed for the individual job holons and resource holons to estimate the future status of HMS through the simulation. A procedure is also proposed to reduce the calculation time for the simulation.
(3) Some case studies of the real-time scheduling have been carried out to verify the effectiveness of the proposed methods in comparison with the previous method. It was shown, through case studies, that the proposed methods are effective to improve the objective function values of the individual holons.

References

1. Fujii, S., Kaihara, T., Utsunomiya, T., Sashio, K.: A study on self-organization functions for agile manufacturing in square arrayed machining centers. In: Proc. of 2004, Japan-USA symposium on flexible automation CD-ROM (2004)
2. Ueda, K., Ohkura, K.: A Biological Approach to Complexity in Manufacturing Systems. In: Proc. of the 27th CIRP Int. Seminar on Manufacturing Systems, pp. 69–78 (1995)
3. Iwata, K., Onosato, M., Koike, M.: Random manufacturing system: A new concept of manufacturing systems for production to order. Annals of the CIRP 43(1), 379–384 (1994)
4. Iwamura, K., Tanimizu, Y., Sugimura, N.: Real-time Scheduling for Holonic Manufacturing System -Coordination Among Holons Using Effectiveness Values-. In: Proc. of the 17th International Conference on Production Research CD-ROM (2003)
5. Iwamura, K., Morishita, Y., Tanimizu, Y., Sugimura, N.: A study on a real-time scheduling for holonic manufacturing system -A decision making based on estimation of future status of holons-. In: Proc. of 2004 Japan-USA Symposium on Flexible Automation CD-ROM (2004)
6. Iwamura, K., Okubo, N., Tanimizu, Y., Sugimura, N.: Real-time scheduling for holonic manufacturing systems based on estimation of future status. In: Proc. of the 18th International Conference on Production Research CD-ROM (2005)
7. Sugimura, N., Tanimizu, Y., Iwamura, K.: A Study on Real-time Scheduling for Holonic Manufacturing System. CIRP Journal of Manufacturing Systems 33(5), 467–475 (2004)

Adaptive Planning for Supply Chain Networks

Michael Andreev[1], George Rzevski[1], Petr Skobelev[1], Peter Shveykin[1], Alexander Tsarev[2], and Andrew Tugashev[2]

[1] Magenta Technology Ltd., 1A, Osipenko str., Samara, Russia, 443110
skobelev@magenta-technology.ru
http://www.magenta-technology.com
[2] Knowledge Genesis Ltd., 221, Sadovaya str., Samara, Russia 443001
tsarev@kg.ru
http://www.kg.ru

Abstract. This paper describes methodology, toolset and case studies of adaptive planning for supply chain networks based on the holistic approach, multi-agent technology and ontological modeling. The set of tools for the development of adaptive planners can be used for a wide range of applications. Case studies are included describing applications inr adaptive airport logistics, factory planning, laundry scheduling and pharmaceutical logistics.

Keywords: adaptive planning, holistic approach, demand-resource network, multi-agent system, ontology, semantic networks.

1 Introduction

The adaptive planning is a continuous, event-driven, real-time planning and re-planning process [1-2]. In contrast to the simple incremental planning, it makes not only the use of simple open time slots, but also employs the conflict-driven reasoning for the implementation of plan changes by "shift", "swap" or "drop". In the adaptive planning, every new event (such as a new order arrival, a cancellation of already allocated orders, the availability of a new resource, a failure of existing resources, or changes of network objectives) can trigger a partial or even the full change of the previously accepted plan, occasionally with long ripple effects.

The adaptive planning is compatible with fundamental ideas of the holistic approach [3] where a number of autonomous "wholes" can dynamically form a new higher-order entity, which begins to operate as a new autonomous "whole". Constituent "parts" of the newly formed "whole" can revert to working autonomously as "wholes", if required. The holistic approach fully matches the key principles of "vertical" self-organization when local interactions form higher-order structures which, in turn, affect local interactions [4].

Holistic ideas and distributed, agent-based decision making provide a powerful mechanism for modeling Prigogin's self-accelerating reactions with a full set of non-linear thermodynamic effects [5]. The system is able to change the whole plan within a short period of time because local parts of a schedule dynamically form higher-order components able to work autonomously and take decisions in negotiation with other

V. Mařík, V. Vyatkin, A.W. Colombo (Eds.): HoloMAS 2007, LNAI 4659, pp. 215–224, 2007.

components. For example, in road transportation scheduling the agent of a journey, as a "whole", can decide to replace a truck without consulting agents of orders allocated to the journey; the agents of orders, in turn, may decide to leave the journey to which they were allocated if they can get better options and if their action will increase the global value.

This approach provides an opportunity for building complex adaptive systems exhibiting emergent intelligence, which helps to make better decisions faster by specific kind of spontaneous autocatalytic reactions [6].

Our previous developments were focused mainly on transportation, including ocean and truck logistics [7-9]. In this paper we will introduce a new toolset for building adaptive planners which is aimed at a wide range of applications and is currently under development. We will illustrate the approach by giving examples of applications which have been prototyped on the basis of the new toolset.

2 Open Demand-Resource Networks

The fundamental concept of the proposed approach is an *Open Demand and Resource Network* (ODRN), which is a network of interlinked demands and resources in which nodes can be dynamically added or removed [10].

An ODRN can be used to represent a variety of types of supply-chain networks which may contain whole factories or just constituent components like robots, machine tools and conveyors; transportation fleets or trucks, journeys, orders, cross-docks, shops, etc. Each single object in the network can be represented by an agent with its own objectives, preferences and constraints. Agents can take a role of either a demand or a resource, and they are continuously active selling or buying services and searching for the best possible match between demands and supplies. Take, for instance, transportation logistics: a single journey (a trip from point A to point B) may occasionally play a role of a resource for a new order and on other occasions, a role of a demand for trucks and drivers. As demands and resources are matched, agents build temporary links between respective objects of the ODRN, which may be changed when new events occur. These links form a network of object instances which are referred to as the Scene of a supply-chain network and which in fact represents the current situation of the virtual market of demands and resources. A scene is constructed using concepts from Ontology, which is a semantic network of classes of objects (concepts), their relations, their attributes and their behaviors. Ontology represents conceptual problem domain knowledge.

The network model of a supply-chain is not necessarily flat and can be organized as a set of pre-defined worlds (networks representing self-contained parts of the supply chain) and also as a set of hierarchical structures of objects dynamically configured by agents. For example a supply chain consisting of factories, transportation fleets and warehouses may be decomposed into a number of constituent supply-chain networks each representing an autonomous virtual world consisting of robots and machine tools; trucks and journeys; and storage locations, respectively. The degree of nesting is not limited and gives an opportunity to increase the complexity of the network when needed. It is important to note that agents assigned to higher order objects do not control the constituent agents – they can only specify and, if required, change their goals, preferences and constraints, in other words, they act as holons. For example, if the risk factor for the whole fleet is very high, the fleet agent can identify most risky trucks and initiate re-scheduling of their operations.

Agents can have several different criteria for decision making, such as the service level, costs, delivery time and risks and they perpetually search for appropriate trade-offs between different criteria. Balancing of criteria is controlled by the use of virtual money. For example, an agent can negotiate and win a better delivery time by paying more for a resource and possibly increase the risk of delivery, if this happens to be less important.

Every object of an ODRN (for example, a journey) can be constructed dynamically from other objects (for example, orders and trucks) by agent negotiation. The constituent objects of the new object are in a state of not-stable equilibrium and delegate the decision making activities to the agent assigned to the new higher-order agent (for example, to the journey). The main idea here is that agents of consolidated objects do not have to compete for the attention of the system dispatcher for time quanta with other agents. Instead they delegate their decision making tasks to a single agent, which acts on their behalf. If for any reason constituent agents are not satisfied with decisions of their representative, the consolidation structure may break up.

An important feature of an ODRN is the mechanism for adding and canceling a demand or resource. For instance, a cross-dock in a supply chain network can be closed at any time because of reconstruction, fire, terrorist attacks or other reasons. For the adaptive planner all situations of this kind will be covered by the event "loss of a resource". Agents of all goods assigned to the cross-dock that is lost are activated and informed that the links to this cross-dock are now unavailable and that they need to find a new appropriate resource. As a result agents will start negotiating new allocations and all affected goods will finally be reassigned to other cross-docks. This feature enables modeling of internal contingencies and, what is more important, of the impacts of external unpredictable factors.

At any time users can visualize ODRN and navigate through the network investigating which demands are linked to which resources and vice versa.

Links between demands and resources are not symmetrical because they reflect the level of satisfaction of each agent. As new events occur the less satisfied agents are continuously trying to improve their allocations and thus break less satisfactory links.

3   The Adaptive Planning Toolset

The architecture of the Adaptive Planning Toolset, as shown in Fig. 1, contains the following modules:

Pattern Generator – generates clusters based on a historical analysis of data, which can be used for demand forecasting, the analysis of state of resources, etc. For example, if a big order is coming every Friday it is reasonable to book specific resources for implementation of this order tentatively in advance. And if the order has not arrived as expected the customer can be alerted and/or resources can be released.

Adaptive Scheduler – processes events flow and creates schedules in real time. The Adaptive Scheduler works in close cooperation with the Pattern Generator. For example, the Pattern Generator may recognize a big cluster of orders in the input flow of events and trigger the process of consolidation of these orders and as a result the re-scheduling of resources for this group with a view to providing a better quality of scheduling results – if time is available.

Network Designer – configures the supply-chain network and describes the initial state of the network manually or automatically, extracting data from different sources (data bases, xls or xml files, etc). For this purpose the user needs to select and load appropriate ontology, which is used as a dictionary of concepts and relations in the process of specifying the concrete customer network. If not all concepts and relations required to specify the new network are available, domain ontology needs to be expanded using the Ontology Editor.

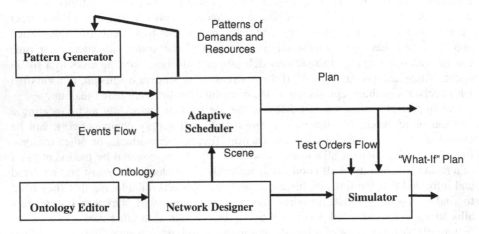

Fig. 1. The Architecture of the Adaptive Planning Toolset

Ontology Editor – helps to build or edit ontology of a supply-chain network, which is required for constructing specific networks using the Network Designer. Ontology contains classes of objects and their relations, attributes and behaviors. Examples include: for objects (factory, cross-dock, etc), relations (resource "is booked" for a demand), attributes (value of an order) and behavior (business processes).

Simulator – is the tool for playing What-If games. At any moment the current state of the supply-chain network can be loaded on to Simulator to answer various questions like, for example, what will happen if a new big orders arrived unexpectedly. Another option is to reconfigure the network (changing geography of main resources or making a new type of equipment available) and to run different scenarios of network optimization in parallel with the continuous scheduling of orders as they arrive.

In future there will also be an opportunity for Evolutionary Design of the supply chain by running the Simulator in parallel with the Scheduler and automatically generating suggestions how to adapt the network in response to the changes in demand and supply.

4 Case Studies

4.1 Airport Logistics: Adaptive In-Flight Catering

The problem was to plan and simulate the food supply to the aircraft and the delivery from the aircraft heating ovens to passengers. The purpose of the simulation was to investigate the impact of a new type of food heating equipment and to develop business processes on board with the aim of reducing costs and providing more efficient individual service for passengers.

The key idea was that the pre-selection of the meal type (for example, a fish or meat choice) in advance, in the course of booking of seats via Internet, or during the check-in stage at the airport, or on the board of the aircraft, may improve the schedule of food heating and delivery on board of the aircraft (Fig. 2).

The operation chain included detailed on-board activities such as heating of meal and delivering individual casseroles to each passenger. Caterers tend to supply big packs of casseroles. The use of consolidation allowed focusing on the important problem of specific local parts of the supply chain in order not to waste time on interactions among the multitude of individual objects.

Since catering is driven by the end customer demands, which affects individual meals, changes in the meal demands create and destroy consolidations in the supply chain. For example, when a passenger changes the selected meal, the agent representing the changed meal leaves its current consolidation and joins another one that is more appropriate.

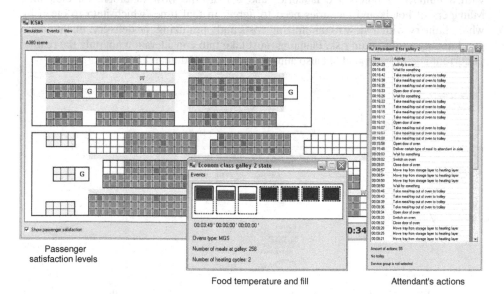

Fig. 2. Screens of the in-flight catering simulator

During the first stages of the on-board supply chain meals are processed as consolidated racks or trays. Meals are delivered on trolleys, transferred to ovens where they are heated and then transferred to trolleys for each aisle. Considering each meal separately at these stages of the supply chain is not necessary.

During the final stage of the service cycle, when the meals are delivered to the end customers they can be grouped into racks or oven trays, if processed at the same time. A rack and a tray are planned as a consolidated object (object consisting of many constituent objects – individual meals). If a passenger changes his/her order, it can lead to deconsolidation of previously created groups and to the new groupings.

Simulation was also used to check the consequences of failures and errors. In conventional systems a failure usually implies the complete re-planning. In simple agent-based systems, if many individual items use the broken-down resource, such as oven, it takes time for all individual agents to find a new available resource and, in addition, during re-scheduling the plan is unstable. The Adaptive Planner however uses consolidated objects, which implies that the re-scheduling is normally done in a single transaction. If rescheduling of a consolidated object causes problems to an individual constituent object, the agent assigned to this object may decide to leave the group and join another that is more appropriate.

The results of simulation have shown a number of benefits of new catering equipment and the improved value proposition for airline companies.

4.2 Adaptive Laundry

One of the more complex problems in a hotel chain business is the cleaning and laundering of items such as bed-sheets, pillow-slips, duvets, towels, etc. Consider a map with a number of hotels and laundries and a real-time flow of orders for cleaning. Managers of hotels and laundries need to agree, in real time, which item to clean in which laundry with a view to minimizing costs and optimizing the delivery, maintaining good quality at minimum risk. Planning must take into consideration not only the reality of current guest turnaround but also annual statistics and demand forecasts.

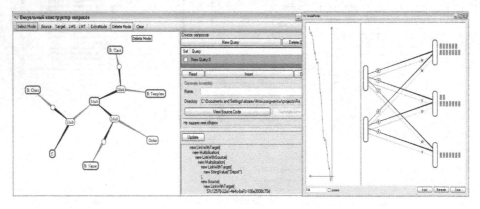

Fig. 3. Ontology Editor (on the left) and Scene Visualization (on the right)

Each laundry has its own configuration of equipment and is likely to have a different business process, which may include: sorting the dirty stock, loading it into washing machines, washing, drying, sorting of washed garments, ironing and packing.

Additional requirements are that garments of different colors are not allowed to be washed together. Also, garments of different sizes have different drying times, thus it is better to group them by size in order to make up more optimal schedule.

The Adaptive Planner assigns an agent to each key element of a laundry, including washing machines, dryers, ironers, etc. Each order that arrives to the system creates an agent for several linked operations on the time line. Each operation uses certain equipment and has certain properties pertaining to the product to be processed. Information about laundry equipment, their operation and their attributes is entered into ontology for each laundry type. Based on this information demand agents negotiate the best available time slots of resources (workers, machines and other equipment) according to their objectives (Fig. 3).

Agents can group several segments on a time line of a resource belonging to different orders to achieve more efficient scheduling. Consolidated operations have a practical value as long as production items are more efficiently processed when grouped by certain properties like size, weight and color. The consolidated objects are usually kept unbroken even when a complete rescheduling is necessary. In such cases consolidation can greatly increase the quality and performance of scheduling.

The incoming dirty garment flow is normally unknown until the bags are unpacked. Therefore the initial plan is created on the basis of real orders and approximate statistics and can be very rough. As production begins, the garment types loaded into machines are entered into the system to correct the initial tentative plan. If the entered real data does not match the initially planned incoming flow, a rapid rescheduling follows.

It should be noted that people who enter corrections cannot do that for each item because this would take more time than the loading. They can enter only the type of the sorting group and its weight. This is fully compatible with the load consolidation concept. The new data is entered as a consolidated group and the agent assigned to the group interacts with agents assigned to other consolidated groups. This reduces greatly the number of interactions needed to obtain a new stable schedule and has a high significance value in the case when a new loading happens each 2 minutes.

The results of simulation showed that the adaptive planning can bring a considerable value to the customer in reducing costs, improving quality of service and delivering all items on time.

4.3 Adaptive Factory

Traditional ERP systems are using classical waterfall Push or Pull schemes of operations. In the Push scheme supply is driving the whole production plan of the year. In the Pull scheme the production plan is demand-driven. The problem is that in reality it is required to combine both schemes dynamically.

For example a factory can get a new big order for product A from a customer and consolidate it with previous orders for this type of product. The consolidation will decrease the cost of production and it may even induce other customers to buy the product A with a good discount. As the demand for product A increases, it may trigger a further consolidation and therefore a further reduction in production costs. The process has all the properties of the autocatalytic reaction which self-accelerates the system transition to a new state potentially near a strong attractor.

Model
structure

Dynamic factory
production plan

Changing
inventory state

Inventory
agent

Orders

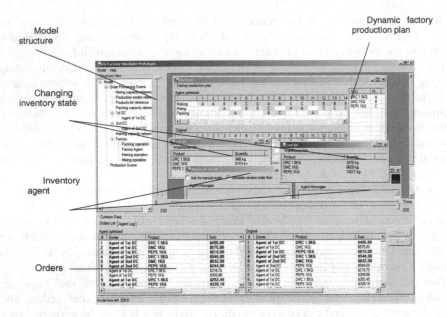

Fig. 4. Screen of adaptive factory simulator

Examples of screens of the Adaptive Factory Scheduler are shown in Fig. 4 and 5.

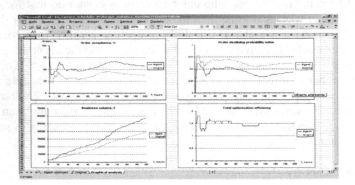

Fig. 5. KPIs Screen of the adaptive factory simulator

Simulation results show that such self-accelerating reaction based on the dynamic pricing model can significantly reduce costs and improve efficiency of all factory operations.

4.4 Adaptive Pharmaceutics

A multi-agent system for providing social services to the citizens on the basis of social passports and smart cards is described in [11]. One of the most complex problems that have been solved by the system was the provision of free medication to welfare recipients (war veterans, retired citizens, disabled persons). The scheduler planed supplies to hospitals, clinics and drugstores that serve a large region with more than 3 million citizens.

This system provides each clinical department with a possibility to plan medications individually for each welfare recipient taking into account changes in his/her health condition, the date of next visit, etc. Data from different departments is consolidated into one general order (for this clinic), and orders from different clinics are then consolidated into a regional order. The bigger the order the more substantial discount can be obtained from medical suppliers and the saved money is used either for ordering more expensive and more efficient medications or for saving budget resources.

To obtain this kind of consolidation the Adaptive Planner has to continuously schedule and reschedule supplies based on changes in demand and supply conditions and the feedback from medical staff and individual patients. Pricing of each type of medication is dynamically adjusted to reflect the size of the order and delivery dates.

5 Conclusions

The adaptive planning is of great interest to supply chain management due to the number of its unique features:

- individual approach to every demand and resource;
- near optimal and well-balanced solutions for very complex networks where combinatorial search is not effective;
- a fast response time to unpredictable events because there is no need to revise the whole schedule every time;
- the dynamical pricing model allows negotiation with clients in real time;
- the easy customization to different requirements.

The development of adaptive planners is however a complex process. It requires knowledge-based tools, distributed decision making with parallel computation, learning and adaptation. With the help of tools described in this paper the complexity and the costs of the development process can be reduced significantly. As a result, adaptive planning can bring a significant value to businesses by providing better service level for clients, reducing operating costs, increasing resource utilization and minimizing risks.

References

[1] Rzevski, G., Skobelev, P.: Magenta Technology: A Family of Multi-Agent Intelligent Schedulers. In: Workshop on Software Agents in Information Systems and Industrial Applications (SAISIA). Fraunhofer IITB (February 2006)
[2] Rzevski, G., Skobelev, P.: Agent Method and Computer System For Negotiating in a Virtual Environment, Patent No: WO 03/067432 A1. Published (14.08.2003)
[3] Van Brussel, H., Wyns, J., Valckenaers, P., Bongaerts, L., Peeters, P.: Reference architecture for holonic manufacturing systems: PROSA. Computers in Industry 37(3), 255–274 (1998)

[4] Kuppers, G.: Self-organization - The Emergence of Order. From local interactions to global structures. no 2, PDF (July 1999), http://www.uni-bielefeld.de/iwt/sein/paper

[5] Nicolis, G., Prigogine, I.: Exploring Complexity. W H Freeman, New York (1939)

[6] Rzevski, G., Skobelev, P.: Road Transportation i-Scheduler with Emergent behavior. In: Emergent Intelligence, Springer, Heidelberg (2007) (in publication)

[7] Himoff, J., Skobelev, P., Wooldridge, M.: Magenta Technology: Multi-Agent Systems for Ocean Logistics. In: Proceedings of The Fourth International Conference on Autonomous Agents and Multi Agent Systems (AAMAS 2005). Holland (July 2005) (2005)

[8] Himoff, J., Rzevski, G., Skobelev, P.: Magenta Technology: Multi-Agent Logistics i-Scheduler for Road Transportation. In: Proceedings of The Fifth International Conference on Autonomous Agents and Multi Agent Systems (AAMAS 2006). Japan (May 2006) (2006)

[9] Glashenko, A., Inozemtzev, S., Grachev, I., Skobelev, P.: Magenta Technology: Case Studies of Magenta i-Scheduler for Road Transportation. In: Proceedings of The Six International Conference on Autonomous Agents and Multi Agent Systems (AAMAS 2007) Hawaii (May 2007) (2007) (in publication)

[10] Vittikh, V.A., Skobelev, P.O.: Multi-Agent Models of Matching in Open Demand and Resource Networks. Automatics and Telemechanics 1, 177–185 (2003)

[11] Vittikh, V., Gritsenko, E., Karavaev, M., Skobelev, P., Tsarev, A., Shamashov, M.: Multi-Agent System for Social Services based on Social Passports and Smart Cards of Citizen. In: Proceedings of The Six International Conference on Autonomous Agents and Multi Agent Systems (AAMAS 2007). Hawaii (May 2007) (2007) (in publication)

An Agent Based Modelling Approach for Stochastic Planning Parameters

Wilhelm Dangelmaier, Benjamin Klöpper, and Alexander Blecken

Heinz Nixdorf Institute, University of Paderborn,
Fürstenallee 11, 33102 Paderborn, Germany
{whd,kloepper,blecken}@hni.upb.de
http://www.hni.upb.de/cim

Abstract. Many planning problems are influenced by stochastical environmental factors. There are several planning algorithms from various application domains which are able to handle stochastic parameters. Correct information about these stochastic parameters has impact on the quality of plans. There is a lack of sufficient research on how to obtain this information. In this paper, we introduce a Multiagent System (MAS) that is able to model stochastic parameters and to provide up-to-date information about these parameters. Due to their access to locally available informations expert agents are used, which apply the paradigm of Bayesian Thinking in order to provide high quality information to planning agents.

1 Introduction

Uncertain or probabilistic factors are inherent to many realistic planning tasks such as production planning, vehicle scheduling and routing, and investment planning amongst others. Examples for uncertain factors include but are not limited to:

- from production planning: machine failures or scrap rate.
- from vehicle scheduling: traffic jam or vehicle breakdowns.
- from investment planning: saving rates or the development of markets.

The planning task itself can be characterized as the task of coming up with a sequence of activities or actions in such a way that a goal state is achieved. It is desirable that this sequence is optimal or at least sufficiently good according to some quality metric, e.g. costs or execution times. Both, the achievement of the goal state and the resulting quality metric are heavily influenced by stochastic factors. Thus, it is necessary to include this uncertainty into the planning process and provide accurate information about these factors to the planning entity, regardless whether it may be a human or an automated planner. By applying the Bayesian Thinking paradigm, we can estimate stochastic variables with partial knowledge of their influences and their conditional probability distributions. Furthermore, established planning techniques are able to include probabilistic

V. Mařík, V. Vyatkin, A.W. Colombo (Eds.): HoloMAS 2007, LNAI 4659, pp. 225–236, 2007.

information. In this paper we introduce a multiagent system in which expert agents can provide information about uncertain factors in planning problems by performing distributed probabilistic inferences. The remainder of this paper is structured as follows: In the next section we will describe the problem addressed in this contribution in a more detailed manner. The third section gives an overview of the relevant techniques of probabilistic reasoning and planning techniques. The concept of Bayesian expert agents which can provide a posteriori information about the uncertain factors of a planning problem is introduced in the fourth section. Section five describes an application scenario for this kind of planning. The application scenario is taken from the field of logistics, where a vehicle has to find a shortest path in order to fulfil a transport job.

2   Problem Statement

This section introduces our model for planning problems under uncertainty. We understand a planning problem as a repeated decision problem with an underlying discrete time model. In each step a decision which available activity should be carried out is required. The course of events and situations during the execution of a plan is directed by several factors. The first and only controllable factor are the activities or actions carried out in the plan. These activities intend to change the former states. The change in the states is caused by the effects of an activity, e.g. by physical forces created by the activity. The actual effects of an activity are influenced by both the environment's and the executing system's state. Overall the planning problem is defined by the tuple (A, S, I, E) where:

- A is the set of possible activities
- S is the set of possible states
- E is the set of possible effects of the activities
- I is the set of possible influences towards the activity effects

Figure 1 illustrates the structure of the planning problem. Possible activities are mapped to links, and situations resulting from actions are mapped to nodes. The nodes encompass three elements: the environmental influences on an action, the effects of an action under consideration of environmental influences, and the situation that results from the effects. The root of the tree is atomic and contains only the initial situation for the given planning problem. Technically we are looking for the following transition functions:

- $T : S \times A \to I$
- $T' : I \times A \to E$
- $T'' : E \times S \to S$

The function T determines the environmental influences towards the effects of an actvity performed in a specific situation. When the actual influences are known, T' defines the effects an influenced action has to the system and its environment. Finally, T'' determines the resulting next situation from the former situation and the effects. The problem tackled in this paper is the implementation of the transition functions T, T', T'' in order to include this information into a planning process. Since most of the uncertain factors depend on the enviromental influences, the use of expert knowledge about the environment is of crucial importance.

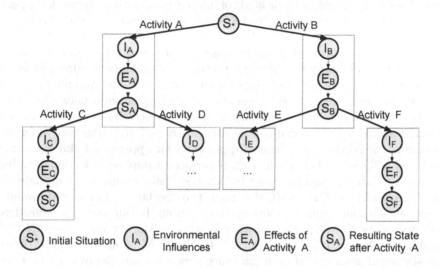

Fig. 1. A Plan Tree

3 Related Work

This section gives a short overview of related work. We will focus on techniques, which can cope with uncertainty and estimation problems. A subsection provides a selection of planning approaches able to cope with uncertainty and probabilistic variables.

3.1 Probabilistic Reasoning

The techniques of probabilistic reasoning can be applied to implement the transition functions T, T', and T''. Pearl [17] describes the application and potential of so-called Bayesian Networks. Bayes theorem allows more precise calculation of a posteriori probability distribution on the basis of former a priori probabilities, when some additonal knowledge about the world is given. This *knowledge about the world* is refered to as evidence. Hard and soft evidence are distinguished, where hard evidence denote a fact that is known for sure and a soft evidence means that an a posteriori probability for the fact is available. A Bayesian Network is a directed, acyclic graph (G,V) with directed edges $e \in G$ and nodes $v \in V$. Nodes represent discrete or continuous variables. A directed edge $e \in G$ from node X_i to node X_j denotes that variable X_j depends on X_i. This dependency is quantified by the conditional probability distribution $P(X_i|Parents(X_i))$ for each node in the network [4]. Bayesian Networks with both discrete and continuous variables are called hybrid networks. According to Jensen [11], Gaussian distributions are the only applicable continuous probabability distributions. Other distributions cannot be used for the lack of mathematical concepts. There are four kinds of inference a Bayesian Network supports: diagnostic inference, intercausal inference, mixed inference, and causal inference, which is most relevant for our problem. Causal inference forecasts events depending on the knowledge about possible causes. Inference can be performed in two ways: exactly and approximately. The runtime and memory requirement for exact inference is always NP-hard. Application of dynamic programming improves both runtime and memory requirements for singly connected networks. A further algorithm that is feasible for singly connected networks is Pearl's Message Passing Algorithm [17], which can be used for causal and diagnostic inference. Because of the NP-hardness several approaches for approximate inference were developed [19]. Some of these algorithms are prior sampling, rejection sampling, likelihood weighting, and inference by Markov chain simulation, especially the Markov chain Monte Carlo (MCMC) algorithm. So far, we introduced probability models without explicit representation of time. In our work, we considered two approaches with explicit time representation: Markov processes (MP) [12] and dynamic Bayesian Networks (DBN) [16]. Both, MP and DBN model time as time slices and assume that each time slice contains a number of non-observable variables X_t and a number of observable variables E_t. A process, spanning over a number of time slices, is called a Markov process, when the state of the current time slice depends only on a finite number of predecessor time slices. The Markov property avoids the need for consideration of an infinite number of predecessor time slices. First order MP can be described by an initial distribution $P(X_0)$ and a transition probability $P(X_{t+1}|X_t)$. The concept of DBN extends Markov processes by a sensor model $P(E_t|X_t)$. The sensor model is the connection between the non-observable variables X_t and the observable variables E_t. The full joint distribution of a DBN that is based on a first order MP is be given by:

$$P(X_0, X_1, ..., X_t, E_1, ...E_t) = P(X_0) \prod_{i=1}^{t} P(X_i|X_{i-1})P(E_i|X_i). \qquad (1)$$

Four kinds of inference in DBN can be distinguished: Filtering (calculation of the current belief state for X_t), Forecasting (calculation of a future state), Smoothing (calculation of a distribution of former time slice k: $X_k|e_{1:t}, 1 \leq k < t$), and finding the most likely sequence of states, which lead to the current state. For planning problems, filtering and forecasting are most relevant since filtering determines the belief state of the current situation while forecasting estimates the future development of the DBN. Thus, the combination of the two inference processes can enable an estimation based on current knowledge.

Due to the structural similarity of Bayesian Networks and plan trees, it is obvious to use Bayesian Networks to implement the transition functions of the plan tree. The nodes and node elements can be mapped to variables in a Bayesian Network. Conditional probability functions define the actual transition functions.

3.2 Planning Algorithms

In artificial intelligence *planning* is defined as the task of finding a sequence of actions which lead from a given initial state to a desired state. Conventional planners assume deterministic environments, where change only happens when the planning agents act and the result of actions is known certainly in advance. However, more recent research tries to relax this assumption [3]. Planning algorithms under consideration of random variables is the objective of some of this research. Examples of such planning algorithms are Buridan [13], C-Buridan [8], DRIPS [9], and Weaver [2]. Weaver has the most advanced representation of stochastic variables. It combines conditional planning and probabilistic reasoning. Weaver includes exogenous events, which influence actions and dynamically constructs a Bayesian Network to calculate the joint probability distribution of the plan. Nevertheless, Weaver does not include external knowledge about the environment and is restricted to a priori knowledge included in the action definition. There are algorithms related to logistics which can handle stochastic information as well. Examples are given in [18] (which is similar to the application example in this paper) and [15]. These domain specific algorithms have the same shortcomings as the domain independent AI planner – they do not incorporate up-to-date information about the stochastic nature of the environment.

4   Agent Based Modelling of Stochastic Parameters

In this section we introduce our concept of a distributed agent-based modelling of stochastic planning parameters. The basic idea is to provide expert knowledge about aspects of the environment to agents. Planning agents can query the expert agents about some aspects of the environment. These queries provide a posteriori information which the agents generate during the planning process. This information includes how and which actions will be performed and what the status of the planning agents (respectively the system the agent generates the plan for) is. Figure 2 illustrates the genreal principle of the agent-based approach for probabilistic planning. It follows the *planning as search* paradigm, which implies that planning problems can be solved by state-space search (see [19]). After the initialization of the given planning problem the planning agent repeatedly selects a node from the plan tree and a respecitve activity in order to expand the tree towards the goal state. For each situation and activity couple, the planning agent can query a number of expert agents. Depending on the information embedded in the queries the expert agents return the current a posteriori probability distributions of a subset of effects of the activity. The planning agent uses this information to calculate the successor state of the currently selected state and activity. The planning process terminates when either a satisfying goal

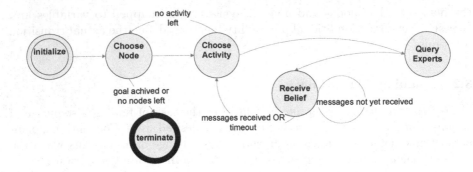

Fig. 2. Agent Based Probabilistic Planning as Finite State Machine

state is found or if no further expansion of the plan tree is possible - in this case, the planning process has failed.

There several reasons to use an agent based approach to model the stochastic parameters of planning problems. First, the fragmentation helps to reduce the complexity of the modelling task. It is much easier to provide a probabilistic model for a small section of the real world then providing a large model for the world at once. Furthermore, the inference process can easily be distributed on several physical machines in order to speed up the processing times. Of course, the planning process must be executed concurrently in order to realize a speed up.

Finally the most important advantage of the agent based modelling approach is the possibility to embed the expert agents in the environment. Doing so, facts of the world are acessible for the expert agent by sensors. Thus, they have direct access to hard evidences which will help to calculate precise a posteriori probabilities. If an agent is embedded in an enviroment for a long time, it is able to record historical data about the various probability variables in his world model and can start to learn the structure and probability distributions of the network autonomously.

4.1 Modelling the Expert Knowledge

Information is provided to the expert agents in form of hybrid Bayesian Networks. In these hybrid networks continuous variables have Gaussian distributions. Figure 3 shows an example of such a Bayesian Network. A problem that arises from the network structure is that the continuous variables can have discrete child nodes. Continuous parents are discretisized for inference. The resulting conditional distribution of the child nodes maps combinations of intervals of the continuous parent variables to likelihoods of the characteristics of the discrete variable according to laws of probability theory. For the opposite case of a continuous variable with discrete parent nodes, Jensen [10] claims that only conditional Gaussian distributions can be handled by the network. If the parent nodes are independent and if the distribution of the child node can be represented as a linear combination of the normally distributed parent nodes, it is possible to calculate a joint probability distribution of the continuous child node using the reproduction and transformation properties of Gaussian distributions:

$$P(C) \approx \mathcal{N}\left(\sum_{i=1}^{n} p_i \mu_i, \sqrt{\sum_{i=1}^{n}(p_i \sigma_i)^2}\right) \tag{2}$$

Figure 3 shows a Bayesian Network from our application example – the shortest path problem. An important property of Bayesian Networks of expert agents is displayed: The existence of only one queried variable. In this case, the *ride duration* is the queried variable. The restriction of one queried variable per network also limits the time required for inference to polynomial time in not singly connected networks. If the planning agent is interested in more than one stochastic variable, the expert agents must perform an inference process for each queried variable. Since the number of planning relevant stochastic variables is much smaller than the number of variables in an expert network, this procedure saves computation time: For a given number of queried variables, the inference time is simply multiplied with a constant factor. However, this procedure reduces the accuracy of the inference, since side effects between variables from other Bayesian Networks are not considered.

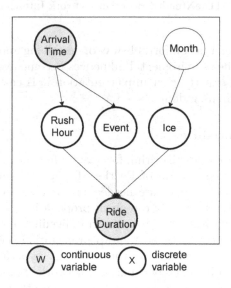

Fig. 3. An Expert Network

We implemented a generic agent class able to perform the inference procedure described in the following section. We used the development framework JADE [1]. Each expert agent can be provided with an XML-file describing the expert knowledge. We call the document type XBIF (eXtended Bayesian Network Interchange), which is an extension to Cozman's XMLBIF [5]. The extension was necessary, because XMLBIF does not support continuous variables.

```
1   <!-- DTD for XBIF v.01 -->
2   <!ELEMENT XBIF ( NETWORK )*>
3       <!ATTLIST BIF VERSION CDATA #REQUIRED>
4   <!ELEMENT NETWORK ( ( PROPERTY | VARIABLE | DEFINITION )* )>
5   <!ATTLIST NETWORK NAME ID #REQUIRED TEMPLATE CDATA #IMPLIED
6               TOPOLOGY CDATA #IMPLIED>
7   <!ELEMENT VARIABLE ( ((OUTCOME | INTERVAL) |  PROPERTY )* ) >
8       <!ATTLIST VARIABLE
9       NAME ID #REQUIRED
10      TYPE (discrete|continuous|continuous_time) "discrete">
11  <!ELEMENT OUTCOME (#PCDATA)>
12  <!ELEMENT INTERVAL (#PCDATA)>
13  <!ELEMENT DEFINITION ( GIVEN | (TABLE | FUNCTION) | PROPERTY )* >
14   <!ATTLIST DEFINITION FOR CDATA #REQUIRED>
15  <!ELEMENT FOR (#PCDATA)>
16  <!ELEMENT GIVEN (#PCDATA)>
17  <!ATTLIST GIVEN MEAN_VALUES CDATA #IMPLIED STD_DEVS CDATA #IMPLIED>
18  <!ELEMENT TABLE (#PCDATA)>
19  <!ELEMENT FUNCTION ( PARAM* )>
20   <!ATTLIST FUNCTION TYPE (gaussian) "gaussian">
21  <!ELEMENT PARAM (#PCDATA)>
22   <!ATTLIST PARAM NAME CDATA #REQUIRED>
23  <!ELEMENT PROPERTY (#PCDATA)>
```

Listing 1.1. DTD eXtended Bayesian Network Interchange Format

With the XBIF format a comfortable way of describing and modelling stochastic parameters and their enviromental influences become available. In combination with the JADE expert agent implementation it is easy to implement our concept in various planning domains.

4.2 Inference Procedure

We decided to implement an algorithm for exact inference in our prototype. The algorithm is a simplified version of Pearl's Message Passing Algorithm. Only mechanisms for causal inference are needed in our case, because there is only one queried node. Therefore, only top-down propagation is required. According to Pearl this is the calculation of the a posteriori likelihood for a queried variable depending on its parents. As no bottom-up propagation (i.e. calculation of the a posteriori likelihood depending on the children) is performed, the network does no longer need to be a singly connected network. Thus, we allow influence variables on the highest level to be connected to more than one child node, e.g. the node arrival time in figure 3. For a more detailed description of the inference procedure implemented in our application example see [7].

4.3 Interaction Between Agents

The planning agents are supposed to query the expert agents about the stochastic parameters of their planning problem. In order to get the most accurate information the query includes information on which action is supposed to be carried out as well as where and when it is supposed to be carried out. Figure 4 illustrates the querying process in case of the shortest path problem. The plan itself is modelled as a Dynamic Bayesian Network and the stochastic parameters, which are constantly required for decision making are updated in every time slice.

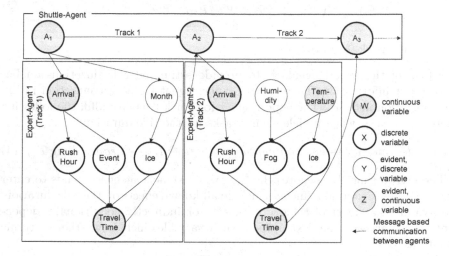

Fig. 4. Interaction of Agents

5   Application Scenario

Our concept of expert agents providing information about stochastic parameters of planning problems is demonstrated as a MAS in a railway scenario for logistics. In [6] we introduced a MAS for transport planning in a demand driven railway scenario. A number of vehicle agents compete against each other to get a transport order. An important subtask during the competition is the search for an optimal path. The MAS was extended in order to cope with uncertain travel times on tracks. We called the resulting planning algorithm *Belief Dijkstra*.

5.1   The Vehicle Agent

One important task of the vehicle agents in our MAS is the calculation of a shortest path between two stations in the transportation network. For this task the vehicle agent performs the Dijkstra algorithm. The new version of our MAS works no longer with fixed ride durations, but treats ride durations as probability variables. We define the following variable within our model:

- $A_{i,j}$ is the time when a vehicle agents enters track $tr_{i,j}$,
- $I_{i,j}$ the influences to the ride duration on track $tr_{i,j}$

The vehicle agents use the distribution of the travel time $T_{i,j}$ on track $tr_{i,j}$ in a modified version of the Dijkstra algorithm, which we call Belief Dijkstra. If $T_{i,j}$ indicates an improvement of a shortest path, $tr_{i,j}$ is temporarily saved as the predecessor of $tr_{j,k}$. The vehicle agent calculates the distribution of the arrival time $A_{j,k}$ at $tr_{j,k}$ on basis of $T_{i,j}$:

$$\sigma_{A_{j,k}} = \sqrt{\sigma^2_{A_{i.j}} + \sigma^2_{T_{i.j}}} \quad and \quad \mu_{A_{j,k}} = \mu_{A_{i.j}} + \mu_{T_{i.j}} \tag{3}$$

5.2   The Track Agents

The task of the expert agents is to provide estimated ride durations on basis of input information. There is one expert agent for each connection in the transportation network. The expert agent for track t has to fulfill the following inference process, when vehicle agent v asks for the ride duration:

$$Arrival\ Time\ A_{i,j} \rightarrow environmental\ influences\ I_{i,j} \rightarrow Travel\ Time\ T_{i,j} \quad (4)$$

The arrival time $A_{i,j}$ denotes the time when vehicle agent v intends to enter track $tr_{i,j}$. The external influences include all known effects on the ride duration. We assume that most of them are directly or indirectly conditionally dependent on the arrival time. Examples of such variables include weather or traffic situations.

5.3   Finding the Shortest Path

The vehicle agents use the distributions of ride durations as input for the path-finding algorithm. Therefore, the agents must be provided with these distributions. The vehicle agents can query one of the expert agents for the distribution of $T_{i,j}$. The vehicle agent sends the arrival time at track 1 to the corresponding expert agent. The expert agent can calculate the conditional probability distribution auf $T_{i,j}$ and sends it to the vehicle agent. The vehicle agent is able to calculate the distribution of $A_{i,j}$ and to proceed with the next track and track expert. The vehicle agents combine the local Bayesian networks of the agent system dynamically to a distributed Bayesian network, in which the inference process is also performed distributedly. The Belief Dijkstra has the same complexity as the conventional Dijkstra: $O(n^2 + m)$ with n nodes and m edges in the transportation network. If the starting time or the probability distribution for the starting time is given and cannot be varied, every track agent is queried exactly once. The number of queries can be reduced by exclusion of obviously unfavorable tracks based on their length and the maximum travel speed.

5.4   Evaluation

In order to evaluate the system, we used three different railway networks with 100, 150, and 300 stations. In several planning and simulation runs the *Belief Dijkstra* was compared to a classical Dijkstra algorithm, using average travel times. The *Belief Dijkstra* resulted in shorter routes, Figure 5 shows the travel time savings for six different start and destination combinations. For more details about the MAS see [7].

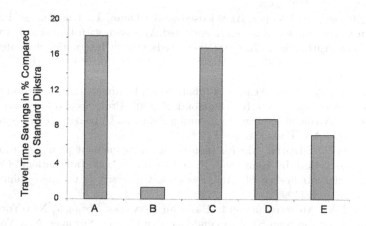

Fig. 5. Travel Time Savings by Belief Dijkstra

6   Conclusion

In this paper we introduced how a MAS can be used to model the stochastic parameters of planning problems and how agent interactions can help to improve the plan. The application of expert agents allows to model extensive information about the stochastic influences from the environment during the planning. The paradigm of Bayesian Thinking was used to provide the information in a most accurate and up-to-date manner. In our opinion, the overall idea of our approach is generally applicable. We intend to use expert agents in a variety of other application scenarios, e.g. the planning of the energy management of a railway shuttle and the selection of a controller implementation in a reconfigurable engine control.

References

1. Bellifemine, F., Rimassa, G., Poggi, A.: JADE - A FIPA-compliant agent framework. In: Proceedings of the 4th International Conference and Exhibition on the Practical Application of Intelligent Agents and Multi-Agents, London, pp. 97–108 (1999)
2. Blythe, J.: Planning Under Uncertainty in Dynamic Domains. PhD thesis, Carnegie Mellon University Computer Science Department (May 1998)
3. Blythe, J.: An Overview of Planning Under Uncertainty. In: Wooldridge, M.J., Veloso, M. (eds.) Artificial Intelligence Today. LNCS (LNAI), vol. 1600, pp. 85–110. Springer, Heidelberg (1999)
4. Charniak, E.: Bayesian Networks without Tears. AI MAGAZINE (1991)

5. Cozman, Gagliardi, F.: XMLBIF: version 0.3 (2001),
   http://www.cs.cmu.edu/javabayes/Home/index.html
6. Dangelmaier, W., Franke, H.: Decentralized management for transportation-logistics: A multi agent based approach. Integrated Computer-Aided Engineering 10(2), 203–210 (2003)
7. Dangelmaier, W., Klöpper, B., Wienstroer, J., Timm, T.: The Shortest Path Problem in Uncertain Domains - an Agentbased Approach with Bayesian Networks. In: Abraham, Ajith, Chen, Yuehui. (Hrsg.) (eds.) Sixth International Conference Intelligent Systems Design and Applications, vol. 2, pp. 943–948. IEEE Computer Society Press, Los Alamitos (2006)
8. Draper, D., Hanks, S., Weld, D.: Probabilistic planning with information gathering and contingent execution. In: Hammond, K. (ed.) Proc. Second International Conference on Artificial Intelligence Planning Systems, University of Chicago, Illinois, pp. 31–37. AAAI Press, Stanford (1994)
9. Haddawy, P., Suwaridi, M.: Decision-theoretic refinement planning using inheritance abstraction. In: Hammond, K. (ed.) Proc. Second International Conference on Artificial Intelligence Planning Systems, University of Chicago, Illinois, AAAI Press, Stanford (1994)
10. Jensen, F.V.: An Introduction to Bayesian Networks. Springer, New York (1996)
11. Jensen, F.V.: Bayesian Networks and Decision Graphs. Springer, New York (2001)
12. Krylov, N.V.: Introduction to the Theory of Random Processes. Amer. Math. Society, Graduate Studies in Mathematics 43 (2002)
13. Kushmerick, N., Hanks, S., Weld, D.: An algorithm for probabilistic planning. Artificial Intelligence 76(1-2), 239–286 (1995)
14. Lauritzen, S., Spiegelhalter, D.J.: Local computations with probabilities on graphical structures and their application to expert systems. Journal of the Royal Statistical Society B 50(2), 157–224 (1988)
15. Liu, B., Lai, K.K.: Stochastic programming models for vehicle routing problems. In: Focus on computational neurobiology, pp. 13–27. Nova Science Publisher, Inc. Commack (2004)
16. Murphy, K.P.: Dynamic Bayesian Networks: Representation, Inference and Learning. Doctoral Thesis. UMI Order Number: AAI3082340 (2002)
17. Pearl, J.: Probabilistic Reasoning in Intelligent Systems - Networks of Plausible Inference. Morgan Kaufmann, San Francisco (1988)
18. Polychronopoulos, G.H., Tsitsiklis, J.N.: Stochastic Shortest Path Problems with recourse. Networks 27(2), 133–143 (1996)
19. Russell, Norvig, S., Peter.: Artificial Intelligence - A Modern Approach, 2nd edn. Prentice-Hall, Englewood Cliffs (2003)

A Holonic Metamodel for Agent-Oriented Analysis and Design

Massimo Cossentino[1,2], Nicolas Gaud[1], Stéphane Galland[1], Vincent Hilaire[1],
and Abderrafiâa Koukam[1]

[1] Multiagent Systems Group,
System and Transport Laboratory
University of Technology of Belfort Montbéliard
90010 Belfort cedex, France
{massimo.cossentino,nicolas.gaud,stephane.galland,
vincent.hilaire,abder.koukam}@utbm.fr
http://set.utbm.fr
[2] ICAR Institute,
National Research Council,
Palermo, Italy
http://www.pa.icar.cnr.it/~cossentino

Abstract. Holonic multiagent systems (HMAS) offers a promising software engineering approach for developing applications in complex domains characterized by a hierarchical structure. However the process of building MASs and HMASs is mostly different from the process of building more traditional software systems and it introduces new design and development issues. Against this background, this paper introduces organization-oriented abstractions for agent-oriented software engineering. We propose a complete organizational meta-model as the basis of a future complete methodology that will spread from requirements analysis to code production. In addition to dealing with this last aspect, we introduce our platform, called Janus, that we specifically designed to implement and deploy holonic multiagent systems by adopting concepts like role and organization as the leading issues of the analysis-development process.

Keywords: Agent Oriented Software Engineering, Holonic Modeling, Methodology, Holonic multiagent systems.

1 Introduction

Sociological concepts have always been a source of inspiration for multiagent researches and recently the agent community has been returning the favor by exploring the potential of agent-based models for studying sociological phenomena (e.g. [1,2,3]). The result of this interaction has been the formalization of a number of sociological, psychological and philosophical concepts with important applications in engineering agent systems. *Holon* and organizational concepts like *Role* and *Organization* are examples of these important concepts. For a

V. Mařík, V. Vyatkin, A.W. Colombo (Eds.): HoloMAS 2007, LNAI 4659, pp. 237–246, 2007.

successful application and deployment of MAS, methodologies are essential [4]. Methodologies try to provide an explicit frame of the process to model and design software applications. Several methodologies have been proposed for MAS [5] and some of them with a clear organizational vision (e.g. [6]). Most of these methodologies recognize that the process of building MASs is mostly different from the process of building more traditional software systems. In particular, they all recognize (to varying extents) the idea that a MAS can be conceived in terms of an organized society of individuals in which each agent plays specific roles and interacts with other agents [7,6]. However, most of them consider agents as atomic entities thus rendering them inappropriate for Holonic MAS (HMAS). In our approach the role is emphasized as a fundamental entity spreading from requirements to implementation. Notice that some of the most known implementation platforms (Jade [8], FIPA-OS [9] and some others) usually do not support the role concept. In our point-of-view the role element offers a number of advantages, e.g. a greater reusability, modularity of developed solutions, and finally encourages a quicker development with less code bugs.

The approach presented in this paper is based on a meta-model for HMAS. It provides a step-by-step guide from requirements to code and it can model a system at different levels of details by using a suite of refinement methods. We propose a meta-model, namely HoloPASSI, as a basis of extension of the PASSI methodology [10] to deal with the analysis and design of HMAS.

The goal of this paper is not to describe the complete methodological process but it rather provides some organization-oriented abstractions that will become the basis of this process. The elements of the meta-model are organized in three different domains. The problem domain deals with the user's problem in terms of requirements, organization, role and ontology. The Agency Domain addresses the holonic solution to the problem described in the previous domain. Finally, the Solution Domain describes the structure of the code solution in the chosen implementation platform. The platform Janus that was developed in our labobatory is selected. It is specifically designed to implement and deploy HMAS. This paper is organized as follows. Section 2 briefly summarizes previous works on Holonic Systems and outlines the key points behind the concept of holon. Section 3 will detail the Problem, Agency and Solution domains of our meta-model.

2   Theoretical Background

The concept of holon is central to our discussion and therefore a definition of what is a holon should be helpful before proceeding. In multiagent systems, the vision of holons is much closer to the one that MAS researchers have of *Recursive* or *Composed* agents. A holon constitutes a way to gather local and global, individual and collective points of view. A holon is thus a self-similar structure composed of holons as sub-structures and the hierarchical structure composed of holons is called a *holarchy*. A holon can be seen, depending on the level of observation, either as an autonomous "atomic" entity or as an organization of holons (this is often called the *Janus effect*).

Two overlapping aspects have to be distinguished in holons: the first is directly related to the holonic nature of the entity (a holon, called super-holon, is composed of other holons, called sub-holons or members) and deals with the government and the administration of a super-holon. This aspect is common to every holon and thus called the *holonic* aspect. The second aspect is related to the problem to solve and the work to be done. It depends on the application or application domain. It is therefore called the *production* aspect.

Holonic Systems have been applied to a wide range of applications, Manufacturing systems [11,12], Health organizations [13], Transportation [14], Adaptive Mesh Problem [15], Cooperative work [16] to mention a few. Thus it is not surprising that a number of models and frameworks have been proposed for these systems, for example PROSA [17], MetaMorph [12]. However, most of them are strongly attached to their domain of application and use specific agent architectures. In order to allow a modular and reusable modeling phase that minimizes the impact on the underlying architecture, a meta-model based on an organizational approach is proposed. The adopted definition of role comes from [18]: *"Roles identify the activities and services necessary to achieve social objectives and enable to abstract from the specific individuals that will eventually perform them. From a society design perspective, roles provide the building blocks for agent systems that can perform the role, and from the agent design perspective, roles specify the expectations of the society with respect to the agents activity in the society"*. However, in order to obtain generic models of organizations, it is required to define a role without making any assumptions on the agent which will play this role. To deal with this issue the concept of capacity was defined [19]. A capacity is a pure description of a know-how. A role may require that individuals playing it have some specifics capacities to properly behave as defined. An individual must know a way of realizing all required capacities to play a role.

3   Engineering Holons

As PASSI, the HoloPASSI methodology introduces three domains. The first is the problem domain dedicated to the description of a problem independently of a specific solution. The second is the agency domain which introduces agent concepts to describe an agent solution on the basis of the elements of the problem domain. The third and last domain is the solution domain which includes the elements used to implement at the code level the solution described in the second domain. The following sub-sections describe these three domains. The HoloPASSI meta-model is described by an UML class diagram in figure 1. Each domain is separated by a dashed line.

3.1   Problem Domain

The PASSI, and then HoloPASSI, methodologies are driven by requirements. Thus the starting phase is the *Functional Requirements* and *Non Functional Requirements* analysis. (Functional) Requirements can be identified by using

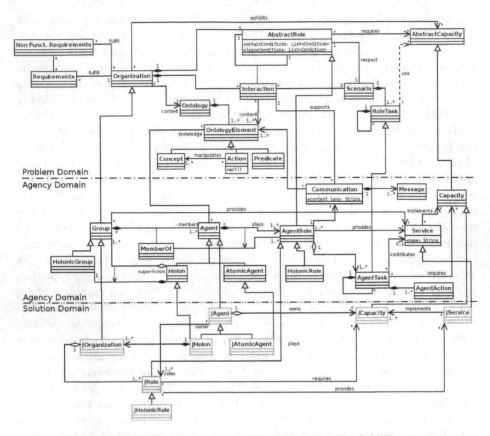

Fig. 1. The Organizational Meta-Model of HoloPASSI

classical techniques such as use cases. Each requirement is associated to an *Organization* (see figure 1). An *Organization* is defined by a set of *AbstractRoles*, their *Interactions* and a common context. The associated context (and therefore the operating environment too) is defined according to an ontology. An ontology is described in terms of *concepts* (categories, entities of the domain), *predicates* (assertions on concepts properties), *actions* (performed in the domain) and their relationships. The aim of an organization is to fulfill one or more (functional and non functional) requirements. An *Interaction* is composed of the event produced by a first role, perceived by a second one, and the reaction(s) produced by the second role. The sequence of events from one to the other can be iterated several times and includes a not a priori specified number of events and participants. These roles must be defined in the same organization. Figure 2 details an example of an organization and its associated ontology. The *Project Management* organization in figure 2(a) defines two roles *Manager* and *Employee*, and two interactions *Supervise* and *Assigns*. The context of the organization is defined according to the domain ontology described in figure 2(b). As described by

John H Holland: "The behavior of a whole complex adaptive system[*cas*] is more than a simple sum of the behaviors of its parts; *cas* abound non linearity" [20]. The notion of capacity was introduced to control and exploit these additional behaviors, emerging from roles interactions, by considering an organization as able to provide a capacity. It describes what an organization is able to do. Organizations used to model roles interactions offer a simple way to represent how these capacities are obtained from the roles.

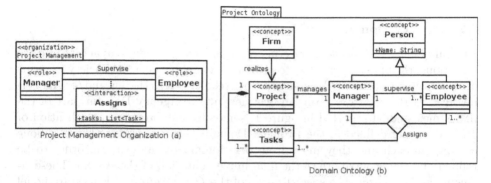

Fig. 2. Organization and Ontology description using two specific UML profiles for class diagram

Let us now consider our previous example of the Project Management organization. The role *Manager* requires for example the capacity of choosing between various employee the most appropriate one to fulfill a task. Each entity wishing to play the *Manager* role must have an implementation of this capacity (through a service for instance implementing a classical algorithm). The choice between various employees effectively depends on personal characteristics of the entity (e.g. Acquaintances, Beliefs). Basing the description of role behavior on capacities, thus gives to the role more genericity and modularity.

An *AbstractRole* is the abstraction of a behavior in a certain context defined by the organization and confers a status within this context. The status is defined as a set of rights and obligations made available to the role, and also defines the way the entity playing the role is perceived by other entities playing another role in the same organization. Specifically, the status gives the playing entity the right to exercise its capacities. To clearly understand this status aspect, let us return to our preceding example. The status of *Manager* gives the right to use his authority to assign a task to one of his subordinates. No *Employee* will be surprised if a *Manager* uses his authority, because the way under which *Employee* perceive their responsible (status), gives him this right. Another important aspect is that the role (and not the individual, like an agent or a holon, who plays the role) belongs to the organization. This means that the same individual may participate to an organization by playing one or more roles that are perceived as different (and not necessarily related) by the organization. Besides, the same individual can play the same or a different role in other organizations.

The goal of each *AbstractRole* is to contribute to (a part of) the requirements of the organization within which it is defined. The behavior of a *AbstractRole* is specified within a *Scenario*. Such a scenario describes how a goal can be achieved. It is the description of how to combine and order interactions, external events, and RoleTasks to fulfill a (part of a) requirement (the goal). A *RoleTask* is the specification of a parameterized behavior in form of a coordinated sequence of subordinate units (a *RoleTask* can be composed of other *RoleTasks*). The definition of these units can be based on capacities, required by the role.

3.2   Agency Domain

After modeling the problem in terms of organizations, roles, capacities and interactions, the objective is, now, to provide a model of the agent society in terms of social interactions and dependencies between entities (Holons and/or Agents) involved in the solution. From an overview at the Agency Domain part of the HMAS meta-model reported in figure 1, some elements are the specialization of other elements defined in the Problem Domain. They constitute the backbone of our approach and they move from one domain to the other in order to be refined and they contribute to the final implementation of the system. These elements are: (*i*) *Group* is a specialization of the *Organization*. It is used to model groups of *Agents* that cooperate in order to achieve a goal. This element is further specialized in the *HolonicGroup* element that is a group devoted to contain roles taking care of the holon internal decision-making process (composed-holon's government). (*ii*) *AgentRole* is the specialization of *AbstractRole*. An *AgentRole* interacts with the others using communications (that are a more refined way for interacting compared to the simple Interactions allowed to the AbstractRole). Several *AgentRoles* are usually grouped in one *Agent* that is in turn a member of the *Group*. An *AgentRole* can be responsible for providing one of more services. (*iii*) *Capacity* is the specialization of the *AbstractCapacity*. It finds an implementation in the *Service* provided by roles and it is used to model what is required by an *AgentTask* in order to contribute in providing a service. (*iv*) *AgentTask* is the specialization of the *RoleTask*. It is aggregated in *AgentRole* and contributes to provide (a portion of) an *AgentRole*'s service. At this level of abstraction, this kind of task is no more considered atomic but it can be decomposed in finer grained *AgentActions*.

A very important element of the MAS meta-model is newly introduced in the Agency Domain; this is the *Agent*. An *Agent* is an entity which can play a set of roles defined within various organizations; these roles interact each other in the specific context provided by the agent itself. The *Agent* context is given by the knowledge, the capacities and the environment. Roles share this context by the simple fact of being part of the same agent. For instance, this means that an agent can play the role of *Buyer* in an organization and later the same agent can sell the goods it had just acquired thus playing for the same organization a different role (*Seller*); conversely, the same agent can also play roles that belong to another organization (for instance devoted to monitoring businesses) and thus it can play a role (*AffairMonitor*) to trace the results and the performance exploited during the first acquisition process. It is worth to note that the agent is still not an implementing element but rather it needs further refinements; only when it will become a JAgent (in the Solution Domain) it can really be coded. Figure 3(a) depicts the context defined by an agent as an interaction space for the roles it plays. These roles, in turn, belong to different organizations, each one defining its own context. An agent in our approach defines a particular context of interaction between roles belonging to different organizations. This aspect is depicted in figure 3(a).

The concept of *Holon* is specialized from the *Agent*. Naturally our definition of holon integrates the *production* and *holonic* aspects previously described in section 2 and it merges them within an organizational approach. A holon is thus a set of roles that can be defined on various organizations interacting in the specific context provided by the agent. A holon can play several roles in different organizations and be composed of other holons. A composed holon (super-holon) contains at least a single instance of a *holonic organization* to precise how members organize and manage the super-holon and a set (at least one) of *production organizations* describing how members interact and coordinate their actions to fulfill the super-holon tasks and objectives. An atomic (non composed) holon is an AtomicAgent. Figure 3(b) illustrates this definition of holon.

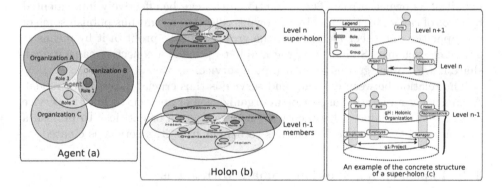

Fig. 3. Agent and Holon symbolic representation, and an example of the concrete structure of a super-holon

The holonic aspect considers how members organize and manage the super-holon. A specific organization, called *Holonic organization*, is defined to describe the government of a holon and its structure (in terms of authority, power repartition). Depending on the level of abstraction, a super-holon can be considered as an atomic entity (let's say level n) or as an organization of holons (let's say level n-1). In the same manner several different holons could be seen as interacting individuals, parts of some organization or as parts of a super-holon. These interactions usually happen in form of communications. Interactions between layers, instead, can happen in two ways: i) (internal) interactions of roles of the same agent if the same agent plays different roles within a holon. For instance, an agent can be the Head delegated to accept some contract (a role of the holonic organization, played at level n) but also the worker which will do part of the work related to that contract in the production organization at level n-1; the Agent existence in this case enables the interactions among the different roles. ii) (external) interactions (mostly communications) between roles at different layers of several agents. For instance the Head (layer n) responsible for accepting a contract asks worker roles (layer n-1) to provide the service.

Figure 3(c) illustrates the concrete structure of a super-holon *Project 1* composed of a *production* organization called *g1:Project* and an instance of the holonic organization.

An agent should be able to estimate the agent's competences in order to identify the most appropriate collaborators. The Capacity concept allows us to represent the competences of an agent or of a set of agents. A Capacity describes what an *Agent* should be able to do in order to satisfy the requirements it is responsible for. This means that the set of Capacities obtained by refining the AbstractCapacity of the Problem Domain, becomes the specification of the system requirements in the Agency Domain. Indeed, Capacities describe what the holon is capable of doing at an abstract level, independently of how it does it (this is a concern dealt by the Service concept).

A service implements a capacity thus accomplishing a set of functionalities on behalf of its owner: a role. These functionalities can be effectively implemented by a set of capacities required by the owner role. A role can thus publish some of its capacities and other members of the group can take profit of it by means of a service exchange. Similarly a group, able to provide a collective capacity can share it with other groups by providing a service.

The relation between capacity and service is thus crucial in our meta-model. A capacity is an internal aspect of an organization or an agent, while the service is designed to be shared between various organization or entities. To publish a capacity and thus allow other entities to benefit from it, a service is created.

3.3   Implementing Solution Domain with Janus

This part of the model is related to the Holon Implementation Model; its objective is to provide an implementation model of the solution. This part is thus dependent on the chosen implementation and deployment platform. A platform called *Janus*[1] was built in our lab. It is specifically designed to deal with the holonic and organizational aspects. The goal of Janus is to provide a full set of facilities for launching, displaying, developing and monitoring holons, roles and organizations.

The two main contributions of Janus are its native management of holons and its implementation of the notion of *Role*. In contrast with other platforms such as MadKit [21], JADE, FIPA-OS, the concept of Role in Janus is considered as a first class entity. It thus allows the user to directly implement organizational models without making any assumptions on the architecture of the holons that

---

[1] http://www.janus-project.org

will play the role(s) of this organization. An organization is defined by a set
of roles and a set of constraints to instantiate these roles (e.g. maximal number of authorized instances). Thus, organizations designed for an application
can be easily reused for another. Janus so promotes reusability and modularity,
moreover the use of organizational design patterns is strongly encouraged. Each
organization is a singleton and it can be instantiated by several groups. Group is
the runtime context of interaction. It contains a set of roles and a set of Holons
playing at least one of these roles. In addition to its characteristics and its personal knowledge, each agent/holon has mechanisms to manage the scheduling
of its own roles. It can change dynamically its roles during the execution of the
application (leave a role and request a new one). The life-cycle of each agent is
decomposed into three main phases : activation, life, termination. The life of an
agent consists in consecutively execute its set of roles and capacities. To describe
the personal competences of each agent/holon, Janus implements the concept of
JCapacity that is an abstract description of a competence; each agent can be
equipped from its birth or can dynamically acquire an implementation of a new
JCapacity (this function is still under development). In addition to the integration of these personal characteristics, a holon provides an execution context for
roles and capacities.

4   Conclusion

This article focuses on the key issues related to the identification of appropriate
abstractions for organizational software engineering and to the basis of a suitable methodology from requirement to implementation of complex applications
in terms of HMAS. In so doing, the two main contributions of this article are a
complete organizational meta-model for the analysis and design of complex systems, and a specific platform, *Janus*, designed to easily implement and deploy
models issued from the HoloPASSI meta-model. It fully implements organizational and holonic concepts. However it is also able to support more "traditional"
multiagent systems.

This work is a part of larger effort to provide a whole methodology and its
supporting set of tools for the analysis, design and implementation of complex
applications. Future works will deepen the meta-model concepts and associate
a methodology to guide the developer during his work of modeling and implementing a complex (and possibly holonic) multi-agent system.

References

1. Carley, K., Prietula, M. (eds.): Computational Organization Theory (1994)
2. Epstein, M., Axtell, R.: Growing Artificial Societies: Social Science from the
   Ground Up. MIT Press, Cambridge (1996)
3. Prietula, M., Carley, K., Gasser, L.: Simulating Organizations: Computational
   Models of Institutions and Groups. AAAI Press, Stanford (1998)
4. Gasser, L.: Mas infrastructure definitions, needs, prospects. In: Infrastructure for
   Agents, Multi-Agent Systems, and Scalable Multi-Agent Systems (01)

5. Iglesias, C., Garijo, M., Gonzalez, J.: A survey of agent oriented methodologies. In: Rao, A.S., Singh, M.P., Müller, J.P. (eds.) ATAL 1998. LNCS (LNAI), vol. 1555, pp. 313–327. Springer, Heidelberg (1999)
6. Zambonelli, F., Jennings, N., Wooldridge, M.: Developing multiagent systems: the gaia methodology. ACM Trans. on Software Engineering and Methodology 12(3) (2003)
7. Jennings, N.: On agent-based software engineering. Artificial Intelligence 177(2), 277–296 (2000)
8. Bellifemine, F., Poggi, A., Rimassa, G.: JADE: a FIPA2000 compliant agent development environment. In: Agents, 216–217 (2001)
9. Poslad, S., Buckle, P., Hadingham, R.: FIPA-OS: the FIPA agent platform available as open source. In: Practical Application of Intelligent Agents and Multi-Agent Technology (PAAM 2000), 355–368 (2000)
10. Cossentino, M.: IV: From Requirements to Code with the PASSI Methodology. In: Agent-Oriented Methodologies, 79–106 (2005)
11. Wyns, J.: Reference architecture for Holonic Manufacturing Systems - the key to support evolution and reconfiguration. PhD thesis, Katholieke Universiteit Leuven (1999)
12. Maturana, F.: MetaMorph: an adaptive multi-agent architecture for advanced manufacturing systems. PhD thesis, The University of Calgary (1997)
13. Ulieru, M., Geras, A.: Emergent holarchies for e-health applications: a case in glaucoma diagnosis. In: IEEE IECON 02. vol. 4, 2957–2961 (2002)
14. Bürckert, H., Fischer, K., Vierke, G.: Transportation scheduling with holonic mas - the teletruck approach. In: Conf. on Practical Applications of Intelligent Agents and Multiagents, pp. 577–590 (1998)
15. Rodriguez, S., Hilaire, V., Koukam, A.: Towards a methodological framework for holonic multi-agent systems. In: Workshop of Engineering Societies in the Agents World, pp. 179–185 (2003)
16. Adam, E.: Modele d'organization multi-agent pour l'aide au travail cooperatif dans les processus d'entreprise: application aux systemes administratif complexes. PhD thesis, Univ. de valenciennes et du hainaut-cambresis (2000)
17. Brussel, H.V., Wyns, J., Valckenaers, P., Bongaerts, L., Peeters, P.: Reference architecture for holonic manufacturing systems: Prosa. Computers in Industry 37, 255–274 (1998)
18. Dignum, V., Dignum, F.: Coordinating tasks in agent organizations. or: Can we ask you to read this paper? In: Coordination, Organization, Institutions and Norms Engineering Societies in the Agents' World (2006)
19. Rodriguez, S., Gaud, N., Hilaire, V., Galland, S., Koukam, A.: An analysis and design concept for self-organization in holonic multi-agent systems. In: Brueckner, S.A., Hassas, S., Jelasity, M., Yamins, D. (eds.) ESOA 2006. LNCS (LNAI), vol. 4335, pp. 15–27. Springer, Heidelberg (2007)
20. Holland, J.: Hidden order: how adaptation builds complexity (1995)
21. Ferber, J., Gutknecht, O., Michel, F.: From agents to organizations: an organizational view of multi-agent systems. In: Giorgini, P., Müller, J.P., Odell, J.J. (eds.) Agent-Oriented Software Engineering IV. LNCS, vol. 2935, pp. 214–230. Springer, Heidelberg (2004)

Using Adaptable Design to Classify Interactions Within a Distributed Control Architecture

Christopher Dan Fletcher, Robert William Brennan, and Peihua Gu

Schulich School of Engineering
University of Calgary, 2500 University Drive NW
Calgary, Alberta T2N 1N4, Canada
{cdfletch,rbrennan,pgu}@ucalgary.ca

Abstract. In this paper we apply Adaptable Design (AD) theory to the problem of fault monitoring and recovery in real-time distributed control systems. The approach draws on the close match between the functional architecture of a modular mechanical design and the functional architecture of distributed mechatronic systems and is based on the classification of interactions between the modules in these systems. The results of this work show that AD theory is applicable to fault monitoring and recovery in real-time distributed control and also has the potential for broader applications in the design of distributed mechatronic systems.

1 Introduction

Recently, there has been considerable interest in applying the techniques of object-oriented and agent-based systems to real-time industrial control problems. This level of control has traditionally been the domain of programmable logic controllers and embedded controllers, however advances in agent- and holonic-based planning and scheduling systems (Shen et al, 2006; McFarlane and Bussmann, 2003) have inspired a new generation of real-time distributed intelligent control research (Brennan, 2007).

Despite the promising early work in this area, some key challenges remain. For example, Hall et al. (2005) identify four barriers to wide-spread adoption of these systems: (1) lack of skills in distributed system design, (2) lack of a methodology to predict the aggregate behaviour of agents, (3) the cost of adoption and implementation, and (4) lack of mature global standards.

In this paper, we focus on the second area: the lack of formal design methodologies for these systems. More specifically, we are concerned with design for safety and the application of an analysis technique that allows the developer to monitor the overall health of a particular distributed control system design. Recent work in Adaptable Design focuses on the identification, classification, and quantifiable description of the many interactions (both functional and physical) within a mechanical design context (Fletcher et. al. 2006). This paper shows the first work in applying the ideas from Adaptable Design to the distributed control architecture for interaction classification. Also proposed is a scheme for fault monitoring and detection in distributed control architectures based on these ideas.

V. Mařík, V. Vyatkin, A.W. Colombo (Eds.): HoloMAS 2007, LNAI 4659, pp. 247–256, 2007.

We begin with an overview of the basic requirements for real-time distributed control in Section 2 with a focus on the requirements for safe operation. The paper builds on a general architecture for fault monitoring and recovery proposed in (Brennan and Norrie, 2002), which is summarised in Section 3 along with an analysis technique based on Adaptable Design theory that is used in conjunction with this architecture. Section 4 describes how this approach can be applied to the problem of fault monitoring and recovery, and Section 5 gives an example of the analysis. We conclude the paper with a discussion of the ongoing work in this area and its broader application to the second challenge noted by Hall et al. (2005).

2 Requirements for Real-Time Distributed Control

The motivation for our work in distributed real-time control systems follows from three key requirements of these systems: (i) control application development, (ii) reconfiguration, and (iii) fault monitoring and recovery. In this section we focus on the third area: please refer to (Brennan, 2007) for more details on real-time distributed control application configuration and reconfiguration.

Monitoring and fault recovery is a key requirement of any industrial control system, so it is not surprising that it is also critical for distributed real-time control system design. The purpose of monitoring is to ensure that the control system performs as intended. In other words, this involves ensuring that no unidentified, or latent, faults occur. Fault monitoring is basically the process of watching for failures and errors that may occur when the system is running or that are present (but possibly undetected) in the system itself. Since software does not "break" or "wear" (though, arguably, data may "wear" by becoming obsolete), the notion of "component failures" has little relevance for control software. Errors, however, are a different matter: i.e., an error is an inherent characteristic of the system. As a result, this concept is more relevant to software systems since errors are often manifested in program "bugs".

Systematic errors can be, and almost always are, present in control software. As well, random failures can, and typically do, occur in the controlled system. Given these eventualities, the control system must be capable of recovering from the resulting faults. As a result, the types of responsibilities that our control system will have are: (i) diagnosis of program execution, (ii) monitoring for exceptions that are thrown by function block code during execution, and (iii) monitoring the system state for inconsistencies (e.g., deadline control).

In the next section, we briefly summarize the basic architecture used to support fault monitoring and recovery (details are reported in (Brennan and Norrie, 2002)) and introduce a new analysis technique that can be used in conjunction with this architecture.

3 Background

3.1 Holonic Control Architecture

As noted previously, the architecture to manage fault monitoring and recovery in distributed control systems is based on the architecture proposed in (Brennan and

Norrie, 2002). This is a layered architecture that was inspired by the notion of "holonic agents" (Marik, 2001). Through their work with the IEC 61499 function block model, members of the Holonic Manufacturing Systems Consortium (HMS, 2007) came to the realization that the best approach is to encapsulate the function block solution into higher-level software when and where it is required to enable more sophisticated reasoning and a richer knowledge representation than function blocks alone. These resulting holonic agents can then integrate a holonic part (for hard real-time) and software agent part (responsible for higher level, soft real-time or non-real-time intelligent decision-making).

This architecture extends this idea to a multi-layer architecture consisting of four temporally decomposed layers of agents and devices illustrated in Figure 1 (Brennan and Norrie, 2002): execution control (EC), control execution (CE), execution (E), and hardware. As one moves down the layers, time scales become shorter and real-time constraints change from soft to hard real-time; as well, the degree of agency decreases (i.e., higher-level agents are more sophisticated but slower, while lower-level agents are fast and light-weight).

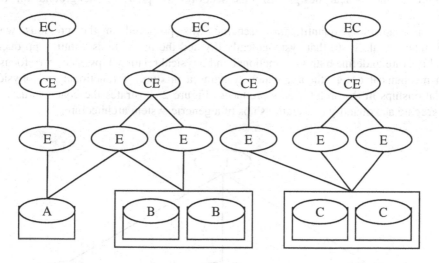

Fig. 1. Holonic control architecture

The EC and CE layers shown in Figure 1 support two fundamental system requirements: control application management, and fault detection and recovery. Since the real-time holonic control system is intended to meet hard real-time requirements, a temporal decomposition of the agents used for this purpose is necessary.

The EC layer is composed of agents, or "holonic units" (i.e., the ovals shown in Figure 1), that are responsible for arranging control applications for execution as well as planning for reconfiguration, fault monitoring and fault detection. In general, CE holonic units are responsible for controlling what is being executed. In other words, the CE holonic units are concerned with distributing execution control code to the appropriate resources (shown as rectangles in Figure 1), performing basic monitoring and alerts, and handling low-level fault recovery procedures. In cases where more sophisticated fault recovery decision-making is required, the CE layer will consult with holonic units in the EC layer (who may even have to consult higher-level agents).

3.2 Quantifying the Adaptability of a Design

Given the modular nature of the holonic architecture described in the previous section, it seems reasonable that recent work on design and analysis techniques for modular and adaptable design would be a good match to our problem domain. In particular, previous work by the authors on the quantification of adaptability focuses on developing a convenient way to classify the interactions within a product's architecture (Fletcher et. al. 2006). The adaptability quantification scheme aims to identify, classify, and describe the complex functional and physical relationships found in mechanical design. In this section, we provide background on this approach.

An adaptability quantification scheme was proposed in the previous work (Fletcher et. al. 2006) that systematically divided the interactions within a product's architecture to define both the functional and physical relationships. The work focuses on mechanical design theory, which contains a mixture of functional and physical relationships in the architectures produced. Figure 2 illustrates the concepts used to segregate and quantify the relationships of a generic system architecture.

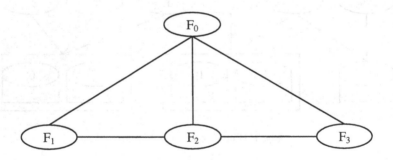

Fig. 2. Generic system architecture

The product architecture is made up of four elements, F_0, F_1, F_2, and F_3, which form the vertices of the architecture diagram. These vertices of the diagram represent the individual building blocks of a Distributed Control (DC) network. In the context of the distributed control architecture, the functional elements in the above diagram (F_0, F_1, F_2, and F_3) represent the subsystems of the distributed control architecture. There is not a distinction at this point between physical and non-physical (hardware and/or software) system elements. The links between vertices of the diagram represent the connections and interactions of the network building blocks.

The previous work in Adaptable Design (Fletcher et. al. 2006) divided the interactions between the DC building blocks of the architecture diagram into four categories. Two categories are related to the physical portion of the product architecture only, and the remaining two categories are related the functional portion of the architecture.

The physical relationships between the blocks are divided into two categories: the interface characteristics and the interaction characteristics. The interface characteristic is used to describe the relative sophistication of the physical interface required for the correct function of the system. The interaction characteristic is used to describe, also in relative terms, the degree of collusion across the interface.

The functional relationships in the architecture are categorized in the exact same manner, although with a different inherent meaning. The functional interface characteristic describes the relative design effort needed to produce the necessary engineering plans to produce the physical interface. In the case of distributed control, the "engineering plans" can be thought of as the control application and the system architecture. The functional interaction characteristic describes (relatively as well) the required engineering work to ensure that the blocks of the realized product architecture interface properly to ensure the correct operation of the final product.

Figure 3 shows the example system architecture with two parameters per system block link. The diagram on the left shows the links graphically which can be quantified in a matrix form as shown on the right. The matrix format is a convenient means of encapsulating the information gathered. In the mechanical design context, the two parameters (X and Y) would represent the interface and interaction between the elements. The subscripts denote only which functional or physical blocks are the parameters relate to. $X_{1,2}$ for instance would represent the interface characteristic between blocks 1 and 2 of the system architecture diagram of figure 2. For the DC architecture, the parameters X and Y would represent any two relevant interactions or information streams between the system components. Again, the subscripts denote only which two system components are described by the characteristic chosen.

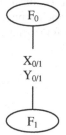

	F_0	F_1	F_2	F_3
F_0	1	$Y_{0/1}$	$Y_{0/2}$	$Y_{0/3}$
F_1	$X_{0/1}$	1	$Y_{1/2}$	n/a
F_2	$X_{0/2}$	$X_{1/2}$	1	$Y_{2/3}$
F_3	$X_{0/3}$	n/a	$X_{2/3}$	1

Fig. 3. Interfaces between functional elements

4 Applying Adaptable Design to the Holonic Architecture

The method for describing the interactions in a mechanical design environment can be easily adapted into a more general form to be used in the DC network fault detection scheme presented in this work.

The application of the system architecture block interaction characterization is most easily presented using the following example illustrated in Figure 4. For a DC network, the system architecture contains the entire hierarchy required to operate the system: Control Execution (CE) blocks, Execution Control (EC) blocks, Execution (E) blocks, and finally the individual physical process blocks that are to be controlled (A, B, and C). Assuming a linear process, i.e.: A to B to C, the DC network architecture shown in Figure 1 can be constructed.

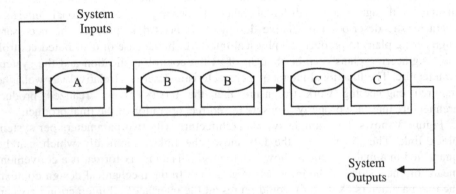

Fig. 4. A distributed control network

The equations presented in this section represent only how the data gathered in the application of the adaptability measures could be used to monitor DC networks. Using the adaptability quantification concepts in the DC networks case, any number of factors can be tracked through the network. Both physical and informational data can be tracked with this model to monitor the state of the DC network at any point and time. The equations that follow provide a schematic of how this information could be used only.

Using the linear process model, the physical transformations that occur at the 'B' stage require inputs from the 'A' blocks, and the 'C' blocks require the outputs of the 'B' blocks. The transformations can be conceptualized using the following simple equations:

$$\lfloor A_{outputs} \rfloor = [System\_Inputs] \times \lfloor A \rfloor = B_{Inputs}$$

$$\lfloor B_{outputs} \rfloor = \lfloor B_{inputs} \rfloor \times [B] = \lfloor C_{inputs} \rfloor$$

$$[System\_Outputs] = \lfloor C_{inputs} \rfloor \times [C]$$

$$[System\_Outputs] = [[[System\_Inputs] \times [A]] \times [B]] \times [C]$$

The above equations relate the physical processes to successive transformations of the original data set (System Inputs) into the final System Outputs configuration. For the DC network case that can utilize many different streams of both informational and physical knowledge, the following data structure is proposed to aid in the fault detection within a DC network.

$$[N_{output}] = [i_1 + i_2 + i_3 + \ldots i_l + p_1 + p_2 + p_3 + \ldots + p_m]^T$$

Where the indices 'i' (1 through L) represents the information states of the output, and the indices 'p' (1 through M) represent the physical state of the output. The segregation of the information and physical states of the system can be modelled on the work done in Adaptable Design: it is useful for the data to be divided into interface and interaction categories, though with the proposed structure, there is no practical limit to the number of data streams that can be recorded for analysis.

An example of information interface could be the result of one system component (such as a fault detection component) sending a query to another system element to verify that it is communicating properly with the rest of the system. This could be a binary type information stream with a nominal value of 1.

An example of information interaction could be the correct transformation of information across a system block. In the proposed structure, there is not a limit to the number of streams that can be analyzed. A physical interface information stream could be the result of a request by one system component to verify that a physical system block is communicating successfully with the rest of the system.

An example of a physical interaction information stream could be the correct physical transformation performed across a system block. In addition throughput data for a given process can be included as a data stream. This would allow the system to monitor the volume performance of a given process in time. In the proposed structure, there is not a limit to the number of physical interaction information streams that can be analyzed.

5 Applying the AD Approach to Fault Monitoring

The Output state vector provides a data structure that is suited to record any number of pertinent states of the output from a functional block of the system architecture. Information type states could include various signals used by the DC network. By gathering and analyzing the information at the conclusion of an operation in the linear system model, information regarding the performance of the system can be obtained.

For instance, in steady state operation, the output parameters of each step can be equal to the values as determined in the design of the network. If you expect a certain component to be communicating with the network at the end of a particular step, and the information stream values of the vector are zero, an error of some type has occurred in the network.

By looking at the variation of the data structure in time, fault detection should be achieved. If the architecture of the system undergoes an unplanned change – a component or software failure of some sort – the vector of information describing the overall state of the output will change. By analyzing the changes of the output vectors throughout the system with pre-set rules, failures in either the software or the physical components of the system may be localized. This type of fault detection detects changes in the system states only. It would be up to the designer to set out the system states while the network is in proper operation. As the indices are dictated by the system designer, the information will be related to specific parts of the architecture. A failure detected in a single (or multiple) indices can be instantaneously tied to the exact location (in the system architecture) of the failure.

$$[A\_Variation]_{t_1 \to t_2} = [A_{output}]_{t=2} - [A_{output}]_{t=1}$$

In the above example, two separate physical processes can independently provide the entire 'A' transformation necessary for the proper operation of the linear process. In normal operation, the A output information vector will record the sum of the transformations performed by the individual holons. In the case of the complete failure of one of the 'A' holons, the information vector will undergo an abrupt change at the next time step that the entire system is queried for its state. This structure will allow the system to detect failures that do not necessarily result in a complete system shutdown, but result in the system performing its tasks in a sub-optimal manner.

Small random fluctuations in the steady state operation of a DC network are expected, as the inputs to the system may be seen to vary in time. A set of threshold values may be set up to compare with the variation data set:

$$if : [Variation] > [Threshold] \text{ a failure has occurred}$$

$$if : [Variation] < [Threshold] \text{ a failure has not occurred}$$

This step will stop the fault detection element from returning false failure readings if the variations in the state of the system are below the limits as prescribed by the system designer.

System stability can easily be examined using this data structure. Small random fluctuations in the steady state operation of a DC network are expected, as the inputs to the system may be seen to vary in time. As the derivative of the variation vector in time increases, this would indicate decreasing system stability. By keeping the data in a non-aggregated format, the stability of specific areas within the network may be seen. That is to say that a potential area of instability can be localized for further study and modification.

Through the capture and analysis of many information streams, it is possible to localize to a high degree any system failures that may occur. This will aid in the fault recovery operations as the system operators will be able to ascertain the local presence of any system faults.

6 Next Steps

In this paper we have shown that Adaptable Design theory can be used to classify interactions between the modules of distributed control architecture: these interactions can then be used to enable fault monitoring and recovery. This approach was inspired by the close match between the functional architecture of a modular mechanical design (which this AD approach was developed for) and the functional architecture of a distributed mechatronic system (Fletcher et. al. 2006).

Although AD theory looks promising for the specific problem of fault monitoring and recovery in distributed control systems, it also has the potential to be applicable to a wider range of problems in this area: especially those relating to distributed control system design. For example, recent work on AD (Fletcher et. al. 2006) has focused on how to design mechanical artefacts that are more adaptable: i.e., capable of a wider range of functions and configurations. AD could be equally applicable to the problem of adaptability (i.e., re-configurability) in real-time control. In particular, the basic models used in this paper could potentially be extended to be used to assess how re-configurable a particular distributed control system design is in the same manner that is used to assess the adaptability of a mechanical design in (Fletcher et al., 2006). As well, since existing AD models focus heavily on the interface between modules, it is likely that these models could be used to provide insights into the design of software modules in distributed control and holonic systems. This could prove useful as a general design tool that could be used to make decisions about how to decompose the overall control problem into software modules (i.e., how to determine appropriate levels of granularity and coupling between modules).

Our ongoing work is focusing on the development of quantitative models for the analysis of adaptable designs in both mechanical and mechatronic systems. It is hoped that this work will lead to contributions in the design of real-time distributed control systems and holonic control systems.

References

Brennan, R.W.: Towards real-time distributed intelligent control: a survey of research themes and applications, IEEE Transactions on Systems, Man and Cybernetics, Part C (Applications and Reviews) (in press, 2007)

Brennan, R.W., Norrie, D.H.: Managing fault monitoring and recovery in distributed real-time control systems. In: 5th IEEE/IFIP International Conference on Information Technology for Balanced Automation Systems in Manufacturing and Services, Cancun, Mexico, pp. 247–254 (2002)

Fletcher, D., Gu, P., Brennan, R.W.: Product and design adaptability quantification. In: Proceedings of the 16th CIRP International Design Seminar, Kananaskis, Alberta, Canada (2006)

Hall, K.H., Staron, R.J., Vrba, P.: Experience with holonic and agent-based control systems and their adoption by industry, in Holonic and Multi-Agent Systems for Manufacturing. In: Second International Conference on Industrial Applications of Holonic and Multi-Agent Systems, pp. 1–10 (2005)

Holonic Manufacturing Systems Consortium (2007), Website http://hms.ifw.uni-hannover.de/

Marik, V., Pechoucek, M.: Holons and agents: recent developments and mutual impacts. In: Twelfth International Workshop on Database and Expert Systems Applications, pp. 605–607. IEEE Computer Society, Los Alamitos (2001)

McFarlane, D.C., Bussmann, S.: Holonic manufacturing control: Rationales, developmentsand open issues. In: Deen, S.M. (ed.) Advances in the HolonicApproach to Agent-Based Manufacturing, pp. 303–326. Springer, Heidelberg (2003)

Shen, W., Wang, L., Hao, Q.: Agent-based distributed manufacturing process planning and scheduling: a state-of-the-art survey. IEEE Transactions on Systems, Man and Cybernetics, Part C (Applications and Reviews) 36, 563–577 (2006)

Application of the Holonic Approach in Distributed Control Systems Designing

Dariusz Choinski, Witold Nocon, and Mieczyslaw Metzger

Faculty of Automatic Control, Electronics and Computer Science,
Silesian University of Technology,
ul. Akademicka 16, 44-100 Gliwice, Poland
{dariusz.choinski, witold.nocon, mieczyslaw.metzger}@polsl.pl

Abstract. Design of a multidisciplinary project is a complicated process requiring cooperation of different designers specialized in particular branches of engineering. The paper proposes a holonic approach to testify that a solution of distributed control systems is compliant with dynamically changing technology rules with ontology-based decomposition. The proposed holarchy includes a multi-agent system considering also its hybrid control architecture connected with a self-organization database. The proposed approach was implemented for a biotechnological pilot-plant continuously working as a platform for several process investigations.

Keywords: Design methodologies, multi-agent systems, knowledge ontologies, holonic systems, industrial applications.

1 Introduction

Design of a multidisciplinary project is a complicated process requiring cooperation of different designers specialized in particular branches of engineering (technology, construction, power supply, control etc. – see for example [1], [2], [3]). Every entity of the system being designed is not only an element of the designed hierarchical structure, but is also assessed and validated with respect to the stated requirements. Those requirements address a reliable operation of the particular elements of the technological system and of the control system, realization of the supervisory control goals and adaptation of the plant to the changing technological or marketing requirements. Therefore, every entity of this structure may be a subject of research and design of a new solution, and usually, this solution has a complex structure that takes into account many technological or control algorithm aspects. Those actions are usually grouped into stages: selection, modification: upgrade/reduction and validation. Selection requires such a projection of the structure so that the selected subsystem fully realizes those functions. Modification requires mutual bindings between particular subsystems to be projected. The main problem is validation, which requires a new structure to be realized within the existing structure, so that the new functions do not violate the previously designed and used functions. Therefore, the validation stage must usually be preceded with a reduction stage, for summarizing entities to an appropriate level of

V. Mařík, V. Vyatkin, A.W. Colombo (Eds.): HoloMAS 2007, LNAI 4659, pp. 257–268, 2007.

abstraction. Such a presentation of the problem enables employment of a holonic system paradigm (see, e.g. [4], [5], [6]). Realization of this paradigm requires a data model that represents a set of concepts within a component and the relationships between those concepts, namely an ontology [7]. The ontology-based division into subsystems may further be exploited by extending each subsystem with a software part. The paper proposes a holonic approach to validation of distributed control systems considering also its hybrid architecture. The proposed holarchy includes a multi-agent system (MAS) [8], [9], [10], connected with a self-organization database [11] and ontology-based technology rules decomposition.

2 Problem Under Consideration

In the considered control system, the software possesses a hierarchical structure, as shown in Fig. 1.

The considered object with a Distributed Control System (DCS) is modeled as a Hybrid Control System (see for example [12], [13]) that is in turn described as a state machine augmented with differential equations [14]. The state can change in two ways:

- instantaneously by discrete transition described by sequences S of actions from source state to target state,
- in a time pass according to a trajectory of the state variables change as a function f of input and output variables.

Object states are divided into the two following sets: $\Omega -$ contains continuous state variables with boundaries depended on physical process parameter constrains, measurement ranges and capabilities of actuators; Φ - contains values describing events for transition conditions. Φ is further divided into two subsets: Φ_c for controllable events and subset Φ_u for uncontrollable events. Agents are responsible for transitions, therefore Φ describes the agent sensors and Ω describes common agent effectors. Controllable events are defined as such, that the process operator is capable of instantaneously disable those event, thus preventing a process failure from occurring. Uncontrollable events on the other hand may not be simply disabled by the operator. In case of such events occurring, the object state must be transferred into other region (see switching between Ω_i, Ω_{i+1} and Ω_{i+2} in Fig. 1). The logic of the control agent implements continuous control, hence it enables a transition into a different state of the process using a time pass according to a trajectory of the state variables defined by function f of input and output variables. Therefore, it is necessary to model complex interactions within DCS. Those interactions and collaborations are examined as a software system with a complex autonomy, intelligence and coordination mechanisms. This software is represented as a hierarchical Multi-Agent System (MAS), (Fig. 1). It consists of the following agents: Control Agent, Supervisory Agent and Expert Agent. The employed technology has been selected in such a way, so that the structure may be implemented both in industrial standard environments and in the Internet.

The Control Agent, being close to the controlled object realizes all the necessary standard control functions like feedback control, emergency shutdown or changes of sequential production cycles. The Supervisory Agent on the other hand is capable of analyzing the plant operations in a wider context, hence addition functions are implemented. In particular, once the Control Agent system is no longer capable of dealing with a certain process disturbance or failure, the Supervisory Agent will try to sequentially change the state of the process in order to deal with the problem. It may therefore move the object into another object state Ω. Certain process disturbances, failures or emergencies however will require an expert knowledge for the problem to be dealt with successfully.

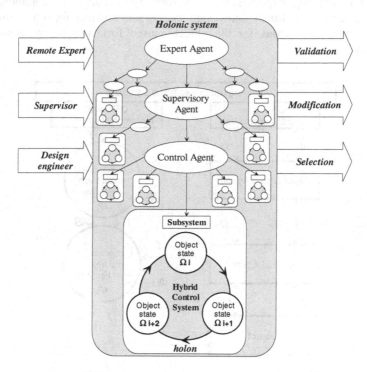

Fig. 1. Holarchy in MAS control system

The Expert Agent will therefore enable remote expert to assess the state of the process. To provide the remote expert access to the plant, certain conditions must be met. First, Internet must be employed for communication, and second, the remote expert must not be exposed to the real complexity of the process. Issues such as power supply, particularities of different feedback loops or control of different effectors should not burden the expert unless those particular issues are important for the problem to be resolved.

The distinction of different subsystems coupled to the software of the hierarchical control system results in a holonic system. In addition, because software agents are used in the hierarchical control system, a multi-agent system is in fact employed.

Fig. 2 presents cooperation in hierarchical MAS system in detail. The consideration as hybrid states automaton allows decomposition of complex object with control
hierarchical system and analysis of this system separately for time-driven and event-
driven part. The Supervisory Agent, working in an event-driven regime, may instantaneously move the object into another state using a discrete transition described by
sequences S of actions from source state to target state. Control Agent uses a trajectory for state transition and all the closed-loop and open-loop control algorithms are
implemented in this agent, hence this part of the control system is time-driven. This
agent's knowledge is based on the implemented control algorithms and realises
function f and subset Φ_u as control actions. The agents cooperation set includes: com-
petitions for changing Expert and Supervisory Agent decisions, collaboration for
maximizing agents benefits by knowledge sharing and hostility for robust implementation of actions dangerous for the object caused for example by measurement
malfunctions.

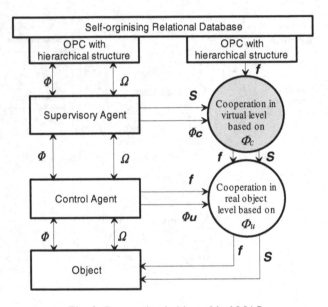

Fig. 2. Cooperation in hierarchical MAS

3 Proposed Solutions

Formalism of the technological, electrical and automatic control system design is
commonly realized by CAD software compatible with the IEC 61346 standard [15].
This standard specifies rules for structuring and reference designations. The structure
defines dependencies and relations between objects that are considered in the process
of designing, construction, realising, operation, exploitation and disposal. A set of
mutually connected objects is a system. Information about objects and about the system may be chosen based on different aspects. Therefore, the structure of the system

and of the particular objects may be described in many different ways. The standard provides three examples of structures: function-oriented, location-oriented and product-oriented. On the other hand, the function aspect may further be divided into the control, process and power supply aspects. Particular structures are organized for holarchy and should specify the information regarding the subsystems, content of the particular documents and composition of reference designations (Fig. 3). Based on the ontology consistent with the IEC 61346 standard, subsystems are distinguished that usually share a common power supply, are placed close together and have a similar goal. In a real process, a great number of subsystems may be distinguished, and it should be remembered that particular systems may belong to a number of different subsystems.

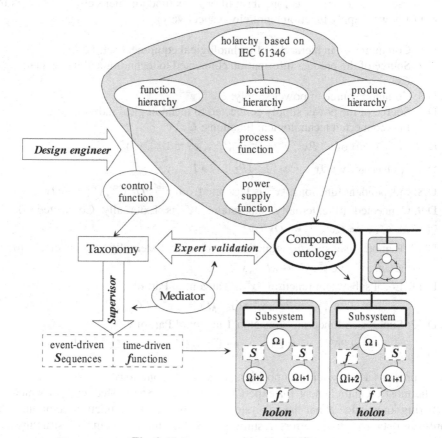

Fig. 3. Holons composition for MAS

4 Ontology-Based Subsystem Topology Semantics

Even the not complicated system design has a multilevel tree of reference designations, which is usually incomprehensible without associated diagrams. The main aim of the proposed ontology is to make physical meaning of the subsystems as a collection of formal axioms based on primitive relation incorporated only in the reference designation tree and the distances in hierarchy

The set of reference designations prepared in accordance with the IEC 61346 standard is a basis for the division into subsystems according to the component ontology. The mereology starts taking a relation 'Cx,y' to express that individuals x and y are connected, as was introduced by Clarke [16] as a Calculus. This Calculus may state ontology describing topology based on reference designation according to IEC 61346.

For particular individuals we can present the following mereological definitions (where superscript '*' is for all references designation, '-' is for subset of product, '+' is for subset of location, '=' is for subset of process function hierarchy and '==' is for subset of power supply function hierarchy respectively):

D 1: Common root in hierarchy of technological equipment set: Cx^+,y^+

D 2: Source of the product information connected to technological individual: Cx^+,y^-

D 3: Common source of power supply: $Cx^{==},y^{==}$

D 4: Source of the power supply connected to technological individual: $Cx^{==},y^+$

D 5: Interconnected technological functions: $Cx^=,y^=$

D 6: 'x is a Part of y': $Px^*,y^* = (\forall z^*)(Cz^*,x^* \supset Cz^*,y^*)$

D 7: 'x Overlaps y': $Ox^*,y^* = (\exists z^*)(Pz^*,x^* \bullet Pz^*,y^*)$

D 8: Independent functions: '$x^{==}$ is Discrete from $y^{==}$': $DRx^{==},y^{==} = \neg Ox^{==},y^{==}$

D 9: Connected to externally subsystem: 'x^+ is Externally Connected to y^+': $ECx^+,y^+ = Cx^+,y^+ \bullet \neg Ox^+,y^+$

D 10: Remote subsystem function: '$x^=$ is Externally Connected to y^+': $ECx^=,y^+ = Cx^=,y^+ \bullet \neg Ox^=,y^+$

D 11: Local subsystem function: '$x^=$ is Tangential Part of y^+': $$TPx^=,y^+ = Px^=,y^+ \bullet (\exists z^=)(ECz^=,x^= \bullet ECz^=,y^+)$$

D 12: Supervised function: '$x^=$ is Non Tangential Part of y^+': $$TPNx^=,y^+ = Px^=,y^+ \bullet \neg(\exists z^=)(ECz^=,x^= \bullet ECz^=,y^+)$$

Fig. 3 presents a subsystem composition based on this ontology.

The most crucial element for expert validation is a Static Mediator [2] which, by gathering knowledge about the subsystems and by gathering function taxonomy, ensures limitation of basic errors resulting from bad understanding of structure and states of the system. This Static Mediator constitutes an interface between the inside of the holonic system and the outside Expert Agent software.

The Mediator guides the transformation of the XML string to an XML object. Due to this transformation, the environment possesses a build-in XML object, that has all the properties and methods needed for reading, writing and handling of any XML document using DOM (Document Object Model) standard.

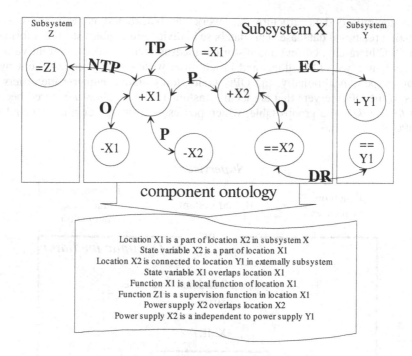

Location X1 is a part of location X2 in subsystem X
State variable X2 is a part of location X1
Location X2 is connected to location Y1 in externally subsystem
State variable X1 overlaps location X1
Function X1 is a local function of location X1
Function Z1 is a supervision function in location X1
Power supply X2 overlaps location X2
Power supply X2 is a independent to power supply Y1

Fig. 4. Ontology based subsystem composition

Using only the Static Mediator would not fulfil all the requirements stated by the control system. This is because the remote expert using the Expert Agent for validation is usually an expert in technology or economy, and is not familiar with particularities of the DCS. Such a system usually comprises a great amount of measurement devices, actuators or regulators. Most of those devices ensure proper values of technological parameters but, from the point of view of a particular test, are usually irrelevant. From the same point of view, the way of obtaining either on-line or off-line measurements is not relevant, as long as the data is acquired with a given period of time and the time of acquiring this data and mutual relations between different parameters are known. This creates a separation of viewpoints: the expert performing the tests and the local operator (control engineer) do not share the same point of view. Therefore, employment of standard distant supervisory and visualization systems for purposes of expert investigations is not effective. Utilization of such systems would involve too much unnecessary information that would be specific only to the given local control system used. This system however is necessary for the proper and reliable pilot-plant operation and must not be disturbed.

In order to eliminate those inconveniences the Dynamic Mediator concept has been formed (Fig. 5).

This mediator employs the OPC standard (www.opcfoundation.org) for presenting the hierarchical structure of the Hybrid Control System. This structure may change dynamically, or may present different projections of the same system with different levels of details included. This structure enables a hierarchy of system access be created by using a collection of holons gathered in collaborating groups.

The centralized data structure that works as blackboard is realised as a self-organizing relational database. This database is divided into tables storing information about OPC hierarchy, current and historical measurements with the current values of readings bound with OPC items and in addition, write-to-OPC requests sent by the Remote Expert. Additionally, the OPC table stores unique numeric identifiers and names of the OPC servers that are locally installed. Those values are stored because, using *foreign key*, the groups table, which possesses a storage engine is bound with the OPC Servers table.

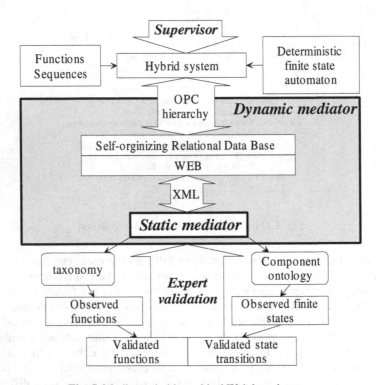

Fig. 5. Mediators in hierarchical Web based system

In the next table the following information is stored: unique identifiers (as *primary key*) of the OPC groups defined in the ontology. This table is bound by *foreign key* with the OPC Servers table. Hence the hierarchical structure and data coherence is maintained, which is one of the most important problems for this application. The data structure in the OPC standard stores no information about the mutual data binding – it is a typical hierarchical structure. The tree structure of data represented in the OPC server hierarchy does not correspond to the holonic structure. However, it stores the key information about the control system state (Ω). Therefore, a mechanism is needed for updating bindings between the relational database and the hierarchical information structure and system to subsystems division.

The table storing OPC items, also stores information about OPC items defined in the Dynamic Mediator application. The dynamic hierarchical structure OPC Items and

Groups gather information about holons and about collaboration between holons. When the remote expert subscribes interesting items, it may define its own control algorithm operating on items that where defined in the OPC server for reading, and calculating values that are overwritten in items defined for writing. Items selected by the subscription, supplemented with the control algorithm, constitute the current configuration, which may be saved in the database.

5 Concluding Remarks - Application for the Biotechnological Pilot-Plant

The implemented user interface [21] for the expert validation allows reading of the hierarchical structure of items in database, selection of those that are interesting for the Internet user, monitoring of current state and historical data and the realization of control algorithms that utilize this data. In addition, visualization and coupling of dynamically loaded clips to the measurements is also realized. The database is polled about all OPC servers, groups and items connected to the hybrid control system and corresponding to particular subsystem chosen by graphical user interface. The structure of items, written in XML, is displayed as a tree, from which the Expert Agent may choose items corresponding to the interested holons and functions. The database returns an answer which is inserted into the script including additional tags, and is saved into an XML variable as a string value. This variable is sent to the client application as OPC Data, where it is properly processed.

The biotechnological process pilot-plant designed and operated in the Institute of Automatic Control serves as a platform for investigations regarding activated sludge process in aquatic environment. Apart from the standard activated sludge process, bioaugmentation process may also be investigated. The pilot-plant consists of a biological reactor and a settler, together with a number of controls (pumps, mixers, heater) and measurements, together with a programmable logic controller capable of running advanced control algorithms (based on control systems of different vendors). The four most vital parameters of the activated sludge that are measured on-line are: pH value, oxidation-reduction potential (Redox), carbon dioxide concentration (CO_2) and dissolved oxygen concentration (Ox). Off-line measurements are available using IR spectrophotometer and UV/VIS spectrophotometer with a thermostatic flow-through cuvette and an automatic aspiration system.

Depending on the particular set of control algorithms applied, the structure of the biological process involved may be changed. For example, the plant may be operated as a continuous or sequencing activated sludge process, the later involving cyclic utilization of the biological reactor for reaction and settling phases, the former involving continuous sedimentation of activated sludge in the settler with recycle of the thickened sludge back to the reactor. Depending on control of pumps interchanging the sludge between the reactor and the settler, the biological reactor may either be operated as a chemostat (constant volume of liquid in the reactor) or as a turbidostat (constant concentration of biomass in the reactor). Investigations regarding batch processes may require a predefined initial concentration of biomass in the reactor, therefore the settler should be used as a buffer for the sludge and the reactor should be operated with changing level. And last but not least, bioaugmentation of biomass in the plant may or may not be involved.

Moreover, some experiments may require a sequence of configurations to be enforced in a specified time regime. Such sequences are referred to as scenarios. A particular configuration of the plant should be prepared prior to commencing experiments by a remote researcher. To burden the researcher with preparing those conditions however, would make the whole process of remote experimentation unacceptably complicated and dangerous for the plant. The remote researcher would have to posses all the information about the local control systems, together with its particularities and constraints. A strictly control-engineering knowledge with control logic implementation language would also be required in order to enforce the proper configurations and scenarios.

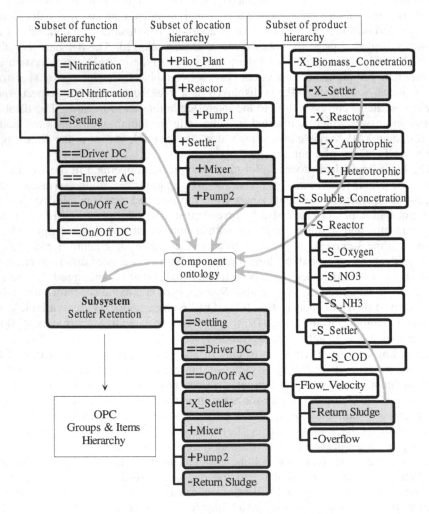

Fig. 6. The subsystem construction example

Fig. 6 presents an example of subsystem composition for the "Settler Retention" subsystem in which sequential control of biomass concentration in the biological reactor is considered. A possibility of such control is highly desired for its ability to proactively deal with disturbances reaching a wastewater treatment plant.

In order to realize such control the proper measurements and actuators must be chosen in a proper place. Therefore, based on a specified ontology, the proper elements from the three subsets (function, location, product) are selected (highlighted in Fig. 6). By carefully examining this graph and the process it becomes evident, that in order to control the given variable in the reactor, the controller must influence a different part of the object, namely the settler (represented as a function =Settling). Two actuators that are needed in order to control the retention time in the settler are: mixer (Location: +Mixer; Function: ==Driver DC) and a recycle pump (Location: +Pump2; Function: = On/Off AC). Those two actuators enable control of the biomass concentration in the recycle (Product: -X_Settler) that, together with the return sludge flow rate (Product: -Return_Sludge), directly influence distribution of biomass in the biotechnological system. Note, that in this case a process variable that is controlled is regarded as a product.

The biotechnological pilot-plant exhibits similar problems regarding the Distributed Control System as an industrial process being developed. It is prone to changes and modifications, hence it serves as a good training ground for employing a holonic approach to maintaining the DCS during process development stage.

Acknowledgements. This work was supported by the Polish Ministry of Scientific Research and Information Technology, using funds for 2006-2008, under grant no. N514 006 31/1739.

References

1. Marquardt, W., Nagl, M.: Workflow and information centered support of design processes—the IMPROVE perspective. Computers and Chemical Engineering 29, 65–82 (2004)
2. Ulieru, M., Brennan, R.W., Walker, S.S.: The holonic enterprise: a model for Iternet-enabled global manufacturing supply chain and workflow management. Integrated Manufacturing Systems 13(8), 538–550 (2002)
3. Kotak, D., Wu, S., Fleetwood, M., Tamoto, H.: Agent-based holonic design and operations environment for distributed manufacturing. Computers in Industry 52, 95–108 (2003)
4. Koestler, A.: The Ghost in the Machine. Macmillan, New York (1968)
5. Holonic manufacturing systems consortium (2000), web site
   http://hms.ifw.uni-hannover.de
6. Babiceanu, R.F., Chen, F.: development and applications of holonic manufacturing systems: a syrvey. Journal of Intelligent Manufacturing 17, 111–131 (2006)
7. Borst, P., Akkermans, H., Top, J.: Engineering ontologies. Int. J. Human – Computer Studies 46, 365–406 (1997)
8. Wooldridge, M., Jennings, N.R.: Intelligent agents: theory and practice. The Knowledge Engineering Practice 10(2), 115–152 (1995)
9. Pechoucek, M., Thompson, S.G.: Agents in Industry: The Best from the AAMAS 2005 Industry Track. IEEE Intelligent Systems, 86–95 (March/April 2006)

10. Marik, V., McFarlane, D.: Industrial Adoption of Agent-Based Technologies. IEEE Intelligent Systems, 27–35 (January/February 2005)
11. Choiński, D., Nocoń, W., Metzger, M.: Multi-agent System for Hierarchical Control with Self-organising Database. In: Nguyen, N.T., et al. (eds.) KES-AMSTA 2007. LNCS(LNAI), vol. 4496, pp. 655–664. Springer, Heidelberg (2007)
12. van der Schaft, A.J., Schumacher, J.M.: Compositionality issues in discrete, continuous, and hybrid systems. International Journal of Robust and Nonlinear Control 11(5), 399–539 (2001)
13. Cassandras, C.G., Pepyne, D.L., Wardi, Y.: Optimal control of a class of hybrid systems. IEEE Transactions on Automatic Control 46(3), 398–415 (2001)
14. Lynch, N., Segala, R., Vaandrager, F.: Hybrid I/O automata. Information and Computation 185, 105–157 (2003)
15. International Electrical Commision: IEC 61346-1, Industrial Systems, installations and equipment and industrial products - Structuring principles and reference designations, 1st edn. (1996)
16. Clarke, B.L.: Individuals and Points. Notre Dame Journal of Formal Logic 26(1), 61–75 (1985)
17. IEC Technical Committee TC65/WG6, IEC61499 Industrial Process Measurement and Control – Specification IEC Draft (2000)
18. Hall, K.H., Staron, R.J., Vrba, P.: Holonic and Agent-Based Control. In: Proceedings of the 16-th IFAC Triennal World Congress, CD, Elsevier, Amsterdam (2005)
19. Vyatkin, V., Hanisch, H.M.: Verification of distributed control systems in intelligent manufacturing. Journal of Intelligent Manufacturing 14, 123–136 (2003)
20. Official National Instruments LabVIEW website: http://www.ni.com/labview/
21. Kraska, J.: An Internet-Based Mobile Control Algorithms Master Thesis, Institute of Automatic Control, Silesian University of Technology (in polish) (2006)

Design and Implementation of Adaptive Agents for Complex Manufacturing Systems

Jens Zimmermann and Lars Mönch

University of Hagen
Chair of Enterprise-wide Software Systems
Universitätsstraße 1, 58097 Hagen, Germany
{Jens.Zimmermann,Lars.Moench}@fernuni-hagen.de

Abstract. In this paper, we extend the Product-Resource-Order-Staff-Architecture (PROSA) for holonic manufacturing systems towards ensuring adaptive behavior of agent-based manufacturing control systems. PROSA suggests the usage of decision-making and staff agents. Staff agents support the decision-making agents. We introduce adaptive staff agents. Adaptive staff agents make sure that the parameters of production control algorithms are adjusted properly in a situation-dependent manner. We describe the architecture of adaptive staff agents and their interaction with the other agents of the manufacturing control system. We present an example for using adaptive staff agents in the semiconductor manufacturing domain.

Keywords: Agent-based Production Control, Adaptability, Architecture, Semiconductor Manufacturing.

1 Introduction

Complex manufacturing systems are characterized by an over time changing and diverse product mix, prescribed due dates, a huge number of machines, a large number of routes, and disturbances. We have to take into account these properties in course of designing and implementing manufacturing control systems, i.e., these systems have to be adapted without large efforts to changing conditions of the manufacturing process. Usually, this is a challenging task and therefore, most of the manufacturing control approaches in practice (and in the academic world) are static, i.e., the approaches are not able to adapt to changing circumstances.

It appears that software agents are an appropriate way to develop distributed scheduling systems that can adapt to various circumstances of the manufacturing process because they are goal-oriented, decision-making entities by definition. In this paper, we discuss the question how we have to design and construct adaptive agent-based manufacturing control systems for the complex manufacturing systems domain. A lot of papers are published that deal with learning in agent-based systems. However, most of the papers discuss these questions from a conceptual point of view, concrete architectures, applications, and computational results usually are not available. After the successful design and implementation of the agent-based system

V. Mařík, V. Vyatkin, A.W. Colombo (Eds.): HoloMAS 2007, LNAI 4659, pp. 269–280, 2007.
© Springer-Verlag Berlin Heidelberg 2007

FABMAS for the semiconductor manufacturing control domain [8,9] we try to improve the performance of FABMAS by adding situation-depended control strategies. In this paper, we describe the results and findings of our research efforts.

The paper is organized as follows. In Section 2, we describe the problem researched in this paper and discuss related literature. We describe the architecture for adaptive staff agents in Section 3. Section 4 provides information on using adaptive staff agents in production control for semiconductor manufacturing.

2 Problem and Related Literature

Manufacturing systems can be controlled by different control strategies (e.g. dispatching rules, scheduling approaches, negotiation-based approaches). Adaptive manufacturing control has to take the behavior of the manufacturing system into account. Most of the control approaches are given by heuristics due to the NP-hardness of many production control problems [12]. Therefore, the control strategies require a certain parameter setting. We suggest the usage of a parameterization approach. Appropriate parameter settings are highly situation dependent. Attributes are necessary to describe a situation. These situation attributes are used to determine appropriate parameterization attributes. A parameterization of a production control strategy φ can be described as a mapping ω_φ

$$\begin{aligned} \omega_\varphi : D_1 \times ... \times D_n &\to R_1 \times ... \times R_k \\ (a_1,...,a_n) &\mapsto (w_1,...,w_k) \end{aligned} , \tag{1}$$

where we denote by

D_i :   the domain of situation attribute i,

a_i :   a concrete realization of situation attribute i,

R_i :   the range of parameterization attribute i,

w_i :   a concrete realization of a parameterization attribute i.

A typical parameterization task consists of determining a set of appropriate situation attributes, a set of parameterization attributes, and the concrete form of ω_φ. This mapping can be represented, for example, by regression equations, neural networks, case-based reasoning (cf. [12] for applications of neural networks and case-based reasoning in manufacturing) or inductive decision trees [15]. The mapping function requires a set of situation attribute values in order to describe a specific situation. It returns concrete values for the parameterization attributes.

The load of a manufacturing system or the due date setting regime are examples for situation attributes. The maximum number of negotiation cycles in an auction may serve as an example for a parameterization attribute.

Different machine learning techniques for adaptive manufacturing control problems are described in the literature. Piramuthu *et al.* [13] consider inductive decision trees to select appropriate dispatching rules among a set of given rules. Neural networks and case-based reasoning techniques to parameterize dispatching rules are described by Pinedo in [12]. Learning in multi-agent-systems is considered in [17]. A multi-agent-system reinforcement learning approach for a job shop scheduling problem is discussed in [2]. A similar technique is applied in [1] to a flow shop scheduling problem. It is difficult to estimate the reward of certain manufacturing control decisions in complex manufacturing systems. Therefore, it is hard to implement reinforcement learning methods. Approaches based on genetic algorithms for the selection of appropriate dispatching rules within multi-agent-systems are considered in [4,5]. The advantages of machine learning techniques applied to holonic and multi-agent-systems are discussed in [10]. All the papers discuss several aspects of the realization of adaptive manufacturing control behavior for sometimes very specific problems. So far, it appears that architecture issues and questions of implementing agents with adaptive behavior for manufacturing control are not discussed in very detail in the literature.

We use the PROSA architecture [16] to design multi-agent-systems for manufacturing control. PROSA differentiates between decision-making and staff agents. Decision-making agents make manufacturing control decisions (on routing and sequencing of jobs). Staff agents support the decision-making agents in course of their activities. They encapsulate scheduling and monitoring abilities. Heuristics for manufacturing control require usually a sophisticated parameter setting to achieve good results. Therefore, we need agents that analyze situations, update ω_φ, and select appropriate values of the parameterization attributes. Staff agents in PROSA do not offer explicitly this functionality. Therefore, the goal for the remainder of this paper consists in describing adaptive staff agents.

3 Architecture of Adaptive Staff Agents

In this section, we describe first the incorporation of adaptive capabilities. Then we introduce adaptive staff agents and parameterization agents. Finally, we discuss the implementation of adaptive staff agents in more detail.

3.1 Incorporation of Adaptive Capabilities

The adaptation process requires the selection of appropriate situation parameters a_i. A situation is completely described by the values of its situation parameters. Staff agents solve specific problems (for example assignment and sequencing problems for jobs waiting in front of machines) for the decision-making agents. In order to solve manufacturing problems, the following generic functionality is provided by staff agents [6,9]:

1. prepare the problem solution,
2. calculation of internal parameters of the problem solution method,
3. feed the problem solution method with data and parameters,
4. solution of the problem,
5. interruption of the solution process in an event or time- driven manner,
6. provide the results of the problem to other agents,
7. treatment of exceptions during the decision-making process.

Two steps are necessary to prepare the solution of a certain problem (1). In the first step, the relevant data for the problem solution method is collected. In the second step, external parameters provided by the decision-making agents for the problem solution are treated. During the calculation of the internal parameters (2), a data-dependent selection of the parameters for the problem solution method is carried out.

We are interested in reusing problem solution capabilities. Due to a certain degree of parallelism in each manufacturing system (for example, because of parallel machines) many algorithms can applied several times. Therefore, we do not implement the corresponding algorithms as part of a certain staff agent. It is necessary to provide data and parameters for the algorithms. Each algorithm is encapsulated by a class. When a certain problem solution capability is required by a staff agent, a new instance of the algorithm class is created. We need agents that provide the same functionality as staff agents but the functionalities (1), (2), and (3) have to be extended by additional features. These capabilities are:

(1.1) situation detection,

(1.2) update of ω_φ,

(1.3) storing of ω_φ,

(2.1) using ω_φ to determine concrete values of the parameterization attributes,

(3.1) feed the values of the parameterization attributes from (2.1) into the problem solution method.

The functionality (1) is refined by (1.1). We determine the values of situation attributes using data of the manufacturing process for describing the current situation. When the current values of the situation attributes a_i are outside the range D_i, ω_φ is invalid and we have to update it in (1.2). Changing ω_φ means, for example, learning of a new decision tree or neural network or determining a new regression equation. The updated mapping has to be stored (1.3). The mapping ω_φ is used in (2.1) to determine new values for parameterization attributes. In (3.1), we communicate these new values to the problem solution methods.

We may consider two different ways to incorporate these additional features. We can integrate them directly into a staff agent. In this case, we call the resulting staff agent adaptive staff agent. The second way consists in considering a staff agent for the problem solution and an additional agent for performing the new tasks (1.1) to (3.1). We call this agent parameterization agent. In this case, a parameterization agent can be used by several staff agents. Note that the first approach is decentralized whereas the second approach is more centralized.

The problem solution method is used in two different ways. It can be used to solve the problems of the decision-making agents with an appropriate parameter setting based on ω_φ. Secondly, it is sometimes necessary to assess the quality of parameterization settings during an update of ω_φ. In this case, we also have to solve a sequence of problems with fixed, but not necessary good, parameter settings in order to find settings that lead to a good solution quality. We determine basically tuples $\left(a_1,...,a_n,\omega_\varphi\left(a_1,...,a_n\right)\right)$.

3.2 Adaptive Staff Agents

Each adaptive staff agent only solves problems of its decision-making agent because of the decentralized data. The update of ω_φ is performed in a decentralized manner separately by each adaptive staff agent. This is a disadvantage of the decentralized adaptive staff agent approach. The benefits of this approach are given by low communication costs and the overlapping of problem solving and update cycles.

Multi-agent-systems usually consist of several runtime environments. A runtime environment provides the infrastructure for agent execution and allows the agents a concurrent execution on the same host [6]. A communication of tuples $(a_1,...,a_n,\omega_\varphi(a_1,...,a_n))$ between adaptive staff agents located at different runtime environments is possible and reduces the time necessary for the update of ω_φ for each single adaptive agent. However, additional communication and coordination efforts are required. The usage of adaptive staff agents is depicted for decision-making agents that are located at two different agent runtime environments in Figure 1.

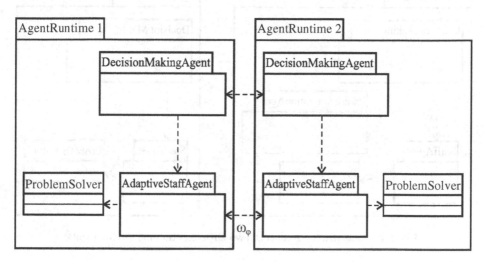

Fig. 1. Adaptive Staff Agents at Two Different Runtime Environments

3.3 Parameterization Agents

The main idea of the second approach consists in a separation of the problem solution and the process of using and updating ω_φ. Staff agents solve the problems and use the functionality of a parameterization agent for determining appropriate values of the parameterization attributes. When $\omega_\varphi(a_1,...,a_n)$ is unknown for a certain tuple $(a_1,...,a_n)$ the parameterization agent determines a parameter setting via an ad hoc strategy either by using default parameters or by an exhaustive search for appropriate parameter values. In the latter case, a repeated solution of the original problem with different parameter values is necessary.

The centralized calculation of appropriate parameter settings for collections of agents by a single parameterization agent is the advantage of this approach. The communication of $\left(a_1,...,a_n,\omega_\varphi\left(a_1,...,a_n\right)\right)$ is not necessary because only one ω_φ has to be updated.

Because of the centralized approach more different situations of the manufacturing process are possible. Hence, it is harder to find appropriate values for the parameterization attributes. The response time of the parameterization agents is much longer as in case of adaptive staff agents. Problems arise especially in case of multiple requests that force the parameterization agent to apply the ad hoc strategy several times.

Figure 2 shows the usage of a parameterization agent within a multi-agent-system that consists of two different agent runtime environments. Note that the parameterization agent communicates only with the problem solution entity (called problem solver) on its own runtime environment in order to update ω_φ.

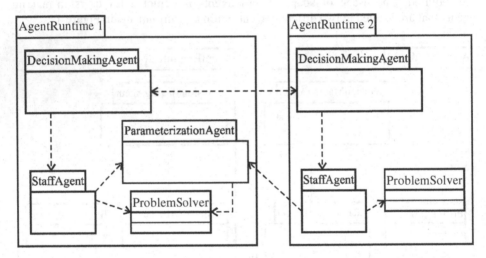

Fig. 2. Parameterization Agents at Two Different Runtime Environments

3.4 Design and Implementation of Adaptive Staff Agents

Because of the limitations of parameterization agents we study only adaptive staff agents in the remainder of this paper in more detail. We implement the adaptive agents based on the ManufAg agent-based framework [6]. ManufAg is a generalization and abstraction of the FABMAS multi-agent-system. It is based on the .NET remoting framework and is implemented in the C# programming language. In ManufAg, an agent mainly consists of a set of behaviors defining the reaction of the agent to different circumstances like incoming messages or events. An agent observes events generated by the environment and can act within that environment.

Additional behavior classes have to add to build an adaptive staff agent from a ManufAg staff agent. An appropriate mapping ω_φ has to be chosen. This mapping has to be integrated into the additional behavior classes of the agent. When an update of ω_φ is required the adaptive staff agent initiates it. For this purpose, an appropriate parameterization for a specific situation is determined. Therefore, an adaptive staff agent proposes several parameter combinations, initiates the solution of the problems for specific parameter settings, and assesses the performance of a certain parameterization by taking into account the performance measure value.

The software architecture of a single agent is based on a role-based approach [11]. An agent has its primary role that can not be changed during lifetime. Nevertheless, the agent can adopt and discard roles during runtime if necessary. Therefore, the characteristic of an agent can differ on demand. A new role can provide the agent with new features like services, goals, and actions; it may assign new behaviors to the agent. These behaviors define when and why an agent acts on special events like incoming messages, environmental or agent state changes. Staff agents provide the following behaviors in ManufAg [6]:

- Prepare_Solution,
- Parameterize_Algorithm,
- Solve_Or_Interrupt,
- Communicate_Solution.

The preparation phase of a certain solution activity is modeled within the behavior Prepare_Solution. The necessary data for the problem solution is collected. The parameterization of a certain problem solution method with external or internally determined parameters is carried out by the Parameterize_Algorithm behavior. The solution of the related manufacturing control problem is done by the Solve_Or_Interrupt behavior. The decision-making agent can stop the solution process after a certain amount of time. This is an important feature for "anytime" algorithms that provide a feasible solution for each $t > 0$. The staff agent sends information to other agents when it obtains a solution for a certain problem. This task is performed by the Communicate_Solution behavior. Adaptive staff agents require the more advanced functionality of (1.1), (1.2), (1.3), (2.1), and (3.1).

The additional behavior Detect_Situation is implemented for situation detection. The new behavior class Update_Mapping is used for the update of ω_φ. Using ω_φ is done by the slightly modified behavior Parameterize_Algorithm. The behavior Update_Mapping is started after Detect_Situation. When ω_φ is provided by a machine learning scheme the update is performed by a training of the machine learning scheme. We depict the adaptive staff agent architecture in the UML class diagram in Figure 3. Each adaptive staff agent needs data structures to store ω_φ. An appropriate software representation is straightforward for closed expressions like regression equations. In case of machine learning schemes a related internal representation has to be avoided. Here, we use a wrapper encapsulation of the machine learning approach in an object and store only a reference on this object within the adaptive staff agent.

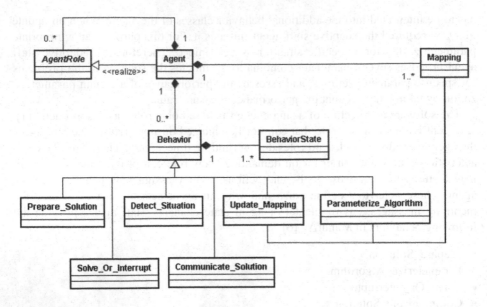

Fig. 3. Adaptive Staff Agent Architecture

4   Example from the Semiconductor Manufacturing Domain

To test the adaptive staff agent approach, we develop a multi-agent-system based on ManufAg [6] for the control of semiconductor wafer fabrication facilities (wafer fabs). We emulate a manufacturing process with batch processes (the processing of different jobs at the same time on the same machine), sequence-dependent set-up times, and re-entrant process flows [14]. Beside the adaptive staff agents we consider tool group agents that represent the machines of a tool group. Furthermore, we also use job and batch agents.

We dispatch the bottleneck batch tool group via the apparent tardiness cost (ATC) rule [12]:

$$I_{bi}(t) = \sum_{i=1}^{n_{bi}} \left[\frac{w_{ij}}{p_i} \, exp\left\{ -\frac{max\{d_{ij} - p_i - t + max(r_{bi} - t, 0), 0\}}{k \, \overline{p}} \right\} \right] \frac{n_{bi}}{B}. \tag{2}$$

Here, we denote by $I_{bi}(t)$ the ATC priority index of batch b from job family i at time t. Only jobs of the same family can be batched together. Batch b consists of n_{bi} jobs. Its maximum batch size is B. We denote by r_{bi} the maximum ready times of the jobs that form the batch. The maximum ready time is the earliest time where all jobs of the batch are available for processing.

The processing time of job family i is denoted by p_i, w_{ij} is used for the weight of job j of family i, d_{ij} denotes the corresponding due date. The notation $\overline{p}$ is used for the average processing time of all jobs waiting in front of the tool group. It becomes clear from (2) that ATC combines the shortest processing time (SPT) rule with a slack-based rule. The slack is scaled by a parameter k. It this well known that ATC is a dispatching rule that leads to a small total weighted tardiness (TWT). TWT is the sum of the weighted tardiness values of all completed jobs. The weighted tardiness is calculated as the product of the job weight and the tardiness of the job. The tardiness is given as the difference between the completion time and the due date maximized with zero. TWT is related to on-time delivery performance.

The performance of the dispatching approach is influenced by an appropriate choice of the scaling parameter k. Proper values for k have to be selected based on the batch machine factor μ, the tightness T, $\tilde{T}$ and the range R, $\tilde{R}$ of the due dates and arrival times of the jobs on the batching tool group. The single parameterization attribute is given by k. We obtain

$$a_1 = \mu, a_2 = T, \ a_3 = \tilde{T}, \ a_4 = R, \ a_5 = \tilde{R}, \tag{3}$$

and

$$w_1 = \omega_\varphi(a_1, a_2, a_3, a_4, a_5) = k. \tag{4}$$

The batch machine factor measures the average number of batches on a single machine. T and $\tilde{T}$ specify the position of the due dates and the arrival times on the time horizon. R and $\tilde{R}$ are basically estimators of the variance of the due dates and the arrival times. We use an adaptive staff agent to determine situation-dependent scaling parameters k. The adaptive staff agent forms batches, assigns batches to machines, and sequences them.

ω_φ is given by an inductive decision tree. The decision tree takes as an input a situation described by $(a_1, ..., a_5)$. Based on this input the inductive decision tree makes a decision and returns the output value for k. The decision tree is a data structure containing leaves, indicating a class, and decision nodes specifying tests that have to be carried out on the attributes (i.e., the input factors) of the test case in order to branch in other sub trees. The structure of a learned decision tree is a collection of disjoint hyper cubes that are created by partitioning the domains of attributes into intervals.

We use the software FuzzyModel Construction 1.0 to construct the inductive decision tree. We perform an event-driven update of ω_φ after each 1000 parameterization decisions.

We use two simulation models of wafer fabs to carry out the experiments. The first model is a reduced variant of the MIMAC Testbed Data Set 1 [3] with 146 machines that are organized into 37 tool groups. Among the tools are batching tools. The model contains two routes with 100 and 103 steps respectively. The process flow is highly reentrant. We denote this model by Model A. The second model is the full MIMAC Testbed Data Set 1. It contains over 200 machines within 80 tool groups. and two process flows with 210 an 245 processing steps respectively. It is called Model B.

We consider the total weighted tardiness (TWT) of the completed jobs and the cycle time (CT) as performance measures. The measure CT of a job is defined as the difference between the completion time and the ready time of the job.

We compare the adaptive dispatching approach with an approach that uses the fixed scaling value *k=1*. This approach is called naive approach. We also perform an exhaustive search that uses a large number of *k* values from the interval *[0.1, 5.0]* and selects the *k* that leads to the smallest TWT value of the jobs on the entire job shop level. This method is called global approach. For comparison reasons we also use a similar approach related to the jobs on a single batching tool group where we make the decisions on choosing *k* based on local TWT values (local approach).

We present some results of the simulation study in Table 1. We show all performance measure values relative to the values obtained from a FIFO dispatched wafer fab.

Table 1. Results of Computational Experiments for TWT and CT

	Model A		Model B	
Approach	TWT	CT	TWT	CT
Naive	0.7651	0.9818	0.7397	0.9770
Global	0.5883	0.9588	-	-
Local	0.6961	0.9752	0.7056	0.9710
Adaptive agents	0.6994	0.9752	0.7176	0.9710

We see from Table 1 that the adaptive agent approach leads to better results than the naive parameter setting strategy. It is slightly outperformed by the local approach. As expected, the global approach leads to the best results for Model A.

We cannot obtain results for the global approach for Model B with reasonable amount of time. This is caused by the fact that we have to run many simulations to find appropriate values for the scaling parameter. The time needed to perform a single simulation for a horizon of three month is for Model B around four minutes. At least 20 simulation runs (each for a fixed *k* value) are required to obtain reasonable results for the global approach. In case of the local approach, the amount of time needed for computation is smaller because repeated simulation runs are not required. However, a repeated calculation of job priorities (each for a fixed *k* value) based on expression (2) is required.

Therefore, both the local and the global approach are time-consuming and therefore not practicable for real-world situations as can be found in the semiconductor industry.

5 Conclusions and Future Research

In this paper, we discussed different possibilities to incorporate adaptability in agent-based manufacturing control systems. We decided to put adaptive capabilities directly into the staff agents from the PROSA architecture. We described the architecture of single adaptive staff agents. We presented the results of a case study where we apply adaptive staff agents to parameterize a certain class of dispatching rules used in semiconductor manufacturing.

There are several directions for future research. We have to extend the ontology [7] by adding constructs that allow for an update of ω_φ. Furthermore, so far little is known on an appropriate frequency of ω_φ updates. Here, experiments with hybrid strategies, i.e. an appropriate mix of event and time-driven updates seem to be useful. The update decision should be made by the adaptive staff agents. However, carry out the details is part of future research.

References

1. Brauer, W., Weiß, G.: Multi-machine Scheduling - A Multi-Agent Learning Approach. In: Proceedings of the Third International Conference on Multi-Agent Systems (ICMAS), IEEE Computer Society, pp. 42–48. IEEE Computer Society Press, Los Alamitos (1998)
2. Csaji, B.C., Kadar, B., Monostori, L.: Improving Multi-Agent Based Scheduling by Neurodynamic Programming. In: Mařík, V., McFarlane, D.C., Valckenaers, P. (eds.) Holo-MAS 2003. LNCS (LNAI), vol. 2744, pp. 110–123. Springer, Heidelberg (2003)
3. Fowler, J.W., Feigin, G., Leachman, R.: Semiconductor Manufacturing Testbed: Data Sets (1995)
4. Geiger, C.D., Uzsoy, R., Aytuk, H.: Rapid Modeling and Discovery of Priority Dispatching Rules: An Autonomous Learning Approach. Journal of Scheduling 9(1), 7–34 (2006)
5. Maione, B., Naso, D.: Evolutionary Adaptation of Dispatching Agents in Heterarchical Manufacturing Systems. International Journal of Production Research 39(7), 1481–1503 (2001)
6. Mönch, L., Stehli, M.: ManufAG: a Multi-Agent-System Framework for Production Control of Complex Manufacturing Systems. Information Systems and e-Business Management 4(2), 159–185 (2006)
7. Mönch, L., Stehli, M.: An Ontology for Production Control of Semiconductor Manufacturing Processes. In: Schillo, M., Klusch, M., Müller, J., Tianfield, H. (eds.) Proceedings First German Conference on Multiagent System Technologies (MATES). LNCS (LNAI), vol. 2831, pp. 156–167. Springer, Heidelberg (2003)
8. Mönch, L., Stehli, M., Zimmermann, J.: FABMAS - an Agent Based System for Semiconductor Manufacturing Processes. In: Mařík, V., McFarlane, D.C., Valckenaers, P. (eds.) HoloMAS 2003. LNCS (LNAI), vol. 2744, pp. 258–267. Springer, Heidelberg (2003)
9. Mönch, L., Stehli, M., Zimmermann, J., Habenicht, I.: The FABMAS Multi-Agent-System Prototype for Production Control of Waferfabs. Design, Implementation, and Performance Assessment. Production Planning & Control 17(7), 701–716 (2006)
10. Monostori, L.: AI and Machine Learning Techniques for Managing Complexity, Changes and Uncertainties in Manufacturing. Engineering Applications of Artificial Intelligence 16(4), 277–291 (2003)
11. Odell, J., Parunak, H.V.D., Fleischer, M.: Modeling Agent Organizations Using Roles. Software and Systems Modeling 2, 76–81 (2003)
12. Pinedo, M.: Scheduling Theory, Algorithms, and Systems. Prentice Hall, New Jersey (2002)
13. Piramuthu, S., Raman, N., Shaw, M.J., Park, S.H.: Integration of Simulation Modelling and Inductive Learning in an Adaptive Decision Support System. Decision Support Systems 9, 127–142 (1993)

14. Schömig, A., Fowler, J.W.: Modeling Semiconductor Manufacturing Operations. In: Proceedings of the 9th ASIM Dedicated Conference Simulation in Production and Logistics, pp. 55–64 (2000)
15. Utgoff, P.E.: Decision Trees. The MIT Encyclopedia of Cognitive Sciences, Bradford (1998)
16. Van Brussel, H., Wyns, J., Valckenaers, P., Bongaerts, L., Peeters, P.: Reference Architecture for Holonic Manufacturing Systems: PROSA. Computers in Industry 37(3), 225–276 (1998)
17. Weiß, G. (ed.): Adaption and Learning in Multi-Agent Systems. LNCS (LNAI), vol. 1042. Springer, Heidelberg (1996)

Dynamic Configuration and Management of e-Supply Chains Based on Internet Public Registries Visited by Clusters of Software Agents

Konrad Fuks, Arkadiusz Kawa, and Waldemar Wieczerzycki

Poznan University of Economics,
al. Niepodleglosci 10, 60-967 Poznan, Poland
{konrad.fuks, arkadiusz.kawa, w.wieczerzycki}@ae.poznan.pl

Abstract. There are three main contributions of the work presented in this paper. First, a particular approach to develop and manage multi-agent environments is presented. It is based on so called agent clusters which group agents that mutually cooperate to perform a particular mission, e.g. to build and manage supply chains, to negotiate details of order. Second contribution is the presentation of public registry model. Authors have widened RosettaNet approach to public registries. Third, the integration of agent cluster model and public registry model is presented. New approach shows how agent technology can automate information exchange process within public registry.

Keywords: Agent clusters, e-Supply Chains, RosettaNet Document Exchange Standards, e-Business Registries.

1 Introduction

Globalization entails necessity of easily configured and reconfigured supply chains. Enterprises which are subjects of supply chains must have well-defined access to the information generated by their suppliers and customers. Additionally, one has to emphasize that information flow must assemble all links of the supply chain, not only the closest partners. Information scope must start from suppliers' suppliers and end on customers' customers. This kind of information flow allows for fast and precise reaction of whole supply chain in changing environment conditions. Very important role in this scenario plays standardization of exchanged information within supply chain. Applied standard must be elastic and interoperable to meet needs of all trading partners. Large companies with highly developed back-end systems as well as small and medium enterprises should have possibility to utilize and generate information within their supply chains. This very important need for information can be satisfied by combining agent technology with e-business registries [10].

Agent technology is one of the most prominent and attractive technologies in computer science at the beginning of the new millennium [2]. Using software agents, especially to support e-commerce automation is a very promising direction. Additionally, nowadays business partnership is very often created dynamically and

V. Mařík, V. Vyatkin, A.W. Colombo (Eds.): HoloMAS 2007, LNAI 4659, pp. 281–292, 2007.
© Springer-Verlag Berlin Heidelberg 2007

maintained only for the required period of time such as a single transaction. For this reason agent technology can be useful for e-supply chain configuration, reconfiguration and management based on e-markets [3, 8].

To conduct B2B transactions properly agents must have access to well defined and structured business information. Therefore e-business registries can solve this problem. E-business registries – electronic platforms build for information exchange between supply chain's or supply network's enterprises. This kind of registries should be based on well-defined uniform information exchange standard. Therefore e-business registries secure coherent communication between trading partners. Nowadays one of the most popular meta-language for building e-business registries is XML (eXtensible Markup Language) and its descent standards. Usage of XML ensures system interoperability of the e-business registry and its openness for new trading partners (single enterprises or whole supply chains).

The paper is a continuation of work presented at the last HoloMas Conference [12]. Its structure is as follows.

In Section 2 multi-agent environment supporting collaboration of agents is briefly reminded. First, basic concepts of the approach are given. Next management problems concerning agents collaboration are described. The approach discussed in this section is inspired by selected mechanisms of the database technology which plays the role of a core technology in the development of business information systems [12].

Section 3 presents a new model of *RosettaNet* based public registries. In the beginning premises and environment of the model are described. In the second part of this section general interaction model and registry information model are presented.

In Section 4 integration of models presented in the above sections is given. Authors start from presentation of integration premises and agent types in the public registries. Section ends with exemplification of agent usage within public registries.

Section 5 concludes the paper.

2 Clusters of Collaborating Agents

We start with the presentation of mechanisms of multi-agent environment which support and facilitate cooperation among agents visiting the same environment. It is worth to emphasize that agent technology background is fully compatible with FIPA specification [4, 5, 6].

The main idea of the proposed multi-agent environment design is the use of so called agent clusters [12]. Before we introduce agent clusters, we have to define some basic concepts. Web servers built in agent technology (e.g. e-markets, e-auctions) can be accessed in practice by an arbitrary number of agents (e.g. representing many businessmen) which work independently, or collaborate with other agents, e.g. to dynamically re-configure electronic supply chains. Depending on whether agents collaborate or not, and how tight is their collaboration, we distinguish two levels of agents grouping: *constellations* and *clusters*. A constellation C_i groups agents which aim to achieve the common goal, typically to buy or sell products or services. Agents belonging to the same constellation can communicate with each other and be informed about progress of business efforts by the use of typical communication channels. Constellations are logically independent, i.e. an agent belonging to a single constellation is not influenced by the evolution of other constellations. It is possible for a single agent to contribute simultaneously in many constellations, thus the intersection between two constellations need not be empty. In this case, however, actions performed in the scope of one constellation are logically independent from actions performed in other constellations.

Agents belonging to the same constellation can collaborate tightly or loosely, depending on whether they represent the same business party, e.g. enterprise (possibly extended by business partners), corporation, or they represent different business parties, aiming to find new business opportunities. Tightly collaborating agents are grouped into the same agent cluster AC_i. Thus, a cluster is an agents subset of a corresponding constellation, with the restriction that a single agent A_i belongs in the scope of a single constellation exactly to one cluster, in particular, to a single-agent cluster. Of course, if the agent is included in many constellations, say n, then it belongs to n clusters.

A *semi-transaction* is a flat, ordered set of operations on the same business data repository (in particular - database operations) performed by agents of the same cluster, which is atomic, consistent and durable. In other words, a semi-transaction is the only unit of communication between a virtual agent representing component agents of a single cluster, and the business data management system (or DBMS).

Formally, a semi- transaction is defined as a triple:

$$ST = (Tid, Cid, ACid) \tag{1}$$

where *Tid* is a transaction identifier, *Cid* is an identifier of the encompassing constellation, and *ACid* is an identifier of the cluster to which *ST* is assigned.

Now we focus on operations which can be performed on semi-transactions being contexts of agent clusters activity.

Every semi-transaction is started implicitly by *initialize(T_i)* operation, which is performed automatically by the agent environment on the very beginning of respective cluster activity, i.e. after first data operation is requested by one of cluster members. This cluster member is called a *transaction leader*. *initialize(T_i)* is also triggered automatically, directly after one of cluster members performs explicit *commit(T_i)* operation, or implicit *auto-commit(T_i)* operation. All consecutive transactions of the same cluster are executed in a serial order.

After a semi-transaction is initialized by the transaction leader, other cluster members can enter it at any moment of the transaction execution, by the use of explicit *connect(T_i)* operation, which is performed in asynchronous manner. Once connected to the transaction, any member of a cluster can perform *disconnect(T_i)* operation, provided there is still at least one agent assigned to this transaction. *disconnect(T_i)* operation brakes the link between transaction T_i and the agent, which can next:

1. close its session,
2. suspend its operations for a particular time moment and re-connect to the same cluster later,
3. wait until transaction commits and connect to a next semi-transaction of the same cluster,
4. continue to work in different cluster in the scope of another semi-transaction, provided the agent belongs to more than one cluster.

In cases: 1, 2 and 4, *disconnect(T_i)* operation plays the role of *sub-commit* operation, which means that the respective agent intends to commit its own operations, and leaves the final decision whether to commit or not the semi-transaction to its recent collaborators (agents).

Operations introduced up till now concern a single semi-transaction. Next two operations: *merge(T_i)* and *split()* are special, since they concern two semi-transactions. They are extremely important for supporting typical business activities (e.g. on e-markets). *Semi-transaction T_j* can merge into transaction T_i by the use of *merge(T_i)* operation, provided the members of a cluster assigned to T_i allow for it. After this operation, transaction T_j is logically removed from the agents environment, i.e. operation *abort(T_j)* is automatically triggered by the environment, and all T_j operations are logically re-done by transaction T_i. These actions are only logical, since in fact operations of T_j are just added to the list of T_i operations, and T_i continues its execution, however, the number of agents assigned to it is now increased. It means that until the end of T_i execution, the agents cluster assigned previously to T_j is merged into the cluster assigned to T_i. Of course, *merge(T_i)* operation is only allowed in the scope of the same constellation. Obviously *merge(T_i)* can be useful when an access conflict between two clusters of the same constellation arises. But in terms of business activities this operation allows to couple representatives of business parties which decide to cooperate (e.g. negotiate cooperation conditions, browse proposals of business contracts and other documents, or even electronically sign them finally). Its use is more detailed further in this section.

Similarly to *merge* operation, *split()* operation can be used in order to avoid access conflicts. *split()* operation causes that a single semi-transaction T_i is split into two transactions: T_i and T_j. After *split()* operation, a subset of cluster members, originally assigned to T_i, is re-assigned to newly created transaction T_j. Also all operations performed by re-assigned agents are logically removed from transaction T_i and redone in transaction T_j directly after its creation. Notice, that in practice this operation can be useful if cooperation of representatives of two business parties for some reasons fails, and they decide for example to autonomously analyze the e-market to look for new parties offering them better cooperation conditions.

Contrarily to *merge* operation which is always feasible, provided members of the other cluster allow it, *split* operation can be done only in particular contexts. Speaking very briefly, a semi-transaction can be split if two sub-clusters, which intend to separate their further actions, have operated on disjoint subsets of data, before *split* operation is requested. If the intersection between the data accessed is not empty, *split* operation is still possible, provided the data have been accessed by the two sub-clusters in a compatible mode (in a classical meaning).

Finally, there are two typical operations on transactions: *commit* and *abort* which are performed in the classical manner (according to the database technology).

3 Public Registry Model (*PRM*)

Premises of the Model

In this section we propose a new approach to public registries. In order to better illustrate the model and to relate it to practical aspects (existing solutions) authors utilized as backbone of the public registry model *RosettaNet* standards.

Themes of this paper don't bring up detailed description of *RosettaNet* standards[2]. We have focused our work on public registry model presentation and interactions between trading partner within public registry.

Main value of the presented model is addressed to SMEs because they mostly left behind well-defined information exchange in the supply networks. SMEs comprise over 95% of enterprises and two thirds of private sector employment in OECD countries [9]. This statistic shows how important is active participation of those enterprises in building supply chains and/or supply networks.

Environment of the Model
1. *RosettaNet* standards do not define registry building specification. Public registries can be built with UDDI or ebXML standards.
2. All trading partners have the same level of public registry control and possibilities of its components usage.
3. Public registry is maintained by Public Registry Host (PRH) with support of *RosettaNet* as a standard body.
4. Public Registry data is well-defined for specific market, thanks to PRH knowledge about the market.
5. PRH should be *RosettaNet* member due to good knowledge about standards.
6. Back-end system in trading partner's IT infrastructure is not obligatory. Information can be processed in machine or human readable format.
7. Trading partners can join PRM alone to search market for new suppliers and clients or adapt PRM to their own supply chains.

General Interaction Model
Interaction between entities starts after successful public registry modeling and implementation by Public Registry Host (PRH). PRH decides which registry standard to use (ebXML, UDDI, other). PRH deploys all needed data (potential business scenarios and connected with them documents, messages and business interaction models ($BS/D/M^3$)) into Public Registry (PR). All deployed data should result from *RosettaNet* standards. Also before deployment all data must be validated with *RosettaNet* centrally maintained Validation Tool. When PR is ready to use Trading Partners (TPs) can create their own profiles within registry. All needed data structure for TPs profiles is specified by PRH on registry modeling stage. Well defined and structured profiles allow TPs to search for possible business contacts [7]. TPs profiles serve also as a base for authentication process in all further business information exchanges. Trading Partners communicate with each other using *RosettaNet* protocols and documents. For wide adoption of PRM authors assumed that access to Public Registry is granted for all TPs (new and well familiar with *RosettaNet* standards).

---

[2] In order to better understanding of *RosettaNet* standards authors encourage readers to acquaint with information on *RosettaNet* web portal – www.rosettanet.org.

[3] *BS/D/M* – all possible business scenarios and related with them documents, messages, business interaction models published by PRH. All these entities are based on *RosettaNet* standards. Documents and messages are stored in XML files and related XML Schemas. Business models are UML diagrams.

Additionally within Public Registry can be stored statistic data about business scenarios utilization among TPs. Such data can be very helpful in PR improvements and developments. RosettaNet may also use this statistics as base for fundamental standards development and upgrades.

Registry Information Model
Presented information model relies on modular approach for BS/D/M creation. We propose two level classification of BS/D/M stored in the PR:

- General Level – PRH creates BS/D/M according to possessed knowledge about the market and *RosettaNet* standards. In the PR should be stored all possible variants of BS/D/M divided into well-described modules. Nature of each module relies on differences between possible business scenarios within specific market domain.
- Trading Partner Level – level of individual TPs registries. Smaller, constrained bases of BS/D/M General Level modules or self – created by *RosettaNet* familiar TPs BS/D/M according to *RosettaNet* standards. Additionally TPs can add their own constrains to General Level BS/D/M but those new modules must be validated by PRH. Validation is conducted with centrally maintained by *RosettaNet* Validation Tool [TPIR – PIP].

We have distinguished three possible scenarios of good PRM utilization. First two scenarios refer mostly to SME sector. Third scenario focuses on *RosettaNet* familiar enterprises, involvement of those entities in PRM adoption is very important because they create foundations of *RosettaNet* standard utilization.

1. In the first scenario TP is new to *RosettaNet* standards and does not have proper IT infrastructure (back – end systems and/or human staff) for final BS/D/M preparation. TP operates mainly on General Level BS/D/M and information is manually processed within its company by using RosettaNet complaisant forms. PRH has here very important role of advisor and supervisor in TP's B2B transactions. On the one hand PRH advises in choosing proper General Level module / modules of BS/D/M, on the other hand it supervises first steps of TP's PR transactions.

2. Second scenario is addressed to those SMEs which are new to *RosettaNet* standards and have well trained IT stuff. Back – end system is not required but its possession can significantly improve business information processing. TPs without back – end system manually process information using RosettaNet complaisant forms. TPs can work on General Level BS/D/M, constrain or expand them accordingly to their business needs. All changes in BS/D/M must be validated before usage. Lower level of PRH support is required in this scenario.

3. Third scenario entities are *RosettaNet* familiar enterprises. They can either utilize all needed General Level modules of BS/D/M from PR or create their own BS/D/M due to their *RosettaNet* standard knowledge. Of course all acquired form General Level BS/D/Ms can be additionally constrained or expanded, but before final utilization they must be validated. PRH supports TPs with comprehensive information about General Level modules.

4 Application of Agent Technology to Public Registry Model

In this section we propose the adaptation of agent technology, especially agent clusters into Public Registry Model (PRM).

The approach stipulates that information about Trading Partners included in PRM can be also successfully applied in creating dynamic and flexible supply chains. Hence, this new proposal expands the present opportunities offered by *RosettaNet* standards.

Thanks to embedding agent technology in PRM, automation of comparing, reorganizing and verifying BS/D/M scenarios is greatly facilitated.

Premises of the Approach
- There is a need to automate some of the operations in PRM, such as: checking, comparing and reorganizing BS/D/M scenarios.
- Enterprises have limited opportunities to automatically search, select and choose future TPs.
- Supply chains are characterized by the integration of activities, operations and functions carried out at different supply stages scattered in various corners of the world. At present supply chains compete with one another.
- There is a need to create temporal and dynamic supply chains aimed at executing a single transaction.
- The aim of supply chain configuration problem is to find a feasible configuration with which the supply chain can achieve a high level of performance [1].

Environment of the New Approach
- Public Registry serves as a base for searching new TPs and creating stable, temporal and dynamic supply chains.
- PRM is expanded with multi-agent environment and each TP is represented by specific group of software agents.
- Agents are divided into two constellations: PRH constellation and TPs constellation.
- Access to Public Registry is granted for all TPs' software agents, but level of privileges of each agent can differ.
- TPs' agents collaborate with each other and consequently add value to established supply chain.

Types of Agents Used in PRM
Two types of software agents representing both PRH and TPs can be distinguished. PRH is represented by the following software agents:

a. Leader Agent – it creates the agent cluster, it is an axis of the whole process, and it groups other agents which can cooperate to perform a particular task. It's also responsible for building temporary Trading Partners Registries and extending TPs registries with reorganized BS/D/Ms.

b. Validating Agent – it cooperates with *RosettaNet Validation Tool*, checks and validates BS/D/Ms (whether they are compatible with *RosettaNet* standards).

c. Notifying Agent – notifies TPs' agents when a new scenario appears and informs about the progress of the validation of created by TPs BS/D/M.
d. Error Handling Agent – is responsible for informing TPs about validation failure and inserting errors to error registry.

TPs are represented by the following software agents:

a. Searching Agent – it's responsible for picking the right TPs for specific scenario that would be compatible with the requirements given by delegating it TP.
b. Coordinating Agent – this agent is the most complex one, since it can manage multi-task processes, it cooperates with and manages other agents, it represents the entity which coordinates the whole supply chain and all the processes connected with it, it creates the sub-cluster.
c. Offering Agent – it represents particular entities (e.g. supplier, logistic service provider, insurance company) which take part in creating a specific supply chain.
d. Validating Agent of TP – is responsible for checking and comparing BS/D/Ms and for contact with Validating Agent of PRH (if changes are introduced to BS/D/M).

Exemplification of Using Agent Clusters in PRM

A sample process of building new supply chain within PRM will be introduced in this section.

Let's imagine that a TP-A (e.g. a trading network) wants to find a potential business partners for delivery and distribution of 100 pallets of fresh juice, a weekly cycles, from a distributing center in the California to 30 supermarkets scattered in the US, for no more than $15 for a pallet and in deferred payment of 30 days. The scenario discussed above is quite complex and hence several entities such as producer, supplier, logistic service provider, insurance company will have to be employed in order to succeed with the realization of the scenario.

The Searching Agent (SA) of TP-A starts searching potential TPs appropriate for this specific business scenario. If the searching process is successful SA informs Leader Agent (LA) of PRH about need of a new agent cluster to be created (*initialize* operation, cf. Section 2). LA designates for leader of new created cluster Coordinating Agent (CA) of TP-A. CA invites to the cluster Offering Agents (OAs) of potential TPs (*connect* or *disconnect* operation, cf. Section 2). OA, which do not compete with one another, can start cooperation to place better offer to cluster leader (CA).

Agents merge (cf. Section 2) with one another in order to create temporal and dynamic supply chains (sub-clusters) that would be able to compete with other OAs of TPs or supply chains (sub-clusters). Each sub-cluster has its own CA which supervises the procedures and it selects and integrates potential OAs within specific cluster. Each OA can initiate sub-cluster creation and become CA. The offers of particular agents (OAs) can merge but they can also split depending on the offer details changeability of other clusters, e.g. price, delivery terms, etc. If after negotiation a different SA can propose the same price but better delivery terms, the CAs of this cluster and its sub-clusters have to react in new circumstances and find an alternative OAs that would fill the split gap.

Particular OAs or sub-clusters of OAs, who are subject to CA, work independently on their tasks. For example, OA of a logistic service provider searches for the proper means of transport and empty spaces in warehouses and distribution stores. Before starting the negotiation process between CA of the cluster, CAs of the sub-clusters and independent OAs the CA has to gather all the offers from OAs and pick the best ones.

Next parts of the process are seven stages of TPs agents operation on the Public Registry. To better illustrate those operations experimental environment with the following conditions were created:

- There are two business sides of the process. One is TP-A (cluster leader). Other is TP-B – group of TPs which have united into one sub-cluster to place the best offer to TP-A.
- TP-B is represented by group of its Leaders Agents. Agents of other TPs in sub-cluster only communicate with agents of sub-cluster Leader.
- TP-B entities have to unify their BS/D/Ms within sub-cluster (see stage 2, 3, below). This operation is crucial for business cooperation between TP-A and TP-B in connection with need of one coherent version of BS/D/Ms in TP-A and TP-B registries.

Agent operations on PR are divided into seven stages:

1. Validating Agent (VA) of TP-A communicates with VA of TP-B and informs which BS/D/Ms are required for cooperation (e.g. Notify Of Shipment Receipt, Distribute Inventory Report, Request Shipping Order, Notify of Shipment Documentation). VA of TP-B checks if these BS/D/Ms are in sub-cluster's TP's registries and expands this list of required BS/D/Ms if needed with proper BS/D/Ms from sub-cluster's TP's registries. If there not all BS/D/Ms are present in sub-cluster's TPs registries then proper BS/D/Ms are acquired from other side registry/registries. On this stage only presence of required BS/D/Ms is checked.
2. VA of sub-cluster Leader communicates with PRH's LA to commission temporary Trading Partner Level Registry creation for unified BS/D/Ms. PRH's LA creates temporary registry and grants administration privileges to sub-cluster Leaders agents. Other TPs agents can only communicate with sub-cluster Leader agents and delegate them for administrative work on registry.
3. VA of sub-cluster Leader groups all BS/D/Ms into topical sub-registries (e.g. Notify Of Shipment Receipt sub-registry) in temporary Trading Partner Lever Registry.
4. Each sub-registry's BS/D/Ms are compared with each other to elaborate one unified version of BS/D/M. Authors bring up fragment of standard RosettaNet "Notify Of Shipment Receipt" XML document as an example of unification process. This stage consists of three steps[4]:
   - Firstly leading VA compares all proper BS/D/M's XML documents with each other to determine which fields are missing (see below code example – comparing of two documents is shown, bolded field is missing). Lists of missing fields for each TP with each document are prepared.

---

[4] (...) symbol placed in code samples shows that there is additional XML code. This procedure was applied due to transparency of the process is increased.

Example of a "Notify Of Shipment Receipt" XML document code. Partner Interface Processes, RosettaNet Standard.

```
Document 1.

( ... )
<ShipmentReceipt schemaVersion="">
           ( ... )
           <ReportDateTime>2007-02-
15T08:30:00+08:00</ReportDateTime>
           <ShipmentIdentifier>String</ShipmentIdentifier>
           <ShipmentReceiptLineItem schemaVersion="">
                 ( ... )
                 <uuom:UnitOfMeasure
( ... )>1BF</uuom:UnitOfMeasure>
           </ShipmentReceiptLineItem>
           <dl:TrackingReference schemaVersion="">
           ( ... )
           </dl:TrackingReference>
           <TransportedBy schemaVersion="">
           ( ... )
           </TransportedBy>
     </ShipmentReceipt>
( ... )


Document 2.

( ... )
<ShipmentReceipt schemaVersion="">
           ( ... )
           <ReportDateTime>2007-02-
15T08:30:00+08:00</ReportDateTime>
           <ShipmentIdentifier>String</ShipmentIdentifier>
           <ShipmentReceiptLineItem schemaVersion="">
                 ( ... )
           </ShipmentReceiptLineItem>
           <dl:TrackingReference schemaVersion="">
           ( ... )
           </dl:TrackingReference>
           <TransportedBy schemaVersion="">
           ( ... )
           </TransportedBy>
     </ShipmentReceipt>
     ( ... )
```

- Secondly TPs' VAs informs leading VA about fields which are obligatory in their BS/D/Ms (c.f. Section 3). Above lists are expanded with information about it (additional ids are added). This model of reorganizing and unifying XML documents is based on simple rule concerning obligatory fields in XML documents: *Obligatory field can't be removed from document.*
- Thirdly leading VA is reorganizing each XML document if needed. Reorganization can take the form of two opposing processes – simple adding and removing fields (XML makers). When VA removes fields it must check if this field is obligatory (c.f. above rule).

If BS/D/M was changed, it has to be validated by PRH's VA. If the validation is successful, then PRH's Notifying Agent informs TP-B's VA about it. If it isn't, then PRH's Error Handling Agent transfers this information to TP-B's VA and inserts the errors to Error Registry. In this case TP-B's VA starts reorganizing process again but must take all errors into consideration.

5. On this stage VA of TP-A communicates with PRH's LA to commission temporary Trading Partner Level Registry creation for this cluster needs. PRH's LA creates temporary registry and grants administration privileges to TP-A's agents. TP-B's agents can only communicate with TP-A's agents and delegate them for administrative work on registry.

6. VA of TP-A groups own and unified TP-B's BS/D/Ms into topical sub-registries (e.g. Notify Of Shipment Receipt sub-registry) in temporary Trading Partner Lever Registry.

7. Each sub-registry's BS/D/Ms are compared and unified analogical to stage 4.

After unification of BS/D/Ms TPs' VAs inform TPs' CAs about process results. If reorganization were successful each CA inform its delegating entity (TP, TP's back-end system, other agent) about it and cooperation along with RosettaNet standards between TPs starts. When reorganization ends with failure cluster Leader may search for other potential partners and invite their OAs into cluster or simply may inform PRH's LA to cancel the cluster, its related sub-clusters and temporary registries.

When cooperation between TPs ends all temporary registries may be included in Trading Partner Level Registry as sub-registries with proper identifier of cooperation (involved TPs identifiers, type of cooperation, etc.). These sub-registries may be used as base for future cooperation between the same TPs or other TPs.

Of course, all the procedures take place in accordance with *RosettaNet* standards. Trading Partners communicate with one another using *RosettaNet* rules (cf. Section 3).

5 Conclusions

The following main advantages of the proposed approach can be distinguished:

- Agent clusters allow unrestricted collaboration among agents of the same business party, as well as safe and controlled cooperation among different business parties.
- Public Registries and agent technology give the opportunity to integrate smaller supply chains into global supply network.
- Enterprises can automatically search, select and choose future TPs.
- Thanks to embedding agent technology in PRM, automation of comparing, reorganizing and verifying BS/D/M scenarios is greatly facilitated.
- Agents can be able to support efficient supply chain configuration, including partners who offer one another the best cooperation possibilities and conditions at a given time.
- There is a possibility to create temporal and dynamic supply chains aimed at executing a single transaction.

Of course, the approach presented in this paper is general and it can take place not only within supply chains but also in other areas of cooperation within e-business.

Nowadays authors work also on advanced negotiation mechanism. It will allow VAs to negotiate which fields of BS/D/Ms XML documents are really required and which can be omitted.

Next interesting direction of research is cooperation between TPs and/or TPs' agents from different public registries based on the same standard (e.g. *RosettaNet*).

References

[1] Blomqvist, E., Levashova, T., Öhrgen, A., Sandkuhl, K., Smirnov, A., Tarassov, V.: Configuration of Dynamic SME Supply Chains Based on Ontologies. In: 2nd Int. Conference on Industrial Applications of Holonic and Multi-Agent Systems, Holomas (2005)

[2] Call for Participation: In: 4th International Joint Conference AAMAS on Autonomous Agents and Multiagent Systems, www.agtivity.com

[3] Denkena, B., Zwick, M., Woelk, P.O.: Multiagent-Based process Planning and Scheduling in Context of Supply Chains. In: 1st Int. Conference on Industrial Applications of Holonic and Multi-Agent Systems, Holomas (2003)

[4] Foundation for Intelligent Physical Agents, FIPA Abstract Architecture Specification, www.fipa.org/specs/fipaSC00001L/

[5] Foundation for Intelligent Physical Agents, FIPA Communicative Act Library Specification, www.fipa.org/specs/fipa00037/

[6] Foundation for Intelligent Physical Agents, FIPA ACL Message Structure Specification, www.fipa.org/specs/fipa00061

[7] ebXML Registry Information Model v2.0, http://www.oasis-open.org/committees/regrep/documents/2.0/specs/ebrim.pdf

[8] Labarthe, O., Tranvouez, E., Ferrarini, A., Espinasse, B., Montreuil, B.: A Heterogeneus Multi-agent Modelling for Distributed Simulation of Supply Chain. In: 1st Int. Conference on Industrial Applications of Holonic and Multi-Agent Systems, Holomas (2003)

[9] OECD SME and Entrepreneurship Outlook – 2005 edn. www.oecd.org/document/15/0,2340,en_2649_33956792_35096847_1_1_1_1,00.html

[10] Ulieru, M.: The Holonic Enterprise: Modelling Holarchies as Mass to Enable Global Collaboration. In: Mařík, V., McFarlane, D.C., Valckenaers, P. (eds.) HoloMAS 2003. LNCS (LNAI), vol. 2744, Springer, Heidelberg (2003)

[11] Trading Partner Implementation Requirements Standard, RosettaNet Standards, portal.rosettanet.org/cms/sites/RosettaNet/Standards/RStandards/tpir/index.html

[12] Wieczerzycki, W.: Polymorphic Agent Clusters – The Concept to Design Multi-agent Environments Supporting Business Activities. In: Mařík, V., Brennan, R.W., Pěchouček, M. (eds.) HoloMAS 2005. LNCS (LNAI), vol. 3593, Springer, Heidelberg (2005)

A Multiagent Control System for Shop Floor Assembly

Gonçalo Cândido and José Barata

New University of Lisbon – Faculty of Sciences and Technology
UNINOVA, New Technology Development Institute,
Quinta da Torre, 2825-114 Caparica, Portugal
{gmc, jab}@uninova.pt

Abstract. Current globalization associated to new customers' needs are decreasing products' life-cycle and pushing researchers to find new ways to provide shop floor assembly systems with agility to adapt to this new volatile reality. This document describes a multiagent implementation to control a shop floor system, with increased plug and play capabilities and providing fast system (re)configuration. In this approach, each shop floor component was agentified enhancing its adaptability and interaction competences to respond to environmental requests. Each agent representing a shop floor component can be aggregated to form a coalition that coordinates higher level processes (complex skills) based on the ones available in its members. An ontology is used to ensure an accurate information exchange, as well as to define the domain and relations between entities. This approach also shows how to adapt legacy systems to support innovative approaches.

Keywords: multiagent systems, agile shop floor, distributed control, ontology.

1 Introduction

The main objective of this document is to describe a multiagent control architecture applied to a shop floor assembly cell. Due to the lack of implementations in real production platforms, this proof-of-concept approach tries to show that multiagent paradigm is a good choice to develop reconfigurable and agile control systems. This paradigm is already adopted to handle problems of complexity, autonomy, distributivity, intelligence, integration, etc. [1]

In the last years, the manufacturing world has deeply felt the effects of globalization on all its different levels. The consumers demand high quality and highly customized products with dynamically variable volumes and a minimum possible time-to-market. The actual manufacturing world has to deal with several critical issues, such as 1) long time for system design and installation, 2) complex and time-consuming re-engineering phase, 3) extremely centralized/hierarchical applications, 4) no scalability, 5) no fault-tolerance, 6) incompatibility between different vendors' equipment and legacy systems, 7) shop floor isolated from higher level business environments, etc.

Some manufacturing paradigms try to face these concerns, such as Flexible and Reconfigurable Manufacturing Systems [2], Evolvable Assembly Systems [3-4] and

V. Mařík, V. Vyatkin, A.W. Colombo (Eds.): HoloMAS 2007, LNAI 4659, pp. 293–302, 2007.

Holonic Manufacturing [5-7] paradigms. Multiagent systems approach is one of the most adopted technologies to deploy these paradigms' applications.

There are already a few multiagent implementations and methodologies available for this subject [8-10], however the industrial world is still reticent to use this approach. The main reasons for this situation are: 1) Paradigm misunderstanding due to lack of practical test-cases, 2) unawareness about manufacturing requirements changes, 3) lack of experience in multiagent systems by actual integrators, 4) risk of investment in a disruptive technology, etc.

As the work being described in this paper can help to prove, multiagent systems can provide 1) modularization of shop floor components improving reutilization, 2) distributed control, 3) reconfiguration rather than reprogramming, 3) simultaneous production of different products, and 4) legacy equipment integration.

The next chapter presents the NovaFlex shop floor cell used as a test-bench; the third chapter consists on an overview about the chosen architecture and development methodologies; the forth chapter details the support ontology; the fifth chapter describes the multiagent system entities and relations between them. At last, the final conclusions are presented.

2 NovaFlex Shop Floor Environment

The NovaFlex manufacturing system is installed at the Intelligent Robotic Centre in UNINOVA and is composed of two assembly robots, an automatic warehouse and a transport system that connects all the modules, as indicated in Fig. 1.

One robot cell consists of a 5-axis ABB IRB-2000 robot with an exchange tool device, and a tools' magazine with capacity to store 4 grippers. This legacy system has no direct TCP/IP connection. The unique external communication with the controller is by using proprietary ABB protocols (ADLP-10 and ARAP 2.0) through a RS232 connection.

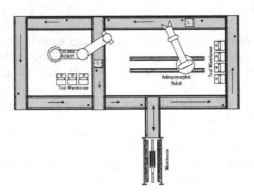

Fig. 1. NovaFlex subsystem layout

The other robot is a Bosch SCARA SR800, also with an exchange tool device, and another tools magazine with capacity to store 4 grippers. In this case, the external communication method is even more inadequate. In fact, the unique interaction possibility is through read/write commands sent by a serial connection, adapted to translate current-loop to RS232, using the programming language BAPS.

The transport system is currently controlled by a Beckhoff CX-1000 PLC that already provides direct TCP/IP connection. This PLC controls the several conveyors, transfer units, and pallet fixers used to hold the pallet with precision for assembly purposes. For external communication, it was used the proprietary ADS Java library that can be easily integrated in the agents' source code, and allows reading and update of variables inside the PLC.

3 System Overview

In this approach, each shop floor component is abstracted by an agent (Fig. 2) – a process frequently called agentification. This way, each component is enhanced with more autonomy, intelligence and interoperability. The approach follows some guidelines from the CoBASA reference architecture [10].

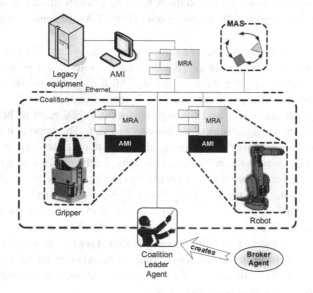

Fig. 2. Multiagent basic Architecture

Each shop floor component is abstracted as a Manufacturing Resource Agent (MRA) that is recognized in the multiagent system as the entity that controls a specific equipment instance or module. An MRA is generic enough to adapt to any instance of a determined type of equipment, just by querying the ontology about its own configuration parameters. In order to maintain MRAs independent from particular controller implementations details, they interact with an Agent-Machine Interface (AMI). An AMI is basically a software wrapper that is able to translate generic requests, described in Agent Communication Language (ACL) messages [11] exchanged with its MRA, to corresponding equipment actuators, in order to execute a physical action. The AMI is also responsible for the lower level control, reporting to its MRA a detected fault/error during running time. This approach enables the integration of legacy systems. Resuming, the AMI executes the skills exposed by the MRA. It is important to emphasise that the AMI it is not necessary in case of equipment modules that already include computational power able to support agents. In this case the MRA is included in the computational device and the MRA directly accesses the input/output ports required to control the module. This is a very important aspect when dealing with a manufacturing environment composed of distributed intelligent devices.

By publishing its skills, which is done by registering them in a shared database (Directory Facilitator (DF) present in FIPA architecture [12]), different entities can request available skills. Still, by aggregation of some skills, new more complex skills can be offered. Using a Broker Agent, the integrator can analyze the system. He can choose which skills he wants to aggregate and launch a Coalition Leader Agent (CLA) to automatically coordinate the interactions between skills' providers with the intention to support a new complex skill. A CLA is a pure software entity that knows how to coordinate different MRAs, and even other CLAs, to support the execution of complex skills.

In order to allow different agents to understand each other, the ontology that describes shop floor assembly domain also defines the interaction parameters and vocabulary to be used during agents' interactions. All the agents enclose this part of the ontology in order to create and understand ACL messages content.

Once the agents are active and sharing their skills, they need to be invoked in a particular sequence to manufacture the desired product. The approach chosen to this implementation was to provide each pallet that transports either raw materials or the final product with decision capabilities. This way, each physical pallet is abstracted by a *Pallet Agent* that knows how to execute its own process sequence. The sequence can be inserted by the user through each *Pallet Agent* GUI, or loaded from a file. This approach allows different products being produced at the same time in the same shop floor environment. Even if the process plan needs to change, the integrator simply needs to update the file to be loaded in each *Pallet Agent* – no programming neither configuration are needed in the assembly equipment. Also, in reengineering phase, if some equipment needs to be added/substituted/removed, the other components do not need to be reprogrammed to adapt to this change.

4   Ontology

An ontology can be defined as a "data model that represents a domain and is used to reason about the objects in that domain and the relations between them" [13]. The construction of an ontology is based on the creation and consensus of terms and relations among those terms, which allow the creation of an abstraction level above specific implementations.

During the system's development, an ontology, as generic as possible, was developed to describe the shop floor assembly domain and be used as knowledge source for the multiagent system (see Fig. 3). By adding to this ontology some instances corresponding to real equipment present in *NovaFlex* environment, it is possible to have a global view about the current system modules, features and relations between them. To develop this same ontology it was used *Protégé* tool [14], added with *OntoViz* (ontology visualization purposes) [15] and *OntologyBeanGenerator* (automatic generation of Java files representing the ontology) [16] plugins. The application visual interface allows an intuitive development/update of the ontology, in addition to support the automatic translation to files that can be used by the agents.

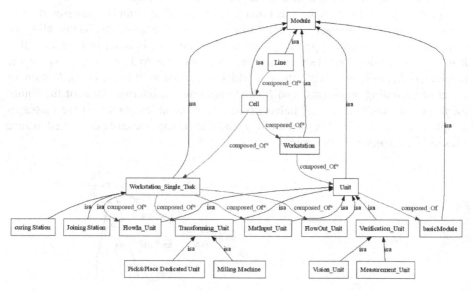

Fig. 3. Partial view of the shop floor assembly ontology

4.1 Skills

An important concept present in ontology is the definition of skills. By definition, skill is the ability to perform actions that are then needed to support the manufacturing process. Skills can have different abstraction levels, i.e. a complex skill is generated through the aggregation of other skills, basic/or complex ones (see Fig. 5.a). The complex skills' instances present in the ontology identify which basic skills are necessary in order to provide it.

Each equipment instance defines which skills that specific entity can support. When a MRA searches the ontology for its configuration parameters, having its serial number and type of equipment as search constrains, it will update the skills it can support. In order to make them visible to other agents, the just configured MRA will register its own skills on DF. In fact, two different instances can provide the same skill, e.g. two robots can provide a *MoveLinear* skill that can be requested in a similar way.

```
((action
     (agent-identifier
        :name IRB2000-3948@Goncalo:1099/JADE
        :addresses (sequence http://Goncalo:7778/acc))
     (RobotAction
        :RobotRequest MoveLinear
        :RobotStatus Ready
        :RobotArgs (sequence -865.1 -147.9 900.0 180 -90.0 1.2)))))
```

Fig. 4. ACL message sent to a RobotAgent requesting a MoveLinear (example)

Each skill has an according action model that defines the parameters needs to be exchange during a request for its execution. Each type of equipment possesses its own message template to interact with external entities. This template can handle all kinds of requests for a specific type of equipment. For instance, in order to interact with a *RobotAgent* (a MRA that abstracts a common robot), the ACL message contains the parameters *RobotRequest* (definition of which particular skill to execute), *RobotArgs* (a set of according arguments) and *RobotStatus* (current internal status of the equipment, or error code in case of failure) (see Fig. 4 for an example). These messages templates are also defined in the ontology, and can be automatically converted to Java files to be interpreted by the agents.

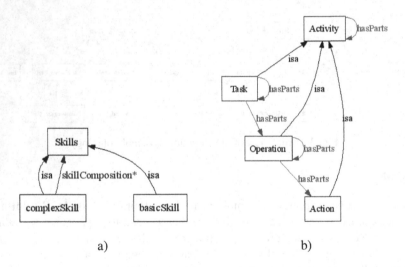

a)   b)

Fig. 5. a) Skills levels' relations, b) Activity types

An action is a subtype of activity (see Fig. 5.b), and each MRA can handle a set of actions. An operation consists on the aggregation of different actions, however it is still needed the coordination of these actions to really grant the according operation. In this approach, the actions' coordination (complex skill execution) is provided by the CLA.

5 Multiagent System

The agent platform chosen to develop the application was taken in consideration regarding systems features as maintenance, current activity, evolution, popularity, accessibility, and others. JADE [17], at starting date of development, was found has the one that best corresponds to this proof-of-concept immediate goals [18].

5.1 Manufacturing Resource Agents

The MRA can be defined as a manufacturing component extended with agent skills, which corresponds to its agentification in order to be able to participate in an agents' society [10]. Since all equipment intricacies are wrapped by the use of an AMI, the MRA is abstract enough to adapt to different instances of a type of equipment; e.g. the two robots present in the *NovaFlex* environment (ABB IRB-2000 and Bosch Turbo Scara SR800) are abstracted exactly by the same MRA source code, being only differentiated after querying the ontology by its configuration parameters and discovering the according AMI to make the lower level connection to hardware.

As said before, each MRA comprises the interaction Java classes that allow the agent to understand other agents and interact with them whenever it is necessary. Once the messages' semantics are described, it is necessary to define an interaction protocol. The fundamental interaction protocol adopted was the standard FIPA Request Interaction Protocol [19], due to simple message exchange requirements and for simplicity purposes. These can still be combined to perform more complex message exchanges. Some interactions depend on previous ones and available action results, i.e. sometimes a response to an incoming request is put on hold until an intermediate interaction provides some results. This behaviour implies a constant share of information between self-interested agents.

Even with functional distinctive capabilities between MRA types, all of them share identical functionalities, e.g. query shop floor ontology, search and registry of skills/agents in DF, deregistration on shut down, response to external requests according to internal status and skills available, intuitive GUI, etc.

5.2 Agent-Machine Interface

Since the AMI is used to make the lower level interaction with the hardware, it runs on the machine that is connected to that particular device.

The transport system is controlled by a single PLC, however each element is considered as an autonomous entity i.e. an agent. Therefore, each one of these elements (conveyors, transfer units and pallet fixers) has its own AMI that has access to the PLC, through an Ethernet connection and using the manufacturer's communication library, in order to read/write variables needed during an action execution. This variable update will actuate a lower level control program, described in IEC 61131 languages inside the PLC, so that the physical action can be executed. This approach emulates a system where each component has its own controller, what would improve system's plug-and-play capabilities.

Each one of the robots present in NovaFlex environment has its own controller cabinet, both using a serial connection as communication interface to access internal functions. Since each robot controller also controls grippers' actions and tools ware-houses sensors, all these MRAs use an AMI with privileges over the serial connection to execute the arriving request. Though, each MRA is totally autonomous from others that also share the same AMI.

Again, this approach emulates the case of each component possessing its own controller.

5.3 Broker Agent

A broker is an agent that is responsible for the creation of coalitions. It gathers infor-mation from the environment and, based on user preferences, supervises/assists the process of creating the coalition [10].

Manufacturing components are the basic blocks from which everything is built up. This way, a shop floor can be seen as a society of manufacturing components that, while cooperating with each other, can provide more complex skills, based on the aggregation of their individual basic skills.

The Broker Agent allows the integrator to choose which components, and accord-ing skills, to aggregate in order to provide a possible new complex skill. The Broker Agent GUI displays the components currently available in the environment allowing the integrator to navigate into its skills and see catalog parameters of that specific equipment, by querying the ontology. In order to create a new coalition, the user can easily pick a set of manufacturing components, and launch a CLA to coordinate its members in order to provide one or more complex skills. Note that, for now, the coa-lition structure is an integrator's responsibility, since it is assumed that he knows the physical system. In this agent's GUI, the integrator can also dismantle an existing coalition, by sending an end coalition message to the CLA responsible for it.

5.4 Coalition Leader Agents

A coalition is an aggregated group of agentified manufacturing components interact-ing in order to generate combined functionalities that can be more complex than the simple sum of their individual capabilities [10].

After gathering coalition members' skills, the CLA searches the ontology for any complex skills possible to be supported with those. If some complex skill can be per-formed by coordination of coalition members, the CLA will register this new skill in the DF in order to advertise it to others and waits requests for it. Since it is a pure software agent, the CLA simply needs to match the new complex skill with the ac-cording behaviour, available in its library, and launch its execution every time it is requested to. A complex skill execution behaviour usually consists on a sequential and conditional invocation of skills provided by coalition members.

5.5 Pallet Agent

All the manufacturing components and coalitions of them represented in the multi-agent system are considered as service providers. These services are the bricks that constitute the production process. For each pallet active in the system, carrying raw material or fixtures for subassemblies, there is a Pallet Agent abstracting it.

The Pallet Agent basically consists on an execution engine that follows a particular process plan adequate for that specific instance. This agent's GUI allows the user to define a process plan using the skills currently available in the system (skills' explorer and parameters entry panel), save it or simply load a previously defined plan. After the process plan is defined, the Pallet Agent will follow it by requesting the skills' providers sequentially in order to accomplish its production objectives (see Fig. 6).

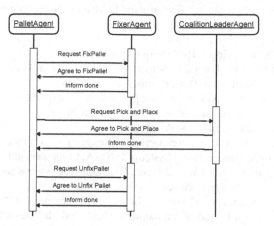

Fig. 6. Pallet Agent interaction example

This approach allows a fast adaptation to a production change. Every time a new production goal is defined, the integrator only needs to update each pallet process type, using the agent's GUI. It is not needed any kind of reprogramming.

6 Conclusions

This paper summarizes the multiagent application developed to control a quasi industrial assembly cell. The chosen approach increases the plug-and-play capability of components to enter or leave the system with minor variations in the production process, enabled by components' modularization and embedded intelligence. The production process can also be easily and promptly updated during run-time just by reconfiguration, being possible to have different products being produced at the same time in the same line. It was also proved that legacy systems can be simply integrated by the use of a software wrapper. Note that this application, even being a proof-of-concept implementation, actually runs on a real shop floor cell. By running it on a real environment, it is possible to observe and easily acquire its major benefits when compared with current industrial manufacturing applications.

Therefore, it was proven that autonomy, intelligence and interoperability capabilities are shop floor components' fundamental requirements to develop agile and reconfigurable assembly systems.

Acknowledgements. The authors would like to thank Filipe Feijão for co-authoring system's development and active contribution on this document.

References

1. Wooldridge, M.J.: An introduction to Multiagent Systems. J.Wiley, New York (2002)
2. ElMaraghy, H.A.: Flexible and Reconfigurable Manufacturing Systems Paradigms. International Journal of Flexible Manufacturing Systems. Springer-Verlag 17, 261–276 (2006)
3. Onori, M., Barata, J., Frei, R.: Evolvable Assembly Systems Basic Priciples. In: Proceedings of BASYS'06, Springer, Heidelberg (2006)
4. Maraldo, T., Onori, M., Barata, J., Semere, D.: In: Evolvable Assembly Systems: Clarifications and Developments to Date, Kashiwa, Japan (2006)
5. Holonic Manufacturing Systems [website]. Available at: http://hms.ifw.uni-hannover.de/
6. Concepts for Holonic Manufacturing [website]. Available at: http://www.mech.kuleuven.be /goa/concepts.htm
7. Van Brussel, H., Wyns, J., Valckennaers, P., Bongaerts, L., Peeters, P.: Reference Architecture for Holonic Manufacturing Systems. PROSA. Computers in Industry 37(3) (1998)
8. Bussman, S., Jenning, N.R., Wooldridge, M.: Multiagent systems for manufacturing control: a design methodology. Springer, Heidelberg (2004)
9. Pechoucek, M., Marik, V.: Review of Industrial Deployment of Multi-Agent Systems, submitted for pub. on Journal of Autonomous Agents and Multiagent Systems (2006)
10. Barata, J.: Coalition Based Approach for Shop Floor Agility – A Multiagent approach. Edições Orion, Amadora – Lisboa (2005)
11. FIPA ACL Message Structure Specification (2002) [website]. Available at: http://www.fipa.org/specs/fipa00061/SC00061G.html
12. FIPA Agent Management Specification (2002) [website]. Available at: http://www.fipa.org/specs/fipa00023/SC00023K.html
13. Wikipedia - Ontology (computer science) definition [website]. Available at: http://en.wikipedia.org/wiki/Ontology_computer_science
14. Protégé website [website]. Available at: http://protege.stanford.edu/
15. Protégé-Wiki: OntoViz [website]. Available at: http://protege.cim3.net/cgi-bin/wiki.pl?OntoViz
16. Protégé Ontology Bean Generator plugin [website]. Available at: http://protege.cim3.net/cgi-bin/wiki.pl?OntologyBeanGenerator
17. Java Agent Development Framework (2006) [website]. Available at: http://jade.tilab.com
18. Leszczyna, Rafai: Evaluation of Agent Platforms. Cybersecurity and New Technologies for Combating Fraud, Institute for the Protection and Security of the Citizen, Joint Research Centre, Ispra, Italy (2004)
19. FIPA Request Interaction Protocol Specification (2002) [website]. Available at: http://www.fipa.org/specs/fipa00026/SC00026H.html

MagentaToolkit: A Set of Multi-agent Tools for Developing Adaptive Real-Time Applications

George Rzevski[1], Petr Skobelev[2], and Vyacheslav Andreev[2]

[1] Magenta Technology, Gainsborough House, 59 - 60 Thames Street, Windsor,
Berkshire Sl4 1TX, UK
`george.rzevski@magenta-technology.com`
[2] Magenta Development, 1a Osipenko St., Samara, 443010, Russia
Tel.: +7 846 270 66 85
`skobelev@magenta-technology.ru`

Abstract. MagentaToolkit is a set of multi-agent tools based on the adaptive problem solving method, which is capable of solving complex problems characterized by a large number of variables of high variety and dynamics caused by the occurrence of unpredictable events. The Toolkit comprises a Multi-Agent Engine, Virtual Market and Ontology Editor. The Toolkit speeds up substantially the application development process and can be used by programmers without expertise in multi-agent technology. The paper contains the description of MagentaToolkit, outlines principles of application design and operation and presents examples of adaptive applications developed for clients.

Keywords: Holistic Approach, Agent, Ontology, Contract Net, Swarm Intelligence, Multi-Agent Systems, Semantic Networks.

1 Introduction

MagentaToolkit is a set of multi-agent tools for developing large-scale adaptive, real-time, multi-agent applications capable of solving problems that are too complex to be tackled by conventional software tools.

The Toolkit follows the holistic approach [1]; it provides help with constructing Open Resource and Demand Networks (ORDN) where demands and resources can join or leave network dynamically, in real time [2]. The Toolkit gives programmers a general and powerful methodology for the development of a variety of real time resource allocation applications [3], [4]. The methodology integrates the use of agents with Demand and Resource roles and semantic networks to formally represent the input situation, events affecting the system and results of ongoing matching and re-matching between agents. A Virtual Market Engine - an extension to a more generic Multi-Agent Engine - is one of the core components of Magenta Toolkit, specifically aimed at supporting ORDN applications and providing adaptive real time solutions.

To the best of our knowledge this is the first commercially available toolkit of its kind. Multi-agent platforms available for downloading JADE (http://jade.tilab.com/) and Cougaar (http://www.cougaar.org/) are more generic and provide basic functional

V. Mařík, V. Vyatkin, A.W. Colombo (Eds.): HoloMAS 2007, LNAI 4659, pp. 303–313, 2007.

frameworks. As a result they require from programmers a considerable competence and effort to deliver ready-to-use multi-agent system with adaptive behavior.

After outlining the class of complex problems for which MagentaToolkit has been developed, the paper reviews the principles of adaptive problem solving, describes the design of the Toolkit, provides a methodology for developing applications and presents a selection of commercial projects where MagentaToolkit was used.

2   Complex Problems

Many important classes of practical problems, for example, the design and configuration of complex engineering systems, resource allocation, planning and scheduling, multi-criteria decision making and search for the most effective message routing in communication networks are very complex, particularly if they are characterized by a high level of dynamics, have many users with conflicting interests, require data to be processed in real time, under conditions of uncertainty due to the occurrence of unpredictable events. Complexity of these problems makes application of well-known constraint programming methods of resource allocation, planning and scheduling very difficult in practice [5].

The transportation logistics [6] is a perfect example of a very complex problem as there is a need to take into account potentially conflicting requirements of participants, including operators, customers, truck owners, truck drivers, truck loaders and their unions, as well as logistic resources, or groups of resources, such as, trucks of different capacities with and without trailers, routes and warehouses; also, solutions are constrained by various rules and regulations on safety, working hours, etc. In addition, as any logistics expert knows, the situation on the ground changes all the time with new orders arriving, some of them urgent and/or from important customers; previously scheduled orders get cancelled or their destination changes; trucks fail; drivers or loaders do not report on duty; roads get congested and deliveries delayed.

Modern decision support systems are required to enable several users to cooperate on each decision, which implies the notification of users about changes made by other users, including cancellations of previously agreed decisions, and alignment of contradictory instructions issued by different decision makers.

In complex situations it is very difficult, or impossible, to formulate realistic mathematical optimization algorithms, which leads to the introduction of empirical rules, which are situation-oriented and are very often broken by users.

The recent increase in complexity of markets created a considerable interest in the use of multi-agent systems for solving resource allocation problems [7]. Many multi-agent prototypes and proof-of-concept systems have been successfully developed and there is now a strong need for general design principles and implementation tools capable of supporting the development of full scale industrial solutions.

3   Adaptive Problem Solving

In contrast to conventional software such as centralized schedulers, planners and optimizers, the proposed Toolkit follows principles of distributed adaptive problem solving outlined below.

An agent is assigned to each object participating in the problem solving process with a task of negotiating for its client (object) the best possible operating conditions. For this purpose we provide programmers with Virtual Market Engine with already pre-implemented and generic enough Roles of Demands and Resources and also with protocols of their negotiations which allow running hundreds and thousands of agent negotiations in parallel a-synchronically or synchronically. For example, Order Agents are given tasks of obtaining the most cost-effective trucks for cargo transportation, and Truck Agents are charged to negotiate the full loading of trucks.

In case of partial matching, agents may attempt to improve the deal if a new opportunity presents itself at a later stage. The process continues as long as it is necessary to obtain full matches, or until the occurrence of the next event (e.g., a new order) which requires agents to re-consider previously agreed deals in some parts of the previously derived solution.

Agent negotiations are controlled using domain knowledge which is far more comprehensive than "rules" used in conventional planners, and normally includes expertise of practicing operators; certain constraints and if-then-else rules may be considered as recommendations and not as instructions and agents may be allowed to evaluate their effectiveness and decide if they should be used. In some cases agents send messages to users asking for approval to ignore ineffective rules or to stress nonessential constraints.

The power of distributed adaptive method is particularly evident when the problem contains a very large number of objects with a variety of different attributes; when there is a frequent occurrence of unpredictable events that affect the problem solving process; and when criteria for matching demands to resources are complex (e.g., balancing risk, profits and level of services, which may differ for different participants).

As the process is incremental, a change of state of one agent may lead to changes of states of many other agents. As a result, at some unpredictable moment in time a spontaneous self-accelerated chain reaction of agent state changes may take place, and after a relatively short transient time the overall structure will switch its state practically completely, transferring from one attractor to another. Once the resulting structure has settled at the new attractor, the incremental changes will continue.

Such a distributed adaptive problem solving process appears to exhibit autonomy and intelligence, known as "swarm intelligence" [8].

Attempts to implement swarm intelligence for solving complex problems were made before – mainly, by analogy with bee swarms or ant colonies [9]. However practical implementation of this approach requires a special event-driven operational system able to support hundreds of thousands or, occasionally, millions of agents, each with associated decision making logic; comprehensive tools are also needed for constructing domain knowledge semantic networks, as well as problem situation models configured as networks, as described below. Once implemented, such problem solving systems exhibit all characteristics of the class of complex adaptive systems [10], [11] with the typical for them phenomena of catastrophes, bifurcations, self-organization and emergent behavior, features that have been observed in Prigogin's thermodynamics [10].

4 Components of the Toolkit

The Toolkit comprises the following key components: (a) Multi-Agent Engine, which provides runtime support for agents; (b) Virtual Market, which is an extension of the Engine; it supports rather more complex agent roles, including those of Demands and Resources; (c) Ontology Management Toolset, which supports the construction and update of Ontology as well as building of Scenes (problem situation network models.

Multi-Agent Engine is an executive system, supporting quasi-parallel and asynchronous operation of agents. Main Multi-Agent Engine components are a dispatcher, which manages agent control, and a subsystem which supports messaging between agents. Agents represent a multitude of continuously executing co-programs, each gaining control in turn and returning it to the dispatcher after processing a state. The system supports work of hundreds of thousands of agents on a single server. The Engine has an important capability of managing pro-activity of agents by allocating control to agents that can achieve the best deals in negotiations (as determined by a prior auction) or to those that are closest to a critical event, e.g., a failure, (which is determined by the analysis of the appropriate Scene). This feature is known as balancing agent activities and it plays an important role when there are many parallel activities in the system. In such cases there is a need to restrict the number of agents that can be pro-active in order to reduce the negotiation time and eliminate time-consuming reconsideration of decisions, as big number of active-in-parallel agents causes many unnecessary conflicts, the so-called "noise". The principle of activity balancing, built on the basis of the hormones paradigm, solves these problems, giving priority to the limited number of agents, allowing them to take decisions and provide required answers relatively quickly.

Virtual Market is an extension of the Engine for supporting ORDN, which provides an advanced construction of agents and extended agent role classes, such as Demand Role and Resource Role, and modified Contract Net protocol of their interactions. Agent design includes "agent personality" and memory, in which it can store part of a Scene. Agent personality is a procedure for managing agent roles and updating agent memory. Agent personality can be used for developing special types of agents called "deliberative agents" that can plan their activities as opposed to "reactive agents" that can only react and respond. Virtual Market agents can get notifications about the occurrence of events and changes in scenes either from yellow pages services or by way of comparing situations in the current scene before and after awakening in pro-activity phase.

An important virtual market component is an extended FIPA Iterated Contract Net Protocol (http://www.fipa.org/), which allows a multitude of agents to negotiate with each other in parallel and asynchronously. The protocol extension allows the execution of additional iterations not only to the initiator, but also to a participant; if the agent state or agent goals have changed, or a new event has arrived, the participant can repeatedly send the updated proposal to the initiator without starting the protocol for the second time.

Ontology Management Toolset is a set of tools for the creation and editing of Ontology (object and relation classes) and Scenes (problem situation models, describing specific object and relation instances as networks). The toolset enables developers and users to create objects for Ontology and Scenes (classes and instances, respectively), build relations between them, delete objects and relations, generate the list of relations for each defined object, and check if there are relations between objects, etc. Using ontology management toolset a user can specify both the problem situation and events and add this information into the system. In the course of their work agents analyze the current Scene and build new relations as part of the problem solving. If a real-world situation changes and new objects or relation classes are required, the user can use the toolset to expand the ontology. Occasionally, changes in Ontology necessitate changes in agent decision-making rules which can be implemented using an appropriate editor, though often this will not be required.

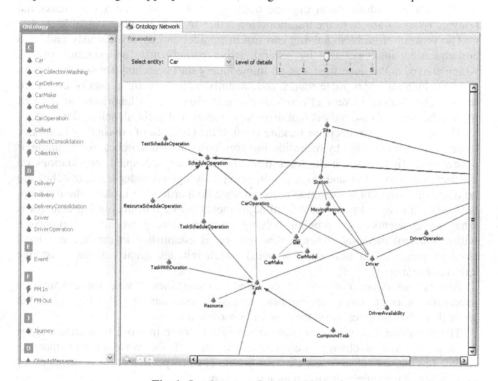

Fig. 1. Ontology as a Semantic Network

All components are implemented in Java and the Toolkit provides a capability for creating programs for industrial applications in both web and desktop options.

5 How Adaptive Multi-agent Applications Work

Adaptive multi-agent applications developed using MagentaToolkit work as follows.

The system consists of a set of continuously functioning agents that may have contradictory or complimentary interests.

Basic roles of Agents, based on the extended Contract Net protocol, are Demand and Supply roles; each agent is engaged in selling to other agents its services or buying services it needs.

Current problem solution is represented as a set of relations between agents, which describe the current matching of services; for example, a schedule is a network of orders, trucks and routes and relations between them.

The arrival of a new event into the system is triggered by the occurrence of a change in the external world; for example, when a truck breaks down, a truck failure event arrives into the system.

The agent representing the object affected by the new event undertakes to find all affected agents and notify them of the event and the consequences; for example, the agent of the broken truck undertakes to find the transportation orders linked to the failed truck and inform them that the truck is not available; the agent breaks the relevant relations and frees the transportation orders to look for other available trucks.

The process of problem solving can run in parallel and asynchronously and, as a consequence, simultaneously by several active participants; for example, orders, which arrived at the same time, can all immediately start searching for suitable trucks or begin building appropriate routes, concurrently with the assignments of drivers to trucks. This feature is very effective because it eliminates a laborious building of truck schedules only to find out that drivers are not available for all selected routes.

The driving force in decision-making is often the presence of conflicts, which have to be exposed and settled by reconsidering previously agreed matches; for example, if a new order finds out that the truck time slot is already occupied, negotiations on conflict resolution start and, as a result, previously agreed order-truck matches are adjusted (the time slot is moved to accommodate both orders) or broken (the time slot is freed). This capability to make local adjustments before introducing big changes is what makes agents-based problem solving so much more powerful in comparison with traditional methods. When a new relation is established in the Scene a local event is generated (a new route is built) which initiates agent activities just like external event does.

Agents can either compete or cooperate among themselves; for example, a successful order placement pre-defines successful placement of following orders but all of them may be given opportunities for consolidation.

The dispatcher may give agents an opportunity to try to improve their state and the consequent wave of changes may cause a clash with the wave of new matches initiated by the arrival of a new external event. The prospective clash is managed by controlling of the supply of virtual money to agents.

The stronger relations between agents are, the higher the level of order in the system (the lesser the level of chaos) and probably the better, more stable is the solution represented by these relations. If there are no relations between agents, the system is in complete chaos.

The system is in a perpetual state of processing either reacting to the arrival of new events or improving the quality of previously agreed matches. The stable solution is reached when there are no agents that can improve their states and there are no new events. This solution may or may not be final depending on whether new events continue to occur.

MagentaToolkit considers any complex problem as a virtual market in which agents simultaneously and asynchronously make deals that result in establishing new or changing previously agreed relations between agents. It is not important to the system whether agents represent real or abstract objects or what the nature of relations is. Relations can be established between trucks and orders, or records and clusters, or even words and their meanings [9], [10], [11]. Every relation, if necessary, may be adaptively reconsidered in real time: a new order may change the schedule of already allocated orders; a new record may cause previously accommodated records to leave a cluster; and a new sentence may change the meaning of a previous fragment of text.

Solutions developed using MagentaToolkit fall into the class of open, non-linear and dissipative systems, built on the principle of "energy flow" (virtual money). As the number of relations increases in the system, the level of complexity of the resulting network goes up and, at a certain point, the need may arise to appoint additional agents to represent certain self-contained parts of the network whose nodes are already represented by agents.

6 Examples of Applications

6.1 Collaborative Design of an Airplane Wing

During the collaborative design of a very large mechanical structure such as an airplane wing, which may consist of more than 10,000 parts, there is often a need for design changes to be carried out. The problem is that changing one wing component may lead to the whole chain of modifications to its neighboring components to ensure that they fit perfectly together. The current practice is to identify design conflicts once a month by a clash-analysis program running on a grid of powerful machines and requiring about two weeks to check all possible clashes for the complete wing. The procedure is to check every component against every other component irrespective if they are mutually connected or not, which generates a huge volume of data for processing. The problem will become even more complex in the future when the clash analysis will include electric, magnetic, stressing and other aspects of design.

Magenta solution was developed using the Toolkit as follows. Wing ontology was constructed using Ontology Management Toolset with classes of wing components as nodes and relations, including neighborhood, as links. Using the same toolset a Scene was constructed for the specific wing which contained more than 1.5 million object instances and relations. It was possible to load into the Scene only objects from the existing CAD system and relations only of the type "part-of". Even that was sufficient to establish a network of geometric wing object instances and relations of the type "neighbor".

Every wing component that was subjected to re-design was immediately checked (in real time) for clashes. This was done by creating an agent for the altered component with the task to compare component sizes prior and post re-design and to find all wing components that may be affected by the change; searching the wing Scene for neighbor relations yielded rapid identification of potential clashes. An agent is then assigned to each identified neighboring component with the task to evaluate implications of re-design. The wave of newly created agents, each evaluating the implications of changes, can spread across the Scene in all directions and agents can carry out evaluations in parallel and asynchronously. If a design change does not affect a neighbor, the wave in the corresponding direction of the wing Scene fades. This reduces the processing effort considerably in comparison with the previous clash analysis. Magenta clash analysis solution required several hours to complete the task which previously required two weeks.

6.2 Design of a Web-Portal for Healthy Life-Style

Designing a healthy life-style web portal closely resembles the classical problem of configuring a system consisting of a large number of components to meet a set of constraints, for example, working out a computer configuration which meets all user requirements and fits into a given price range.

The objective of the portal was to collect from the users their preferences (medical, religious, cost-related and taste-related) and to build for them a healthy and balanced daily meal and exercise plan. Producing a meal plan can be described as a task to configure a menu within a set of constraints taking into account available products. If users did not like the system generated solutions, they could ask for modifications or make changes by themselves. If users changed the recommended menu during the day and entered changes into the system, they received, in real time, a modified plan for the rest of the day. Recommendations always took care of the appropriate balance between meals and exercises, particularly if user-generated changes led to exceeding the limit on calories.

The healthy life-style portal was designed using MagentaToolkit and associated adaptive problem solving method. The first task was to construct Ontology of healthy life-style containing object classes, relation classes and object attributes, such as user, meal, breakfast, drink and walk. For each user a Scene was constructed containing object/relation/attribute instances, which described specific user preferences.

The menu, daily rations and the daily exercise program were viewed as a network of object/relation instances, which could be at any moment modified by agents or the user, in real time; for example, let us assume that the user obtained from the portal his/her daily meal plan, balanced up to 2000 calories per day. If the user did not like one of the items offered for breakfast, say, skimmed cottage cheese, he/she could change it, for instance, for an omelet. In response, the system created the event of change, which activated the agent of the changed item. The agent of the changed item got in touch with the agent of the daily menu, which initiated a search for an item on the menu to delete in order to maintain the meal plan below the upper calorie limit.

The benefits of the suggested approach are obvious: the ability to handle trade-offs between the diet and physical exercises, or between different meal items (for example, between meat and red wine), and a possibility to add business or family events or any other factor, which affect the daily plan. In fact, the adaptive method appears to be the only method capable of handling the problem of a healthy life-style without simplifications normally imposed by conventional, algorithmic methods. The problem, being very complex, requires a coordinated examination of every event affecting the daily plan and a resolution of conflicts by negotiations "back" and "forward", involving balancing of contradictory interests, change of previously made decisions, mutual concessions and so on.

6.3 Ocean and Truck Schedulers

The most complex applications built on the basis of Magenta Toolkit were built for transportation logistics.

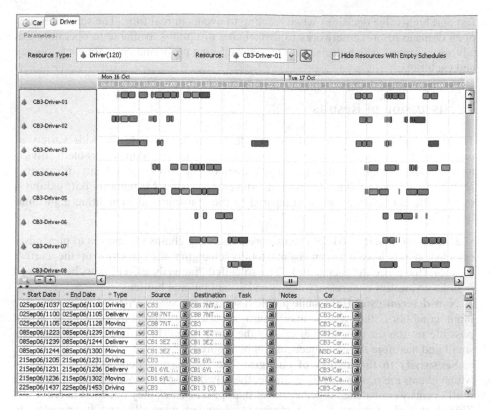

Fig. 2. A Transportation Logistics Solution

One of the first Magenta adaptive solutions for transportation logistics was the creation of Ocean i-Scheduler [12]. Ocean i-Scheduler was developed as a decision support system for managing very large tankers transporting oil across the globe, eg, from Venezuela to Japan and from Middle East to Europe and US. The key problem is to manage tankers operation in real time, which amounts to considering the current vessel positions and analyzing options for every new event (new order, delay in delivery, failure of vessels, etc) taking into account market trends, specific features of every order and contract agreement with every client, position of competitors, cost of fuelling in different ports, etc. Ontology and Scenes of the Ocean i-Scheduler contain deep domain knowledge about tankers, countries and ports, shipment regulations, owner preferences and know-how of logistics to mention just a few elements. The Ocean i-Scheduler is now in full-scale operation by a world-leading company in oil transportation.

One of the most complex adaptive solutions based on MagentaToolkit is Truck i-Scheduler [13]. Currently it is able to schedule more than 1000 orders per day for UK- or US-wide transportation networks with the fleet of 300 – 500 trucks taking into consideration different types of trucks, geography of depots, distances between delivery points, cross-docks, regulations for drivers, consolidation of goods, etc. Truck i-Scheduler also operates in a decision-support mode helping operators to take fast and high-value decisions when reacting to events in real time. The scheduler uses open demand-resource networks to investigate all options available to operators and advises operators which decision to take considering profit and costs for each journey and each truck.

7 Discussion of Results

The case studies described above were selected to demonstrate the wide variety of problems that can be solved using MagentaToolkit and the adaptive problem solving method. The examples differ not only in content but also in complexity, illustrating scalability of the Toolkit. Applications developed using MagentaToolkit, exhibit a rather different behavior when compared to the conventional monolithic algorithm-based systems:

High nonlinearity: Trivial events may cause long chains of changes to previously established relations between agents totally changing the structure of the current solution (the schedule, menu, etc). The so called "butterfly effect" must be managed in order to prevent unnecessary delays and computational burdens.

Non-determinism: If the same problem solving process is repeated under the same input conditions, the system may return somewhat different results, as it is not possible to stop the execution at exactly the same time. The differences are normally small and therefore the consequences can be ignored.

Sensitivity to the history of changes: The results may depend on the order in which events are processed; for example, the schedule or menu would look differently if all events were batched together rather than processed as they occurred in real time. This feature is present in real systems scheduled manually and it provides an opportunity to compare real-time with batch scheduling.

Evolutionary irreversibility: The outcome of a decision depends on conditions prevailing at the time when the decision was taken; therefore the process of constructing a solution in a stepwise manner is irreversible. For example, if an order, processed yesterday, is cancelled today and then introduced again, the second allocation of resources to the same order may be totally different from the first. This feature reflects reality of business decisions.

Self-organization: The system responds to every change in the external or internal worlds by adjusting relations between agents (in other words, adjusting matching of resources to demands) to reflect the new situation; this is the key feature which makes Magenta multi-agent applications *adaptable*.

Substantial dialogs with users: Users can influence how the application works at any time by changing agent goals, modifying Ontology or by selecting options suggested by the system; also, agents can pro-actively communicate with the user.

Emergent Intelligence: The system exhibits intelligence much higher than that of individual agents; the system intelligence, also known as Swarm Intelligence emerges from agent interactions. This is another key feature of MagentaToolkit; the tool enables the amplification of certain useful properties due to an intensive teamwork of swarms of agents.

Flexibility in decision-making and high reliability: Any changes in any system component, such as failures or delays, do not cause the system to fail; in response, agents always manage to find a satisfactory solution. The system reacts in the same way to resource "unavailability" whatever the reason: resource sale, resource failure, a terrorist attack, fire or anything else.

High efficiency: In response to an event the system adapts only that part of the global structure that is necessary, which reduces the time of the reaction and makes it precisely directed.

Self-checking and self-restoring after failures: The system is not very sensitive to mistakes in data inputs and even to mistakes in algorithms, because decisions are continuously being improved through the process of agent negotiations.

References

1. Van Brussel, H., Wyns, J., Valckenaers, P., Bongaerts, L., Peeters, P.: Reference architecture for holonic manufacturing systems PROSA. Computers in Industry 37(3), 255–274 (1998)
2. Vittikh, V.A., Skobelev, P.O.: Multi-Agent Models of Matching in Open Demand and Resource Networks. Automatics and Telemechanics 1, 177–185 (2003)
3. Rzevski, G., Himoff, J., Skobelev, P.: Magenta Technology: A Family of Multi-Agent Intelligent Schedulers. Workshop on Software Agents in Information Systems and Industrial Applications (SAISIA), Fraunhofer IITB (February 2006)
4. Rzevski, G., Skobelev, P.: Agent Method and Computer System For Negotiating in a Virtual Environment, Patent No: WO 03/067432 A1. Published (14.08.2003)
5. Dechter, R.: Constraint Processing. Morgan Kaufmann, San Francisco (2003)
6. Jacques, R.: Recent Trends in Logistics and the Need for Real-time Decision Tools in the Trucking Industry. Proceedings of the 34th Hawaii International Conference on System Sciences (2001)
7. Chevaleyre, Y., Endriss, U., Estivie, S., Maudet, N.: Welfare engineering in practice: On the variety of multi-agent resource allocation problems. In: Engineering Societies in the Agents World V, pp. 335–347. Springer, Heidelberg (2005)
8. Swarm Intelligence. Scientific American (2001)
9. Thompson, J.: Ant Colony Optimisation. School of Mathematics, Cardiff University, SWORDS (2004)
10. Nicolis, G., Prigogine, I.: Exploring Complexity. W H Freeman, New York (1939)
11. Kuppers, G.: Self-organization. The Emergence of Order. From local interactions to global structures, no 2, PDF (July 1999), http://www.uni-bielefeld.de/iwt/sein/paper
12. Himoff, J., Skobelev, P., Wooldridge, M.: Magenta Technology: Multi-Agent Systems for Ocean Logistics. In: Proceedings of 4th International Conference on Autonomous Agents and Multi Agent Systems (AAMAS 2005) Holland (July 2005) (2005)
13. Himoff, J., Rzevski, G., Skobelev, P.: Magenta Technology: Multi-Agent Logistics i-Scheduler for Road Transportation. In: Proceedings of 5-th International Conference on Autonomous Agents and Multi Agent Systems (AAMAS 2006), Japan (May 2006) (2006)

On Practical Implementation of Holonic Control Principles in Baggage Handling Systems Using IEC 61499

Geoff Black and Valeriy Vyatkin

Department of Electrical and Computer Engineering
University of Auckland, Auckland, New Zealand
gbla004@ec.auckland.ac.nz, v.vyatkin@auckland.ac.nz

Abstract. IEC 61499 Functional Blocks is an upcoming architectural framework for the design of complete distributed industrial automation systems and their reusable components. This paper presents a multi-agent distributed control approach for a baggage handling system using IEC 61499 Functional Blocks. In particular, it focuses on demonstrating a distributed control system that is scalable, reconfigurable and fault tolerant. The design follows the Automation Object approach, which ends up in a functional block representing a single section of conveyor, such that the structure (and consequently the behaviour) of the conveyor network is entirely defined by the interconnection of these blocks within the IEC 61499 design environment. The use of distributed simulation to achieve predictive control is demonstrated as a part of the control system design.

Keywords: IEC 61499, Functional Blocks, Distributed control, Simulation.

1 Introduction

Tracking and distribution of luggage through airports requires a range of interconnected systems. For a general treatment of the processes involved see [1].

While there are a number of commonly deployed options for moving bags around, in this work we consider the systems built from conveyors. In its most basic form, a conveyor is a moving belt that transfers objects from one end to the other. Each conveyor must be equipped with a motor to drive the belt and most conveyors have at least one Photo-Eye (PE) to detect the presence of bags. In most practical uses of conveyors it is necessary to direct the flow of objects in a more sophisticated manner than simple end-to-end transfer. This is achieved by joining together multiple conveyors in chains. Bags may be diverted from certain conveyors and merged into others, and these actions must be appropriately directed so as to move objects to their correct destinations.

Figure 1 shows a simple conveyor chain that demonstrates most of the important actions of Baggage Handling Systems (BHS). Bags enter the system and are moved by conveyor through a scanner that identifies bags, usually by RFID or Barcode. The bags then move to a merge point, where a controller must manage bag traffic to avoid collisions. Further along is a diverter, which may eject bags from the main flow, in

V. Mařík, V. Vyatkin, A.W. Colombo (Eds.): HoloMAS 2007, LNAI 4659, pp. 314–325, 2007.

this case causing them to loop back to the merge point. After the divert, is a metering section where short sections of conveyor are stopped and started in order to control the distance between adjacent bags. If bags are not diverted they will eventually exit the chain.

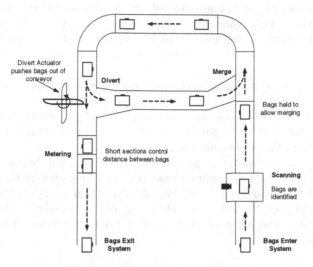

Fig. 1. Simple Conveyor Chain

A real BHS will contain many conveyors controlled to achieve the actions described above and coordinated at a higher level to achieve correct delivery of bags to the a waiting aircraft or baggage claim point.

Current controllers for BHS are based on conventional industrial control hardware and programming techniques. This includes a heavy reliance on Programmable Logic Controllers (PLC) for low level manipulation of actuators based on sensor data. The software used in PLCs is generally monolithic, increasing the difficulty of modification and maintenance and reducing scalability. Although with modern tools the PLC code may be quite modular, there is still a considerable manual component to the task of reconfiguring the code for a new BHS.

In this paper we investigate the use of the emerging IEC 61499 architecture for implementation of intelligent distributed control systems of BHS. The need for manufacturing processes to become increasingly flexible, fault-tolerant and reconfigurable is well recognised. In recent times these efforts have begun to coalesce into a few patterns that start to form usable frameworks for construction of multi-agent manufacturing systems. In [7] Vrba presents an architecture for simulation of agent-based control of manufacturing systems, where Functional Blocks occupy only the real-time control and hardware integration space, with a higher level agent layer required for cooperative tasks. While IEC 61499 Functional Blocks are already recognised as a good fit for these specific parts of a multi-agent implementation, most approaches to the creation of holonic manufacturing architectures rely on a specialised multi-agent platform such as JADE or JACK.

Modeling and simulation of distributed systems in IEC 61499 is growing in maturity. In [9] Frey and Hussain provide a summary of the approaches and challenges involved. As originally planned for IEC 61499 but so far lacking in full implementation, this paper aims to show that many of the requirements for building holonic agents are inherent in the IEC 61499 standard. We attempt to show an IEC 61499 implementation of holonic control, eventually to be executed directly on embedded devices. This represents a step toward industrial application of holonic principles, demonstrating that Functional Blocks can combine simulation, real-time control and predictive control options with sufficient communication between agents to achieve cooperative behaviours. It is emphasised that the scheme presented is fully executable on currently available embedded control hardware supporting the Java IEC 61499 runtime.

In fitting with the strong emphasis on reusability and portability, it is a key goal of this work that standard functional blocks and the design environment is used where possible to achieve the desired outcome.

This paper the introduces a general purpose 'Conveyor Section' Automation Object that may be used to construct models of real conveyor systems for baggage handling. The following sections explain the functional block architecture for the conveyor model and controller, including use of the simulation components for predictive control. The paper concludes with a brief description of tools, proposed future work and conclusions.

2   The Conveyor as an Automation Object

The concept of an 'Automation Object', explored in [2] and in particular in [3], and defined as *'a collection of data and knowledge elements belonging/relevant/describing physical building blocks of automated manufacturing system'*, extends the modularity of software or hardware to the modularity of the whole entity, which combines mechanical, electrical and intelligent (software) components. According to [3], IEC 61499 is an appropriate architecture to organize the IT (*information technology*) side of Automation Objects.

The example BHS shown in Figure 1 has already been described as being constructed of a set of 'conveyor sections' connected end to end, or in merge or divert configurations. These physical sections would appear the most obvious unit to represent as a Automation Object component and this is the approach taken here.

If we imagine a fully featured conveyor component, able to perform any of the actions described above, it would look something like the general purpose conveyor section shown in Figure 2. This contains the mechanical conveyor components required for merge and divert, the sensors for detecting bags and measuring belt speed, and a motor with drive to make the belt move. It also includes an embedded controller that makes control decisions based on sensor data and from information exchanged with other conveyors networked connected by network.

In the case of a real reusable conveyor section 'module' it is highly unlikely that a single module would be able to perform all the actions described, but it is convenient from an Object Oriented perspective to describe the functionality in its most general form and restrict/hide functions as appropriate.

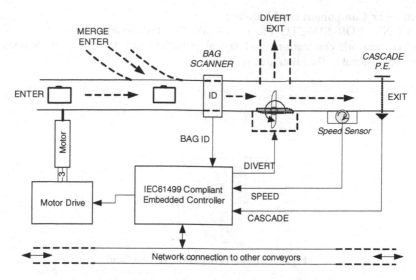

Fig. 2. A Fully Featured Conveyor Module

A control system for a conveyor-based BHS is an appropriate demonstration of distributed control because a conveyor is an easily definable module that is intuitively suited to a reconfigurable application. A BHS control system using IEC 61499 functional blocks may provide advantages in several areas, thanks to the following characteristics required for useful and easy modular design with easy reuse - defined interfaces, transparent networking for event and data transfer between remote objects and the ability to execute on a growing range of platforms. The following sections cover the development of a reusable conveyor component for modeling and simulated control.

3 Conveyor Section Model

A Conveyor section model was developed to eventually to form part of a complete conveyor Automation Object. The generalised conveyor section of Figure 2 was the initial model for this component. The goal was to create a reusable component that could describe a section of conveyor at several levels from its logical connection to other sections, to its dimensions and other physical parameters.

It was desired that a network of conveyors could then be modelled by simply making connections between appropriately parameterised conveyor blocks in the Functional Block Development Kit (FBDK) design environment. Our design generally follows the object-oriented Model-View-Control design patterns, introduced in [5] and exemplified in [6]. The model has a multilevel structure where the low level operations are wrapped in composite blocks that hide details, provide connectivity and present a clean interface for the designer to create system models without detailed knowledge of low level functionality.

A Conveyor Component for Modeling

The CONVEYOR_SIMCTL block has all the functionality required to define conveyor network connections and layout, simulate the network and demonstrate distributed control of the simulated network.

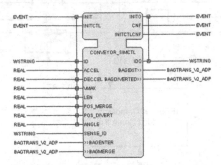

Fig. 3. CONVEYOR_SIMCTL Interface

The CONVEYOR_SIMCTL interface is shown in Figure 3. This block requires explicit assignment of most parameters that define its physical dimensions and behaviour. The designer can choose to use this block as is, assigning each value, or more conveniently the generalised block will be refined by encapsulation within a composite block that sets default values and hides some functionality, analogous to a sub-classing operation.

Connecting Blocks with Interfaces (BAGTRANS_ADP)

To simplify the connection of conveyor sections, CONVEYOR_SIMCTL, makes use of IEC 61499 adapters. Adapters bundle together a defined set of events and data signals so that the designer has to manage only a single connection. It also forces the interaction between two blocks to conform to a particular specification, making the scheme similar to interfaces as implemented by Java and other object-oriented languages. More details on the benefits of Adapters in functional block designs can be found in [6], Chapter 16.

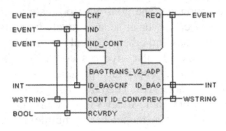

Fig. 4. The BAGTRANS_ADP adapter

Figure 4 shows the BAGTRANS_ADP adapter. This represents the only interface between adjacent conveyors. The adapter provides signal and event ports to allow for transfer of bags between conveyors, notification of readiness to receive bags and construction of paths.

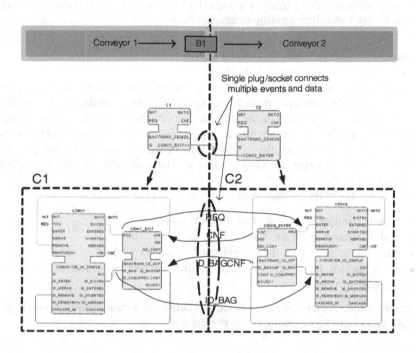

Fig. 5. Bag Transfer Logic

Figure 5 demonstrates the transaction of a bag exiting from Conveyor 1 on the left to Conveyor 2 on the right. C1 and C2 are very simplified conveyor models showing only the required bag transfer logic used by the controllers for each conveyor.

When a bag reaches the end of C1, the EXITED event is triggered and the BAG_ID output is set appropriately. This event is directed through the BAGTRANS adapter to the ENTER event input of C2. If C2 is able to accept a bag (i.e. it is moving, not blocked) then it will respond by triggering the ENTERED event which connects through the adapter back to the REMOVE input of C1 indicating that the bag is to be removed. Any block that properly implements this bag transfer interface will be able to connect to these blocks and achieve bag transfer.

The set of events and signals currently implemented are only those required for simulation of bag movement and for propagation of path signals. A more complete solution could include additional event and signal paths for diagnostics or management without any effect on the top level model.

Simulation and Predictive Control
The CONVEYOR_SIMCTL composite block contains several types of blocks to perform simulation, prediction and control.

Simulator

A simulation block models the movement of the belt and motor and supplies a simulated encoder output. Using the belt model, it also simulates the progress of any bags on the conveyor. This block packages the simulated sensor signals from these blocks and publishes them using a standard PUBLISH block, making these signals available to any subscriber wanting to access them.

Predictor

As suggested in [4], the use of distributed predictive simulation for control is a natural development from the functional block based simulation used for testing purposes. Therefore, while the conveyor model is designed for pure simulation, it can also be used to implement a *predictor* - a simulation synchronised with the environment. It is the job of the predictor to take sensor inputs and produce a sufficiently accurate recreation of system state for the controller to operate correctly. In the case of the baggage handling conveyor, the only sensors available are the velocity sensor for the belt and the photo-eye.

The major tasks of the predictor are;

- Detect and measure bags based on PE sensors
- Match detected bags to known bags in the system
- If a bag is identified, then match the ID to a known bag
- For known bags, continuously predict current positions using measured conveyor velocity

The action of the predictor is exemplified in Figure 7 where a visualisation shows the predictor accurately regenerating the system state.

The Controller

The controller block is responsible for management of a single conveyor section and uses the estimated bag positions from the predictor along with available path information to attempt to deliver bags closer to their final destination.

The challenge for the controller in the distributed configuration is that it only has direct information about its own conveyor section and limited data from adjoining sections, whereas a centralised controller may freely use information from throughout the network. This did not prove to be a problem for the control actions implemented so far. If further functionality requires more global information then there are a couple of possible solutions. First is to explicitly add more connections to other conveyors as required to provide information about state, demand, etc. The second option would be to sparingly use global broadcast of some events and values.

The control behaviours so far achieved are briefly described.

Cascade Stop - This is a simple behaviour in which a conveyor will not attempt to deliver a bag to a subsequent section if the subsequent section is blocked. This behaviour is achieved by direct connection between adjacent conveyor sections via the BAGTRANS interface. Each section indicates its ability to receive bags by setting its ENTERREADY or MERGEREADY outputs. The preceding or merging section simply sees a Boolean on its EXITRDY input and responds accordingly by stopping until it becomes enabled. Although the EXITRDY input is generated remotely and may be received via a network channel, the ladder logic for this behaviour is simply:

```
CASCADE      EXITRDY                 cascadeStop
-----|  |-------|/|------------------( )
```

Economy Stop - To save power a conveyor section may stop when it is not carrying any bags.

Bag metering - To prevent bags getting confused or misdirected, it is important that a reasonable gap is maintained between each. This can be achieved by a conveyor stopping or slowing to put extra gap between bags. This behaviour is a natural extension of the Cascade Stop, depending on what criteria the entering conveyor has for allowing incoming bags.

Merge Control - When two streams of traffic merge, it is necessary for one stream to wait for a gap in the other before delivering each bag. This is one of the more important aspects of bag management in a BHS as incorrect merging can easily result in collisions or misordering of bags resulting in lost bags. In the functional block controller, it is implemented in a simple manner using the same BAGTRANS RCVRDY signal to indicate readiness for merge traffic.

Path Finding - In order for a conveyor network to be useful, each bag must be delivered to the correct destination. In conventional conveyor control systems this is done by a central controller that has a complete model of the network layout and can perform a tree search of possible paths between points. The distributed IEC 61499 based controller instead uses the connections between conveyor sections to construct valid paths from each conveyor to each reachable exit. The approach is similar to that described in [7] where paths are generated starting at network exit points and terminating at entry points, with each conveyor component appending its own details to the partially generated path and passing the result on to its immediate peers. This process builds 'path strings' for each reachable network node that define all the possible future choice combinations from that node.

Modeling Conveyor Networks
The purpose of creating the reusable general purpose conveyor block is to be able to connect them together to define and model the behaviour of a chain of conveyors. Let us take the example of the conveyor chain shown in Figure 1 and examine how it can easily be modelled using the CONVEYOR_SIMCTL functional block, with each block representing a single conveyor section.

For simplicity some of the actions of the conveyor chain are omitted, such as the scanner and metering sections. To further simplify the example, the CONVEYOR_SIMCTL blocks are encapsulated into CONV_BASIC blocks that hide much of the detail of the CONVEYOR_SIMCTL block by assigning default values to most parameters. The structure of the network is defined simply by the connection of the ENTER, EXIT, MERGE and DIVERT ports. Figure 6 shows a fragment of a IEC 61499 Resource that models the chain from Figure 1, laid out similarly to the original example. Note that only the adapter connections are shown, with all other signals hidden.

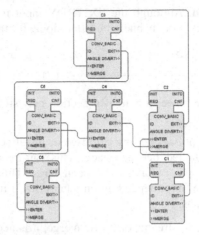

Fig. 6. Function block model of conveyor chain from Figure 1

4 Visualisation

To provide intuitive information about a conveyor system as represented by functional blocks, it is very useful to have some a method of displaying the network in a way that resembles a real conveyor system. The FBDK contains building blocks for simple visualisation of common industrial system components such as solenoids, linear actuators and drills. The representation of the conveyor network was seen as limited by the FBDK's visualisation components because while the conveyors are

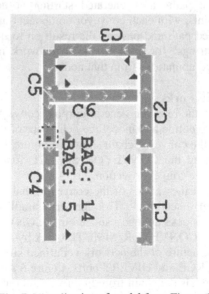

Fig. 7. Visualisation of model from Figure 6

generally static, the bags they carry are dynamic and will vary in number per conveyor. To avoid these limitations an OpenGL based visualiser was created that runs entirely outside the FBDK. This visualiser displays the conveyor sections and bags in real-time, including the state of sensors and actuators.

Figure 7 shows a visualisation generated from the model of Figure 6. In this case a single bag is present in the model with the actual simulated bag position indicated by the small solid box and the predicted position by the larger dotted outline.

5 Conveyor Testbed

With the BHS controller able to control the delivery of bags in the simulated environment presented, the next step is to realise the Conveyor Component as a working physical device. The current setup is based on the Festo MPS500 Modular Production System. The Transport Station comprises a four section conveyor loop each equipped with a motor and a photo eye to detect work pieces on the belt.

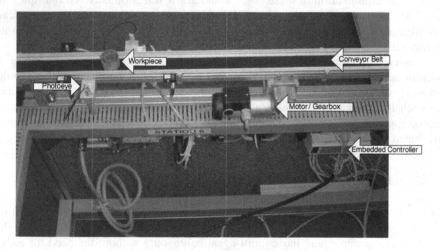

Fig. 8. Conveyor Section of MPS Transport Station

As supplied, the MPS Conveyor is centrally controlled via a bus-connected PLC. In the distributed arrangement, each conveyor section is controlled by an embedded controller capable of executing the IEC 61499 runtime. The two controller types deployed so far are the Elsyst Netmaster II and the Tait Control Systems Mo'Intelligence. Both of these units execute IEC 61499 system configurations using the Functional Block Run Time (FBRT).

6 Future Work

The next stage in this work is to successfully demonstrate the predictive controller working on the conveyor testbed described above. Extensions to the conveyor loop will allow more complete testing of the path finding and merge controllers on the physical model.

The current conveyor loop limits the variety of control that can be performed. An immediate goal is the extension of the loop to allow multiple material flow paths by the addition of extra conveyor sections with diverters and merge points. The final goal will be to demonstrate the validity of the controller design on a real BHS, replacing existing PLCs with multiple embedded controllers.

Currently there is a lack of automation of the process of deploying the IEC 61499 system configurations to the appropriate embedded controllers. It would be desirable that the IEC 61499 system configuration was able to automatically allocate to remote devices using an auto discovery process. This is not part of the standard, but could achieved using other established protocols, e.g. proposed by the Foundation for Intelligent Physical Agents (FIPA).

The path-finding scheme is very basic and suggests many obvious enhancements. The path strings could also incorporate path metrics, such as length or average processing time, in order to assist in 'cost' prediction for a given path sequence. Appropriate combination of these costs would allow selection between multiple valid paths. In the case of baggage handling, this could allow automatic, dynamically reconfigurable bag routing from arbitrary entry point to arbitrary output without any central control system needed to determine path.

A critical requirement for Airport BHS is reliability and recovery from failure. An inherent advantage of the approach described is that each controller contains identical software, so swap out of controllers should be simple. However, a more formal approach is required to determine the response of the distributed system to failure. It may be appropriate to attempt to implement the methods presented in [8] for recovery in distributed IEC 61499 systems including provision of automatic failover redundancy.

7 Conclusion

This paper has demonstrated IEC 61499 Functional Blocks as a suitable design tool for a distributed control task. The transparent networking capabilities of the standard made it easy to implement basic multi-agent behaviours without the need for custom networking code. The use of adapters proved valuable in the creation of a top level reusable component that hides complexity from the system designer and minimises the number of visible connections between components.

Following from [4] the use of predictive control was implemented by adapting simulation components to work in a closed loop with the environment.

The availability of hardware able to directly execute IEC 61499 designs makes it an attractive choice for applications requiring control, simulation or a mixture of the two as demonstrated here.

Acknowledgements

This work has been supported by the research grant 3607028/9273 of the University of Auckland, and by Technology for Industry Fellowship provided by TechNZ. The authors are grateful to John Fitzgerald of Glidepath Ltd. for fruitful discussions.

References

[1] Vickers, K., Chinn, R.W.: Passenger terminal baggage handling systems. Systems Engineering of Aerospace Projects, 249 (1998)

[2] Special Issue on Automation Objects, Int. J. Manufacturing Research 1 (2007)

[3] Vyatkin, V., Hanisch, H.-M., Karras, S., Pfeiffer, T., Dubinin, V.: Rapid Engineering and Re-Configuration of Automation Objects Using Formal Verification. Int. J. Manufacturing Research 1(4), 382–404

[4] Hirsch, M., Vyatkin, V., Hanisch, H. M.: IEC 61499 Function Blocks for Distributed Networked Embedded Applications. In: Proceedings of 4th IEEE Conference on Industrial Informatics (INDIN 2006), Singapore (2006)

[5] Christensen, J.H.: IEC 61499 architecture, engineering methodologies and software tools. In: Proceedings of 5th IFIP International Conference on Information Technology for Balanced Automation System. Manufacturing and Services, Cancun, Mexico (September 2002)

[6] Vyatkin, V.: IEC 61499 Function Blocks for Embedded and Distributed Control Systems Design, p. 297 O3NEIDA - Instrumentation Society of America (2007)

[7] Vrba, P.: MAST: manufacturing agent simulation tool Emerging Technologies and Factory Automation. In: Proceedings of ETFA '03. IEEE Conference, September 16-19, 2003, pp. 282–287 (2003)

[8] Froschauer, R., Auinger, F., Grabmair, G., Strasser, T.: Automatic control application recovery in distributed IEC 61499 based automation and control systems Distributed Intelligent Systems: Collective Intelligence and Its Applications, DIS 2006. In: IEEE Workshop on June 15-16, 2006, pp. 103–108 (2006)

[9] Frey, G., Hussain, T.: Modeling techniques for distributed control systems based on the IEC 61499 standard - current approaches and open problems. Discrete Event Systems. In: 8th International Workshop on July 10-12, 2006, pp. 176–181 (2006)

Zero Downtime Reconfiguration of Distributed Automation Systems: The εCEDAC Approach

Martijn N. Rooker[1], Christoph Sünder[2], Thomas Strasser[1],
Alois Zoitl[2], Oliver Hummer[2], and Gerhard Ebenhofer[1]

[1] PROFACTOR Research, Im Stadtgut A2,
4407 Steyr-Gleink, Austria
{martijn.rooker, thomas.strasser, gerhard.ebenhofer}@profactor.at
[2] Vienna University of Technology, Automation and Control Institute, Gußhaustr. 27-29,
1040 Vienna, Austria
{suender, zoitl, hummer}@acin.tuwien.ac.at

Abstract. Future manufacturing is envisioned to be highly flexible and adaptable. New technologies for reconfigurable systems and their adaptations are preconditions for this vision. Without such solutions, engineering adaptations of Industrial Process Measurement and Control Systems (IPMCS) will exceed the costs of engineered systems by far and the reuse of equipment will become inefficient. Especially the reconfiguration of control applications is not sufficiently solved. This paper gives an overview of the use of reconfiguration applications for downtimeless system evolution of control applications on basis of the standard IEC 61499. A new approach for the reconfiguration of IEC 61499 based control application and the corresponding modeling is discussed. This new method significantly increases engineering efficiency and reuse in component-based IPMCS.

Keywords: Reconfiguration, Architectures, Holonic Systems.

1 Introduction

The decisive factor for the market success of the manufacturing industry is a fast and flexible reaction to changing customer demands—companies must show a high degree of changeability. New paradigms like "Flexible production up to small lot-sizes", "Mass Customization" or "Zero Downtime Production" will achieve these requirements but demand completely new technologies [1]. Changeability, which describes the ability of companies being flexible concerning customer demands, impacts all levels of product manufacturing. In particular these are the agility at a strategic level, the transformability at a factory level and the reconfigurability at the manufacturing system level [2]. The state-of-the-art in manufacturing systems is inadequate to meet the above mentioned requirements. Current manufacturing systems are either tailored towards a specific product at high volume production and can hardly be adapted to new products or are flexible and programmable but technology specific and only for single items or small batch production. Another relatively new approach which is

V. Mařík, V. Vyatkin, A.W. Colombo (Eds.): HoloMAS 2007, LNAI 4659, pp. 326–337, 2007.
© Springer-Verlag Berlin Heidelberg 2007

flexible and programmable but less technology specific and also not adaptable concerning the above mentioned requirements is the usage of "Multi Machining Technology Integration Production Systems" [21] which are characterized by the static implementation and combination of different technologies within one production system. To reach the above mentioned changeability at the machine level it can be postulated that a change from product and technology rigid manufacturing systems towards product and technology flexible, modular, easy to setup component-based production systems is necessary. Consequently perpetuated this means future plants will produce their products on manufacturing systems which will be designed and setup just prior to production of goods. Machining, assembly and transport systems of such production systems are also designed and setup by the utilization of various flexible autonomous and intelligent mechatronic components just before usage within the production line. The consequences of the above mentioned attempt are extensive and many technological breakthroughs will be necessary. Beside others the development of an adequate automation system for heavily interacting distributed real-time systems can be seen as a major task. Current architectures of IPMCS do not conceptual support reconfiguration and distribution which are necessary for the above mentioned systems [15]. Distributed embedded real–time systems for industrial automation and control of plants that evolve towards downtimeless adaptable systems will play a key role to realize the roadmaps towards adaptive manufacturing [2] of products, goods and services in 2020. Most value will then be added in engineering and performing a system evolution (the change from one system state to another) rather than in engineering and performing "normal operation".

The challenge and aim of this paper is to present an approach for modeling of reconfiguration control applications based on the IEC 61499 standard. Section 2 discusses general reconfiguration issues. Section 3 gives an overview of state-of-the-art in reconfiguration of control applications. Section 4 summarizes the main features and characteristics of IEC 61499 as reference model for distributed automation and control systems with special focus of the management capabilities for reconfiguration. In Section 5 an approach for the controlled reconfiguration of control applications is introduced. Especially the modeling of reconfiguration control applications based on the IEC 61499 reference model is topic of Section 6. First tests at the Odo Struger Laboratory at Vienna University of Technology (Automation and Control Institute) will be presented in Section 7. The summary of this work concludes the paper.

2   General Reconfiguration Issues

In industrial informatics, reconfiguration of software modules and components has been discussed many times, for instance in [6][7][8]. Agile software processes like the extreme programming method recognize change as an essential part of the software life–cycle [9].

2.1   Basic vs. Dynamic Reconfiguration

Within the scope of this paper, reconfiguration is described best as altering a systems operation in order to meet changes in requirements. Quite a simple reconfiguration method—hence further denoted as basic reconfiguration—is to stop current operation, apply all necessary changes to the system and restart the desired operation again (coldstart). But this approach is not sufficient to meet the constraints mentioned in section 1. The opposite of basic reconfiguration is termed dynamic reconfiguration. Brinkschulte et al. [10] define dynamic reconfiguration as reconfiguration of an application while it is running. What therefore further distinguishes dynamic from basic reconfiguration is provision for timeliness constraints [3]. Dynamic reconfiguration considers timeliness as crucial facet of correctness. With respect to control applications this means that timeliness requirements put on the whole application must be preserved while parts of it are modified.

2.2 Classification of Dynamic Reconfiguration

Within the topic of dynamic reconfiguration a big variety of opportunities arises. This especially demands means of classification for the different approaches within this field. Wermelinger [11] has formulated 3 essential questions that have to be answered for dynamic reconfiguration:

1)   What kind of modifications can be done?
2)   How are they performed?
3)   When may the changes be performed?

The first two questions concern the reconfiguration model (model of system architecture and modification process) as well as the features of the underlying operating system and/or the runtime environment. Question 3 is of special interest. The answer to this question certainly is that those parts of an automation system that will undergo changes have to be in a consistent state before. But consistency is not only a prerequisite for reconfiguration. Quite on the contrary, consistency is an important attribute of systems that must be preserved over reconfiguration in order to avoid unnecessary disruption of the system environment. This requires transfer of state information from the current system state to the desired state after reconfiguration. Rasche and Polze [12] give an idea of how correct state information can be ensured against different use cases of reconfiguration.

3   State-of-the-Art Reconfiguration Approaches

Today common automation systems predominantly rely on the programming paradigms of the standard IEC 61131–3 [13] dedicated to systems based on programmable logic controllers (PLCs). The common paradigm within IEC 61131 is a device centered engineering methodology. Aspects of distribution have to be considered from the beginning of the engineering phase. Current IEC 61131–3 based engineering tools such as [14] already enable online code exchange for single devices at task level, including transfer of variable values. But there are still a number of drawbacks like undeterministic switching points in time (due to cyclic execution policy), lack of fine granularity (reconfiguration at task level), jitter effects (task reconfiguration influences other tasks) or the possibility of inconsistent states (e.g. leading to deadlocks) [15]. The International Electrotechnical Commission (IEC) addresses these issues by the standard IEC 61499 [16], which extend the Function Block (FB) model of IEC 61131–3 in order to meet the requirements of engineering distributed automation systems. The most important concepts of IEC 61499 are an event–driven execution model, a management interface capable of basic reconfiguration support and the application centered engineering methodology. The major benefit of this approach is a separation of concerns: first the whole application is programmed as a FB network like in centralized systems, afterwards the components of this network (the function blocks) are mapped to the devices of the real system where they are executed. Doing so facilitates the movement of functionality from one controller to another as mentioned in section 1, since only the mapping is concerned while the original application remains unchanged. Furthermore, the enhanced support of distribution enables the idea of component–based automation in the sense of entities of software and hardware [17]. A more detailed description of IEC 61499 and its aptitude for reconfiguration purposes can be found in [18]. Various researchers have developed reconfiguration methodologies based on IEC 61499: the research project TORERO [19] focuses on plug–and–play and self–(re)configuration of field devices in a so–called total lifecycle approach utilizing IEC 61499 for modeling control logic. But still the system has to be stopped for deployment of code to the devices. Thramboulidis et al. [20] use Real-time–UML as a meta-model between the design models of IEC 61499 and their implementation models to support dynamic reconfiguration of control applications. Brennan et al. [3] propose an agent–based reconfiguration approach, extending the IEC 61499 FB model: they introduce a second state–machine within the basic FB together with a reconfiguration agent and a second event and data flow for reconfiguration purposes. All these approaches rely on a technology that is outside the scope of IEC 61499 (e.g. Universal Plug and Play, agents or Realtime–UML), they do not consider utilizing the basic reconfiguration functionality provided by the management model outlined in the next section.

4   IEC 61499 as Reference Model for Reconfigurable Control

The new standard IEC 61499 [16] serves as a reference architecture developed for distributed, modular, and flexible control systems. It specifies an architectural model for distributed applications in IPMCS in a very generic way and extends the FB model of its predecessor IEC 61131-3 (Function Block Diagram FBD) with additional event handling mechanisms and concepts for distributed systems. The standard builds a good basis to overcome the above mentioned problems according to reconfiguration processes in current IPMCS. The following sections describe some fundamental issues of IEC 61499 that make this standard suitable as reference architecture for building zero-downtime IPMCS by using the concept of reconfiguration applications. More detailed information is available from [4] and [5].

4.1   Execution Control by Events

The FB model of IEC 61499 defines FBs that are characterized by the occurrence of two Input/Output (I/O) types: events and data. The execution is triggered by events, needed data have to be valid at the inputs of the FB before an event arrives. Only if an event occurs at a FB input, the runtime environment has to process the execution of this FB. Therefore it is clearly understandable whether an application is active or not and even exactly which part is currently processed.

4.2 Distribution Model

One of the main intentions of IEC 61499 is enabling distributed applications. The system model consists of devices connected by a communication network and applications. These may be distributed within devices or resources, located within devices. The engineering process starts with the top-level functionality that has to be realized without reference to the concrete hardware structure. The last step within the engineering cycle is the mapping of the applications to concrete hardware components; independent whether the application is executed by one device or distributed to several devices.

4.3 Management Interface of IEC 61499 Devices

The configuration of a distributed automation and control system based on IEC 61499 can be enabled by the use of management functions which can be included in each device. For this purpose the standard defines a management application, represented by a management FB. By using this FB combined with a remote application, access between different IEC 61499 compliant devices is possible. The IEC 61499 Compliance Profile for Feasibility Demonstrations (available from [5]) describes a concrete interface of a management FB and an appropriate remote application. The following standardized management functions can be used to interact with a device ([16], Part 1-Table 6, 8). Especially the management of software components (i.e. FBs) regarding to their execution is a very important item in reconfiguration processes. A FB instance operates according to a state machine (see [16], Part 1-Fig. 24) that includes an initialization and operation state controlled by management commands: Create, Start, Stop/Kill and Delete.

5 Engineering Method for Reconfiguration of IPMCS

To overcome the limitations of current embedded industrial automation and control engineering methods, we propose an application centered engineering method for efficient component-based modeling of applications for controlled, fault–tolerant and safe system reconfiguration of IPMCS. The execution of a reconfiguration will become a normal operational state of such systems, while dependability and Quality of Service (QoS) of the reconfigured system are not endangered and migration is cost–efficient. Thus important steps towards Adaptive Manufacturing will be realized. The top–level approach focuses on replacing state–of–the–art "ramp down—stop—download—restart—ramp up" methods with a simple continuous system evolution, which is controlled by a reconfiguration control application that is modeled with components in the same way as control applications are. Reconfiguration control can be either executed from an engineering environment or—if constraints regarding fault tolerance, real–time and safety have to be met—can be distributed to different controllers. For safe and fault–tolerant control and reconfiguration execution the reconfiguration application is verified together with hardware capability descriptions of the different devices in the network leading to trustable QoS judgment.

5.1 Modeling Cycle for Control and Reconfiguration Control Applications

The following engineering process provides a method for handling system reconfiguration of IPMCS by an efficient support for engineering of control applications and reconfiguration control applications. This engineering method consists of the following four major parts as depicted in Fig. 1:

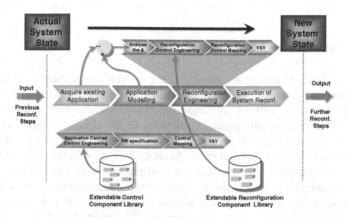

Fig. 1. Modeling cycle for control and reconfiguration control applications

1. *Acquire existing application:* Collect all data necessary for describing the current system state and deliver it as input to the application modeling. The data consists of the system model including applications currently running in the system, the hardware configuration of the system (used devices and network structure), the mapping of the applications to the different devices and the hardware capability descriptions.
2. *Application Modeling:* Modeling of the new control application based on the existing ones by adding/removing components, their interconnections and specification of application properties (e.g. real–time constraints). The next step is the configuration of the hardware structure with devices and network connections. After this the modeled application parts are mapped to the according devices they should be executed on. The final step is the verification and validation of the control application in order to determine if the specified constraints will be met.
3. *Reconfiguration Engineering:* With the Delta Analysis differences between the current running control application and the newly modeled one are determined. These differences serve as input and starting point for the modeling of the reconfiguration control application that will change the existing application to the new one. The reconfiguration control properties and parameters are specified in the same way as control application properties (according to step 2). Similar to the mapping of the control application the reconfiguration application parts are mapped to the devices. The final step is the verification of the reconfiguration control application together with device capabilities in order to determine if reconfiguration constraints will be met and the running application is disturbed as less as possible.

4. *Execution of System Reconfiguration:* To execute evolution control applications the use of basic reconfiguration services at runtime platforms based on IEC 61499 management commands is necessary. The first step is to instantiate the reconfiguration control application on the according devices. Next the execution of the reconfiguration control application is done, i.e. the currently running control application is transformed into the new control application. The main services are: control application component load/remove, connect/disconnect, query parameters, write parameters, query component state and write component state. To finish the evolution procedure the reconfiguration control application will be removed after successfully executing all commands and all changes are finished.

6 Reconfiguration Methodology

The process of reconfiguring a control system without downtimes sets high demands on the underlying concepts and methodologies: Applications within the automation system have to work without disturbances; the reconfiguration process has to be adapted to the special environmental conditions of the affected application part. Any failure during the reconfiguration process has to be managed at least to such a degree, that the system is left in a defined state. As described the standard IEC 61499 already includes basic management commands for configuration and reconfiguration of applications. This section proposes useful extensions to the management model of IEC 61499 enhancing the reconfiguration abilities of IEC 61499 with special regard to remaining compliant to the ideas of the standard. The main idea of this new methodology is to control the reconfiguration of control logic (part of the control application) by an application, the so called reconfiguration application. The reconfiguration application does not differ from any other application and can therefore be modeled in the same manner. But it will have an impact on the control application, which means that it will include management commands that influence FBs and their interconnections in a defined manner. The basic idea of reconfiguration applications is described by Sünder et. al. [15]. The presented engineering methodology builds on these results, particularly with regard to the setup and characteristics of reconfiguration applications.

6.1 Reconfiguration Control Terminology and Definitions

At this point it is suitable to define a few terms used later on for the development of an appropriate engineering methodology for dynamic reconfiguration processes:

- *Region of Interest (ROI):* a specific part of an IEC 61499 application that will be target for a specific reconfiguration. A reconfiguration application is assigned to this specific part. The definition of this region is given by the following cases of system changes:
  - Creating/Deleting a FB: the suggested ROI is the FB itself plus the corresponding halves of the surrounding function blocks (either output or input side) it is connected with, as there is a significant temporal order of operations (a FB cannot be deleted unless all of its connections have been deleted).
  - Creating/Deleting a connection: the suggested ROI consists of the corresponding halves of source and target FBs of the connection and the interconnections.

- Creating/Deleting a parameter: quite similar to connections, but without a source FB. The suggested ROI only consists of the left half of the target FB and the parameter itself.
- *System evolution*: the whole process of transforming the current control application into the desired control application (instead of the state–of–the–art method "ramp down—download new control application—ramp up again").
- *Reconfiguration Execution Control Function Blocks (RECFB)*: special function blocks encapsulating reconfiguration functionality (e.g. a whole reconfiguration application). Within the execution of *RECFB* 3 reconfiguration control execution phases can be distinguished (see Fig. 2):
  - RINIT Sequence: contains all preparation work that is needed to enable a controlled change of applications.
  - RECONF Sequence: encapsulates all operations necessary to change from the old state to the new one. This for instance includes reading of internal states, calculation of the new internal states and writing the internal state to the new FB in case of a simple FB exchange with awareness to consistency. The final step of this sequence is the switch to the new FB.
  - RDINIT Sequence: responsible for cleaning up after reconfiguration (e.g. deleting connections and function blocks not needed anymore). One RECFB concerns to one ROI.

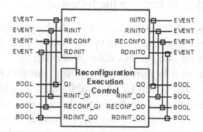

Fig. 2. Reconfiguration Execution Control Function Block (RECFB)

- *Reconfiguration Control Application*: application (i.e. a special IEC 61499 based FB network) built of *RECFBs*, that carries out the whole system evolution process on an ordinary IEC 61499 system.

6.2 Reconfiguration Engineering Method

The use of reconfiguration applications describes control of the dynamic reconfiguration within a ROI. The main intentions for the introduction of an evolution engineering method handling these reconfiguration applications are:

- *Complexity*: The use of reconfiguration applications includes a reasonable amount of complexity. The bigger the ROI the more complex the whole reconfiguration application will be. Also in the case of distributed applications that have to be changed a certain extent of complexity is added to the system. By using small ROIs, the complexity remains quite low.

– *Scalability*: There has to be a way to compose larger evolution scenarios from several steps. The RECFBs give the possibility to build composite RECFBs in the same way as in "normal" applications using the same means.

– *Reusability*: As scalability is possible, the use of libraries for often used scenarios within typical application scopes will be useful. The concept enables such standardized RECFBs and their simple usage within composite RECFBs, again in the same way as in "normal" applications. The main idea is to maintain the fundamental principles of IEC 61499 (application centered engineering, component-based architecture, event–driven execution and the management model) for evolution engineering. Fig. 3 illustrates a reconfiguration control application containing 3 RECFBs. Each contains a reconfiguration application performing reconfiguration on the associated ROI in the IEC 61499 application shown in the lower part of the figure. The interconnection of the RECFBs defines the way of executing the three steps. In the shown example only one RECFB is active at the same time (serial execution). In detail, each RECFB runs through the three phases of Initialization, Reconfiguration and Deinitialization before the next RECFB is triggered. By using the QI and QO data variables of the RECFBs, the internal sequences of the RECFBs communicate in a very simple manner. If one sequence fails, the next step will not be executed.

The presented engineering methodology handles the two main tasks of reconfiguration applications according to Fig. 3 in the following way:

– It performs runtime adaptations on the control application of a distributed automation system, corresponding to the upper half of Fig. 3. This includes transfer of state information from one system state to another.

– It performs runtime–checks during execution to ensure correct operation. In case of failures the system must be left in a tolerable state, this may include undo functionality for abortive reconfiguration steps. Such failure recovery strategies also require backup and restore mechanisms for state information, corresponding to the lower half of Fig. 3. In our approach these topics are handled on different levels. First of all within one reconfiguration application the issues of recovery have to be handled internally. Second also within reconfiguration control applications this issue has to be modeled. The example in Fig. 3 only provides a stop of later RECFBs in case of an error by use of the simple QI/QO construct.

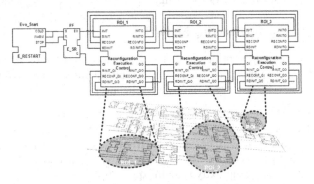

Fig. 3. Regions of interest during the evolution process

Another important aspect for reconfiguration is real-time constrained execution. IEC 61499 leaves issues such as timeliness open and delegates appropriate specifications to compliance profiles and runtime implementations respectively. There exists no barrier to apply such a capability of the runtime environment to the presented engineering methodology. So if the underlying runtime system features timeliness (i.e. deterministic behavior), it can also be applied to the evolution process (doing so certainly the complexity is further increasing).

7 First Tests and Concept Validation

First tests in the "Testbed for Highly Distributed Control" for the proposed engineering concept have been performed at the Odo Struger Laboratory of the Automation and Control Institute (ACIN), Vienna University of Technology. These tests gave us the possibility of validating our reconfiguration concepts. In detail, reconfiguration of a prototypic implementation of an advanced execution environment, a linear servo drives has been performed during operation, in this case the movement of the axis according to a position profile. The control program for the linear servo drive consists of the velocity and the position closed-loop control. The tests have been provided for both of these two parts of the control program and have been investigated for the change of the control algorithm. For instance a proportional control algorithm has been exchanged by a new one including an integral part or in addition a derivative part. The scenario for the velocity closed-loop control was the exchange of the control algorithm without changes in the hardware. So the ROI for this scenario was restricted to the FB including the control algorithm and its surrounding.

During the RECONF sequence an appropriate algorithm has to be applied to avoid disturbances, in this example the output fitting method has been used [22]. In the second scenario the position closed-loop control has been exchanged and also the hardware configuration has been changed. An additional controller has been introduced and the new position controller has been applied to the new controller. The results of the second scenario are presented in Fig. 4.

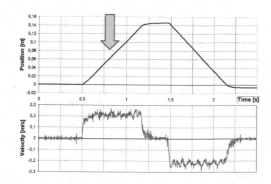

Fig. 4. Reconfiguration with output-fitting at time 0.75 s

The linear axis performs a ramp. During the ramp up sequence the reconfiguration takes place, depicted by the green arrow in Fig. 4. In the lower part of Fig. 4 the corresponding velocity of the linear axis gives an impression of the performance of the reconfiguration. There is no influence visible in the velocity graph (of course also in the position graph), although the control algorithm of the position controller has been changed and the position controller itself has been moved to another device within the network. This first result shows that the proposed reconfiguration approach is sufficient for providing dynamic reconfiguration of lower level control applications in distributed IPMCS.

8 Summary and Conclusion

This paper presents an approach for structured modeling of reconfiguration control applications of IPMCS based on the IEC 61499 standard. It shows that means of the IEC 61499 standard's management model, with little extensions, are sufficient for dynamic reconfiguration of applications. This means that both runtime adaptations and failure recovery can be modeled the same way as ordinary applications. A huge amount of state information can be gathered and transferred via data and event flow between application and reconfiguration application. This information can easily be saved to and restored from internal variables of the RECFBs. Necessary extensions of the management model concern state information hidden in function block internals (local variables, ECC states, etc.). The results of a first test case for a closed-loop controller reconfiguration on a linear servo drive have shown its practical use.

Acknowledgments. This work is supported by the FIT–IT: Embedded Systems program, an initiative of the Austrian federal ministry of transport, innovation, and technology (bm:vit) within the εCEDAC–project under contract FFG 809447. Further information about the project is available at: www.ecedac.org

The authors would like to thank the European Commission and the partners of the Innovative Production Machines and Systems (I*PROMS) Network of Excellence for their support under the Sixth Framework Program (Contract No. 500273). Further information about I*PROMS is available at: www.iproms.org

References

1. European Commission, MANUFUTURE A Vision for 2020, Report of the High-Level Group (November 2004)
2. Koren, Y., Heisel, U., Jovane, F., Moriwaki, T., Pritshow, G., Ulsoy, G., van Brussel, H.: Reconfigurable Manufacturing Systems. Annals of the International Institution for Production Engineering Research (CIRP) 48/2, 527–539 (1999)
3. Brennan, R.W., Fletcher, M., Norrie, D.H.: An agent-based approach to reconfiguration of real-time distributed control systems. IEEE Journal of Robotics and Automation 18(4), 444–451 (2002)
4. Lewis, R.W.: Modeling control systems using IEC 61499. IEE Publishing (2001) ISBN Number: 0 85296 796 9
5. Christensen, J. H.: HOLOBLOC, INC. - Resources for the New Generation of Automation and Control (Access Date May 2005) www.holobloc.com

6. Brennan, R.W., Zhang, X., Xu, Y., Norrie, D.H.: A reconfigurable concurrent function block model and its implementation in real-time java. Integrated Computer-Aided Engineering 9, 263–279 (2002)
7. Bussmann, S., McFarlane, D.: Rationales for Holonic Manufacturing Control. In: 2nd International Workshop on Intelligent Manufacturing Systems, Leuven (1999)
8. Burmester, S.: Modeling reconfigurable mechatronic systems with mechatronic UML. in MDAFA - Model Driven Architecture: Foundations and Applications (2004)
9. Mens, T., Wermelinger, M., Ducasse, S., Demeyer, S., Hirschfeld, R., Jazayeri, M.: Challenges in software evolution. in Principles of Software Evolution. In: Proc. Eighth Int. Workshop, Sept. 5–6, pp. 13–22 (2005)
10. Brinkschulte, U., Schneider, E., Piciorag̃a, F.: Dynamic real-time reconfiguration in distributed systems: timing issues and solutions. Object-Oriented Real-Time Distributed Computing, ISORC 2005. In: Proceedings of Eighth IEEE International Symposium, May 18–20 2005, pp. 174–181 (2005)
11. Wermelinger, M.: A hierarchic architecture model for dynamic reconfiguration, in Software Engineering for Parallel and Distributed Systems. In: Proceedings of Second International Workshop, Boston, USA, May 17-18, 1997, pp. 243–254 (1997)
12. Rasche, A., Polze, A.: Dynamic reconfiguration of component-based real-time software. in Object-Oriented Real-Time Dependable Systems WORDS 2005. In: Proceedings of 10th IEEE International Workshop, Feb. 2–4 2005, pp. 347–354 (2005)
13. International Electrotechnical Commission. IEC 61131-3: Programmable controllers - Part 3: Programming languages. In: International Standard, 2nd Revision, Geneva (January 2003)
14. logiCAD. The IEC 61131, Technology Platform. kirchner SOFT GmbH
15. Sünder, C., Zoitl, A., Favre-Bulle, B., Strasser, T., Steininger, H., Thomas, S.: Towards reconfiguration applications as basis for control system evolution in zero-downtime automation systems. appears in Intelligent Production Machines and Systems. In: IPROMS 2006. IPROMS NoE Virtual International Conference (June 3-14, 2006)
16. International Electrotechnical Commission. IEC 61499: Function Blocks, Parts 1–4, International Standard / Technical Report, 1st edn. Geneva (2004/2005)
17. Ferrarini, L., Lorentz, K.: A case study for modeling and design of distributed automation systems, in Advanced Intelligent Mechatronics. In: Proceedings. IEEE/ASME International Conference on, July 22-24, 2003, pp. 1043–1048 (2003)
18. Strasser, T., Zoitl, A., Auinger, F., Sünder, C.: Towards engineering methods for reconfiguration of distributed automation systems based on the reference model of IEC 61499, in Industrial Applications of Holonic and Multi-Agent Systems. In: 2nd Int. Conf. on, Copenhagen, Denmark (August 22-24, 2005)
19. Lorentz, K.: Torero newsletter no. 2. TORERO Consortium, Tech. Rep, [Online]. (access date 28-03-2006) (January 2004) Available: http://www.uni-magdeburg.de/iaf/cvs/torero
20. Thramboulidis, K., Doukas, G., Frantzis, A.: Towards an implementation model for FB-based reconfigurable distributed control applications. In: Proceedings of 7th IEEE International Symposium on Object-Oriented Real-Time Distributed Computing, pp. 193–200 (2004)
21. Abele, E., Wörn, A., Stroh, C., Elzenheimer, J.: Multi Machining Technology Integration in RMS. In: CIRP sponsored 3rd Conference on Reconfigurable Manufacturing, University of Michigan, Ann Arbor, MI (May 2005)
22. Guler, M., Clement, S., Wills, L.M., Heck, B.S., Vachtsevanos, G.J.: Transition management for reconfigurable hybrid control systems. IEEE Control Systems Magazine 23(1), 1 (2003)

Holonic Multiagent-Based System for Distributed Control of Semi-industrial Pilot Plants

Mieczyslaw Metzger and Grzegorz Polaków

Faculty of Automatic Control, Electronics and Computer Science
Silesian University of Technology,
Akademicka 16, 44-100 Gliwice, Poland
{mieczyslaw.metzger, grzegorz.polakow}@polsl.pl

Abstract. Semi-industrial pilot plants are the best experimental domain for advanced control systems testing with the real-world instrumentation. At the same time, inexpensive flexible process real-time simulators and virtual soft controllers are indispensable in the research and education field. Integrating control instrumentation of varying manufacturers, plant simulators, and virtual controllers into uniform system capable of flexible research and educational experiments is a complex problem to solve. A tool is needed to describe and organise knowledge on such integrated structure involving many communication channels and using distributed processing power. In the presented case-study, holarchy paradigm is applied, resulting in an untypical holonic multiagent system. The concept, architecture and development of application framework for the system are presented thoroughly in the paper.

Keywords: system integration, distributed control, multi-agent, holonic system, producer-distributor-consumer networking.

1 Introduction

Over the past years automation systems designed for industrial plants became complex and distributed and usually consist of many components such as instrumentation, software and networking. A growing need for appropriate research and education techniques for such complex control systems results in creation of more advanced methods and tools. For example, real-time simulation plays an important role in the development of industrial process simulators [1]. Such kind of tools (virtual plants) can be very useful for operator's training, testing specialised control software and especially for testing industrial controllers as well as virtual soft controllers.

Software simulation-based experiments are not expensive, but they consider only limited part of the real world, depending on the model's level of detail. Hence, such a method of investigation is suitable for initial tests only. Testing control software and hardware with the real-world processes gives more realistic results that take into account all possible problems occurring in industrial reality. Unfortunately, experiments with the real world industrial processes are not only very expensive, but are also limited by possibility of production disturbance and potential financial losses. A concept

V. Mařík, V. Vyatkin, A.W. Colombo (Eds.): HoloMAS 2007, LNAI 4659, pp. 338–347, 2007.
© Springer-Verlag Berlin Heidelberg 2007

of specialised semi-industrial pilot plants – designed specifically for control systems investigation, can be considered a compromising solution. Such method of experiments conducting is less expensive than the one based on industrial processes during normal production. Moreover, it ensures nearly the same potential that is provided by an experimentation with real full-scale industrial processes (industry standard control instrumentation). Such laboratory with semi-industrial pilot plants has been developed for a few years [2]. The plants, which are of different types and distributed in several laboratory rooms, are attractive subject of investigation in the field of industrial network-based distributed control systems. Although the experiments with the pilot plants are less expensive than with the industrial ones, their costs are still considerably notable for educational entities. Hence, it can be very interesting to expand the number of plants' users by the Internet. It has to be considered that a lot of experimenters (local and remote) will carry out theirs investigations simultaneously using different plants, different instrumentation (for example not connected to particular plant), and different industrial networking. Realisation of such demands is a very difficult control issue. An untypical holonic multi-agent system is proposed as a solution to the problem.

Basic concepts of multiagent systems are discussed for example in [3],[4],[5], while industrial applications of multi-agent systems are presented in [6],[7],[8]. The word "holon" was proposed by Koestler [9] to describe an elementary unit of organisation in biological and social systems, whereas standardisation of holonic systems for manufacturing is proposed by HMS consortium [10]. Over the last decade several survey papers (see e.g. [11],[12]) as well as industry application papers (see e.g. [13],[14]) have been presented. It is not standard yet, but in several publications (see e.g [15], [16]) applications of FIPA communication connected with functional blocks (FB) programming are proposed.

A holonic multi-agent system, which is proposed in this paper, is developed in the LabVIEW (LV) environment [17]. Although LV is not designed with agentural applications on mind, it is well-equipped for programming an artificial intelligence (neural networks, fuzzy logic, DB) and co-operation tasks (XML). Also, programming in the LV environment is done with the G graphical language, which is as powerful and versatile as any typical text-based C and C++ languages. It should be noticed that the LV's supplier offers wide choice of instrumentation for measurement and distributed control. It appears to be the reason of the broad popularity of the LV environment in research and educational fields. Although function blocks for the basic TCP/IP client-server communication exist in the LV environment by default, any more advanced communication schemes (like producer-distributor-consumer) adequate and necessary for multi-agent communication have to be developed additionally [18].

2 Hardware Architecture

System under consideration consists of six physical semi-industrial plants, designed to enable research in the following industrial process domains: biological, heating, pH neutralisation, sedimentation, combustion, and hydraulics. Detailed information on functionalities of these plants is available in [2].

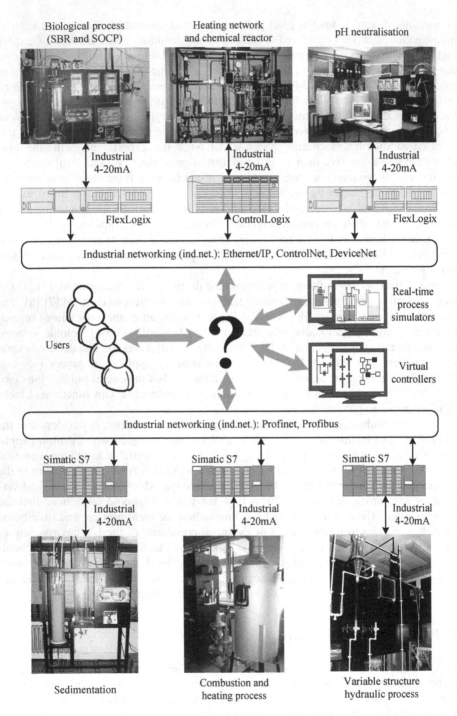

Fig. 1. Physical structure of system under consideration

Each of the six plants is hardwired to the separate commercial programmable logic controller (PLC) using classical industrial standard (4-20mA current loop or 0-10V signal). Three of the PLCs are Siemens Simatic S7 controllers and other three are various models of Rockwell Logix series. S7 controllers are connected together with the Profinet and Profibus network, while Logix controllers communicate with the DeviceNet, ControlNet and EtherNet/IP protocols. Physical structure of the system is shown in Fig. 1. Additionally, not shown in the figure, there are multiple desktop personal computers (PC) present in the vicinity of the plants, connected to each of the PLCs with available means (specialised network interfaces and networking/integration software: RSLinx, MPI, OPC). All these PCs are linked to the existing Ethernet-based local area network.

Requirement of a system integration is an effect of the specific character of the pilot plants. Being part of the technical university resources, the system is expected to be useful both in research and education. It is a usual situation, when researchers or instructors need a process from the specific domain, connected to the exact model (or even specific unit) of the commercial programmable logic controller. These interconnection requirements are very dynamic, as they change between any classes and researches conducted by students, instructors, and researchers using the system.

As a result, the most required functionality of the integrated system is possibility of connecting any available controller to any of the existing plants. Additionally, it is desirable to seamlessly integrate software instrumentation with the existing hardware, where software instruments are virtual controllers and processes simulators. There exist solutions for varying vendors' industrial networks interconnection like specialised PLC modules, PC cards (see for example Anybus cards and modules for Profibus-DeviceNet transmission [19]), and network bridges (such as proposed in [20] or [21]). Unfortunately such solutions are usually limited to two network standards only and require extensive configuration, so they can not provide required degree of integration.

Such uncommon structure of the system and additional specific requirements of its quick and flexible reconfiguration, are describable with the holarchy theory ([10]). Each of the semi-industrial plants together with its linked programmable logic controller can be treated as a holon. Requests of students, instructors and researchers are external rules. Intelligent agents employed by holons dynamically reconfigure the structure of inter-holon connections to form clusters of holons, which fit to the current constraints given by the rules. The hardware of the system is logically embedded in the holons, only unified interface of the agents is presented to other members of the holarchy. This makes it possible to integrate software instruments with the system, as they can be embedded in the uniformed holons, too. Achieved logical structure of the system is presented in the Fig. 2.

While idea of the holonic integration of the system is very attractive, it requires extensive development of the unified inter-holon interface. A protocol of real-time process data exchange between boundaries of existing industrial networks is needed, and. a method of holons synchronisation and appropriate agent language are required. Proposed structure of the interface and progress of the development of all its layers is presented in the following section.

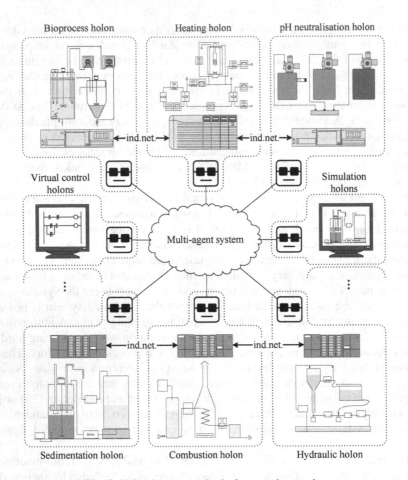

Fig. 2. Holarchy as a method of system integration

3 Communication Framework

A need for exchange of sampled process data between holons not physically interconnected through the specialised industrial networks, implies a necessity of developing a
method for such data transmission by the network of inter-holon connections. Therefore, interface agents have to be equipped with double communicational skills. On the
one hand, advanced high level protocol is needed, so the holons are able to synchronise knowledge on the logical structure of the holarchy and on the other hand a low
level real-time process data transmission protocol is required. When compared to the
usually investigated holonic manufacturing systems, presence of the real-time protocol at the level of holon communication is a notable distinction. That is because
sampled continuous processes are controlled by algorithms in the form of recursive
difference equations, which in each iteration require knowledge of values of all input

variables to be valid. On the contrary, manufacturing systems are not time critical – required periods of data exchange are large enough to be fulfilled by nearly any networking protocol.

Required structure of the holon's interface is shown in Fig. 3. As it is seen, internal structure of a holon is layered, each layer of the structure has corresponding level of communication. Structure of the interface agent is also layered to support the two types of communication. Upper level of agent's thread is connected with cooperation control protocol, while lower one deals with the real-time data transmission.

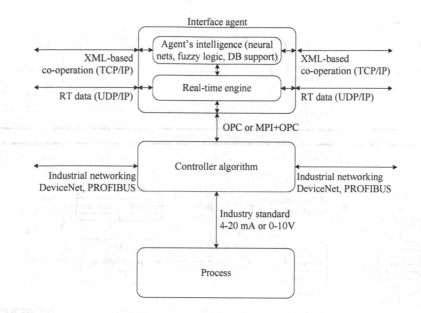

Fig. 3. Anatomy of holon

3.1 Real Time Engine

An Ethernet-based protocol for real-time transmission of numerical values between LabVIEW developed software agents was developed earlier and is described thoroughly in [18].

The protocol was designed specifically for cyclical exchange of data between equally privileged network peers. Whole transmission framework is built according to the producer-distributor-consumer paradigm. Each of the interface agents is connected to scheduling agent, which manages timing of the communication performing the role of the distributor. Main task of the distributor is storing the list of variables (each variable consist of a textual identifier and a value) and making it available to the interface agents performing the roles of producers and consumers. The list of identifiers is served constantly and may be downloaded by agents at any moment (usually once, when agent is started). List of values of variables is broadcasted cyclically. Period of broadcast cycle defines sampling time of all continuous signals in the system.

Each specific broadcast synchronises cycles of work of distributed plants. Diagram of the real-time framework is presented in the Fig. 4. Continuous black arrows show the flow of control in agents' threads; grey dashed lines indicate data flow inside and between agents.

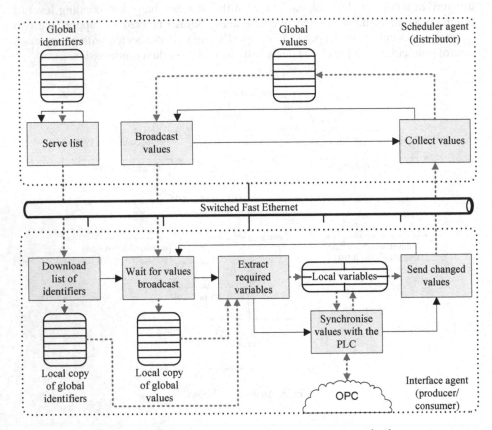

Fig. 4. Control and data flow in real-time agent communication

A presumption taken into account during framework design was compatibility with the existing Ethernet-based local area network. To ensure compatibility with existing network traffic, protocol was designed to run in the application layer i.e. on top of TCP and UDP protocols. List of the variables' textual identifiers is transmitted with the TCP, because it is served on demand (TCP supports two-way request-answer transmission). Raw values are transmitted with the UDP protocol, because of its low control data overhead and capability of broadcasting, which is required in producer-distributor-consumer communication scheme.

It is sometimes pointed that Ethernet's transmission times are non determined because of used CSMA/CD method. Therefore, it should be noted that Ethernet networks built using switching technology does not use that algorithm and only source of possible data loss is overloading switches' internal packet queues. Keeping queues safe from overfilling (by limiting amount of traffic in the network) allows to ensure that each time of packet transmission is determined. Summarising: presented framework is real-time capable when running on top of not overloaded Ethernet network built with the switching technology only.

Distributor application is developed using LabVIEW and it is required to be running on one of the computers in the local network. Cooperation between distributor and the interface agents is made easy with the predeveloped set of functional blocks, which make transforming any LabVIEW program into framework capable agent trivial. Details on the framework operation, available G language functional blocks, network transmission formats and distributors manual are included in [18]

3.2 Co-operation Engine

Cooperation engine is superordinated to all the layers in the holon's structure, including interface agent's real-time engine layer. The role of cooperation engine is synchronising internal state of the holon with the state of the holarchy which is defined by current constraints.

Changes of the structure of the holarchy are unpredictable and unscheduled, yet they are very important for the proper functionality of the system. Therefore it is proposed to implement transmission of this kind of information with the reliable TCP protocol. All advanced agent and holonic knowledge languages can be successfully implemented with the LabVIEW thanks to Internet Toolbox supplied by National Instruments. The toolbox contains (among others) complete XML support with the full functionality of the Document Object Model including namespaces support. In combination with the artificial intelligence methods supported by LabVIEW (neural networks, fuzzy logic, database integration, etc.) it is easy to develop a custom program able to synchronise holon with the rest of the holarchy.

Additional possibilities are enabled by the web server embedded in the distributor application (not marked in the Fig. 4). The framework is supplied with the set of server side scripts enabling Web Services providing full access to all the variables of the system. This channel of system communication is preferred as the method of inputting holarchy constraints using standard web browser.

3.3 Interface Agent – PLC Connection

Each of the six plants of the system is connected to one of designated desktop PCs. Linking method depends on the specific PLC and include dedicated interface cards and retail integration software (e.g. RSLinx). Despite of the specific linking method, each of the links ends with the OPC standard compliant data server providing access to the internal variables of the PLC programs (which include plants process data).

Interface agents are resident and execute their threads in the computers directly connected to the process plants. Versatility of the typical PC (in contrary to the limited PLCs) allows for execution of LabVIEW developed software. There exist programmable logic controllers able to execute directly LabVIEW applications (National Instruments FieldPoint series), but in the case of presented system it does not apply.

Applications executed by the PLCs present in the system have to react to changes of the logical role of the holarchy. Proposed method of implementing such reaction capability is to develop separate subprograms fulfilling every possible role of the specific plant in the holarchy. Then, all the subroutines have to be merged into single application for the PLC. Subprogram to being executed at the moment has to be chosen by the application basing on the value of variable. In such configuration, interface agent is able to choose subprogram of the PLC by simple modification of this specific variable. It is visible at the diagram in the Fig. 3 – agent's cooperation engine is able to communicate with the PLC through the real-time variables layer.

3.4 Industrial Networking

Industrial networks present physically in the system do not connect all of the holons, dividing them into two clusters. It is possible to employ the networks for communication in the range of the two clusters, however it would require careful developing of the PLC programs, so they supported two channels of real-time transmission (both industrial networks and holon layer) when needed. Such situation would complicate development process, so it was decided that industrial networks are not used for plant integration anymore

Since industrial networking is not used to transfer process data it is possible to utilise them in other ways. There are lessons and researches, where industrial networking is not the *tool for* but *subject of* the investigation. Proposed structure of the holarchy supports such researches, because user has access to parallel real-time communication on higher level than industrial networks. Ethernet-based real-time transmission may be used to supervise industrial communication. Such approach turns existing industrial networks into additional holons being another research and education plants.

4 Concluding Remarks and Future Work

Holonic approach to the presented system turned out to fulfil all required duties, so presented system is successful implementation of the holarchy paradigm in the process automation. Currently, only real-time protocol of the holons layer is codified and regulated to the extent comparable to retail software products. Other layers (i.e. PLC programs and cooperation layer of the holons) were developed as custom prototype applications, so only loose hints and advices are presented in the paper. A work is still ongoing to develop a general methodology and tools for those layers.

It is also planned to implement holarchy paradigm at even lower level of the system. Each of the currently developed plant holons is planned to be modelled as a holarchy consisting of holons embedding elemental components of the process control system (i.e. actuators, sensors, and algorithms).

Acknowledgments. This work was supported by the Polish Ministry of Scientific Research and Information Technology.

References

1. Metzger, M.: Fast-mode real-time simulator for the wastewater treatment process. Water Science and Technology 30(4), 191–197 (1994)
2. Metzger, M.: Virtual controllers improve Internet-based experiments on semi-industrial pilot plants. In: Proceedings of the 16th IFAC Triennal World Congress, Elsevier, Amsterdam (2005) CD

3. Wooldridge, M., Jennings, N.R.: Intelligent agents: theory and practice. The Knowledge Engineering Practice 10(2), 115–152 (1995)
4. Jennings, N.R., Sycara, K., Wooldridge, M.: A Roadmap of Agent Research and Development. In: Autonomous Agents and Multi–Agent Systems, vol. 1, pp. 7–38. Kluwer Academic Publishers, Boston (1998)
5. Ferber, J.: Multi–agent systems – an introduction to distributed artificial intelligence. Addison–Wesley, London, UK (1999)
6. Van Dyke Parunak, H.: A practitioners' review of industrial agent applications. In: Autonomous Agents and Multi-Agent Systems, vol. 3, 4, pp. 389–407 (2000)
7. Marik, V., McFarlane, D.: Industrial Adoption of Agent-Based Technologies. IEEE Intelligent Systems, 27–35 (January/February 2005)
8. Pechoucek, M., Thompson, S.G.: Agents in Industry: The Best from the AAMAS 2005 Industry Track. IEEE Intelligent Systems, 86–95 (March/April 2006)
9. Koestler, A.: The Ghost in the Machine. Macmillan, New York (1968)
10. HMS: Holonic manufacturing systems consortium web site (2000), http://hms.ifw.uni-hannover.de
11. Giret, A., Botti, V.: Holons and agents. Journal of Intelligent Manufacturing 15, 645–659 (2004)
12. Babiceanu, R.F., Chen, F.: development and applications of holonic manufacturing systems: a syrvey. Journal of Intelligent Manufacturing 17, 111–131 (2006)
13. Fletcher, M., Brennan, R.W., Norrie, D.H.: Modelling and reconfiguring intelligent holonic manufacturing system with Internet-based mobile agents. Journal of Intelligent Manufacturing 14, 7–23 (2003)
14. Kotak, D., Wu, S., Fleetwood, M., Tamoto, H.: Agent-based holonic design and operations environment for distributed manufacturing. Computers in Industry 52, 95–108 (2003)
15. Hall, K.H., Staron, R.J., Vrba, P.: Holonic and Agent-Based Control. In: Proceedings of the 16th IFAC Triennal World Congress, Elsevier, Amsterdam (2005) CD
16. Vyatkin, V., Hanisch, H.M.: Verification of distributed control systems in intelligent manufacturing. Journal of Intelligent Manufacturing 14, 123–136 (2003)
17. Official National Instruments LabVIEW website, http://www.ni.com/labview/
18. Polaków, G., Metzger, M.: Agent-Based Approach for LabVIEW Developed Distributed Control Systems. In: The 1st KES Symposium on Agent and Multi-Agent Systems, Wroclaw, Poland. LNCS, Springer, Heidelberg (to appear, 2007)
19. Official HMS Anybus website, http://www.anybus.com/
20. Kalogeras, A.P., Gialelis, J.V., Alexakos, C.E., Georgoudakis, M.J.: Vertical Integration of Enterprise Industrial systems Utilizing Web Services. IEEE Trnasactions on Industrial informatics 2(2), 120–128 (2006)
21. Hadellis, L., Koubias, S., Makios, V.: An integrated approach for an interopearable industrial networking architecture consisting of heterogenous fieldbuses. Computers in Industry 49, 283–298 (2002)

Collision Avoidance Algorithms: Multi-agent Approach

Pavel Vrba[1], Vladimír Mařík[1,2,3], Libor Přeučil[2], Miroslav Kulich[3],
and David Šišlák[2]

[1] Rockwell Automation Research Center
Pekařská 695/10a, 15500 Prague, Czech Republic
{pvrba, vmarik}@ra.rockwell.com
[2] Department of Cybernetics, Czech Technical University in Prague
Technická 2, 166 27 Prague 6, Czech Republic
{marik, preucil, sislak}@labe.felk.cvut.cz
[3] Center of Applied Cybernetics, Czech Technical University in Prague
Technická 2, 166 27 Prague 6, Czech Republic
{marik, kulich}@labe.felk.cvut.cz

Abstract. The paper deals with the methods for detection and avoidance of collisions of autonomously moving vehicles utilizing the principles and techniques of multi-agent systems. Three different scenarios are discussed: (i) movement of AGVs in 2D space with fixed trajectories, (ii) movement of autonomous robots in an open 2D space and (iii) collision-free flights of unmanned aerial vehicles. For each category, an agent-based solution is proposed. Presented experiments show that the cooperative approach to detecting and avoiding collisions based on negotiation and goal sharing of agents, representing vehicles, seems to be highly efficient. The multi-layer architecture combining cooperative approach with algorithms based on dynamic no-access zones for avoiding non-cooperative vehicles provides good results in generating collision-free flight corridors.

1 Introduction

A robot is a computer controlled integrated system, capable of autonomous and goal-oriented interaction with real environment according to man instructions. The interaction requires that the robot is able to perceive its environment, make decisions and carry out actions in the outer world. There is an increasing number of applications that cannot be solved just by using a single robot, but require deployment of larger number of robots to ensure distributed perception, distributed action and distributed goal-oriented decision making. For instance, the assembly of highly complex machinery in hardly accessible terrain or space, activities carried out during nuclear power plant failures or rescue and military operations fall in these categories. Consideration of groups of robots makes sense also in situations where it is effective to physically and spatially distribute the perception, decision-making and action tasks – small specialized robots for instance carry out the exploitation of contaminated or hardly accessible areas, information is processed by other robots (often not able to move in space)

V. Mařík, V. Vyatkin, A.W. Colombo (Eds.): HoloMAS 2007, LNAI 4659, pp. 348–360, 2007.
© Springer-Verlag Berlin Heidelberg 2007

while the physically intensive operation (barrier removal, pipe cut off or mine defusing) is usually performed by large powerful robots possibly in coordinated manner.

In all examples mentioned above there is a notion of *autonomous* or *unmanned vehicles* that have to be able to autonomously move in an unknown and dynamically changing environment while collaborating on common goals. This introduces a new category of theoretical and technical problems linked for example with communication, decision-making on the basis of partial knowledge, coordinated movement etc. This paper focuses on the mutual *collision detection and avoidance* problem. Collision can be considered as a state when the movement trajectories of two or more vehicles cross at the same time in a particular point in the environment. The collision detection means the ability of a vehicle to discover the possible collision beforehand. When discovered, the vehicles may apply different algorithms for re-planning their paths to avoid the collision point.

The paper discusses different categories of this problem from the viewpoint of the characteristics of the environment in which the vehicles move:

1. 2-D area with predefined paths that the vehicles must follow. Typical example of this category are the AGVs (Autonomous Guided Vehicles) deployed in factories and warehouses moving along predefined network of paths embedded in a factory's floor usually in form of magnetic stripes or rails.
2. 2-D area where the vehicles can move in any direction in two-dimensional space. The representatives of this large category are for instance robots cooperatively exploring unknown environment, robots playing soccer (http://www.robocup.org), AGVs with freedom in movement etc.
3. 3-D area where the vehicles can freely move in three-dimensional space. This category includes for example UAVs (Unmanned Aerial Vehicles) [4] and UUV (Unmanned Undersea Vehicles) [5] usually deployed in military missions. Routing of commercial jet planes is another example.

To effectively solve collision avoidance problem in a cooperative manner, robots have to be able to:

- communicate with each other using the common language, common negotiation mechanisms and common knowledge representation formats (ontology); in this case it is referred to as *cooperative collision avoidance*, otherwise when the robots cannot communicate for any reason, we talk about *non-cooperative collision avoidance*
- share knowledge about their location in the environment and anticipated direction of movement and keep this knowledge consistent and up-to-date in order to minimize the communication channels load in time critical moments
- reason about the movement plans of neighboring robots to detect possible collision situation and avoid it by re-planning the movement trajectory

2 Multi-agent Approach to Collision Avoidance

Organizational structures and control algorithms of multi-robotic system are more and more often designed and implemented using the methods and principles known from the domain of *multi-agent systems* [9]. These two research domains have evolved relatively separately from each other, nevertheless the technological enhancements over the last few years, like smaller and cheaper robotic platforms, faster processor, more sophisticated sensors, wireless communication, new results in the multi-agent research domain, etc. lead to their convergence. The algorithms developed originally for highly distributed agent decision-making are now being applied for control of activities of robot groups. It is mainly the algorithms for distributed action planning, acquaintance models for social knowledge modeling [7] and negotiation mechanisms and protocols for inter-agent communication [8].

When designing a multi-agent system representing the community of robots, the agent should represent an independent functional part, usually the robot as a whole or its functional subsystem (in this case a single robot is represented by more agents). Subsequently, an appropriate software environment, so-called agent platform, where the agents exist have to be chosen. The agent platform should provide the white pages services holding information on registered agents and their addresses and the Directory Facilitator (yellow pages) where the agents register their services and search for suitable service providers. The agent negotiation is usually based on contract-net-protocol [2] or various auction mechanisms. An important aspect is sharing of semantic information, especially about surrounding environment in form of environment maps used by robot to localize itself, other robots, available paths or obstacles.

2.1 Collision Avoidance in 2-D Space with Fixed Trajectories

First category of collision detection and avoidance problem refers to the movement of AGVs (Automated Guided Vehicles) used in factories or warehouses for transportation of products or materials. This is a special case where there is a built-in network of magnetic or optical stripes or rails in the factory's shop floor which the AGV is able to observe and move along [10]. The network can be viewed as a graph with edges representing particular segments of network the AGVs travel through and vertices representing two different types of nodes: (i) a junction point where two or more segments cross and (ii) a work station representing source and/or destination place on factory floor between them the transportation is done. The work station is for instance a CNC machine, assembly machine, buffer storage station, etc.

Figure 1 shows an example of AGV transportation system with two work stations (W1 and W2) and a network of segments designed to provide redundant transportation paths between the two work stations. It is supposed that the idle AGVs wait in a special dedicated segment(s) (s5 in Fig. 1). Although the AGV can move through a particular segment in any direction, there obviously cannot be two AGVs moving in the same segment in opposite directions.

A primary collision situation appears at the junction point, which only one AGV can go through at the same time. This is a case of agv5 and agv4 in Figure 1 that have to go through junction j2 in a sequence – thus agv4 have to wait until agv5 enters segment s4 and leaves the area around the junction. A secondary collision situation happens when two AGVs approaching a junction intend both to continue in segment occupied by the other one. As depicted in Figure 1, the collision is around the junction j1, where the agv1 in segment s1 wants to enter segment s2, which is occupied by agv2 that intends to go to segment s1. A possible solution to avoid this collision is that one AGV avoids to third segment (agv2 avoiding to s3 in Fig. 1),

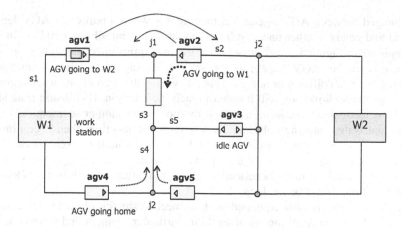

Fig. 1. Possible collisions in AGV transportation system

waits until the second AGV passes the junction and then continues in the released segment as intended.

The proposed AGV agent is equipped with a complex behavior allowing it to negotiate with the work station agents about products transportation, navigate through the network to get to a particular work station as fast as possible, detect and avoid possible collisions with other AGVs and even dynamically detect and avoid obstacles in the paths. When instantiated, the AGV agent is given the XML description of the network comprising of the location of all nodes (X, Y coordinates), their type (work station, junction or curve) and their interconnection via segments. The AGV agent translates this description into an internal object model that is used to pre-compute all the possible routes to work stations from each junction node. This information is then used by the AGV to compute the length of an anticipated path between the source and the destination workstation and also for the navigation when determining the optimal direction at the junction point [13].

For the primary collision situation mentioned above, the first AGV agent that approaches a junction point declares itself as a *master*, while informing the second AGV that it became a *slave*. Additionally, the master AGV includes an estimation of the time period needed to go through the junction point. Then, the master AGV goes through the junction as the first one and, after the estimated period passes, the slave AGV moves through as the second one. It may happen that both AGVs reach the junction point at the same time and thus both declare themselves as masters. In this case, the AGV agent with the lower priority of carried work piece or, if priorities are same, the one whose name is second according to alphabetical ordering freely gives up and becomes a slave.

Detecting and avoiding secondary type of deadlock is a bit more complicated issue. When the AGV approaches a junction node it determines what direction to choose, i.e. to which segment to continue to get to intended workstation by shortest path. However, a collision may happen in this segment if there is already another AGV moving toward the same junction. To detect such a situation the AGV should know in advance, if the segment is free or not. For this purpose, each AGV agent is equipped with knowledge about the position and direction of all other AGVs. This information is exchanged between AGV agents via messages – when a particular AGV leaves a segment and enters another one, it informs about this event all other AGVs. In situation depicted in Figure 1, agv2 in segment s2 that approached junction j1 is aware that there is another AGV (agv1) in segment s1 moving toward the j1 junction. To detect if there is a collision or not, the first AGV asks the second one what segment it plans to go to and how long will it take to reach the junction. If collision state shown in Fig. 1 is recognized, the agv2 avoids it by moving to another segment (s3) where it stops and waits until the colliding AGV passes the junction; then it continues as intended. In non-collision situation, the AGV just waits until the second one leaves the junction point. In both cases, the first AGV considers the waiting time period and decides if it would be more beneficial to take an alternative path to intended work station if waiting would be too long.

The AGV agent is also equipped with a mechanism for obstacle detection and avoidance. When the AGV hits an obstacle in particular segment and there is no other AGV in front moving in that segment in same direction, it marks the segment as blocked in its internal model of environment, turns back and informs all other AGV agents that the segment is blocked and should be avoided. However, if there is another AGV in front, the first AGV uses a ping-like mechanism to test whether the in-front-AGV is failed or not. If there is no response within some period of time (1s), the first AGV assumes that it hit the failed AGV – it turns back and again informs all other AGVs that the segment is blocked. When response is received (the asked AGV includes information about its own position in segment), the first AGV determines if it hit an obstacle or the in-front-AGV and reacts appropriately.

2.2 Collision Avoidance in Open 2-D Space

Starting from graph-bounded collision avoidance, the more general problems incorporate situations with freely bounded vehicles. Solution of this class of tasks is typically required for systems providing large portion of autonomy and intelligence – self guided vehicles represented mainly by autonomous robots. On contrary to the previous case, these robots have no pre-determined motion trajectories in majority of cases as these are built up dynamically "on the fly" and dependent on the shape and structure of the operating environment at a time.

As the *Freely Moving Vehicles Avoidance (FMVA)* stand for a general case, previous feature of no predetermined motion trajectories allows us to classify the possible approaches to solutions of the problem into two base categories as:

1. *ExPost Collision Avoidance (EPCA)* methods which belong mainly to classical approaches of how to resolve collision situations after their appearance, or whenever their occurrence is predetermined by the vehicle behavior (and therefore can be recognized in advance). The EPCA methods are always used to correct existing and/or foreseen collision situations.

2. *Predictive Collision Avoidance (PCA)* methods are located on the edge of planning approaches, which are extended towards cooperation of planning procedures for separate vehicles. The predictive collision avoidance is typically capable of extinguishing collisions due to insufficiently coordinated plans for diverse autonomous entities. These methods are mainly applied prior to execution of the planned trajectory of the vehicle or robot.

The former EPCA methods rely of the knowledge of the robot path, which is typically predetermined either by technical constrains or pre-computed by a path planner. So far, the situation may be similar to the previous case with cable or rail-guided vehicles. The suitable collision resolution approaches can therefore be similar to the previous case. The advantage of the EPCA methods is seen in limited need of the vehicle to stick necessarily on the pre-planned trajectory (like on a guiding rail), but allows it to perform collision avoidance maneuver anywhere on its trajectory (if not constrained by other obstacles). This situation does not require relying exclusively on avoidance methods based on *scheduling* of vehicles on trajectory vertices. Moreover, performing the meeting maneuvers whenever needed allows the vehicle to achieve much higher efficiency of the collision avoidance (shorter paths, less traffic congestions in bottlenecks, no delays due to vehicle wait-states, etc.) and therefore improved efficiency of path planning procedures as well.

The EPCA approach sketched above requires executing the meeting maneuvers that can generally occur either in case of a vehicle colliding with an unexpected obstacle or in case of two independent, non-communicating vehicles. The former situation can be handled by a simple reactive behavior of the vehicle control system, for instance by executing a wall following procedure until the original path is reached. The latter case requires more sophisticated approach. Meeting of two independent autonomous vehicles brings together two autonomous behaviors which are bound together only through observations of the common environment (that can include also other entities). It is straightforward that design of such a behavior needs to avoid falling into an endless loop or a deadlock when trying to resolve the meeting maneuver. All previously mentioned situations denote so called *non-cooperative collision avoidance*.

An alternative approach bounds both the behaviors together by a communication link. This enables to perform proper negotiation procedure [6] to ensure correct behavior by a *cooperative collision avoidance procedure*. The most common solution of this kind incorporates the *master-slave* approach in which all the entities negotiate priorities and in a stepwise manner undertake top-down decisions and resolve possible deadlocks. Extension of the preceding situations for multiple obstacles and/or mobile entities is then easy.

On the other hand, the PCA approaches are bidding to prevent possible collisions already in the phase of a path planning. As this kind of behavior is generic for a standard path planner and builds an inseparable functional part of an autonomous vehicle, execution of the path re-planning procedures during the autonomous vehicle mission differs. The dynamic re-planning in result tends to respond to the current state of the operating environment as well as to the current level of knowledge about the environment. Lack of these knowledge or a certain change in the environment status may then invoke re-planning, representing a goal oriented behavior. This can typically include also avoidance of collisions of expected and unexpected sort. If the collision is prevented by a proper plan, it has been the expected one (derivable from the current level of knowledge about the environment). The other cases cover the unexpected ones, which could not have been discovered from the so far existing data or behavioral intentions of the other entities present. The latter can be corrected by execution of the re-planning procedure with the goal to update the vehicles' behavior with respect to last discovered facts.

In general case, the PCA approaches can be used to fulfill reactive behaviors if executed in a fast loop, but also to resolve cooperative tasks and scheduling problems in long term. This is widely used to ensure cooperated and coordinated behaviors for multiple mobile entities.

Another class of tasks that belongs to the fundamental test-bench problems of intelligent robotics and that is similar to collision avoidance problems is the task of *cooperative exploration* of an unknown environment by multiple robots. One of the problems of exploration is the creation of the map of the unknown environment while optimizing available resources. The resources can be for instance the task execution time, total trajectories driven, minimum energy costs, number of resolved collisions, percentage of explored space overlaps, etc.

Having a common map containing actual shape and structure of the surrounding environment as well as positions of all the participating robots, following questions arise:

- Where the places of interest are – places, which visiting provides the best profit for understanding of the environment and which consideration in the following tasks can lead to best possible performance.
- How to assign the exploration of the places of interest to particular robots so that the possible collisions and overlapping of explored areas is kept to minimum in order to achieve the best efficiency of the system performance with respect to the overall cost function.

The cost function is in the frontier-based approach [15] usually expressed as the distance of a robot to selected place of interest and its distance to other candidate places selected by other robots [1]. If an observation gain of visiting the selected place by the robot is high, the profit of visiting the neighboring places by other robots is decreased. The assignment of robots to particular places of interest, called *frontiers*, can be viewed as multi-robot and multi-goal optimization problem, which is well-suited subject for the agent-based approach. In the proposed solution, each physical robot is represented by a single agent. The negotiation-based algorithm is initiated by a *triggering* agent recognizing significant event like detection of close-to-collision state, substantial change in the observed part of the environment or simply a time stamp. First, all the agents compute their utility values for all known frontiers and share this knowledge with the others. A single robot-frontier pair with the best cost function is determined and excluded from the subsequent rounds of negotiations. The number of negotiation rounds obviously corresponds to number of participating robots. Although, the given procedure does not provide generally optimal solution to the problem (which remains *NP-hard*), experimental results prove a good quality of the proposed method.

2.3 Collision Avoidance in 3-D Space

The distributed collision avoidance problem extended to third dimension is characteristic for the domain of unmanned aerial vehicles (UAVs). The work presented in [12] suggests multi-layer collision avoidance architecture based on multi-agent technology. Each UAV is controlled by a single agent wrapping several different avoidance algorithms. Both cooperative and non-cooperative methods are optimally combined for planning runtime trajectory of the UAV with respect to series of time-specific way-points. There is no central planner providing collision-free flight plans – the plans for each UAV are individually held and modified in case of detected collision by the UAV agents themselves.

The multi-layer avoidance collision architecture contains the CSM (Collision Solver Manager) as a main controller able to combine all the available cooperative and non-cooperative collision solvers. Each collision solver is responsible for both collision detection and collision solving. Different solvers provide different quality of the avoidance solution, but require different amount of time to find a solution. Thus, based on the priority of solvers, the CSM assigns specific time slot to each solver so that the strict time constraints are met.

Cooperative avoidance is based on interaction between airplanes that exchange their flight plans. Two different collision solvers are implemented – *rule-based* and *utility-based*. The former one is implemented according to the Visual Flight Rules defined by FAA (http://www.faa.gov) – it determines the collision type on the basis of the angle between direction vectors of aircrafts and then applies a predefined maneuver to avoid the specific collision. This is done by both planes independently because the second aircraft also detects a possible collision with the first plane.

The utility-based avoidance mechanism finds a solution for a pair of airplanes. One of the airplanes is regarded as a master entity (usually the first one that identifies a collision) and the second one as slave entity. The slave planning agent is requested by the master to generate a set of flight plan changes using different combinations of seven parameterized maneuvers – straight flight (no change), turn right, turn left, turn up, turn down, speed and slow down. The set is ordered according to the utility value computed for each configuration considering for example total length of the flight plan, time deviations for mission way-points, fuel status, possible damage, etc. The set is sent back to the master aircraft that generates its own set of plans and tries to combine both sets together to find a collision solution selected from Cartesian product of generated plans. The candidates for solution are again ordered in increasing manner by product of utility quotients of flight plan pair. Each pair candidate is tested for a collision and if there is no collision between participants, candidate is selected as collision solution. The slave entity is then requested to change its flight plan according to selected collision solution.

Non-cooperative avoidance is applied when the communication between planes is not possible for instance due to broken communication module of the aircraft. The proposed algorithm is based on the *dynamic no-flight zones* computed for each object detected by the onboard radar. First, the collision point is determined as intersection of the current UAV's flight plan and the predicted flight trajectory of the non-cooperative object. Second, the collision point is wrapped by the no-flight zone, which shape is derived from object's possible future flight trajectory taking into account the minimal turning radius, maximal climbing/descending angle, etc. The UAV's planner module then tries to determine such flight path that doesn't intersect any detected no-flight zone using A* algorithm.

3 Experiments

The proposed agent-based solution of presented AGV transportation system is part of the Manufacturing Agent Simulation Tool (MAST) developed at Rockwell Automation Research Center in Prague [14]. This tool provides agent-based simulation and control solution for the material-handling domain, mainly the transportation of products and materials on the factory floor. Originally, the transportation using conveyor belts was considered – a library of agent classes representing basic material-handling components, like workstation, conveyor belt and diverter was developed. To enhance the capabilities of MAST to simulate AGV-based transportation, the AGV agent class, with capabilities described in Section 2.1, has been added.

Figure 2 shows a screenshot of the MAST tool with an example of AGV network connecting four workstations. When the "source" workstation agent needs to deliver a product to another "destination" workstation, it first queries the Directory Facilitator to obtain a list of AGV agent names. Second, it initiates the contract-net-protocol in which the AGV agents give their bids in terms of time estimate for moving from current position to the source workstation plus from source to destination workstation. The source workstation selects the best bid and awards the contract to selected AGV agent. Several experiments with different number of AGVs working under different conditions (blocked paths, failed AGVs) have been carried out. It has been shown that solving head-to-head deadlocks might become very complicated if there are multiple AGVs involved at the same time (not only two as described earlier) and that a simple, but efficient solution is to fix a direction in which the AGVs can move in each segment.

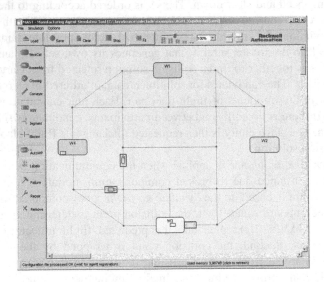

Fig. 2. AGV-based transportation system with four workstations and three AGVs as part of the Manufacturing Agent Simulation Tool

The presented robot exploration algorithm was implemented in the Gerstner Laboratory at the Czech Technical University in Prague and experimentally verified with a squad of four fully autonomous mobile robots (see Figure 3). RCS control architecture [3] was used to control the robots, while communication among them was performed by means of A-globe multi-agent platform [11]. Furthermore, SICK LMS 200 laser rangefinder stood as a main sensor for gathering information about the working environment and for collision detection and avoidance.

Fig. 3. G2bots during exploration

The tests were performed in both simulated and real environments with different numbers of robots varying from two to four. Numerous frequencies of negotiation procedure (i.e. the process of generation, evaluation, and assignment of frontiers) were evaluated during these tests. The best results were obtained for frequency 5 seconds. Generated paths are smooth, while probability of collision is low for this value. Figure 4 shows a typical run – explored environment and robots' trajectories in an early stage of exploration (left) and the same after exploration completed. Notice that although the violet and yellow trajectories intersect several times, no collisions need to be solved because the robots moved to cross points in different stages of exploration.

The multi-layer collision avoidance architecture presented in the section 2.3 has been evaluated on huge set of experiments. The experiments have been carried out using multi-agent system simulating air traffic built on to of A-globe platform [12]. The simulation system is extended to integrate several external data sources. One of them provides position of civil real aircrafts (10 minutes delayed) operating in selected area in the U.S. Randomly generated UAVs controlled by agents fulfill their missions in the same air space. Simulated UAVs are configured to use utility-based

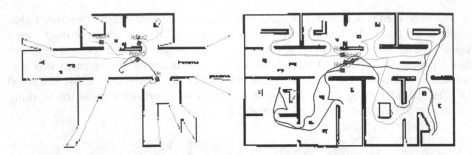

Fig. 4. Exploration of an unknown space by four robots: detected obstacles (black), found frontiers (yellow), unreachable frontiers (brown), actual plans (green), already traversed trajectories (thick curves)

cooperative collision avoidance method with other agent-based UAV (can communicate with it) and use dynamic no-flight zones non-cooperative method against imported air-traffic (can use only position reported by on-board radar) at the same time.

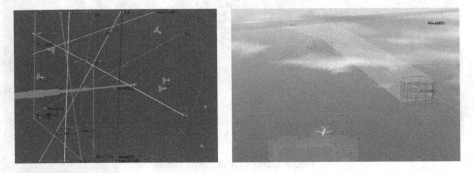

Fig. 5. Operation of agent-controlled UAVs over LA with imported civil real air-traffic

The screenshots from the simulation are shown in the Figure 5. Left screen is taken from the top view and provides small part of the simulated area. Right screen is three-dimensional view from one of the simulated aircraft. There is captured the situation when one of the agent-controlled plane monitors its local neighbor, builds the prediction of future trajectory from the historical data and detects possible collision with civil plane. It just re-plan it flight corridor to not to collide with civil plane and re-negotiate new corridor with other cooperative (agent-controlled) UAVs.

4   Conclusion

Multi-agent technology provides good background for solving collision detection and avoidance issues. The collaborative approach seems to be highly desired – the agents representing vehicles can mutually inform themselves about their goals and intentions for future movement and thus can solve a possible collision much more efficiently than in non-collaborative case.

The following principles common for agent-based collision avoidance solutions can be identified:

1) *Master and slave*: when collision is detected, one of the vehicles is determined as a master while the second one is slave. Master then proposes a solution to avoid the collision and requests the slave to accept it.
2) *Collision metrics*: a utility value or cost of each candidate solution is computed and the most convenient one is adopted. Various negotiation protocols play an important role in exchanging this kind of information.
3) *Dynamic no-access zones*: an estimated collision point with each detected non-cooperative object is surrounded by dynamically updated no-access (no-flight) zone and the trajectory is planned to avoid all the zones.

As expected, avoiding collisions in 2D is much easier than in 3D. In the simplest case, the vehicle can stop itself and wait until the colliding vehicle passes the estimated collision point (as in case of AGVs described in Sect. 2.1); in a collaborative scenario, the master vehicle can command the slave to drive away.

The presented multi-layer architecture for generating collision-free flight corridors in 3D space is designed to optimally combine different cooperative and non-cooperative methods for planning and re-planning runtime trajectory of the UAV in the fully distributed manner. The cooperative methods are used to avoid the mutual UAVs collisions while the non-cooperative one based on dynamic no-access zones help to avoid other non-cooperative aircrafts. We envision that the application of this complex architecture also in 2D scenarios will offer even more sophisticated and efficient methods to detect and resolve collisions.

Acknowledgements

The support of the Ministry of Education of the Czech Republic, under the Project No. 1M0567 to Miroslav Kulich is also gratefully acknowledged.

Effort on three-dimensional collision avoidance is sponsored by the Air Force Office of Scientific Research, Air Force Material Command, USAF, under grant number FA8655-06-1-3073[1].

References

1. Burgard, W., Moors, M., Stachniss, C., Schneider, F.: Coordinated Multi-Robot Exploration. IEEE Transactions on Robotics 21(3), 376–378 (2005)
2. Bussmann, S., Jennings, N.R, Wooldridge, M.: Multiagent Systems for Manufacturing Control: A design Methodology. In: Ishida T (ed) Springer, Heidelberg (2004)

---

3. Chudoba, J., Mázl, R., Přeučil, L.: A Control System for Multi-Robotic Communities. In: ETFA 2006 Proceedings, pp. 827–832. IEEE, Piscataway (2006)
4. Department of Defence, US: Unmanned Systems Roadmap 2005-2030 (2005)
5. Fletcher, B.: Autonomous Vehicles and the Net-Centric Battlespace. In: International Unmanned Undersea Vehicle Symposium, April 2000, Newport, RI, USA (2000)
6. Fujimori, A., Teramoto, M., Nikiforuk, P., Gupta, M.: Cooperative Collision Avoidance Between Multiple Mobile Robots. Journal of Robotic Systems 17(7), 347–363 (2000)
7. Mařík, V., Pěchouček, M., Štěpánková, O.: Social Knowledge in Multi-Agent Systems. In: Luck, M., Mařík, V., Štěpánková, O., Trappl, R. (eds.) ACAI 2001 and EASSS 2001. LNCS (LNAI), vol. 2086, pp. 211–245. Springer, Heidelberg (2001)
8. Mařík, V., Pěchouček, M., Vrba, P., Hrdonka, V.: FIPA Standards and Holonic Manufacturing. In: Deen, S.M. (ed.) Agent Based Manufacturing: Advances in the Holonic Approach, pp. 89–121. Springer, Heidelberg (2003)
9. Ortiz, C.L., Vincent, R., Morisset, B.: Task Inference and Distributed Task Management in the Centibots Robotic System. In: Proceedings of the Fourth International Joint Conference on Autonomous Agents and Multiagent Systems, pp. 860–867. ACM, New York (2005)
10. Reveliotis, S.A.: Conflict Resolution in AGV Systems. IIE Transactions 32(7), 647–659 (2000)
11. Šišlák, D., Rehák, M., Pěchouček, M., Pavlíček, D.: Deployment of A-globe Multi-Agent Platform. In: Proceedings of the Fifth International Joint Conference on Autonomous Agents and Multiagent Systems (2006)
12. Šišlák, D., Rehák, M., Pěchouček, M., Pavlíček, D., Uller, M.: Negotiation-based Approach to Unmanned Aerial Vehicles. In: Proceedings of the IEEE Workshop on Distributed Intelligent Systems: Collective Intelligence and Its Applications, pp. 279–284. IEEE Computer Society, Washington, DC (2006)
13. Vrba, P.: MAST: Manufacturing Agent Simulation Tool. In: Proceedings of IEEE Conference on Emerging Technologies and Factory Automation, Lisbon, Portugal, vol. 1, pp. 282–287 (2003)
14. Vrba, P., Mařík, V.: Simulation in Agent-Based Control Systems: MAST Case Study. In: Proceedings of 16th IFAC World Congress, Prague (2005)
15. Yamauchi, B.: A frontier-based approach for autonomous exploration. In: Proceedings of the 1997 IEEE International Symposium on Computational Intelligence in Robotics and Automation, Monterey, CA, pp. 146–151 (1997)

Creating Contract Templates for Car Insurance Using Multi-agent Based Text Understanding and Clustering

Igor Minakov[1], George Rzevski[2],
Petr Skobelev[1], and Simon Volman[1]

[1] Magenta Development, 1a Osipenko St., Samara, 443010, Russia
{minakov,skobelev,volman}@magenta-technology.ru
[2] Magenta Technology, Gainsborough House, 59 - 60 Thames Street, Windsor, Berkshire
Sl4 1TX, UK
george.rzevski@magenta-technology.com

Abstract. The paper discusses the problem of automated processing and classification of unstructured text and proposes a new approach based on the multi-agent technology. The proposed method was successfully used to develop a system for a large UK insurance company capable of analysing and classifying 25000 documents related to car insurance, as well as creating template contract documents. The paper describes the system, presents testing results and discusses perspectives.

Keywords: Template building, problem domain ontology, multi-agent text understanding, semantic network comparison, text mining, data mining, classification, clustering.

1 Introduction and Problem Definition

Contemporary companies work with a very large number of documents, dealing with contracts, emails, business letters, licenses, manuals, financial and technical reports etc. Even for a medium-size company, the number of documents is so high, that it is impossible to process them manually without electronic document circulation or CRM systems. In addition to performing usual tasks, there is often a need for tools for deeper analysis, including semantic search and comparison of documents, grouping of documents with similar meanings and even an automatic document generation.

The method and supporting system described in this paper was developed for a client, one of the five biggest insurance companies in the UK, which had the following problem. Since car insurance premiums depend on many parameters, including client's gender and age, their education level, yearly income, class of the car and driving history, their lawyers created over the last 20 years more than 25,000 documents related to car insurance contracts. The task given to our team was to analyse these documents, classify them according to their semantic similarity and create a contract template for each group of documents. Contract templates were expected to include the most frequent clauses from the constituent documents within the group to be used in future as a basis for all new contracts. A part of the task was also to analyse and classify available contracts from the competitive insurance

V. Mařík, V. Vyatkin, A.W. Colombo (Eds.): HoloMAS 2007, LNAI 4659, pp. 361–370, 2007.

companies, and take these results into account during the creation of templates. The initial estimate was that there would be around 100 groups of documents, and that the whole work would take approximately 16 man-years of highly qualified law experts. Our task was to automate this process thus saving time and money.

2   The Solution

The existing systems and algorithms, which are capable of clustering documents (even the best ones, like LSA [1], Scatter/Gather [2] and STC [3]), have a number of limitations [4], as follows. Some of them require "seed" document in each group, some require expert pre-analysis, including desired number of resulting groups and others produce inadequate results because they use keywords-based rather than semantic searches and therefore produce a considerable noise and irrelevant results. To the best of our knowledge there are no other algorithmic or multi-agent based methods that could handle text understanding, clustering and template creation.

Therefore we have used Magenta multi-agent technology for all tasks of the requirement specification. First, our previously developed ontology and multi-agent based method for text understanding was used to represent the document meaning as a semantic network. Then, our multi-agent clustering method was applied to classify documents; and, finally, a heuristic method was developed to create templates based on groups of semantically similar documents.

2.1   Ontology

The proposed method is knowledge-based rather than data-driven. Conceptual knowledge of the domain of car insurance is contained in Ontology, which is constructed in a semi-automatic way, as follows. Using the ontology constructor [5] an expert inputs a set of domain documents (in our case – insurance contracts), and the system suggests hierarchy of objects, attributes and relations, which the expert can adjust manually. The heuristics are similar to those, used in [6] and [7]. For the car insurance domain ontology includes more than 400 objects (like "document", "agreement", "contractor", "terms of contract"), on the average, six attributes per object (like "amount", "class of car", "car parameters", "contract lengths", "warranty conditions" etc), and 37 relations (like "have", "between", "part of contract", "belongs to", "guarantee" etc).

2.2   Semantic Analysis

Using the domain knowledge from ontology, a multi-agent text understanding engine, described in [8, 9], assigns to each document a Semantic Descriptor, which describes the meaning of the document in the form of a semantic network (Fig. 1). The expression "meaning of the document" is used here to denote the meaning of the most relevant and important information contained in the document. For example, from the fragment of a semantic network shown in Fig. 1 it is possible to deduce that it describes a certificate for options, which belongs to a party of the agreement and that options belong to the registered holder. By similar analysis it is quite easy to interpret any semantic network and to determine the meaning of the document and, therefore, its possible future use. Also to be able to use standard clustering methods, in addition to semantic descriptors, keywords and key clauses are created for each document.

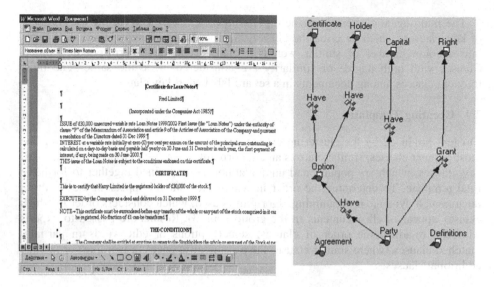

Fig. 1. A fragment of a semantic descriptor for an insurance contract

2.3 Clustering of Documents

Once semantic descriptors for all documents have been built, a multi-agent clustering engine, described in [10, 11], creates clusters of documents with similar meaning. The use of semantic descriptors helps to interpret reasons behind grouping documents together.

As a result we get a hierarchical structure where each document, or cluster of documents, can belong to several clusters, the criterion being the similarity of their semantic descriptors, as shown in (Fig. 2).

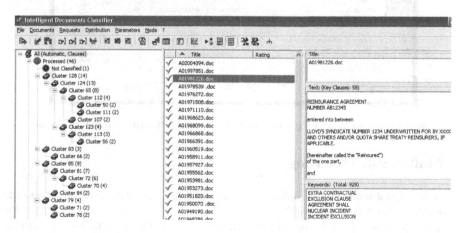

Fig. 2. An example of document clusters for car insurance

The multi-agent clustering engine represents each cluster as a record with number of key clauses, which describe the cluster. A procedure of comparing clauses takes into account number of similar words in clauses and their corresponding order. Clauses with high degree of similarity are considered to be the same. The most frequent clauses among documents in a set are labelled as key clauses.

2.4 Creating Templates

Clusters produced by the clustering engine are analysed with a view to finding the most popular clauses, similar clauses and abnormalities for each group of clusters. All key clauses, which are popular and unique/abnormal are joined together to form the final template. To determine the order in which they should appear in the resulting document, a dynamic programming algorithm is used, which considers order in which clauses appear in all documents in the group (Fig. 3). Results are passed to experts who can re-adjust the order of clauses, select options or edit words in partially matched clauses (where similar clauses have some differences in wording) or include additional clauses.

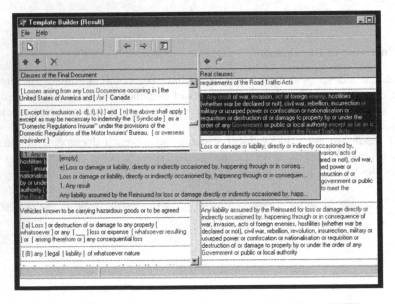

Fig. 3. Creating a template based on a set of key clauses from a cluster of documents

3 Multi-agent Technology

The multi-agent technology employed for semantic analysis (text understanding) and clustering is described here briefly to enable the reader to comprehend the logic of the method. A more detailed description can be found in [9, 10] and a detailed comparison with other methods, alongside with performance analysis and number of real-life applications can be found in [7, 11]. It is worth mentioning, that multi-agent applications are designed following holistic approach by building open Resource and

Demand Networks, where demand agents and resource agents can join or leave the network dynamically, in real time [12]. In this application Demand and Resource Agents are assigned to records and clusters for clustering, and to words and their possible meanings for text understanding, respectively. The input situation, called the initial Scene, is formally represented as a network of instances of concepts from ontology. The semantic analysis engine and clustering engine are event driven. Results of ongoing matching and re-matching of resources to demands are represented as intermediate scenes and the final result as the final scene.

3.1 Multi-agent Text Understanding

The method consists of the following four steps (see Figure 4): (1) Morphological Analysis; (2) Syntactic Analysis; (3) Semantic Analysis; (40 Pragmatics.

The process is as follows. The whole text is divided into sentences. Sentences are fed into the meaning extraction process one by one and the first three stages are applied to each sentence. After the text is parsed, the resulting semantic descriptor enters the forth stage – pragmatics.

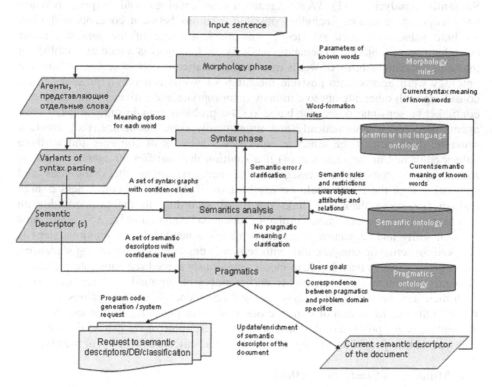

Fig. 4. General scheme of the multi-agent text understanding method

Morphological Analysis - An agent is assigned to each word in the sentence; (1) Word Agents access ontology and acquire relevant knowledge on morphology; (2) word agents execute morphological analysis of the sentence and establish characteristics of each word, such as gender, number, case, time, etc.; (3) if morphological analysis results in polysemy, i.e., a situation in which some words could play several roles in a sentence (a noun, an adjective or a verb), several agents are assigned to the same word each representing one of its possible roles thus creating several branches of possible sentence parsing results.

Syntactical Analysis – (1) Word agents access ontology and acquire relevant knowledge on syntax; (2) word agents execute syntactical analysis where they aim at identifying the syntactical structure of the sentence; for example, a subject searches for a predicate of the same gender and number, and a predicate looks for a suitable subject and objects. Conflicts are resolved through a process of negotiation; a grammatically correct sentence is represented by means of a syntactic descriptor; (3) if results of the syntactical analysis are ambiguous, i.e., several variants of the syntactic structure of the sentence under consideration are feasible, each feasible option is represented by a different syntactic descriptor; if no syntactic descriptor is valid, then several options with high enough level of correctness (i.e. more than 80% of grammatically possible links are present in the syntactic descriptor) are selected for the next stage.

Semantic Analysis - (1) Word agents access ontology and acquire relevant knowledge on semantics, including possible relations between concepts and valid attribute values; (2) each selected grammatical structure of the sentence under consideration is subjected to semantic analysis; this analysis is aimed at establishing the semantic compatibility of words in each grammatically correct sentence; from the ontology word agents learn possible meanings of words that they represent and by consulting each other attempt to eliminate inappropriate alternatives by building least contradictive semantic descriptor based on the problem domain ontology; (3) once agents agree on a grammatically and semantically correct sentence, they create a semantic descriptor of the sentence, which is a network of concepts and attribute values contained in the sentence; (4) if a solution that satisfies all agents cannot be found, agents compose a message to the user explaining the difficulties and suggesting how the issues could be resolved or, if the level of correctness is high enough (i.e. more than 80% links are valid according to the problem domain ontology), agent select most probable decision autonomously; (5) each new grammatically and semantically correct sentence generated in the previous steps is checked for semantic compatibility with semantic descriptors of preceding sentences; in the process agents may decide to modify previously agreed semantic interpretations of words or sentences by returning to earlier stages of negotiation (described above) with their new knowledge; this may improve confidence in certain options and may result in the reconstruction of semantic descriptors for preceding sentences; (6) when all sentences are processed, the final semantic descriptor of the whole document is constructed thus providing a computer readable semantic interpretation of the text.

3.2 Multi-agent Clustering Method

The method is conceptually simple and elegant. An agent is assigned to every data element (record, document, text segment) and given the task to seek similar data elements with a view to forming a cluster. Agents fulfil their tasks by sending invitations to other agents and by responding to received invitations. Each agent is looking after its own interests and will join other agents in a cluster only if it suits its objectives. Once a cluster is formed an agent is assigned to it with the task to attract suitable data elements. Agents of data elements belonging to a cluster form temporary virtual communities, which can be organised in many different ways.

In a simple case, records try to find clusters with the maximum density. In more complex cases, metrics can include number of records, number of sub-dimensions for a cluster, time of life in the cluster, type of attributes etc. The search always starts with the nearest candidate and extends gradually. When a record finds a proper cluster, it makes an offer and waits for a reply. The cluster considers record's locality, calculates its variant and either accepts or rejects the offer. Thus instead of a centralised optimal top-down decision of a classic clustering algorithm, the multi-agent approach builds solutions in a stepwise manner, bottom-up. The matching of records to clusters is based on a current local balance of interests of a particular record and a particular cluster. If both parties agree, the record enters the cluster, if not – the record searches for other options.

The stages of dynamic clustering process for a simple 2D case are shown in Fig. 5. Stage a – the first record arrives. Stage b – the second record arrives; the two records form a cluster. Stage c – the third record arrives; the first cluster and the third record form another cluster. Stage d – the second cluster invites the records from the first cluster to join it; records decide to accept invitation because the switch offers them certain advantages; the first cluster is dismantled; the fourth record arrives. Stage e – a new cluster is formed. Stage f – a new cluster invites the records from the inner cluster to join it and they accept; a new record arrives. Stage g – a new record arrives and the process is repeated. Stage h – the final cluster is formed.

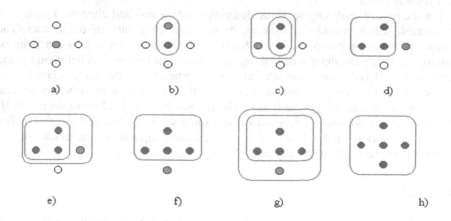

Fig. 5. The stages of forming a cluster

In general, agents trade with each other in the environment called Virtual Market where decisions are made by agent negotiations involving exchange of virtual money. Each agent has a specified sum of monetary units, which it may use to pay joining fees or leaving penalties, if any.

Various microeconomic models can be used to control the clustering process. For example, a charge for joining a cluster may be in accordance with the "club model" (the charge does not depend on the situation, richness of a record or on the number of the club members) or according to the "shareholder model" (the amount depends on the situation). In the latter case, a record may increase its capital entering or leaving the cluster at the right time.

Clusters and records conduct perpetual negotiation, with parties agreeing to meet requested demands or meeting each other half-way, for example, by mutual concessions. As a result of negotiation records may leave clusters and join new ones causing further adjustments, known as a ripple effect. The decentralised decision process combined with microeconomics enables balancing of factors such as the accuracy, cost and time effectiveness.

Multi-agent clustering method enables users to guide the clustering process by specifying clustering rules. Agents representing records or clusters use these rules whenever they have to decide whether particular records and clusters should be matched. For example, the rule of maximising density can be combined with rules on restrictions to the number of clusters to which a record can belong, on the number of records a cluster can contain, on how rich a cluster can be, or what the lifespan of a cluster should be. Various combinations of rules result in different clustering outcomes: few big clusters, a large number of small clusters, very dense clusters, clusters with dispersed records, clusters that are robust, clusters that are dynamic, etc.

The clustering processes for a stable data structure resembles crystallisation processes – first records create elementary structures at the bottom level and then structures themselves get involved in clustering, forming ever more complicated structures, only to stop when available records are exhausted. The clustering outcome is a high-level structure, which is more or less stable, but is modified in real time as new records arrive.

For the task of analysing semantic descriptors of records and clusters, a metrics is introduced, which provides a measure of semantic proximity of descriptors. The metrics is based on ontology. Using heuristic methods distances between pairs of ontology concepts are determined taking into account factors such as belonging to the same parents, having the same attributes and connected by the same relation. The metrics is valid for the comparison of two records but not for comparison of several records because transitivity rule is not valid (if document A is close to document B, and document B is close to document C, we cannot say how close are A and C). The lack of transitivity makes the use of conventional algorithmic methods for the comparison of semantic proximity impossible.

4   Testing

Tests of the proposed method were conducted using documents which were previously manually processed by lawyers of the client company and divided into groups according to their semantic similarity. Templates were previously manually created based on this analysis. Tests consisted of (1) the construction of problem domain ontology based on the full set of documents; (2) creation of semantic descriptors for each document using Magenta semantic analysis engine; (3) clustering of semantic descriptors using Magenta clustering engine; and (4) creating templates for each cluster in semi-automatic mode with the help of the expert who was not involved in the preparation of the test set.

Table 1. Comparing experts manual test analysis with system result

# of Docs	# of Groups* (auto/ manual)	Max hierarchy level (auto / manual)	Average number of docs in a group (auto / manual)	Same and similar groups (%)	Template validity level (%)
11	7 / 9	4/3	2/2	94 %	96 %
43	23/14	5/2	4/3	91 %	90 %
125	54/28	9/3	6/4	87 %	81 %
864	279 / 43	13/3	5/14	88 %	79 %

shows overall number of groups rather that only high-level groups

The testing generated several interesting observations: The smaller the number of documents, the better is the result of manual analysis (which is to be expected). Experts on average prefer to simplify the document structure; therefore the number of hierarchical levels and the number of groups produced in manual mode is considerably lower, groups usually being: "very similar, quite similar, more or less similar, and non-similar". In all tests one or several groups specified by expert (usually on top levels of hierarchy, i.e. more generalised) were the same as those produced in automatic mode. Differences were caused by the system feature to include a document into every cluster with which the document is semantically similar, while human experts prefer to assign such documents to only one cluster. This difference in the assignment of documents to clusters is the reasons for the increasing divergence between manual and automatic results over time – when there are many documents, human experts have difficulties with identifying and remembering similarities. In groups, which were found both by Magenta engines and human experts, there were many more documents that were missed by experts (approx. 35%), than documents that were wrongly assigned (11%) or missed by clustering engines and found by experts (7%). To summarise testing results, system even in the purely automatic mode, without any human guidance, gave results with approximately 90% agreement in grouping and 80-85% in template building. In practical testing, when Magenta engines were fully implemented and the system was fully deployed in the client's company, the results were as follows. The processing of approximately 25,000 instances of car insurance contracts, each of 30 pages, which was estimated to require 16 man-years, was done by the system based on the method described in this paper in 40 man-months, i.e. the productivity gain of almost five times.

5 Conclusion

Multi-agent method for semantic analysis and clustering of documents described in this paper has been applied to practical non-trivial problems and achieved results many times better than those accomplished by experts. To the best of our knowledge there are no published applications of either conventional or multi-agent systems that have achieved comparable (or indeed any) results. The success of the Magenta method is based on the following main features: (1) ontological modelling of the problem domain; (2) reformulation of the semantic analysis and clustering problems into problems of the allocation of meaning to words and clusters to records, respectively; (3) distributed creation of solutions in a event-driven, stepwise manner through a process of knowledge-based (rather than data-driven) negotiation (exchange of messages) between autonomous agents rather than by the predetermined algorithmic procedures; (4) creation of a powerful run-time engine capable of supporting communication links and decision making logic for hundreds of thousands agents; (5) implementation of user-friendly ontology editors and user interfaces for users. Authors have applied the method to a variety of practical problems for which there were no known solutions, including semantic search, generation of logistics rules and fault and fraud detection.

References

1. Dumains Susan, T., Furnas George, W., Landauer Thomas, K.: Indexing by Latent Semantic Analysis. Bell Communications Research 435 South St. Morristown, NJ 07960. University Of Western Ontario, Richard Rashman
2. Cutting, D.R., Karger, D.R., Pedersen, J.O., Tukey, J.W.: Scatter/Gather: A Cluster-based Approach to Browsing Large Document Collections. In: SIGIR '92, pp. 318–329 (1992)
3. Eli, Z.O.: A Phrase-Based Method for Grouping Search Engine Results. University of Washington, Department of Science & Engineering
4. Steinbach, M., Karypis, G., Kumar, V.: A Comparison of Document Clustering Techniques. In: Sixth ACM SIGKDD International Conference on Knowledge Discovery and Data Mining, Boston, MA, USA, August 20-23, 2000, ACM Press, New York (2000)
5. Andreev, V., Iwkushkin, K., Minakov, I., Rzevski, G., Skobelev, P.: The Constructor of Ontologies for Multi-Agent Systems. In: 3rd International Conference 'Complex Systems: Control and Modelling Problems', Samara, Russia, September 4-9, 2001, pp. 480–488 (2001)
6. Morin, E.: Automatic acquisition of semantic relations between terms from technical corpora. In: Proc. Of the Fifth Int. Congress on Terminology and Knowledge Engineering (TKE-99), TermNet-Verlag, Vienna (1999)
7. Faure, D., Poibeau, T.: First experiments of using semantic knowledge learned by ASIUM for information extraction task using INTEX. In: Staab, S., Maedche, A., Nedellec, C., Wiemer-Hastings, P. (eds.) Proceedings of the Workshop on Ontology Learning. 14th European Conference on Artificial Intelligence ECAI'00, Berlin, Germany (2000)
8. Andreev, V., Iwkushkin, K., Karyagin, D., Minakov, I., Rzevski, G., Skobelev, P., Tomin, M.: Development of the Multi-Agent System for Text Understanding. In: 3rd International Conference 'Complex Systems: Control and Modelling Problems', Samara, Russia, September 4-9, 2001, pp. 489–495 (2001)
9. Minakov, I., Rzevski, G., Skobelev, P.: Automated Text Analysis. Patent Application No. 305634, UK (2004)
10. Minakov, I., Rzevski, G., Skobelev, P.: Data Mining. Patent Application No. 0403145.6, UK (2004)
11. Rzevski, G., Skobelev, P., Minakov, I., Volman, S.: Dynamic Pattern Discovery using Multi-Agent Technology. In: Proceedings of the 6th WSEAS International Conference on Telecommunications and Informatics (TELE_INFO '07), Dallas, Texas, USA, March 22-24, 2007, pp. 75–81 (2007)
12. Skobelev, P.O.: Holonic Systems Simulation. In: Proc. of the 2nd International Conference "Complex Systems: Control and Modelling Problems", Samara, June 20-23, 2000, pp. 73–79 (2000)

Multi-agent-Based Diagnostics of Automotive Electronic Systems

Dušan Pavlíček, Michal Pěchouček, Vladimír Mařík, and Ondřej Flek

Gerstner Laboratory, Czech Technical University in Prague,
Technická 2, 166 27, Prague 6, Czech Republic
{pavlicd,pechouc,marik}@labe.felk.cvut.cz

Abstract. The diagnostic system discussed in this paper provides an agent-based approach to advanced on-board diagnostics of operation and communication failures occurring in an electronic automotive system. To facilitate development and testing of agent-based automotive diagnostics, a software simulator of automotive electronics systems, also based on multi-agent technology, has been implemented, allowing the developers to simulate various automotive system failures. The paper presents both the proof-of-concept on-board diagnostics system and the simulation layer used for its development and testing. The following topics are covered: simulation of the hardware units, simulation of user-invoked hardware failures, distributed detection and diagnostics of the failures, and visualization. The proposed automotive diagnostics approach can be deployed on real automotive electronics hardware.

1 Introduction

Graceful degradation or *fault tolerance* in terms of automotive electronic systems is the ability of the system to classify all detected failures occurring in the system according to their seriousness and potential impact and selectively disable only the affected parts of the system while the rest of the system can remain in operation. Prediction of future propagation of the detected failure across the electronic system may also be involved in this process. Such behavior allows far more precise and adequate reaction to failures than just one-shot disabling of the entire system.

Effective estimation of the severity of system failure and of the possible impact and future development of the problem also allows the diagnostic system to present the vehicle driver with relevant information at the right moment, ensuring safe operation of the vehicle on one hand, and avoiding unnecessary distraction and/or overburdening of the driver with excessive information on the other.

The approach discussed in this paper uses multi-agent technology to address this issue. An on-board automotive diagnostics system based on such approach is presented. Since developing such system directly on real-world automotive electronics hardware would not be economically acceptable, a test-bed capable of simulating the functionality of automotive systems and modeling of their various

V. Mařík, V. Vyatkin, A.W. Colombo (Eds.): HoloMAS 2007, LNAI 4659, pp. 371–382, 2007.
© Springer-Verlag Berlin Heidelberg 2007

failures had to be implemented. Multi-agent technology proved very efficient in this task, too. Thus, the proof-of-concept on-board automotive diagnostics system and the simulation test-bed are each implemented by a separate layer of agents. The two layers are very loosely coupled. It is assumed that if the agent-based approach to automotive diagnostics proves viable, the simulation layer could be replaced by real-world automotive electronics and the diagnostics layer deployed to such hardware without significant modifications.

The key strengths of multi-agent systems are their distributed nature and parallelism. This makes them particularly suitable for application in the field of simulation of complex electronic systems, as well as their diagnostics. Another advantage of multi-agent systems in general is their modularity and natural support for reconfiguration. This provides the diagnostic layer with the ability to reconfigure itself dynamically to reflect a changed configuration of the diagnosed system. In the simulation layer, dynamic loading and unloading of selected hardware devices at run-time upon user's request is possible, facilitating simulation of various hardware configurations without the need to restart the system.

The fact that the actual hardware layer is simulated by software agents is highly beneficial for many reasons. The user has full control over simulation of failures occurring in the system and thus can simulate various failure scenarios. Thanks to the agent introspection and easy ad-hoc modification available to the user, the simulation layer can serve not only as a powerful platform for development and testing of automotive diagnostics systems but, as a by-product, can also be used as an advanced test-bed for a number of other tasks, including hardware performance and stability testing, behavior analysis, internal hardware algorithm design and optimization etc.

The discussed proof-of-concept diagnostic system involves four types of failure diagnostics, including prediction of both direct and indirect immediate influence of the detected failures on individual hardware units in the system. Two major types of failures can be detected: failures affecting output signals of hardware units (i.e. their internal failures) and failures of communication links between the units.

2   System Overview

The presented software system consists of four major parts:

- entity execution manager (see section 3)
- simulated hardware layer (see section 4)
- diagnostic layer (see section 6)
- visualization module (see section 7)

The system is built on top of the A-globe [1], [4] multi-agent platform which provides infrastructure for basic agent functionality (environment simulation, yellow pages services, message transport etc.), and A-globeX Simulation layer responsible for executing predefined scenarios, managing central virtual simulation clock updates and so forth. For portability reasons as well as for fast development and easy maintenance purposes, the entire system is written in Java.

All entities in the system (simulated hardware units, diagnostic agents, visualization module, internal system modules etc.) have the form of autonomous agents. There are currently approx. 180 agents running in the implemented scenario (a door-locking electronic subsystem). The entire multi-agent system is fully distributed and asynchronous by its nature. Agents in A-globe "live" on containers, i.e. software platforms that provide their "inhabitants" with basic agent-oriented infrastructure.

There are two types of containers:

- a single central **master container**, populated by system agents including the Visio Agent as well as agents responsible for simulation of the scenario environment and flow of time, particularly the Car Agent.
- multiple **client containers**, each of them hosting a single scenario agent, either a simulated hardware unit (electronic control unit – ECU, sensor, switch, BUS) or a diagnostic agent (monitoring, data flow, data consistency, prediction).

Each container can run on a separate computer and therefore all agents communicate strictly by using messages sent through the network. The message transport layer is provided to the agents by the individual A-globe containers. In order to find each other in the network, agents use directory services ("yellow pages") provided also by the containers.

Communication with the server container (environment simulation and visio) is performed by a special type of system messages called *topics*. Unlike standard messages, topics can be sent only from the server to client containers or vice versa, but never between client containers only. Topics can also be broadcast, e.g. when the server container sends system time updates to client containers.

3   Dynamic Scenarios

A particular simulation scenario to be executed (i.e. startup configuration of simulated hardware units and diagnostic agents) is created dynamically. Static XML files hold only information about all usable agent types, including their global parameters. All the rest of the process of scenario loading (and possible subsequent modification) is controlled by the user at run-time. The Entity Execution Manager allows the user to choose interactively which simulated hardware units will be loaded when the given scenario is executed (by pressing the Start Scenario button in the Entity Manager).

Moreover, upon user's request selected simulated hardware units can also be loaded or unloaded dynamically during run-time. The Entity Execution Manager handles loading and unloading of all corresponding diagnostic agents automatically.

This feature can be used e.g. for dynamic reconfiguration of the simulated system: adding new hardware units or introducing alternative versions of particular hardware units during run-time.

4   Simulated Hardware Layer

All hardware units (electronic control units – ECUs, sensors, switches and BUSes) are simulated by dedicated agents. One type of agent is used for simulation of BUS units, while another type is used for simulation of ECUs, switches and sensors.

Note that if the diagnostic system is deployed on real hardware, the entire simulated hardware layer would be replaced by actual hardware devices, similarly as in [2], [3].

Communication between hardware units is simulated by sending messages among corresponding agents. Each transmitted signal is physically represented by a message sent between the corresponding agents.

While the common functionality of all agents simulating hardware devices is implemented by the same code, internal behavior of each ECU, switch or sensor is defined by a reference to algorithm specific for each hardware unit. Such algorithm defines responses to particular incoming signals depending on the current internal state of the given hardware unit. Internal state of a simulated hardware unit is stored in a set of internal variables, e.g. VarBool, VarInt, VarCounter etc. that are involved in the internal algorithms (i.e. body) of the simulated hardware units. The advantage of these variables over standard built-in Java variables (boolean, int etc.) is that any change of their value can trigger an event and thus they can be monitored easily. Also, their value can be imported and exported which makes it possible to import and export the current state of the entire simulated hardware unit. Time dependencies within the internal algorithms are handled by so called timers (VarTimer), internal variables that expire after a predefined period of time. When timer expiration occurs, the internal algorithm is notified about it and it can take an appropriate action.

Simulated hardware units not only communicate with each other via signals but some of them must also react to changes of their environment. For example, sensors repetitively read values of physical phenomena they are dedicated to, and almost all simulated hardware units need to be aware of flow of simulated time. The real-world environment is simulated by a central Car Agent. This agent not only handles the flow of central simulation time but also keeps information of the current physical status of all car parts related to the scenario.

Interaction of hardware units with the environment is implemented by sending a special type of system messages from the central Car Agent to the hardware agents and vice versa if needed (e.g. Door Control Units physically moving door lock motors).

The topology of the network of hardware devices is defined statically. For each signal, one or more sender-receiver pairs of units are defined. This way, the entire system topology is fully described. As a by-product, a number of other types of information can be derived from this elementary description, such as all input and output signals for a particular hardware unit. These automatically derived types of data are subsequently used for diagnostic and visualization purposes.

5 Failure Simulation

In order to provide the various diagnostic agents with relevant data to operate on, it was necessary to allow the user to introduce failures into the simulated hardware system.

All failure types are simulated within the simulated hardware layer, more specifically inside hardware unit agents. Therefore diagnostic agents are not directly aware of any failures introduced by the user and they have to detect them by actual observation of behavior of the hardware system they are deployed on.

The user can introduce two main types of failures:

- failures of **hardware units** (signal drop-out, invalidation, alteration)
- failures of **communication links** between devices (signal drop-out)

Failures of a hardware unit are implemented in the output module of the agent. After the internal logic module of the agent generates an outgoing signal, this signal can be either dropped, invalidated (wrong data format) or altered (modified data value) by the output module before it is actually sent through the network, depending on the user's input. Notice that the internal logic module is unable to influence this process.

Failures of communication links are implemented in the input module of the agent. Before an incoming signal is processed by the internal logic module of the agent, it can be dropped by the input module, depending on the user's input. If a signal is dropped, it never reaches the internal logic module and therefore it is never actually processed. Again, notice that the internal logic module is unable to influence this process.

6 Diagnostic Layer

There are currently four types of agent-based diagnostics implemented:

- Monitoring Layer (see section 6.1)
- Data Flow Layer (see section 6.2)
- Data Consistency Layer (see section 6.3)
- Prediction Layer (see section 6.4)

They all observe the same underlying simulated hardware system from different perspectives and provide the user with a wide range of diagnostic results.

6.1 Monitoring Layer

Each hardware unit (simulated by an agent on the hardware layer) is accompanied by one dedicated Monitoring Agent.

Whenever the Entity Execution Manager loads a new simulated hardware unit to the system, it also loads a corresponding Monitoring Agent.

The Monitoring Agent possesses a reference model of behavior of the hardware unit it monitors. For easy code management and development efficiency reasons, the current implementation of the reference model uses the same algorithms (and even the same source code classes) as the actual simulated hardware units.

If the diagnostic system was deployed on real hardware and the agents on the simulated hardware layer were replaced by actual hardware devices, these reference behavior algorithms would have to be updated in order to match the behavior of the real hardware as closely as possible.

The Monitoring Agent "listens" to all input and output signals of the hardware unit it monitors, it processes all the input signals with the reference algorithm and it compares its results with the actual output signals that the monitored hardware unit produced in response to the given input signals. If any differences between the real hardware and the reference model are detected, they are classified as follows:

- signal **drop-out** – the reference algorithm generated an output signal but the hardware unit did not
- signal **invalidation** – an output signal was generated by the hardware unit but the signal data is in wrong (illegible) format
- signal **alteration** – both the reference algorithm and the hardware unit produced an output signal but the signal data values differ

It is obvious that the Monitoring Agent and the monitored hardware unit must be well synchronized for this diagnostic method to provide reliable results.

Apart from the forementioned functionality, the Monitoring Agent also detects whether the monitored hardware unit receives and sends all signal types regularly as expected. If a particular signal type is not received or sent by the monitored hardware unit within a predefined period of time, a signal timeout is detected and classified as either input or output signal drop-out.

6.2   Data Flow Layer

While the Monitoring Agents are responsible for observing the operation of hardware units, the Data Flow Agents focus on reliability of communication links between hardware units.

Each Data Flow Agent is dedicated to a particular signal type.

Whenever the Entity Execution Manager loads a new simulated hardware unit into the system, it also loads all Data Flow Agents responsible for monitoring all input and output signal types of that hardware unit, unless the particular Data Flow Agents have been loaded previously together with other hardware units.

A Data Flow Agent assigned to monitor the flow of a particular signal type "listens" to all signals of that type sent through the hardware network. The Data Flow Agent checks whether all sent signals (of the particular type) reach their destination successfully. If a sent signal is not received within a predefined time period, a signal timeout is detected and reported as a failure of the communication link between the sender and the receiver.

Note that if the sender stops generating the output signal as a result of internal failure, the Data Flow Agent will not pay attention to it. This is the responsibility of the corresponding Monitoring Agent.

6.3   Data Consistency Layer

Consistency Agents check whether a certain type of information, or *property* (carried by a certain type of signal), that is shared among several hardware units, is consistent across all of these units.

Each Consistency Agent is dedicated to monitoring consistency of a certain property, i.e. certain type of signal across the entire system.

Whenever the Entity Execution Manager loads a new simulated hardware unit to the system, it also loads all Consistency Agents responsible for monitoring all properties (represented by input and/or output signals) of that hardware unit, unless the particular Consistency Agents have been loaded previously together with other hardware units.

If any inconsistency of a particular property is detected, the Consistency Agent uses the static topology definition of the hardware system to generate description of the hardware unit sequence through which the property is propagated and identifies all hardware units whose property value differs from the value of the first unit in the sequence (the originator), e.g. the sensor. The Consistency Agent also compares property values of all pairs of adjacent hardware units to identify the exact locations where the change of the propagated property value – i.e. failure – occurred. This information can also be used to classify the nature of the failure: if the value change occurs between the input and output of the same hardware unit, it is clear that we are dealing with a failure of the actual hardware unit; if the value change occurs between the output and input of two different hardware units, it indicates that the failure is located on the way between these units, most likely within their communication link.

The advantage of this diagnostic method is that Consistency Agents don't need any knowledge of internal behavior of the observed hardware units and they regard them as black boxes.

6.4   Prediction Layer

The prediction diagnostic layer continually receives reports of failures detected by other diagnostic layers and generates prediction on possible direct or indirect influence of the detected failures on other parts of the entire hardware system.

This type of diagnostics can be called *forward diagnostics* as it simulates spreading of failures in a forward direction through the system.
This diagnostic layer consists of two major parts:

- a single Prediction Coordinator
- multiple Prediction Units – one agent for each ECU

When a Monitoring Agent (monitoring diagnostic layer) or a Data Flow Agent (data flow diagnostic layer) detects a failure in the hardware system, it notifies the Prediction Coordinator. The failure report contains the following items: signal name, signal sender and receiver, an *isActive* flag and a *failureID* (used internally by the prediction diagnostic layer).

If the reported failure is active and is new for the Coordinator (i.e. it is not being processed already), the Coordinator assigns a unique ID to the failure and activates the Prediction Unit that corresponds to the receiver of the faulty signal.

Each Prediction Unit contains the same model of the ECU's internal behavior as the corresponding Monitoring Agent. When the Prediction Unit is activated, it starts to receive regular internal state updates from the respective Monitoring Agent and it applies them to its own copy of the ECU's internal logic model, thus keeping it up-to-date.

Apart from activating the Prediction Unit of the receiver ECU, the Coordinator also sends this agent a copy of the failure report for processing.

Upon receiving a failure report, the Prediction Unit runs various instances of the faulty signal through the ECU's internal behavior model. The signal instances contain different data values, depending on the data type of the signal:

- boolean – **true, false**
- three-state boolean – **true, false, undefined**
- integer – a few selected numeric values representatively covering the entire range of data values of the particular signal, e.g. minimal and maximal value etc.

It is crucial that before each input signal is processed, the internal behavior model is reset to a state corresponding to the latest state update received from the respective Monitoring Agent.

The Prediction Unit agent checks whether any of the processed input signal instances results in generation of any output signal. Depending on the results of this procedure, the Prediction Unit agent sends the Coordinator all output signals of the ECU's internal behavior model that are marked either as active or inactive, depending on the fact whether they were or were not generated in response to the particular failure (identified by a unique ID).

If an output signal is marked as active in this step, it means it may be influenced by the particular faulty input signal and thus may also become faulty.

Note that all currently active failures (i.e. faulty input signals) are also processed whenever the Prediction Unit receives a new state update from the Monitoring Agent.

When the Prediction Coordinator receives results from any of the Prediction Unit agents, it handles them in a very similar way to how it handles failure reports received from any diagnostic agent. It sends them to the corresponding Prediction Units (signal receivers) as a failure report. This way the potential failure iteratively spreads through the system.

When a particular failure is deactivated, i.e. the Prediction Coordinator receives a failure report from a diagnostic agent having the isActive field set to **false**, the Coordinator tries to find the received failure report in its list of currently active failures and thus identify the (previously assigned) ID of the failure. When the failure ID is found, a report on this failure's deactivation is propagated through all involved Prediction Units.

7   Visualization Module

The visualization module is implemented as an agent located on the server container. It provides the following modules and functionality:

- interactive GUIs allowing the user to interact with the hardware system
- hardware system topology viewer
- signal sniffer (filterable via the filter tree)
- tools for failure control
- visualization of diagnostic results

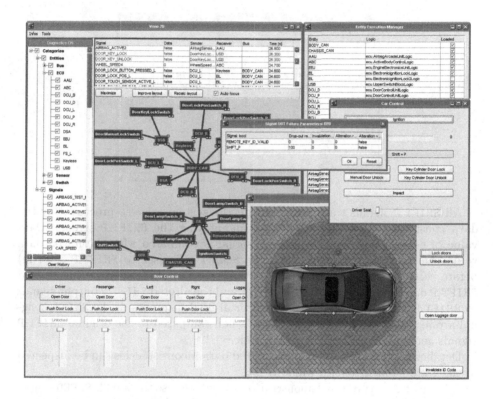

8   Use Case

This section provides a brief demonstration of the diagnostic functionality. Introduction of a simple failure to the simulated automotive system and the response of the diagnostic layer is shown.

Let us choose the **SHIFT_P** signal for now. This signal is generated by the *Shift Switch* unit, then it is sent to the *Engine Electronics Unit* (*EEU*) which passes it on to the *Electronic Ignition Lock* unit (*EIL*).

We set both the invalidation and alteration probability rate of the **SHIFT_P** output signal of the *EEU* to 50 percent.

Once the failure parameters are applied, we can use the signal sniffer window to observe the randomly invalidated or altered SHIFT_P signals generated by the *EEU*.

Monitoring agents dedicated to observation of the *EEU* and *EIL* units start to detect the randomly occurring signal failures at the output (*EEU*) or input (*EIL*) of the respective unit. This is indicated to the user by lighting up the corresponding red diagnostic "diodes" in the visualization of the two hardware units.

The user can also inspect detailed descriptions of the detected failures for each unit. Failures that are no longer active are displayed in gray.

Signal Failure Info: EEU			
Signal IN	Failure type	From [s]	To [s]
Signal OUT	Failure type	From [s]	To [s]
SHIFT_P	altered: false/true	2954.200	
SHIFT_P	invalid	2942.500	2946.500
SHIFT_P	altered: false/true	2938.500	2939.200
SHIFT_P	invalid	2936.200	2936.500
SHIFT_P	invalid	2930.500	2934.500
SHIFT_P	altered: false/true	2930.200	2930.500
SHIFT_P	invalid	2921.200	2930.200
SHIFT_P	invalid	2915.200	2918.500
SHIFT_P	altered: false/true	2914.500	2915.200

Clear inactive

All SHIFT_P signals transmitted within the system are also processed by the data consistency agent responsible for monitoring the SHIFT_P signals. Data value of each instance of the SHIFT_P signal is compared with the initial data value that was generated by the *Shift Switch* unit (set to SHIFT_P = true) before reaching the *EEU* and *EIL* units. Since the *EEU* sets the invalidated SHIFT_P output signals to SHIFT_P = ??? and the altered SHIFT_P output signals to SHIFT_P = false, these invalidated or altered instances of the SHIFT_P signal are regarded as data inconsistencies when compared to the original SHIFT_P signals generated by the *Shift Switch* unit.

Detailed information about the detected data inconsistencies can be inspected in the *Data inconsistencies* window.

For the next part of the demonstration we will choose the WHEEL_SPEED signal. This signal is generated by four independent *Wheel Speed Sensors*. The four independent signals are all received by the *Active Body Control* unit (*ABC*) which uses them for calculation of the speed of the car. The resulting car speed is them sent to the *EIL* in the form of the CAR_SPEED signal.

We set the drop-out probability rate of the WHEEL_SPEED1 input signal of the *ABC* to 100 percent. This setup can be regarded as a simulation of a broken communication link between the *Wheel Speed Sensor 1* and the *ABC*: WHEEL_SPEED1 signals are sent from the *Wheel Speed Sensor 1* successfully but they are not received by the *ABC*.

The WHEEL_SPEED1 signal lost on its way is detected by the data flow agent responsible for monitoring all WHEEL_SPEED1 signals.

Property	Sequence	Data	Inc. Entities	Inc. Pairs	From [s]	To [s]
ShiftP	ShiftSwitch(out) » EEU(in) » EEU(out) » EIL(in)	true » true » ??? » ???	EEU(out), EIL(in)	EEU(in) » EEU(out)	2986.800	
ShiftP	ShiftSwitch(out) » EEU(in) » EEU(out) » EIL(in)	true » true » ??? » ???	EEU(out), EIL(in)	EEU(in) » EEU(out)	2981.300	2984.300
ShiftP	ShiftSwitch(out) » EEU(in) » EEU(out) » EIL(in)	true » true » true » ???	EIL(in)	EEU(out) » EIL(in)	2975.200	2975.300
ShiftP	ShiftSwitch(out) » EEU(in) » EEU(out) » EIL(in)	true » true » true » false	EIL(in)	EEU(out) » EIL(in)	2972.200	2972.300
ShiftP	ShiftSwitch(out) » EEU(in) » EEU(out) » EIL(in)	true » true » true » false	EIL(in)	EEU(out) » EIL(in)	2963.200	2963.300
ShiftP	ShiftSwitch(out) » EEU(in) » EEU(out) » EIL(in)	true » true » true » ???	EIL(in)	EEU(out) » EIL(in)	2957.200	2957.300
ShiftP	ShiftSwitch(out) » EEU(in) » EEU(out) » EIL(in)	true » true » true » ???	EIL(in)	EEU(out) » EIL(in)	2946.500	2946.600
ShiftP	ShiftSwitch(out) » EEU(in) » EEU(out) » EIL(in)	true » true » true » false	EIL(in)	EEU(out) » EIL(in)	2939.200	2939.300
ShiftP	ShiftSwitch(out) » EEU(in) » EEU(out) » EIL(in)	true » true » true » false	EIL(in)	EEU(out) » EIL(in)	2934.500	2934.600
ShiftP	ShiftSwitch(out) » EEU(in) » EEU(out) » EIL(in)	true » true » true » ???	EIL(in)	EEU(out) » EIL(in)	2918.500	2918.600
ShiftP	ShiftSwitch(out) » EEU(in) » EEU(out) » EIL(in)	true » true » true » false	EIL(in)	EEU(out) » EIL(in)	2909.200	2909.300
ShiftP	ShiftSwitch(out) » EEU(in) » EEU(out) » EIL(in)	true » true » true » ???	EIL(in)	EEU(out) » EIL(in)	2903.200	2903.300

Also, the monitoring agent dedicated to the *ABC* detects that no WHEEL_SPEED1 signals are coming from the *Wheel Speed Sensor 1* which is indicated to the user by lighting up the corresponding red diagnostic diode.

Let us now focus on the prediction diagnostic layer. Hardware units that are identified by this layer as potentially affected by the detected failure are marked by a lit-up orange diode. The prediction is updated with each change of state of the system.

Let us assume that the car is currently parked and the ignition is turned off. In such situation, the units identified as potentially affected are the *ABC* and *EIL*. The *ABC* does not currently receive any updates of the WHEEL_SPEED1 signal, therefore it is directly affected by the failure we introduced earlier. Because of that, the speed of the car that the ABC calculates and sends to the *EIL* may also be incorrect. Therefore the *EIL* is indirectly influenced by the given failure.

If we now turn the ignition on, the state of the system changes, the prediction is updated and all *Door Control Units* (*DCUs*) are now also marked as potentially affected by the failure. The reason why this happens is that the *EIL* sends a request to all the *DCUs* to lock all the doors (signal DOOR_DEMAND_LOCK) when the ignition is on and the speed of the car exceeds 20 km/h. The ignition is on now but since the *EIL* may receive an incorrectly calculated car speed from the

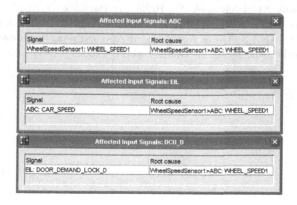

ABC, proper generation of the DOOR_DEMAND_LOCK signal may be influenced by this failure. Therefore all the *DCUs* are indirectly influenced now as well because they may not receive the DOOR_DEMAND_LOCK signal correctly.

9 Conclusion

Agent technology proved not only very promising in the area of diagnostics of automotive electronic systems, but also very efficient in simulation of such systems for the purpose of development and testing. The distributed multi-agent system is particularly useful for modeling various scenarios both in terms of online hardware reconfiguration and failure simulation. The natural modularity of the agent-based simulation and diagnostics is a key feature and benefit of the proposed solution. Also, the distributed and parallel approach to failure detection and diagnostics increases its robustness and enables easy and effective deployment of the described technology even in large-scale electronic systems.

The implemented failure prediction considers only the current state of the underlying hardware system. One of our future goals is to extend the implementation so that the prediction would also consider selected *future* states of the system and based on the results of the individual prediction passes. The system would then automatically suggest to the user what action to take in order to minimize the number of hardware devices influenced by the detected failure.

References

1. A-globe: A-globe Agent Platform (2006), http://agents.felk.cvut.cz/aglobe
2. Maturana, F.P., Staron, R.J., Hall, K.H.: Methodologies and tools for intelligent agents in distributed control. IEEE Intelligent Systems 20(1), 42–49 (2005)
3. Provan, G.M., Chen, Y.-L.: Agent-based, distributed diagnosis for shipboard systems. In: BASYS '02: Proceedings of the IFIP TC5/WG5.3 Fifth IFIP/IEEE International Conference on Information Technology for Balanced Automation Systems in Manufacturing and Services, Deventer, The Netherlands, pp. 281–288. B. V. Kluwer, Dordrecht (2002)
4. Šišlák, D., Rehák, M., Pěchouček, M., Rollo, M., Pavlíček, D.: A-globe: Agent development platform with inaccessibility and mobility support. In: Unland, R., Klusch, M., Calisti, M. (eds.) Software Agent-Based Applications, Platforms and Development Kits, Berlin, pp. 21–46. Birkhauser Verlag (2005)

Performance in Industrial Holonic Systems

Vadim Ermolayev[1] and Wolf-Ekkehard Matzke[2]

[1] Zaporozhye National Univ., 66, Zhukovskogo st., 69063 Zaporozhye, Ukraine
vadim@ermolayev.com
[2] Cadence Design Systems, GmbH, Mozartstr. 2, D.85622 Feldkirchen, Germany
wolf@cadence.com

We are glad to present the papers of the special session on Performance in Industrial Holonic Systems[1] (Pi-HolS 2007) at the 3^d International Conference on Industrial Applications of Holonic and Multi-Agent Systems[2] (HoloMAS 2007). The session brought together researchers and practitioners in the areas of holonic and multi-agent systems, knowledge engineering, and performance management to share their views and experience in design, development, deployment, and application of technologies for measuring, assessing and optimizing the performance of industrial systems based on holonic principles.

A holon in a broad philosophical sense is an entity which is a whole and a part of the whole at the same time. A very close paradigm of a holistic approach advocates for the fact that the properties of the whole system can not be described using only the properties of its parts. In such a holonic system some distinct integral properties appear. These emerging properties represent new qualities of the non-mechanistic union of the system's constituents. The following aspects of a holonic paradigm are of particular academic and practical interest:

– The model of an organization capturing its self-configurability, self-development, and dynamic character
– Deliberate collaboration
– Ambient intelligence

One natural choice for modeling a holonic system and implementing software for it is the choice of an intelligent software agent and agency paradigms. Another way may be the use of self-configurable compositions of (Semantic) Web Services. These software engineering approaches, though distinct, have at least one important feature in common – formal shared representation of Domain semantics.

Pi-HolS collected primarily the contributions related to industry. Indeed, a holon and a holonic system are suitable metaphors for implementing and deploying intelligent software in a vastly wide variety of industrial applications. The spectrum is as broad as starting with *Emergency Response*, covering *Agile Manufacturing*, *e-Commerce*, *Traffic Control*, and ending with *Engineering Design*. Holons are especially attractive in representing self-configuring, self-optimizing, collaborative dynamic systems. Our special focus of interest in such systems is their performance and performance management. Both the performance of actions and artifacts in the real world and the performance of their software models are interesting.

---

[1] http://ermolayev.com/pi-hols/
[2] http://cyber.felk.cvut.cz/HoloMAS/2007/

V. Mařík, V. Vyatkin, A.W. Colombo (Eds.): HoloMAS 2007, LNAI 4659, pp. 383–386, 2007.
© Springer-Verlag Berlin Heidelberg 2007

We have grouped these papers loosely in three categories: vision, technologies, and applications. This grouping formed the basics of our scientific program.

The paper by Ermolayev and Matzke emphasizes that industrial business performance management is very much intuitive, high-level, and does not possess a rigorous and grounded engineering methodology yet. This vagueness appears to be one of the main reasons for current dissatisfaction in industry. The paper proposes the vision of how a rigorous engineering methodology for business performance management in microelectronic engineering design may look like. It is motivated that the underlying framework has to be holonic. The authors suggest that the solution has to: be based on a sound Domain ontology of performance; use dynamic distributed planning technique and simulations to predict the performance of a design system; use the methodology which is sensitive to the specificities of a particular design system. The main contribution of the paper is the elaboration of the definition of performance and performance management resulting in the ontology of performance. By this it makes a visionary attempt to solve the "performance paradox"[3] originally pointed to by Meyer and Gupta.

The session offers two papers reporting on the development of technologies: ontology matching for competence management and the use of software agents and ontologies for process monitoring.

The paper by Tarasov et al reports on the technology of competence profile matching for collaborative production networks. Their research is motivated by the observation that manufacturers, distributors, and dealers form production networks to implement their need to collaborate. It is noticed that production networks provide significant advantages in production variety, flexibility and lead time. The challenge of modeling and supporting such networks is matching the best capable partners and configuring them in a collaboration network. The authors report on the novel technology for solving the task. This technology is based on ontology matching technique and uses ontology management, context management, and profiling. The authors claim that using ontological representation of competences allows identifying those team members who are best suited for the task. Developing and maintaining competence profiles of all the relevant parties associated with production can significantly reduce network composition and actual production times. Hence, the performance of the resulting team composition in terms of the efficiency of composition and operation becomes close to optimal.

The paper by Pirttioja et al proposes the approach extending process monitoring with the help of information agents handling semantic data in the form of ontologies. According to their work an operator of a process automation system can configure monitoring tasks executed by a group of agents. These tasks are composites because comprise several process observations and their logical relations. It is demonstrated that delegation of monitoring tasks to agents enhances the performance of the human operator both in terms of efficiency and effectiveness. Agents working on his behalf let him supervising the process at a higher level of abstraction instead of routinely following a large amount of simple measurement data. Agents cooperate in a multi-agent system to setup and execute user configured monitoring tasks. This paper

---

[3] Meyer and Gupta noticed [1] that "organizational control is maintained by not knowing exactly what performance is".

bridges our technology and application streams by presenting the test case from an industrial paper making process.

Pi-HolS application stream offers three papers in three different Domains: manufacturing, emergency response, and engineering design.

The paper by Bal and Hashemipour presents the implementation of Virtual Reality - based simulations with holonic control for the assessment of the performance of a manufacturing system. It is emphasized that the proposed methodology is targeted to small and medium size enterprises which have expertise limits and substantial cost constraints. The paper presents the application implemented in a medium-sized die-casting factory demonstrating the efficiency of the approach. In this application the overall performance of the factory has been tested for implementation of a robot-arm integrated die casting cell with holonic control architecture. Presented approach allowed to investigate the best course of action for enterprise's investment decisions with the least disruption to existing production activities.

The paper by Narzisi et al reports on the experimental work using PLAN C for assessing the performance of emergency response. PLAN C is an Agent-Based Model platform for urban disaster simulation and emergency planning. It features a variety of reality-based agents interacting on a realistic city map and can simulate the complex dynamics of emergency responses in different urban catastrophe scenarios. Work reported here focuses on the incorporation of specific subpopulations of person agents, reflecting the existence of individuals with specific defining characteristics and needs, and their interactions with the available resources. Performance of these subpopulations is compared in both point-source attack and distributed disaster scenarios of varying magnitudes. The effect of varying topologies of available resources, like different hospital maps, provides particular insight into the dynamics that can emerge in this complex system. PLAN C produces interesting emergent behavior of such artificial populations. This behavior is realistically adequate as it complies with the literature on emergency medicine.

The paper by Sohnius et al presents the approach to assess the performance of an engineering design system in the field of microelectronics using holonic simulation. Instead of measuring some input and output parameters of the system and applying metrics to them, the authors build a fine-grained model of the entire design system and simulate the course of a design process in a design system using a multi-agent system. Simulation comprises essentially two phases: planning and execution. In the planning phase, the agents use the knowledge of the design system to generate a work breakdown structure, do resource assignment and derive a schedule from these. At the execution phase the agents simulate the actual course of the execution of the previously created plan. The planning phase uses a more abstract, higher level description of the tasks to be executed which allows for planning with reasonable computational effort. Whereas the execution phase uses a finer grained model that supports detailed features like iterative activities. The advantage of this approach is that one gets both the clarity and the lower algorithmic complexity in planning and the precise and detailed information from the execution. Performance metrics are then applied to the detailed results of these simulations. The paper presents the simulation part of the framework.

We believe that this quality selection of research papers may be interesting for those readers who are interested in theoretical and practical aspects of performance in industrial holonic systems. The balance of the theoretical rigor and the selection of grounding industrial applications may attract attention both from academia and industry.

Reference

1. Meyer, M.W., Gupta, V.: The Performance Paradox. In: Cummings, L.L., Staw, B. (eds.) Research in Organizational Behavior, pp. 309–369. JAI Press, Greenwich, Conn. (1994)

Towards Industrial Strength Business Performance Management

Vadim Ermolayev[1] and Wolf-Ekkehard Matzke[2]

[1] Zaporozhye National Univ., 66, Zhukovskogo st., 69063 Zaporozhye, Ukraine
vadim@ermolayev.com
[2] Cadence Design Systems, GmbH, Mozartstr. 2, D.85622 Feldkirchen, Germany
wolf@cadence.com

Abstract. Business performance management today does not possess a rigorous and grounded engineering methodology capable of delivering reliably measured values to backing up decision making. Much more it is the art of executive gurus who listen to their backbone experience and take their decisions using intuitive and heuristic approaches. This vagueness appears to be one of the main reasons for current dissatisfaction in industry. In this paper we express our vision of how a rigorous engineering methodology for business performance management in engineering design may look like. Our research work in PSI[1] and PRODUKTIV+[2] projects strongly suggests that the underlying modeling framework has to be holonic. We consider that the solution has to: (i) be based on a sound Domain ontology of performance; (ii) use dynamic distributed planning technique and simulations to predict the performance of a design system; (iii) use the methodology which is sensitive to the specificities of a particular design system.

Keywords: Business performance, engineering design, microelectronics, performance ontology, performance measurement and management methodology, simulation.

1 Introduction

Given the popularity of "performance" in modern society it is not surprising that performance management is very much en-vogue in virtually every area of human activity. Journalists, management consultants, and performance management solution providers alike seem to be overly excited by the topic. But performance management as a rigorous discipline is still in an embryonic state. In fact, *"performance management as an identifiable subject for academic study and research arguably*

---

[1] Performance Simulation Initiative (PSI) is the internal R&D project of Cadence Design Systems, GmbH.
[2] Reference System for Measuring Design Productivity of Nanoelectronic Systems (PRODUKTIV+) is the project partially funded by German Federal Ministry of Education and Research (http://www.edacentrum.de/produktivplus).

V. Mařík, V. Vyatkin, A.W. Colombo (Eds.): HoloMAS 2007, LNAI 4659, pp. 387–400, 2007.

began in the mid-1990" [1]. We find myriads of papers on performance management, we find a significant and fast growing performance management market, but we don't find a mature, or even a suitably grounded framework of the non-linear management of performance. Despite significant research efforts, the result is not the shortly expected one. Probably the main reason for this unsatisfactory situation is the highly interdisciplinary nature of performance management research, involving many fields of varying states of maturity and methodological practice. Disciplines that play a vital role in performance management research are for example: economics, engineering science, management theory, cultural anthropology, information technologies, psychology, education, artificial intelligence, philosophy, and so on. Additionally, there are professionals missing that are particularly skilled in integrating multiple research disciplines into a single required perspective. The metaphor of a holon comes to mind after saying that. Indeed, a mechanistic sum of skills required to solve performance management challenge does not give a satisfactory result. However, an intelligently combined and orchestrated (holonic) constellation of capabilities may bring us closer to the desired outcome.

In this paper we shall try to systematically describe the ingredients which, in their carefully combined proportion, may help in pursuing the solution. Indeed, the problem of performance management is that today it does not possess a rigorous and grounded engineering methodology capable of delivering reliably measured values to backing up decision making. Much more it is the art of executive gurus who listen to their backbone experience and take their decisions using intuitive and heuristic approaches[3].

We are not that ambitious to envision an ultimate and a universal "philosopher stone" [2] for any industry. Instead, we base the vision on our several year research and development experience in devising performance management methodology and intelligent tool support for engineering design in microelectronic and integrated circuits industry. All the statements of this paper are thereby applicable to engineering design performance in this industrial sector. Of course, the approach may seem generic enough to be applied in different domains.

The paper is structured as follows. Section 2 argues that performance management at strategic or executive level severely lacks important bits of the necessary knowledge to produce robust assessments. It is required to apply rigorous engineering approaches at design process level and simulate design system actions in order to proactively maintain its performance at the desired level. Section 3 is focused on the knowledge engineering aspect. Our approach to developing a descriptive Domain theory of performance is introduced. Section 4 expresses our views on how performance may be reliably measured based on the taken ontological approach. Section 5 sketches our vision of a performance engineering methodology based on the simulation of the performance of a design system. Section 6 provides concluding remarks.

---

[3] Of course it is stated that such methods are based on the assessments using Key Performance Indicators (http://en.wikipedia.org/wiki/Key_performance_indicators, checked on March 1, 2007).

2 Strategic Management Versus Engineering Approach

Today's trends in engineering design in microelectronics and integrated circuits show that mastering a new sub-micron technology slightly ahead of the competitors is not sufficient to feel yourself on the safe side. It is also required that your design system (denoted later in Section 3.3) demonstrates the "best-in-class" performance. Among the other performance "indicators" to be gained at a high level, a design system should be flexible and responsive enough to be capable of meeting and compensating sudden changes. For example, changing factors may be: time-to-market constraints, design specification, technology. Unpredicted distorting external influences like sudden reorganization of a design team, increased number of design activity iterations due to the changes in the quality requirements, or factual unavailability of a required resource may also influence a design system. Another important feature of a design system in the Era of glocalisation[4] is the increasing geographical and cultural distribution bringing up new challenges to performance management. Indeed, provided that the parts of a design system are spread globally over time zones, the proper time management may substantially increase "round-the-clock" performance. If the particularities of local traditions and cultures are properly accounted for different groups the performance may be increased due to the savings in communication and synchronization overhead, etc.

Today's performance measurement and management practices are based mostly on strategic level benchmarking – finding a place of your company among the others on the industry sector bench. The prevailing methodology is the use of one or another sort of balanced scorecards [3]. Such a benchmarking, though providing reasonably sound indications of what is good or bad in terms of performance, does not help much in revealing the reasons. Moreover, these measures are based on the past and do not help predicting what will happen in the future. They also do not account for the changes in the business, its flexibility and the role of collaboration, which are important factors in engineering design performance. In order to make more grounded and predictive assessments, to engineer design performance at the required level, we have to apply the measures at the level of engineering design processes and use much finer grained bits of information for that. A negative consequence of taking this way in performance assessment and management is that the volume and the complexity of data to be processed are far too high to perform such an analysis by hand before the changes pass the point of no return. Therefore, a methodology and an intelligent software tool capable to automate such analyses is required as one of the important factors ensuring better performance of a design system.

The objective of the PSI and PRODUKTIV+ projects is to develop such a methodology and a tool capable to discover the "abyssal" reasons for the weaknesses of a design system and accounting for the pro-activity of human designers and the stochastic character of the external factors. The approach is to simulate a design system as a social and self-regulating team of autonomous actors having differing professional and cultural backgrounds. Hence, holonic principles become very relevant. One of the central points in modeling a design system is to adequately

---

[4] *Glocalisation* – a portmanteau of *globalisation* and *localisation* (http://en.wikipedia.org/wiki/Glocalisation, checked on March 1, 2007).

represent a designer as a locus of a goal-directed behavior and a design team as a dynamic social structure. A holon, comprising the computational models of actors, design teams, design tools in frame of an organization and possessing useful emerging properties of these combinations, may be efficiently used as an adequate model of a design system. Further on, a software agent can be naturally used as an appropriate implementation model for a designer, a design tool, or a resource and a multi-agent system (MAS) – as a model for an adaptable collaborative social structure like a design team or an organization at strategic management level. More details on how design systems are simulated and how their performance is accessed in PSI and PRODUKTIV+ may be found in [4].

3   Towards the Definition and the Ontology of Performance

"Performance" is one of the most prominent buzzwords today. For example, Google yields approximately 468.000.000 hits for "performance"[5]. Assuming a positive correlation between the number of hits on the World Wide Web and the importance of a concept in contemporary society, "performance" is definitely among the top terms used. To compare, the search for an undeniably important concept like "human" results in 467.000.000 hits[6], which is slightly below "performance".

Performance is everywhere and in everything one does – cradle-to-grave. There are seemingly countless word-combinations with the word "performance" in it. To give a glimpse of this, here are a few examples of what is available: high-performance baby wipes (from cradle!), kindergarten performance, performance school, performance university, performance bike, performance agreements, performance poetry, performance period, network performance, environmental performance, computer performance, performance objectives, performance agreements, performance appraisal, performance art, performance grave (to grave!)... So, why becomes "performance" that popular? And, being such an ultra-popular concept these days, doesn't "performance" become almost completely meaningless? If anything, what is it that people are trying to say when they speak of "performance"?

3.1   The Notion of Performance

Perhaps the definition of "performance" will lead to some hints. This, so far, turned out to be a naive hope. More then ten years ago Meyer and Gupta [5] pointed out that there is "*massive disagreement as to what performance is*". A recent linguistic search and analysis of existing definitions of "performance" conducted in the PSI project highlights two main points: (i) there are many definitions of "performance" and new ones are continuously added; and (ii) "performance" definitions proffered by the performance proponents – whether from academia or industry – suffer from the lack of rigor and consensus. On the contrary, the trend towards opting for 'seductively vague' definitions continues unbroken to this day. A selection of few examples chosen from the vast supply of "performance" definitions is as follows.

---

[5] http://www.google.com.ua/search?q=performance, checked on March 1, 2007.
[6] http://www.google.com.ua/search?q=human, checked on March 1, 2007.

Baldvinsdottir et al [6]: *"Performance is defined as carrying out tasks in a situation that allows optimal outcome."* The issue that immediately arises with this definition is the exact meaning of "a situation that allows optimal outcome". Seemingly, the authors have chosen to employ a tautological conception of optimality. Under such a conception everything is adjusted to everything else given all relevant constraints. Saying that a situation allows for optimal outcome means that it allows exactly what it allows given all situational constraints. However, an important hint in this definition is that *performance is tightly linked to carrying out tasks in an optimal way.*

Faulk II [7]: *"Performance is defined as the accomplishment of job duties as required by the organization."* This is a much too narrow definition. For example, what about any accomplishments above and beyond the required job duties? According to the above definition those accomplishments would not be attributed to "performance". However intuitively we know that this can't be the case. In fact, what is done above and beyond the job duties is often percept as a major contribution to "performance". Despite that, a hint that we shall collect is: *an organization requires that tasks (arising of the job duties or beyond) are well-performed to optimize its own performance at a higher level.*

Hall [8]: *"Performance is defined as the combination of competence in job skills and high levels of productivity."* This attempt of a definition combines two disparate concepts – competence, which is a human ability and productivity, which is a neo-classical economic metric - into a single "mechanism" called "performance". What is the author trying to define here? A hint to answer might be: *there are various sorts of performance aspects applicable to different parts of the puzzle. For example, a level of skill may characterize the performance of an actor, while productivity may be used as an integral performance characteristic of a process.*

Melchert and Winter [9]: *"Performance is defined as valued contribution to reach the goals of an organization."* This is just another approach of defining "performance" that is seemingly both limited and inadequate. Who valuates a contribution? What happens if a contribution is not valued? From the above definition it follows that any contribution that is not considered to be a valued contribution – by whomever – does not add to performance. This will be true, regardless of the significance a contribution has to reach the goals of the organization. Isn't it too bad if it is just not valued? For example, if ten men months have been spent to find out that the development approach taken was a complete crap, was it good or bad performance? We tend to answer positively, though such an answer doesn't make assessments easier. A rational hint in this definition, however, is that *a methodology of performance assessment needs to be based on a sort of a problem solving methodology.*

O'Donnell and Duffy [10] suggest *"In summary, the research in performance has been hindered by a lack of clarity on its meaning."* We agree wholeheartedly with this statement, but there is always hope:

Harkema [11]: *"Performance is defined as a number or series of activities directed toward an outcome."* This definition comes closest to encompassing all of the wide and varied sorts of "performance". Yet it is not perfect, as it contains the ambiguous phrase *"number or series of"*. Furthermore, *"directed"* seem to indicate some "outside" control or intention. This is an unnecessary restriction, which results in a too-narrow definition of "performance".

In a situation like this, it is advisable to go back to the roots and use the etymology of "performance". In addition it is sensible to pin down dictionary definitions. This information can then be used as a framing device for denoting the concept of a performance in a comprehensive way. According to the Chambers Dictionary of Etymology [12], "performance" was formed around 1500 AD from the English "*perform*" and the suffix "*-ance*". "*Perform*" is derived from the Old French "*par*" (completely) + "*fornir*" (to provide, furnish). The suffix "*-ance*" labels "performance" as a noun of action. As for the standard dictionary definitions we have: (1) the Oxford-English-Dictionary-Online[7] defines "performance" as "*the action of performing*" or "*something performed*", (2) the Merriam-Webster-Online Dictionary[8] refers to "performance" as "*the execution of an action*", or "*something accomplished*", and (3) the American Heritage Dictionary[9] says "*the act of performing*", or "*the state of being performed.*"

The etymology and the standard dictionary definitions of "performance" suggest that "performance" is derived from the root concept (or summum-genus) for intentional action. Therefore, we arrive at the following definition of performance: *Performance is intentional action.*

This definition of "performance", though too abstract and not much better than the one by Harkema, is valid under all circumstances and for all context-specific situations. However, all other "performance"-related concepts have to be defined as specialization of this root-concept. This is of central importance as the "performance" of something is always context based. More details will be given in Section 3.3. It should further be noted that not all actions are intentional. The notion of intentional action can be contrasted with accidental as well as with unintentional action.

3.2 Performance Management

It is self-evident that any means, which supports the realization of intentions, is relevant in the context of performance. Management is said to be such a means. Therefore, performance should be managed. In a nutshell, this is what performance management is all about.

From the point of general concept, management has two basic dimensions. One, "linear management", centers on striving to continually improve practices and processes. Along this dimension, managers plan, budget, organize, staff, direct, supervise, control, etc. Linear management is solely applicable to situations of relative stability. For historical reasons (industrial society), most of the contemporary management knowledge is about linear management. An example for a linear management technique is Total Quality Management (TQM). The other dimension, "non-linear management", centers on coping with change. Along this dimension managers pro-actively respond to and anticipate change by aligning, motivating, and inspiring humans. Non-linear management has to be adaptive, whereas linear management is mainly plan-driven ("plan-pushed"). Non-linear management has to be "environmentally-pulled", that is, managers are directed more by responses to their

---

[7] http://www.oed.com/, checked on March 1, 2007.

[8] http://www.m-w.com/, checked on March 1, 2007.

[9] http://www.bartleby.com/61/, checked on March 1, 2007.

environment than to a central command authority. Linear management prescribes what to do. Non-linear management enables how to determine what to do. Unmistakably, non-linear management is considerably more difficult than linear management. Examples for non-linear management techniques can be found under the topic of "agility" (the ability to perceive changes and establish appropriate techniques to cope with them).

Ubbesen[10] provides the following metaphor to describe the significant difference between linear and non-linear management: *"We could imagine that we have a line, and then we put a cross at one end and write the word problem. In accordance with our ordinary way of thinking, the word solution should consequently be placed at the other end. What do we do if the good solution is somewhere outside the line? As a matter of fact, creative consciousness is not bound to the line, it moves within a larger field of solution methods."* Remarkably, this metaphor hints to look at the problem solving methodologies developed in Artificial Intelligence (AI).

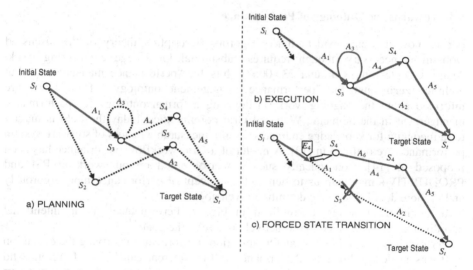

Fig. 1. Search for the path with optimal performance in the solution space. The shortest arches stand for the best performance.

Indeed, if we would like to devise an optimal composition of design activities in a design process (Fig. 1) at planning phase, we most certainly risk to be mistaken. The combination of A_1 and A_2 (Fig. 1a) results in theoretically the shortest path $S_i \xrightarrow{A_1} S_3 \xrightarrow{A_2} S_t$. However, the reality at execution phase may reveal that A_3 should be added several times before A_2 to improve the quality of results delivered by A_1 (Fig. 1b). In fact, it may well happen that a longer path skipped at planning, e.g. $S_i \rightarrow S_2 \rightarrow S_5 \rightarrow S_t$, may appear to be the optimal one with respect to performance. A different continuation of the process instead of making iterations ($S_i \xrightarrow{A_3} S_3 \xrightarrow{A_4} S_4 \xrightarrow{A_5} S_t$) may in fact appear to be even more attractive.

---

[10] http://www.aaa.dk/aaa/ledelse-og_organisationsudvikling.eng.pdf, checked on March 1, 2007.

Another complication is the case when following the optimal planned path is no longer possible because of an external event forcing state transition (Fig. 1c). Both cases b) and c) require non-linear management methodology in order to be optimally resolved – dynamic re-planning, re-scheduling, possibly, design team reconfiguration, reaching agreements, coping with external events and other disturbances.

In today's business reality both management dimensions are present and necessary. However, the ratio between them is what makes the difference. Change was always with us, it always will be. But the pace and breadth of change may exceed the capability of linear response methods that worked before. That is linear management tends to "ignore" or "discourage" change until serious problems vent in a "volcanic eruption". With change more rampant today than ever, companies are required to utilize increasingly non-linear management techniques. However, the reality looks quite different. Most companies are "over"-managed in the linear sense and "under"-led in the non-linear sense.

3.3 Towards the Ontology of Performance

For us now it seems evident that a rigorous description theory of the discussed Domain is necessary, though requires substantial knowledge engineering work. Again, Google returns around 23,400,000 hits for "performance management", but nothing (**zero** hits) for "performance management ontology". Though we are informed about the ongoing work on devising a formal ontology for performance management in the Semantic Web and Grid communities, today the field is mainly terra incognita for knowledge engineers. Some measurable factors of software system performance are outlined in [13]. A model of a Grid workflow performance has been proposed in [14]. Consequently such a theory based on our work in PSI and PRODUKTIV+ may help us to denote the concept of performance more rigorously and in more detail than in the definition given above.

In engineering design, as outlined in Fig. 2, Performance[11] is an intentional coordinated action targeted to pro-actively reaching the goals[12].

Performance is exhibited by an Organization. Performance is driving the execution of Tasks in design Projects. Performance is the inherent capability of Actors who form design Teams. A closely related concept is a Design System. In microelectronics a Design System is often understood as the configuration of a collection of software tools and IP libraries used in design processes to support them. We suggest broadening this simplified definition and consider a Design System *a holonic system providing the environment in which design processes are performed*. This environment comprises Actors rationally collaborating in design Teams, a normative framework providing regulations and policies, material resources, and Tools.

Performance is assessed using various Indicators. These Indicators may be taxonomized by their relationship to the concepts possessing Performance. For example, ActorRelatedIndicators are applied to assess Performance exhibited by Actors (like a *skill level*), ProcessRelatedIndicators are used to assess the Performance

---

[11] Concept names are given with capitalized first letter.

[12] An important point is that the goals pursued by different players: Actors, Teams, Organizations, may be coherent or conflicting. The parties have to reach agreements on their goals and to coordinate their actions to obtain better Performance.

demonstrated in processes (like *productivity*), etc. Indicators have measurement rules associated with them – Metrics in Fig. 2. These rules may, however, be quite complex.

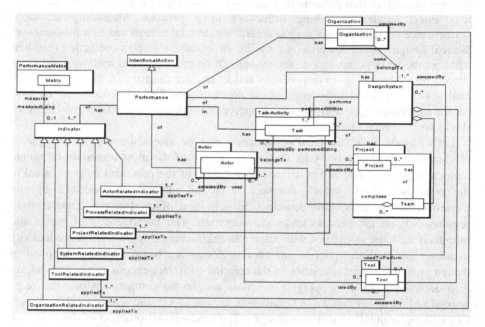

Fig. 2. The outline of Performance Ontology

This outline of the performance ontology is grounded in the PSI Ontologies Suite [15] and relies on its formal definitions of the Domain o dynamic engineering design processes structured in Task-Activity, Actor, Resource, and Project ontologies.

4 Measuring Performance

Today's industrial performance management frameworks are based on the strategic-level analysis of the carefully collected practices. They use statistical methods and knowledge mining techniques to devise the heuristics further on applied to coining out their performance indicators. It proves to be rather efficient for answering some important questions. For instance, a company's performance may be compared to the collected practices with quite a good ratio of statistical correlation if the knowledge base of these good and bad practices is sufficiently representative. According to the performance management literature (e.g., [16]), the most popular frameworks for performance measurement and management (PMM) are Balanced Scorecards, Business Excellence Model, Performance Prism. In microelectronic and integrated circuits design a popular methodology is the one by Numetrics [17]. The method of all these approaches to assess performance is the way to measure the abovementioned indicators. However, even if the knowledge of performance indicator metrics is properly defined and managed (which is unfortunately not the case), such a high-level heuristic benchmarking approach does not help much in understanding the reasons of the strengths and weaknesses of a design system. The simulation of the behavior of a design system may be more helpful. Suppose, there is a way to simulate designer teams executing design projects in a design system, Suppose also, such a simulation may inject sudden disturbing influences in a process. Measuring simulated performance in such settings may to a certain extent be considered as a prediction of the real design system behavior in a similar environment. Such a prediction may hint what are the weak points in a design system. Of course the model used in simulations should be calibrated to more precisely reflect the peculiarities of the system under analyses. Fine grained knowledge of the previously performed actions may be used for the calibration. Generally, a similar approach is applied in devising trend lines for stocks and financial markets.

Let's observe how simulated performance may be assessed using the example of productivity. Productivity by its very nature is one of the most important economic metrics of performance and is defined by the ratio of the produced output (value) to the consumed input (value). As such, it is an integral characteristic of any transformation process. This neo-classical definition of productivity imposes rigid requirements on the process under consideration. The homogeneity of inputs and outputs is the most severe one with respect to engineering design. Known productivity measurement methodologies in engineering design are based on the assessment of design complexity characteristics in the creation of homogeneous input- and output-measures. They do it by applying heuristic weights to compared parameters (e.g., normalized transistor count[13] in Semiconductor and Electronic Systems (SES) design, FP, KSLOC counts[14] in software design). The fundamental problem of this approach is that complexity characteristics need to be invariant both to the type of a process and to the transformed design artifact. If those characteristics are not invariant, measurement scales tend to lack well-defined units. Consequently the properties of the measurement scale, the labeling of the units, and the interpretation of the values derived are of very limited practical use. Furthermore, in non-deterministic environments, like a design system, such measures are not very reliable, even if proposed. It is therefore important to build a measure which addresses the homogeneity requirement with respect to inputs and outputs and which is invariant to the dynamic characteristics of a process. Such a measure may be based on the integral process utility indicators like for example the ratio of the Earned Value to the Planned Value or to the Actual Cost at a Sign-off Stage. This implies that productivity of a design process may be assessed by the utility asset produced and accumulated by designers in a team. The more utility produced by a designer – the more relatively productive he or she is. Hence, more productive designers are characterized by the higher volume of accumulated Units of Welfare (UoW). It is assumed in PSI modeling framework that designers receive incentives adequately to their produced value. UoW earning and spending mechanisms in PSI are based on contracting deals stricken in several types of negotiations [21].

---

[13] Measuring IC and ASIC Design Productivity. White Paper. Numetrics Management Systems, 5201 Great America Parkway, Suite 320 Santa Clara, CA 95054, 2000.

[14] FP stands for Functional Point, KSLOC – for kilo lines of source code.

5 Towards Performance Measurement and Management Methodology

Krause [18] has analyzed the following weaknesses of the contemporary performance management (PM) approaches pointing to them as to the reasons of dissatisfaction in industry: (i) strategic PM approaches are driven by "lagging" but not "leading" measurement methods; (ii) resulting PM methodologies and systems tend to be static[15]; (iii) there is a significant "abstraction" gap between strategic PM approaches and available knowledge acquisition and representation methodologies; (iv) PM is traditionally based on rigid organizational structuring but not on desired properties of the required business processes; (v) the "metrics" are not transparent, are vague and do not clearly reveal the method of measurement and the sources of data. Our experience suggests adding: (vi) the role of a human designer and his pro-active collaboration in a design team is neglected; (vii) existing frameworks do not allow revealing the "abyssal" reasons for the weaknesses of a design system. Answering "why" questions requires a sort of a paradigmatic shift in modeling and assessing a design system and the design processes performed. In addition to building and measuring high-level heuristic performance indicators we need to acquire and use a deeper knowledge about the processes and their performers to make the assessments more justified. These bits of knowledge should cover engineering design processes and their support by technical, human, and organizational components comprising the aspects of design complexity, designers' competencies and abilities, concurrency and iteration of design tasks, dependencies, interfaces and collaboration effects at required level of detail.

Fig. 3 shows the differences in performance management methodologies. Traditional ones are applied at strategic management level. The Performance Measurement and Management Methodology (PM^3) we develop in PSI and PRODUKTIV+ occupies the niche between business and project management layers. PM^3 uses agent-based design process simulation as its basic method. One of the topical distinctions of PM^3 is that the model of a design system is calibrated before performance assessments are done. Calibration is the adjustment of the model by accounting the specifics of the design system. It is performed in the series of simulations of design processes. Using simulation allows us conducting the following kinds of experiments: (i) performance benchmarking based on the full records of the accomplished design processes; (ii) performance assessment based on the comparative analysis of the ideally simulated process performed by the team of agents and the record of the same process in real life; (iii) performance management based on the incremental simulation and comparison to what happens in the managed real life design process. The latter two modes allow us to understand why a real life process demonstrated worse performance than the corresponding ideal one, to verify if the process is stable with respect to different kinds of disturbing influences by injecting these influences in simulations, and to suggest grounded improvement recommendations for the design system. Evidently, PM^3 and the prototype software tool require a domain model which is much more detailed than a traditional one.

---

[15] ... and linear.

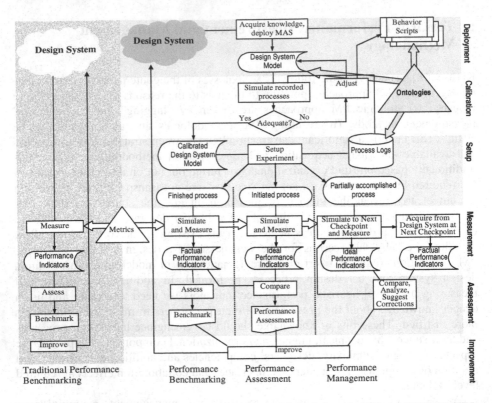

Fig. 3. Performance Measurement and Management Methodology in PSI and PRODUKTIV+ (simplified) compared to traditional frameworks

ontologies [15] play a central role in it. Fig. 3 shows that ontologies are intensively exploited in PM[3]. They provide formal specifications of the domain used in agent behavior scripts, design process records, the specification of a design system.

In order to obtain a qualitative assessment of a design system performance by simulation [19], we use the acquired knowledge and data [20] to represent a design process in a procedural way accounting for a high degree of process dynamics [15].

6 Concluding Remarks

In this paper we expressed our vision of how an engineering methodology may be devised and applied to performance assessment and management in microelectronic engineering design. We stressed that engineering approach is required to make industry satisfied with its performance management methodology. The approach we suggest has to combine the contributions from different disciplines. Knowledge engineering provides a rigorous Domain theory in the form of performance ontology. Distributed artificial intelligence contributes with the agent-based software engineering methodologies and the theoretical foundation for distributed dynamic planning and scheduling. Management science draws the frames for the understanding how the key performance indicators may look like and provides the requirements for an industrial strength performance measurement and management methodology. We also advocate the simulation approach for performance management capable of making predictive analyses of a design system. The weakest spot in the outlined methodology is still performance metrics. It remains one of the main focuses of the ongoing research in PSI and PRODUKTIV+ projects.

References

1. Thorpe, R., Beasley, T.: The characteristics of performance management research – Implications and challenges. Int. J. of Productivity and Performance Management 53(4), 334–344 (2004)
2. Matzke, W.-E.: Engineering Design Performance Management – from Alchemy to Science through ISTa. In: Kachek, R., Mayr, H., Liddle, S. (eds.) Proc. 4th Int. Conf. on Information Systems Technology and its Applications, ISTA 2005, Palmerston North, New Zealand, May 23-25. LNI, vol. 63, pp. 154–179. Gesellschaft für Informatik, Bonn (2005)
3. Kaplan, R.S., Norton, D.P.: The Balanced Scorecard: Measures that Drive Performance. Harvard Business Review, 71–80 (January-Feburary 1992)
4. Sohnius, R., Jentzsch, E., Matzke, W.-E.: Holonic Simulation of a Design System for Performance Analysis. In: Marik, V., Colombo, A.W., Vyatkin, V. (eds.) Proc. 3d Int. Conf. on Industrial Applications of Holonic and Multi-Agent Systems (HoloMAS 2007), September 3-5, Regensburg, Germany (2007)
5. Meyer, M.W., Gupta, V.: The Performance Paradox. In: Cummings, L.L., Staw, B. (eds.) Research in Organizational Behavior, pp. 309–369. JAI Press, Greenwich, Conn. (1994)
6. Baldvinsdottir, G., et al.: The Role of Trust in Accounting Research. In: Proc. 26th Annual Congress of the European Accounting, April 2-4, Seville (2003)
7. Faulk II, L.H.: Pay Satisfaction Consequences: Development and Test of a Theoretical Model. Dissertation, Louisiana State Univ. (2002)
8. Hall, D.: Power Strategy Tool Kit - Part 2: Managing the performance. Learning & Leading with Technology 31(2), 36–41 (2003)
9. Melchert, F., Winter, R.: The Enabling Role of Information Technology for Business Performance Management. In: Meredith, B., Shanks, G., Arnott, D., Carlsson, S. (eds.) Decision Support in an Uncertain and Complex World. Proc. 2004 IFIP Int. Conf. on Decision Support Systems (DSS2004), Prato, Italy, pp. 535–546 (2004)
10. O'Donnell, F.J., Duffy, A.H.B.: Modelling Design Development Performance. Int. J. of Operations & Production Management 22(11), 1198–1221 (2002)
11. Harkema, S.: Reflections on the Consequences of the Application of Complexity Theory for New Pproduct Introductions. In: Frizelle, G., Richards, H. (eds.) Tackling Industrial Complexity: the Ideas that Make a Difference. Papers from the 2nd Int. Conf. of the Manufacturing Complexity Network, April 9-10, 2002, pp. 467–482. U. of Cambridge, UK (2002)
12. Barnhart, R.K. (ed.): Chambers Dictionary of Etymology. Chambers Harrap Publishers Ltd. Edinburgh (1988)
13. Lera, I., Juiz, C., Puigjaner, R.: Performance-Related Ontologies and Semantic Web Applications for On-Line Performance Assessment of Intelligent Systems. Science of Computer Programming 61, 27–37 (2006)

14. Truong, H.-L., Dustdar, S., Fahringer, T.: Performance Metrics and Ontologies for Grid Workows. Technical report TUV-1841-2004-28, Technical University of Vienna, (September 20, 2004)
15. Ermolayev, V., Jentzsch, E., Karsayev, O., Keberle, N., Matzke, W.-E., Samoylov, V., Sohnius, R.: An Agent-Oriented Model of a Dynamic Engineering Design Process. In: Kolp, M., Bresciani, P., Henderson-Sellers, B., Winikoff, M. (eds.) Agent-Oriented Information Systems III. 7th Int. Bi-Conf. W-shop AOIS 2005, Utrecht, Netherlands, July 26, 2005, and Klagenfurt, Austria, October 27, 2005, pp. 168–183 (revised selected papers)(2006)
16. Carlucci, D., Marr, B., Schiuma, G.: The Knowledge Value Chain: How Intellectual Capital Impacts on Business Performance. Int. J. Technology Management 27(6, 7), 575–590 (2004)
17. Collett, R.: Benchmarking IC Development Capability – What to Measure? Fabless Forum. Fabless Semiconductor Association 11(2) (2004)
18. Krause, O.: Beyond BSC: a process based approach to performance management. Measuring Business Excellence 7(3), 4–14 (2003)
19. Gorodetsky, V., Karsayev, O., Konushy, V., Jentzsch, E., Matzke, W.-E., Ermolayev, V.: Multi-agent Software Tool for Management of Design Process in Microelectronics. In: Nishida, T., Klusch, M., Sycara, K., Yokoo, M. (eds.) Proc. IEEE/WIC/ACM Int. Conf. on Intelligent Agent Technology (IAT-06), Hong Kong, December 18-22, 2006, pp. 773–776. ACM Press, New York (2006)
20. Sohnius, R., Ermolayev, V., Jentzsch, E., Keberle, N., Matzke, W.-E., Samoylov, V.: Managing Concurrent Engineering Design Processes and Associated Knowledge. In: Ghodous, P., Dieng-Kuntz, R., Loureiro, G. (eds.) Leading the Web in Concurrent Engineering. Proc. 13th ISPE Int. Conf. on Concurrent Engineering: Research and Applications, Antibes, French Riviera, September 18-22, 2006. Frontiers in AI and Applications, vol. 143, pp. 198–205. IOS Press, Amsterdam (2006)
21. Ermolayev, V., Keberle, N.: A Generic Ontology of Rational Negotiation. In: Karagiannis, D., Mayr, H.C. (eds.) Information Systems Technology and its Applications. 5th Int. Conf. ISTA'2006, Klagenfurt, Austria, May 30-31, 2006. LNI, vol. 84, pp. 51–66. Gesellschaft für Informatik, Bonn (2006)

Ontology-Based Competence Management for Team Configuration

Vladimir Tarasov[1], Thomas Albertsen[1], Alexey Kashevnik[2], Kurt Sandkuhl[1],
Nikolay Shilov[2], and Alexander Smirnov[2]

[1] School of Engineering at Jönköping University, P.O. Box 1026,
55111 Jönköping, Sweden
{Vladimir.Tarasov,Thomas.Albertsen,Kurt.Sandkuhl}@jth.hj.se
[2] St.Petersburg Institute for Informatics and Automation of the RAS, 39, 14 line,
199178 St.Petersburg, Russia
{alexey,nick,smir}@iias.spb.su

Abstract. When manufacturers, distributors and dealers need to collaborate, they form production networks because this provides significant advantages in production variety, flexibility and lead time. Production processes in such networks often spawn different specific tasks that are to be solved by the network members. This requires creation of a team able to tackle the identified problem. When dealing with multiple organizations and multiple processes within a complicated production network, trying to find a member that has required competence can be a laborious, time-consuming process. Developing and maintaining competence profiles of all the relevant parties associated with production can significantly reduce the time. The paper proposes an approach to team configuration based on competence profiles. The approach utilizes such technologies as ontology management, context management and profiling. Using ontological representation makes it possible to identify those team members who are best suited for the task by ontology matching.

Keywords: build-to-order production network, competence management, competence profile, ontology, context.

1 Introduction

Increasing global competition and toughening requirements from customers cause major changes in the world economy. One of the outcomes of these changes is the growing rate of collaboration between manufacturers. This can be explained by the fact that network-like organizations consisting of a large amount of nodes are usually more flexible and robust when compared with hierarchically organized large-scale companies, which is essential for the build-to-order (BTO) strategy.

Although the advantage described above is clear, networked structures raise a number of problems to solve. One of them is configuration of a team that is able to carry out a specific task arisen from a production process. Collaborative design of a product in dispersed groups of engineers is one example of such a task, which may arise in a

V. Mařík, V. Vyatkin, A.W. Colombo (Eds.): HoloMAS 2007, LNAI 4659, pp. 401–410, 2007.

production network. This task creates plenty of challenges, for example knowledge sharing, coordination support or secure tool integration [8].

When dealing with multiple organizations and multiple processes within a complicated production network, trying to find a member that has suitable competence for a required task can be a laborious, time-consuming process. Developing and maintaining a competence management system for all the relevant parties that are potential candidates for such teams can significantly reduce the time. Furthermore, linking such a competence management system to key decision points and frequent problems can further enhance effectiveness of the production network [9]. The proposed approach is to apply ontology engineering to modeling competences of potential team members.

There are a number of technologies, including Web intelligence and business intelligence, which are relevant for the identified situation. *Web intelligence* and *business intelligence* provide for strategies that can enable implementation of the main behavioural principles of a production network. Web intelligence deals with advancement of Web-empowered systems, services, and environments. It considers issues of Web-based knowledge processing and management; distributed inference; information exchange and knowledge sharing [19]. The purpose of business intelligence is an effective support of consumer and business processes. Achieving this goal involves development of services for consumer needs recognition, information search, and evaluation of alternatives [18]. Business intelligence relies on modern information technologies dealing with data and knowledge. Currently, knowledge often referred to as corporate knowledge in the contexts of the business and manufacturing is the key resource in the modern era of information.

As to competence management, a number of research projects have, to a certain extent, used the concept of storing information concerning competence of individuals in a structured form. In the CRAI model, a general approach has been presented for development of competence management systems. The model formalizes the concept of competence and provides guidelines for how a competence management system should be deployed [6]. Another project where competence profiles have been used in order to simplify and speed up the search for fitting candidates and thus to support a more efficient personnel management is described in [2]. In this project at Daimler Chrysler AG, a competence management system was implemented using ontologies and data warehouse technology to be able to compare competence profiles with profiles for staff hiring. This system is used for team staffing for projects, capturing and planning of training requirements and succession planning. An approach to create an ontology for combing the perspectives of competence management and technology enhanced workplace learning is described in [12]. This article describes a general idea of the ontology and discusses how this ontology could be implemented.

The next chapter will introduce the approach to a competence profiles management that could be used for team configuration. Chapter 3 will describe the structure of an enterprise competence profile while the individual competence profile is presented in chapter 4. The conclusion presents a summary and an outlook on future work.

2   Competence Profile Management

It is very important to share and exchange knowledge on available competences in a production network. This should be achieved at both technical and semantic levels.

The interoperability at the technical level is addressed in a number of research efforts that usually employ such approaches as SOA (service-oriented architecture) and standards as WSDL and SOAP. The semantic level interoperability in a production network is also paid significant attention. The most widely known example is probably the Semantic Web initiative aiming at using ontologies for knowledge and terminology description [13].

An approach presented in this paper also relies on the ontological representation for knowledge sharing. The conceptual model of the proposed ontology-based competence management is based on the ideas of knowledge logistics [14] and competence modeling [16] developed earlier. In our approach, ontologies are used to describe competence profiles of enterprises and their employees. As a result it is possible to treat all available knowledge on competencies as one distributed knowledge base.

The architecture of the knowledge management platform is shown in Fig. 1. The system is accessed by the BTO production network stakeholders via the Web-service interface (intended for applications) or via a user interface (intended for humans) when a new team should be configured. The access is done in a certain context describing current scenario and other specific information. Contexts are important because the dynamic nature of the BTO production networks requires considering the current situation in order to provide for actual knowledge or information. The context represents additional information, which helps to identify specifics of the current situation, and defines a narrow domain the user of the competence management platform works with.

Competence profiles for each company together with its specialists are represented as an ontology. Competence profiles are subdivided into enterprise and individual ones and contain such information as the production network member's capabilities and capacities, preferred ways of interaction, skills of staff members, etc. The platform provides an access to competence profiles of the production network members through their ontologies. Provided that competences required from companies or specialists are described as subparts of the BTO ontology, the system can search for potential team members by matching the identified parts to ontologies representing competence profiles.

3 Enterprise Competence Profiles

Competences of a company are described in an enterprise competence profile. These competencies are important for determining which company is capable of carrying out a specified task and, hence, can be chosen as a team member. Company competence is determined by available production facilities and previous experience of carrying out tasks. Fig. 2 depicts a structure of the developed profile for companies in a BTO production network. The enterprise competence profile consists of the following parts: General Information, Specific Information, Activity History, Company Preferences, Detectable Company Preferences, and Feedback.

The *General Information* part describes general information about a company. It contains a name of company, identifier of company in the system, date of the company foundation, and URL to the company web page.

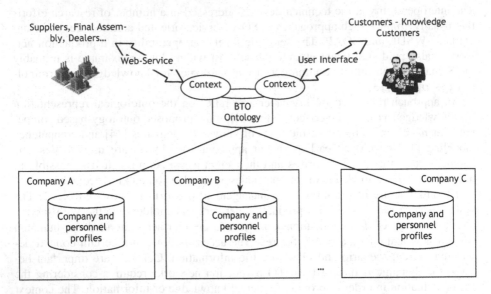

Fig. 1. Conceptual model of competence profiles management

Specific Information is a set of tuples describing information about company facilities. Each tuple contains the following properties:

- Facility ID – an identifier of a facility in the system;
- Facility Name – a name of a facility;
- Location – geographical location of a facility, it can be taken into account for estimating rapidity and quality of request processing in a particular situation;
- Time – time zone of a facility;
- Capabilities – production capabilities of a facility; this property stores several options from a list of all the options for the domain;
- List of Languages – represent languages for contacting a facility;
- Rights – determine knowledge area, which a facility can access, for example a facility that produces 'tires' should not be able to access information about glass production;
- Group – a facility can be part of a group, based on its capabilities;
- Phone Number, E-mail – contact information.

Activity History is also a set of tuples. Each tuple contains the following properties:

- Request – a request to a company, it can be employed for further reuse of sets of solutions to the same or similar requests to the system;
- Set of Solutions, Decision – are used to analyze performance of a company (other companies can see solutions generated in particular situations) and to identify detectable company preferences (via analyzing differences of selected decisions from other offered alternative solutions);

- Company Preferences* – store company preferences at the moment of request initiation. They contain a snapshot of all the properties of the category "Company Preferences";
- Detectable Company Preferences* – store detectable company preferences at the moment of request initiation. They contain a snapshot of all the properties of the category "Detectable Company Preferences";
- Specific Information* – stores specific information about a facility at the moment of request initiation. It contains a snapshot of all the properties of the category "Specific Information".

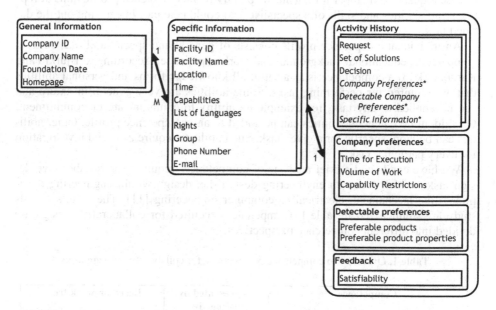

Fig. 2. Enterprise competence profile

The *Company Preferences* part describes company preferences, which can be obtained manually. These preferences are used for choosing a particular company when a set of solutions is generated. They contain company preference for work execution time (e.g. short-term or long-term orders), volume of work (e.g. serial production or mass production), and capability restrictions. The latter stores several capabilities and logical restrictions from a list of all the capabilities for the domain (for example if a company performs operation A, it necessarily performs operation B).

Detectable Company Preferences describe automatically detectable company preferences. These preferences are used for choosing a company when generating a set of solutions for a particular order, e.g., products which the company prefers to produce and their properties.

The last part, *Feedback*, contains information about quality of the company performance – if a company keeps its promises.

Companies can determine themselves which categories of a profile are visible for other companies.

4 Individual Competence Profiles

Although company capabilities are important, real work is done by humans. Therefore it is as important to know competence of the company's human resources in order to choose a qualified member for a team. The individual competence profile aims at representing abilities and skills of a specialist who could take part in carrying out the defined task.

An individual competence profile consists of general and special abilities, cultural competence, educational background, and work experience. According to Bjurklo and Kardemark [3] a competence is as a set of all knowledge forms and personal abilities that are required for performing tasks. Some abilities are very general in nature and can be applied to any task, for example an ability to communicate or commitment. Once identified, general abilities can be added to any competence profile. Other abilities can be more specific for a given task. Such abilities require a special investigation for every particular task.

We have conducted a brief analysis of competences required for collaborative design tasks, which focus on engineering design, i.e. design within engineering disciplines like mechanical, electrical or computer engineering [11]. The results of this study are summarized in table 1. Competences required for collaborative design are divided into different competence perspectives.

Table 1. Overview to competence perspectives for collaborative design tasks

Competence	Represented by perspective	Based on work from
Problem solving competence	General Competences	Bjurklo and Kardemark [3], Pahl and Beitz [10]
Planning and designing competences	General Competences	Bjurklo and Kardemark [3], Pahl and Beitz [10]
Competences in the field of engineering in question	Occupational Competences	FOET-99 [1] and ISCO-88 [7]
Different technical competences in this engineering area	Occupational Competences	FOET-99 [1] and ISCO-88 [7]
Competence for team work and different roles	General Competences	Bjurklo and Kardemark [3], Ullman [17], Grudin [4]
Language competences, competences in integrating different social backgrounds	Cultural Competences	Hammer et al. [5]

We utilize ontologies to represent competence profiles because this method allows for capturing the rich semantics of competence and accommodation of the results obtained in the areas of human resource management and statistics. An individual competence profile is divided into three parts according to the perspective.

The General Competence part includes general competences as proposed by Bjurklo and Kardemark. They represent abilities general in nature and applicable to any task. The more specific abilities, which are needed for performing tasks related to collaborative design, encompass design skills identified in [10] and teamwork abilities pointed out in [4], [17]. This profile part are subdivided into problem solving competences, planning and designing competences, and competences for team work. Each competence is graded against a scale when creating a profile. Team roles competence is also graded according to the experience level of a person acting in this role. An example of an individual competence profile showing some abilities of the general competence part is given in Fig. 3. This profile was created during modeling of a software design team [15].

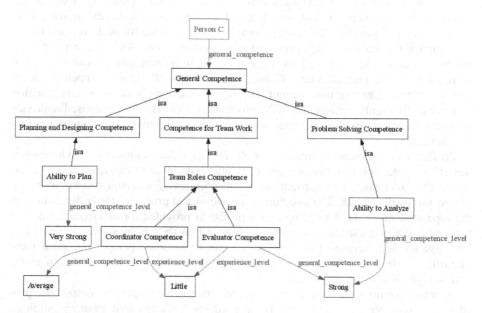

Fig. 3. Relations between some concepts of the general competence part of person C's profile

The Cultural Competence part considers cultural competences, which are described based on intercultural sensitivity. Hammer et al. [5] describe the concept of intercultural sensitivity, which shows how people can perceive cultural differences and act in multicultural environments. The intercultural sensitivity is subdivided into ethnocentric orientations – denial, defense (reversal), minimization, and ethnorelative ones – acceptance, adaptation, integration. As soon as geographically distributed design groups may include people from different cultural backgrounds, this profile part also contains language competence. It includes languages, spoken by a person, which can be related to a language level ranging from a beginner to a native speaker.

The Occupational Competence part shows what knowledge and skills the person has acquired during his/her work and education. These skills reflect competences in the field of expertise in question and different technical competences in this area. This profile part is based on statistical classifications: the Classification of fields of education and training, 1999 (FOET 1999), [1] and International Standard Classification of Occupations, 1988 (ISCO-88) [7]. FOET 1999 is used to represent educational areas studied by an individual and relevant for engineering design. Each detailed field of education or program/subject is related to appropriate educational levels and countries where the education took place. The person's present and past jobs are represented with the occupational groups from ISCO-88.

5 Conclusions

The paper proposes an approach to building a competence management platform that could be used for team configuration. It is based on the ontological knowledge representation for knowledge sharing, profiling and also incorporates context management. Competence profiles describe network members and provide for such information as their capabilities and capacities, preferred ways of interaction, skills of specialists, etc. When a team should be created for a given task, competence profiles can be used to search for suitable team members. Context management allows the competence management platform to take into account specific information about the current situation that is usually highly dynamic for BTO production networks. The proposed approach provides for an easier more accurate way of team configuration in complex production networks.

Profiles can represent enterprise as well as indi vidual competences. The former describes production facilities of a company and experience of carrying out particular tasks. The latter takes into account skills and abilities of a person that could be required for a defined task. The structure of an individual profile is partly dependant on the type of work to do. An example of a profile is provided for collaborative design tasks in engineering fields. This example is based on the findings from an empirical investigation and literature from CSCW. The most important competence areas were identified starting from the nature of design work, problem solving in design teams and working in distributed groups.

As soon as ontologies are used as the representation technique for competence profiles, it is possible to identify potential candidates for a required team by ontology matching[1]. Once competence profiles describing potential team members are created, one can compare their profiles to a specific production task represented by parts of the BTO ontology. Research into different ontology matching techniques enabling team configuration by using ontology-based profiles is one of the next logical steps in our future work.

Acknowledgments. Cooperation between SPIIRAS and Jönköping University was supported by the Swedish Foundation for International Cooperation in Research and Higher Education under grant # IG2003-2040. Part of this research has been done in the project "ICT for the formation of business relationships with developing countries" funded by Swedish International Development Agency within the SPIDER program, 2004 - 2006. Other parts have been carried out in the Integrated Project

---

[1] Here, by ontology matching, we rather mean matching of different subparts of the same ontology.

FP6-IST-NMP 507592-2 "Intelligent Logistics for Innovative Product Technologies" sponsored by European Commission, projects funded by grants # 05-01-00151 and # 06-07-89242 of the Russian Foundation for Basic Research, projects # 16.2.35 of the research program "Mathematical Modelling and Intelligent Systems", # 1.9 of the research program "Fundamental Basics of Information Technologies and Computer Systems" of the Russian Academy of Sciences (RAS), as well as projects of the scientific program of St. Petersburg Scientific Center of RAS, and of the Science and High School Committee of St. Petersburg Government.

References

1. Andersson, R., Olsson, A.-K.: Fields of Education and Training. Manual (1999), http://europa.eu.int/comm/eurostat/ramon/nomenclatures/index.cfm?TargetUrl=LST_NOM
2. Biesalski, E., Abecker, A.: Similarity Measures for Skill-Profile Matching in Enterprise Knowledge Management. In: 8th International Conference on Enterprise Information Systems (ICEIS), Paphos - Cyprus May 2006, pp. 23–27 (2006)
3. Bjurklo, M., Kardemark, G.: Social tests in a model for controlling the enhancement of competence. Journal of Human Resource Costing and Accounting 3(2), 51–64 (1998)
4. Grudin, J.: Computer-Supported Cooperative Work: History and Focus. IEEE Computer, Los Alamitos (May 1994)
5. Hammer, M.R., Bennett, M.J., Wiseman, R.: Measuring intercultural sensitivity: The intercultural development inventory. International Journal of Intercultural Relations 27(4), 421–443 (2003)
6. Harazallah, M., Biero, G., Vernadat, F.: Analysis and Modeling of Individual Competencies: Toward Better Management of Human Resources. IEEE Transactions on Systems, Man, and Cybernetics-Part A: Systems and Humans 36(1), 187–207 (2006)
7. International Labour Organization. International Standard Classification of Occupations, 1988 (ISCO-88) (2004),
   http://www.ilo.org/public/english/bureau/stat/isco/isco88/index.htm
8. Jacucci, G., Pawlak, A., Sandkuhl, K. (eds.): The Knowledge Perspective in Industrial Collaborative Engineering. 3 Intl. Workshop on Collaborative Engineering. Sopron, Hungary (2005)
9. Lesser, I., Butner, K.: Knowledge and the Supply Chain. Inside Supply Management 16(4), 12 (2005)
10. Pahl, G., Beitz, W.: Engineering Design: A Systematic Approach. Springer, London (1996)
11. Sandkuhl, K., Lundqvist, M., Tarassov, V.: Competence Model for Collaborative Design. In: Proceedings of the 4 Intl. Workshop on Collaborative Engineering, Prague, Czech Republic (2006)
12. Scmidt, A., Kunzmann, C.: Towards a Human Resource Development Ontology for Combining Competence Management and Technology-Enhanced Workplace Learning. In: Meersman, R., Tari, Z., Herrero, P. (eds.) On the Move to Meaningful Internet Systems 2006: OTM 2006 Workshops. LNCS, vol. 4278, pp. 1078–1087. Springer, Heidelberg (2006)
13. Semantic Web (2006), Web site http://www.semanticweb.org
14. Smirnov, A., Pashkin, M., Chilov, N., Levashova, T.: Knowledge Logistics in Information Grid Environment (The special issue in Zhuge, H. (ed.) Semantic Grid and Knowledge Grid: The Next-Generation Web). International Journal on Future Generation Computer Systems 20(1), 61–79 (2004)

15. Tarasov, V., Lundqvist, M.: Modelling Collaborative Design Competence with Ontologies. International Journal of e-Collaboration (to appear, 2007)
16. Tarassov, V., Sandkuhl, K., Henoch, B.: Using ontologies for representation of individual and enterprise competence models. In: Proceedings of the Fourth IEEE International Conference on Computer Sciences Research, Innovation and Vision for the Future, RIVF 2006, Ho-Chi-Minh City, Vietnam, pp. 205–212 (2006)
17. Ullman, D.G.: The Mechanical Design Process. McGraw-Hill Book Co., Singapore (1997)
18. Vrechopoulos, A.P., Pramataris, K.C., Doukidis, G.I.: Utilizing information processing for enhancing value: towards a model for supporting business and consumers within an Internet retailing environment. In: Proceedings of 12th International Bled Electronic Commerce Conference, Bled, Slovenia (1999)
19. Zhong, N., Liu, J., Yao, Y.: In Search of the Wisdom Web. Computer 35, 27–31 (2002)

Information Agents Handling Semantic Data as an Extension to Process Monitoring Systems

Teppo Pirttioja[1], Ilkka Seilonen[2], Antti Pakonen[3], Aarne Halme[1], and Kari Koskinen[2]

[1] Helsinki University of Technology, Automation Technology Laboratory,
P.O. Box 5500, 02015 TKK, Espoo, Finland
{teppo.pirttioja,aarne.halme}@tkk.fi
[2] Helsinki University of Technology, Computer and Information Systems in Automation,
P.O. Box 5500, 02015 TKK, Espoo, Finland
{ilkka.seilonen, kari.o.koskinen}@tkk.fi
[3] VTT Technical Research Centre of Finland
P.O. Box 1000, 02044 VTT, Espoo, Finland
antti.pakonen@vtt.fi

Abstract. An approach to extend process monitoring with the help of information agents (IA) handling semantic data is presented in this paper. According to this approach, an operator of a process automation system can configure monitoring tasks that a group of IAs performs proactively. The monitoring tasks are assumed to be composites which refer to several process observations and their logical relations. The purpose of these composite monitoring tasks is to enhance the work of the operator by letting him to supervise process phenomena at a higher level of abstraction instead of following a large amount of simple measurement data. The monitoring agents operate as a multi-agent system consisting of agents with capabilities to combine both numerical and symbolic information from several data sources. The agents can setup and execute user configured monitoring tasks cooperatively. The approach is illustrated with test scenarios using data from an industrial paper making process.

Keywords: Process monitoring, information agents, semantic data.

1 Introduction

This paper is motivated by the increasing requirements of the work of process operators and possible solutions to these requirements with the help of new information technology. The volume of measurement data from controlled processes has increased which makes the monitoring task harder. Same time the need for cost reduction requires better monitoring performance. The monitoring work might be supported better by raising the abstraction level of the monitoring tasks implemented in automation systems [15]. The monitoring tasks could have a larger scope, i.e. refer to measurement and other related data in various separate systems, and more versatile monitoring logic, i.e. handling of logical relations between various observations.

V. Mařík, V. Vyatkin, A.W. Colombo (Eds.): HoloMAS 2007, LNAI 4659, pp. 411–420, 2007.
© Springer-Verlag Berlin Heidelberg 2007

The purpose of this paper is to present an approach for extending process monitoring systems with agents handling semantic data. The aim of the approach is to facilitate automation of some monitoring tasks, which require combination of numerical measurement data with symbolic information about the controlled process. IAs based on the BDI-agent model [1], [4], [18] and utilization of semantic data models [4], [6] are proposed as a suitable implementation method for extended monitoring functionality. The BDI-agent model is used for modeling and executing the application logic of the extended monitoring tasks configured by the operator. Semantic data models are used for modeling symbolic information about the process and its state. Combination of symbolic data with numerical monitoring data is expected to provide better information for the operator about the state of the monitored process. This paper presents an overview of the whole of the approach. Details of the approach have been described in other publications [14], [16], [17], [19].

The paper is outlined as follows. Chapter 2 will discuss process monitoring and the possible role of semantic data and IAs as its extensions. A specification of an extension to a process monitoring system utilizing the mentioned techniques is presented in Chapter 3. Illustrating demonstrations are described in Chapter 4 followed by conclusions in Chapter 5.

2 Process Monitoring, Semantic Data and Information Agents

2.1 Process Monitoring

Monitoring the production process is one of the main tasks of process operators together with pre-planned control operations and disturbance control. The objective of monitoring is to evaluate if the process is behaving according to its objectives and detect possible deviations as early as possible. The requirements of this work have become harder in recent years due to ever increasing demands of cost reductions.

The main sub-tasks of process monitoring include selection of observed data, interpretation of results and decision-making about the need to act [15]. An important difficulty in data interpretation is the complex relationships between various phenomena in the process. Some deviations are difficult to observe and can only be noticed via inferences combining several information sources. The operators have expertise for performing these tasks. However, the large amount and low abstraction level of measurement data combined with limited human perception makes monitoring an error-prone task.

Process monitoring systems could be developed with capabilities to assist the data selection and interpretation sub-tasks of monitoring through so-called indirect management [9]. An essential idea in this approach is let the operator to configure a part of his expertise to the monitoring system and automate it. The data selection sub-task could be partly automated according to user defined rules which reflect his understanding of the expected behavior of the process. The low abstraction level of measurement data could partly be raised through creation of symbolic data from it [20]. However, this functionality needs to be designed carefully so that the user can trust it and the application can be maintained. It is also necessary to integrate it with existing monitoring systems.

2.2 Semantic Data in Monitoring

Semantic data models, e.g. ontologies represented with OWL [13] provide a mechanism to represent symbolic information that may be expected to be useful also in process monitoring. Semantic data can represent additional information about the process (e.g. about structure of the process, control activities, etc.) and offer a more abstract to view to observations detected from numerical measurement data.

The data handled in monitoring can be classified to three groups: numerical measurement data, symbolic data about the process and metadata about the services providing the data. Creation of symbolic data from numerical one can be useful when trying to interpret measurements [3]. Again, combination of both numerical and symbolic inferences may be useful in solving of complex problems [5]. Symbolic modeling of lower-level monitoring services can enable composition of higher-level monitoring functions [11].

Development of indirect management type of monitoring functions is likely to require combination of all the previously mentioned types of data. In situation interpretation sub-task of monitoring symbolic data inferred from numerical measurements is likely to be useful when creating an overview of a situation. While planning of data selection for monitoring symbolic information about the structure and behavior of the process and available data services could be used in order to ensure the scope and precision of observations.

2.3 Information Agents in Monitoring

IAs are a particular type of multi-agent systems whose purpose is to assist human users in accessing data that they need in their activities. IAs are expected to reduce the information overload that some users are facing [10]. They are expected to do this by proactively working for the interests of their users.

The functions of IAs in assisting their users have been proposed to include e.g. planning of information access operations and interpreting intermediate results. Eventually IAs could compose an answer to a query through a distributed problem-solving process [12]. Combination of BDI-agent model and ontologies has been proposed as one suitable implementation technique for IAs [4]. In monitoring IAs have been proposed to be applied to several functions, e.g. communication of process events to operators [2] and flexible definition of alarm conditions [9].

The properties of IAs seem to match at least partially the requirements of process monitoring. The operators need assistance in order to cope with the increased amount of monitoring information. Proactive operation of IAs could be useful for this purpose. However, in order to implement IAs for monitoring suitable methods for representing process data and handling it in IAs need to be designed. BDI-agent model and integration of ontologies with numerical data could be useful starting points for a design.

3 Information Agents Based Monitoring

3.1 System Overview

In this study the purpose of the IAs in assisting process monitoring is to improve the monitoring functionality available to operators through user-configurable extended monitoring tasks with higher abstraction level. An operator configures extended monitoring tasks according to his expertise and the IAs proactively run them and provide the user with abstracted feedback leaving out unnecessary details [16], [17].

The IAs operate as an extension to existing automation and information systems at a process plant as illustrated in Fig. 1. The information agents are intermediate agents that operate between the user interface and lower-level monitoring functions and other data sources. The operation of the IAs include conversation with the human user, composition of the extended monitoring tasks from the lower-level monitoring services and possibly cooperation with other IAs.

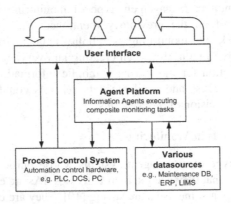

Fig. 1. Architecture of a process monitoring system extended with IAs

In order to be able to perform their tasks, the IAs are designed according to the BDI-agent model [1], [9], [18] as illustrated in Fig. 2. Data access and composition modules enable receiving and combination of data from several data sources. With further levels of data processing modules it is possible to create symbolic data from numerical one and make inferences from the received, combined and created data. The user configured monitoring tasks are represented as plans which are run parallelly by the BDI-interpreter. The plan execution is guided by goals, which represent the monitoring objectives configured to the monitoring tasks by the operator. The goal-oriented operation scheme is expected to select the focus of the monitoring tasks according to the intentions of the operator.

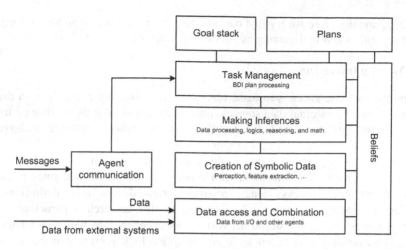

Fig. 2. Architecture of an IA

3.2 Data Access and Combination

The purpose of data access and combination is to collect data from separate external data sources and transform it into a suitable symbolic form for the monitoring tasks of the IA. This functionality is aimed for fulfilling the so-called location transparency requirement of information access in monitoring. For those data sources that naturally produce symbolic events, e.g., maintenance database and electronic diary for operator notes, there is still need to convert data to unite syntax and semantics. Ontologies representing the structure, events and behavior of the monitored process can be used for this purpose. A more detailed description of the data access and combination functionality is available in [14].

3.3 Creation of Symbolic Data

The purpose of creation of symbolic data is to transform a part of the numerical information, e.g., perceptions from physical world, into a symbolic form so that the monitoring tasks can combine it with other symbolic data and make inferences from it. This functionality is aimed for fulfilling the so-called format transparency requirement of information access in monitoring. The use of symbolic data is expected to make inferences less sensitive to noise which is always present in time-series data. Furthermore, symbolic and semantically meaningful data is needed to effectively integrate the whole production enterprise and it also might be produced by lower level devices in the future [7].

There are numerous ways to create symbolic data from the sensed inputs, e.g. using data mining, classification, and rule discovery techniques [3], and recently wavelets have been demonstrated to be effective in producing meaningful symbolic information [8]. Although there has been a great deal of research about methodologies of creating symbolic information, implementations to real life are not so numerous. This might be mainly because complex analyzing algorithms are too laborious to maintain, and therefore we try find out how to generate enough symbolic information requiring still as less maintaining as possible to keep the approach feasible.

3.4 Making Inferences

The purpose of inferences is to make observations, which are not evident in the data received from the external data sources, but which an operator would deduce from it. This functionality is aimed for fulfilling the so-called existence transparency requirement of information access in monitoring.

There are many possible ways in which useful new information can be produces from the data available from monitored process, e.g. user defined rules presenting relations between process values, relations from device type definitions, and correlations that data mining tools discover. In this research a particular type of making inferences, i.e. constraint networks, was experimented with (see Chapter 4.3 and [19] for details). Constraints are used to express logical criteria on the acceptable state of the process as configured by the user. The conditions can refer to any data available to the IAs. The IAs automate the consistency checking of the constraints. The constraints are expected to provide a relatively easily configurable method for expressing a part of operator's knowledge which he applies during monitoring.

3.5 Task Management

The purpose of task management is let users configure their monitoring tasks, run the tasks parallelly and provide them with necessary feedback through a suitable conversation. This functionality is aimed for fulfilling the requirement of flexibility in monitoring.

The task management can be designed according to the BDI-agent model in which the interpreter runs several extended monitoring tasks parallelly. The tasks are user configured combinations of data access and combination, symbolic data creation and inference making operations. The execution of the monitoring tasks is managed according to the goals they are fulfilling. It is expected that this kind of a control structure enables IAs to focus their attention to those monitoring tasks that are most relevant to the user taking into account the process state as described in the available data. More comprehensive descriptions of the task management functionality are in [16], [17].

4 Demonstrations

4.1 Monitoring of Maintenance Events

The first test scenario demonstrates the data access and combination capabilities of an IA [16]. Currently factories have various heterogeneous data sources containing important information about operational issues of a process. Especially, maintenance operations may dramatically change the functionality of the process, but as maintenance events are rather rare operators do not bother login to a separate system for checking them. Fig. 3 illustrates our first demonstration where an IA seeks maintenance events from a specified time period and uses a semantic plant model to link events to the corresponding time-series data.

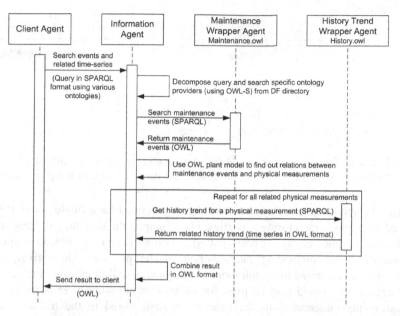

Fig. 3. Example where an IA decomposes a multi-ontology query into two sub-queries that *Wrapper Agents* (capable of answering to a single ontology query) are capable of answering. About SPARQL see [21].

Background for this scenario is that maintenance personnel registers maintenance operations to certain physical devices (address space relates to devices) and operators work with process measurements (control loop related address space) and there is no direct relation between these two. It is valuable for the user that an IA checks if there are registered maintenance events and links them to the corresponding time-series values using a semantic plant model. In short, the plant model used here expresses that maintained devices have some kind of relation to physical process quantities which again relate to process measurements.

4.2 Monitoring of Process Fluctuations

The second test scenario demonstrates the operation of one possible symbolic data creation capability of an IA. Within the normal operation of a specific process area it is desired that physical quantities are steady and near their normal operation points. Fluctuation from this steady state may be judged to be undesirable, and it would be beneficial for the operator to get information about the change events that happen in the process quantities.

With statistical methods it is possible to quite robustly detect change events from time series data, even when there is not so much a priori information about the characterization of the measured value. Figure 4 shows an example of real measurements where *change events* (level changes in this case) are detected with statistical methods.

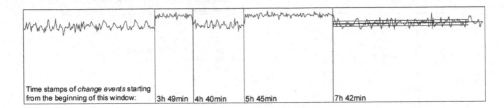

<table>
<tbody>
<tr><td>Time stamps of change events starting
from the beginning of this window:</td><td>3h 49min</td><td>4h 40min</td><td>5h 45min</td><td>7h 42min</td></tr>
</tbody>
</table>

Fig. 4. Example of an IA using statistical signal processing to generate symbolic *change event* information (vertical lines in the figure) for time-series data measured from a physical process

After the symbolic change events have been generated for a single value, they may be used for various monitoring activities. For example, the user may request an IA to watch over some change event pattern within numerous physical quantities representing some interesting phenomenon in the process. Alternatively change events may be registered to launch more thorough temporal monitoring tasks.

Change events could also be used for navigation aid when user is trying to find interesting phenomenon from the time-series data stored in the history database. Currently, most history databases offer time or stored values as basis for navigation. If symbolic change events would also be available for navigation, user could jump to next or previous change event stored in the system. Depending on the characteristics of a process quantity this could be a useful shortcut to bypass steady, and usually not so interesting, time periods.

4.3 Monitoring of Measurement Consistency

The third test scenario demonstrates the inference and task management capabilities of an IA [19]. The test scenario concerns about the pH control in bleaching of mechanical pulp in a paper mill. The operator of the process has rules of thumb about the acceptable values of process measurements. Deviations may indicate malfunctions of pH sensors.

The operator configures the extended monitoring task by defining a set of constraints describing his monitoring logic, e.g. the flow of sodium hydroxide must be greater than the flow of sulphur dioxide (see [19] for details). The task definition is passed to an IA which identifies the needed data sources, sets up communication with them and builds data structures needed for checking the constraints (see Fig. 5). The communication and inferences of the task are activated by the BDI-interpreter of the IA when needed. Feedback is provided to the user if the constraints are not satisfied.

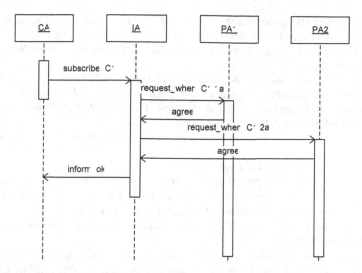

Fig. 5. Part of the operation in the pH monitoring test scenario in which an IA decomposes an user configured constraint (C1) to two simpler constraints (C1.1a and C1.2a)

5 Conclusions

In this paper an approach for extending process monitoring systems with IAs handling semantic data has been presented. The approach proposes the so-called BDI-model combined with processing of semantic data as a suitable implementation model for the extended process monitoring functions. It is stated that the BDI-model would be able to help gaining the flexibility and configurability that is needed in future monitoring applications. The approach has been illustrated with test scenarios using data from an industrial paper making process. The presented approach can be seen as a start for extended monitoring applications but more research remains to be done. Maybe one of the most crucial aspects for the future is the trust issue, i.e. how you can trust an autonomous system monitoring your plant.

In the future, the creation and utilization of symbolic data needs to be studied more thorough, e.g., detecting event patterns, producing better data combination and inferences. Novel studies are needed to show that we can produce useful results also with a limited set of symbolic data available in real world situations.

References

1. Bratman, M.E., Israel, D.J., Pollack, M.E.: Plans and Resource Bounded Practical Reasoning. Computational Intelligence 4, 349–355 (1988)
2. Bunch, L., Breedy, M., Bradshaw, J.M., Carvalho, M., Suri, N., Uszok, A., Hansen, J., Pechoucek, M., Marik, V.: Software Agents for Process Monitoring and Notification. In: ACM Symposium on Applied Computing, pp. 94–99 (2004)
3. Daw, C.S., Finney, C.E.A., Tracy, E.R.: A review of symbolic analysis of experimental data. Review of Scientific Instruments 74(2), 915–930 (2003)

4. Dickinson, I.: BDI Agents and the Semantic Web: Developing User-Facing Autonomous Applications. Doctoral thesis, University of Liverpool, England (2006)
5. Goonatilake, S., Khebbal, S. (eds.): Intelligent Hybrid Systems. John Wiley & Sons, Chichester (1995)
6. Grigoris, A., Van Harmelen, F.A: Semantic Web Primer. MIT Press, Cambridge (2004)
7. Kalogeras, A., Gialellis, J., Alexacos, C., Georgoudakis, M., Koubias, S.: Vertical Integration of Enterprise Industrial Systems Utilizing Web Services. IEEE Trans. Industrial Informatics 2(2), 120–128 (2006)
8. TKhatkhate, A., Ray, A., Keller, E., Gupta, S., Chin, S.C.: Symbolic time-series analysis for anomaly detection in mechanical systems. IEEE/ASME Transactions on Mechatronics 11(4), 439–447 (2006)
9. Koskinen, T., Nieminen, M., Paunonen, H., Oksanen, J.: The Framework for Indirect Management Features of Process Control User Interfaces. In: 10th International Conference on Human - Computer Interaction, Crete, Greece (2003)
10. Maes, P.: Agents that Reduce Work and Information Overload. Communications of the ACM 37, 30–40 (1994)
11. Misono, S., Koide, S., Shimada, N., Kawamura, M., Nagano, S.: Distributed Collaboraitve Decision Support System for Rocket Launch Operation. In: IEEE/ASME International Conference on Advanced Mechatronics, Monterey, California, USA, IEEE Computer Society Press, Los Alamitos (2005)
12. Oates, T., Nagendra Prasad, M.V., Lesser, V.R.: Cooperative Information-Gathering: A Distributed Problem-Solving Approach. IEEE Proceedings on Software Engineering, Special Issue on Agent-based Systems 144, 72–88 (1997)
13. OWL Web Ontology Language: W3C Recommendation, http://www.w3.org/TR/olw-ref/
14. Pakonen, A., Tommila, T., Pirttioja, T., Seilonen, I.: OWL Based Information Agent Services for Process Monitoring. In: 12th IEEE International Conference on Emerging Technologies and Factory Automation (ETFA 2007), Patras, Greece, IEEE Computer Society Press, Los Alamitos (submitted, 2007)
15. Paunonen, H.: Roles of Informating Process Control Systems. Tampere University of Technology, Tampere, Finland (1997)
16. Pirttioja, T., Pakonen, A., Seilonen, I., Halme, A., Koskinen, K.: Multi-Agent Based Information Access Services for Condition Monitoring in Process Automation. In: 3rd IEEE International Conference on Industrial Informatics (INDIN 2005), Perth, Australia (2005)
17. Pirttioja, T., Halme, A., Seilonen, I., Koskinen, K., Pakonen, A.: Multi-Agent System Enhanced Supersision of Process Automation. In: IEEE 2006 Workshop on Distributed Intelligent Applications, Prague, Czech Republic, IEEE Computer Society Press, Los Alamitos (2006)
18. Rao, A.O., Georgeff, M.P.: BDI Agents: From Theory to Practice, Technical Note 56, Australian Artificial Intelligence Institute, Melbourne, Australia (1995)
19. Seilonen, I., Pirttioja, T., Pakonen, A., Halme, A., Koskinen, K.: Indirect Process Monitoring with Constraint Handling Agents. In: 4th International IEEE Conference on Industrial Informatics (INDIN 2006), Singapore (2006)
20. Seppälä, J., Salmenperä, M.: Intelligent Visualisation of Pocess State Using Service Oriented Architecture. In: 16th IFAC World Congress, July 4th - 8th, 2005, Czech Republic (2005)
21. SPARQL Query Language for RDF: W3C Working Draft http://www.w3.org/TR/rdf-sparql-query/

Applications of Virtual Reality in Design and Simulation of Holonic Manufacturing Systems: A Demonstration in Die-Casting Industry

Mert Bal and Majid Hashemipour

Department of Mechanical Engineering, Eastern Mediterranean University, T.R.N.C., via.
Mersin 10, Turkey
{mert.bal,majid.hashemipour}@emu.edu.tr

Abstract. This paper presents the concepts and the techniques of implementation of Virtual Reality (VR) - based simulations into the design of the Holonic Manufacturing Systems. An integrated methodology is presented, which has been developed for modelling and simulations of a manufacturing system with holonic control with the aid of VR. The main focus is given to the implementation in small and medium size enterprises (SMEs) using limited expertise and minimum costs. To demonstrate the effectiveness of the presented method, an application in a medium-sized die-casting factory is presented. The overall performance of the factory has been tested for implementation of a robot-arm integrated die casting cell with holonic control architecture. In this regard, the best course of action for enterprise's investment decisions has been investigated with the least disruption to existing production activities.

Keywords: Virtual Reality, Holonic Manufacturing, 3-D Modelling, Simulation.

1 Introduction

The small and medium size manufacturing industry is entering a phase of change which is being spurred by the quality and cost demands of the end-user. Modern manufacturing systems must have sufficient responsiveness in order to efficiently adapt their behaviours to a wide range of circumstances [1].

Several technologies have been developed for realization of the agility in manufacturing enterprises. These include; Flexible Manufacturing Systems (FMS) and Computer Integrated Manufacturing (CIM) systems, which consist of various programmable manufacturing hardware and information system components. They have been useful in improving manufacturing design and cooperation, supporting changes in the production schedules, various manufacturing and assembly operations, enhancing product service and repair.

However, many conventional CIM systems suffer from the limitations of scalability, robustness and re-configurability because of the centralized control. It is often difficult for some of these systems to cope with different information, expertise and decision-making in the increasingly competitive global market due to their traditional centralized control architectures [2].

V. Mařík, V. Vyatkin, A.W. Colombo (Eds.): HoloMAS 2007, LNAI 4659, pp. 421–432, 2007.

Hence the researches apply methods in order to be able to implement evolution in manufacturing control systems. One such method is Holonic Manufacturing System (HMS), as a new intelligent manufacturing paradigm, to organize manufacturing activities in decentralized control architecture and meet the agile, scalable and fault tolerant requirements. The HMS overcomes many difficulties faced by existing conventional, rigid CIM systems [3].

On the other hand, the design of such highly automated manufacturing systems with suitable control architectures require high expertise, and careful decisions in order to ensure that the system will successfully satisfy the demands of an ever-changing market. One promising approach is 'digital factory' / 'virtual production' for designing automated manufacturing systems with the objective of reducing time and costs [4].

The Virtual Reality (VR), providing a digital environment with the sense of reality and an impression of 'being there', has been increasingly employed in various applications of design and manufacturing. The VR-based simulations provide company managers and system analysts with an environment to understand the implementation and solve problems in manufacturing applications before being employed in practical manufacturing, thereby, preventing costly mistakes [5].

Under this framework, various VR-based modelling and simulation tools have been developed [6]. They are a highly valuable support to manufacturing enterprises in design and simulations of machine systems, robotic work cells, design of factories [7, 8], process planning [5, 9], facility layout planning [10] and information requirements analysis [11].

In addition, several commercial software packages such as, VisFactory™, DELMIA™ has been developed for the use of VR in manufacturing applications. DELMIA package provides authoring applications such as QUEST™, that provide platforms to develop and create virtual manufacturing environment to address the various aspects of manufacturing discrete-event simulation [12].

Most of these tools are dedicated to manufacturing systems with rigid, conventional centralized control architectures. However, it should be recognized that, the VR has a great potential in modelling and simulations of the de-centralized manufacturing control architectures, such as HMS.

A number of researchers realize the importance of this concept and have engaged in developing methods of graphical modelling and simulation of HMSs, though, based on the VR technology, which offers great advantages to visualization and simulation of manufacturing systems, quite few real industrial applications have been reported in the literature [13].

The objective of this paper is to present a methodology and an industrial framework for VR-based modelling and simulations for use in a wide range of manufacturing industry. The model presented here makes use of VR simulations in combination with the modelling techniques of decentralized manufacturing control architecture based on Multi-Agent Systems (MAS) for capturing the design requirements of HMSs.

A prototype tool has been developed and presented with a case study, which has been performed in a firm in die-casting industry. For this study, a model of an automated die-casting cell with holonic control architecture has been generated and simulated for various operating conditions. The overall system has been investigated with the aim of maximizing the performance of the enterprise.

2 Modelling and Simulation of Holonic Manufacturing Systems

The design and implementation of HMS for the real industrial applications require risky, careful decisions to ensure that the highly automated manufacturing system will successfully satisfy the demands of an ever-changing market. The behaviour of a HMS is not deterministic. Yet the direct experimental testing of it with the physical manufacturing/control environment being involved is not only extremely expensive, but non-realistic as well [14]. Hence, the companies need methods and tools for modelling and simulation of such complicated systems in a quick, cost-effective, error and risk free way [15].

There are various simulation methods and tools available for design and analysis of HMS. Some of them are state of art in modelling the MAS in addition to simulation of manufacturing systems with HMS control architecture, while some of them are commercial tools in graphical visualizations of the factories and complex manufacturing systems. Generally, commercial software packages require long trained experts for operations and the high purchase costs, which are not affordable by SMEs [16].

The HMS consortium developed an interactive, visual simulation tool of a Holonic material flow. The tool targets an automated workshop production, where the material flow is carried out by Automated Guided Vehicles (AGVs) [3]. As result of the research effort under the Intelligent Manufacturing Systems (IMS) framework Rockwell Automation in cooperation with different partners has designed and developed MAST (Manufacturing Agent Simulation Tool) a graphical visualization tool for multi agent systems. The main target is the materials handling domain and it is built on the JADE standard FIPA platform. In MAST, the user is provided with the agents for basic material handling components as for instance manufacturing-cell, conveyor belt, diverter and AGVs. The agents cooperate together via message sending using common knowledge ontology developed for material handling domain.

MAST represents the state of the art in graphical simulation tools for modelling and simulation of multi agent systems in manufacturing control, however and due to the fact that only material handling systems are targeted the tool does not cover complex application from a 3-D geometric viewpoint such as the robotic manipulation [17, 18].

2.1 Virtual Reality in the Design and Simulation of HMSs

By definition, the VR is referred to as a knowledge and computer-based system that integrates the real world activities with 3-D virtual models and simulations. The VR technology provides a sense of reality, which is considerably useful in representing the manufacturing activities as the user and the information support elements are put in direct relation with the operation of the system in a realistic environment [19].

In the manufacturing domain, by simulating the production in 'virtual world', multiple products and complex shop floor system designs can be evaluated before investing in a costly prototype. Hence this leads to the development of production facilities and processes in a much faster, more efficient, cost effective and error free way [20].

There is great potential in applying the 'interactive' VR technology to help developing applications of HMS for complex and costly implementations of industrial automation [21]. Although these applications can also be simulated in conventional discrete event simulators, it is not possible to visualize the true meanings of the outcomes and their implications on the shop floor operations. Although looking closer to being real, animated simulation is symbolic and hence is not capable of allowing users to interface with the modelled physical world as accurately as VR [22].

Manufacturing systems modellers often encounter difficulties in transforming the real world's multidimensional, visual and dynamic characteristics into the one dimensional, textual and static representation required by traditional languages [16]. Specifically, they lack the modelling capability of the user's complex reaction resulting from her perceptions built upon the real-time information supplied.

The structured analysis diagrams tend to become complex and difficult to understand by those other than the original creator of the diagram. Most users find the diagrams too abstract to understand easily the system under analysis. VR constitutes an effective communication means since it is constructed by the images that resemble their real correspondents and it executes motion elements taken from reality. Even the line personnel can participate in its construction. The relevant information can be gathered at an early stage, resulting in the early detection of any inconsistency, thus reducing the complexity of data communication for the development of HMSs.

The VR-based methodology and the system model proposed in this paper, takes into account the simulation of holonic control by VR, where all controlled operational behaviour of manufacturing are visualized in a 3D environment, with the aim of enhancing the design process of HMS.

3 Proposed System Framework

The HMS design and simulation methodology presented in this paper, takes into account the identification, implementation of holonic control, within virtually modelled real manufacturing systems. A desktop VR system allows the users to interact intuitively with the virtual environment and its objects, as if they were real, by immersing them in a realistic 3-D environment.

The proposed approach looks to exploit simulation in a much wider range of applications with significant benefits in the design and development of agile manufacturing systems. To this end a number of integration mechanisms are facilitated in supporting processes in a typical design and development life cycle.

These include:

(i)   Creating VR manufacturing environments based on the functional and holonic control requirements,

(ii)   Identification of holons and holarchies for modelling holonic control
         architectures, exchanging the control requirement/design information
         between VR simulation and the holonic operations environment;

(iii)   Performing distributed control of manufacturing devices and execution
         of control functions in VR operations environment with holonic
         architectures with runtime support application verification.

The VR-based framework presented, shown in Figure 1, is built upon design and
integration two major environments; these are namely, Design Environment and
Operations Environment.

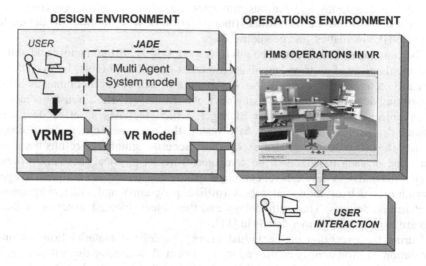

Fig. 1. The structure of the proposed system framework

3.1 Design Environment

The integrated Design Environment focuses on building a 'virtual factory', based on
its VR and HMS models.   The VR model represents the 3-D nature of the
manufacturing system for simulations in the virtual world. Various manufacturing and
assembly operations are simulated throughout the movements and interactions of the
3-D graphical VR objects. A modelling environment is employed for constructing a
'virtual factory' by creating a 3-D graphical model based on object-oriented
modelling paradigm. The virtual factory comprises an initial model, which is
constructed by a built-in module; VR Model Builder (VRMB).

VRMB has been developed for the construction of an initial model of the 'virtual
factory' that simulates the shop floor operations in a 3-D virtual environment. The
virtual factory consists of pre-modelled VR artefacts, having object-oriented
characteristics. Each VR object represents an entity in the virtual factory such as
machines, lathes, labour, storage, raw material, order etc.

The object oriented modelling framework through VRMB consists of three sub-models: object model, functional model and dynamic model.

The object model constitutes the static layout model of the factory, which consists of manufacturing devices having their positions in the layout. To represent such a factory layout model, the VRMB makes use of 'reference virtual factory models', which provide various object models of the manufacturing shop floor devices.   In designing a virtual factory model, the most important measure should be the reusability of the components because a virtual device can be used for many different factory configurations. To achieve reusability, the tool constructs a virtual device into an object oriented model. Such that the main class of the device can adapt to different factory configurations and various attributes undertake inherent properties of the device, such as device controller (interpretation and execution of device-level commands), kinematics, and geometric shape.

The functional model covers the job flow model of the virtual factory and aimed to describe the flow of parts and auxiliary resources (pallets and tools) between devices. In reality, a transfer happens by the combination of device-level commands between co-working devices (giving and taking devices). In the VRMB, a transfer is modelled as an object, called the Transfer Manager, which includes a set of device-level commands enabling the transfer. As a result, the users can check the mechanical validity of each transfer and also expect more accurate simulation results because the total time of each transfer will be computed from its physical mechanism (device-level commands). A device-level command can be considered as a program to operate a machine, such as industrial robots (offline programs) and other programmable mechatronic devices. The methodology and the object oriented structure of the VR MB are explained in further details in [11].

During the execution of the virtual factory model the material flow within the simulation environment is controlled by the event flow among the VR objects. The event flow is defined as a result of decisions on possible transfers based on the system state according to the production schedules. Due to the object-oriented modelling, the behaviour of triggered objects cause state changes in the VR environment.

The HMS model involves the interaction of holons, which are defined as "an autonomous and cooperative building blocks of a manufacturing system for transforming, transporting, storing and/or validating information and physical objects". A holon in a holarchy is characterized by autonomy and cooperation consists of a physical component and an informational component. The intelligent software agents as they are autonomous, cooperative and distributed in nature, they are employed to build the communication and cooperation part of dynamic interactive holons. The holonic agent in this research is an extended JADE agent, which is fully implemented in Java language [23]. The JADE is an open source agent platform that provides a library of Java classes that allow creating agents with application-specific attributes and behaviour with capabilities to send and receive FIPA messages. The agents are designed compatible to FIPA interaction protocols [24].

3.2 Operations Environment

The Operations Environment consists of an interactive platform for visualizing the HMS operations in 3-D graphical VR environment, receiving the user requests upon several manufacturing operations, editing parameters of production processes and collecting statistics regarding the performance of the tested system.

The Operations Environment consists of two main modules; VR-Based Emulation Module (VR-EM), which is intended to emulate the behaviour of the physical manufacturing system being controlled by using the VR model, and a holonic control module (HCM), which is used to implement holonic control architectures in Java-JADE environment. The structure of the Operations Environment is shown in Figure 2.

VR-EM provides a communication link between the dynamic objects in the VR model and HCM throughout TCP/IP sockets, which provide data transfer between software platforms. The "VR to Reality Interface", is a platform in which progress in simulation time is proportional to real-world time while the simulation executes.

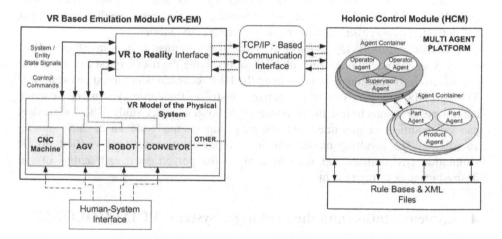

Fig. 2. The structure of the Operations Environment

The HCM contains platforms where the holons run and carry out negotiation over the manufacturing tasks in the agent container platforms. In the Operations Environment, the physical component of a holon is characterized by the VR model of a manufacturing device. The VR model encapsulates all the properties of the device and executes its operations through visual representations. The informational component of a holon is a Java class that extends the Agent class provided by the JADE framework. The behaviour of each holon uses multi-threaded programming, over the concept of JADE's behaviour, to allow the execution of several actions in parallel. The holons acquire knowledge from the system under study, from the user editable XML files that contain the information regarding the manufacturing operations process plans, machine/operator skills, production requirements, quality control parameters etc. Also a rule base is provided for supporting the decision making process of the holons. The communication between distributed holons is done over the Ethernet network, the messages being encoded using the FIPA-ACL communication language.

During run time operation, the HCM receives messages from the VR-EM regarding the occurrence of several states in the manufacturing environment, such as; status of the operations and failure of machines and other resources. HCM prepares and sends the control signals to the emulation module for taking the actions necessary for the states occurred within the simulated model. For example, in the case of new order arrival, the HCM produces feasible and optimal schedules for the arrived order and informs the emulation module for the schedule of routing the order to the corresponding machines/stations. When the operation of an order on that machine is about to be completed, the emulation module, gives another feedback to the holonic control module for defining the schedule for the upcoming operations of the same order.

In the case of occurrence of a disturbance such as machine failure, rush order arrival etc.., the VR-EM sends an online message to the corresponding operational holon to start the necessary action in order to recover the failure.

The main part of the Operations Environment is a 'human system interface' (HIS), which is an interactive platform with GUI for receiving the user requests upon several manufacturing operations and visualizing the HMS operations in virtual environment. Through HIS, users are free to interactively visualize the entire system and generate certain perturbations to test the response of the system under study. The VR models can be modified, re-generated and instantly implemented into an already running simulation. The resulting model, which is iteratively upgraded, is verified in VR simulation environment and used to analyze the performance and agility of the desired manufacturing system.

4   Implementation and the Prototype System: VCIM-HOLONIC

For the realization of the presented framework, an analysis tool; VCIM-HOLONIC has been designed and is currently being developed as a software system to realize the features outlined in each phase of the methodology. The prototype tool is an information system framework, which is built on top of Open GL in C++ language. The agents that build up the HMS models are coded in Java, with the support of JADE platform.

For demonstration of the methodology, a sample implementation has been performed in a medium size die-casting manufacturer company in Turkey. The company invests for integration of fully automated die casting cells into production plant in order to increase production volume and quality. In this study, we have focused on developing a VR model of the current implementation in the factory and testing HMS control architecture in order to find a scalable and re-configurable control architecture model, which is most appropriate for such a medium size company.

The fully automated cell consists of a die-casting machine with an ABB robot arm as operator, an automatic ladling device, a camera for detection of defects, a hydraulic trimming press, and an automated palletizing device for storage of the finished castings in racks for cooling as well as delivery of the cooled parts to the robot arm for trimming.

An object library serving as a repository of virtual reference models has been developed to help the modelling of the physical domains. The operations of the cell have been simulated under a centralized cell controller and an holonic control architectures for analysis.

For the implementation of the proposed tool into the real manufacturing plant, we adopt the Agile and Adaptive Holonic control architecture (ADACOR) approach developed by P.Leitao [25]. The main focus of the ADACOR architecture is reaction of the dynamic manufacturing systems to the disturbances, such as; rush orders, adding/removing machines, machine/robot breakdowns, which are highly frequent in the die-casting manufacturing. Details of the ADACOR architecture and its operations can be found in [25].

Five main holon classes: Product, Part, Operator, Cell supervisor and Coordinating and Quality Monitoring Holon have been defined for this study. The Product holon represents every product registered to the factory catalogue and holds the production information. It contains specifications such as process plan, production routing, which cells to go through. A Product holon receives the manufacturing order, decomposes it into separate operations and process them in order to prepare a short- term process plan, which involves alternative routings and process plans for any given order according to the current state of the factory and its production requirements. The Part holons represent the particular stages of the production orders launched to the factory. The Operator holons constitute the physical resources and operators available. The Cell Supervisor Holons are responsible of monitoring the schedules of the die casting cells. They hold a general image of the entire work cell and aids in combining the schedules of individual Operator holons. The Coordinating and Quality Monitoring Holon (CQMH) has been employed as a coordinator of the overall production activities for monitoring the performance of the resources according to the specified quality control parameters and output rate. CQMHs periodically monitor the current status of the production by the quality control parameters. They can detect the disturbances and immediately initiate the corrective actions that are needed to be taken. The quality control holons are responsible for each production cell. The structure and operation of CQMH will be explained more detailed in our further publications.

Through the VR simulations, the fully die-automated cell is analyzed for the response of the decentralized control. The interactive 3-D environment, provided by VR, allows viewing the response of the overall factory in the case of changes in the configurations. For instance, an automated cell or equipment is added to the initial model, while all other cells were in manual operation. Other cells and automation hardware have been added in order to see the response of the system with the holonic control architecture. The VR model of the developed automated cell is shown in Figure 3.

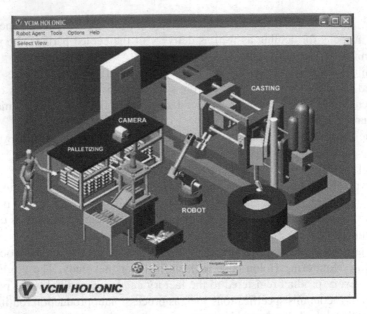

Fig. 3. A snapshot of the developed prototype tool VCIM-HOLONIC, employed for the implementtation into holonic control of a fully automated die-casting cell

5 Conclusions

A VR-based methodology and a practical system framework for design and implementation of HMS are presented in this paper. The methodology implements an inexpensive software tool supported by 3-D computer simulations in order to provide easy applicability to SMEs with little prior computer experience and high initial investments. The proposed VR-based system architecture enhances the design, analysis and testing phases of automation system implementations into manufacturing enterprises, and supports the educational activities in the field of automation and design of complex manufacturing control systems.

A case study has been performed in a medium size company in die-casting industry to demonstrate the implementation of the presented methodology into a real manufacturing environment.

As a result of analysis, through VR-based simulations of automated die-casting cells with holonic control architectures, it has been observed that the VR environment provides excellent visual animation where certain patterns (e.g. inventory build-up, blockages in flow) can be quickly seen. This is an important feature, especially in demonstrating the response of HMS to the factory management.

Also, by employing VR into the design process of HMS, physical configuration of the floor and study the effects of changes (e.g. distance between machines, speed of material handling systems) can be done very easily. The VR environment has provided an ability to quickly conduct controlled and repeatable experiments; Ability to implement identical production lines providing side-by-side comparative visual feedback on the operational differences.

Acknowledgments. The authors wish to thank the North Cyprus Ministry of Education for the grant awarded to the project of "Developing Virtual Reality based simulation systems for design and testing of flexible manufacturing systems in SMEs".

References

1. Kidd, P.T: Agile manufacturing: Forging new frontiers. Addition-Wesley, England (1994)
2. Brennan, R.W., Norrie, D.H.: Metrics for evaluating distributed manufacturing control systems. Computers in Industry 51, 225–235 (2003)
3. Holonic Manufacturing System (HMS) consortium web site (2000), http://hms.ifw.uni-hannover.de/
4. Park, S.C.: A methodology for creating a virtual model for a flexible manufacturing system. Computers in Industry 56, 734–746 (2005)
5. Okulicz, K.: Virtual reality-based approach to manufacturing process planning. Journal Production Research 42(17), 3493–3504 (2004)
6. Mujber, T.S., Szecsi, T., Hashmi, M.S.J.: Virtual reality applications in manufacturing process simulation. Journal of Materials Processing Technology 155-156, 1834–1838 (2004)
7. Bal, M., Hashemipour, M., Manesh, H.: A Virtual Reality - Based Methodology of Design and Testing of Flexible Manufacturing Systems for Small and Medium Size Enterprises: A Demonstration in Die-Casting Industry. In: Proceedings of AMPT 2006, Las Vegas, USA (2006)
8. Korves, B., Loftus, M.: Designing an immersive virtual reality interface for layout planning. Journal of Materials Processing Technology 107, 425–430 (2000)
9. Peng, Q., Hall, F.R., Lister, P.M.: Application and evaluation of VR-based CAPP system. Journal of Materials Processing Technology 107, 153–159 (2000)
10. Iqbal, M., Hashmi, M.S.J.: Design and analysis of a virtual factory layout. Journal of Materials Processing Technology 118, 403–410 (2001)
11. Bal, M., Manesh, H.F., Hashemipour, M.: Virtual-reality-based information requirements analysis tool for CIM system implementation: a case study in die-casting industry: International Journal of Computer Integrated Manufacturing. iFirst Article, 1–14 (2007)
12. DELMIA: Dassault Systems, http://www.delmia.com
13. Kotak, D., Wu, S., Fleetwood, M., Tamoto, H.: Agent-based holonic design and operations environment for distributed manufacturing. Computers in Industry 52, 95–108 (2003)
14. Marik, V., Fletcher, M., Pechoucek, M.: Holons & Agents: Recent Developments and Mutual Impacts. In: Mařík, V., Štěpánková, O., Krautwurmová, H., Luck, M. (eds.) ACAI 2001, EASSS 2001, AEMAS 2001, and HoloMAS 2001. LNCS (LNAI), vol. 2322, pp. 233–267. Springer, Heidelberg (2002)
15. Saint-Germain, B., Valckenaers, P., Brussel, H.V., Hadeli, Bochmann, O., Zamfirescu, C., Verstraete, P.: Multi-agent Manufacturing Control: An Industrial Case Study. In: Proceedings of the 7th IFAC Workshop on Intelligent Manufacturing Systems, Budapest, Hungary, pp. 227–232 (2003)
16. Erenay, O., Hashemipour, M., Kayaligil, S.: Virtual Reality in Requirement Analysis for CIM System Development Suitable for SMEs. Int. Journal of Production Research 40(15), 3693–3708 (2002)

17. Vrba, P.: MAST: Manufacturing Agent Simulation Tool. In: Proceedings of IEEE Conference on Emerging Technologies and Factory Automation, Lisbon, Portugal, vol. 1, pp. 282–287 (2003)
18. Lastra, J.L.M., Torres, L.E., Colombo, A.W.: A 3D Visualization and Simulation Framework for Intelligent Physical Agents. In: Mařík, V., Brennan, R.W., Pěchouček, M. (eds.) HoloMAS 2005. LNCS (LNAI), vol. 3593, pp. 23–38. Springer, Heidelberg (2005)
19. Burdea, G.C.: Invited Review: The Synergy Between Virtual Reality And Robotics. IEEE Transactions On Robotics And Automation 15(3), 400–410 (1999)
20. Moore, P.R., Pu, J., Hg, H.C., Wong, C.B., Chong, S.K., Chen, X., Adolfsson, J., Olofsgard, P., Lundgren, J.O.: Virtual Engineering: an integrated approach to agile manufacturing machinery design and control. Mechatronics 13, 1105–1121 (2003)
21. Bal, M., Hashemipour, M., Manesh, H.: Agent-Based Holonic Virtual Worlds For Design And Operations Of Agile Manufacturing Systems. In: Proceedings of International Conference of Intelligent Manufacturing - IMS 2006, Sakarya, Turkey (2006)
22. Kotak, D., Bardi, S., Gruver, W.A., Zohrevand, K.: Comparison of hierachical and holonic shop floor control using a virtual manufacturing environment. In: Proceedings of IEEE international Conference on System, Man and Cybernetics, Nashville, TN, vol. 3, pp. 1667–1672 (2000)
23. JADE: Java Agent DEvelopment Framework (JADE), http://jade.cselt.it/
24. Foundation for Intelligent Physical Agents: FIPA Abstract Architecture Specification (2001), http://www.fipa.org/specs/fipa00001/
25. Leitao, P., Restivo, F.: ADACOR: A holonic architecture for agile and adaptive manufacturing control. Computers in Industry 57, 121–130 (2006)

Resilience in the Face of Disaster: Accounting for Varying Disaster Magnitudes, Resource Topologies, and (Sub)Population Distributions in the PLAN C Emergency Planning Tool

Giuseppe Narzisi[1], Joshua S. Mincer[1], Silas Smith[2], and Bud Mishra[1]

[1] Courant Institute of Mathematical Sciences, New York, NY 10012, USA
{narzisi,joshua.mincer,mishra}@nyu.edu
[2] NYU School of Medicine, NYC Poison Control Center, New York, USA
smiths11@med.nyu.edu
http://bioinformatics.nyu.edu/Projects/planc

Abstract. PLAN C, an Agent-Based Model platform for urban disaster simulation and emergency planning, features a variety of reality-based agents interacting on a realistic city map and can simulate the complex dynamics of emergency responses in different urban catastrophe scenarios. Work reported here focuses on the incorporation of specific subpopulations of person agents, reflecting the existence of individuals with specific defining characteristics and needs, and their interactions with the available resources. Performance of these subpopulations are compared in both point-source attack and distributed disaster scenarios for disasters of different magnitudes. Specific "recovery points" can be derived both for total- and sub-populations, which estimate the duration of a response system's/city's vulnerability. The effect of varying topologies of available resources, i.e. different hospital maps, provides particular insight into the dynamics that can emerge in this complex system. PLAN C produces interesting emergent behavior which is often consistent with the literature on emergency medicine of previous events.

Keywords: PLAN C, Agent-Based Modeling, Complex Systems, Disaster Management.

1 Multi-agent and Complex Systems: Application to Disaster Management

A central problem in disaster management is the complexity inherent in an emergency response. As such, planners often rely on experience gained from previous events or drills, where possible, coupled with expert opinion. Such thinking informs policies governing operations for hospitals, responders, ambulances, etc. There exists, however, no practical way to test these policies and their effects within the global dynamic of the everyday milieu, i.e. a city with all of its resources and interacting population. The resulting gap between the theory of

V. Mařík, V. Vyatkin, A.W. Colombo (Eds.): HoloMAS 2007, LNAI 4659, pp. 433–446, 2007.
© Springer-Verlag Berlin Heidelberg 2007

disaster management and its practice is thus largely due to the fact that the real-world environment is fundamentally a *Complex System* whose intricacies cannot be reduced without sacrificing realism. Predicting the dynamics of this system, and in particular the experience of a disaster for particular subpopulations of individuals is therefore a nontrivial task.

Complex Systems are often characterized by agents capable of interacting with each other dynamically, often in non-linear and non-intuitive ways. Attempts to characterize their dynamics often results in partial differential equations that are difficult, if not impossible, to solve. One powerful technique for analyzing such complex systems is agent-based modeling (ABM) [16]. ABM has seen an exponential growth in the last few years for understanding the dynamical behavior of complex systems [16], including applications to economics [18], social science [6], biology, [5,1] and several other real-world domains. It has been recently applied with success also in the area of Disaster Management and Preparedness (evacuation, traffic, epidemic, health-care, etc). In such models, the system is represented by a collection of autonomous decision-making entities called "agents". A large multi-agent system can reproduce very complex dynamics even if the individual agents and their interactions follow simple rules of behavior. Emergent behaviors may be even more unpredictable and even counterintuitive when the agents are embedded and forced to interact in a real-world environment that introduces more communication channels, constraints, and behavioral rules.

Related works. Though several mathematical and computational approaches have been proposed in recent years for public health and emergency response planning, no unified framework yet exists. These methods differ in various characteristics including: underlying modeling technology, level of details and assumptions, population size, scale and realism of the environment, etc. PLAN C has been developed in order to avoid various limitations of the following (not exhaustive) list of competing agent-based modeling and simulation tools: *InterSim* [17] is an epidemic model that uses a powerful mathematical model for modeling the agent interactions and the time course of the disease (e.g., the SEIRS model), but it lacks a realistic environment in which the simulation evolves. *EpiSim* [2], by contrast, is a highly detailed epidemic simulation system, but it is rather expensive in terms of computational time. Also, it can be difficult to collect reliable statistics from a significantly large number of simulation runs. Furthermore, it lacks an interactive user interface that could enhance its practical applicability. *DrillSim* [10] and *PedSim* [8] are two examples of evacuation models with topological constraints where the scale is restricted to evacuation plans of a floor of a building with a limited number of active agents. For example Drillsim was used in [9] to analyze a scenario with a total of twenty-eight evacuee agents. In [8] PedSim is used to suggest practical ways of minimizing the harmful consequences during evacuation of 400 people. It was found that a set of columns placed asymmetrically in front of the exit door can considerably reduce the number injuries.

1.1 PLAN C

Integral to the Large Scale Emergency Readiness (LaSER) project of NYU's Center for Catastrophe Preparedness and Response (CCPR[1]), is the development of a robust, agent-based model of the dynamics of urban catastrophes that permits evaluation of different biological, chemical, radiological, and other hazardous scenarios, alone or in combination, and their disaster dynamics. PLAN C[2] [11,12,13,14] (Planning with Large Agent-Networks against Catastrophes), a modeling and simulation tool for catastrophic events, has been designed and tested in other areas of disaster preparedness. Built on top of the Java version of Repast 3.1 [15], it aims to integrate theories, algorithms, techniques, and technologies from essential preparedness disciplines in order to improve planning for and response to the public health and medical consequences of a mass casualty event. Using this robust and flexible modeling platform, public health, medical, or emergency management professionals can simulate, analyze, and predict consequences of a catastrophe, and thereby improve the capabilities of both the government and the private sectors to prepare for and respond to large-scale incidents. The agent-based modeling (ABM) paradigm provides a natural way to describe the behavior of the agents and also facilitates easier transfer of domain specific knowledge into the model.

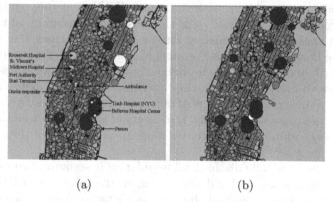

(a)   (b)

Fig. 1. PLAN C snapshots: (a) point-source scenario and (b) distributed scenario. People are labeled by small circles; color changes from green to red, signifying a high and low health level, respectively. Ambulances and first responders are labeled by small yellow circles. Larger circles signify hospitals; circle size correlates with resource level. Color represents the state of the hospital (available, critical, or full); color stays white, irrespective of state, until the first disaster patient is admitted.

PLAN C is constructed at the micro-level but permits macro-level behavior to emerge from the individual interactions of all of the agents (and their interactions, via messaging, with authorities). Behavior is not artificially imposed in

---
[1] http://www.nyu.edu/ccpr/
[2] http://www.bioinformatics.nyu.edu/Projects/planc

a top-down approach. In this way, the ABM technology on which PLAN C is founded is consistent with the underlying philosophy of disaster response planning: namely, planning for what people, individually and as a whole population, will do in an emergency, not what the emergency planner would like them to do [4]. Detailed descriptions of person and hospital agents, which are specifically analyzed in this research paper, are given in the appendix. A more thorough description of the PLAN C model can be found in [12,13].

PLAN C results can be analyzed at both the macro- and micro- levels. Collective results and system dynamics at the global level (e.g. average health, fatality rate, average distress, etc.) in different emergency scenarios can be addressed. At the micro-level, analysis of selected individual agent traces allows for greater spatio-temporal resolution of disaster dynamics in a "post-debugging" process. For instance, the behavior of the hospital closest to the disaster may be compared with one further away. Similarly, the experience of a particular disaster survivor may be compared with that of a victim, perhaps enabling a finer delineation of the factors contributing to survival.

2   Simulation Results

Previous studies employed a homogeneous population of person agents. The present article reports the incorporation into PLAN C of subpopulations with special characteristics, specifically, physical disability. Dynamics of the subpopulations are analyzed and compared for a point-source attack (i.e. a sarin gas attack at the Port Authority Bus Terminal in Manhattan, NY) as well as a hypothetical distributed scenario (i.e. a previously concentrated population exposed to an agent with delayed onset of symptoms that is now distributed throughout Manhattan). Furthermore, disasters of different magnitudes vis a vis the number of casualties are considered. Finally, the effects of varying the topology of available resources (hospitals) on disaster outcome are considered for the point-source attack.

Modeling the physically disabled subpopulation is accomplished by stochastically tagging individuals with a disability factor, the value of which is initialized probabilistically from a uniform distribution between 0 and 0.5 and remains constant, reflecting the chronic nature of the disability. Thus, the range of 0 to 0.5 means that a particular disabled person can move at most half as fast as a normal person, all other factors, such as health level, being equal.

The health level (a real number in the interval $[0, 1]$) of each person in the population is initialized according to four major categories of illness defined respectively by the following probabilities and ranges: $dead_{pr} = 0.05 - [0, 0.2]$, $severe_{pr} = 0.2 - [0.2, 0.5]$, $light_{pr} = 0.3 - [0.5, 0.8]$, $no\text{-}symptoms = 0.45 - [0.1, 1]$. The incorporation of people with mild or no symptoms captures explicitly the effect of the "worried well": people who do not actually need medical treatment but nonetheless consume available resources.

All simulations involve 20 ambulances, 5 onsite responder units and 30 hospitals. Unless otherwise stated, a total number of 10 simulations are run for each set of initial conditions. Thus, a point on the graph represents a mean value, for that specific tick, of the parameter value found in 10 independent runs.

3   Point-Source Attack

The first scenario is a point-source sarin gas attack at the Port Authority Bus Terminal in Manhattan. 25% of the exposed population (either 1000, 5000, or 10000 people) suffer from impaired mobility, covering anything from low level disability (e.g., extremes of age) to chronic physical disabilities (e.g., wheelchair-bound). The emergency response and population dynamics are followed for a period of 2 days and 2 hours (3000 ticks/minutes), representing a reasonable amount of time before external aid arrives.

Different Disaster Magnitudes. Fig.2(a) features the fraction of the total population treated by each tick for disasters of different magnitudes, i.e. increasing size of the total exposed population. This parameter is an important performance measure of the emergency response system, as it characterizes its ability and efficiency in absorbing and treating disaster casualties. As seen in the figure, in the case of 1000 exposed people, 70% of the population has received treatment in the first 800 minutes of the disaster aftermath. This number decreases somewhat as the total exposed population increases. These values attest to the resilience of the city-wide emergency response system in that most victims have been seen and treated well within the first 24 hours of the disaster event. Significantly, these results compare well with actual events. The Madrid terrorist bombings of March 11, 2004 resulted in 2062 casualties. Of these, 1430 (about 70%) were treated within the first 810 minutes post event [3]. The fatality rate per tick as a percentage of the total population is graphed in the inset plot of Fig. 2(a). This value increases nonlinearly with increasing disaster magnitude.

Subpopulation Dynamics. A finer level of detail is attained by analyzing the fraction of each subpopulation (normal and physically disabled) accessing medical treatment at each tick. As seen in Fig. 2(b), the first thing to note is that all curves are sloping downward by 3000 minutes, and in fact well before that time. All along, many people who are not very sick but nonetheless seek out medical treatment (i.e. the "worried well") receive treatment, if necessary, and are discharged relatively quickly. This fraction shows itself in the difference between the fraction of people receiving treatment at a given tick (Fig. 2(b)) and the total fraction that has received treatment by that tick (Fig. 2(a)). There are others who require a longer stay in the hospital. As these sicker patients recover and begin to be discharged in significant numbers, the curves shown in Fig. 2(b) begin to slope downwards until all have been discharged.

Passing this point represents that the population as a whole is on the way to recovery. The timing of this recovery point is significant. A population that features an earlier point is recovering faster. In this light, the results in Fig. 2(b) shows that the normal subpopulation as a whole recovers faster than the physically disabled population for all disaster magnitudes. Within the normal population,

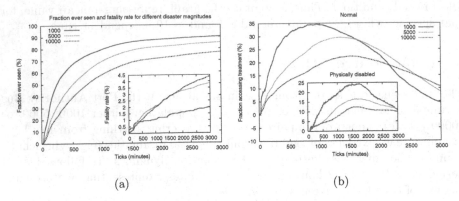

(a)   (b)

Fig. 2. Point-source attack: (a) fraction of the total population treated by each tick and fatality rate dynamics (inset plot) for the total population for different disaster magnitudes; (b) fraction of the normal and physically disabled subpopulations treated at each tick for different disaster magnitudes

the point of recovery shifts to later times as disaster magnitude increases, illustrating the intuitive notion that a population recovers more slowly from a disaster of larger magnitude. Interestingly, the recovery point is fairly constant for the physically disabled subpopulation, suggesting that its ability to recover is compromised even at smaller disaster magnitudes.

Different hospital topology structures. Analysis in the aftermath of the Madrid bombings suggested that there probably existed an over-triage to the closest hospital. Namely, many noncritical patients presented to the nearest hospital [3]. In light of this conclusion, it is interesting to study the effects of the closest hospitals on disaster outcome. One way to do this is to remove sequentially hospitals close to the disaster site, i.e. to change the hospital topologies. Results in this section report on three such scenarios. In the first simulation, the closest hospital, St. Vincent's Midtown Hospital (415 W. 51st St) is removed. The second simulation features removal of this and the next closest hospital, Roosevelt Hospital (1000 Tenth Ave.). Finally, the third simulation features the additional removal of Bellevue Hospital (462 First Ave.). Fig. 1(a) shows the specific locations of these four hospitals in the map.

The fraction of each subpopulation (normal and physically disabled) accessing treatment at each tick is graphed in Fig. 3(a) for these three scenarios (and the original point-source attack with all hospitals operating). For the physically disabled population, removal of the hospitals has little effect. A relatively small, but interesting effect is seen early on for the normal subpopulation. Removal of the first hospital has very little effect, and this is consistent with the fact that St. Vincent's Midtown Hospital, while the closest, is a relatively small facility. The additional removal of Roosevelt Hospital, however, leads paradoxically to an increase in the number of individuals receiving treatment early in the simulation

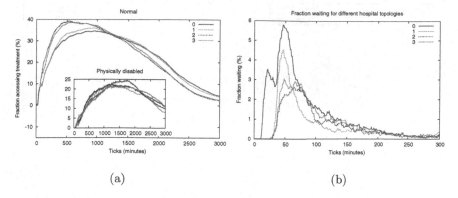

(a)   (b)

Fig. 3. Hospital topologies: (a) dynamics for the fraction accessing treatment for the normal and the physically disabled (inset plot) individual for the removal of 0, 1, 2, and 3 specific hospitals near the disaster site. (b) dynamics for the total fraction of people waiting for admission.

and also results in an earlier recovery point. Further removal of Bellevue Hospital Center results in a slight decrease in these numbers and a slightly delayed recovery point.

This trend is confirmed by analyzing the fraction of the total population that is waiting for admission to a hospital at each tick. As seen in Fig. 3(b), the number of people waiting early (first 300 minutes) in the simulation decreases significantly as the closest two hospitals are removed. Taken together, these results highlight a counterintuitive emergent phenomenon: removal of the two closest hospitals results in better performance. Further consideration suggests a reason: their removal somehow allows for a better distribution of people among the available hospitals by removing the incentive for people to move in a counterproductive fashion by crowding the closest two hospitals.

A confirmation of this hypothesis is seen in Fig. 4, which plots for each of the 30 hospitals the number of people either admitted to the hospital for treatment or waiting for admission in each minute. Each plot corresponds to the removal of 0, 1, 2, or 3 specific hospitals. As seen in Fig. 4(a), for the removal of no hospitals, crowds of people leaving the Port Authority in the aftermath of the disaster initially reach St. Vincent's Midtown, evidenced by the early green spike in the figure. A short time later, people also arrive at Roosevelt Hospital, evidenced by the early red spike. Roosevelt Hospital, due to its large size, continues to attract a large fraction of the total population throughout the simulation. Note that the hospital curves are similar in shape to the curves for the fraction accessing treatment at each tick. They feature similar recovery points and slope downwards as the sicker people recover and are discharged. Fig. 4(b) confirms the hypothesis that dynamics do not significantly change with the removal of the closest hospital, St. Vincents Midtown. As seen there, the early spike seen for St. Vincents in Fig. 4(a) is no longer present, while the dynamics overall are

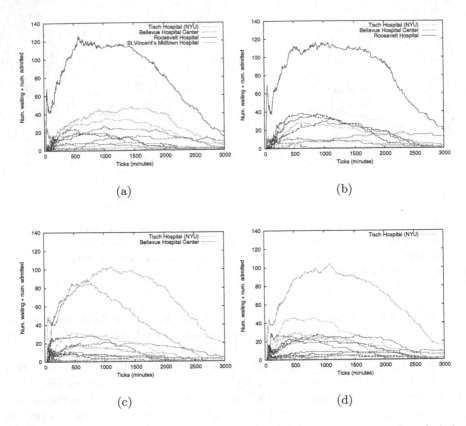

Fig. 4. Dynamics for the number of people either admitted or waiting for admission at each hospital for the case of removal of 0 (a), 1 (b), 2 (c), or 3 (d) nearby hospitals in the point-source attack scenario

similar to Fig. 4(a), with Roosevelt Hospital playing a dominant role. As seen in Figs. 4(c) and 4(d), people's movements change dramatically once Roosevelt Hospital is also removed. Instead of moving northward, people move east to Tisch Hospital (gray curve) and nearby Bellevue Hospital (pink curve), which is no longer seen in Fig. 4(d) as it has also been removed. Moving east instead of north results in the better outcome seen in Figs. 3(a) and 3(b). This is understood in light of the greater number of resources that are found there. For example, Tisch and Bellevue are both large hospitals in close proximity to one another, as compared with Roosevelt and St. Vincent's Midtown, whose combined resources are less. Furthermore, movement east places people closer to larger hospitals on Manhattan's East Side.

These results are particularly illustrative of the usefulness of PLAN C in emergency planning. While suggesting that the distribution of hospitals in Manhattan as given may not be optimal for a specific disaster scenario, they also suggest that emergency managers, through risk communication or other means, can guide people's movements in particular directions and to particular hospitals to improve outcome. Moreover, the map for a given city may not necessarily be a given constraint. Different configurations for the resource locations can be designed and PLAN C could be employed to determine the optimal layout for a given scenario, enabling planners to redesign an entire city or a particular locale for optimal robustness in the face of a specific disaster.

4   Distributed Scenario

In contrast to the point-source attack studied above, the current section focuses on a distributed scenario in which the individuals are positioned randomly throughout Manhattan. The hypothetical situation is one in which a large number of people were congregated at some earlier point in time. All were exposed to a hypothetical agent that does not reveal itself symptomatically until a later time. As the simulation starts, a certain number are already dead, and the city-wide health system is becoming aware of the nature of the situation. The parameters for the hypothetical agent vis a vis health decline are made identical to those of the sarin scenario in order to facilitate comparisons between a point-source and distributed attack. The distributed scenario does not feature onsite responders or ambulances, as PLAN C does not currently include ambulances that can respond to particular emergency calls.

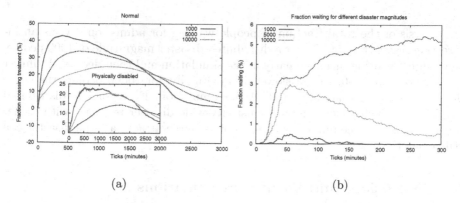

(a)   (b)

Fig. 5. Distributed scenario: (a) fraction of the normal and physically disabled subpopulations treated at each tick for different disaster magnitudes; (b) dynamics for the total fraction of people waiting for admission

Fig. 5(a) highlights the fraction of the normal and physically disabled subpopulations that are receiving medical treatment at each tick for disasters of different magnitudes. Comparison with the point-source attack (Fig. 2) demonstrates a robustness of the physically disabled population not seen previously. Namely, the recovery point (maximum) is earlier for disasters of lesser magnitude, whereas in the point-source attack it was constant. This robustness in the distributed scenario is expected. There is less competition for the same hospital resources as people distribute more equitably to a variety of hospitals. This more equitable distribution is seen when comparing Fig. 6, which plots the number of people admitted or waiting for admission at each hospital, with the analogous figure for the point-source attack (Fig. 4(a)). From the point of view of the city-wide health system, the ability to absorb disaster casualties is significantly compromised in a point-source attack as compared with a distributed scenario.

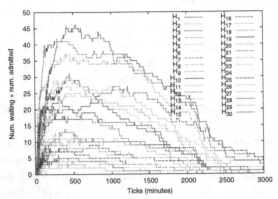

Fig. 6. Distributed scenario: dynamics for the number of people either admitted or waiting for admission at each hospital (represented by a different trace)

Analysis of the total fraction of people waiting for admission reveals an interesting result (Fig. 5(b)). For a distributed disaster magnitude of 1000 people, the number waiting increases early in the simulation and then decays. A similar form is seen for 5000, with a slower decay. Finally, for 10000 people, the curve does not decay in the early part of the simulation. Even for the distributed simulation, which yields a more robust city-wide disaster response with earlier recovery points as compared with the point-source attack, a large disaster can still stress the system.

5   Conclusions and Future Investigations

Results presented here illustrate the feasibility of incorporating special subpopulations within the PLAN C framework, capable of simulating disasters of various magnitudes (10000 casualties). Analysis of the system dynamics in disasters of varying topologies, both in terms of the spatial distribution of subpopulations (point-source versus distributed scenario) as well as the locations of the available resources (hospitals), can reveal counterintuitive emergent phenomena, such as the fact that removing hospitals close to the disaster site can improve overall outcome of the system. A significant finding is that "recovery points" can be discerned, both for total- and sub-populations. When carried forward with disasters of larger magnitude or of longer duration (e.g. infectious diseases), these points can be determines in order to estimate the duration of a response system's/city's vulnerability. Proactive use of PLAN C in planning would attempt to maximize system resilience and earlier recovery points by optimizing various facets of disaster response. Emergency managers, urban planners and public health officials can refine existing emergency plans and policies using PLAN C's versatile, innovative platform.

Among the many lines of investigation which we plan to address, particularly relevant are the following: 1) greater realism can be incorporated by the introduction of social networks linking individuals across subpopulations with consequent dynamics that may prove very different as normal individuals alter their dynamics to aid "friends" or family members who suffer from some impairment such as physical disability; 2) validation of PLAN C's realism in order to build confidence in its use as a tool for disaster planning; 3) automatic computation of optimal configurations (locations) for the available resource (i.e. hospitals) through the use of multi-objective evolutionary algorithms [14].

Acknowledgments. We would like to thank Lewis Nelson, Dianne Rekow and Ian Portelli for their contribution to the clinical aspect of the study design and development. We also thank Venkatesh Mysore, Ofer Gill, Jee Woong Byeon and Raoul-Sam Daruwala who contributed to the implementation in Repast. The work was supported by New York University's Center for Catastrophe Preparedness and Response, through its U.S. Department of Homeland Security grant #2004-GT-TX-0001.

References

1. Athale, C.A., Deisboeck, T.S.: The effects of egf-receptor density on multiscale tumor growth patterns. Journal of Theoretical Biology 238(4), 771–779 (2006)
2. Barrett, C.L., Eubank, S.G., Smith, J.P.: If smallpox strikes portland.. Scientific American 292(3), 42–49 (2005)
3. de Gutierrez Ceballos, J.P., Turegano Fuentes, F., Perez Diaz, D., Sanz Sanchez, M., Martin Llorente, C., Guerrero Sanz, J.E.: Casualties treated at the closest hospital in the madrid, march 11, terrorist bombings. Crit Care Med. 33(1), S107–112 (2005)
4. der Heide, E.A.: The importance of evidence-based disaster planning. Annals of Emergency Medicine 47(1), 34–49 (2006)
5. Emonet, T., Macal, C.M., North, M.J., Wickersham, C.E., Cluzel, P.: AgentCell: a digital single-cell assay for bacterial chemotaxis. Bioinformatics 21(11), 2714–2721 (2005)
6. Epstein, J.M.: Generative Social Science: Studies in Agent-Based Computational Modeling, vol. 2. Princeton University Press, Princeton (2007)
7. Rathlev, N.K., et al.: Time series analysis of variables associated with daily mean emergency department length of stay. Annals of Emergency Medicine 49(3), 265–271 (2007)
8. Helbing, D., Farkas, I., Vicsek, T.: Simulating dynamical features of escape panic. Nature 407, 487 (2000)

9. Massaguer, D., Balasubramanian, V., Mehrotra, S., Venkatasubramanian, N.: Multi-agent simulation of disaster response. In: Proceedings of the First International Workshop on Agent Technology for Disaster Management, ATDM (2006)
10. Massaguer, D., Balasubramanian, V., Mehrotra, S., Venkatasubramanian, N.: Synthetic humans in emergency response drills. Demo paper in AAMAS (2006)
11. Mysore, V., Gill, O., Daruwala, R.-S., Antoniotti, M., Saraswat, V., Mishra, B.: Multi-agent modeling and analysis of the brazilian food-poisoning scenario. In: The Agent Conference (2005)
12. Mysore, V., Narzisi, G., Nelson, L., Rekow, D., Triola, M., Shapiro, A., Coleman, C., Gill, O., Daruwala, R.-S., Mishra, B.: Agent modeling of a sarin attack in manhattan. In: Proceedings of the First International Workshop on Agent Technology for Disaster Management, ATDM (2006)
13. Narzisi, G., Mysore, V., Nelson, L., Rekow, D., Triola, M., Halcomb, L., Portelli, I., Mishra, B.: Complexities, catastrophes and cities: Unraveling emergency dynamics. In: Schärfe, H., Hitzler, P., Øhrstrøm, P. (eds.) ICCS 2006. LNCS (LNAI), vol. 4068, Springer, Heidelberg (2006)
14. Narzisi, G., Mysore, V., Mishra, B.: Multi-objective evolutionary optimization of agent based models: an application to emergency response planning. In: Computational Intelligence - CI 2006, pp. 224–230. ACTA Press (2006)
15. North, M.J., Collier, N.T., Vos, J.R.: Experiences creating three implementations of the repast agent modeling toolkit. ACM Transactions on Modeling and Computer Simulation 16(1), 1–25 (2006)
16. PNAS. Adaptive Agents, Intelligence, and Emergent Human Organization: Capturing Complexity through Agent-Based Modeling, 99(3) (May 2002)
17. Schwehm, M., Leary, C., Duerr, H.-P., Eichner, M.: InterSim: A network-based outbreak investigation and intervention planning tool. In: Schärfe, H., Hitzler, P., Øhrstrøm, P. (eds.) ICCS 2006. LNCS (LNAI), vol. 4068, Springer, Heidelberg (2006)
18. Tesfatsion, L., Judd, K. (eds.): Handbook of Computational Economics, Agent-Based Computational Economics, vol. 2. Elsevier, Amsterdam (2006)

Appendix: PLANC's Agent Behavior Description

PLAN C is an innovative agent-based framework for simulating large scale disasters in urban settings which features: (i) large number of computational actors/agents (Person, Hospital, On-Site Responder, Ambulance and Catastrophe); (ii) flexible number of parameters for describing the agents' behavior and interaction, the time course of the disease, environmental factors, etc.; (iii) communication channels to exchange information (e.g., health/resource levels, hospital operation mode, etc.); among similar and differing agents; (iv) realistic models of medical/responder units and catastrophe chemical agent effects; and (v) integrated urban topologies (streets, subways, hospitals, etc), via publicly available GIS (geographical information system) data. PLAN C involved collaborative participation from a multi-disciplinary team including medical, sociological and legal experts from the NYU's CCPR (Center for Catastrophe Preparedness and Response). Because of the focus of the present paper, we present detailed descriptions of the Person and the Hospital agents.

Hospital Agent

The hospital is a stationary agent that is an abstraction of any medical facility that can play a role at the time of a catastrophe. The hospital uses a simple triage policy with three operation modes (*available, critical* and *full*). The transition from one state to another is based on the available number of beds and resources. The hospital is realistically modeled to include an Emergency Department (ED), inpatient beds, isolation beds, and critical care capacity in the form of an Intensive Care Unit (ICU) and ventilators.

The hospital mode directly influences several decisions (*triage*): whom to turn away, whom to admit, whom to treat, how much resources to allocate to a person requiring treatment, who can be discharged, and who can be moved from the ED to an inpatient or ICU bed. In the available mode, the hospital admits all persons present for treatment; in the critical mode, only critically ill people can be admitted; in the full mode, no new people can be admitted. Among the several parameters which influence the way the hospital operates, the following are particularly relevant. Thirty major hospitals have been included, and the number of hospital beds was used as an indicator of the capacity of the hospital.

Probability of admission. This equation captures the assumption that increased hospital efficiency results in a higher probability of admitting additional people in each tick. Conversely, as the number of occupied beds increases, the admission probability decreases:

$$P_r(admit) = \frac{Eff_H \times rate_p \times tick_{size}}{1 + |H|_{occ}} \tag{1}$$

where Eff_H is the efficiency of the hospital H (defined later), $tick_{size}$ is the number of minutes per tick of the simulation ($= 1$), $rate_p$ ($= 50$) is the number of people per minute that can be attended to (admitted + treated + discharged), and $|H|_{occ}$ is the number of total occupied beds in the hospital.

Hospital efficiency. The efficiency, regulated by the following rule, directly influences many decisions, such as the amount of treatment given to a person as well as the number of persons admitted or treated at each tick, also it indirectly affects the waiting time at the hospital and mean hospitalization time:

$$Eff_H = \frac{1}{1 + \left(\frac{|H|_{occ} + S_H}{|H| + |ED|} \right)} \tag{2}$$

$|H|_{occ}$ is defined as before, while $|H|$ and $|ED|$ are respectively the total number of inpatient and ED beds and S_H is the level of *sickness* inside the hospital, defined as $S_H = \sum_{i:p \in H} (1 - h_p)$, where h_p is the health level of the person p. The intuitive notion behind this equation is that the efficiency of the hospital should decrease as bed occupancy and the overall sickness of the inpatient population increases. We are currently studying different variations of these formulas to better model these processes.

Average time in ED. The average time a person spends in th ED before being moved to an inpatient bed is defined by the following equation:

$$Avg_t^{ED} = base_t \times (1 + |Ed|_{occ} + \frac{S_{ED}}{|ED|}) \qquad (3)$$

where $base_t$ (= 5) is a user parameter defining the base value for the average time in the ED, S_{ED} is the total sickness of people in the ED. This formula and the previous one are consistent with the time series analysis in [7].

Person Agent

The affected population is modeled as reactive *selfish* agents with *bounded rationality* and *stochastic behavior*. The person's initial goal is to reach the original destination (home or place of work) from the initial location. After the event, health begins to deteriorate such that at a certain health-level, governed by environmental and personality factors, the person decides to head to a hospital. The person agent maintains information about destination (home/work or hospital), current health level $h_l \in [0, 1]$, current level of medical intervention $m_l \in [0, 1]$; location and current capacity of known hospitals. An agent may talk to any agent in its neighborhood (defined as everybody in the same location on the map), and exchange information about the known list of hospitals, the disease type, etc.

Level of worry and compliance. Each person has specific personality traits defined through the degree of worry/fear $w_l \in [0, 1]$, which represents the innate level of irrationality in the agent, and the level of compliance $c_l \in [0, 1]$, which captures the instruction-abiding trait of a person; Both w_l and c_l are initialized uniformly random in $[0, 1]$ but they also change during the simulation as a consequence of the interactions between the agents: when two agents talk to each other they both update the variables w_l and c_l according to the current values of the other agent computing the mean value.

Level of distress. The degree of worry and the health level are combined together to define the perceived level of distress of a person: $s_l = w_l \times (1 - h_l)$. The simple intuition behind this formula is the following: if the health level is high then with low probability the degree of worry can generate distress. This parameter influence many decisions of the person agent, for example, higher the level of distress suffered by a person, higher the probability of selecting the nearest hospital even when it is full.

Disability factor. The disability factor d_l reflects the chronic nature of the disability of the person. This parameter which is initialized randomly in $[0, l]$, where l is used to decide the degree of disability, is then used as a multiplication factor with other characteristics parameter of a person. In this paper, the speed of a disabled person is updated proportionally to d_l.

Holonic Simulation of a Design System for Performance Analysis

Richard Sohnius, Eyck Jentzsch, and Wolf-Ekkehard Matzke

Cadence Design Systems, GmbH, Mozartstr., 2, 85622, Feldkirchen, Germany
{rsohnius,jentzsch,wolf}@cadence.com

Abstract. In this paper, we present our approach to assess the performance of an engineering design system in the field of microelectronics using a holonic simulation. Instead of measuring some input and output parameters of the system and applying some metrics to them as common performance assessment approaches do, we build a model of the entire system and simulate the course of the design process using a multi agent system. The performance metrics are then applied to the detailed results of this simulation. The main focus of this paper thereby lies in the simulation part of the approach which we designed to have two parts: a planning phase and an execution phase.

Keywords: Design system, assessment, simulation, holonic simulation, Produktiv+, PSI, performance, productivity, dynamic engineering design process, ontology, multi-agent system, microelectronics.

1 Introduction

It is well known that the design of microelectronic devices gets more and more complex [1]. To keep design time and cost of such devices in reasonable boundaries, the performance of the system carrying out designs needs to be increased. However, one can not improve what can not be measured. Thus, a reliable and comprehensible way to measure engineering design performance needs to be developed.

Applying mainstream workflow and project management tools has proven to be not suitable in the domain of engineering design. Therefore, we develop a new approach based on a holonic simulation of the design system with a multi agent system. It is capable of modeling, simulating and assessing design systems. For that, it uses cooperating intelligent agents and acts as a decision support tool by allowing to measure productivity and other performance related indicators and by helping to improve performance by analyzing bottlenecks and weak spots of a design system.

The approach is developed in the Performance Simulation Initiative (PSI) which is an internal R&D project of Cadence Design Systems, GmbH [2]. Further development is done in a joint research project between AMD Saxony LLC, Robert Bosch GmbH, Infineon Technologies AG and Cadence Design Systems GmbH. It is called PRODUKTIV+[1] and is partially funded by the German government.

---

[1] http://www.edacentrum.de/produktivplus

V. Mařík, V. Vyatkin, A.W. Colombo (Eds.): HoloMAS 2007, LNAI 4659, pp. 447–454, 2007.
© Springer-Verlag Berlin Heidelberg 2007

Additionally, scientific institutes are incorporated as subcontractors namely UH-IMS (Hannover), OFFIS (Oldenburg), FSU-metheval (Jena), Fraunhofer-IIS/EAS (Dresden), and UTU-TI (Tübingen).

2   The Motivation

A considerable weakness of mainstream process modeling approaches is the consequence of their strength. Indeed, the majority of process modeling frameworks provides sophisticated means to describe a rich variety of process structures [3]. They do it in a rigorous, but rather a static manner. Unfortunately, this fits only to well-defined processes, for example in manufacturing. However, design processes are of a different kind: They "… are frequently chaotic and non-linear, and have not been well served by project management or workflow tools" [4].

Commercial offerings like those of Numetrics Management Systems, Inc [5] provide a benchmarking service to assess development capabilities and analyze the design cycle to identify which phases are having the greatest impact on productivity and cycle time performance. However, their model of a design process is based on the black box principle. Their evaluation uses only integral characteristics which are lagging [6]. The weak point is that such an approach does not allow "what-if" analysis reliably.

Other approaches like those described in [7], [8], [9], [10] take into account the nature of continuous process evolution but neglect the source of this evolution: the human beings involved in the process and pro-actively driving it.

The approach presented in this paper not only models the process, the organization and its environment but also the humans performing this process and combines them into one simulation of the whole system. Whereby, the software agents representing the human engineers collaborate in this multi-agent simulation to create the ambient intelligence required. As a whole, this is capable of much more than the sum of its parts. This leads us to the notion of a "holonic simulation".

The rest of the paper is structured as follows: section 3 describes the model used, section 4 reports on the simulation in detail, section 5 outlines the evaluation and verification and is followed by the conclusion and outlook in section 6.

3   The Model

The approach comprises three steps. It uses a suite of ontologies, a set of metrics, and dynamic behavioral models (Fig. 1). A description of the ontologies can be found in [11].

As in any assessment process, the first step, denoted "measurement", is collecting information. In this case, very detailed information about the elements of the design system is acquired. This data is used to fill the model of the design system with its parameters. The model consists of several parts: an ontology specifying the elements, their properties and relationships, a behavioral specification describing the algorithmic parts of the model and the metrics specification.

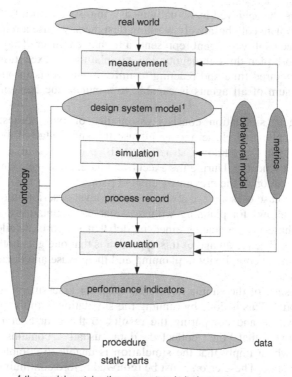

procedure

data

static parts

¹ the model contains the parameters in its instances

Fig. 1. The Assessment Flow

At the next step, denoted "simulation", the design system with the given parameters is simulated and the parameters are adjusted so that the results fit observable results and properties. With a simulation model calibrated this way it is possible to gain very detailed data about the process (the process record). More details on the simulation can be found in the next section.

In the last step, denoted "evaluation", this record together with the initial data can be analyzed and evaluated resulting in the desired performance indicators and measures. This methodology also allows other kinds of analyses. For example "what if" analyses which can be used to answer questions like: "how much do I gain if I buy this new computer?", "which technology to use in the upcoming project?", "design a part in house or buy it from a vendor?", "can I handle the new technology with my tools?", "what quality will my product most likely have?" or "where can I save some time or costs with minimal impact on quality? [12]

4 Simulation

Simulation is a major step in the assessment process. It reproduces the course of the project and provides information on each single step and that with a level of detail which could never be achieved by actually measuring. As a naturally fitting paradigm to model and simulate collaboratively working designers, we use a multi-agent system [11]. Thereby, each software agent represents a human engineer. They are responsible for creating a work plan through negotiation, simulating the execution of the plan by estimating the required time and reacting to unforeseen events through cooperation. In the end, the sum of all agents is capable to simulate the behavior of the actual design system.

The multi-agent simulation consists essentially of two phases: planning and execution. In the planning phase, the agents use the knowledge of the design system to first create a work breakdown structure (WBS), do a resource assignment and derive from this a schedule. During the execution phase, the agents simulate the actual course of the execution of the previously created plan.

The planning phase uses a more abstract, higher level description of the tasks to be executed which allows for planning with reasonable computational effort. Whereas the execution phase uses a finer grained model that supports detailed features like iterative activities. The advantage of this approach is that one gets both the clarity and the lower algorithmic complexity in planning and the precise and detailed information from the execution.

Before the results of the simulation can be used for assessment, it is necessary to calibrate the model. This is done by running the simulation with the parameter values collected in advance and comparing the results to the course of the real project. Experience shows that the collected data usually contains mistakes and inconsistencies which imply that the simulation is unable to complete or completes with senseless results. These errors must be removed before continuing.

4.1 Planning

The aim of the planning phase in the simulation is the same as that of planning in real life: getting a clear plan for the project which fits its peculiarities and tells you what do to and in which time frame. And as in real life, the plan does not contain all the details of the execution as they are either unknown or not interesting at that point. Instead, it shows the tasks to be done at a level of abstraction that still shows basic actions. This allows experts to verify the plan. At the same time, it leaves out details like small iterations which would make the plan too large to be clearly comprehensible.

A particular challenge is the algorithm that does the planning. Traditionally, AI planning algorithms use considerably large building blocks and optimize resource assignment and the schedule. This works fine as long as the plan can be assumed to have a large similarity to previous plans. In the particular case of engineering design this is not the case. From project to project, the designs do vary in many if not all aspects. Furthermore, the design system – everything that is required to perform a design process – changes as well: new technologies are being developed, new tools used, new computers introduced and the most important aspect of such a design system – the designers – change too. Therefore, we have chosen a different approach: we create a detailed model for each activity including the requirements as skills, tools, and files, the outcome and the effort depending on the different aspects. Based on that knowledge and the knowledge about the particularities of the design and the design system, we create a graph that shows all feasible ways to reach the project goal. Then we use heuristics to try and select the best path based on a given optimization function (Fig. 2). The figure shows a small section of the resulting graph with activities as rectangles and results as ellipses. The gray nodes have been chosen as plan whereas white nodes have been discarded. In this example, the logic design (RTL Development, Verification, Debug) is done on the shown block (MEM IF) but Synthesis is done on higher hierarchy level (not shown) and therefore has been discarded for this block. This not only results in a plan customized to fit the given design and design system but also allows optimizing the plan for different criteria as project runtime, total effort, cost or any weighted combination.

This plan is then the basis for the second phase, the simulation of the execution of the project. But it can of course also be used directly: for example as a template for a future project by direct export to MS Project or by comparing multiple plans which are the result of different optimization criteria or different resource setups. It is for example possible to compare generated plans optimized for project run time and for budget to get an idea in which cost-time window a project can be executed.

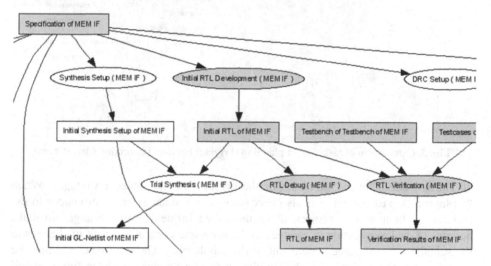

Fig. 2. WBS Graph; section of graph generated in planning. Ellipses stand for results, rect-angles for tasks. Darker entries show the selected path.

4.2 Execution

The second phase of the simulation is the execution phase: the agents execute the plan using the non-simplified, detailed activity description. Thereby, it introduces small iterations, communication overhead and quality of results into the simulation which allows for a much more detailed analysis and assessment of the project. Among other things, this allows for detailed checks in the case of inconsistencies between the simulated project and the real course of the project. This can either hint at mistakes in the modelling of the design system or at problems in the real design system which makes it less efficient than the model assumed.

The main difference between planning and execution, besides a more detailed effort model, are the iterations. Tasks which have to be executed in an alternating iterative way like verification and debugging are planned as parallel tasks. During the execution phase, these tasks are then split into small activities which are executed in an iterative loop – verification, debugging, verification ... – until the quality of the result is sufficient – for example, the verification cannot find any more bugs.

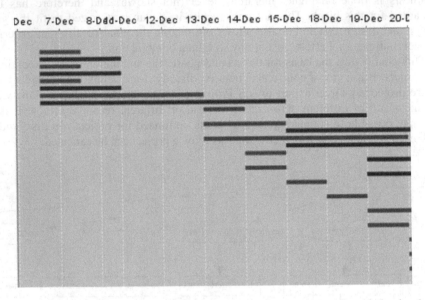

Fig. 3. Comparison of task time in planning (brighter bars) and execution (darker bars)

The simulation of the execution of the project also has other advantages. When "replaying" a past project, it is also necessary to introduce external influences to the simulation. In a normal project, these unforseen influences like changes in staff, updates to the specification or changes to the tools and computers result in changes to the schedule, the resource assignment or the whole plan. These influences cannot be introduced at the beginning of the simulation as this knowledge of the future would result in adaptions to the plan that no manager could forsee and therefore in an unrealistic simulation. Instead, these influences must get known to the simulation at the same moment as in the real course of the project. And as in the real world, the simulation, that means the agents, have to react to these influences and make adaptions to the plan or in the worst case do a complete replanning for the project from this point in time on.

This can also be used to analyze the stability of a given plan and/or a design system: By randomly introducing typical events in the simulation of project, it is possible to observe how severe the impact of such influences is and to find out where the design system is most vulnerable. Such simulations must of course be repeated many times and the results have to be statistically analyzed [12].

5 Evaluation

We developed testcases to evaluate the suite of ontologies and the simulation. A testcase is a real or a fictive project for which at least all the initial data instances required for design system modeling (Fig. 1) are available. Acquiring a testcase allows to verify that the ontology is capable of storing all initial data and to start MAS-based simulation. Ideally, a testcase also provides a complete project execution record which is required for the calibration step and for the verification of the simulation results. Amongst the set of testcases are very simple and fictive ones describing a tiny digital and a tiny analog design. We used them to verify and refine the model and the ontologies. Others are based on digital real world projects. There are fictive ones as well designed for demonstration purposes, as real world projects usually may not be disclosed.

For calibration the MAS is fed with the project definition and the knowledge base. Using these, it creates a new WBS. The result is then compared to the original structure, differences are analyzed, and corrections are made until the both roughly match. At subsequent stages the MAS simulates project execution and again the results are compared to the original project course. Project log replay simulations and calibration experiments proved that the methodology is effective and practical.

6 Conclusions and Outlook

From our experiences so far, we can tell that this approach requires a considerable amount of effort to develop in detail but it has shown promising results already. A first prototype with a working planning phase has been implemented and creates reasonable plans for the test cases. A more detailed task model and the execution phase of the simulation are currently under development.

We will continue developing the prototype and at the same time enlarge the set of test cases. Once we have a first complete implementation of the whole approach, we plan to conduct a series of tests to assess the precision of the results. After that, we shall concentrate on different use cases like "what if"-analyses and we shall automate conducting and analyzing whole series of random simulations.

References

1. Moore, G.E.: Cramming more components onto integrated circuits. Electronics 38(8), 114–117 (1965)
2. Matzke, W.-E.: Engineering Design Performance Management – from Alchemy to Science through ISTa. In: Kaschek, R., Mayr, H.C., Liddle, S. (eds.) Proc. 4th Int. Conf on Information Systems Technology and its Applications (ISTA'2005), (May 23-25, 2005), Palmerston North, New Zealand, pp. 154–179 (2005)
3. van der Aalst, W.M.P., ter Hofstede, A.H.M., Kiepuszewski, B., Barros, A.P.: Workflow Patterns. Distributed and Parallel Databases 14(1), 5–51 (2003)
4. Neal, D., Smith, H., Butler, D.: The evolution of business processes from description to data to smart executable code – is this the future of systems integration and collaborative commerce? Research Services Journal: 39–49 (March 2001)

5. Collett, R.: Benchmarking IC Development Capability – What to Measure? Fabless Forum, Fabless Semiconductor Association, 11(2) (2004)
6. Krause, O.: Beyond BSC: a process based approach to performance management. Measuring Business Excellence 7(3), 4–14 (2003)
7. Jacome, M.F.: Design Process Planning and Management for CAD Frameworks. Dissertation at the Carnegie Mellon University, Pittsburgh, Pennsylvania (1993)
8. Sutton, P.R.: A Framework and Discipline Independent Approach to Design System Management. Dissertation at the Carnegie Mellon University, Pittsburgh, Pennsylvania (1997)
9. Gilmore, S., Kloul, L.: A Unified Tool for Performance Modelling and Prediction, Reliability Engineering and System Safety, vol. 89(1), pp. 17–32. Elsevier Science, Amsterdam (2005)
10. Heller, M., Schleicher, A., Westfechtel, B.: A Management System for Evolving Development Processes. Integrated Design and Process Technology, IDPT-2003 (2003)
11. Ermolayev, V., Jentzsch, E., Karsayev, O., Keberle, N., Matzke, W.-E., Samoylov, V., Sohnius, R.: An Agent-Oriented Model of a Dynamic Engineering Design Process. In: Kolp, M., Bresciani, P., Henderson-Sellers, B., Winikoff, M. (eds.) AOIS 2005. LNCS (LNAI), vol. 3529, pp. 168–183. Springer, Heidelberg (2006)
12. Sohnius, R., Jentzsch, E., Matzke, W.-E., Ermolayev, V.: An Approach for Assessing Design Systems; Design System Simulation and Analysis for Performance Assessment, to appear In: Cardoso, J., Cordeiro, J., Filipe, J (eds.) Proceedings of ICEIS 2007 – Ninth International Conference on Enterprise Information Systems (2007)

Author Index

Lecture Notes in Artificial Intelligence (LNAI)

Vol. 4441: C. Müller (Ed.), Speaker Classification. X, 309 pages. 2007.

Vol. 4438: L. Maicher, A. Sigel, L.M. Garshol (Eds.), Leveraging the Semantics of Topic Maps. X, 257 pages. 2007.

Vol. 4434: G. Lakemeyer, E. Sklar, D.G. Sorrenti, T. Takahashi (Eds.), RoboCup 2006: Robot Soccer World Cup X. XIII, 566 pages. 2007.

Vol. 4429: R. Lu, J.H. Siekmann, C. Ullrich (Eds.), Cognitive Systems. X, 161 pages. 2007.

Vol. 4428: S. Edelkamp, A. Lomuscio (Eds.), Model Checking and Artificial Intelligence. IX, 185 pages. 2007.

Vol. 4426: Z.-H. Zhou, H. Li, Q. Yang (Eds.), Advances in Knowledge Discovery and Data Mining. XXV, 1161 pages. 2007.

Vol. 4411: R.H. Bordini, M. Dastani, J. Dix, A.E.F. Seghrouchni (Eds.), Programming Multi-Agent Systems. XIV, 249 pages. 2007.

Vol. 4410: A. Branco (Ed.), Anaphora: Analysis, Algorithms and Applications. X, 191 pages. 2007.

Vol. 4399: T. Kovacs, X. Llorà, K. Takadama, P.L. Lanzi, W. Stolzmann, S.W. Wilson (Eds.), Learning Classifier Systems. XII, 345 pages. 2007.

Vol. 4390: S.O. Kuznetsov, S. Schmidt (Eds.), Formal Concept Analysis. X, 329 pages. 2007.

Vol. 4389: D. Weyns, H.V.D. Parunak, F. Michel (Eds.), Environments for Multi-Agent Systems III. X, 273 pages. 2007.

Vol. 4386: P. Noriega, J. Vázquez-Salceda, G. Boella, O. Boissier, V. Dignum, N. Fornara, E. Matson (Eds.), Coordination, Organizations, Institutions, and Norms in Agent Systems II. XI, 373 pages. 2007.

Vol. 4384: T. Washio, K. Satoh, H. Takeda, A. Inokuchi (Eds.), New Frontiers in Artificial Intelligence. IX, 401 pages. 2007.

Vol. 4371: K. Inoue, K. Satoh, F. Toni (Eds.), Computational Logic in Multi-Agent Systems. X, 315 pages. 2007.

Vol. 4369: M. Umeda, A. Wolf, O. Bartenstein, U. Geske, D. Seipel, O. Takata (Eds.), Declarative Programming for Knowledge Management. X, 229 pages. 2006.

Vol. 4343: C. Müller (Ed.), Speaker Classification. X, 355 pages. 2007.

Vol. 4342: H. de Swart, E. Orłowska, G. Schmidt, M. Roubens (Eds.), Theory and Applications of Relational Structures as Knowledge Instruments II. X, 373 pages. 2006.

Vol. 4335: S.A. Brueckner, S. Hassas, M. Jelasity, D. Yamins (Eds.), Engineering Self-Organising Systems. XII, 212 pages. 2007.

Vol. 4334: B. Beckert, R. Hähnle, P.H. Schmitt (Eds.), Verification of Object-Oriented Software. XXIX, 658 pages. 2007.

Vol. 4333: U. Reimer, D. Karagiannis (Eds.), Practical Aspects of Knowledge Management. XII, 338 pages. 2006.

Vol. 4327: M. Baldoni, U. Endriss (Eds.), Declarative Agent Languages and Technologies IV. VIII, 257 pages. 2006.

Vol. 4314: C. Freksa, M. Kohlhase, K. Schill (Eds.), KI 2006: Advances in Artificial Intelligence. XII, 458 pages. 2007.

Vol. 4304: A. Sattar, B.-h. Kang (Eds.), AI 2006: Advances in Artificial Intelligence. XXVII, 1303 pages. 2006.

Vol. 4303: A. Hoffmann, B.-h. Kang, D. Richards, S. Tsumoto (Eds.), Advances in Knowledge Acquisition and Management. XI, 259 pages. 2006.

Vol. 4293: A. Gelbukh, C.A. Reyes-Garcia (Eds.), MICAI 2006: Advances in Artificial Intelligence. XXVIII, 1232 pages. 2006.

Vol. 4289: M. Ackermann, B. Berendt, M. Grobelnik, A. Hotho, D. Mladenič, G. Semeraro, M. Spiliopoulou, G. Stumme, V. Svátek, M. van Someren (Eds.), Semantics, Web and Mining. X, 197 pages. 2006.

Vol. 4285: Y. Matsumoto, R.W. Sproat, K.-F. Wong, M. Zhang (Eds.), Computer Processing of Oriental Languages. XVII, 544 pages. 2006.

Vol. 4274: Q. Huo, B. Ma, E.-S. Chng, H. Li (Eds.), Chinese Spoken Language Processing. XXIV, 805 pages. 2006.

Vol. 4265: L. Todorovski, N. Lavrač, K.P. Jantke (Eds.), Discovery Science. XIV, 384 pages. 2006.

Vol. 4264: J.L. Balcázar, P.M. Long, F. Stephan (Eds.), Algorithmic Learning Theory. XIII, 393 pages. 2006.

Vol. 4259: S. Greco, Y. Hata, S. Hirano, M. Inuiguchi, S. Miyamoto, H.S. Nguyen, R. Słowiński (Eds.), Rough Sets and Current Trends in Computing. XXII, 951 pages. 2006.

Vol. 4253: B. Gabrys, R.J. Howlett, L.C. Jain (Eds.), Knowledge-Based Intelligent Information and Engineering Systems, Part III. XXXII, 1301 pages. 2006.

Vol. 4252: B. Gabrys, R.J. Howlett, L.C. Jain (Eds.), Knowledge-Based Intelligent Information and Engineering Systems, Part II. XXXIII, 1335 pages. 2006.

Vol. 4251: B. Gabrys, R.J. Howlett, L.C. Jain (Eds.), Knowledge-Based Intelligent Information and Engineering Systems, Part I. LXVI, 1297 pages. 2006.

Vol. 4248: S. Staab, V. Svátek (Eds.), Managing Knowledge in a World of Networks. XIV, 400 pages. 2006.

Vol. 4246: M. Hermann, A. Voronkov (Eds.), Logic for Programming, Artificial Intelligence, and Reasoning. XIII, 588 pages. 2006.

Vol. 4223: L. Wang, L. Jiao, G. Shi, X. Li, J. Liu (Eds.), Fuzzy Systems and Knowledge Discovery. XXVIII, 1335 pages. 2006.

Vol. 4213: J. Fürnkranz, T. Scheffer, M. Spiliopoulou (Eds.), Knowledge Discovery in Databases: PKDD 2006. XXII, 660 pages. 2006.

Vol. 4212: J. Fürnkranz, T. Scheffer, M. Spiliopoulou (Eds.), Machine Learning: ECML 2006. XXIII, 851 pages. 2006.

Vol. 4211: P. Vogt, Y. Sugita, E. Tuci, C.L. Nehaniv (Eds.), Symbol Grounding and Beyond. VIII, 237 pages. 2006.